2009/10
FACTS & FIGURES

TABLES FOR THE CALCULATION OF DAMAGES

2009/10 FACTS & FIGURES

TABLES FOR THE CALCULATION OF DAMAGES

Compiled and Edited by:

Members of the Professional Negligence Bar Association

General Editor: Robin de Wilde Q.C.

Editors:

Michael Jarvis, FCA
Peter Jennings
Leslie Keegan
Simon Levene
Tejina Mangat
Harry Trusted

SWEET & MAXWELL

THOMSON REUTERS

Published in 2009 by Thomson Reuters (Legal) Limited
(Registered in England & Wales, Company No 1679046.
Registered Office and address for service:
100 Avenue Road, London NW3 3PF)
trading as Sweet & Maxwell Limited

Designed and typeset by J&L Composition, Scarborough, North Yorkshire
Printed in Great Britain by TJ International Ltd, Padstow, Cornwall

No natural forests were destroyed to make this product:
only farmed timber was used and re-planted.

ISBN—13 978-1-84703-901-9

A CIP catalogue record for this book is available from the British Library.

Thomson Reuters (Legal) Limited
2009

ACKNOWLEDGMENTS

HMSO gave us kind permission to use Table A3 (Life tables), Table A8 (The Ogden Tables), Table C2 (Real and nominal interest rates and price inflation), Table F5 (Average earnings index), Table F6 (Average weekly earnings), Table F7 (Average earnings statistics), and the material from the NHS leaflet HC13, NHS charges. The Inland Revenue and HMSO gave us permission to use the material in Table L2 (Taxation of car and fuel benefits).

We are grateful to Adrian Gallop, Government Actuary, for his assistance in preparing A3 (Life tables and projected life tables).

Crown Copyright is reproduced with the permission of HMSO.

We are extremely grateful to Victoria Wass of Cardiff Business School for putting together the step-by-step guide to finding the annual estimates for hourly pay in ASHE 6115 at B6.

Permission to use the tables from Kemp & Kemp: The Quantum of Damages at C3 (Special investment account rates), C8 (Judgment debt interest rates), E1 (Retail price index) and E2 (Inflation table) was given by Sweet & Maxwell Ltd.

We are grateful to Rodney Nelson Jones of Field Fisher Waterhouse and Butterworths for allowing us to use and to develop his table for the calculation of special damage interest in C4.

Permission to use Table C9 (Judicial rates of interest) was given by W. Green.

Tim Higginson of Dixon Wilson has for many years been involved in the meticulous preparation and updating of various annually changing tables in sections C, F, G, H and L. We thank him once again.

FTSE gave us permission to use the FTSE 100 Index at Table D1.

We are grateful to Barclays Capital for the use of their table at D2 (Barclays Equity Index).

We are grateful to Peter Dickerson of Baker Tilly for helping us with Table D3 (Index-linked stock).

Our thanks go to Robert Owen of Hewitt for preparation of the Inflation Table at E2.

Halifax Plc provided the up-to-date material for Tables E3 and E4 showing House price indices.

We are grateful to Keith Carter and Lynn Sandercock of Keith Carter & Associates for the research undertaken in preparing the tables in F4 to F7.

We are grateful to the Family Law Bar Association for their permission to use these tables taken from At a Glance (and its electronic companion @ a Glance): Tables F8 (Public sector comparable earnings), I1 and I2 (Social security benefits) and I6 (Foster care allowances).

We are very grateful to Paul Stagg for his input into the benefits material in I1.

We wish to thank David Coldrick of Wrigleys for preparing Table I4.

We are grateful to Niall Baker and Ian Potter of Irwin Mitchell for their assistance in reworking Tables J1, J2, J3 and J4.

We would like to thank Master Lush of the Court of Protection for his help.

We are grateful to Spire Healthcare who kindly provided us with their hospital charges, Table K4.

Permission to produce the Code of Best Practice on Rehabilitation at K6 and K7 was given to us by the Bodily Injury Claims Management Association.

Permission to use Table L1 (AA motoring costs) was given by the AA Motoring Trust.

Our thanks go to Nicholas Leviseur for preparing the notes on the Motability Scheme at L3.

We are grateful to Emap Consumer Media Limited, publishers of *Parker's Car Price Guide* and Haymarket Consumer Media, publishers of *WhatCar?* on whose figures the calculations in Table L4 are based.

Table M2 (Perpetual calendar) is reproduced with permission from the International Management Diary published by Collins Debden Australia.

FOREWORD TO THE FIRST EDITION

by the Hon. Mr Justice Bell

The assessment of damages for personal injuries and consequential losses has become a matter of increasingly intricate calculation. Detailed schedules of damages and counter-schedules are vital to the proper portrayal of claim and defence to claim but they are arduous and time consuming to compile. Much the same building blocks of information and aids to calculation are required over and over again. This volume has gathered many of the most frequently used building blocks and aids together in a readily accessible form and those who prepare, argue and settle such cases should be grateful for it. Robin de Wilde and his committee have put a lot of work into what is in fact a manual of very practical assistance and they are to be congratulated on a new venture which should mature year by year with the help of your own suggestions.

May 1996

INTRODUCTION TO THE FOURTEENTH EDITION

> "I believe that banking institutions are more dangerous to our liberties than standing armies. If the American people ever allow private banks to control the issue of their currency, first by inflation, then by deflation, the banks and corporations that will grow up around the banks will deprive the people of all property until their children wake-up homeless on the continent their fathers conquered."
>
> *Thomas Jefferson, 1802*

Continuity is all. We remain the same, being Peter Jennings, Simon Levene, Harry Trusted, Tejina Mangat, Michael Jarvis, FCA, and Leslie Keegan. As always, it is our aspiration to make the calculation of damages as simple as it can possibly be. Sometimes, it is not so easy.

The financial background

We understated the severity of the recession/depression in the Introduction to last year's edition. In the words of Mervyn King, the occasionally maligned Governor of the Bank of England, we are in "the worst financial crisis since the First World War."[1] The idea that the Bank of England's Minimum Lending Rate would be 0.5% is incredible. Other effects are also dramatic. The Stock Market has been down as low as 3,500. Vast sums have been paid into the National Savings & Investments (run by the Government) in excess of £8.6 billion, by private individuals, since the beginning of the year. People may not trust politicians, but now they trust banks even less. We are all going to have to work longer, whether we want to or not, and many young people are going to have enormous trouble in finding employment at all.

The Discount Rate

Over the past year this has come to reflect the real state of the market less and less. We noted in the Introduction last year the effect of the Government's reluctance to make the alteration on litigants' unwillingness to accept lump sum awards. In an excellent article to be found in the Journal of Personal Injury Law[2] the last Government Actuary makes these points about the discount rate:

> ". . . what is really more urgently needed is a fundamental review of the setting of the discount rate. At the moment changes to the Ogden tables would be just tinkering with the problem. As we have seen, the discount rate of 2½% is significantly too high, even for price-linked amounts and should in my view be reduced to 1½% or even 1%. For earnings-linked payments and cost of care, a discount rate of 0% or less even −1%, although I can imagine some disbelief in the Courts at the idea of a negative discount rate." (p.20)

[1] It is often forgotten that for the United Kingdom, 1913 was a year of a great financial and banking crisis, only rescued by the arrival of the First World War in August 1914. The crisis was far worse than that of 1929–1933. Hence Mervyn King's comparison.

[2] "Fair Compensation Needs Actuaries", Chris Daykin [2009] J.P.I.L. 48.

"For periodical payments to come fully into their own, I believe we will need to see different indexation for different elements of the award and more flexibility to review and to adjust the periodical payments in the light of changing circumstances and make one-off payments, to address particular needs." (p.21)

The discount rate has remained unchanged since 2001, while the Special Account Rate has been reduced from 6% a year ago to ½% as of July 1, 2009, and the average yield from index-linked gilts (which was used as the basis for setting the discount rate) is now less than half the level that it was in 2001. This is not joined-up economics.

Apologies and regrets

Sometimes in the course of a year after publication I receive telephone calls, emails or correspondence pointing that we have got things wrong. There is one matter to admit, as well as others, doubtless, which we ought to confess and avoid. In the Average Earnings section (Table F7) we published the average earnings rather the median earnings, whereas in the original documents, both figures are available, though the median is more useful (for reasons, see the website of the Office of National Statistics). I am grateful to Jeremy Watt of Trevor Gilbert & Associates for drawing this to our attention. Other errors to be found in Table A4 have been corrected.

What is new?

Not as much as in previous years. As the effects of *Thompstone* and the Periodical Payments Orders become more refined and more popular, we have provided a short *vade mecum* of the points to look for in a draft Order. Practitioners will not sign off a case without an Independent Financial Adviser, but knowing what to ask for and why is always helpful. We are grateful to Harry Trusted and to Jennifer Stone of the Nestor Partnership, who assisted him with her experience (Table B5).

In view of the number of claims involving members of the Armed Forces, we have introduced the PULHHEEMS system of measuring physical and mental grading for service personnel (Table M4).

We have attempted to improve the financial information section and refine our presentation of a P45. Michael Jarvis continues to look after the financial calculations and the pension calculations, which range through Tables F, G and H.

David Coldrick has further revised his work on Personal Injury Trusts.

Cases of Interest

At the risk of boring those who have every new case delivered to their Inbox daily, the last year has brought the folliwng interest cases:

(1) *Peters v East Midlands Strategic Health Authority* [2009] EWCA Civ 145 is one of significance. It appears to have buried both *Sowden* and *Crofton* for a while, even if they are not "entombed in the urns and sepulchres of mortality".[3] Lord Justice Dyson, speaking for the whole Court, held that the trial judge was not wrong to have regard to the possibility of legislative change as a relevant factor in deciding whether it was reasonable for those representing the claimant to opt for private funding rather than rely on the Council [para.87].

[3] Lord Justice Crew in the Earl of Oxford's case.

(2) *Cobham Hire Services Ltd v Benjamin Eeles* [2009] EWCA Civ 204 is also important. It limits the amount that may properly be awarded by way of an interim payment, where a large award might interfere with the trial judge's freedom to make an appropriate Periodical Payments Order.

(3) In *Manning v Kings College Hospital NHS Trust* [2009] EWHC 693 (QB), Stadlen J. gave useful guidance on issue-based costs orders.

(4) The Court of Appeal in *Fletcher v A Train & Sons Limited* gave the Claimant permission to appeal to the House of Lords on the issue of the correct calculation of multipliers in Fatal Accidents Act claims. The House of Lords would have revisited an issue decided 30 years ago in *Cookson v Knowles*,[4] but the matter was compromised before the appeal was heard – the Respondents presumably making the Appellant an offer she could not refuse.

Bernie Ecclestone

Since the First Edition of this book, Mr Bernie Ecclestone has been a popular and useful comparator in claims for loss of earnings. Tragically, his position in the *Sunday Times* Rich List has slumped to No.24, reflecting the catastrophic decline in his fortune from £2.4 billion to £1.466 billion. There is no suggestion in any newspaper that these figures are to be taken seriously.

However, Mr Ecclestone, plainly against his will, has been divorced by his wife and private matrimonial lawyers are now engaged in sorting out the consequences. We will leave it to our colleagues at the Family Law Bar Association to establish the accuracy of the *Sunday Times* Rich List. Never a conspicuous spender, the King Jog *de nos jours*[5] will probably never agonise over the source of his next meal.

Meanwhile, another star has entered the firmament, namely a Mr Bob Diamond, Chief Executive of Barclays Bank, who, it has been announced in the newspapers, earned in 2007 at least £21.1 million in the course of his employment. As a result of the sale of part of his shareholding in one company (BGI) being sold by Barclays Bank to a hedge fund, he is going to receive a further £22 million in 2009. When the First Edition Introduction was written in 1996, Mr Ecclestone's earnings of £30 million or so in 1993 seem substantial but, in comparison to Mr Diamond's £21.1 million in 2007 and £22 million in 2009, he clearly has a challenger.

Despite the pleasure they give the public and the excellent value for money that they represent, neither Mr Ecclestone[6] nor Mr Diamond appear in the relevant Table of Public Sector Comparative Earnings (Table F8).

Envoi

The delicate reader, who has been brave enough to read this far, now encounters the usual encomia on those who respond and point out errors and suggest improvements. The idea that people continue to buy, read and use this volume is heartwarming to the sensitive and delicate souls of your editors.

[4] [1977] A.B. 913.

[5] Nickname of the First Earl of Durham, 1792–1840, who once remarked that one could "jog along on £40,000 a year" – about £3,500,000 at today's rates.

[6] *The Times* of July 4, 2009 carried an unfortunate interview with Mr Ecclestone, in which he argued that autocracy or tyranny is more efficient than democracy, with unfortunate references to one Herr Adolf Hitler. He may be good at making money, but he has little understanding of either basic political ideas, history or the nature of psychopathic monsters. As he was not able to discriminate between Napoleon and Stalin, his own deficiences were only too apparent. He might consider asking his wife for a lesson on mid-twentieth century Croatian history.

Every year, as we start our progress towards publication, we lie awake at night worrying whether we can justify what we have done and whether anyone will wish to renew their subscription. As evidence that you have done so, we are grateful for suggestions, corrections and improvements.

218 Strand Chambers
Third Floor
218, Strand
London WC2R 1AT

Robin de Wilde, Q.C.
rdewilde@218strand.com
July 2009
020 7353 3936

INTRODUCTION TO THE FIRST EDITION

Schedules of Damages have become more complex. These tables are intended as an assistance to those who have to check the details which support a Schedule. The Tables themselves come from a variety of primary sources. In one volume they should be easier to use.

The task of compiling this volume has proved more onerous than any of the members of the Committee assigned to the task would have imagined. The discussions as to what should be included or excluded became intense. When dealing with comparative and comparable earnings, should not Mr Bernie Ecclestone of Formula One Promotions and International Sports World receive a mention? He was paid in 1993 the sum of £30,750,109 and became easily the highest paid director by £8,000,000 or so. He is not included in the Table of Comparable Earnings.

We are also conscious that the application of each Table may or may not be easy depending on the contents. We do not intend to triple the size of the volume by setting out worked examples, but would refer the reader to the appropriate text books. It is intended as a source book, easily to hand, so that the practitioner may find what is needed quickly and easily in a single volume.

As this is our first foray into the world of tables, we appreciate that some matters will have been omitted that should be included and some of that which is included should not be present. We rely on our readers to tell us what is wanted and needed, so that the next annual update can be improved. The intention is that each edition is published in late January or early February of each year, incorporating the declarations announced in the Budget in November the previous year.

We have plundered shamelessly from a variety of sources. The final stimulus has been the Family Law Bar Association's "At A Glance" annual publication, but it is designed for practitioners in a different world, facing other demands and needs.

We are also grateful to Mr Justice Bell, who attended the final Advisory Committee Meeting and agreed to write a Foreword to this venture.

We conclude with the thought expressed by the historian Edward Gibbon in *The Decline and Fall of the Roman Empire*, when he states in a footnote about one Emperor that:

"Twenty-two acknowledged concubines and a library of sixty-two thousand volumes, attested the variety of his inclinations; and from the productions which he left behind him, it appears that the former as well as the latter were designed for use rather than ostentation."

These Tables, too, are designed for use rather than ostentation.

199 Strand
London WC2R 1DR
May 1996

Robin de Wilde, Q.C.

CONTENTS

Group M—Other Information

Group A
Ogden Tables and Related Materials

A1: 2.5% Discount Tables "At a Glance"

The following two tables comprise the 2.5 per cent columns from Ogden Tables 1–26.

If 2.5 per cent is the appropriate discount factor, these tables contain all the appropriate multipliers.

Readers are reminded that the figures for loss of earnings must be adjusted in accordance with Section B of the Explanatory Notes to the Ogden Tables (Contingencies Other than Mortality) reproduced in Part A8. Multipliers already adjusted for these contingencies are set out in Table A4.

2.5% Discount Tables "At a Glance" – MALE

	Table 1 Pecuniary loss for life	Table 3 Loss of earnings to age 50	Table 5 Loss of earnings to age 55	Table 7 Loss of earnings to age 60	Table 9 Loss of earnings to age 65	Table 11 Loss of earnings to age 70	Table 13 Loss of earnings to age 75	Table 15 Loss of pension from age 50	Table 17 Loss of pension from age 55	Table 19 Loss of pension from age 60	Table 21 Loss of pension from age 65	Table 23 Loss of pension from age 70	Table 25 Loss of pension from age 75
0	35.15							6.75	5.43	4.29	3.31	2.47	1.76
1	35.19							6.94	5.59	4.41	3.40	2.53	1.81
2	35.05							7.10	5.71	4.51	3.47	2.59	1.84
3	34.90							7.26	5.84	4.61	3.55	2.64	1.88
4	34.75							7.43	5.97	4.71	3.62	2.69	1.91
5	34.59							7.60	6.11	4.81	3.70	2.75	1.95
6	34.43							7.77	6.24	4.92	3.78	2.80	1.99
7	34.26							7.95	6.38	5.03	3.86	2.86	2.03
8	34.08							8.13	6.53	5.14	3.94	2.92	2.06
9	33.91							8.31	6.67	5.25	4.02	2.98	2.10
10	33.72							8.50	6.82	5.36	4.11	3.04	2.14
11	33.53							8.70	6.98	5.48	4.19	3.10	2.18
12	33.34							8.90	7.13	5.60	4.28	3.16	2.22
13	33.14							9.10	7.29	5.72	4.37	3.23	2.27
14	32.93							9.31	7.45	5.85	4.46	3.29	2.31
15	32.72							9.52	7.62	5.97	4.56	3.36	2.35
16	32.51	22.77	24.72	26.41	27.86	29.09	30.11	9.74	7.79	6.10	4.66	3.42	2.40
17	32.29	22.33	24.33	26.05	27.54	28.80	29.85	9.96	7.97	6.24	4.75	3.49	2.44
18	32.07	21.88	23.93	25.70	27.22	28.51	29.58	10.19	8.15	6.37	4.85	3.56	2.49
19	31.85	21.43	23.52	25.34	26.89	28.22	29.32	10.42	8.33	6.52	4.96	3.64	2.54
20	31.63	20.96	23.11	24.97	26.56	27.92	29.04	10.67	8.52	6.66	5.06	3.71	2.58
21	31.40	20.48	22.68	24.59	26.23	27.61	28.77	10.92	8.71	6.81	5.17	3.79	2.63
22	31.16	19.99	22.25	24.20	25.88	27.30	28.48	11.17	8.91	6.96	5.29	3.87	2.68
23	30.92	19.49	21.80	23.81	25.52	26.98	28.19	11.43	9.12	7.12	5.40	3.95	2.74
24	30.67	18.98	21.35	23.40	25.16	26.65	27.89	11.70	9.33	7.27	5.51	4.03	2.79
25	30.42	18.45	20.88	22.98	24.78	26.31	27.58	11.97	9.54	7.43	5.63	4.11	2.84
26	30.15	17.91	20.40	22.55	24.40	25.96	27.26	12.25	9.75	7.60	5.75	4.19	2.89
27	29.89	17.35	19.91	22.12	24.01	25.61	26.94	12.53	9.98	7.77	5.88	4.28	2.95
28	29.61	16.78	19.40	21.67	23.61	25.25	26.61	12.83	10.21	7.94	6.00	4.37	3.01
29	29.33	16.20	18.89	21.21	23.20	24.88	26.27	13.13	10.45	8.12	6.14	4.46	3.07
30	29.05	15.61	18.36	20.74	22.78	24.50	25.92	13.44	10.69	8.31	6.27	4.55	3.12
31	28.75	15.00	17.82	20.26	22.35	24.11	25.57	13.76	10.93	8.49	6.40	4.64	3.18
32	28.46	14.37	17.27	19.77	21.91	23.72	25.21	14.08	11.19	8.68	6.54	4.74	3.25
33	28.15	13.73	16.70	19.27	21.46	23.21	24.84	14.42	11.45	8.88	6.69	4.84	3.31
34	27.83	13.08	16.12	18.76	21.00	22.90	24.46	14.76	11.71	9.08	6.83	4.94	3.37
35	27.51	12.40	15.53	18.23	20.53	22.47	24.08	15.11	11.98	9.28	6.98	5.04	3.44
36	27.18	11.71	14.92	17.26	20.05	22.04	23.68	15.47	12.26	9.49	7.13	5.14	3.50
37	26.85	11.01	14.30	17.14	19.56	21.60	23.28	15.84	12.55	9.71	7.29	5.25	3.57
38	26.50	10.28	13.66	16.57	19.05	21.14	22.86	16.22	12.84	9.93	7.45	5.36	3.64
39	26.15	9.54	13.00	15.99	18.54	20.68	22.44	16.61	13.15	10.16	7.61	5.47	3.71
40	25.79	8.78	12.33	15.40	18.01	20.20	22.01	17.01	13.46	10.39	7.78	5.59	3.78
41	25.42	8.00	11.64	14.79	17.47	19.72	21.57	17.43	13.78	10.63	7.95	5.71	3.86
42	25.05	7.20	10.94	14.17	16.92	19.22	21.12	17.85	14.11	10.88	8.13	5.83	3.93
43	24.67	6.38	10.22	13.53	16.35	18.72	20.66	18.29	14.45	11.13	8.32	5.95	4.01
44	24.28	5.53	9.48	12.88	15.77	18.20	20.19	18.74	14.80	11.40	8.50	6.08	4.09
45	23.88	4.67	8.73	12.22	15.19	17.67	19.71	19.21	15.16	11.67	8.70	6.21	4.17
46	23.49	3.79	7.95	11.54	14.58	17.14	19.23	19.70	15.54	11.95	8.90	6.35	4.26
47	23.08	2.88	7.16	10.84	13.97	16.59	18.74	20.21	15.93	12.24	9.11	6.49	4.35
48	22.68	1.94	6.34	10.13	13.35	16.04	18.24	20.73	16.33	12.55	9.33	6.64	4.44
49	22.27	0.99	5.51	9.40	12.71	15.47	17.73	21.28	16.76	12.86	9.56	6.79	4.54
50	21.86		4.65	8.66	12.06	14.90	17.22	21.86	17.20	13.20	9.80	6.95	4.64
51	21.44		3.78	7.90	11.40	14.32	16.70		17.66	13.54	10.04	7.12	4.74
52	21.02		2.87	7.11	10.71	13.72	16.17		18.15	13.90	10.30	7.30	4.85
53	20.59		1.94	6.31	10.02	13.11	15.63		18.65	14.28	10.57	7.48	4.96
54	20.15		0.99	5.48	9.30	12.48	15.07		19.17	14.67	10.85	7.67	5.08

2.5% Discount Tables "At a Glance" – MALE *continued*

	Table 1 Pecuniary loss for life	Table 3 Loss of earnings to age 50	Table 5 Loss of earnings to age 55	Table 7 Loss of earnings to age 60	Table 9 Loss of earnings to age 65	Table 11 Loss of earnings to age 70	Table 13 Loss of earnings to age 75	Table 15 Loss of pension from age 50	Table 17 Loss of pension from age 55	Table 19 Loss of pension from age 60	Table 21 Loss of pension from age 65	Table 24 Loss of pension from age 70	Table 25 Loss of pension from age 75
55	19.70			4.63	8.56	11.84	14.50		19.70	15.07	11.14	7.86	5.20
56	19.23			3.76	7.81	11.18	13.92			15.48	11.43	8.06	5.32
57	18.76			2.86	7.03	10.50	13.32			15.90	11.73	8.26	5.44
58	18.28			1.94	6.24	9.81	12.71			16.34	12.04	8.47	5.57
59	17.79			0.98	5.42	9.11	12.09			16.81	12.37	8.69	5.70
60	17.30				4.59	8.39	11.46			17.30	12.72	8.92	5.84
61	16.82				3.73	7.65	10.82				13.09	9.17	6.00
62	16.34				2.84	6.91	10.18				13.50	9.43	6.16
63	15.86				1.93	6.14	9.52				13.93	9.72	6.34
64	15.37				0.98	5.35	8.85				14.39	10.03	6.52
65	14.88					4.53	8.16				14.88	10.35	6.72
66	14.39					3.69	7.46					10.70	6.93
67	13.88					2.82	6.73					11.06	7.15
68	13.36					1.92	5.99					11.45	7.38
69	12.84					0.98	5.22					11.86	7.62
70	12.30						4.43					12.30	7.87
71	11.76						3.61						8.14
72	11.21						2.77						8.44
73	10.67						1.89						8.78
74	10.13						0.97						9.16
75	9.61												9.61
76	9.10												
77	8.61												
78	8.14												
79	7.69												
80	7.25												
81	6.83												
82	6.42												
83	6.02												
84	5.63												
85	5.26												
86	4.91												
87	4.58												
88	4.27												
89	4.00												
90	3.74												
91	3.49												
92	3.25												
93	3.04												
94	2.87												
95	2.71												
96	2.56												
97	2.41												
98	2.26												
99	2.12												
100	1.97												

2.5% Discount Tables "At a Glance" – FEMALE

	Table 2 Pecuniary loss for life	Table 4 Loss of earnings to age 50	Table 6 Loss of earnings to age 55	Table 8 Loss of earnings to age 60	Table 10 Loss of earnings to age 65	Table 12 Loss of earnings to age 70	Table 14 Loss of earnings to age 75	Table 16 Loss of pension from age 50	Table 18 Loss of pension from age 55	Table 20 Loss of pension from age 60	Table 22 Loss of pension from age 65	Table 24 Loss of pension from age 70	Table 26 Loss of pension from age 75
0	35.67							7.18	5.85	4.69	3.67	2.80	2.04
1	35.70							7.39	6.01	4.81	3.77	2.87	2.10
2	35.58							7.56	6.15	4.92	3.85	2.93	2.14
3	35.45							7.74	6.30	5.04	3.94	2.99	2.18
4	35.32							7.92	6.44	5.15	4.03	3.06	2.23
5	35.18							8.10	6.59	5.27	4.12	3.12	2.27
6	35.03							8.29	6.74	5.39	4.21	3.19	2.32
7	34.88							8.49	6.90	5.51	4.30	3.26	2.37
8	34.73							8.69	7.06	5.63	4.40	3.33	2.42
9	34.57							8.89	7.22	5.76	4.49	3.40	2.46
10	34.41							9.10	7.38	5.89	4.59	3.47	2.51
11	34.24							9.31	7.55	6.02	4.69	3.54	2.57
12	34.07							9.52	7.73	6.16	4.80	3.62	2.62
13	33.89							9.75	7.91	6.30	4.90	3.70	2.67
14	33.71							9.97	8.09	6.44	5.01	3.78	2.72
15	33.53							10.21	8.27	6.58	5.12	3.86	2.78
16	33.34	22.89	24.87	26.60	28.11	29.40	30.50	10.45	8.46	6.73	5.23	3.94	2.84
17	33.15	22.45	24.49	26.26	27.80	29.12	30.25	10.69	8.66	6.89	5.35	4.02	2.89
18	32.95	22.01	24.09	25.91	27.48	28.84	30.00	10.94	8.86	7.04	5.47	4.11	2.95
19	32.75	21.55	23.68	25.55	27.16	28.55	29.74	11.20	9.06	7.20	5.59	4.20	3.01
20	32.54	21.08	23.27	25.18	26.83	28.26	29.47	11.46	9.27	7.36	5.71	4.28	3.07
21	32.33	20.60	22.84	24.80	26.49	27.95	29.19	11.73	9.49	7.53	5.84	4.38	3.14
22	32.11	20.11	22.40	24.41	26.15	27.64	28.91	12.01	9.71	7.70	5.96	4.47	3.20
23	31.89	19.60	21.96	24.01	25.79	27.32	28.62	12.29	9.93	7.88	6.10	4.56	3.26
24	31.66	19.08	21.50	23.60	25.43	26.99	28.33	12.58	10.16	8.05	6.23	4.66	3.33
25	31.42	18.55	21.02	23.18	25.05	26.66	28.02	12.87	10.39	8.24	6.37	4.76	3.40
26	31.18	18.00	20.54	22.75	24.67	26.32	27.71	13.17	10.63	8.42	6.51	4.86	3.47
27	30.93	17.45	20.05	22.31	24.28	25.96	27.39	13.48	10.88	8.61	6.65	4.97	3.54
28	30.67	16.88	19.54	21.86	23.88	25.60	27.07	13.80	11.13	8.81	6.80	5.07	3.61
29	30.41	16.29	19.02	21.40	23.46	25.23	26.73	14.12	11.39	9.01	6.95	5.18	3.68
30	30.15	15.69	18.49	20.93	23.04	24.86	26.39	14.46	11.65	9.21	7.10	5.29	3.75
31	29.87	15.07	17.95	20.45	22.61	24.47	26.04	14.80	11.92	9.42	7.26	5.40	3.83
32	29.59	14.44	17.39	19.95	22.17	24.07	25.68	15.15	12.20	9.64	7.42	5.52	3.91
33	29.30	13.80	16.82	19.45	21.72	23.67	25.32	15.50	12.49	9.86	7.58	5.64	3.99
34	29.01	13.14	16.23	18.93	21.26	23.25	24.94	15.87	12.78	10.08	7.75	5.76	4.07
35	28.71	12.46	15.63	18.39	20.78	22.83	24.56	16.25	13.07	10.31	7.92	5.88	4.15
36	28.40	11.76	15.02	17.85	20.30	22.39	24.16	16.63	13.38	10.55	8.10	6.00	4.23
37	28.08	11.05	14.39	17.29	19.80	21.95	23.76	17.03	13.69	10.79	8.28	6.13	4.32
38	27.76	10.32	13.74	16.72	19.29	21.49	23.35	17.43	14.01	11.04	8.47	6.26	4.41
39	27.43	9.58	13.08	16.14	18.77	21.03	22.93	17.85	14.34	11.29	8.65	6.40	4.50
40	27.09	8.81	12.41	15.54	18.24	20.55	22.50	18.28	14.68	11.55	8.85	6.54	4.59
41	26.74	8.02	11.71	14.92	17.70	20.06	22.06	18.72	15.03	11.82	9.05	6.68	4.68
42	26.39	7.22	11.01	14.30	17.14	19.57	21.61	19.17	15.39	12.10	9.25	6.83	4.78
43	26.04	6.39	10.28	13.66	16.57	19.06	21.16	19.64	15.76	12.38	9.46	6.97	4.88
44	25.67	5.55	9.54	13.00	15.99	18.54	20.69	20.12	16.14	12.67	9.68	7.13	4.98
45	25.30	4.68	8.77	12.33	15.40	18.01	20.22	20.62	16.53	12.97	9.91	7.29	5.09
46	24.93	3.79	7.99	11.64	14.79	17.48	19.73	21.13	16.93	13.28	10.14	7.45	5.19
47	24.55	2.88	7.19	10.94	14.17	16.93	19.24	21.66	17.35	13.61	10.38	7.62	5.30
48	24.16	1.95	6.37	10.22	13.54	16.36	18.74	22.21	17.78	13.94	10.62	7.79	5.42
49	23.77	0.99	5.53	9.48	12.89	15.79	18.23	22.78	18.23	14.28	10.88	7.97	5.54
50	23.37		4.67	8.73	12.23	15.21	17.71	23.37	18.70	14.64	11.14	8.16	5.66
51	22.96		3.79	7.96	11.55	14.61	17.18		19.18	15.01	11.42	8.35	5.79
52	22.55		2.88	7.16	10.85	14.00	16.63		19.67	15.39	11.70	8.55	5.92
53	22.13		1.95	6.35	10.14	13.37	16.08		20.19	15.78	11.99	8.76	6.05
54	21.70		0.99	5.51	9.41	12.73	15.51		20.71	16.19	12.29	8.97	6.19

2.5% Discount Tables "At a Glance" – FEMALE *continued*

	Table 2 Pecuniary loss for life	Table 4 Loss of earnings to age 50	Table 6 Loss of earnings to age 55	Table 8 Loss of earnings to age 60	Table 10 Loss of earnings to age 65	Table 12 Loss of earnings to age 70	Table 14 Loss of earnings to age 75	Table 16 Loss of pension from age 50	Table 18 Loss of pension from age 55	Table 20 Loss of pension from age 60	Table 22 Loss of pension from age 65	Table 23 Loss of pension from age 70	Table 24 Loss of pension from age 75
55	21.26			4.66	8.66	12.07	14.93		21.26	16.60	12.60	9.19	6.33
56	20.81			3.78	7.90	11.40	14.33			17.03	12.91	9.41	6.48
57	20.35			2.87	7.11	10.71	13.72			17.48	13.24	9.63	6.62
58	19.88			1.94	6.30	10.01	13.10			17.94	13.58	9.87	6.78
59	19.41			0.99	5.48	9.29	12.47			18.43	13.93	10.12	6.94
60	18.94				4.63	8.56	11.83			18.94	14.31	10.38	7.11
61	18.46				3.76	7.80	11.17				14.70	10.66	7.29
62	17.98				2.86	7.03	10.50				15.12	10.95	7.47
63	17.49				1.94	6.24	9.82				15.55	11.25	7.67
64	17.00				0.98	5.43	9.12				16.01	11.57	7.88
65	16.50					4.59	8.41				16.50	11.90	8.09
66	15.99					3.73	7.67					12.26	8.32
67	15.47					2.84	6.92					12.62	8.55
68	14.93					1.93	6.14					13.00	8.79
69	14.38					0.98	5.34					13.40	9.03
70	13.81						4.52					13.81	9.28
71	13.22						3.68						9.54
72	12.63						2.81						9.82
73	12.03						1.91						10.12
74	11.43						0.98						10.45
75	10.84												10.84
76	10.27												
77	9.71												
78	9.17												
79	8.65												
80	8.15												
81	7.66												
82	7.19												
83	6.73												
84	6.28												
85	5.85												
86	5.44												
87	5.06												
88	4.69												
89	4.36												
90	4.05												
91	3.77												
92	3.51												
93	3.28												
94	3.08												
95	2.89												
96	2.72												
97	2.55												
98	2.40												
99	2.25												
100	2.11												

A2: Nil Discount Tables "At a Glance"

MALE (0%)

	Table 1 Pecuniary loss for life	Table 3 Loss of earnings to age 50	Table 5 Loss of earnings to age 55	Table 7 Loss of earnings to age 60	Table 9 Loss of earnings to age 65	Table 11 Loss of earnings to age 70	Table 13 Loss of earnings to age 75	Table 15 Loss of pension from age 50	Table 17 Loss of pension from age 55	Table 19 Loss of pension from age 60	Table 21 Loss of pension from age 65	Table 23 Loss of pension from age 70	Table 25 Loss of pension from age 75
0	86.63							37.30	32.51	27.80	23.20	18.76	14.52
1	85.96							37.37	32.56	27.83	23.21	18.75	14.50
2	84.86							37.27	32.45	27.72	23.11	18.65	14.41
3	83.76							37.16	32.35	27.62	23.00	18.55	14.31
4	82.65							37.04	32.23	27.51	22.90	18.45	14.22
5	81.53							36.93	32.12	27.40	22.79	18.35	14.12
6	80.42							36.81	32.01	27.28	22.68	18.24	14.03
7	79.30							36.70	31.89	27.17	22.58	18.14	13.93
8	78.18							36.58	31.78	27.06	22.47	18.04	13.84
9	77.06							36.47	31.67	26.95	22.36	17.94	13.74
10	75.95							36.35	31.55	26.84	22.25	17.84	13.65
11	74.83							36.24	31.44	26.73	22.15	17.74	13.56
12	73.71							36.12	31.33	26.62	22.04	17.64	13.46
13	72.59							36.01	31.21	26.51	21.93	17.53	13.37
14	71.48							35.89	31.10	26.40	21.83	17.43	13.27
15	70.36							35.78	30.99	26.29	21.72	17.33	13.18
16	69.25	33.58	38.37	43.07	47.63	52.01	56.16	35.66	30.88	26.18	21.62	17.23	13.09
17	68.14	32.59	37.37	42.07	46.62	51.00	55.14	35.55	30.77	26.08	21.52	17.14	13.00
18	67.04	31.59	36.38	41.07	45.63	50.00	54.13	35.45	30.66	25.97	21.42	17.04	12.91
19	65.95	30.60	35.39	40.08	44.64	49.01	53.13	35.35	30.56	25.87	21.32	16.95	12.83
20	64.87	29.62	34.41	39.10	43.65	48.01	52.13	35.25	30.47	25.78	21.22	16.86	12.74
21	63.79	28.63	33.42	38.11	42.66	47.02	51.13	35.16	30.37	25.68	21.13	16.77	12.66
22	62.71	27.65	32.43	37.12	41.67	46.03	50.14	35.07	30.28	25.59	21.04	16.68	12.57
23	61.63	26.66	31.45	36.14	40.69	45.04	49.14	34.98	30.19	25.50	20.95	16.59	12.49
24	60.55	25.67	30.46	35.15	39.70	44.05	48.14	34.88	30.09	25.40	20.85	16.50	12.41
25	59.47	24.68	29.47	34.16	38.71	43.06	47.14	34.78	29.99	25.30	20.76	16.41	12.32
26	58.38	23.70	28.49	33.18	37.72	42.06	46.15	34.69	29.90	25.21	20.67	16.32	12.24
27	57.31	22.71	27.50	32.19	36.73	41.07	45.15	34.60	29.81	25.12	20.58	16.23	12.16
28	56.24	21.72	26.52	31.21	35.75	40.09	44.16	34.51	29.72	25.03	20.49	16.15	12.08
29	55.17	20.74	25.53	30.23	34.76	39.10	43.17	34.43	29.64	24.95	20.41	16.07	12.00
30	54.10	19.75	24.55	29.24	33.78	38.12	42.18	34.35	29.55	24.86	20.32	15.99	11.92
31	53.03	18.77	23.57	28.26	32.80	37.13	41.19	34.27	29.47	24.77	20.23	15.90	11.85
32	51.97	17.78	22.59	27.28	31.82	36.15	40.20	34.19	29.38	24.69	20.15	15.82	11.77
33	50.91	16.80	21.60	26.30	30.84	35.17	39.21	34.11	29.30	24.61	20.07	15.74	11.69
34	49.85	15.81	20.62	25.32	29.86	34.19	38.23	34.03	29.22	24.52	19.99	15.66	11.62
35	48.78	14.83	19.64	24.34	28.88	33.21	37.24	33.96	29.14	24.44	19.90	15.58	11.54
36	47.73	13.84	18.66	23.36	27.90	32.23	36.26	33.88	29.07	24.36	19.82	15.50	11.46
37	46.67	12.86	17.68	22.39	26.93	31.25	35.28	33.81	28.99	24.28	19.74	15.42	11.39
38	45.62	11.87	16.70	21.41	25.95	30.27	34.30	33.74	28.92	24.21	19.67	15.34	11.32
39	44.56	10.89	15.72	20.43	24.98	29.30	33.32	33.68	28.85	24.13	19.59	15.27	11.25
40	43.52	9.90	14.74	19.45	24.00	28.32	32.34	33.62	28.78	24.06	19.52	15.20	11.18
41	42.48	8.92	13.76	18.48	23.03	27.35	31.37	33.56	28.72	24.00	19.45	15.13	11.11
42	41.44	7.93	12.78	17.50	22.06	26.38	30.40	33.51	28.66	23.93	19.38	15.06	11.04
43	40.40	6.94	11.80	16.53	21.09	25.41	29.43	33.46	28.60	23.87	19.31	14.99	10.97
44	39.37	5.95	10.82	15.56	20.12	24.45	28.46	33.42	28.55	23.81	19.25	14.92	10.91
45	38.35	4.97	9.84	14.59	19.16	23.49	27.50	33.38	28.51	23.76	19.19	14.86	10.85
46	37.34	3.98	8.86	13.62	18.20	22.53	26.55	33.36	28.48	23.72	19.14	14.81	10.79
47	36.34	2.99	7.88	12.65	17.24	21.58	25.60	33.35	28.45	23.68	19.10	14.76	10.74
48	35.34	1.99	6.91	11.69	16.29	20.63	24.66	33.35	28.44	23.66	19.06	14.71	10.69
49	34.37	1.00	5.93	10.72	15.33	19.69	23.72	33.37	28.44	23.64	19.03	14.67	10.64
50	33.40		4.95	9.76	14.39	18.76	22.79	33.40	28.45	23.64	19.01	14.64	10.60
51	32.44		3.96	8.80	13.44	17.83	21.87		28.48	23.64	19.00	14.61	10.57
52	31.49		2.98	7.83	12.49	16.90	20.95		28.51	23.66	19.00	14.60	10.54
53	30.55		1.99	6.87	11.55	15.97	20.04		28.56	23.68	19.00	14.59	10.52
54	29.61		1.00	5.90	10.60	15.03	19.12		28.61	23.71	19.01	14.57	10.49

MALE (0%) *continued*

	Table 1 Pecuniary loss for life	Table 3 Loss of earnings to age 50	Table 5 Loss of earnings to age 55	Table 7 Loss of earnings to age 60	Table 9 Loss of earnings to age 65	Table 11 Loss of earnings to age 70	Table 13 Loss of earnings to age 75	Table 15 Loss of pension from age 50	Table 17 Loss of pension from age 55	Table 19 Loss of pension from age 60	Table 21 Loss of pension from age 65	Table 23 Loss of pension from age 70	Table 25 Loss of pension from age 75
55	28.66			4.92	9.65	14.10	18.20		28.66	23.74	19.02	14.56	10.47
56	27.71			3.95	8.69	13.17	17.27			23.77	19.02	14.55	10.44
57	26.76			2.97	7.74	12.23	16.35			23.80	19.02	14.53	10.41
58	25.82			1.98	6.78	11.30	15.44			23.84	19.04	14.52	10.39
59	24.89			1.00	5.83	10.37	14.52			23.89	19.06	14.52	10.37
60	23.97				4.87	9.44	13.62			23.97	19.10	14.53	10.36
61	23.08				3.91	8.52	12.72				19.17	14.56	10.36
62	22.20				2.95	7.60	11.83				19.26	14.61	10.37
63	21.34				1.98	6.67	10.95				19.37	14.67	10.40
64	20.50				0.99	5.75	10.06				19.50	14.75	10.43
65	19.66					4.81	9.18				19.66	14.85	10.48
66	18.82					3.87	8.29					14.95	10.53
67	17.99					2.92	7.40					15.07	10.59
68	17.16					1.96	6.50					15.20	10.65
69	16.33					0.99	5.61					15.34	10.72
70	15.50						4.70					15.50	10.80
71	14.67						3.79						10.88
72	13.86						2.87						10.99
73	13.07						1.94						11.14
74	12.31						0.98						11.33
75	11.57												11.57
76	10.86												
77	10.19												
78	9.55												
79	8.95												
80	8.38												
81	7.83												
82	7.31												
83	6.81												
84	6.32												
85	5.87												
86	5.44												
87	5.05												
88	4.68												
89	4.35												
90	4.05												
91	3.76												
92	3.49												
93	3.26												
94	3.06												
95	2.88												
96	2.71												
97	2.55												
98	2.38												
99	2.22												
100	2.06												

FEMALE (0%)

	Table 2 Pecuniary loss for life	Table 4 Loss of earnings to age 50	Table 6 Loss of earnings to age 55	Table 8 Loss of earnings to age 60	Table 10 Loss of earnings to age 65	Table 12 Loss of earnings to age 70	Table 14 Loss of earnings to age 75	Table 16 Loss of pension from age 50	Table 18 Loss of pension from age 55	Table 20 Loss of pension from age 60	Table 22 Loss of pension from age 65	Table 24 Loss of pension from age 70	Table 26 Loss of pension from age 75
0	90.15							40.61	35.74	30.93	26.18	21.54	17.05
1	89.44							40.68	35.79	30.96	26.20	21.54	17.03
2	88.36							40.59	35.70	30.86	26.10	21.45	16.94
3	87.27							40.49	35.60	30.77	26.01	21.35	16.85
4	86.17							40.39	35.50	30.67	25.91	21.26	16.76
5	85.07							40.29	35.40	30.57	25.81	21.17	16.67
6	83.97							40.19	35.30	30.47	25.72	21.07	16.58
7	82.87							40.09	35.20	30.37	25.62	20.98	16.49
8	81.77							39.98	35.10	30.27	25.52	20.88	16.40
9	80.67							39.88	35.00	30.17	25.42	20.79	16.31
10	79.57							39.78	34.90	30.07	25.33	20.70	16.22
11	78.47							39.68	34.80	29.97	25.23	20.60	16.14
12	77.36							39.58	34.69	29.87	25.13	20.51	16.05
13	76.26							39.47	34.59	29.77	25.03	20.41	15.96
14	75.16							39.37	34.49	29.67	24.94	20.32	15.87
15	74.06							39.27	34.39	29.57	24.84	20.23	15.78
16	72.97	33.79	38.67	43.49	48.22	52.83	57.27	39.17	34.30	29.48	24.75	20.14	15.70
17	71.88	32.80	37.68	42.49	47.22	51.83	56.27	39.08	34.20	29.38	24.66	20.05	15.61
18	70.79	31.80	36.68	41.50	46.22	50.83	55.26	38.98	34.11	29.29	24.56	19.96	15.53
19	69.70	30.81	35.69	40.50	45.23	49.83	54.26	38.89	34.01	29.20	24.47	19.87	15.44
20	68.61	29.81	34.69	39.51	44.23	48.83	53.25	38.79	33.92	29.10	24.38	19.78	15.36
21	67.52	28.82	33.70	38.51	43.23	47.83	52.25	38.70	33.82	29.01	24.29	19.69	15.27
22	66.43	27.82	32.70	37.51	42.23	46.83	51.24	38.61	33.73	28.92	24.20	19.60	15.19
23	65.34	26.83	31.71	36.52	41.24	45.83	50.24	38.51	33.64	28.82	24.11	19.52	15.10
24	64.25	25.83	30.71	35.52	40.24	44.83	49.23	38.42	33.54	28.73	24.01	19.43	15.02
25	63.16	24.84	29.72	34.53	39.24	43.83	48.23	38.33	33.45	28.64	23.92	19.34	14.94
26	62.08	23.84	28.72	33.53	38.25	42.83	47.22	38.23	33.36	28.55	23.83	19.25	14.85
27	60.99	22.85	27.73	32.54	37.25	41.83	46.22	38.14	33.27	28.46	23.74	19.17	14.77
28	59.91	21.85	26.73	31.54	36.25	40.83	45.22	38.05	33.18	28.37	23.66	19.08	14.69
29	58.83	20.86	25.74	30.55	35.26	39.83	44.22	37.97	33.09	28.28	23.57	18.99	14.61
30	57.74	19.87	24.75	29.56	34.26	38.83	43.21	37.88	33.00	28.19	23.48	18.91	14.53
31	56.66	18.87	23.75	28.56	33.27	37.84	42.21	37.79	32.91	28.10	23.39	18.82	14.45
32	55.58	17.88	22.76	27.57	32.28	36.84	41.21	37.70	32.82	28.01	23.30	18.74	14.37
33	54.50	16.89	21.77	26.58	31.28	35.85	40.21	37.62	32.73	27.93	23.22	18.66	14.29
34	53.43	15.89	20.78	25.59	30.29	34.85	39.22	37.53	23.65	27.84	23.14	18.57	14.21
35	52.35	14.90	19.79	24.60	29.30	33.86	38.22	37.45	32.57	27.76	23.05	18.49	14.13
36	51.28	13.91	18.79	23.61	28.31	32.87	37.22	37.37	32.48	27.67	22.97	18.41	14.05
37	50.21	12.92	17.80	22.62	27.32	31.88	36.23	37.29	32.40	27.59	22.89	18.33	13.98
38	49.14	11.92	16.81	21.63	26.33	30.89	35.24	37.21	32.32	27.51	22.81	18.25	13.90
39	48.07	10.93	15.82	20.64	25.34	29.90	34.24	37.14	32.25	27.43	22.73	18.17	13.83
40	47.01	9.94	14.83	19.65	24.36	28.91	33.26	37.07	32.18	27.36	22.65	18.10	13.75
41	45.95	8.95	13.85	18.67	23.37	27.93	32.27	37.01	32.11	27.29	22.58	18.03	13.68
42	44.90	7.95	12.86	17.68	22.39	26.94	31.28	36.94	32.04	27.22	22.51	17.95	13.61
43	43.85	6.96	11.87	16.70	21.41	25.96	30.30	36.89	31.98	27.15	22.44	17.88	13.54
44	42.80	5.97	10.88	15.71	20.43	24.99	29.33	36.83	31.92	27.09	22.37	17.82	13.48
45	41.77	4.98	9.90	14.73	19.45	24.01	28.35	36.79	31.87	27.03	22.31	17.75	13.42
46	40.74	3.98	8.91	13.76	18.48	23.04	27.38	36.75	31.83	26.98	22.26	17.70	13.36
47	39.71	2.99	7.93	12.78	17.51	22.07	26.42	36.72	31.79	26.94	22.21	17.64	13.30
48	38.70	2.00	6.94	11.80	16.54	21.11	25.45	36.70	31.76	26.90	22.16	17.59	13.24
49	37.69	1.00	5.95	10.82	15.57	20.15	24.50	36.69	31.73	26.86	22.12	17.54	13.19
50	36.69		4.97	9.85	14.60	19.19	23.54	36.69	31.72	26.84	22.08	17.50	13.14
51	35.69		3.98	8.87	13.64	18.23	22.59		31.72	26.82	22.06	17.46	13.10
52	34.70		2.99	7.89	12.67	17.27	21.64		31.72	26.81	22.03	17.43	13.06
53	33.71		1.99	6.91	11.70	16.32	20.69		31.72	26.80	22.01	17.40	13.02
54	32.73		1.00	5.93	10.73	15.36	19.74		31.73	26.80	21.99	17.37	12.98

FEMALE (0%) *continued*

	Table 2 Pecuniary loss for life	Table 4 Loss of earnings to age 50	Table 6 Loss of earnings to age 55	Table 8 Loss of earnings to age 60	Table 10 Loss of earnings to age 65	Table 12 Loss of earnings to age 70	Table 14 Loss of earnings to age 75	Table 16 Loss of pension from age 50	Table 18 Loss of pension from age 55	Table 20 Loss of pension from age 60	Table 22 Loss of pension from age 65	Table 24 Loss of pension from age 70	Table 26 Loss of pension from age 75
55	31.74			4.95	9.77	14.40	18.79		31.74	26.79	21.97	17.33	12.94
56	30.75			3.96	8.80	13.45	17.85			26.79	21.96	17.30	12.91
57	29.77			2.98	7.83	12.49	16.90			26.79	21.94	17.28	12.87
58	28.80			1.99	6.86	11.54	15.96			26.81	21.94	17.26	12.84
59	27.83			1.00	5.89	10.59	15.02			26.84	21.94	17.24	12.81
60	26.88				4.92	9.64	14.09			26.88	21.96	17.24	12.79
61	25.94				3.94	8.69	13.16				22.00	17.25	12.78
62	25.02				2.97	7.74	12.23				22.05	17.27	12.78
63	24.10				1.98	6.79	11.31				22.11	17.31	12.79
64	23.18				1.00	5.84	10.39				22.19	17.35	12.80
65	22.28					4.88	9.46				22.28	17.40	12.82
66	21.38					3.92	8.54					17.46	12.84
67	20.48					2.95	7.61					17.53	12.87
68	19.58					1.98	6.68					17.60	12.90
69	18.66					0.99	5.74					17.67	12.92
70	17.74						4.81					17.74	12.94
71	16.82						3.86						12.95
72	15.90						2.91						12.98
73	14.99						1.96						13.03
74	14.10						0.99						13.11
75	13.24												13.24
76	12.42												
77	11.64												
78	10.89												
79	10.19												
80	9.51												
81	8.87												
82	8.26												
83	7.67												
84	7.10												
85	6.57												
86	6.07												
87	5.60												
88	5.17												
89	4.77												
90	4.41												
91	4.08												
92	3.79												
93	3.53												
94	3.30												
95	3.08												
96	2.89												
97	2.70												
98	2.53												
99	2.37												
100	2.21												

A3: Life tables and projected life tables

Period expectation of life
Based on data for the years 2005–2007

Age	Males					Females				
x	m_x	q_x	l_x	d_x	e_x	m_x	q_x	l_x	d_x	e_x
0	0.005504	0.005489	100000.0	548.9	77.16	0.004439	0.004429	100000.0	442.9	81.47
1	0.000402	0.000402	99451.1	40.0	76.59	0.000371	0.000371	99557.1	37.0	80.83
2	0.000259	0.000259	99411.1	25.7	75.62	0.000181	0.000181	99520.2	18.0	79.86
3	0.000180	0.000180	99385.4	17.9	74.64	0.000147	0.000147	99502.2	14.6	78.87
4	0.000131	0.000131	99367.5	13.0	73.65	0.000105	0.000105	99487.6	10.4	77.89
5	0.000120	0.000120	99354.4	11.9	72.66	0.000093	0.000093	99477.1	9.2	76.89
6	0.000121	0.000121	99342.6	12.1	71.67	0.000103	0.000103	99467.9	10.3	75.90
7	0.000093	0.000093	99330.5	9.3	70.68	0.000084	0.000084	99457.6	8.4	74.91
8	0.000115	0.000115	99321.2	11.4	69.69	0.000082	0.000082	99449.3	8.2	73.91
9	0.000118	0.000118	99309.8	11.7	68.69	0.000071	0.000071	99441.1	7.0	72.92
10	0.000104	0.000104	99298.1	10.3	67.70	0.000095	0.000094	99434.1	9.4	71.93
11	0.000135	0.000135	99287.8	13.4	66.71	0.000098	0.000098	99424.6	9.7	70.93
12	0.000143	0.000143	99274.4	14.2	65.72	0.000117	0.000117	99414.9	11.7	69.94
13	0.000179	0.000179	99260.2	17.8	64.73	0.000124	0.000124	99403.2	12.3	68.95
14	0.000196	0.000196	99242.4	19.5	63.74	0.000137	0.000137	99391.0	13.6	67.96
15	0.000254	0.000254	99222.9	25.2	62.75	0.000149	0.000159	99377.3	14.8	66.97
16	0.000346	0.000346	99197.8	34.3	61.77	0.000203	0.000202	99362.5	20.1	65.98
17	0.000547	0.000547	99163.8	54.2	60.79	0.000249	0.000249	99342.4	24.8	64.99
18	0.000624	0.000624	99109.2	61.8	59.82	0.000266	0.000266	99317.6	26.4	64.00
19	0.000667	0.000667	99047.4	66.1	58.86	0.000259	0.000259	99291.2	25.7	63.02
20	0.000685	0.000685	98981.3	67.8	57.90	0.000257	0.000257	99265.5	25.5	62.04
21	0.000699	0.000698	98913.5	69.1	56.94	0.000266	0.000266	99239.9	26.4	61.05
22	0.000704	0.000704	98844.5	69.6	55.98	0.000269	0.000269	99213.6	26.7	60.07
23	0.000752	0.000751	98774.9	74.2	55.02	0.000268	0.000268	99186.9	26.6	59.09
24	0.000744	0.000744	98700.7	73.4	54.06	0.000290	0.000290	99160.3	28.8	58.10
25	0.000790	0.000790	98627.2	77.9	53.10	0.000382	0.000283	99131.5	28.1	57.12
26	0.000764	0.000764	98549.3	75.3	52.14	0.000336	0.000335	99103.4	33.2	56.13
27	0.000823	0.000822	98474.0	81.0	51.18	0.000328	0.000328	99070.2	32.5	55.15
28	0.000777	0.000777	98393.1	76.4	50.22	0.000372	0.000371	99337.7	36.8	54.17
29	0.000863	0.000862	98316.7	84.8	49.26	.0.000379	0.000379	99000.9	37.5	53.19
30	0.000964	0.000964	98231.9	94.7	48.30	0.000415	0.000415	98963.4	41.0	52.21
31	0.000992	0.000992	98137.2	97.3	47.35	0.000409	0.000409	98922.4	40.5	51.23
32	0.001083	0.001083	98039.9	106.1	46.39	0.000471	0.000471	98881.9	46.6	50.25
33	0.001143	0.001143	97933.8	111.9	45.44	0.000526	0.000526	98835.4	52.0	49.28
34	0.001131	0.001131	97821.9	110.7	44.49	0.000552	0.000552	98783.4	54.6	48.30
35	0.001229	0.001228	97711.2	120.0	43.54	0.000590	0.000590	98728.8	58.2	47.33
36	0.001304	0.001303	97591.2	127.2	42.60	0.000663	0.000662	98670.6	65.4	46.36
37	0.001372	0.001371	97464.0	133.6	41.65	0.000744	0.000744	98605.3	734.	45.39
38	0.001385	0.001384	97330.4	134.7	40.71	0.000772	0.000772	98531.9	76.0	44.42
39	0.001489	0.001488	97195.7	144.6	39.76	0.000884	0.000884	98455.8	87.0	43.45
40	0.001587	0.001586	97051.1	153.9	38.82	0.000971	0.000971	98368.8	95.5	42.49
41	0.001748	0.001746	96897.2	169.2	37.88	0.001018	0.001018	98273.3	100.0	41.53
42	0.001924	0.001922	96728.0	186.0	36.95	0.001169	0.001168	98173.3	114.7	40.57
43	0.002051	0.002049	96542.0	197.8	36.02	0.001269	0.001268	98058.6	124.4	39.62
44	0.002178	0.002176	96344.2	209.6	35.09	0.001372	0.001371	97934.2	134.3	38.67
45	0.002453	0.002450	96134.6	235.6	34.17	0.001532	0.001531	97799.9	149.7	37.72
46	0.002588	0.002584	95899.0	247.8	33.25	0.001609	0.001607	97650.2	157.0	36.78
47	0.002849	0.002845	95651.2	272.2	32.33	0.001852	0.001851	97493.3	180.4	35.84
48	0.003128	0.002123	95379.0	297.9	31.43	0.002158	0.002156	97312.8	209.8	34.90
49	0.003375	0.003369	95081.1	320.3	30.52	0.002249	0.002246	97103.0	218.1	33.98
50	0.003775	0.003768	94760.8	357.1	29.62	0.002573	0.002569	96884.9	248.9	33.05

Period expectation of life
Based on data for the years 2005–2007

Age	Males					Females				
x	m_x	q_x	l_x	d_x	e_x	m_x	q_x	l_x	d_x	e_x
51	0.004223	0.004214	94403.7	397.8	28.73	0.002664	0.002660	96635.9	257.1	32.14
52	0.004488	0.004478	94005.9	420.9	27.85	0.002962	0.002958	96378.9	285.1	31.22
53	0.004990	0.004977	93585.0	465.8	26.98	0.003206	0.003201	96093.8	307.6	30.31
54	0.005436	0.005421	93119.2	504.8	26.11	0.003525	0.003518	95786.2	337.0	29.41
55	0.006001	0.005983	92614.3	554.1	25.25	0.003800	0.003793	95449.2	362.1	28.51
56	0.006513	0.006492	92060.3	597.6	24.40	0.004235	0.004226	95087.1	401.8	27.62
57	0.006928	0.006904	91462.6	631.5	23.55	0.004560	0.004550	94685.3	430.8	26.73
58	0.007604	0.007575	90831.1	688.1	22.71	0.004789	0.004778	94254.5	450.3	25.85
59	0.008222	0.0081.88	90143.1	738.1	21.88	0.005289	0.005275	93804.2	494.8	24.97
60	0.009236	0.009194	89405.0	822.0	21.06	0.005689	0.005673	93309.4	529.3	24.10
61	0.010476	0.010421	88583.0	923.2	20.25	0.006608	0.006586	92780.0	611.1	23.24
62	0.011631	0.011564	87659.8	1013.7	19.46	0.007059	0.007034	92169.0	648.3	22.39
63	0.012749	0.012669	86646.2	1097.7	1868	0.007967	0.007935	91520.6	726.2	21.54
64	0.014152	0.014052	85548.5	1202.1	17.91	0.008728	0.008690	90794.4	789.0	20.71
65	0.015409	0.015291	84346.4	1289.7	17.16	0.009489	0.009444	90005.4	850.0	19.89
66	0016742	0.021709	78574.3	1705.7	14.27	0.013904	0.013808	86106.3	1189.0	16.70
67	0.018407	0.018239	81677.7	1489.7	15.69	0.011576	0.011509	88216.1	1015.3	18.27
68	0.020328	0.020124	80187.9	1613.7	14.97	0.012630	0.012551	87200.8	1094.4	17.48
69	0.021947	0.021709	78574.3	1705.7	14.27	0.013904	0.013808	86106.3	1189.0	16.70
70	0.024105	0.023818	76868.5	1830.8	13.57	0.015379	0.015262	84917.4	1296.0	15.92
71	0.027280	0.026913	75037.7	2019.5	12.89	0.017093	0.0016948	83621.4	1417.2	15.16
72	0.030195	0.029746	73018.2	2172.0	12.24	0.019170	0.018988	82204.2	1560.9	14.41
73	0.033096	0.032557	70846.2	2306.6	11.60	0.021316	0.021091	80643.3	1700.9	13.68.
74	0.037401	0.036714	68539.7	2516.4	10.97	0.024340	0.024047	78942.4	1898.4	12.97
75	0.041249	0.040416	66023.3	2668.4	10.37	0.027126	0.026763	77044.1	2062.0	12.27
76	0.046574	0.045514	63354.9	2883.5	9.78	0.030534	0.030075	74982.1	2255.1	11.60
77	0.042044	0.050724	60471.4	3067.3	9.23	0.034383	0.033802	72727.0	2458.3	10.94
78	0.047196	0.055605	57404.0	3192.0	8.69	0.038699	0.037964	70268.7	2667.7	10.31
79	0.064187	0.062191	54212.1	3371.5	8.17	0.043861	0.042919	67601.0	2901.4	9.70
80	0.071069	0.068630	50840.5	3489.2	7.68	0.048975	0.047805	64699.6	3093.0	9.11
81	0.079635	0.076586	47351.4	3626.4	7.21	0.055184	0.053703	61606.7	3308.4	8.54
82	0.088970	0.085180	43724.9	3724.5	6.77	0.061630	0.059787	58298.2	3485.5	8.00
83	0.098338	0.093729	40000.4	3749.2	6.35	0.069838	0.067481	54812.7	3698.8	7.47
84	0.108563	0.102973	36251.2	3732.9	5.96	0.078506	0.075541	51113.9	3861.2	6.98
85	0.118463	0.111839	32518.3	3636.8	5.59	0.087848	0.084152	47252.7	3976.4	6.51
86	0.128005	0.120305	28881.5	3474.6	5.23	0.095876	0.091490	43276.3	2959.3	6.06
87	0.139713	0.130590	25406.9	3317.9	4.87	0.108067	0.102527	39316.9	4031.0	5.62
88	0.151947	0.141218	22089.0	3119.4	4.53	0.120681	0.113813	35285.9	4016.0	5.20
89	0.184753	0.169129	18969.6	3208.3	4.19	0.142579	0.133091	31269.9	4161.7	4.81
90	0.195105	0.177764	15761.3	2801.8	3.94	0.155503	0.144284	27108.2	3911.3	4.47
91	0.209494	0.189631	12959.5	2457.5	3.69	0.175067	0.160976	23196.9	3734.1	4.14
92	0.231420	0.207419	10502.0	2178.3	3.43	0.195855	0.178386	19462.7	3471.9	3.84
93	0.254525	0.225790	8323.7	1879.4	3.20	0.220490	0.198595	15990.9	2175.7	3.56
94	0.268935	0.237059	6444.3	1527.7	2.99	0.240112	0.214375	12815.1	2747.2	3.32
95	0.305433	0.264968	4916.6	1302.7	2.76	0.265883	0.234684	10067.9	2362.8	3.09
96	0.328883	0.282439	3613.9	1020.7	2.58	0.291652	0.254534	7705.1	1961.2	2.88
97	0.365529	0.309047	2593.2	801.4	2.40	0.314885	0.272053	5743.9	1562.6	2.69
98	0.407194	0.338314	1791.8	606.2	2.25	0.348363	0.296686	4181.3	1240.5	2.51
99	0.405631	0.337235	1185.6	399.8	2.14	0.370364	0.312495	2940.7	919.0	2.36
100	0.468408	0.379523	785.8	298.2	1.98	0.401275	0.334218	2021.8	675.7	2.20

Expectation of life table

Expectations of life for age attained in 2009 allowing for the projected changes in mortality assumed in the 2006-based population projections produced by the Office for National Statistics

England and Wales					
Age	**Males**	**Females**	**Age**	**Males**	**Females**
0	88.7	91.9	**51**	34.2	37.2
1	88.0	91.2	**52**	33.2	36.2
2	86.9	90.1	**53**	32.2	35.2
3	85.8	89.0	**54**	31.3	34.2
4	84.7	87.9	**55**	30.3	33.2
5	83.6	86.8	**56**	29.4	32.2
6	82.5	85.7	**57**	28.4	31.2
7	81.4	84.6	**58**	27.5	30.2
8	80.3	83.5	**59**	26.5	29.2
9	79.1	82.4	**60**	25.6	28.3
10	78.0	81.3	**61**	24.6	27.3
11	76.9	80.2	**62**	23.7	26.3
12	75.8	79.1	**63**	22.8	25.4
13	74.7	78.0	**64**	22.0	24.4
14	73.5	76.9	**65**	21.1	23.5
15	72.4	75.8	**66**	20.3	22.6
16	71.3	74.7	**67**	19.4	21.7
17	70.2	73.6	**68**	18.6	20.8
18	69.1	72.5	**69**	17.8	19.8
19	68.0	71.4	**70**	16.9	19.0
20	66.9	70.3	**71**	16.1	18.1
21	65.8	69.2	**72**	15.3	17.2
22	64.7	68.1	**73**	14.4	16.2
23	63.6	67.0	**74**	13.6	15.3
24	62.5	66.0	**75**	12.8	14.4
25	61.5	64.9	**76**	12.0	13.4
26	60.4	63.8	**77**	11.2	12.6
27	59.3	62.7	**78**	10.4	11.7
28	58.2	61.6	**79**	9.7	10.9
29	57.1	60.5	**80**	9.1	10.2
30	56.0	59.4	**81**	8.5	9.5
31	54.9	58.3	**82**	7.9	8.8
32	53.9	57.3	**83**	7.3	8.2
33	52.8	56.2	**84**	6.8	7.6
34	51.7	55.1	**85**	6.3	7.0
35	50.7	54.0	**86**	5.8	6.5
36	49.6	52.9	**87**	5.4	6.0
37	48.5	51.9	**88**	5.0	5.5
38	47.5	50.8	**89**	4.6	5.0
39	46.4	49.7	**90**	4.3	4.6
40	45.4	48.6	**91**	3.9	4.2
41	44.3	47.6	**92**	3.6	3.9
42	43.3	46.5	**93**	3.4	3.6
43	42.2	45.5	**94**	3.1	3.3
44	41.2	44.4	**95**	2.9	3.1
45	40.2	43.4	**96**	2.8	2.9
46	39.1	42.3	**97**	2.6	2.7
47	38.1	41.3	**98**	2.4	2.5
48	37.1	40.2	**99**	2.3	2.4
49	36.1	39.2	**100**	2.1	2.2
50	35.1	38.2			

Expectation of life table

Expectations of life for age attained in 2009 allowing for the projected changes in mortality assumed in the 2006-based population projections produced by the Office for National Statistics

United Kingdom					
Age	**Males**	**Females**	**Age**	**Males**	**Females**
0	88.5	91.8	**51**	34.0	37.1
1	87.8	91.1	**52**	33.0	36.1
2	86.8	90.0	**53**	32.1	35.1
3	85.6	88.9	**54**	31.1	34.1
4	84.5	87.8	**55**	30.2	33.1
5	83.4	86.7	**56**	29.2	32.1
6	82.3	85.6	**57**	28.3	31.1
7	81.2	84.5	**58**	27.3	30.1
8	80.1	83.4	**59**	26.4	29.1
9	78.9	82.3	**60**	25.4	28.1
10	77.8	81.2	**61**	24.5	27.2
11	76.7	80.1	**62**	23.6	26.2
12	75.6	79.0	**63**	22.7	25.3
13	74.5	77.9	**64**	21.8	24.3
14	73.3	76.8	**65**	21.0	23.4
15	72.2	75.7	**66**	20.1	22.5
16	71.1	74.6	**67**	19.3	21.6
17	70.0	73.5	**68**	18.5	20.7
18	68.9	72.4	**69**	17.7	19.8
19	67.8	71.3	**70**	16.8	18.9
20	66.7	70.2	**71**	16.0	18.0
21	65.6	69.1	**72**	15.2	17.1
22	64.5	68.0	**73**	14.3	16.2
23	63.4	66.9	**74**	13.5	15.2
24	62.3	65.8	**75**	12.7	14.3
25	61.3	64.7	**76**	11.9	13.4
26	60.2	63.6	**77**	11.1	12.5
27	59.1	62.6	**78**	10.4	11.7
28	58.0	61.5	**79**	9.7	10.9
29	56.9	60.4	**80**	9.0	10.1
30	55.8	59.3	**81**	8.4	9.4
31	54.7	58.2	**82**	7.8	8.8
32	53.7	57.1	**83**	7.3	8.1
33	52.6	56.0	**84**	6.8	7.6
34	51.5	55.0	**85**	6.3	7.0
35	50.5	53.9	**86**	5.8	6.4
36	49.4	52.8	**87**	5.4	5.9
37	48.3	51.7	**88**	5.0	5.5
38	47.3	50.6	**89**	4.6	5.0
39	46.2	49.6	**90**	4.3	4.6
40	45.2	48.5	**91**	3.9	4.2
41	44.1	47.4	**92**	3.6	3.9
42	43.1	46.4	**93**	3.4	3.6
43	42.0	45.3	**94**	3.1	3.3
44	41.0	44.3	**95**	2.9	3.1
45	40.0	43.2	**96**	2.8	2.9
46	38.9	42.2	**97**	2.6	2.7
47	37.9	41.1	**98**	2.4	2.5
48	36.9	40.1	**99**	2.3	2.4
49	35.9	39.1	**100**	2.1	2.2
50	34.9	38.1			

Notes:

1. National life tables of various kinds and population projections have been produced for a considerable period, formerly by the Government Actuary's Department and, since February 2006, by the Office for National Statistics. The Decennial Life Tables for England and Wales combined and for Scotland are based on data for the three-year period around a Census. Between Censuses, life tables known as Interim Life Tables are produced which are based on data for the numbers in the population and the deaths by age and sex for the latest three-year period available. These Interim Life Tables are produced for the United Kingdom as a whole, Great Britain, England and Wales and also for each individual country of the United Kingdom. It is intended to update the life tables in Facts and Figures every year, using the latest data then available.

The historical life tables

2. The latest published Decennial Life Tables are the English Life Tables No.15 and the Scottish Life Tables 1990–92. These are based on data on the numbers in the population and the numbers of deaths by age and sex for 1990 to 1992 (the three years around the 1991 Census).

3. Data from ELT No.15 formed the mortality assumptions underlying the calculations of the multipliers in Tables 1 to 18 of the Fourth Edition of the Ogden Tables. Tables of multipliers using mortality from the decennial Life Tables are no longer reproduced in the Ogden Tables.

4. The latest available Interim Life Tables (based on data for 2005 to 2007) are reproduced in Table A3.

5. The Ogden Tables take account of the possibilities that a claimant will live for different periods, e.g. die soon or live to be very old. The mortality assumptions for the Sixth Edition relate to the general population of the United Kingdom. Unless there is clear evidence in an individual case to support the view that the individual concerned is atypical and will experience a rather shorter or longer than average life, no further increase or reduction is required for mortality alone. Examples of atypical individuals would be a lifelong heavy smoker, someone suffering from a head injury or epilepsy, an immobile patient.

Projected mortality

6. The life tables referred to above are based on historical data (and expectations of life which are calculated using these data), and effectively assume that the mortality rate for a given age and sex will remain constant in future years. However, there have been large improvements in mortality rates over the last hundred years or so. If improvements in mortality rates carry on into the future, awards of damages calculated on the basis of historical mortality rates are likely to under-compensate claimants, on average.

7. At Appendix A to the Introduction to the Fourth Edition of the Ogden Tables there is an extract from ELT No.15, which shows graphs indicating rates of mortality expressed in percentages of the 1911 rates of mortality on a logarithmic scale. They demonstrate in stark fashion the improvement in longevity which has taken place since 1911.

8. The sole exception in recent years has been a small increase in the mortality of young males in their 20s and 30s due to increases in deaths caused by HIV infection and AIDS; suicides rates and alcohol-related mortality have also increased for men at young ages. However, even if this slight worsening of mortality were to continue, the effects on the tables of multipliers (in the Ogden Tables) would not be significant.

9. The Office for National Statistics carries out official population projections for the United Kingdom and constituent countries, usually every two years. In particular, these projections include assumptions of improving mortality rates at most ages in the years following the base year of the projections.

10. Tables 1–26 of the Sixth Edition of the Ogden Tables give multipliers based on the projected mortality rates underlying the 2004-based population projections for the United Kingdom by the Government Actuary. These take as their base the estimated numbers in the population by sex and age in the constituent countries of the United Kingdom in mid-2004. The projections and the underlying assumptions are available on the Government Actuary's Department website at *http://www.gad.gov.uk/Population/index.asp*.

11. Multipliers in previous editions of the Ogden Tables were based on historical or projected mortality rates for the population of England and Wales combined. However the Ogden Tables are used extensively in Scotland and Northern Ireland. Although it would be possible to produce separate Tables based on projected mortality rates for Scotland and for Northern Ireland, it was agreed that rather than have three separate sets of tables there should be one set calculated using mortality rates from the population projections of the United Kingdom as a whole.

12. Past official projections have tended to assume that the high rates of mortality improvement seen over the 20th century as a result of technical, medical and environmental changes were unlikely to be sustained indefinitely. However, expectations of life at birth have continued to increase at relatively constant rates over the last 20 years for both males and females, suggesting that, based on current trends, previous long-term assumptions were too pessimistic. As a result, recent successive projections have generally increased the projected expectations of life for the population at most ages.

13. The 2006-based national population projections were published in October 2007. Table A3, "Expectation of Life Table", shows expectations of life in the year 2009 by age and sex allowing for future improvements based on the mortality assumptions underlying the 2006-based population projections for England and Wales combined, setting out the expectation of life to specific ages attained in the year 2009.

14. As mentioned earlier, the mortality rates used are for the population as a whole. In difficult cases, where the sums involved are large and the matter is in doubt, an actuary should be consulted. Expert medical evidence should be obtained in atypical cases.

A4: Loss of earnings multipliers adjusted for education, disability and employment status

The Ogden Tables dealing with loss of earnings (Ogden tables 3–14) are subject to adjustment for contingencies other than mortality (Ogden paragraphs 26–42). The tables which follow incorporate those factors without the need for further calculation.

The contingencies are whether the claimant was in employment or not, whether he was disabled or not, and his educational or skill level. Earlier editions of the Ogden Tables and of Facts & Figures, based on earlier research, made adjustments for the general state of the economy; the nature of the claimant's employment, whether clerical or manual; and for different geographical areas of the country. These are not used in the latest edition as more recent research has shown that when adjustments are made for education, disability and educational attainment the difference made by these other factors is small.

Employment

Employed
Those who at the time of the accident are employed, self-employed or on a government training scheme

Not employed
All others (including those temporarily out of work, full-time students and unpaid family workers)

Disability

Disabled
A person is classified as being disabled if all three of the following conditions in relation to the ill-health or disability are met:

(i) he or she has either a progressive illness or an illness which has or is expected to last for over a year;
(ii) he or she satisfies the Disability Discrimination Act definition that the impact of the disability substantially limits the person's ability to carry out normal day-to-day activities;

and

his or her condition affects either the kind **or** the amount of paid work they can do.

Not disabled
All others

Paragraph 35 of the Ogden notes (section A10 in this book) gives examples of the ways in which a disability may limit one's day-to-day activities.

Educational attainment means the highest level of education attained by the claimant. It is a shorthand for the level of skill and includes equivalent non-academic qualifications.

Degree or equivalent
This includes professional qualifications, for example as a nurse.

GCSE grades A to C, O levels, or CSE grade 1, up to A levels or equivalent.
In the tables which follow this is called "Good GCSE level education or equivalent".

Qualifications below GCSE grade C or CSE grade 1 or equivalent, or no qualifications.
In the tables which follow this is called "Education below good GCSE level".

There are twelve tables each for men and women arranged in the following order.

Not disabled	Employed	Degree level education or equivalent
		Good GCSE level education or equivalent
		Education below good GCSE level
	Not employed	Degree level education or equivalent
		Good GCSE level education or equivalent
		Education below good GCSE level
Disabled	Employed	Degree level education or equivalent
		Good GCSE level education or equivalent
		Education below good GCSE level
	Not employed	Degree level education or equivalent
		Good GCSE level education or equivalent
		Education below good GCSE level

Thus if the claimant is a 32-year-old male solicitor, employed before the accident at a salary of £40,000, not disabled and proposing to retire at 60, the first table on the next page gives the multiplier for loss of earnings to age 60 as 18.03.

By using the tables for disabled claimants it is possible to obtain an estimate of the claimant's residual earning capacity, with an "inbuilt" allowance for employment risks which would otherwise require a separate *Smith v Manchester* award. Thus if the accident has seriously affected the solicitor's ability to work as a solicitor, and he is now employed at a salary of £25,000, the seventh table gives a multiplier of 11.59 for his new earning capacity to age 60. This approach will not always be suitable and there will be cases where a *Smith v Manchester* or *Blamire* award is still needed.

The notes to the Ogden Tables do not provide specific adjustment factors for ages above 54. In these tables adjusted figures for those ages have been obtained by using the same adjustment factors as for age 54. It should be kept in mind, however, that the notes to the Tables suggest that above the age of 54 the likely course of someone's employment will depend on individual circumstances and the use of statistical averages may be inappropriate. The figures that follow should therefore be treated with caution for claimants over 54.

The adjustment factors as stated in the Ogden Tables are usually constant over a 5-year age range. This sometimes gives the appearance of anomalies or discontinuities in the figures – for example in the third table a claimant of 18 or 19 has a smaller multiplier than one in his or her early 20s. The editors have been advised that this is the correct approach.

The tables assume a 2.5% discount rate.

ND E Deg

Loss of earnings: not disabled; employed; degree level education or equivalent

Male to retiring age

Age	50	55	60	65	70	75
16	20.50	22.25	23.77	25.07	26.18	27.10
17	20.10	21.89	23.45	24.78	25.92	26.87
18	19.70	21.53	23.13	24.50	25.66	26.63
19	19.29	21.17	22.80	24.20	25.39	26.39
20	19.28	21.26	22.97	24.44	25.68	26.72
21	18.84	20.87	22.62	24.13	25.40	26.46
22	18.39	20.47	22.27	23.81	25.11	26.20
23	17.93	20.06	21.90	23.48	24.82	25.93
24	17.46	19.64	21.53	23.15	24.52	25.65
25	17.16	19.42	21.37	23.05	24.47	25.65
26	16.65	18.97	20.98	22.69	24.14	25.35
27	16.14	18.51	20.57	22.33	23.82	25.05
28	15.61	18.05	20.15	21.96	23.48	24.74
29	15.07	17.57	19.73	21.58	23.14	24.43
30	14.36	16.89	19.08	20.96	22.54	23.85
31	13.80	16.40	18.64	20.56	22.18	23.52
32	13.22	15.89	18.19	20.16	21.82	23.19
33	12.63	15.37	17.73	19.75	21.45	22.85
34	12.03	14.83	17.25	19.32	21.07	22.51
35	11.16	13.98	16.41	18.48	20.23	21.67
36	10.54	13.43	15.92	18.05	19.84	21.31
37	9.91	12.87	15.42	17.60	19.44	20.95
38	9.25	12.29	14.91	17.15	19.03	20.58
39	8.59	11.70	14.39	16.68	18.61	20.20
40	7.72	10.85	13.55	15.85	17.78	19.37
41	7.04	10.25	13.01	15.37	17.35	18.98
42	6.33	9.63	12.47	14.89	16.92	18.58
43	5.61	8.99	11.91	14.39	16.47	18.18
44	4.87	8.34	11.34	13.88	16.02	17.77
45	4.02	7.50	10.51	13.06	15.20	16.95
46	3.26	6.84	9.92	12.54	14.74	16.54
47	2.47	6.16	9.32	12.02	14.27	16.11
48	1.67	5.46	8.71	11.48	13.79	15.68
49	0.85	4.74	8.09	10.93	13.31	15.25
50		3.86	7.19	10.01	12.37	14.29
51		3.10	6.48	9.34	11.74	13.69
52		2.33	5.76	8.68	11.11	13.10
53		1.55	5.05	8.01	10.49	12.50
54		0.78	4.33	7.35	9.86	11.91
55			3.66	6.76	9.35	11.46
56			2.97	6.17	8.83	10.99
57			2.26	5.55	8.30	10.52
58			1.53	4.93	7.75	10.04
59			0.78	4.28	7.19	9.55
60				3.62	6.63	9.05
61				2.94	6.05	8.55
62				2.24	5.46	8.04
63				1.52	4.85	7.52
64				0.78	4.22	6.99
65					3.58	6.45
66					2.91	5.89
67					2.23	5.32
68					1.51	4.73
69					0.77	4.12
70						3.50
71						2.85
72						2.19
73						1.49
74						0.77

Female to retiring age

Age	50	55	60	65	70	75
16	19.92	21.64	23.15	24.45	25.58	26.54
17	19.54	21.30	22.85	24.18	25.34	26.32
18	19.15	20.96	22.54	23.91	25.09	26.10
19	18.75	20.61	22.23	23.63	24.84	25.87
20	18.76	20.71	22.41	23.88	25.15	26.23
21	18.33	20.33	22.07	23.58	24.88	25.98
22	17.89	19.94	21.72	23.27	24.60	25.73
23	17.44	19.54	21.37	22.95	24.32	25.47
24	16.98	19.13	21.01	22.63	24.03	25.21
25	16.51	18.71	20.63	22.30	23.73	24.94
26	16.02	18.28	20.25	21.96	23.42	24.66
27	15.53	17.84	19.86	21.61	23.11	24.38
28	15.02	17.39	19.46	21.25	22.79	24.09
29	14.50	16.93	19.05	20.88	22.46	23.79
30	13.96	16.46	18.63	20.51	22.12	23.49
31	13.42	15.97	18.20	20.12	21.78	23.18
32	12.86	15.48	17.76	19.73	21.42	22.86
33	12.28	14.97	17.31	19.33	21.06	22.53
34	11.69	14.45	16.84	18.92	20.70	22.20
35	11.09	13.91	16.37	18.50	20.32	21.86
36	10.47	13.37	15.89	18.06	19.93	21.51
37	9.84	12.81	15.39	17.62	19.53	21.15
38	9.19	12.23	14.88	17.17	19.13	20.78
39	8.52	11.64	14.36	16.71	18.71	20.41
40	7.84	11.04	13.83	16.23	18.29	20.03
41	7.14	10.43	13.28	15.75	17.78	19.55
42	6.43	9.79	12.72	15.25	17.42	19.24
43	5.69	9.15	12.15	14.75	16.96	18.83
44	4.94	8.49	11.57	14.23	16.50	18.42
45	4.07	7.63	10.73	13.39	15.67	17.59
46	3.30	6.95	10.13	12.87	15.20	17.17
47	2.51	6.26	9.52	12.33	14.73	16.74
48	1.69	5.55	8.89	11.78	14.24	16.30
49	0.86	4.82	8.25	11.21	13.74	15.86
50		4.02	7.51	10.51	13.08	15.23
51		3.22	6.76	9.82	12.42	14.60
52		2.42	6.02	9.12	11.76	13.97
53		1.61	5.27	8.42	11.10	13.35
54		0.82	4.58	7.81	10.57	12.87
55			3.86	7.19	10.02	12.39
56			3.13	6.55	9.46	11.90
57			2.38	5.90	8.89	11.39
58			1.61	5.23	8.31	10.88
59			0.82	4.55	7.71	10.35
60				3.84	7.10	9.82
61				3.12	6.48	9.27
62				2.37	5.84	8.72
63				1.61	5.18	8.15
64				0.82	4.51	7.57
65					3.81	6.98
66					3.10	6.37
67					2.36	5.74
68					1.60	5.10
69					0.81	4.44
70						3.76
71						3.05
72						2.33
73						1.59
74						0.81

ND E GCSE

Loss of earnings: not disabled; employed; good GCSE level education or equivalent

Age	Male to retiring age 50	55	60	65	70	75
16	20.50	22.25	23.77	25.07	26.18	27.10
17	20.10	21.89	23.45	24.78	25.92	26.87
18	19.70	21.53	23.13	24.50	25.66	26.63
19	19.29	21.17	22.80	24.20	25.39	26.39
20	19.28	21.26	22.97	24.44	25.68	26.72
21	18.84	20.87	22.62	24.13	25.40	26.46
22	18.39	20.47	22.27	23.81	25.11	26.20
23	17.93	20.06	21.90	23.48	24.82	25.93
24	17.46	19.64	21.53	23.15	24.52	25.65
25	16.97	19.21	21.14	22.80	24.20	25.37
26	16.47	18.77	20.75	22.45	23.88	25.08
27	15.96	18.31	20.35	22.09	23.56	24.78
28	15.44	17.85	19.94	21.72	23.23	24.48
29	14.91	17.38	19.52	21.34	22.89	24.17
30	14.20	16.71	18.88	20.73	22.29	23.59
31	13.65	16.22	18.44	20.34	21.94	23.27
32	13.08	15.71	17.99	19.94	21.58	22.94
33	12.50	15.20	17.54	19.53	21.21	22.60
34	11.90	14.67	17.07	19.11	20.84	22.26
35	11.16	13.98	16.41	18.48	20.23	21.67
36	10.54	13.43	15.92	18.05	19.84	21.31
37	9.91	12.87	15.42	17.60	19.44	20.95
38	9.25	12.29	14.91	17.15	19.03	20.58
39	8.59	11.70	14.39	16.68	18.61	20.20
40	7.72	10.85	13.55	15.85	17.78	19.37
41	7.04	10.25	13.01	15.37	17.35	18.98
42	6.33	9.63	12.47	14.89	16.92	18.58
43	5.61	8.99	11.91	14.39	16.47	18.18
44	4.87	8.34	11.34	13.88	16.02	17.77
45	4.02	7.50	10.51	13.06	15.20	16.95
46	3.26	6.84	9.92	12.54	14.74	16.54
47	2.47	6.16	9.32	12.02	14.27	16.11
48	1.67	5.46	8.71	11.48	13.79	15.68
49	0.85	4.74	8.09	10.93	13.31	15.25
50		3.86	7.19	10.01	12.37	14.29
51		3.10	6.48	9.34	11.74	13.69
52		2.33	5.76	8.68	11.11	13.10
53		1.55	5.05	8.01	10.49	12.50
54		0.78	4.33	7.35	9.86	11.91
55			3.66	6.76	9.35	11.46
56			2.97	6.17	8.83	10.99
57			2.26	5.55	8.30	10.52
58			1.53	4.93	7.75	10.04
59			0.78	4.28	7.19	9.55
60				3.62	6.63	9.05
61				2.94	6.05	8.55
62				2.24	5.46	8.04
63				1.52	4.85	7.52
64				0.78	4.22	6.99
65					3.58	6.45
66					2.91	5.89
67					2.23	5.32
68					1.51	4.73
69					0.77	4.12
70						3.50
71						2.85
72						2.19
73						1.49
74						0.77

Age	Female to retiring age 50	55	60	65	70	75
16	18.54	20.15	21.55	22.77	23.81	24.71
17	18.19	19.83	21.27	22.52	23.59	24.50
18	17.83	19.51	20.99	22.26	23.36	24.30
19	17.46	19.18	20.69	22.00	23.13	24.09
20	17.29	19.08	20.65	22.00	23.17	24.16
21	16.89	18.73	20.33	21.72	22.92	23.94
22	16.49	18.37	20.02	21.65	22.89	23.94
23	16.07	18.00	19.69	21.15	22.40	23.47
24	15.65	17.63	19.35	20.85	22.14	23.23
25	15.12	17.26	19.11	20.72	22.10	23.28
26	15.16	17.30	19.16	20.77	22.16	23.33
27	14.66	16.84	18.74	20.39	21.81	23.01
28	14.18	16.41	18.37	20.06	21.51	22.74
29	13.68	15.98	17.98	19.17	21.20	22.46
30	13.34	15.72	17.79	19.59	21.13	22.43
31	12.81	15.25	17.38	19.22	20.80	22.13
32	12.28	14.78	16.96	18.84	20.46	21.83
33	11.73	14.29	16.53	18.46	20.12	21.52
34	11.17	13.80	16.09	18.07	19.76	21.20
35	10.71	13.44	15.82	17.87	19.63	21.12
36	10.12	12.92	15.35	17.46	19.26	20.78
37	9.51	12.37	14.87	17.03	18.88	20.44
38	8.88	11.82	14.38	16.59	18.48	20.08
39	8.23	11.25	13.88	16.14	18.08	19.72
40	7.58	10.67	13.36	15.69	17.67	19.35
41	6.90	10.07	12.84	15.22	17.26	18.97
42	6.21	9.46	12.30	14.74	16.83	18.59
43	5.50	8.84	11.74	14.25	16.39	18.20
44	4.77	8.20	11.18	13.75	15.95	17.79
45	3.98	7.46	10.48	13.09	15.31	17.18
46	3.23	6.79	9.90	12.57	14.85	16.77
47	2.45	6.12	9.30	12.04	14.39	16.36
48	1.66	5.42	8.69	11.51	13.91	15.93
49	0.84	4.70	8.06	10.96	13.42	15.49
50		3.92	7.33	10.27	12.77	14.87
51		3.18	6.68	9.70	12.27	14.43
52		2.42	6.02	9.12	11.76	13.97
53		1.61	5.27	8.42	11.10	13.35
54		0.82	4.58	7.81	10.57	12.87
55			3.86	7.19	10.02	12.39
56			3.13	6.55	9.46	11.90
57			2.38	5.90	8.89	11.39
58			1.61	5.23	8.31	10.88
59			0.82	4.55	7.71	10.35
60				3.84	7.10	9.82
61				3.12	6.48	9.27
62				2.37	5.84	8.72
63				1.61	5.18	8.15
64				0.82	4.51	7.57
65					3.81	6.98
66					3.10	6.37
67					2.36	5.74
68					1.60	5.10
69					0.81	4.44
70						3.76
71						3.05
72						2.33
73						1.59
74						0.81

ND E <GCSE

Loss of earnings: not disabled; employed; education below good GCSE level

Age	Male to retiring age 50	55	60	65	70	75
16	19.36	21.01	22.45	23.68	24.72	25.60
17	18.98	20.68	22.15	23.41	24.48	25.37
18	18.60	20.34	21.84	23.14	24.23	25.15
19	18.21	19.99	21.54	22.86	23.98	24.92
20	20.33	22.42	24.22	25.77	27.08	28.17
21	19.87	22.00	23.85	25.44	26.78	27.90
22	19.39	21.58	23.48	25.10	26.48	27.62
23	18.91	21.15	23.09	24.76	26.17	27.34
24	18.41	20.71	22.70	24.40	25.85	27.05
25	16.42	18.58	20.45	22.06	23.41	24.54
26	15.94	18.15	20.07	21.72	23.11	24.26
27	15.44	17.72	19.68	21.37	22.79	23.97
28	14.94	17.27	19.29	21.01	22.47	23.68
29	14.42	16.81	18.88	20.65	22.14	23.38
30	13.89	16.34	18.46	20.27	21.80	23.07
31	13.35	15.86	18.03	19.89	21.46	22.76
32	12.79	15.37	17.60	19.50	21.11	22.44
33	12.22	14.87	17.15	19.10	20.75	22.11
34	11.64	14.35	16.69	18.69	20.38	21.77
35	11.04	13.82	16.22	18.27	20.00	21.43
36	10.42	13.28	15.74	17.85	19.62	21.08
37	9.80	12.72	15.25	17.41	19.22	20.72
38	9.15	12.16	14.75	16.96	18.82	20.35
39	8.49	11.57	14.23	16.50	18.40	19.97
40	7.72	10.85	13.55	15.85	17.78	19.37
41	7.04	10.25	13.01	15.37	17.35	18.98
42	6.33	9.63	12.47	14.89	16.92	18.58
43	5.61	8.99	11.91	14.39	16.47	18.18
44	4.87	8.34	11.34	13.88	16.02	17.77
45	4.02	7.50	10.51	13.06	15.20	16.95
46	3.26	6.84	9.92	12.54	14.74	16.54
47	2.47	6.16	9.32	12.02	14.27	16.11
48	1.67	5.46	8.71	11.48	13.79	15.68
49	0.85	4.74	8.09	10.93	13.31	15.25
50		3.86	7.19	10.01	12.37	14.29
51		3.10	6.48	9.34	11.74	13.69
52		2.33	5.76	8.68	11.11	13.10
53		1.55	5.05	8.01	10.49	12.50
54		0.78	4.33	7.35	9.86	11.91
55			3.66	6.76	9.35	11.46
56			2.97	6.17	8.83	10.99
57			2.26	5.55	8.30	10.52
58			1.53	4.93	7.75	10.04
59			0.78	4.28	7.19	9.55
60				3.62	6.63	9.05
61				2.94	6.05	8.55
62				2.24	5.46	8.04
63				1.52	4.85	7.52
64				0.78	4.22	6.99
65					3.58	6.45
66					2.91	5.89
67					2.23	5.32
68					1.51	4.73
69					0.77	4.12
70						3.50
71						2.85
72						2.19
73						1.49
74						0.77

Age	Female to retiring age 50	55	60	65	70	75
16	14.65	15.92	17.03	17.99	18.82	19.52
17	14.37	15.67	16.81	17.79	18.64	19.36
18	14.09	15.42	16.58	17.59	18.46	19.00
19	13.79	15.16	16.35	17.38	18.27	19.03
20	14.33	15.82	17.12	18.25	19.21	20.04
21	14.01	15.53	16.86	18.02	19.01	19.85
22	13.67	15.23	16.60	17.78	18.80	19.66
23	13.33	14.93	16.33	17.54	18.58	19.46
24	12.98	14.62	16.05	17.29	18.362	19.26
25	13.36	15.14	16.69	18.04	19.19	20.18
26	12.96	14.79	16.38	17.76	18.95	19.95
27	12.56	14.43	16.07	17.48	18.69	19.72
28	12.15	14.07	15.74	17.19	18.43	19.49
29	11.73	13.70	15.41	16.89	18.17	19.25
30	11.77	13.87	15.70	17.28	18.64	19.79
31	11.31	13.46	15.34	16.96	18.35	19.53
32	10.83	13.04	14.96	16.63	18.05	19.26
33	10.35	12.61	14.58	16.29	17.75	18.99
34	9.85	12.17	14.19	15.94	17.44	18.71
35	9.72	12.19	14.35	16.21	17.81	19.15
36	9.18	11.71	13.92	15.83	17.47	18.85
37	8.62	11.22	13.49	15.44	17.12	18.53
38	8.05	10.72	13.04	15.05	16.76	18.21
39	7.47	10.21	12.59	14.64	16.40	17.89
40	7.05	9.93	12.43	14.59	16.44	18.00
41	6.42	9.37	11.94	14.16	16.05	17.65
42	5.78	8.80	11.44	13.71	15.65	17.29
43	5.12	8.22	10.93	13.26	15.25	16.93
44	4.44	7.63	10.40	12.79	14.83	16.55
45	3.79	7.11	9.99	12.47	14.59	16.38
46	3.07	6.48	9.43	11.98	14.16	15.98
47	2.34	5.83	8.86	11.48	13.71	15.59
48	1.58	5.16	8.28	10.96	13.26	15.18
49	0.80	4.48	7.68	10.44	12.79	14.77
50		3.78	7.07	9.90	12.32	14.34
51		3.07	6.45	9.35	11.83	13.91
52		2.33	5.80	8.79	11.34	13.47
53		1.58	5.14	8.21	10.83	13.02
54		0.81	4.52	7.72	10.44	12.72
55			3.82	7.10	9.90	12.24
56			3.10	6.47	9.35	11.75
57			2.35	5.83	8.78	11.25
58			1.59	5.17	8.21	10.75
59			0.81	4.49	7.62	10.23
60				3.80	7.02	9.70
61				3.08	6.40	9.16
62				2.35	5.77	8.61
63				1.59	5.12	8.05
64				0.81	4.45	7.48
65					3.77	6.89
66					3.06	6.29
67					2.33	5.67
68					1.58	5.04
69					0.80	4.38
70						3.71
71						3.02
72						2.30
73						1.57
74						0.80

ND NE Deg

Loss of earnings: not disabled; not employed; degree level education or equivalent

Age	Male to retiring age 50	55	60	65	70	75	Age	Female to retiring age 50	55	60	65	70	75
16	19.36	21.01	22.45	23.68	24.72	25.60	**16**	19.23	20.89	22.35	23.61	24.70	25.62
17	19.21	20.92	22.41	23.68	24.77	25.67	**17**	18.86	20.57	22.06	23.35	24.46	25.41
18	19.04	20.82	22.36	23.68	24.80	25.74	**18**	18.49	20.24	21.76	23.09	24.23	25.20
19	18.86	20.70	22.30	23.67	24.83	25.80	**19**	18.10	19.89	21.46	22.82	23.98	24.98
20	18.66	20.57	22.22	23.64	24.85	25.85	**20**	17.71	19.55	21.15	22.54	23.74	24.75
21	18.23	20.19	21.89	23.34	24.57	25.60	**21**	17.26	19.14	20.78	22.20	23.42	24.46
22	17.79	19.80	21.54	23.03	24.30	25.35	**22**	16.81	18.73	20.41	21.86	23.11	24.17
23	17.35	19.41	21.19	22.72	24.01	25.09	**23**	16.35	18.31	20.02	21.51	22.79	23.87
24	16.89	19.00	20.83	22.39	23.72	24.82	**24**	15.88	17.88	19.64	21.15	22.46	23.57
25	16.42	18.58	20.45	22.06	23.41	24.54	**25**	15.40	17.45	19.24	20.79	22.13	23.26
26	15.86	18.07	19.98	21.62	23.00	24.15	**26**	14.87	16.97	18.79	20.38	21.74	22.89
27	15.30	17.56	19.51	21.18	22.59	23.76	**27**	14.34	16.48	18.34	19.96	21.34	22.52
28	14.74	17.04	19.03	20.73	22.17	23.36	**28**	13.80	15.98	17.89	19.53	20.94	22.14
29	14.16	16.51	18.54	20.28	21.74	22.96	**29**	13.26	15.48	17.42	19.10	20.54	21.76
30	13.58	15.98	18.05	19.82	21.31	22.55	**30**	12.71	14.98	16.95	18.67	20.13	21.38
31	12.99	15.43	17.55	19.36	20.88	22.14	**31**	12.18	14.50	16.52	18.27	19.77	21.04
32	12.39	14.89	17.04	18.89	20.44	21.73	**32**	11.64	14.01	16.08	17.87	19.40	20.70
33	11.78	14.33	16.53	18.42	20.00	21.31	**33**	11.09	13.52	15.63	17.46	19.03	20.35
34	11.17	13.77	16.02	17.94	19.55	20.89	**34**	10.54	13.02	15.18	17.05	18.65	20.00
35	10.54	13.20	15.49	17.45	19.10	20.46	**35**	9.97	12.51	14.72	16.63	18.26	19.65
36	9.89	12.59	14.93	16.92	18.60	19.99	**36**	9.36	11.95	14.21	16.16	17.83	19.23
37	9.22	11.98	14.36	16.39	18.10	19.51	**37**	8.75	11.40	13.70	15.68	17.38	18.82
38	8.55	11.36	13.79	15.85	17.59	19.02	**38**	8.13	10.83	13.18	15.20	16.94	18.40
39	7.88	10.74	13.21	15.31	17.08	18.53	**39**	7.51	10.26	12.65	14.72	16.49	17.98
40	7.20	10.11	12.63	14.77	16.57	18.05	**40**	6.87	9.68	12.12	14.23	16.03	17.55
41	6.48	9.43	11.98	14.15	15.97	17.47	**41**	6.16	9.00	11.46	13.59	15.41	16.94
42	5.76	8.75	11.33	13.53	15.38	16.89	**42**	5.46	8.32	10.81	12.96	14.79	16.34
43	5.04	8.07	10.69	12.92	14.79	16.32	**43**	4.76	7.65	10.16	12.33	14.18	15.74
44	4.32	7.40	10.05	12.30	14.20	15.75	**44**	4.06	6.98	9.52	11.70	13.57	15.15
45	3.60	6.72	9.41	11.69	13.61	15.18	**45**	3.37	6.32	8.88	11.09	12.97	14.56
46	2.88	6.04	8.77	11.08	13.02	14.61	**46**	2.67	5.63	8.20	10.41	12.30	13.89
47	2.16	5.37	8.13	10.48	12.44	14.05	**47**	1.98	4.95	7.53	9.75	11.65	13.24
48	1.44	4.69	7.50	9.88	11.87	13.50	**48**	1.31	4.28	6.87	9.10	11.00	12.59
49	0.72	4.02	6.86	9.28	11.30	12.94	**49**	0.65	3.63	6.22	8.46	10.36	11.96
50		3.35	6.23	8.68	10.73	12.40	**50**		2.99	5.59	7.83	9.73	11.33
51		2.64	5.53	7.98	10.02	11.69	**51**		2.27	4.77	6.93	8.77	10.31
52		1.92	4.77	7.18	9.19	10.83	**52**		1.61	4.01	6.08	7.84	9.32
53		1.22	3.98	6.31	8.26	9.85	**53**		0.97	3.17	5.07	6.69	8.04
54		0.58	3.23	5.49	7.36	8.89	**54**		0.43	2.43	4.14	5.60	6.82
55			2.73	5.05	6.98	8.56	**55**			2.05	3.81	5.31	6.57
56			2.22	4.61	6.60	8.21	**56**			1.66	3.47	5.02	6.31
57			1.69	4.15	6.20	7.86	**57**			1.26	3.13	4.71	6.04
58			1.14	3.68	5.79	7.50	**58**			0.85	2.77	4.40	5.77
59			0.58	3.20	5.37	7.13	**59**			0.43	2.41	4.09	5.49
60				2.71	4.95	6.76	**60**				2.04	3.76	5.20
61				2.20	4.52	6.39	**61**				1.65	3.43	4.92
62				1.68	4.07	6.01	**62**				1.26	3.09	4.62
63				1.14	3.62	5.62	**63**				0.85	2.75	4.32
64				0.58	3.15	5.22	**64**				0.43	2.39	4.01
65					2.67	4.82	**65**					2.02	3.70
66					2.18	4.40	**66**					1.64	3.38
67					1.66	3.97	**67**					1.25	3.04
68					1.13	3.53	**68**					0.85	2.70
69					0.58	3.08	**69**					0.43	2.35
70						2.61	**70**						1.99
71						2.13	**71**						1.62
72						1.63	**72**						1.24
73						1.11	**73**						0.84
74						0.57	**74**						0.43

ND NE GCSE

Loss of earnings: not disabled; not employed; good GCSE level education or equivalent

Age	Male to retiring age					
	50	**55**	**60**	**65**	**70**	**75**
16	19.36	21.01	22.45	23.68	24.72	25.60
17	19.15	20.86	22.34	23.61	24.69	25.60
18	18.93	20.70	22.23	23.54	24.66	25.59
19	18.70	20.52	22.11	23.47	24.62	25.58
20	18.45	20.34	21.97	23.38	24.57	25.56
21	18.03	19.96	21.64	23.08	24.30	25.31
22	17.59	19.58	21.30	22.77	24.02	25.06
23	17.15	19.19	20.95	22.46	23.74	24.80
24	16.70	18.79	20.59	22.14	23.45	24.54
25	16.23	18.37	20.22	21.81	23.15	24.27
26	15.69	17.87	19.76	21.37	22.74	23.88
27	15.13	17.36	19.29	20.94	22.33	23.49
28	14.57	16.84	18.81	20.49	21.91	23.09
29	14.00	16.32	18.33	20.04	21.49	22.70
30	13.42	15.79	17.84	19.59	21.07	22.29
31	12.84	15.26	17.35	19.13	20.64	21.89
32	12.24	14.71	16.85	18.67	20.21	21.48
33	11.64	14.16	16.34	18.20	19.77	21.06
34	11.04	13.61	15.83	17.73	19.33	20.65
35	10.42	13.04	15.31	17.25	18.88	20.22
36	9.77	12.44	14.75	16.72	18.38	19.75
37	9.11	11.84	14.19	16.19	17.88	19.27
38	8.45	11.23	13.62	15.66	17.38	18.79
39	7.78	10.61	13.05	15.13	16.87	18.31
40	7.11	9.99	12.47	14.59	16.36	17.83
41	6.41	9.34	11.86	14.01	15.81	17.30
42	5.71	8.69	11.25	13.43	15.26	16.77
43	5.01	8.03	10.64	12.85	14.71	16.24
44	4.31	7.38	10.02	12.27	14.16	15.71
45	3.60	6.72	9.41	11.69	13.61	15.18
46	2.88	6.04	8.77	11.08	13.02	14.61
47	2.16	5.37	8.13	10.48	12.44	14.05
48	1.44	4.69	7.50	9.88	11.87	13.50
49	0.72	4.02	6.86	9.28	11.30	12.94
50		3.35	6.23	8.68	10.73	12.40
51		2.64	5.53	7.98	10.02	11.69
52		1.92	4.77	7.18	9.19	10.83
53		1.22	3.98	6.31	8.26	9.85
54		0.58	3.23	5.49	7.36	8.89
55			2.73	5.05	6.98	8.56
56			2.22	4.61	6.60	8.21
57			1.69	4.15	6.20	7.86
58			1.14	3.68	5.79	7.50
59			0.58	3.20	5.37	7.13
60				2.71	4.95	6.76
61				2.20	4.52	6.39
62				1.68	4.07	6.01
63				1.14	3.62	5.62
64				0.58	3.15	5.22
65					2.67	4.82
66					2.18	4.40
67					1.66	3.97
68					1.13	3.53
69					0.58	3.08
70						2.61
71						2.13
72						1.63
73						1.11
74						0.57

Age	Female to retiring age					
	50	**55**	**60**	**65**	**70**	**75**
16	17.63	19.15	20.49	21.64	22.64	23.49
17	17.23	18.79	20.15	21.34	22.35	23.22
18	16.84	18.43	19.82	21.03	22.06	22.95
19	16.43	18.06	19.48	20.71	21.77	22.67
20	16.02	17.68	19.13	20.39	21.47	22.40
21	15.61	17.31	18.80	20.08	21.19	22.13
22	15.20	16.94	18.45	19.77	20.90	21.86
23	14.78	16.55	18.10	19.45	20.60	21.58
24	14.35	16.17	17.75	19.12	20.30	21.30
25	13.91	15.77	17.39	18.79	19.99	21.02
26	13.50	15.41	17.07	18.50	19.74	20.78
27	13.09	15.04	16.74	18.21	19.47	20.55
28	12.66	14.66	16.40	17.91	19.20	20.30
29	12.22	14.27	16.05	17.60	18.93	20.05
30	11.77	13.87	15.70	17.28	18.64	19.79
31	11.28	13.42	15.29	16.91	18.30	19.48
32	10.78	12.97	14.88	16.54	17.96	19.16
33	10.27	12.51	14.47	16.16	17.61	18.84
34	9.75	12.04	14.04	15.77	17.25	18.51
35	9.22	11.57	13.61	15.38	16.89	18.17
36	8.66	11.05	13.14	14.94	16.48	17.78
37	8.09	10.53	12.66	14.49	16.07	17.39
38	7.52	10.01	12.17	14.04	15.65	17.00
39	6.93	9.47	11.68	13.59	15.22	16.60
40	6.34	8.93	11.19	13.13	14.80	16.20
41	5.65	8.25	10.51	12.46	14.13	15.53
42	4.97	7.57	9.84	11.79	13.46	14.87
43	4.30	6.91	9.18	11.14	12.81	14.22
44	3.64	6.26	8.53	10.49	12.16	13.57
45	3.00	5.62	7.89	9.85	11.53	12.94
46	2.36	4.97	7.24	9.20	10.87	12.27
47	1.74	4.35	6.61	8.56	10.22	11.62
48	1.14	3.74	5.99	7.93	9.59	10.98
49	0.56	3.14	5.39	7.32	8.97	10.35
50		2.57	4.80	6.72	8.36	9.74
51		1.93	4.06	5.89	7.45	8.76
52		1.32	3.30	4.99	6.44	7.65
53		0.80	2.60	4.16	5.48	6.59
54		0.35	1.93	3.29	4.46	5.43
55			1.63	3.03	4.23	5.22
56			1.32	2.76	3.99	5.02
57			1.00	2.49	3.75	4.80
58			0.68	2.21	3.50	4.59
59			0.34	1.92	3.25	4.37
60				1.62	2.99	4.14
61				1.31	2.73	3.91
62				1.00	2.46	3.68
63				0.68	2.18	3.44
64				0.34	1.90	3.19
65					1.61	2.94
66					1.31	2.68
67					1.00	2.42
68					0.68	2.15
69					0.34	1.87
70						1.58
71						1.29
72						0.98
73						0.67
74						0.34

ND NE <GCSE

Loss of earnings: not disabled; not employed; education below good GCSE level

Age	Male to retiring age 50	55	60	65	70	75
16	18.67	20.27	21.65	22.84	23.85	24.69
17	18.37	20.01	21.43	22.65	23.69	24.55
18	18.05	19.74	21.20	22.45	23.52	24.41
19	17.73	19.46	20.97	22.25	23.35	24.26
20	17.40	19.18	20.72	22.05	23.17	24.11
21	16.96	18.78	20.36	21.71	22.86	23.82
22	16.51	18.38	19.99	21.38	22.55	23.52
23	16.06	17.97	19.62	21.03	22.23	23.23
24	15.60	17.55	19.23	20.68	21.90	22.92
25	15.13	17.12	18.85	20.32	21.57	22.61
26	14.65	16.69	18.45	19.96	21.24	22.30
27	14.16	16.24	18.05	19.59	20.90	21.98
28	13.66	15.79	17.64	19.22	20.55	21.66
29	13.16	15.34	17.22	18.84	20.20	21.33
30	12.64	14.87	16.80	18.45	19.84	21.00
31	12.12	14.40	16.37	18.06	19.48	20.66
32	11.58	13.92	15.94	17.66	19.12	20.32
33	11.04	13.43	15.49	17.26	18.74	19.97
34	10.49	12.93	15.04	16.84	18.36	19.62
35	9.92	12.42	14.58	16.43	17.98	19.26
36	9.32	11.88	14.08	15.96	17.54	18.85
37	8.72	11.32	13.57	15.49	17.10	18.43
38	8.10	10.76	13.06	15.01	16.66	18.02
39	7.48	10.19	12.54	14.53	16.21	17.59
40	6.85	9.62	12.01	14.05	15.76	17.17
41	6.17	8.99	11.42	13.49	15.22	16.65
42	5.50	8.36	10.82	12.92	14.69	16.13
43	4.82	7.73	10.23	12.36	14.15	15.62
44	4.14	7.09	9.64	11.80	13.61	15.10
45	3.46	6.46	9.04	11.24	13.08	14.59
46	2.77	5.82	8.44	10.68	12.54	14.07
47	2.08	5.18	7.85	10.12	12.01	13.56
48	1.39	4.54	7.25	9.56	11.48	13.06
49	0.70	3.90	6.66	9.00	10.96	12.55
50		3.26	6.06	8.44	10.43	12.05
51		2.57	5.37	7.75	9.74	11.36
52		1.90	4.70	7.07	9.06	10.67
53		1.22	3.98	6.31	8.26	9.85
54		0.58	3.23	5.49	7.36	8.89
55			2.73	5.05	6.98	8.56
56			2.22	4.61	6.60	8.21
57			1.69	4.15	6.20	7.86
58			1.14	3.68	5.79	7.50
59			0.58	3.20	5.37	7.13
60				2.71	4.95	6.76
61				2.20	4.52	6.39
62				1.68	4.07	6.01
63				1.14	3.62	5.62
64				0.58	3.15	5.22
65					2.67	4.82
66					2.18	4.40
67					1.66	3.97
68					1.13	3.53
69					0.58	3.08
70						2.61
71						2.13
72						1.63
73						1.11
74						0.57

Age	Female to retiring age 50	55	60	65	70	75
16	13.51	14.68	15.70	16.58	17.35	18.00
17	13.30	14.51	15.56	16.47	17.26	17.92
18	13.09	14.33	15.42	16.35	17.16	17.85
19	12.88	14.15	15.26	16.23	17.06	17.77
20	12.65	13.96	15.11	16.10	16.95	17.68
21	12.40	13.75	14.93	15.95	16.83	17.57
22	12.14	13.53	14.74	15.79	16.70	17.46
23	11.88	13.31	14.55	15.63	16.56	17.35
24	11.60	13.07	14.35	15.46	16.41	17.22
25	11.32	12.83	14.14	15.28	16.26	17.09
26	11.05	12.61	13.97	15.15	16.16	17.02
27	10.78	12.39	13.79	15.00	16.05	16.93
28	10.50	12.15	13.60	14.85	15.93	16.84
29	10.20	11.91	13.40	14.69	15.80	16.74
30	9.88	11.65	13.19	14.52	15.66	16.63
31	9.50	11.31	12.88	14.25	15.42	16.41
32	9.10	10.95	12.57	13.97	15.17	16.18
33	8.69	10.59	12.25	13.68	14.91	15.95
34	8.28	10.23	11.92	13.39	14.65	15.71
35	7.85	9.85	11.59	13.09	14.38	15.47
36	7.34	9.37	11.14	12.67	13.97	15.08
37	6.83	8.89	10.69	12.24	13.56	14.68
38	6.32	8.41	10.23	11.81	13.15	14.29
39	5.80	7.93	9.78	11.38	12.74	13.90
40	5.29	7.44	9.32	10.94	12.33	13.50
41	4.69	6.84	8.72	10.33	11.72	12.88
42	4.10	6.25	8.12	9.73	11.11	12.28
43	3.53	5.67	7.54	9.15	10.52	11.68
44	2.97	5.11	6.97	8.57	9.94	11.09
45	2.44	4.56	6.41	8.01	9.37	10.51
46	1.90	4.01	5.84	7.42	8.77	9.91
47	1.40	3.48	5.30	6.86	8.19	9.31
48	0.91	2.97	4.76	6.31	7.63	8.73
49	0.44	2.48	4.25	5.77	7.07	8.17
50		2.01	3.75	5.26	6.54	7.61
51		1.51	3.18	4.62	5.84	6.87
52		1.04	2.58	3.91	5.04	5.99
53		0.62	2.03	3.25	4.28	5.15
54		0.27	1.49	2.54	3.44	4.19
55			1.26	2.34	3.26	4.03
56			1.02	2.13	3.08	3.87
57			0.78	1.92	2.89	3.71
58			0.52	1.70	2.70	3.54
59			0.27	1.48	2.51	3.37
60				1.25	2.31	3.19
61				1.01	2.11	3.02
62				0.77	1.90	2.84
63				0.52	1.69	2.65
64				0.27	1.47	2.46
65					1.24	2.27
66					1.01	2.07
67					0.77	1.87
68					0.52	1.66
69					0.26	1.44
70						1.22
71						0.99
72						0.76
73						0.52
74						0.26

D E Deg

Loss of earnings: disabled; employed; degree level education or equivalent

Age	Male to retiring age 50	55	60	65	70	75
16	13.89	15.08	16.11	16.99	17.74	18.37
17	13.62	14.84	15.89	16.80	17.57	18.21
18	13.35	14.60	15.68	16.60	17.39	18.05
19	13.07	14.35	15.46	16.41	17.21	17.88
20	12.79	14.10	15.23	16.20	17.03	17.72
21	12.45	13.79	14.95	15.95	16.79	17.49
22	12.12	13.48	14.67	15.68	16.54	17.26
23	11.77	13.17	14.38	15.42	16.29	17.02
24	11.42	12.85	14.09	15.15	16.04	16.79
25	11.07	12.53	13.79	14.87	15.79	16.55
26	10.71	12.20	13.49	14.59	15.53	16.30
27	10.34	11.86	13.18	14.31	15.26	16.05
28	9.97	11.53	12.87	14.02	15.00	15.80
29	9.59	11.18	12.56	13.73	14.73	15.55
30	9.21	10.83	12.24	13.44	14.45	15.30
31	8.82	10.48	11.92	13.14	14.18	15.04
32	8.42	10.12	11.59	12.84	13.90	14.77
33	8.02	9.75	11.25	12.53	13.61	14.51
34	7.61	9.38	10.92	12.22	13.33	14.24
35	7.19	9.01	10.57	11.91	13.03	13.96
36	6.77	8.62	10.22	11.59	12.74	13.69
37	6.34	8.24	9.87	11.27	12.44	13.41
38	5.90	7.84	9.51	10.94	12.14	13.12
39	5.46	7.44	9.15	10.60	11.83	12.84
40	5.00	7.03	8.78	10.26	11.52	12.54
41	4.53	6.59	8.37	9.89	11.16	12.21
42	4.04	6.15	7.96	9.51	10.80	11.87
43	3.56	5.70	7.55	9.12	10.44	11.53
44	3.07	5.25	7.14	8.74	10.08	11.18
45	2.57	4.80	6.72	8.35	9.72	10.84
46	2.07	4.34	6.30	7.96	9.36	10.50
47	1.56	3.88	5.88	7.57	8.99	10.15
48	1.05	3.41	5.45	7.18	8.63	9.81
49	0.53	2.94	5.02	6.79	8.26	9.47
50		2.47	4.59	6.39	7.90	9.13
51		2.00	4.19	6.04	7.59	8.85
52		1.55	3.84	5.79	7.41	8.73
53		1.05	3.41	5.41	7.08	8.44
54		0.53	2.96	5.02	6.74	8.14
55			2.50	4.62	6.39	7.83
56			2.03	4.22	6.04	7.51
57			1.54	3.80	5.67	7.19
58			1.05	3.37	5.30	6.86
59			0.53	2.93	4.92	6.53
60				2.48	4.53	6.19
61				2.01	4.13	5.84
62				1.53	3.73	5.50
63				1.04	3.31	5.14
64				0.53	2.89	4.78
65					2.45	4.41
66					1.99	4.03
67					1.52	3.64
68					1.03	3.23
69					0.53	2.82
70						2.39
71						1.95
72						1.49
73						1.02
74						0.52

Age	Female to retiring age 50	55	60	65	70	75
16	14.88	16.17	17.29	18.27	19.11	19.83
17	14.32	15.61	16.74	17.72	18.57	19.29
18	13.75	15.06	16.19	17.18	18.03	18.75
19	13.20	14.51	15.65	16.64	17.49	18.21
20	12.65	13.96	15.11	16.10	16.95	17.68
21	12.48	13.84	15.03	16.06	16.94	17.69
22	12.30	13.71	14.94	16.00	16.92	17.69
23	12.11	13.57	14.84	15.94	16.89	17.69
24	11.91	13.41	14.73	15.87	16.84	17.68
25	11.69	13.25	14.61	15.78	16.80	17.65
26	11.31	12.90	14.29	15.49	16.53	17.40
27	10.92	12.55	13.97	15.20	16.25	17.15
28	10.53	12.19	13.64	14.90	15.98	16.89
29	10.13	11.83	13.31	14.60	15.70	16.63
30	9.73	11.46	12.98	14.29	15.41	16.36
31	9.32	11.09	12.64	13.97	15.12	16.09
32	8.90	10.71	12.29	13.66	14.83	15.82
33	8.47	10.33	11.94	13.34	14.53	15.54
34	8.04	9.93	11.58	13.01	14.23	15.26
35	7.60	9.54	11.22	12.68	13.93	14.98
36	7.15	9.13	10.85	12.34	13.62	14.69
37	6.70	8.72	10.48	12.00	13.30	14.40
38	6.24	8.30	10.10	11.65	12.98	14.10
39	5.76	7.88	9.71	11.30	12.66	13.80
40	5.29	7.44	9.32	10.94	12.33	13.50
41	4.81	7.03	8.95	10.62	12.04	13.24
42	4.33	6.60	8.58	10.28	11.74	12.97
43	3.84	6.17	8.19	9.94	11.44	12.69
44	3.33	5.72	7.80	9.59	11.13	12.42
45	2.81	5.26	7.40	9.24	10.81	12.13
46	2.28	4.80	6.99	8.87	10.49	11.84
47	1.73	4.32	6.56	8.50	10.16	11.55
48	1.17	3.82	6.13	8.12	9.82	11.24
49	0.59	3.32	5.69	7.73	9.48	10.94
50		2.80	5.24	7.34	9.12	10.62
51		2.31	4.85	7.04	8.91	10.48
52		1.76	4.37	6.62	8.54	10.15
53		1.21	3.94	6.29	8.29	9.97
54		0.62	3.47	5.93	8.02	9.77
55			2.93	5.46	7.61	9.40
56			2.38	4.97	7.18	9.03
57			1.81	4.48	6.75	8.65
58			1.22	3.97	6.31	8.26
59			0.62	3.45	5.85	7.86
60				2.92	5.39	7.45
61				2.37	4.92	7.04
62				1.80	4.43	6.62
63				1.22	3.93	6.19
64				0.62	3.42	5.75
65					2.89	5.30
66					2.35	4.83
67					1.79	4.36
68					1.22	3.87
69					0.62	3.37
70						2.85
71						2.32
72						1.77
73						1.20
74						0.61

D E GCSE

Loss of earnings: disabled; employed; good GCSE level education or equivalent

Age	Male to retiring age 50	55	60	65	70	75
16	12.53	13.60	14.52	15.32	16.00	16.56
17	12.28	13.38	14.33	15.15	15.84	16.42
18	12.04	13.16	14.13	14.97	15.68	16.27
19	11.79	12.94	13.94	14.79	15.52	16.12
20	11.53	12.71	13.73	14.61	15.35	15.97
21	11.22	12.43	13.48	14.37	15.13	15.76
22	10.92	12.15	13.22	14.13	14.90	15.55
23	10.60	11.86	12.95	13.88	14.68	15.33
24	10.28	11.57	12.68	13.64	14.44	15.11
25	9.96	11.27	12.41	13.38	14.21	14.89
26	9.60	10.93	12.09	13.08	13.92	14.61
27	9.23	10.59	11.77	12.77	13.62	14.33
28	8.86	10.25	11.44	12.47	13.33	14.05
29	8.49	9.90	11.12	12.16	13.04	13.76
30	8.12	9.55	10.79	11.85	12.74	13.48
31	7.68	9.12	10.38	11.44	12.35	13.09
32	7.24	8.70	9.97	11.04	11.95	12.71
33	6.81	8.28	9.56	10.65	11.56	12.32
34	6.38	7.87	9.15	10.25	11.17	11.94
35	5.95	7.45	8.75	9.86	10.79	11.56
36	5.62	7.16	8.49	9.62	10.58	11.37
37	5.28	6.86	8.23	9.39	10.37	11.17
38	4.94	6.56	7.95	9.15	10.15	10.97
39	4.58	6.24	7.68	8.90	9.93	10.77
40	4.21	5.92	7.39	8.64	9.70	10.56
41	3.84	5.59	7.10	8.38	9.46	10.35
42	3.45	5.25	6.80	8.12	9.23	10.14
43	3.06	4.91	6.50	7.85	8.98	9.91
44	2.66	4.55	6.18	7.57	8.74	9.69
45	2.24	4.19	5.86	7.29	8.48	9.46
46	1.83	3.83	5.56	7.03	8.26	9.27
47	1.39	3.46	5.25	6.76	8.03	9.07
48	0.95	3.08	4.92	6.49	7.79	8.86
49	0.48	2.69	4.59	6.20	7.55	8.65
50		2.28	4.24	5.91	7.30	8.44
51		1.85	3.87	5.58	7.02	8.18
52		1.41	3.49	5.25	6.72	7.92
53		0.95	3.09	4.91	6.42	7.66
54		0.49	2.74	4.65	6.24	7.54
55			2.32	4.28	5.92	7.25
56			1.88	3.90	5.59	6.96
57			1.43	3.52	5.25	6.66
58			0.97	3.12	4.91	6.35
59			0.49	2.71	4.55	6.04
60				2.29	4.19	5.73
61				1.86	3.83	5.41
62				1.42	3.45	5.09
63				0.96	3.07	4.76
64				0.49	2.67	4.43
65					2.27	4.08
66					1.84	3.73
67					1.41	3.37
68					0.96	2.99
69					0.49	2.61
70						2.21
71						1.81
72						1.38
73						0.94
74						0.49

Age	Female to retiring age 50	55	60	65	70	75
16	9.84	10.70	11.44	12.09	12.64	13.12
17	9.71	10.59	11.36	12.02	12.60	13.08
18	9.57	10.48	11.27	11.96	12.55	13.05
19	9.43	10.36	11.18	11.88	12.49	13.01
20	9.28	10.24	11.08	11.81	12.43	12.97
21	9.10	10.10	10.96	11.71	12.36	12.90
22	8.93	9.95	10.84	11.61	12.27	12.84
23	8.74	9.79	10.71	11.50	12.19	12.77
24	8.55	9.63	10.57	11.39	12.09	12.69
25	8.35	9.46	10.43	11.27	12.00	12.61
26	8.14	9.29	10.28	11.15	11.89	12.53
27	7.92	9.10	10.13	11.02	11.79	12.44
28	7.70	8.91	9.97	10.89	11.67	12.34
29	7.46	8.71	9.80	10.75	11.56	12.24
30	7.22	8.51	9.63	10.60	11.43	12.14
31	6.99	8.33	9.49	10.49	11.35	12.08
32	6.76	8.14	9.34	10.38	11.27	12.02
33	6.51	7.94	9.18	10.25	11.17	11.95
34	6.25	7.73	9.01	10.12	11.07	11.87
35	5.98	7.50	8.83	9.98	10.96	11.79
36	5.72	7.30	8.68	9.86	10.88	11.74
37	5.44	7.08	8.51	9.74	10.80	11.69
38	5.14	6.84	8.33	9.61	10.70	11.63
39	4.83	6.59	8.13	9.46	10.60	11.56
40	4.49	6.33	7.92	9.30	10.48	11.48
41	4.14	6.04	7.70	9.13	10.35	11.38
42	3.77	5.74	7.46	8.95	10.21	11.28
43	3.38	5.43	7.21	8.75	10.06	11.17
44	2.96	5.09	6.94	8.54	9.90	11.05
45	2.53	4.74	6.66	8.31	9.73	10.92
46	2.06	4.35	6.33	8.05	9.51	10.74
47	1.58	3.94	6.00	7.77	9.28	10.54
48	1.07	3.52	5.64	7.47	9.03	10.34
49	0.55	3.08	5.27	7.17	8.78	10.14
50		2.62	4.89	6.85	8.52	9.92
51		2.20	4.62	6.70	8.47	9.96
52		1.73	4.30	6.51	8.40	9.98
53		1.21	3.94	6.29	8.29	9.97
54		0.65	3.64	6.21	8.40	10.24
55			3.07	5.72	7.97	9.85
56			2.49	5.21	7.52	9.46
57			1.90	4.69	7.07	9.06
58			1.28	4.16	6.61	8.65
59			0.65	3.62	6.13	8.23
60				3.05	5.65	7.81
61				2.48	5.15	7.37
62				1.89	4.64	6.93
63				1.28	4.12	6.48
64				0.65	3.58	6.02
65					3.03	5.55
66					2.46	5.06
67					1.88	4.56
68					1.27	4.05
69					0.65	3.53
70						2.99
71						2.43
72						1.85
73						1.26
74						0.64

Loss of earnings: disabled; employed; education below good GCSE level

Age	Male to retiring age 50	55	60	65	70	75	Age	Female to retiring age 50	55	60	65	70	75
16	7.29	7.91	8.45	8.91	9.31	9.64	**16**	5.72	6.22	6.65	7.03	7.35	7.63
17	7.48	8.15	8.73	9.23	9.65	10.00	**17**	5.61	6.12	6.57	6.95	7.28	7.56
18	7.66	8.37	8.99	9.53	9.98	10.35	**18**	5.50	6.02	6.48	6.87	7.21	7.50
19	7.82	8.59	9.25	9.82	10.30	10.70	**19**	5.39	5.92	6.39	6.79	7.14	7.43
20	7.97	8.78	9.49	10.09	10.61	11.04	**20**	5.27	5.82	6.29	6.71	7.06	7.37
21	7.95	8.80	9.54	10.18	10.71	11.16	**21**	5.15	5.71	6.20	6.62	6.99	7.30
22	7.92	8.81	9.58	10.25	10.81	11.28	**22**	5.03	5.60	6.10	6.54	6.91	7.23
23	7.87	8.81	9.62	10.31	10.90	11.39	**23**	4.90	5.49	6.00	6.45	6.83	7.16
24	7.82	8.80	9.64	10.37	10.98	11.49	**24**	4.77	5.37	5.90	6.36	6.75	7.08
25	7.75	8.77	9.65	10.41	11.05	11.58	**25**	4.64	5.26	5.80	6.26	6.66	7.01
26	7.45	8.49	9.38	10.15	10.80	11.34	**26**	4.68	5.34	5.92	6.41	6.84	7.21
27	7.15	8.20	9.11	9.89	10.55	11.10	**27**	4.71	5.41	6.02	6.55	7.01	7.40
28	6.85	7.92	8.84	9.63	10.30	10.86	**28**	4.73	5.47	6.12	6.69	7.17	7.58
29	6.55	7.63	8.57	9.37	10.05	10.61	**29**	4.72	5.52	6.21	6.80	7.32	7.75
30	6.24	7.34	8.30	9.11	9.80	10.37	**30**	4.71	5.55	6.28	6.91	7.46	7.92
31	5.97	7.09	8.06	8.90	9.60	10.18	**31**	4.64	5.53	6.30	6.96	7.54	8.02
32	5.69	6.84	7.83	8.68	9.39	9.98	**32**	4.56	5.49	6.30	7.01	7.61	8.12
33	5.41	6.58	7.59	8.46	9.18	9.79	**33**	4.47	5.45	6.30	7.04	7.67	8.20
34	5.13	6.32	7.35	8.23	8.98	9.59	**34**	4.36	5.39	6.28	7.06	7.72	8.28
35	4.84	6.06	7.11	8.01	8.76	9.39	**35**	4.24	5.31	6.25	7.07	7.76	8.35
36	4.57	5.82	6.90	7.82	8.60	9.24	**36**	4.09	5.23	6.21	7.06	7.79	8.41
37	4.29	5.58	6.68	7.63	8.42	9.08	**37**	3.93	5.12	6.16	7.05	7.81	8.46
38	4.01	5.33	6.46	7.43	8.25	8.92	**38**	3.76	5.00	6.09	7.02	7.82	8.50
39	3.72	5.07	6.24	7.23	8.06	8.75	**39**	3.56	4.87	6.00	6.98	7.82	8.53
40	3.42	4.81	6.00	7.02	7.88	8.58	**40**	3.35	4.71	5.90	6.93	7.81	8.55
41	3.12	4.54	5.77	6.81	7.69	8.41	**41**	3.11	4.55	5.79	6.87	7.79	8.56
42	2.81	4.27	5.53	6.60	7.50	8.24	**42**	2.86	4.36	5.66	6.79	7.75	8.56
43	2.49	3.99	5.28	6.38	7.30	8.06	**43**	2.58	4.15	5.52	6.69	7.70	8.55
44	2.16	3.70	5.02	6.15	7.10	7.87	**44**	2.29	3.93	5.36	6.59	7.64	8.52
45	1.82	3.40	4.76	5.92	6.89	7.69	**45**	1.97	3.69	5.18	6.47	7.57	8.49
46	1.48	3.12	4.52	5.72	6.72	7.54	**46**	1.63	3.44	5.01	6.36	7.51	8.49
47	1.13	2.82	4.27	5.51	6.54	7.38	**47**	1.27	3.17	4.81	6.23	7.45	8.47
48	0.77	2.51	4.01	5.29	6.35	7.22	**48**	0.88	2.87	4.60	6.09	7.36	8.43
49	0.39	2.19	3.74	5.06	6.16	7.06	**49**	0.45	2.55	4.36	5.93	7.26	8.39
50		1.86	3.46	4.82	5.96	6.89	**50**		2.20	4.10	5.75	7.15	8.32
51		1.55	3.24	4.67	5.87	6.85	**51**		1.86	3.90	5.66	7.16	8.42
52		1.18	2.92	4.39	5.63	6.63	**52**		1.47	3.65	5.54	7.14	8.48
53		0.82	2.65	4.21	5.51	6.56	**53**		1.05	3.43	5.48	7.22	8.68
54		0.42	2.36	4.00	5.37	6.48	**54**		0.56	3.14	5.36	7.26	8.84
55			1.99	3.68	5.09	6.24	**55**			2.65	4.94	6.88	8.51
56			1.62	3.36	4.81	5.98	**56**			2.15	4.50	6.50	8.17
57			1.23	3.02	4.52	5.73	**57**			1.64	4.05	6.11	7.82
58			0.83	2.68	4.22	5.46	**58**			1.11	3.59	5.71	7.47
59			0.42	2.33	3.92	5.20	**59**			0.56	3.12	5.30	7.11
60				1.97	3.61	4.93	**60**				2.64	4.88	6.74
61				1.60	3.29	4.65	**61**				2.14	4.45	6.37
62				1.22	2.97	4.38	**62**				1.63	4.01	5.99
63				0.83	2.64	4.09	**63**				1.10	3.56	5.60
64				0.42	2.30	3.81	**64**				0.56	3.09	5.20
65					1.95	3.51	**65**					2.62	4.79
66					1.59	3.21	**66**					2.13	4.37
67					1.21	2.90	**67**					1.62	3.94
68					0.82	2.57	**68**					1.10	3.50
69					0.42	2.24	**69**					0.56	3.05
70						1.90	**70**						2.58
71						1.55	**71**						2.10
72						1.19	**72**						1.60
73						0.81	**73**						1.09
74						0.42	**74**						0.56

D NE Deg

Loss of earnings: disabled; not employed; degree level education or equivalent

Age	Male to retiring age 50	55	60	65	70	75	Age	Female to retiring age 50	55	60	65	70	75
16	13.89	15.08	16.11	16.99	17.74	18.37	**16**	13.28	14.43	15.43	16.30	17.05	17.69
17	13.18	14.35	15.37	16.25	16.99	17.61	**17**	13.02	14.20	15.23	16.12	16.89	17.55
18	12.47	13.64	14.65	15.51	16.25	16.86	**18**	12.76	13.97	15.03	15.94	16.73	17.40
19	11.79	12.94	13.94	14.79	15.52	16.12	**19**	12.50	13.74	14.82	15.75	16.56	17.25
20	11.11	12.25	13.23	14.08	14.80	15.39	**20**	12.23	13.50	14.60	15.56	16.39	17.09
21	10.65	11.80	12.79	13.64	14.36	14.96	**21**	11.62	12.88	13.99	14.94	15.77	16.46
22	10.20	11.35	12.34	13.20	13.92	14.52	**22**	11.02	12.28	13.38	14.33	15.15	15.84
23	9.75	10.90	11.90	12.76	13.49	14.09	**23**	10.43	11.68	12.77	13.72	14.54	15.23
24	9.30	10.46	11.47	12.33	13.06	13.66	**24**	9.85	11.09	12.18	13.12	13.93	14.62
25	8.85	10.02	11.03	11.90	12.63	13.24	**25**	9.27	10.51	11.59	12.53	13.33	14.01
26	8.42	9.59	10.60	11.47	12.20	12.81	**26**	8.79	10.02	11.10	12.04	12.84	13.52
27	7.98	9.16	10.17	11.04	11.78	12.39	**27**	8.30	9.54	10.62	11.56	12.36	13.04
28	7.55	8.73	9.75	10.62	11.36	11.97	**28**	7.83	9.07	10.15	11.08	11.88	12.56
29	7.13	8.31	9.33	10.21	10.95	11.56	**29**	7.36	8.60	9.67	10.61	11.41	12.08
30	6.71	7.90	8.92	9.80	10.53	11.15	**30**	6.90	8.14	9.21	10.14	10.94	11.61
31	6.30	7.49	8.51	9.39	10.13	10.74	**31**	6.57	7.82	8.92	9.86	10.67	11.35
32	5.89	7.08	8.11	8.98	9.72	10.34	**32**	6.24	7.51	8.62	9.58	10.40	11.09
33	5.49	6.68	7.71	8.59	9.32	9.94	**33**	5.91	7.20	8.32	9.30	10.13	10.84
34	5.10	6.29	7.31	8.19	8.93	9.54	**34**	5.57	6.88	8.02	9.01	9.86	10.58
35	4.71	5.90	6.93	7.80	8.54	9.15	**35**	5.23	6.57	7.73	8.73	9.59	10.31
36	4.33	5.52	6.54	7.42	8.15	8.76	**36**	4.85	6.19	7.35	8.36	9.23	9.96
37	3.96	5.15	6.17	7.04	7.77	8.38	**37**	4.47	5.81	6.99	8.00	8.87	9.60
38	3.60	4.78	5.80	6.67	7.40	8.00	**38**	4.09	5.44	6.62	7.64	8.51	9.25
39	3.24	4.42	5.44	6.30	7.03	7.63	**39**	3.72	5.08	6.26	7.28	8.16	8.90
40	2.90	4.07	5.08	5.94	6.67	7.26	**40**	3.35	4.71	5.90	6.93	7.81	8.55
41	2.53	3.68	4.67	5.52	6.23	6.81	**41**	2.89	4.22	5.37	6.37	7.22	7.94
42	2.17	3.30	4.28	5.11	5.80	6.38	**42**	2.45	3.74	4.86	5.83	6.65	7.35
43	1.84	2.94	3.90	4.71	5.39	5.95	**43**	2.05	3.29	4.37	5.30	6.10	6.77
44	1.52	2.60	3.53	4.32	4.99	5.53	**44**	1.66	2.86	3.90	4.80	5.56	6.21
45	1.21	2.27	3.18	3.95	4.59	5.12	**45**	1.31	2.46	3.45	4.31	5.04	5.66
46	0.97	2.04	2.95	3.73	4.39	4.92	**46**	1.02	2.16	3.14	3.99	4.72	5.33
47	0.73	1.80	2.73	3.52	4.18	4.72	**47**	0.75	1.87	2.84	3.68	4.40	5.00
48	0.48	1.57	2.51	3.31	3.98	4.52	**48**	0.49	1.59	2.56	3.38	4.09	4.69
49	0.24	1.34	2.29	3.10	3.78	4.33	**49**	0.24	1.33	2.28	3.09	3.79	4.37
50		1.12	2.08	2.89	3.58	4.13	**50**		1.07	2.01	2.81	3.50	4.07
51		0.87	1.82	2.62	3.29	3.84	**51**		0.80	1.67	2.43	3.07	3.61
52		0.63	1.57	2.36	3.02	3.56	**52**		0.58	1.43	2.17	2.80	3.33
53		0.41	1.33	2.10	2.75	3.28	**53**		0.35	1.14	1.83	2.41	2.89
54		0.20	1.10	1.86	2.50	3.01	**54**		0.16	0.88	1.51	2.04	2.48
55			0.93	1.71	2.37	2.90	**55**			0.75	1.39	1.93	2.39
56			0.75	1.56	2.24	2.78	**56**			0.60	1.26	1.82	2.29
57			0.57	1.41	2.10	2.66	**57**			0.46	1.14	1.71	2.20
58			0.39	1.25	1.96	2.54	**58**			0.31	1.01	1.60	2.10
59			0.20	1.08	1.82	2.42	**59**			0.16	0.88	1.49	2.00
60				0.92	1.68	2.29	**60**				0.74	1.37	1.89
61				0.75	1.53	2.16	**61**				0.60	1.25	1.79
62				0.57	1.38	2.04	**62**				0.46	1.13	1.68
63				0.39	1.23	1.90	**63**				0.31	1.00	1.57
64				0.20	1.07	1.77	**64**				0.16	0.87	1.46
65					0.91	1.63	**65**					0.73	1.34
66					0.74	1.49	**66**					0.60	1.23
67					0.56	1.35	**67**					0.46	1.11
68					0.38	1.20	**68**					0.31	0.98
69					0.20	1.04	**69**					0.16	0.86
70						0.89	**70**						0.72
71						0.72	**71**						0.59
72						0.55	**72**						0.45
73						0.38	**73**						0.31
74						0.19	**74**						0.16

D NE GCSE

Loss of earnings: disabled; not employed; good GCSE level education or equivalent

Age	Male to retiring age 50	55	60	65	70	75
16	11.16	12.11	12.94	13.65	14.25	14.76
17	10.78	11.74	12.57	13.29	13.90	14.40
18	10.40	11.37	12.21	12.93	13.54	14.05
19	10.02	11.00	11.84	12.57	13.19	13.71
20	9.64	10.63	11.49	12.22	12.84	13.36
21	9.22	10.21	11.07	11.80	12.43	12.94
22	8.80	9.79	10.65	11.39	12.01	12.53
23	8.38	9.38	10.24	10.98	11.60	12.12
24	7.97	8.97	9.83	10.57	11.19	11.71
25	7.56	8.56	9.42	10.16	10.79	11.31
26	7.09	8.08	8.93	9.66	10.28	10.79
27	6.63	7.60	8.45	9.17	9.78	10.29
28	6.18	7.14	7.97	8.69	9.29	9.79
29	5.74	6.69	7.51	8.21	8.81	9.30
30	5.31	6.24	7.05	7.75	8.33	8.81
31	4.92	5.85	6.65	7.33	7.91	8.39
32	4.54	5.46	6.25	6.92	7.49	7.97
33	4.17	5.08	5.86	6.52	7.09	7.55
34	3.82	4.71	5.48	6.13	6.69	7.14
35	3.47	4.35	5.10	5.75	6.29	6.74
36	3.16	4.03	4.78	5.41	5.95	6.39
37	2.86	3.72	4.46	5.09	5.62	6.05
38	2.57	3.41	4.14	4.76	5.29	5.72
39	2.29	3.12	3.84	4.45	4.96	5.39
40	2.02	2.84	3.54	4.14	4.65	5.06
41	1.79	2.61	3.31	3.91	4.42	4.83
42	1.57	2.39	3.09	3.69	4.19	4.60
43	1.35	2.17	2.87	3.47	3.97	4.38
44	1.14	1.95	2.65	3.25	3.75	4.16
45	0.93	1.75	2.44	3.04	3.53	3.94
46	0.74	1.56	2.26	2.86	3.36	3.77
47	0.55	1.37	2.08	2.68	3.19	3.60
48	0.37	1.19	1.90	2.51	3.02	3.43
49	0.18	1.01	1.73	2.34	2.85	3.26
50		0.84	1.56	2.17	2.68	3.10
51		0.64	1.34	1.94	2.43	2.84
52		0.46	1.14	1.71	2.20	2.59
53		0.29	0.95	1.50	1.97	2.34
54		0.14	0.77	1.30	1.75	2.11
55			0.65	1.20	1.66	2.03
56			0.53	1.09	1.56	1.95
57			0.40	0.98	1.47	1.86
58			0.27	0.87	1.37	1.78
59			0.14	0.76	1.27	1.69
60				0.64	1.17	1.60
61				0.52	1.07	1.52
62				0.40	0.97	1.43
63				0.27	0.86	1.33
64				0.14	0.75	1.24
65					0.63	1.14
66					0.52	1.04
67					0.39	0.94
68					0.27	0.84
69					0.14	0.73
70						0.62
71						0.51
72						0.39
73						0.26
74						0.14

Age	Female to retiring age 50	55	60	65	70	75
16	8.01	8.71	9.31	9.84	10.29	10.68
17	7.75	8.45	9.06	9.59	10.05	10.44
18	7.48	8.19	8.81	9.34	9.81	10.20
19	7.22	7.93	8.56	9.10	9.57	9.96
20	6.96	7.68	8.31	8.85	9.32	9.72
21	6.76	7.49	8.13	8.69	9.17	9.58
22	6.55	7.30	7.96	8.52	9.01	9.43
23	6.35	7.11	7.78	8.36	8.85	9.27
24	6.14	6.92	7.60	8.19	8.69	9.12
25	5.94	6.73	7.42	8.02	8.53	8.97
26	5.73	6.53	7.24	7.84	8.37	8.81
27	5.51	6.34	7.05	7.67	8.20	8.66
28	5.30	6.14	6.87	7.50	8.04	8.50
29	5.08	5.93	6.68	7.32	7.87	8.34
30	4.86	5.73	6.49	7.14	7.71	8.18
31	4.58	5.46	6.22	6.87	7.44	7.92
32	4.30	5.18	5.95	6.61	7.17	7.65
33	4.03	4.91	5.68	6.34	6.91	7.39
34	3.76	4.64	5.41	6.08	6.65	7.13
35	3.49	4.38	5.15	5.82	6.39	6.88
36	3.18	4.05	4.82	5.48	6.05	6.52
37	2.87	3.74	4.50	5.15	5.71	6.18
38	2.58	3.44	4.18	4.82	5.37	5.84
39	2.30	3.14	3.87	4.51	5.05	5.50
40	2.03	2.85	3.57	4.20	4.73	5.18
41	1.77	2.58	3.28	3.89	4.41	4.85
42	1.52	2.31	3.00	3.60	4.11	4.54
43	1.28	2.06	2.73	3.31	3.81	4.23
44	1.05	1.81	2.47	3.04	3.52	3.93
45	0.84	1.58	2.22	2.77	3.24	3.64
46	0.66	1.39	2.03	2.57	3.04	3.43
47	0.48	1.21	1.84	2.38	2.84	3.23
48	0.32	1.03	1.66	2.19	2.65	3.04
49	0.15	0.86	1.48	2.01	2.46	2.84
50		0.70	1.31	1.83	2.28	2.66
51		0.53	1.11	1.62	2.05	2.40
52		0.37	0.93	1.41	1.82	2.16
53		0.21	0.70	1.12	1.47	1.77
54		0.09	0.50	0.85	1.15	1.40
55			0.42	0.78	1.09	1.34
56			0.34	0.71	1.03	1.29
57			0.26	0.64	0.96	1.24
58			0.17	0.57	0.90	1.18
59			0.09	0.49	0.84	1.12
60				0.42	0.77	1.06
61				0.34	0.70	1.01
62				0.26	0.63	0.95
63				0.17	0.56	0.88
64				0.09	0.49	0.82
65					0.41	0.76
66					0.34	0.69
67					0.26	0.62
68					0.17	0.55
69					0.09	0.48
70						0.41
71						0.33
72						0.25
73						0.17
74						0.09

D NE <GCSE

Loss of earnings: disabled; not employed; education below good GCSE level

Age	Male to retiring age 50	55	60	65	70	75	Age	Female to retiring age 50	55	60	65	70	75
16	5.69	6.18	6.60	6.96	7.27	7.53	**16**	4.35	4.73	5.05	5.34	5.59	5.80
17	5.53	6.02	6.45	6.82	7.13	7.39	**17**	4.15	4.53	4.86	5.14	5.39	5.60
18	5.36	5.86	6.30	6.67	6.98	7.25	**18**	3.96	4.34	4.66	4.95	5.19	5.40
19	5.20	5.70	6.14	6.52	6.84	7.11	**19**	3.77	4.14	4.47	4.75	5.00	5.20
20	5.03	5.55	5.99	6.38	6.70	6.97	**20**	3.58	3.96	4.28	4.56	4.80	5.01
21	4.92	5.44	5.90	6.29	6.63	6.90	**21**	3.46	3.84	4.17	4.45	4.70	4.90
22	4.80	5.34	5.81	6.21	6.55	6.84	**22**	3.34	3.72	4.05	4.34	4.59	4.80
23	4.68	5.23	5.71	6.13	6.47	6.76	**23**	3.21	3.60	3.94	4.23	4.48	4.69
24	4.55	5.12	5.62	6.04	6.40	6.69	**24**	3.09	3.48	3.82	4.12	4.37	4.59
25	4.43	5.01	5.52	5.95	6.31	6.62	**25**	2.97	3.36	3.71	4.01	4.27	4.48
26	4.26	4.85	5.37	5.81	6.18	6.49	**26**	2.84	3.25	3.60	3.90	4.16	4.38
27	4.09	4.70	5.22	5.67	6.04	6.36	**27**	2.72	3.13	3.48	3.79	4.05	4.27
28	3.93	4.54	5.07	5.52	5.91	6.23	**28**	2.60	3.01	3.37	3.68	3.94	4.17
29	3.76	4.38	4.92	5.38	5.77	6.09	**29**	2.48	2.89	3.25	3.57	3.84	4.06
30	3.59	4.22	4.77	5.24	5.63	5.96	**30**	2.35	2.77	3.14	3.46	3.73	3.96
31	3.36	3.99	4.54	5.01	5.40	5.73	**31**	2.23	2.66	3.03	3.35	3.62	3.85
32	3.13	3.76	4.31	4.78	5.17	5.50	**32**	2.11	2.54	2.91	3.24	3.51	3.75
33	2.91	3.54	4.09	4.55	4.94	5.27	**33**	1.99	2.42	2.80	3.13	3.41	3.65
34	2.69	3.32	3.86	4.33	4.72	5.04	**34**	1.87	2.30	2.69	3.02	3.30	3.54
35	2.48	3.11	3.65	4.11	4.49	4.82	**35**	1.74	2.19	2.58	2.91	3.20	3.44
36	2.23	2.83	3.36	3.81	4.19	4.50	**36**	1.62	2.07	2.46	2.80	3.09	3.33
37	1.98	2.57	3.08	3.52	3.89	4.19	**37**	1.50	1.96	2.35	2.69	2.98	3.23
38	1.75	2.32	2.82	3.24	3.59	3.89	**38**	1.38	1.84	2.24	2.59	2.88	3.13
39	1.53	2.08	2.56	2.97	3.31	3.59	**39**	1.26	1.73	2.13	2.48	2.78	3.03
40	1.32	1.85	2.31	2.70	3.03	3.30	**40**	1.15	1.61	2.02	2.37	2.67	2.93
41	1.14	1.65	2.10	2.48	2.80	3.06	**41**	1.01	1.48	1.88	2.23	2.53	2.78
42	0.96	1.47	1.90	2.27	2.58	2.83	**42**	0.88	1.34	1.74	2.09	2.39	2.64
43	0.80	1.29	1.71	2.06	2.36	2.60	**43**	0.75	1.21	1.61	1.96	2.25	2.50
44	0.65	1.12	1.52	1.86	2.15	2.38	**44**	0.63	1.09	1.48	1.82	2.11	2.36
45	0.51	0.96	1.34	1.67	1.94	2.17	**45**	0.52	0.97	1.36	1.69	1.98	2.22
46	0.41	0.86	1.25	1.58	1.85	2.08	**46**	0.41	0.86	1.26	1.60	1.89	2.13
47	0.31	0.76	1.15	1.48	1.76	1.99	**47**	0.31	0.76	1.16	1.50	1.79	2.04
48	0.20	0.66	1.05	1.39	1.67	1.90	**48**	0.20	0.66	1.06	1.41	1.70	1.95
49	0.10	0.56	0.96	1.30	1.58	1.81	**49**	0.10	0.56	0.97	1.31	1.61	1.86
50		0.47	0.87	1.21	1.49	1.72	**50**		0.47	0.87	1.22	1.52	1.77
51		0.34	0.71	1.03	1.29	1.50	**51**		0.34	0.72	1.04	1.31	1.55
52		0.23	0.57	0.86	1.10	1.29	**52**		0.23	0.57	0.87	1.12	1.33
53		0.14	0.44	0.70	0.92	1.09	**53**		0.14	0.44	0.71	0.94	1.13
54		0.06	0.33	0.56	0.75	0.90	**54**		0.06	0.33	0.56	0.76	0.93
55			0.28	0.51	0.71	0.87	**55**			0.28	0.52	0.72	0.90
56			0.23	0.47	0.67	0.83	**56**			0.23	0.47	0.68	0.86
57			0.17	0.42	0.63	0.80	**57**			0.17	0.43	0.64	0.82
58			0.12	0.37	0.59	0.76	**58**			0.12	0.38	0.60	0.79
59			0.06	0.33	0.55	0.73	**59**			0.06	0.33	0.56	0.75
60				0.28	0.50	0.69	**60**				0.28	0.51	0.71
61				0.22	0.46	0.65	**61**				0.23	0.47	0.67
62				0.17	0.41	0.61	**62**				0.17	0.42	0.63
63				0.12	0.37	0.57	**63**				0.12	0.37	0.59
64				0.06	0.32	0.53	**64**				0.06	0.33	0.55
65					0.27	0.49	**65**					0.28	0.50
66					0.22	0.45	**66**					0.22	0.46
67					0.17	0.40	**67**					0.17	0.41
68					0.11	0.36	**68**					0.12	0.37
69					0.06	0.31	**69**					0.06	0.32
70						0.27	**70**						0.27
71						0.22	**71**						0.22
72						0.17	**72**						0.17
73						0.11	**73**						0.11
74						0.06	**74**						0.06

A5: Multipliers for fixed periods and at intervals

Introductory notes

1. The purpose of the tables is to provide a means of calculating an appropriate multiplier which will produce the present day equivalent of a cost recurring, either continuously or at fixed intervals, over a given number of years. It does not allow for mortality or contingencies.

2. The three tables are based on discount rates of 1.5 per cent, 2 per cent and 2.5 per cent per annum. The Lord Chancellor has fixed the discount rate under the Damages Act 1996 (June 27, 2001) at 2.5 per cent, leaving open the possibility of a different rate in exceptional cases such as the effect of tax on large sums.

3. It is assumed that yearly loss is incurred at the *end* of each year in which the loss arises. (Continuous loss obviously accrues from day to day throughout the period. Weekly and monthly losses can in practice be treated as continuous.) For example:

   For expenditure assumed to recur every 7 years the expenditure is shown as arising at the end of years 7, 14, and so on.

4. The table contains a number of columns: the number of years; the multiplier for a single payment in *n* years' time; that for a continuous loss over that period of *n* years; that for annual payments in the sense of a series of payments at intervals of 1 year; and those for payments at intervals of 2, 3, 4 and so on years.

5. The multiplier for a single payment in *n* years' time (second column) is the same as the discount factor for deferment for the next *n* years.

6. The table shows a multiplier appropriate to each year in which expenditure is to be incurred, and also cumulative multipliers for expenditure up to the end of that year. For example, at 2.5 per cent discount:

   The multiplier for expenditure at the end of year 10 is 0.781. Thus the current lump sum required to provide £100 in 10 years' time is £78.10.

   And similarly:

   - £100 a year continuously over the next 10 years has a present value of £886;
   - £100 at the end of each of the next 10 years a present value of £875;
   - £100 at the end of 2,4,6,8 and 10 years a present value of £432 (row 10, 2-yearly column);
   - £100 at the end of 3,6 and 9 years a present value of £259 (row 9, 3-yearly column).

   The cumulative multipliers do not include an immediate payment: where one is needed in addition to the recurring payments add 1.00 to the multiplier.

7. The calculations have been rounded to 2 places of decimals.

Multipliers where there is evidence of life expectancy

8. In some cases there is medical evidence (agreed or not) of the particular claimant's life expectancy. As more distant losses have lower present value, the possibility of dying earlier than expected has more effect on the multiplier than that of dying later than expected. The multiplier for life of someone whose life expectancy is *n* years will therefore be lower than the multiplier for a fixed period of *n* years. The difference varies with sex and age. It is not large but at a discount rate of 2.5 per cent it is not negligible.

Reduction of fixed multipliers for mortality

9. For the reasons discussed above in relation to cases where there is evidence of life expectancy, in all cases where the period of loss is dependent on someone's life the multiplier for a fixed period will be slightly higher than the true multiplier. In appropriate cases the fixed term multipliers can be reduced by the method discussed in paragraphs 20–23 of the Ogden notes (section A10 of this book).

10. For example:

The claimant is aged 53 and 7 months. His life expectancy is 30 years. For the first 12 years he will need care at £10,000 a year and incur expenditure on equipment of £5,000 every 4 years. For the remaining 18 years he will need care at £20,000 a year and expenditure on equipment of £6,000 every 3 years.

For a fixed term of 30 years the multipliers at 2.5 per cent – from the following table – are:

First 12 years:	care	equipment	Remaining 18 years:	care	equipment	30 years
	10.39	2.47		10.80	3.47	21.19

The claimant's multiplier for life at 2.5 per cent (Table A1) is 20.33. It is not 21.19, because the possibility of dying earlier than expected affects the multiplier more than the possibility of dying later. The fixed term multipliers for care and equipment are therefore high and need to be reduced by a factor of 20.33/21.19 = 0.96.

Multipliers adjusted for mortality (that is multiplied by 0.96):

First 12 years:	care	equipment	Remaining 18 years:	care	equipment	Life
	9.97	2.37		10.36	3.33	20.33

Modifications

11. Multipliers for continuous loss for periods other than entire years can be obtained by interpolation:

For continuous payments for 10 and 11 years the multipliers are 8.86 and 9.63.

So for weekly payments for $10\frac{1}{2}$ years the multiplier is approximately $\frac{1}{2}(8.86 + 9.63) = 9.25$.

12. Multipliers for payments beginning after a deferred period can be derived by subtraction or by multiplying by a factor from the single payment column:

Multipliers for 5-yearly payments for 15 and for 50 years are 2.36 and 5.40;

So the multiplier for 5-yearly payments from years 20 to 50 inclusive is $5.40 - 2.36 = 3.14$;

Multiplier for one payment after 18 years is 0.641;

So that for 5-yearly payments from years 23 to 68 inclusive is $5.40 \times 0.641 = 3.46$.

13. Multipliers for irregular payments can be found by adding individual figures from the single payment column.

Multipliers at 1.5 per cent discount

	Single payment	Continuous loss	Frequency of payments in years											
n			**1**	**2**	**3**	**4**	**5**	**6**	**7**	**8**	**10**	**12**	**15**	**20**
1	0.985	0.99	0.99											
2	0.971	1.97	1.96	0.97										
3	0.956	2.93	2.91		0.96									
4	0.942	3.88	3.85	1.91		0.94								
5	0.928	4.82	4.78				0.93							
6	0.915	5.74	5.70	2.83	1.87			0.91						
7	0.901	6.65	6.60						0.90					
8	0.888	7.54	7.49	3.72		1.83				0.89				
9	0.875	8.42	8.36		2.75									
10	0.862	9.29	9.22	4.58			1.79				0.86			
11	0.849	10.15	10.07											
12	0.836	10.99	10.91	5.41	3.58	2.67		1.75				0.84		
13	0.824	11.82	11.73											
14	0.812	12.64	12.54	6.23					1.71					
15	0.800	13.44	13.34		4.38		2.59						0.80	
16	0.788	14.24	14.13	7.01		3.45				1.68				
17	0.776	15.02	14.91											
18	0.765	15.79	15.67	7.78	5.15			2.52						
19	0.754	16.55	16.43											
20	0.742	17.30	17.17	8.52		4.20	3.33				1.60			0.74
21	0.731	18.03	17.90		5.88				2.44					
22	0.721	18.76	18.62	9.24										
23	0.710	19.48	19.33											
24	0.700	20.18	20.03	9.94	6.58	4.90		3.22		2.38		1.54		
25	0.689	20.88	20.72				4.02							
26	0.679	21.56	21.40	10.62										
27	0.669	22.23	22.07		7.25									
28	0.659	22.90	22.73	11.28		5.56			3.10					
29	0.649	23.55	23.38											
30	0.640	24.20	24.02	11.92	7.89		4.66	3.86			2.24		1.44	
31	0.630	24.83	24.65											
32	0.621	25.46	25.27	12.54		6.18				3.00				
33	0.612	26.07	25.88		8.50									
34	0.603	26.68	26.48	13.14										
35	0.594	27.28	27.08				5.26		3.70					
36	0.585	27.87	27.66	13.73	9.08	6.76		4.44				2.12		
37	0.576	28.45	28.24											
38	0.568	29.02	28.81	14.30										
39	0.560	29.58	29.36		9.64									
40	0.551	30.14	29.92	14.85		7.31	5.81			3.55	2.80			1.29
41	0.543	30.69	30.46											
42	0.535	31.23	30.99	15.38	10.18			4.98	4.23					
43	0.527	31.76	31.52											
44	0.519	32.28	32.04	15.90		7.83								
45	0.512	32.80	32.55		10.69		6.32						1.95	
46	0.504	33.30	33.06	16.41										
47	0.497	33.80	33.55											
48	0.489	34.30	34.04	16.89	11.18	8.32		5.46		4.04		2.61		
49	0.482	34.78	34.52						4.71					
50	0.475	35.26	35.00	17.37			6.79				3.27			
51	0.468	35.73	35.47		11.65									
52	0.461	36.20	35.93	17.83		8.78								
53	0.454	36.66	36.38											
54	0.448	37.11	36.83	18.28	12.09			5.91						
55	0.441	37.55	37.27				7.23							
56	0.434	37.99	37.71	18.71		9.22			5.15	4.47				
57	0.428	38.42	38.13		12.52									
58	0.422	38.84	38.56	19.13										
59	0.415	39.26	38.97											
60	0.409	39.68	39.38	19.54	12.93	9.63	7.64	6.32			3.68	3.02	2.36	1.70

	Single payment	Continuous loss	Frequency of payments in years												
n			**1**	**2**	**3**	**4**	**5**	**6**	**7**	**8**	**10**	**12**	**15**	**20**
61	0.403	40.08	39.78											
62	0.397	40.48	40.18	19.94										
63	0.391	40.88	40.57		13.32				5.54					
64	0.386	41.27	40.96	20.33		10.01				4.86				
65	0.380	41.65	41.34				8.02							
66	0.374	42.02	41.71	20.70	13.70			6.70						
67	0.369	42.40	42.08											
68	0.363	42.76	42.44	21.06		10.38								
69	0.358	43.12	42.80		14.06									
70	0.353	43.48	43.15	21.42			8.38		5.89		4.03			
71	0.347	43.83	43.50											
72	0.342	44.17	43.84	21.76	14.4	10.72		7.04		5.20		3.36		
73	0.337	44.51	44.18											
74	0.332	44.85	44.51	22.09										
75	0.327	45.18	44.84		14.73		8.70						2.69	
76	0.323	45.50	45.16	22.41		11.04								
77	0.318	45.82	45.48						6.21					
78	0.313	46.14	45.79	22.73	15.04			7.35						
79	0.308	46.45	46.10											
80	0.304	46.76	46.41	23.03		11.34	9.01			5.50	4.34			2.01
81	0.299	47.06	46.71		15.34									
82	0.295	47.35	47.00	23.33										
83	0.291	47.65	47.29											
84	0.286	47.94	47.58	23.61	15.62	11.63		7.64	6.50			3.65		
85	0.282	48.22	47.86				9.29							
86	0.278	48.50	48.14	23.89										
87	0.274	48.78	48.51		15.90									
88	0.270	49.05	48.68	24.16		11.90				5.77				
89	0.266	49.32	48.95											
90	0.262	49.58	49.21	24.42	16.16		9.55	7.90			4.60		2.95	
91	0.258	49.84	49.47						6.76					
92	0.254	50.09	49.72	24.68		12.15								
93	0.250	50.35	49.97		16.41									
94	0.247	50.60	50.22	24.92										
95	0.243	50.84	50.46				9.79							
96	0.239	51.08	50.70	25.16	16.65	12.39		8.14		6.01		3.89		
97	0.236	51.32	50.94											
98	0.232	51.55	51.17	25.39					6.99					
99	0.229	51.78	51.40		16.88									
100	0.226	52.01	51.62	25.62		12.62	10.02				4.82			2.23

1. The single payment column is the appropriate multiplier for one payment in *n* years' time.
2. The continuous loss column is for loss accruing from day to day: in practice it is appropriate for weekly and monthly losses as well.
3. The column headed "1" is for a series of payments at yearly intervals at the *end of each year* for *n* years. If you want an immediate payment as well, add 1.
4. The remaining columns similarly show the multiplier for a series of payments at invervals of 2, 3, 4 and so on years.
5. Thus at 1.5 per cent discount £100 paid after 10 years has a present value of £86.20;
   – £100 a year continuously over the next 10 years has a present value of £929;
   – £100 at the end of each of the next 10 years has a present value of £922;
   – £100 at the end of 2, 4, 6, 8 and 10 years has a present value of £458 (row 10, 2-yearly column);
   – £100 at the end of 3, 6 and 9 years has a present value of £275 (row 9, 3-yearly column);
   – £100 now and after 2, 4, 6 and 8 years (but *not* the 10th year) has a present value of £472 (row 8, 2-yearly column, *plus* 1).

Multipliers at 2 per cent discount

n	Single payment	Continuous loss	Frequency of payments in years											
			1	2	3	4	5	6	7	8	10	12	15	20
1	0.980	0.99	0.98											
2	0.961	1.96	1.94	0.96										
3	0.942	2.91	2.88		0.94									
4	0.924	3.85	3.81	1.89		0.92								
5	0.906	4.76	4.71				0.91							
6	0.888	5.66	5.60	2.77	1.83			0.89						
7	0.871	6.54	6.47						0.87					
8	0.853	7.40	7.33	3.63		1.78				0.85				
9	0.837	8.24	8.16		2.67									
10	0.820	9.07	8.98	4.45			1.73				0.82			
11	0.804	9.88	9.79											
12	0.788	10.68	10.58	5.24	3.46	2.57		1.68				0.79		
13	0.773	11.46	11.35											
14	0.758	12.23	12.11	5.99					1.63					
15	0.743	12.98	12.85		4.20		2.47						0.74	
16	0.728	13.71	13.58	6.72		3.29				1.58				
17	0.714	14.43	14.29											
18	0.700	15.14	14.99	7.42	4.90			2.38						
19	0.686	15.84	15.68											
20	0.673	16.51	16.35	8.09		3.97	3.14				1.49			0.67
21	0.660	17.18	17.01		5.56				2.29					
22	0.647	17.83	17.66	8.74										
23	0.634	18.48	18.29											
24	0.622	19.10	18.91	9.36	6.18	4.59		3.00		2.20		1.41		
25	0.610	19.72	19.52				3.75							
26	0.598	20.32	20.12	9.96										
27	0.586	20.91	20.71		6.77									
28	0.574	21.49	21.28	10.54		5.16			2.86					
29	0.563	22.06	21.84											
30	0.552	22.62	22.40	11.09	7.32		4.30	3.55			2.05		1.30	
31	0.541	23.17	22.94											
32	0.531	23.70	23.47	11.62		5.69				2.73				
33	0.520	24.23	23.99		7.84									
34	0.510	24.74	24.50	12.13										
35	0.500	25.25	25.00				4.80		3.36					
36	0.490	25.74	25.49	12.62	8.33	6.18		4.04				1.90		
37	0.481	26.23	25.97											
38	0.471	26.71	26.44	13.09										
39	0.462	27.17	26.90		8.79									
40	0.453	27.63	27.36	13.54		6.64	5.26			3.19	2.50			1.13
41	0.444	28.08	27.80											
42	0.435	28.52	28.23	13.98	9.23			4.48	3.80					
43	0.427	28.95	28.66											
44	0.418	29.37	29.08	14.40		7.06								
45	0.410	29.79	29.49		9.64		5.67						1.71	
46	0.402	30.19	29.89	14.80										
47	0.394	30.59	30.29											
48	0.387	30.98	30.67	15.18	10.02	7.44		4.86		3.57		2.29		
49	0.379	31.36	31.05						4.18					
50	0.372	31.74	31.42	15.56			6.04				2.87			
51	0.364	32.11	31.79		10.39									
52	0.357	32.47	32.14	15.91		7.80								
53	0.350	32.82	32.50											
54	0.343	33.17	32.84	16.26	10.73			5.21						
55	0.337	33.51	33.17				6.37							
56	0.330	33.84	33.50	16.59		8.13			4.51	3.90				
57	0.323	34.17	33.83		11.06									
58	0.317	34.49	34.15	16.90										
59	0.311	34.80	34.46											
60	0.305	35.11	34.76	17.21	11.36	8.43	6.68	5.51			3.17	2.59	2.01	1.43

	Single payment	Continuous loss	Frequency of payments in years											
n			1	2	3	4	5	6	7	8	10	12	15	20
61	0.299	35.41	35.06											
62	0.293	35.71	35.35	17.50										
63	0.287	36.00	35.64		11.65				4.80					
64	0.282	36.28	35.92	17.78		8.72				4.19				
65	0.276	36.56	36.20				6.96							
66	0.271	36.83	36.47	18.05	11.92			5.78						
67	0.265	37.10	36.73											
68	0.260	37.36	36.99	18.31		8.98								
69	0.255	37.62	37.25		12.17									
70	0.250	37.87	37.50	18.56			7.21		5.04		3.42			
71	0.245	38.12	37.74											
72	0.240	38.36	37.98	18.80	12.41	9.22		6.02		4.43		2.83		
73	0.236	38.60	38.22											
74	0.231	38.84	38.45	19.03										
75	0.226	39.06	38.68		12.64		7.43						2.24	
76	0.222	39.29	38.90	19.26		9.44								
77	0.218	39.51	39.12						5.26					
78	0.213	39.72	39.33	19.47	12.85			6.23						
79	0.209	39.93	39.54											
80	0.205	40.14	39.74	19.68		9.64	7.64			4.63	3.63			1.64
81	0.201	40.35	39.95		13.05									
82	0.197	40.54	40.14	19.87										
83	0.193	40.74	40.34											
84	0.189	40.93	40.53	20.06	13.24	9.83		6.42	5.45			3.02		
85	0.186	41.12	40.71				7.82							
86	0.182	41.30	40.89	20.24										
87	0.179	41.48	41.07		13.42									
88	0.175	41.66	41.25	20.42		10.01				4.81				
89	0.172	41.83	41.42											
90	0.168	42.00	41.59	20.59	13.59		7.99	6.59			3.80		2.40	
91	0.165	42.17	41.75						5.62					
92	0.162	42.33	41.91	20.75		10.17								
93	0.159	42.49	42.07		13.75									
94	0.155	42.65	42.23	20.90										
95	0.152	42.80	42.38				8.14							
96	0.149	42.95	42.53	21.05	13.90	10.32		6.74		4.96		3.17		
97	0.146	43.10	42.68											
98	0.144	43.25	42.82	21.20					5.76					
99	0.141	43.39	42.96		14.04									
100	0.138	43.53	43.10	21.34		10.46	8.28				3.94			1.77

1. The single payment column is the appropriate multiplier for one payment in *n* years' time.
2. The continuous loss column is for loss accruing from day to day: in practice it is appropriate for weekly and monthly losses as well.
3. The column headed "1" is for a series of payments at yearly intervals at the *end of each year* for *n* years. If you want an immediate payment as well, add 1.
4. The remaining columns similarly show the multiplier for a series of payments at intervals of 2, 3, 4 and so on years.
5. Thus at 2 per cent discount £100 paid after 10 years has a present value of £82;
   - £100 a year continuously over the next 10 years has a present value of £907;
   - £100 at the end of each of the next 10 years has a present value of £898;
   - £100 at the end of 2, 4, 6, 8 and 10 years has a present value of £455 (row 10, 2-yearly column);
   - £100 at the end of 3, 6 and 9 years has a present value of £267 (row 9, 3-yearly column);
   - £100 now and after 2, 4, 6 and 8 years (but *not* the 10th year) has a present value of £463 (row 9, 2-yearly column, plus 1).

Multipliers at 2.5 per cent discount

	Single payment	Continuous loss	Frequency of payments in years											
n			1	2	3	4	5	6	7	8	10	12	15	20
1	0.976	0.99	0.98											
2	0.952	1.95	1.93	0.95										
3	0.929	2.89	2.86		0.93									
4	0.906	3.81	3.76	1.86		0.91								
5	0.884	4.70	4.65				0.88							
6	0.862	5.58	5.51	2.72	1.79			0.86						
7	0.841	6.43	6.35						0.84					
8	0.821	7.26	7.17	3.54		1.73				0.82				
9	0.801	8.07	7.97		2.59									
10	0.781	8.86	8.75	4.32			1.67				0.78			
11	0.762	9.63	9.51											
12	0.744	10.39	10.26	5.07	3.34	2.47		1.61				0.74		
13	0.725	11.12	10.98											
14	0.708	11.84	11.69	5.77					1.55					
15	0.690	12.54	12.38		4.03		2.36						0.69	
16	0.674	13.22	13.06	6.45		3.14				1.49				
17	0.657	13.88	13.71											
18	0.641	14.53	14.35	7.09	4.67			2.25						
19	0.626	15.17	14.98											
20	0.610	15.78	15.59	7.70		3.75	2.97				1.39			0.61
21	0.595	16.39	16.18		5.26				2.14					
22	0.581	16.97	16.77	8.28										
23	0.567	17.55	17.33											
24	0.553	18.11	17.88	8.83	5.82	4.31		2.80		2.05		1.30		
25	0.539	18.65	18.42				3.51							
26	0.526	19.19	18.95	9.36										
27	0.513	19.71	19.46		6.33									
28	0.501	20.21	19.96	9.86		4.81			2.65					
29	0.489	20.71	20.45											
30	0.477	21.19	20.93	10.34	6.81		3.98	3.28			1.87		1.17	
31	0.465	21.66	21.40											
32	0.454	22.12	21.85	10.79		5.26				2.50				
33	0.443	22.57	22.29		7.25									
34	0.432	23.01	22.72	11.22										
35	0.421	23.43	23.15				4.40		3.07					
36	0.411	23.85	23.56	11.63	7.66	5.67		3.69				1.71		
37	0.401	24.26	23.96											
38	0.391	24.65	24.35	12.02										
39	0.382	25.04	24.73		8.04									
40	0.372	25.42	25.10	12.40		6.05	4.78			2.87	2.24			0.98
41	0.363	25.78	25.47											
42	0.354	26.14	25.82	12.75	8.40			4.04	3.42					
43	0.346	26.49	26.17											
44	0.337	26.84	26.50	13.09		6.38								
45	0.329	27.17	26.83		8.72		5.10						1.50	
46	0.321	27.49	27.15	13.41										
47	0.313	27.81	27.47											
48	0.306	28.12	27.77	13.72	9.03	6.69		4.35		3.18		2.01		
49	0.298	28.42	28.07						3.72					
50	0.291	28.72	28.36	14.01			5.40				2.53			
51	0.284	29.00	28.65		9.31									
52	0.277	29.28	28.92	14.28		6.97								
53	0.270	29.56	29.19											
54	0.264	29.83	29.46	14.55	9.58			4.61						
55	0.257	30.09	29.71				5.65							
56	0.251	30.34	29.96	14.80		7.22			3.97	3.43				
57	0.245	30.59	30.21		9.82									
58	0.239	30.83	30.45	15.04										
59	0.233	31.06	30.68											
60	0.227	31.30	30.91	15.26	10.05	7.44	5.88	4.84			2.76	2.24	1.72	1.21

	Single payment	**Continuous loss**	**Frequency of payments in years**											
n			**1**	**2**	**3**	**4**	**5**	**6**	**7**	**8**	**10**	**12**	**15**	**20**
61	0.222	31.52	31.13											
62	0.216	31.74	31.35	15.48										
63	0.211	31.95	31.56		10.26				4.18					
64	0.206	32.16	31.76	15.69		7.65				3.64				
65	0.201	32.36	31.96				6.08							
66	0.196	32.56	32.16	15.88	10.46			5.04						
67	0.191	32.76	32.35											
68	0.187	32.94	32.54	16.07		7.84								
69	0.182	33.13	32.72		10.64									
70	0.178	33.31	32.90	16.25			6.26		4.36		2.94			
71	0.173	33.48	33.07											
72	0.169	33.66	33.24	16.41	10.81	8.00		5.20		3.80		2.41		
73	0.165	33.82	33.40											
74	0.161	33.99	33.57	16.58										
75	0.157	34.14	33.72		10.96		6.42						1.88	
76	0.153	34.30	33.88	16.73		8.16								
77	0.149	34.45	34.03						4.51					
78	0.146	34.60	34.17	16.87	11.11			5.35						
79	0.142	34.74	34.31											
80	0.139	34.88	34.45	17.01		8.30	6.55			3.94	3.08			1.35
81	0.135	35.02	34.59		11.25									
82	0.132	35.15	34.72	17.15										
83	0.129	35.28	34.85											
84	0.126	35.41	34.97	17.27	11.37	8.42		5.48	4.63			2.54		
85	0.123	35.53	35.10				6.68							
86	0.120	35.66	35.22	17.39										
87	0.117	35.77	35.33		11.49									
88	0.114	35.89	35.45	17.50		8.54				4.06				
89	0.111	36.00	35.56											
90	0.108	36.11	35.67	17.61	11.60		6.79	5.58			3.18		1.99	
91	0.106	36.22	35.77						4.74					
92	0.103	36.32	35.87	17.72		8.64								
93	0.101	36.42	35.98		11.70									
94	0.098	36.52	36.07	17.81										
95	0.096	36.62	36.17				6.88							
96	0.093	36.72	36.26	17.91	11.79	8.73		5.68		4.15		2.63		
97	0.091	36.81	36.35											
98	0.089	36.90	36.44	18.00					4.83					
99	0.087	36.99	36.53		11.88									
100	0.085	37.07	36.61	18.08		8.82	6.97				3.27			1.43

1. The single payment column is the appropriate multiplier for one payment in n years' time.
2. The continuous loss column is for loss accruing from day to day: in practice it is appropriate for weekly and monthly losses as well.
3. The column headed "1" is for a series of payments at yearly intervals *at the end of each year* for n years. If you want an immediate payment as well, add 1.
4. The remaining columns similarly show the multiplier for a series of payments at intervals of 2, 3, 4 and so on years.
5. Thus at 2.5 per cent discount £100 paid after 10 years has a present value of £78.10;
   - £100 a year continuously over the next 10 years has a present value of £886;
   - £100 at the end of each of the next 10 years has a present value of £875;
   - £100 at the end of 2, 4, 6, 8 and 10 years has a present value of £432 (row 10, 2-yearly column);
   - £100 at the end of 3, 6 and 9 years has a present value of £259 (row 9, 3-yearly column);
   - £100 now and after 2, 4, 6 and 8 years (but not the 10th year) has a present value of £454 (row 8, 2-yearly column, plus 1).

A6: Combination Tables

Introductory notes

1. The following table is a combination of Ogden Tables 27 and 28. This is intended for use when a claimant will suffer a loss over a known number of years, but that loss will not start to run immediately.

2. For example:

   a. The claimant is now thirty years old. He has a reduced life expectation, to the age of 60. For the last ten years of his life, he will need nursing care at a cost of £7,500 a year. His nursing needs will therefore start in twenty years.

   b. At 2.5 per cent discount, the multiplier for a period of ten years is 8.86 [Ogden Table 28].

   c. At 2.5 per cent discount, a loss that will not occur for a further twenty years must be discounted by multiplying it by 0.6103 [Ogden Table 27].

   d. The appropriate multiplier is therefore [8.86 × 0.6103] = 5.41 (to two decimal places).

   But see paras 20–33 of the Ogden notes.

3. The following points should also be remembered:

   a. When applying the multipliers to claims for loss of earnings, Ogden Tables 3–14 only take the ordinary risks of mortality into account. They do *not* take into account any other factors such as educational attainment or disability. A further discount must be made for these risks: see Section B of the Introduction to the Ogden Tables (Contingencies other than Mortality).

   b. Ogden Table 27 (Discounting Factors for Term Certain) gives the discount factor for a period of *complete* years. So in the example above, where the date of trial is May 23, 2009, the need for nursing care will start on May 23, 2029.

   c. Ogden Table 28 (Multipliers for Pecuniary Loss for Term Certain) assumes that the loss will occur regularly throughout the year, e.g. a monthly nursing bill.

Combination grid (Discount rate 1.5%)

Years of loss	Years before loss starts to run 1	2	3	4	5	6	7	8	9	10	12.5	15	20	25	30	35	40	Years of loss
1	0.98	0.96	0.95	0.94	0.92	0.91	0.89	0.88	0.87	0.86	0.82	0.79	0.74	0.68	0.64	0.59	0.55	**1**
2	1.94	1.91	1.88	1.86	1.83	1.80	1.78	1.75	1.72	1.70	1.64	1.58	1.46	1.36	1.26	1.17	1.09	**2**
3	2.89	2.85	2.81	2.76	2.72	2.68	2.64	2.60	2.57	2.53	2.44	2.35	2.18	2.02	1.88	1.74	1.62	**3**
4	3.83	3.77	3.71	3.66	3.60	3.55	3.50	3.45	3.40	3.35	3.22	3.11	2.88	2.68	2.48	2.31	2.14	**4**
5	4.75	4.68	4.61	4.54	4.47	4.41	4.34	4.28	4.21	4.15	4.00	3.85	3.58	3.32	3.08	2.86	2.66	**5**
6	5.66	5.57	5.49	5.41	5.33	5.25	5.17	5.10	5.02	4.95	4.77	4.59	4.26	3.96	3.67	3.41	3.16	**6**
7	6.55	6.45	6.36	6.26	6.17	6.08	5.99	5.90	5.81	5.73	5.52	5.32	4.94	4.58	4.25	3.95	3.66	**7**
8	7.43	7.32	7.21	7.11	7.00	6.90	6.80	6.70	6.60	6.50	6.26	6.03	5.60	5.20	4.83	4.48	4.16	**8**
9	8.30	8.18	8.06	7.94	7.82	7.70	7.59	7.48	7.37	7.26	6.99	6.74	6.25	5.81	5.39	5.00	4.64	**9**
10	9.15	9.02	8.89	8.75	8.62	8.50	8.37	8.25	8.13	8.01	7.71	7.43	6.90	6.40	5.94	5.52	5.12	**10**
11	10.00	9.85	9.70	9.56	9.42	9.28	9.14	9.01	8.87	8.74	8.42	8.12	7.53	6.99	6.49	6.03	5.59	**11**
12	10.83	10.67	10.51	10.35	10.20	10.05	9.90	9.76	9.61	9.47	9.12	8.79	8.16	7.57	7.03	6.53	6.06	**12**
13	11.64	11.47	11.30	11.14	10.97	10.81	10.65	10.49	10.34	10.18	9.81	9.45	8.78	8.15	7.56	7.02	6.52	**13**
14	12.45	12.27	12.09	11.91	11.73	11.56	11.39	11.22	11.05	10.89	10.49	10.11	9.38	8.71	8.08	7.50	6.97	**14**
15	13.24	13.05	12.86	12.67	12.48	12.29	12.11	11.93	11.76	11.58	11.16	10.75	9.98	9.27	8.60	7.98	7.41	**15**
16	14.03	13.82	13.62	13.41	13.22	13.02	12.83	12.64	12.45	12.27	11.82	11.39	10.57	9.81	9.11	8.46	7.85	**16**
17	14.80	14.58	14.36	14.15	13.94	13.74	13.53	13.33	13.14	12.94	12.47	12.01	11.15	10.35	9.61	8.92	8.28	**17**
18	15.56	15.33	15.10	14.88	14.66	14.44	14.23	14.02	13.81	13.61	13.11	12.63	11.72	10.88	10.10	9.38	8.70	**18**
19	16.30	16.06	15.83	15.59	15.36	15.14	14.91	14.69	14.47	14.26	13.74	13.24	12.29	11.41	10.59	9.83	9.12	**19**
20	17.04	16.79	16.54	16.30	16.06	15.82	15.59	15.36	15.13	14.90	14.36	13.84	12.84	11.92	11.07	10.27	9.54	**20**
21	17.77	17.51	17.25	16.99	16.74	16.49	16.25	16.01	15.77	15.54	14.97	14.42	13.39	12.43	11.54	10.71	9.94	**21**
22	18.48	18.21	17.94	17.68	17.41	17.16	16.90	16.65	16.41	16.17	15.57	15.01	13.93	12.93	12.00	11.14	10.34	**22**
23	19.19	18.90	18.63	18.35	18.08	17.81	17.55	17.29	17.03	16.78	16.17	15.58	14.46	13.42	12.46	11.57	10.74	**23**
24	19.88	19.59	19.30	19.01	18.73	18.46	18.18	17.91	17.65	17.39	16.75	16.14	14.98	13.91	12.91	11.98	11.12	**24**
25	20.57	20.26	19.96	19.67	19.38	19.09	18.81	18.53	18.26	17.99	17.33	16.70	15.50	14.39	13.36	12.40	11.51	**25**
26	21.24	20.93	20.62	20.31	20.01	19.72	19.43	19.14	18.86	18.58	17.90	17.24	16.01	14.86	13.79	12.80	11.88	**26**
27	21.90	21.58	21.26	20.95	20.64	20.33	20.03	19.74	19.44	19.16	18.46	17.78	16.51	15.32	14.22	13.20	12.26	**27**
28	22.56	22.23	21.90	21.57	21.25	20.94	20.63	20.33	20.03	19.73	19.01	18.31	17.00	15.78	14.65	13.60	12.62	**28**
29	23.20	22.86	22.52	22.19	21.86	21.54	21.22	20.91	20.60	20.29	19.55	18.84	17.49	16.23	15.07	13.99	12.98	**29**
30	23.84	23.49	23.14	22.80	22.46	22.13	21.80	21.48	21.16	20.85	20.09	19.35	17.96	16.68	15.48	14.37	13.34	**30**
31	24.46	24.10	23.75	23.40	23.05	22.71	22.37	22.04	21.72	21.40	20.61	19.86	18.44	17.11	15.89	14.75	13.69	**31**
32	25.08	24.71	24.34	23.98	23.63	23.28	22.94	22.60	22.26	21.94	21.13	20.36	18.90	17.54	16.29	15.12	14.03	**32**
33	25.69	25.31	24.93	24.57	24.20	23.84	23.49	23.15	22.80	22.47	21.65	20.85	19.36	17.97	16.68	15.48	14.37	**33**
34	26.29	25.90	25.51	25.14	24.77	24.40	24.04	23.68	23.33	22.99	22.15	21.34	19.81	18.39	17.07	15.84	14.71	**34**
35	26.88	26.48	26.09	25.70	25.32	24.95	24.58	24.22	23.86	23.51	22.65	21.82	20.25	18.80	17.45	16.20	15.04	**35**
36	27.46	27.05	26.65	26.26	25.87	25.49	25.11	24.74	24.37	24.01	23.14	22.29	20.69	19.21	17.83	16.55	15.36	**36**
37	28.03	27.61	27.21	26.80	26.41	26.02	25.63	25.25	24.88	24.51	23.62	22.75	21.12	19.61	18.20	16.89	15.68	**37**
38	28.59	28.17	27.75	27.34	26.94	26.54	26.15	25.76	25.38	25.01	24.09	23.21	21.55	20.00	18.57	17.23	16.00	**38**
39	29.15	28.72	28.29	27.87	27.46	27.06	26.66	26.26	25.87	25.49	24.56	23.66	21.97	20.39	18.93	17.57	16.31	**39**
40	29.69	29.26	28.82	28.40	27.98	27.56	27.16	26.76	26.36	25.97	25.02	24.11	22.38	20.77	19.28	17.90	16.62	**40**
41	30.23	29.79	29.35	28.91	28.49	28.06	27.65	27.24	26.84	26.44	25.48	24.55	22.78	21.15	19.63	18.22	16.92	**41**
42	30.77	30.31	29.86	29.42	28.99	28.56	28.14	27.72	27.31	26.91	25.92	24.98	23.18	21.52	19.98	18.54	17.21	**42**
43	31.29	30.83	30.37	29.92	29.48	29.04	28.61	28.19	27.77	27.36	26.36	25.40	23.58	21.89	20.32	18.86	17.51	**43**
44	31.80	31.33	30.87	30.41	29.97	29.52	29.09	28.66	28.23	27.82	26.80	25.82	23.97	22.25	20.65	19.17	17.80	**44**
45	32.31	31.83	31.36	30.90	30.44	29.99	29.55	29.11	28.68	28.26	27.23	26.23	24.35	22.60	20.98	19.48	18.08	**45**
Years of loss	**1**	**2**	**3**	**4**	**5**	**6**	**7**	**8**	**9**	**10**	**12.5**	**15**	**20**	**25**	**30**	**35**	**40**	**Years of loss**

Combination grid (Discount rate 2%)

Years of loss	Years before loss starts to run 1	2	3	4	5	6	7	8	9	10	12.5	15	20	25	30	35	40	Years of loss
1	0.97	0.95	0.93	0.91	0.90	0.88	0.86	0.85	0.83	0.81	0.77	0.74	0.67	0.60	0.55	0.50	0.45	1
2	1.92	1.88	1.85	1.81	1.78	1.74	1.71	1.67	1.64	1.61	1.53	1.46	1.32	1.20	1.08	0.98	0.89	2
3	2.86	2.80	2.74	2.69	2.64	2.59	2.54	2.49	2.44	2.39	2.27	2.16	1.96	1.78	1.61	1.46	1.32	3
4	3.77	3.70	3.62	3.55	3.48	3.41	3.35	3.28	3.22	31.5	3.00	2.86	2.59	2.34	2.12	1.92	1.74	4
5	4.67	4.58	4.49	4.40	4.31	4.23	4.14	4.06	3.98	3.91	3.72	3.54	3.20	2.90	2.63	2.38	2.16	5
6	5.55	5.44	5.33	5.23	5.12	5.02	4.93	4.83	4.73	4.64	4.42	4.20	3.81	3.45	3.12	2.83	2.56	6
7	6.41	6.28	6.16	6.04	5.92	5.80	5.69	5.58	5.47	5.36	5.10	4.86	4.40	3.98	3.61	3.27	2.96	7
8	7.25	7.11	6.97	6.84	6.70	6.57	6.44	6.31	6.19	6.07	5.78	5.50	4.98	4.51	4.08	3.70	3.35	8
9	8.08	7.92	7.77	7.62	7.47	7.32	7.18	7.04	6.90	6.76	6.44	6.13	5.55	5.02	4.55	4.12	3.73	9
10	8.89	8.72	8.55	8.38	8.22	8.06	7.90	7.74	7.59	7.44	7.08	6.74	6.11	5.53	5.01	4.54	4.11	10
11	9.69	9.50	9.31	9.13	8.95	8.78	8.61	8.44	8.27	8.11	7.72	7.34	6.65	6.03	5.46	4.94	4.48	11
12	10.47	10.27	10.07	9.87	9.67	9.48	9.30	9.12	8.94	8.76	8.34	7.94	7.19	6.51	5.90	5.34	4.84	12
13	11.24	11.02	10.80	10.59	10.38	10.18	9.98	9.78	9.59	9.40	8.95	8.52	7.71	6.99	6.33	5.73	5.19	13
14	11.99	11.75	11.52	11.30	11.07	10.86	10.64	10.44	10.23	10.03	9.55	9.09	8.23	7.45	6.75	6.11	5.54	14
15	12.72	12.47	12.23	11.99	11.75	11.52	11.30	11.08	10.86	10.65	10.13	9.64	8.73	7.91	7.16	6.49	5.88	15
16	13.44	13.18	12.92	12.67	12.42	12.18	11.94	11.70	11.47	11.25	10.71	10.19	9.23	8.36	7.57	6.86	6.21	16
17	14.15	13.87	13.60	13.34	13.07	12.82	12.57	12.32	12.08	11.84	11.27	10.73	9.71	8.80	7.97	7.22	6.54	17
18	14.85	14.55	14.27	13.99	13.71	13.45	13.18	12.92	12.67	12.42	11.82	11.25	10.19	9.23	8.36	7.57	6.86	18
19	15.52	15.22	14.92	14.63	14.34	14.06	13.79	13.52	13.25	12.99	12.36	11.77	10.66	9.65	8.74	7.92	7.17	19
20	16.19	15.87	15.56	15.26	14.96	14.66	14.38	14.10	13.82	13.55	12.89	12.27	11.11	10.07	9.12	8.26	7.48	20
21	16.84	16.51	16.19	15.87	15.56	15.26	14.96	14.66	14.38	14.09	13.41	12.77	11.56	10.47	9.49	8.59	7.78	21
22	17.48	17.14	16.81	16.48	16.15	15.84	15.53	15.22	14.92	14.63	13.92	13.25	12.00	10.87	9.85	8.92	8.08	22
23	18.11	17.76	17.41	17.07	16.73	16.41	16.08	15.77	15.46	15.16	14.42	13.73	12.43	11.26	10.20	9.24	8.37	23
24	18.73	18.36	18.00	17.65	17.30	16.96	16.63	16.30	15.98	15.67	14.91	14.19	12.86	11.64	10.55	9.55	8.65	24
25	19.33	18.95	18.58	18.22	17.86	17.51	17.17	16.83	16.50	16.18	15.39	14.65	13.27	12.02	10.89	9.86	8.93	25
26	19.92	19.53	19.15	18.77	18.41	18.05	17.69	17.34	17.00	16.67	15.87	15.10	13.68	12.39	11.22	10.16	9.20	26
27	20.50	20.10	19.71	19.32	18.94	18.57	18.21	17.85	17.50	17.16	16.33	15.54	14.07	12.75	11.55	10.46	9.47	27
28	21.07	20.66	20.25	19.86	19.47	19.09	18.71	18.34	17.99	17.63	16.78	15.97	14.46	13.10	11.87	10.75	9.73	28
29	21.63	21.21	20.79	20.38	19.98	19.59	19.21	18.83	18.46	18.10	17.22	16.39	14.85	13.45	12.18	11.03	9.99	29
30	22.18	21.74	21.32	20.90	20.49	20.09	19.69	19.31	18.93	18.56	17.66	16.81	15.22	13.79	12.49	11.31	10.24	30
31	22.71	22.27	21.83	21.40	20.98	20.57	20.17	19.77	19.39	19.01	18.09	17.21	15.59	14.12	12.79	11.58	10.49	31
32	23.24	22.78	22.34	21.90	21.47	21.05	20.63	20.23	19.83	19.44	18.51	17.61	15.95	14.45	13.09	11.85	10.73	32
33	23.75	23.29	22.83	22.38	21.94	21.51	21.09	20.68	20.27	19.88	18.92	18.00	16.31	14.77	13.38	12.11	10.97	33
34	24.26	23.78	23.32	22.86	22.41	21.97	21.54	21.12	20.70	20.30	19.32	18.38	16.65	15.08	13.66	12.37	11.21	34
35	24.75	24.27	23.79	23.33	22.87	22.42	21.98	21.55	21.13	20.71	19.71	18.76	16.99	15.39	13.94	12.62	11.43	35
36	25.24	24.74	24.26	23.78	23.32	22.86	22.41	21.97	21.54	21.12	20.10	19.13	17.32	15.69	14.21	12.87	11.66	36
37	25.71	25.21	24.72	24.23	23.76	23.29	22.83	22.39	21.95	21.52	20.48	19.49	17.65	15.99	14.48	13.12	11.88	37
38	26.18	25.67	25.16	24.67	24.19	23.71	23.25	22.79	22.35	21.91	20.85	19.84	17.97	16.28	14.74	13.35	12.09	38
39	26.64	26.12	25.60	25.10	24.61	24.13	23.65	23.19	22.74	22.29	21.21	20.19	18.29	16.56	15.00	13.59	12.31	39
40	27.09	26.56	26.04	25.52	25.02	24.53	24.05	23.58	23.12	22.67	21.57	20.53	18.59	16.84	15.25	13.82	12.51	40
41	27.53	26.99	26.46	25.94	25.43	24.93	24.44	23.96	23.49	23.03	21.92	20.86	18.90	17.11	15.50	14.04	12.72	41
42	27.96	27.41	26.87	26.35	25.83	25.32	24.83	24.34	23.86	23.39	22.26	21.19	19.19	17.38	15.74	14.29	12.92	42
43	28.38	27.82	27.28	26.74	26.22	25.71	25.20	24.71	24.22	23.75	22.60	21.51	19.48	17.64	15.98	14.47	13.11	43
44	28.79	28.23	27.68	27.13	26.60	26.08	25.57	25.07	24.58	24.09	22.93	21.82	19.77	17.90	16.21	14.69	13.30	44
45	29.20	28.63	28.07	27.52	26.98	26.45	25.93	25.42	24.92	24.43	23.25	22.13	20.04	18.15	16.44	14.89	13.49	45
Years of loss	1	2	3	4	5	6	7	8	9	10	12.5	15	20	25	30	35	40	Years of loss

Combination grid (Discount rate 2.5%)

Years of loss	Years before loss starts to run 1	2	3	4	5	6	7	8	9	10	12.5	15	20	25	30	35	40	Years of loss
1	0.96	0.94	0.92	0.89	0.87	0.85	0.83	0.81	0.79	0.77	0.73	0.68	0.60	0.53	0.47	0.42	0.37	**1**
2	1.90	1.86	1.81	1.77	1.72	1.68	1.64	1.60	1.56	1.52	1.43	1.35	1.19	1.05	0.93	0.82	0.73	**2**
3	2.82	2.75	2.69	2.62	2.56	2.49	2.43	2.37	2.32	2.26	2.12	2.00	1.76	1.56	1.38	1.22	1.08	**3**
4	3.72	3.63	3.54	3.45	3.37	3.28	3.20	3.13	3.05	2.98	2.80	2.63	2.32	2.05	1.82	1.61	1.42	**4**
5	4.59	4.48	4.37	4.26	4.16	4.06	3.96	3.86	3.77	3.67	3.45	3.25	2.87	2.54	2.24	1.98	1.75	**5**
6	5.44	5.31	5.18	5.05	4.93	4.81	4.69	4.58	4.47	4.36	4.10	3.85	3.40	3.01	2.66	2.35	2.08	**6**
7	6.27	6.12	5.97	5.82	5.68	5.54	5.41	5.28	5.15	5.02	4.72	4.44	3.92	3.47	3.06	2.71	2.39	**7**
8	7.08	6.91	6.74	6.58	6.42	6.26	6.11	5.96	5.81	5.67	5.33	5.01	4.43	3.92	3.46	3.06	2.70	**8**
9	7.87	7.68	7.49	7.31	7.13	6.96	6.79	6.62	6.46	6.30	5.93	5.57	4.93	4.35	3.85	3.40	3.01	**9**
10	8.65	8.43	8.23	8.03	7.83	7.64	7.45	7.27	7.10	6.92	6.51	6.12	5.41	4.78	4.22	3.73	3.30	**10**
11	9.40	9.17	8.95	8.73	8.51	8.31	8.10	7.91	7.71	7.53	7.07	6.65	5.88	5.20	4.59	4.06	3.59	**11**
12	10.13	9.89	9.64	9.41	9.18	8.96	8.74	8.52	8.32	8.11	7.63	7.17	6.34	5.60	4.95	4.38	3.87	**12**
13	10.85	10.58	10.33	10.07	9.83	9.59	9.36	9.13	8.90	8.69	8.17	7.68	6.79	6.00	5.30	4.69	4.14	**13**
14	11.55	11.27	10.99	10.72	10.46	10.21	9.96	9.72	9.48	9.25	8.69	8.17	7.22	6.38	5.64	4.99	4.41	**14**
15	12.23	11.93	11.64	11.36	11.08	10.81	10.55	10.29	10.04	9.79	9.21	8.66	7.65	6.76	5.98	5.28	4.67	**15**
16	12.90	12.58	12.27	11.98	11.68	11.40	11.12	10.85	10.58	10.33	9.71	9.13	8.07	7.13	6.30	5.57	4.92	**16**
17	13.54	13.21	12.89	12.58	12.27	11.97	11.68	11.39	11.12	10.85	10.20	9.59	8.47	7.49	6.62	5.85	5.17	**17**
18	14.18	13.83	13.50	13.17	12.84	12.53	12.23	11.93	11.64	11.35	10.67	10.03	8.87	7.84	6.93	6.12	5.41	**18**
19	14.80	14.44	14.08	13.74	13.40	13.08	12.76	12.45	12.14	11.85	11.14	10.47	9.26	8.18	7.23	6.39	5.65	**19**
20	15.40	15.02	14.66	14.30	13.95	13.61	13.28	12.95	12.64	12.33	11.59	10.90	9.63	8.51	7.52	6.65	5.88	**20**
21	15.99	15.60	15.22	14.85	14.48	14.13	13.79	13.45	13.12	12.80	12.04	11.31	10.00	8.84	7.81	6.90	6.10	**21**
22	16.56	16.16	15.76	15.38	15.00	14.64	14.28	13.93	13.59	13.26	12.47	11.72	10.36	9.16	8.09	7.15	6.32	**22**
23	17.12	16.70	16.30	15.90	15.51	15.13	14.76	14.40	14.05	13.71	12.89	12.12	10.71	9.47	8.37	7.39	6.54	**23**
24	17.67	17.24	16.82	16.41	16.01	15.61	15.23	14.86	14.50	14.15	13.30	12.50	11.05	9.77	8.63	7.63	6.74	**24**
25	18.20	17.76	17.32	16.90	16.49	16.09	15.69	15.31	14.94	14.57	13.70	12.88	11.38	10.06	8.89	7.86	6.95	**25**
26	18.72	18.26	17.82	17.38	16.96	16.55	16.14	15.75	15.36	14.99	14.09	13.25	11.71	10.35	9.15	8.09	7.15	**26**
27	19.23	18.76	18.30	17.85	17.42	16.99	16.58	16.17	15.78	15.40	14.47	13.61	12.03	10.63	9.40	8.30	7.34	**27**
28	19.72	19.24	18.77	18.31	17.87	17.43	17.01	16.59	16.19	15.79	14.85	13.96	12.34	10.90	9.64	8.52	7.53	**28**
29	20.20	19.71	19.23	18.76	18.30	17.86	17.42	17.00	16.58	16.18	15.21	14.30	12.64	11.17	9.87	8.73	7.71	**29**
30	20.68	20.17	19.68	19.20	18.73	18.27	17.83	17.39	16.97	16.56	15.56	14.63	12.93	11.43	10.10	8.93	7.89	**30**
31	21.13	20.62	20.12	19.63	19.15	18.68	18.22	17.78	17.35	16.92	15.91	14.96	13.22	11.68	10.33	9.13	8.07	**31**
32	21.58	21.06	20.54	20.04	19.55	19.08	18.61	18.16	17.71	17.28	16.25	15.27	13.50	11.93	10.55	9.32	8.24	**32**
33	22.02	21.48	20.96	20.45	19.95	19.46	18.99	18.52	18.07	17.63	16.58	15.58	13.77	12.17	10.76	9.51	8.41	**33**
34	22.45	21.90	21.37	20.84	20.34	19.84	19.36	18.88	18.42	17.97	16.90	15.89	14.04	12.41	10.97	9.69	8.57	**34**
35	22.86	22.31	21.76	21.23	20.71	20.21	19.71	19.23	18.76	18.31	17.21	16.16	14.30	12.64	11.17	9.87	8.73	**35**
36	23.27	22.70	22.15	21.61	21.08	20.57	20.06	19.58	19.10	18.63	17.52	16.47	14.56	12.86	11.37	10.05	8.88	**36**
37	23.67	23.09	22.52	21.98	21.44	20.92	20.41	19.91	19.42	18.95	17.81	16.75	14.80	13.08	11.56	10.22	9.03	**37**
38	24.05	23.47	22.89	22.33	21.79	21.26	20.74	20.23	19.74	19.26	18.11	17.02	15.04	13.30	11.75	10.39	9.18	**38**
39	24.43	23.83	23.25	22.68	22.13	21.59	21.06	20.55	20.05	19.56	18.39	17.29	15.28	13.51	11.94	10.55	9.33	**39**
40	24.80	24.19	23.60	23.03	22.46	21.92	21.38	20.86	20.35	19.86	18.67	17.55	15.51	13.71	12.12	10.71	9.47	**40**
41	25.16	24.54	23.94	23.36	22.79	22.23	21.69	21.16	20.65	20.14	18.94	17.80	15.74	13.91	12.29	10.86	9.60	**41**
42	25.51	24.88	24.28	23.68	23.11	22.54	21.99	21.46	20.93	20.42	19.20	18.05	15.95	14.10	12.46	11.02	9.74	**42**
43	25.85	25.22	24.60	24.00	23.42	22.85	22.29	21.74	21.21	20.70	19.46	18.29	16.17	14.29	12.63	11.16	9.87	**43**
44	26.18	25.54	24.92	24.31	23.72	23.14	22.58	22.02	21.49	20.96	19.71	18.53	16.38	14.47	12.79	11.31	9.99	**44**
45	26.51	25.86	25.23	24.61	24.01	23.43	22.86	22.30	21.75	21.22	19.95	18.76	16.58	14.65	12.95	11.45	10.12	**45**
Years of loss	**1**	**2**	**3**	**4**	**5**	**6**	**7**	**8**	**9**	**10**	**12.5**	**15**	**20**	**25**	**30**	**35**	**40**	**Years of loss**

A7: Table of adjustments to multiplier for Fatal Accidents Acts dependency

These tables deal with factors to be applied in fatal accident cases to allow for the possibility that the deceased would not have survived until trial. These tables are derived from the Explanatory Notes of the Ogden Tables, paras 64ff. They are set out here on one page for convenience. (The user will need to consider the current state of authority on the acceptability of this approach.)

PRE-TRIAL damages (factor to be applied to damages from date of accident to trial)

Age of deceased at date of accident	Period from accident to trial (or cessation of dependency if earlier) Male 3	6	9	Female 3	6	9
10	1.00	1.00	1.00	1.00	1.00	1.00
20	1.00	1.00	1.00	1.00	1.00	1.00
30	1.00	1.00	0.99	1.00	1.00	1.00
40	1.00	0.99	0.99	1.00	1.00	0.99
50	0.99	0.99	0.98	1.00	0.99	0.99
60	0.98	0.96	0.94	0.99	0.98	0.96
65	0.98	0.94	0.90	0.99	0.96	0.94
70	0.96	0.91	0.84	0.98	0.94	0.89
75	0.93	0.85	0.75	0.95	0.90	0.83
80	0.89	0.77	0.64	0.92	0.83	0.73

POST-TRIAL damages (factor to be applied to damages from date of trial to retirement age)

Age of deceased at date of accident	Period from accident to trial Male 3	6	9	Female 3	6	9
10	1.00	1.00	1.00	1.00	1.00	1.00
20	1.00	1.00	0.99	1.00	1.00	1.00
30	1.00	0.99	0.99	1.00	1.00	0.99
40	0.99	0.99	0.98	1.00	0.99	0.99
50	0.99	0.97	0.95	0.99	0.98	0.97
60	0.97	0.93	0.87	0.98	0.95	0.92
65	0.95	0.88	0.79	0.97	0.93	0.87
70	0.92	0.81	0.66	0.95	0.87	0.77
75	0.86	0.69	0.51	0.91	0.78	0.64
80	0.78	0.54	0.33	0.84	0.65	0.45

POST-RETIREMENT damages (for the period of dependency after retirement age)

1. First obtain the multiplier for the whole of life dependency by the following steps:
   (a) determine, from 0 per cent tables, the expectation of life which the deceased would have had at the date of trial (or the shorter period for which the deceased would have provided the dependency);
   (b) determine the expected period for which the dependant would have been able to receive the dependency (for a widow, normally her life expectancy from 0 per cent tables; for a child, the period until it reaches adulthood);
   (c) take the lesser of the two periods;
   (d) treat the resulting period as a term certain and look up the multiplier for that period (table A5, continuous loss column).
2. Obtain the multiplier for dependency from date of trial to retirement age. Do not adjust it for contingencies other than mortality. Do not apply the factors in the Post-Trial table above.
3. Subtract the multiplier for dependency to retirement age (2) from the whole life multiplier (1). Multiply by the factor in the Post-trial table above.

   Post-retirement multiplier = [Stage 1 figure *minus* Stage 2 figure] × Post-trial factor.

A8: The Ogden Tables

Actuarial tables with explanatory notes for use in personal injury and fatal accident cases.

Prepared by an Inter-Professional Working Party of Actuaries, Lawyers, Accountants and other interested parties.

Sixth edition prepared by the Government Actuary's Department.

Table of Contents

Introduction to the 6th Edition

"When it comes to the explanatory notes we must make sure that they are readily comprehensible. We must assume the most stupid circuit judge in the country and before him are the two most stupid advocates. All three of them must be able to understand what we are saying."

Sir Michael Ogden QC, on his explanatory notes to the First Edition of the Ogden Tables.[1]

1. This is the second edition published since Sir Michael Ogden's death. The new multipliers provided by the Government Actuary's Department use mortality rates from the latest available population projections, which take account of data following the last National Census. In general, such figures have added about 1% for most younger ages to the previous figures. There are, however, other matters here, which are discussed below and described in detail in the Explanatory Notes.

The purpose of the Ogden Tables

2. The Tables are designed to help in the calculation of future pecuniary losses.

3. The number of cases that actually fall into the multitrack, that is are worth more than £15,000, is small, and estimated by some to be only some 5% of the total claims notified. I express it as 'claims notified' for the practice of insurers has changed and now many cases are settled early without the need for the issue of proceedings.

4. When the Tables were first produced, it was on the basis that the appropriate discount rate should be chosen with regard to the yields on Index Linked Government Stock (ILGS). This was the argument presented to the House of Lords in ***Wells v Wells*** **[1999] 1 A.C. 345** and accepted by them in their speeches. When Lord Chancellor Irvine set the discount rate, he elected not to follow that course, but gave his own reasoning for selecting the discount rate that he chose. This was something that he was entitled to do under the powers granted to him in the Damages Act 1996. He is also required under the Act to keep the discount rate he chooses under constant review, which it is said that both Lord Chancellor Irvine and his successor Lord Falconer constantly did and do.

Mortality

5. For the most part, the new multipliers provided by the Government Actuary's Department use mortality rates from the latest available population projections, which take account of data following the last National Census. In general, such figures have had most effect on the multipliers at younger ages for loss of pension; there has been very little change in the multipliers for loss of earnings and increases of between 0% and 4% for multipliers for pecuniary loss for life compared to those in the Fifth Edition.

Contingencies other than Mortality

6. This is the most significant contribution to this edition of the Ogden Tables. It is based on two recent and interesting pieces of research which consider the impact of contingencies other than mortality on working life. This research was carried out, in two separate exercises, by Professor Richard Verrall, Professor Steven Haberman and Mr Zoltan Butt of City University, London and by Dr Victoria Wass of Cardiff University.

1 Memoirs of Sir Michael Ogden Q.C., *Variety is the Spice of Legal Life*, p.182 (The Book Guild, 2002).

7. The findings of these two pieces of research have been combined to produce the tables which are set out in Section B of this edition of the Ogden Tables and which replace the Section B tables which were introduced in the Second Edition.

8. The Ogden Working Party thinks that these tables are likely to prove useful to lawyers when it comes to assessing the appropriate discount to the working life multiplier for contingencies other than mortality.

9. The research demonstrates that people without disabilities spend more time out of employment than earlier research had suggested. It is therefore appropriate to apply a higher discount for contingencies other than mortality than was indicated in the Section B tables introduced in the Second Edition of the Ogden Tables. The effect of this is that some claims for loss of earnings are likely to come down.

10. The research also demonstrates that the factors, other than gender, which have the most effect on a person's future employment status are: (i) whether the person was employed or unemployed at the outset, (ii) whether the person is disabled or not, and (iii) the educational attainment of the person. Interestingly the research has shown that the effect of factors previously thought important, such as occupation, industrial sector, geographic location and levels of economic activity, are relatively insignificant once educational attainment has been taken into account.

11. Accordingly, the discount to be applied to a working life multiplier (or at least a starting point) can be determined from the tables by looking up the discount factor to be applied to a person of the claimant's gender, age, educational attainment and employment status at the time of injury.

12. The tables now included at Section B may also assist those having to deal with the question of a disabled claimant's residual earnings capacity. Again, unsurprisingly to me, the research has demonstrated that disabled people are more likely to be out of employment than people without disabilities, therefore justifying a higher discount for contingencies other than mortality.

13. Both pieces of research have used the published Labour Force Survey definition of 'disabled'. This means that the range of disabilities covered by 'disabled' is very wide as it includes all people who have said that they have a condition that (a) substantially limits (or will limit due to progressive illness) their ability to carry out day-to-day activities *and* (b) affects either the amount *or* the type of paid work they might do.

14. There will be situations when it will be appropriate to use the factors as set out in the Section B tables to calculate a claimant's residual earning capacity on a multiplier/multiplicand basis. However, in many cases it will be appropriate to increase or reduce the discount in the tables to take account of the nature of a particular claimant's disabilities. There will also be some cases when the *Smith v Manchester Corporation* or *Blamire* approach remains applicable. There may be still cases where a precise mathematical approach is inapplicable.

15. My view is that the findings of this research provide a very useful starting point for lawyers grappling with loss of earnings calculations and provide a basis for a more scientific approach than that which has been taken to date. There are fully worked examples in the Explanatory Notes but, clearly, they cannot cover every factual situation.

16. It also provides yet another justification for the importance of education, if such was ever needed, when faced with the unexpected hazards and problems of life visited on those who are the subject of these tables.

Variable future losses or expenses

17. The tables do not provide an immediate answer when the annual future loss or expense is likely to change at given points in time in the future, for example where a claimant's lost earnings would have increased on a sliding scale or changed due to promotion; or the claimant's future care needs are likely to change, perhaps because it is anticipated that a family carer will not be able to continue to provide help. In such situations it is usually necessary to split the overall multiplier, whether for working life or whole of life, into segments, and then to apply those smaller segmented multipliers to the multiplicand appropriate for each period. The Explanatory Notes now include some guidance on how to use the multipliers in such cases (see paragraphs 22 to 24).

Final remarks

18. We are conscious with each Edition of the Tables that we produce that we are being prescriptive about the way in which calculations are made.

19. When we make suggestions for the method of calculations, each change which is put forward is the result of long and careful debate by the whole Working Party, assisted by others from outside the Working Party, who put forward proposals which we consider.

20. The figures for the Tables themselves are produced by the Government Actuary's Department according to long established principles.

21. All other matters are the subject of careful and detailed analysis by all the members of the Working Party.

22. However, if anyone wishes to put forward further improvements, they are invited to do so. We travel like that Pilgrim on the Golden Journey to Samarkand, conscious of our failures and hoping for enlightenment. If you consider that you can assist us in that process, do not hesitate to write to the Government Actuary or myself.

23. I am grateful to those members of the Working Party (listed inside the front cover) who give up their time and mental energy to attend the meetings.

Robin de Wilde Q.C. 1 March 2007

Explanatory Notes

Section A: General

Purpose of tables

1. The tables have been prepared by the Government Actuary's Department. They provide an aid for those assessing the lump sum appropriate as compensation for a continuing future pecuniary loss or consequential expense or cost of care in personal injury and fatal accident cases.

Application of tables

2. The tables set out multipliers. These multipliers enable the user to assess the present capital value of future annual loss (net of tax) or annual expense calculated on the basis of various assumptions which are explained below. Accordingly, to find the present capital value of a given annual loss or expense, it is necessary to select the appropriate table, find the appropriate multiplier and then multiply the amount of the annual loss or expense by that figure.

3. Tables 1 to 26 deal with annual loss or annual expense extending over three different periods of time. In each case there are separate tables for men and women.

— In Tables 1 and 2 the loss or expense is assumed to begin immediately and to continue for the whole of the rest of the claimant's life, allowing for different potential lifespans, including the possibility of early death or prolonged life. The tables apply to both the deceased and the dependants' lives in fatal accident cases.

— In Tables 3 to 14 the loss or expense is assumed to begin immediately but to continue only until the claimant's retirement or earlier death. The age of retirement is assumed to be 50 in Tables 3 and 4, 55 in Tables 5 and 6, 60 in Tables 7 and 8, 65 in Tables 9 and 10, 70 in Tables 11 and 12, and 75 in Tables 13 and 14.

— In Tables 15 to 26 it is assumed that the annual loss or annual expense will not begin until the claimant reaches retirement but will then continue for the whole of the rest of his or her life. In Table 19 (males) and Table 20 (females) the age of retirement is assumed to be 60. In Table 21 (males) and Table 22 (females) the age of retirement is assumed to be 65 (and similarly for retirement ages 50, 55, 70 and 75). These tables all make due allowance for the chance that the claimant may not live to reach the age of retirement.

Mortality assumptions

4. For the previous edition of the Tables the Working Party agreed that the tables to be published should be based on a reasonable estimate of the future mortality likely to be experienced by average members of the population alive today. The mortality assumptions used in the 5th Edition were taken from the then latest available population projections (the 2002 based population projections) for England and Wales. The Tables are routinely used in Scotland and Northern Ireland. Although it would be possible to produce separate tables of multipliers for Scotland and Northern Ireland using mortality rates from population projections for Scotland and for Northern Ireland the Working Party agreed that rather than have three separate sets of Tables there should be one set calculated using mortality rates from the population projections for the United Kingdom as a whole.

5. On the basis of some reported cases, it appears that tables for pecuniary loss for life, e.g. cost of care, may have been misunderstood. The tables do not assume that the claimant dies after a period equating to the expectation of life, but take account of the possibilities that the claimant will live for different periods, e.g. die soon or live to be very old. The mortality assumptions relate to the general population of the United Kingdom. Unless there is clear evidence in an individual case to support the view that the individual is atypical and will enjoy longer or shorter expectation of life, no further increase or reduction is required for mortality alone.

6. For the purposes of preparing the official national population projections, the Government Actuary makes an estimate of the extent of future improvements in mortality. Tables 1 to 26 in this edition show the multipliers which result from the application of these projected mortality rates (derived from the 2004 based population projections for the United Kingdom, which were published in October 2005 on the GAD website *www.gad.gov.uk*. Details can also be found in the publication *National Population Projections 2004 based. PP2 No.25* from the Office for National Statistics). The actuaries on the Working Party consider that these alternative tables provide a more appropriate estimate of the value of future income streams than tables based on historic mortality which, given the rate at which mortality experience has improved, and continues to improve, are likely to underestimate future longevity to a significant extent. The Working Party therefore recommends the Courts use Tables 1 to 26 contained in this latest edition of the tables.

Use of tables

7. To find the appropriate figure for the present value of a particular loss or expense, the user must first choose that table which relates to the period of loss or expense for which the individual claimant is to be compensated and to the sex of the claimant, or, where appropriate, the claimant's dependants.

8. If, for some reason, the facts in a particular case do not correspond with the assumptions on which one of the tables is based (e.g. it is known that the claimant will have a different retiring age from that assumed in the tables), then the tables can only be used if an appropriate allowance is made for this difference; for this purpose the assistance of an actuary should be sought, except for situations where specific guidance is given in these explanatory notes.

Rate of return

9. The basis of the multipliers set out in the tables is that the lump sum will be invested and yield income (but that over the period in question the claimant will gradually reduce the capital sum, so that at the end of the period it is exhausted). Accordingly, an essential factor in arriving at the right figure is the choice of the appropriate rate of return.

10. The annual rate of return currently to be applied is $2\frac{1}{2}$% (net of tax), as fixed by the Lord Chancellor on 25 June 2001, and reassessed on 27 July 2001, under the provisions of the Damages Act 1996 Section 1. An annual rate of return of $2\frac{1}{2}$% was also set for Scotland by the Scottish Ministers on 8 February 2002. The Lord Chancellor may make a fresh determination of this rate, after receiving advice from the Government Actuary and the Treasury (and, in Scotland, the Scottish Ministers after consultation with the Government Actuary). In order to allow the Tables to continue to be used should a new discount rate be specified, the tables are accordingly shown for a range of possible annual rates of return ranging from $\frac{1}{2}$% to 5%, as in the previous edition. In addition, a 0% column has been included to show the multiplier without any discount for interest (i.e. expectations of life, or the equivalent for different periods). These are supplied to assist in the calculation of multipliers in Fatal Accidents Act cases (see Section D).

11. Section 1(2) of the Damages Act 1996 makes provision for the Courts to make variations to the discount rate if any party to the proceedings shows that it is more appropriate in the case in question. Variations to the discount rate under this provision have, however, been rejected by the Court of Appeal in the cases of ***Warriner v Warriner*** **[2002] 1 W.L.R. 1703** and ***Cooke & Others v United Bristol Health Care & Others*** **[2004] 1 W.L.R. 251**.

12. Previous editions of these tables explained how the current yields on index-linked government bonds could be used as an indicator of the appropriate real rate of return for valuing future income streams. Such considerations were endorsed by the House of Lords in ***Wells v Wells*** and the same argumentation was adopted by the Lord Chancellor when he set the rate on commencement of Section 1 of the Damages Act 1996. In cases outwith the scope of these tables, the advice of an actuary should be sought.

Different retirement ages

13. In paragraph 8 above, reference was made to the problem that will arise when the claimant's retiring age is different from that assumed in the tables. Such a problem may arise in valuing a loss or expense beginning immediately but ending at retirement; or in valuing a loss or expense which will not begin until the claimant reaches retirement but will then continue until death. Tables are provided for retirement ages of 50, 55, 60, 65, 70 and 75. Where the claimant's actual retiring age would have been between two of these retirement ages for which tables are provided, the correct multiplier can be obtained by consideration of the tables for retirement age immediately above and below the actual retirement age, keeping the period to retirement age the same. Thus a woman of 42 who would have retired at 58 can be considered as being in between the cases of a woman of 39 with a retirement age of 55 and a woman of 44 with a retirement age of 60. The steps to take are as follows:

(1) Determine between which retirement ages, for which tables are provided, the claimant's actual retirement age R lies. Let the lower of these ages be A and the higher be *B*.

(2) Determine how many years must be subtracted from the claimant's actual retirement age to get to A and subtract that period from the claimant's age. If the claimant's age is *x*, the result of this calculation is $(x+A-R)$.

(3) Look up this new reduced age in the Table corresponding to retirement age A at the appropriate rate of return. Let the resulting multiplier be *M*.

(4) Determine how many years must be added to the claimant's actual retirement age to get to B and add that period to the claimant's age. The result of this calculation is $(x+B-R)$.

(5) Look up this new increased age in the Table corresponding to retirement age B at the appropriate rate of return. Let the resulting multiplier be *N*.

(6) Interpolate between M and *N*. In other words, calculate:

$(B-R) \times M + (R-A) \times N$

and divide the result by $[(B-R) + (R-A)]$, (or equivalently $[B-A]$).

14. In the example given in paragraph 13, the steps would be as follows:

(1) *R* is 58, *A* is 55 and *B* is 60.

(2) Subtracting 3 years from the claimant's age gives 39.

(3) Looking up age 39 in Table 6 (for retirement age 55) gives 13.08 at a rate of return of $2\frac{1}{2}$%.

(4) Adding 2 years to the claimant's age gives 44.

(5) Looking up age 44 in Table 8 (for retirement age 60) gives 13.00 at a rate of return of $2\frac{1}{2}$%.

(6) Calculating 2 × 13.08 + 3 × 13.00 and dividing by (60 – 58) + (58 — 55) [equals 5] gives 13.03 as the multiplier.

15. When the loss or expense to be valued is that from the date of retirement to death, and the claimant's date of retirement differs from that assumed in the tables, a different approach is necessary, involving the following three steps.

(1) Assume that there is a present loss which will continue for the rest of the claimant's life and from Table 1 or 2 establish the value of that loss or expense over the whole period from the date of assessment until the claimant's death.

(2) Establish the value of such loss or expense over the period from the date of assessment until the claimant's expected date of retirement following the procedure explained in paragraphs 13 and 14 above.

(3) Subtract the second figure from the first. The balance remaining represents the present value of the claimant's loss or expense between retirement and death.

16. If the claimant's actual retirement age would have been earlier than 50, or later than 75, the advice of an actuary should be sought.

Younger ages

17. Tables 1 and 2, which concern pecuniary loss for life, and Tables 15 to 26, which concern loss of pension from retirement age, have been extended down to age 0. In some circumstances the multiplier at age 0 is slightly lower than that at age 1; this arises because of the relatively high incidence of deaths immediately after birth.

18. Tables for multipliers for loss of earnings (Tables 3 to 14) have not been extended below age 16. In order to determine the multiplier for loss of earnings for someone who has not yet started work, it is first necessary to determine an assumed age at which the claimant would have commenced work and to find the appropriate multiplier for that age from Tables 3 to 14, according to the assumed retirement age. This multiplier should then be multiplied by the deferment factor from Table 27 which corresponds to the appropriate rate of return and the period from the date of the trial to the date on which it is assumed that the claimant would have started work. A similar approach can be used for determining a multiplier for pecuniary loss for life where the loss is assumed to commence a fixed period of years from the date of the trial. For simplicity the factors in Table 27 relate purely to the impact of compound interest and ignore mortality. At ages below 30 this is a reasonable approximation but at higher ages it would normally be appropriate to allow explicitly for mortality and the advice of an actuary should be sought.

Contingencies

19. Tables 1 to 26 make reasonable provision for the levels of mortality which members of the population of the United Kingdom alive today may expect to experience in future. The tables do not take account of the other risks and vicissitudes of life, such as the possibility that the claimant would for periods have ceased to earn due to ill health or loss of employment. Nor do they take account of the fact that many people cease work for substantial periods to care for children or other dependants. Section B suggests ways in which allowance may be made to the multipliers for loss of earnings, to allow for certain risks other than mortality.

Impaired lives

20. In some cases, medical evidence may be available which asserts that a claimant's health impairments are equivalent to adding a certain number of years to their current age, or to treating the individual as having a specific age different from their actual age. In such cases, Tables 1 and 2 can be used with respect to the deemed higher age. For the other tables the adjustment is not so straightforward, as adjusting the age will also affect the assumed retirement age, but the procedures described in paragraphs 13 to 15 may be followed, or the advice of an actuary should be sought. In other cases, the medical evidence may state that the claimant is likely to live for a stated number of years. This is often then treated as requiring payment to be made for a fixed period equal to the stated life expectancy and using Table 28 to ascertain the value of the multiplier. In general, this is likely to give a multiplier which is too high since this approach does not allow for the distribution of deaths around the expected length of life. For a group of similarly impaired lives of the same age, some will die before the average life expectancy and some after; allowing for this spread of deaths results in a lower multiplier than assuming payment for a term certain equal to the life expectancy. In such cases, it is preferable to look up the age in the 0% column in Table 1 or 2 for which the value of the multiplier at 0% is equal to the stated life expectancy. The relevant multipliers are then obtained from the relevant tables using this age. Take, for example, an impaired male life which is stated to have a life expectancy of 20 years. By interpolation, the age for which the multiplier in the 0% column in Table 1 is 20 is:

$$(20 - 19.66)/(20.50 - 19.66) \times 64 + (20.50 - 20)/(20.50 - 19.66) \times 65$$

which equals 64.6 years.

The value of the whole of life multiplier is then obtained from the 2.5% column of Table 1 for age 64.6 years:

$$(65 - 64.6) \times 15.37 + (64.6 - 64) \times 14.88$$

which equals 15.08 (compared to 15.78 for the value for a term certain of 20 years using the 2.5% column of Table 28).

Fixed periods

21. In cases where pecuniary loss is to be valued for a fixed period, the multipliers in Table 28 may be used. These make no allowance for mortality or any other contingency but assume that regular frequent payments (e.g. weekly or monthly) will continue throughout the period. These figures should in principle be adjusted if the periodicity of payment is less frequent, especially if the payments in question are annually in advance or in arrears.

Variable future losses or expenses

22. The tables do not provide an immediate answer when the annual future loss or expense is likely to change at given points in time in the future. The most common examples will be where:

(a) the claimant's lost earnings would have increased on a sliding scale or changed due to promotion; or

(b) the claimant's future care needs are likely to change in the future, perhaps because it is anticipated that a family carer will not be able to continue to provide help.

In such situations it is usually necessary to split the overall multiplier, whether for working life or whole of life, into segments, and then to apply those smaller segmented multipliers to the multiplicand appropriate for each period.

There are a variety of methods which could be used for splitting a multiplier, especially where the age at which a payment is increased or decreased, or stops or begins, is one which is tabulated in Tables 1 to 26. The following examples serve to illustrate how multipliers might be split using the "apportionment method". This method can be extended for use in cases where none of the ages at which payments change are tabulated.

Example 1—Variable future earnings

23. The claimant is female, a graduate with a degree, aged 25 at date of settlement/trial. Her probable career progression, in the absence of injury, would have provided her with salary increases at ages 30, 35 and 40; thereafter she would have continued at the same level to age 60, when she would have stepped down from full-time work to work part-time until 70. Post accident she is now incapable of working.

The multiplicands for lost future earnings are:

Age 25 to 30: £16,000 a year

Age 30 to 35: £25,000 a year

Age 35 to 40: £35,000 a year

Age 40 to 60: £40,000 a year

Age 60 to 70: £20,000 a year

The multipliers for each stage of her career are calculated as follows:

(1) The working life will be 45 years and the multiplier from Table 12 for that period taking into account mortality risks but without any discounts for any other contingencies will be 26.66.

(2) The multiplier for a term certain of 45 years (ignoring mortality risks) from Table 28 is 27.17.

(3) The multiplier from Table 28 should be split so that each individual segment of the whole working life period (45 years) is represented by a figure. So, the first 5 years is represented by a multiplier for a term certain of 5 years, namely 4.70; the next 5 years is represented by a multiplier of 4.16 (being the difference between the figure for a term certain of 10 years, namely 8.86 and the figure for a term certain of 5 years, namely 4.70); the next 5 years by 3.68 (i.e. the 15 year figure of 12.54 less the 10 year figure of 8.86); the next 20 years by 10.89 (i.e. the difference between the 35 year figure which is 23.43 and the 15 year figure of 12.54); then, the final 10 years by the balance of 3.74 (the residual figure being 27.17 less 23.43).

(4) Each of those smaller segmented multipliers can be shown as a percentage or fraction of the whole: so, for the first 5 years the segmented multiplier of 4.70 is 17.30% of the whole figure of 27.17, and so on for each segment of the 45 year period.

(5) The working life multiplier from Table 12 can now be split up in identical proportions to the way in which the Table 28 multiplier has been treated above: thus the first 5 year period is now represented by a multiplier of 4.61, which is calculated by taking 17.30% of 26.66. Each segmented multiplier is calculated in the same way.

(6) Having now obtained multipliers for each segment of working life, taking into account mortality risks, it is then necessary to discount those figures for "contingencies other than mortality". The discount factor from Table C (using the column for a female, not disabled, with degree level education) is 0.89. So, the figure of 4.61 for the first 5 year period now becomes 4.10 (i.e. 4.61 × 0.89). Again, treat each segmented multiplier in the same way.

(7) The multiplicand for each segment of working life is now multiplied by the appropriate segmented multiplier to calculate the loss for that period. The sum total of those losses represents the full sum for loss of future earnings (ignoring any mitigation).

(8) The figures are set out in tabular form below and give a total lump sum award of £714,500:

Ages	Period (years)	Table 28	% Split	Table 12	Discounted Multipliers (Table C) (× 0.89)	Net Annual Earnings £	£ Loss
25—30	5	4.70	17.30	4.61	4.10	16,000	65,600
30—35	5	4.16	15.31	4.08	3.63	25,000	90,750
35—40	5	3.68	13.54	3.61	3.21	35,000	112,350
40—60	20	10.89	40.08	10.69	9.51	40,000	380,400
60—70	10	3.74	13.77	3.67	3.27	20,000	65,400
Totals:	45 years	27.17	100.00	26.66	23.72		**714,500**

N.B. the figures in the above table have been rounded at each step of the calculation.

Example 2—Variable future care costs

24. A male aged 20 years at the date of settlement/trial requires personal care support for life. He has a normal life expectation for his age. Significant changes in his care regime are anticipated at age 30 and again at age 50.

The multiplicands for care costs are:

Age 20 to 30: £30,000 a year

Age 30 to 50: £60,000 a year

Age 50 for rest of life: £80,000 a year

The multipliers for each stage of the care regime are calculated as follows:

(1) The life expectation will be 64.87 years (from the 0% column of Table 1) and the multiplier for that period taking into account mortality risks (from Table 1) will be 31.63.

(2) The multiplier for a term certain of 64.87 years (ignoring mortality risks) from Table 28 lies between 32.16 (for 64 years) and 32.36 (for 65 years) and is calculated thus:

$(65 - 64.87) \times 32.16 + (64.87 - 64) \times 32.36 = 32.33$

(3) The multiplier from Table 28 should be split so that each individual segment of the whole period of life expectation is represented by a figure. So, the first 10 years (20–30) are represented by a multiplier of 8.86; the next 20 years (30–50) are represented by a multiplier of 12.33 (being the difference between the 30 year figure of 21.19 and the 10 year figure of 8.86); then, the final years (50 to death) are represented by the balance of 11.14 (being the difference between the term certain multiplier of 32.33 and the 30 year figure of 21.19).

(4) Each of those smaller segmented multipliers can be shown as a percentage or fraction of the whole: so, for the first 10 years the segmented multiplier of 8.86 is 27.40% of the whole figure of 32.33, and so on for each segment of the life period.

(5) The life multiplier from Table 1 can now be split up in the way in which the Table 28 multiplier was treated above and in identical proportions: thus the first 10 year period is now represented by a multiplier of 8.67 which is calculated by taking 27.40% of 31.63.

(6) The figures are set out in tabular form below and give a total lump sum award of £1,855,700:

Age (years)	Table 28 (64.87 years) Split multipliers	% Split (of Table 28) figure	Table 1 (multiplier allowing for mortality)	Care costs £ a year	Total £
20–30	8.86	27.40	8.67	30,000	260,100
30–50	12.33	38.14	12.06	60,000	723,600
50 till death	11.14	34.46	10.90	80,000	872,000
Totals	32.33 (no mortality discount)	100.00%	31.63 life multiplier		**1,855,700**

N.B. the figures in the above table have been rounded at each step of the calculation.

Spouses' pensions

25. If doubt exists whether the tables are appropriate to a particular case which appears to present significant difficulties of substance, it would be prudent to take actuarial advice. This might be appropriate in relation to the level of spouses' benefits, if these are to be assessed, since these are not readily valued using Tables 1 to 26. As a rough rule of thumb, if spouses' benefits are to be included when valuing pension loss from normal pension age, the multipliers in tables 15 to 26 should be increased by 5% for a female claimant (i.e. benefits to the male spouse) and by 14% for a male claimant if the spouse's pension would be half of the pension that the member was receiving at death. If the spouse's pension would be payable at a rate of two-thirds the member's pension at death the multipliers should be increased by 7% for a female claimant and by 19% for a male claimant.

Section B: Contingencies other than mortality

26. As stated in paragraph 19, the tables for loss of earnings (Tables 3 to 14) take no account of risks other than mortality. This section shows how the multipliers in these tables may be reduced to take account of these risks.

27. Tables of factors to be applied to the existing multipliers were first introduced in the Second Edition of the Ogden Tables. These factors were based on work commissioned by the Institute of Actuaries and carried out by Professor S Haberman and Mrs D S F Bloomfield (*Work time lost to sickness, unemployment and stoppages: measurement and application* (1990), Journal of the Institute of Actuaries 117, 533595). Although there was some debate within the actuarial profession about the details of the work, and in particular about the scope for developing it further, the findings were broadly accepted and were adopted by the Government Actuary and the other actuaries who were members of the Working Party when the Second Edition of the Tables was published and have remained unchanged in later editions.

28. Some related work has more recently been published by Lewis, McNabb and Wass (*Methods of calculating damages for loss of future earnings*, Journal of Personal Injury Law, 2002 Number 2). Since the publication of the Fifth Edition of the Ogden Tables, the Ogden Working Party has been involved in further research into the impact of contingencies other than mortality carried out by Professor Richard Verrall, Professor Steven Haberman and Mr Zoltan Butt of City University, London and, in a separate exercise, by Dr Victoria Wass of Cardiff University. Their findings have been combined to produce the tables of factors given in this section.

29. The Haberman and Bloomfield paper relied on data from the Labour Force Surveys for 1973, 1977, 1981 and 1985 and English Life Tables No. 14 (198082). The Labour Force Survey (LFS) was originally designed to produce a periodic cross-sectional snapshot of the working age population and collects information on an extensive range of socio-economic and labour force characteristics. Since the winter of 1992/3, the LFS has been carried out on a quarterly basis, with respondents being included in the

survey over 5 successive quarters. The research of Professor Verrall *et al* and Dr Wass has used data from the Labour Force Surveys conducted from 1998 to 2003 to estimate the probabilities of movement of males and females between different states of economic activity, dependent on age, sex, employment activity and level of disability. These probabilities permit the calculation of the expected periods in employment until retirement age, dependent on the initial starting state of economic activity, disability and educational attainment. These can then be discounted at the same discount rate that is used for obtaining the relevant multiplier from Tables 3 to 14, in order to give a multiplier which takes into account only those periods the claimant would be expected, on average, to be in work. These discounted working life expectancy multipliers can be compared to those obtained assuming the person remained in work throughout, to obtain reduction factors which give the expected proportion of time to retirement age which will be spent in employment.

30. The factors described in subsequent paragraphs are for use in calculating loss of earnings up to retirement age. The research work did not investigate the impact of contingencies other than mortality on the value of future pension rights. Some reduction to the multiplier for loss of pension would often be appropriate when a reduction is being applied for loss of earnings. This may be a smaller reduction than in the case of loss of earnings because the ill-health contingency (as opposed to the unemployment contingency) may give rise to significant ill-health retirement pension rights. A bigger reduction may be necessary in cases where there is significant doubt whether pension rights would have continued to accrue (to the extent not already allowed for in the post-retirement multiplier) or in cases where there may be doubt over the ability of the pension fund to pay promised benefits. In the case of a defined contribution pension scheme, loss of pension rights may be allowed for simply by increasing the future earnings loss (adjusted for contingencies other than mortality) by the percentage of earnings which the employer contributions to the scheme represent.

31. The methodology proposed in paragraphs 33 to 42 describes one method for dealing with contingencies other than mortality, which replaces that set out in earlier editions of the Ogden Tables. If this methodology is followed, in many cases it will be appropriate to increase or reduce the discount in the tables to take account of the nature of a particular claimant's disabilities. It should be noted that the methodology does not take into account the pre-accident employment history. The methodology also provides for the possibility of valuing more appropriately the possible mitigation of loss of earnings in cases where the claimant is employed after the accident or is considered capable of being employed. This will in many cases enable a more accurate assessment to be made of the mitigation of loss. However, there may be some cases when the *Smith v Manchester Corporation* or *Blamire* approach remains applicable or otherwise where a precise mathematical approach is inapplicable.

32. The suggestions which follow are intended as a 'ready reckoner' which provides an initial adjustment to the multipliers according to the employment status, disability status and educational attainment of the claimant when calculating awards for loss of earnings and for any mitigation of this loss in respect of potential future post-injury earnings. Such a ready reckoner cannot take into account all circumstances and it may be appropriate to argue for higher or lower adjustments in particular cases. In particular, it can be difficult to place a value on the possible mitigating income when considering the potential range of disabilities and their effect on post-injury work capability, even within the interpretation of disability set out in paragraph 35. However, the methodology does offer a framework for consideration of a range of possible figures with the maximum being effectively provided by the post-injury multiplier assuming the claimant was not disabled and the minimum being the case where there is no realistic prospect of post-injury employment.

The deduction for contingencies other than mortality

33. Under the proposed new method, multipliers for loss of earnings obtained from Tables 3 to 14 are multiplied by factors to allow for the risk of periods of non-employment and absence from the workforce because of sickness.

34. The new research by Professor Verrall *et al* and Dr Wass referred to in paragraphs 28 and 29 demonstrated that the key issues affecting a person's future working life are employment status, disability status and educational attainment.

35. The definitions of employed/not employed, disabled/not disabled and educational attainment used in this analysis and which should be used for determining which factors to apply to the multipliers to allow for contingencies other than mortality are as follows:

Employed — Those who at the time of the accident are employed, self-employed or on a government training scheme.

Not employed — All others (including those temporarily out of work, full-time students and unpaid family workers).

Disabled — A person is classified as being disabled if all three of the following conditions in relation to the ill-health or disability are met:

(i) has either a progressive illness or an illness which has lasted or is expected to last for over a year,

(ii) satisfies the Disability Discrimination Act definition that the impact of the disability substantially limits the person's ability to carry out normal day-to-day activities

and

their condition affects either the kind or the amount of paid work they can do.

Not disabled — All others.

Normal day-to-day activities are those which are carried out by most people on a daily basis, and we are interested in disabilities/health problems which have a substantial adverse effect on the respondent's ability to carry out these activities.

There are several ways in which a disability or health problem may affect the respondent's day-to-day activities:

Mobility – for example, unable to travel short journeys as a passenger in a car, unable to walk other than at a slow pace or with jerky movements, difficulty in negotiating stairs, unable to use one or more forms of public transport, unable to go out of doors unaccompanied.

Manual dexterity – for example, loss of functioning in one or both hands, inability to use a knife and fork at the same time, or difficulty in pressing buttons on a keyboard.

Physical coordination – for example, the inability to feed or dress oneself, or to pour liquid from one vessel to another except with unusual slowness or concentration.

Problems with bowel/bladder control – for example, frequent or regular loss of control of the bladder or bowel. Occasional bedwetting is not considered a disability.

Ability to lift, carry or otherwise move everyday objects (for example, books, kettles, light furniture) – for example, inability to pick up a weight with one hand but not the other, or to carry a tray steadily.

Speech – for example, unable to communicate (clearly) orally with others, taking significantly longer to say things. A minor stutter, difficulty in speaking in front of an audience, or inability to speak a foreign language would not be considered impairments.

Hearing – for example, not being able to hear without the use of a hearing aid, the inability to understand speech under normal conditions or over the telephone.

Eyesight – for example, while wearing spectacles or contact lenses being unable to pass the standard driving eyesight test, total inability to distinguish colours (excluding ordinary red/green colour blindness), or inability to read newsprint.

Memory or ability to concentrate, learn or understand – for example, intermittent loss of consciousness or confused behaviour, inability to remember names of family or friends, unable to write a cheque without assistance, or an inability to follow a recipe.

Perception of risk of physical danger – for example, reckless behaviour putting oneself or others at risk, inability to cross the road safely. This excludes (significant) fear of heights or underestimating risk of dangerous hobbies.

Three levels of educational attainment are defined for the purposes of the tables as follows:

D Degree or equivalent or higher.

GEA GCSE grades A to C up to A levels or equivalents.

O Below GCSE grade C or CSE grade 1 or equivalent or no qualifications.

The following table gives a more detailed breakdown of the allocation of various types of educational qualification to each of the three categories above and are based on the allocations used in the research by Professor Verrall *et al* and Dr Wass.

Categories of highest educational attainment

D **Degree or equivalent or higher**	**GE-A** **GCSE grades A to C up to A levels or equivalent**	**O** **Below GCSE grade C or CSE grade 1 or equivalent or no qualifications**
Any degree (first or higher) Other higher education qualification below degree level Diploma in higher education	A or AS level or equivalent O level, GCSE grade A–C or equivalent	CSE below grade 1 GCSE below grade C
NVQ level 4 or 5	NVQ level 2 or 3	NVQ level 1 or equivalent
HNC/HND, BTEC higher, etc	BTEC/SCOTVEC first or general diploma OND/ONC, BTEC/SCOTVEC national	BTEC first or general certificate SCOTVEC modules or equivalent
RSA higher diploma	RSA diploma, advanced diploma or certificate	RSA other
Teaching, Nursing, etc	GNVQ intermediate or advanced	GNVQ/GVSQ foundation level
	City and Guilds craft or advanced craft	City and Guilds other
	SCE higher or equivalent Trade apprenticeship Scottish 6th year certificate (CSYS)	YT/ YTP certificate Other qualifications No qualification Don't know

Note: "educational attainment" is used here as a proxy for skill level, so that those in professional occupations such as law, accountancy, nursing, etc who do not have a degree ought to be treated as if they do have one.

36. The research also considered the extent to which a person's future working life expectancy is affected by individual circumstances such as occupation and industrial sector, geographical region and education. The researchers concluded that the most significant consideration was the highest level of education achieved by the claimant and that, if this was allowed for, the effect of the other

factors was relatively small. As a result, the Working Party decided to propose adjustment factors which allow for employment status, disability status and educational attainment only. This is a change from previous editions of the Ogden Tables where adjustments were made for types of occupation and for geographical region.

37. A separate assessment is made for (a) the value of earnings the claimant would have received if the injury had not been suffered and (b) the value of the claimant's earnings (if any) taking account of the injuries sustained. The risk of non-employment is significantly higher post-injury due to the impairment. The loss is arrived at by deducting (b) from (a).

38. In order to calculate the value of the earnings the claimant would have received if the injury had not been suffered, the claimant's employment status and the disability status need to be determined as at the date of the accident (or the onset of the medical condition) giving rise to the claim, so that the correct table can be applied. For the calculation of future loss of earnings (based on actual pre-accident earnings and also future employment prospects), Tables A and C should be used for claimants who were not disabled at the time of the accident, and Tables B and D should be used for those with a pre-existing disability. In all of these tables the three left-hand columns are for those who were employed at the time of the accident and the three right-hand columns are for those who were not.

39. In order to calculate the value of the actual earnings that a claimant is likely to receive in the future (i.e. after settlement or trial), the employment status and the disability status need to be determined as at the date of settlement or trial. For claimants with a work affecting disability at that point in time, Tables B and D should be used. The three left-hand columns will apply in respect of claimants actually in employment at date of settlement or trial and the three right-hand columns will apply in respect of those who remain non-employed at that point in time.

40. The factors in Tables A to D allow for the interruption of employment for bringing up children and caring for other dependants.

41. In the case of those aged under 16 at the date of the accident, the relevant factor from the tables would be chosen on the basis of the level of education the child would have been expected to have attained, had the injury not occurred, together with an assessment as to whether the child would have become employed or not. The relevant factor for age 16 would be chosen using the assessed employment status and educational status likely to be ultimately attained, discounted by the appropriate factor from Table 27 for the number of years from the age at the date of trial to age 16.

42. Tables A to D include factors up to age 54 only. For older ages the reduction factors increase towards 1 at retirement age for those who are employed and fall towards 0 for those who are not employed. However, where the claimant is older than 54, it is anticipated that the likely future course of employment status will be particularly dependent on individual circumstances, so that the use of factors based on averages would not be appropriate. Hence reduction factors are not provided for these older ages.

Table A
Loss of Earnings to Pension Age 65 (Males—Not disabled)

Age at date of trial	Employed			Not employed		
	D	GEA	O	D	GEA	O
16–19	0.90	0.90	0.85	0.85	0.85	0.82
20–24	0.92	0.92	0.87	0.89	0.88	0.83
25–29	0.93	0.92	0.89	0.89	0.88	0.82
30–34	0.92	0.91	0.89	0.87	0.86	0.81
35–39	0.90	0.90	0.89	0.85	0.84	0.80
40–44	0.88	0.88	0.88	0.82	0.81	0.78
45–49	0.86	0.86	0.86	0.77	0.77	0.74
50	0.83	0.83	0.83	0.72	0.72	0.70
51	0.82	0.82	0.82	0.70	0.70	0.68
52	0.81	0.81	0.81	0.67	0.67	0.66
53	0.80	0.80	0.80	0.63	0.63	0.63
54	0.79	0.79	0.79	0.59	0.59	0.59

Table B
Loss of Earnings to Pension Age 65 (Males—Disabled)

Age at date of trial	Employed			Not employed		
	D	GEA	O	D	GEA	O
16–19	0.61	0.55	0.32	0.61	0.49	0.25
20–24	0.61	0.55	0.38	0.53	0.46	0.24
25–29	0.60	0.54	0.42	0.48	0.41	0.24
30–34	0.59	0.52	0.40	0.43	0.34	0.23
35–39	0.58	0.48	0.39	0.38	0.28	0.20
40–44	0.57	0.48	0.39	0.33	0.23	0.15
45–49	0.55	0.48	0.39	0.26	0.20	0.11
50	0.53	0.49	0.40	0.24	0.18	0.10
51	0.53	0.49	0.41	0.23	0.17	0.09
52	0.54	0.49	0.41	0.22	0.16	0.08
53	0.54	0.49	0.42	0.21	0.15	0.07
54	0.54	0.50	0.43	0.20	0.14	0.06

Table C
Loss of Earnings to Pension Age 60 (Females—Not disabled)

Age at date of trial	Employed			Not employed		
	D	GEA	O	D	GEA	O
16–19	0.87	0.81	0.64	0.84	0.77	0.59
20–24	0.89	0.82	0.68	0.84	0.76	0.60
25–29	0.89	0.84	0.72	0.83	0.75	0.61
30–34	0.89	0.85	0.75	0.81	0.75	0.63
35–39	0.89	0.86	0.78	0.80	0.74	0.63
40–44	0.89	0.86	0.80	0.78	0.72	0.60
45–49	0.87	0.85	0.81	0.72	0.64	0.52
50	0.86	0.84	0.81	0.64	0.55	0.43
51	0.85	0.84	0.81	0.60	0.51	0.40
52	0.84	0.84	0.81	0.56	0.46	0.36
53	0.83	0.83	0.81	0.50	0.41	0.32
54	0.83	0.83	0.82	0.44	0.35	0.27

Table D
Loss of Earnings to Pension Age 60 (Females—Disabled)

Age at date of trial	Employed D	Employed GEA	Employed O	Not employed D	Not employed GEA	Not employed O
16–19	0.65	0.43	0.25	0.58	0.35	0.19
20–24	0.64	0.44	0.25	0.58	0.33	0.17
25–29	0.63	0.45	0.25	0.50	0.32	0.16
30–34	0.62	0.46	0.30	0.44	0.31	0.15
35–39	0.61	0.48	0.34	0.42	0.28	0.14
40–44	0.60	0.51	0.38	0.38	0.23	0.13
45–49	0.60	0.54	0.42	0.28	0.18	0.11
50	0.60	0.56	0.47	0.23	0.15	0.10
51	0.61	0.58	0.49	0.21	0.14	0.09
52	0.61	0.60	0.51	0.20	0.13	0.08
53	0.62	0.62	0.54	0.18	0.11	0.07
54	0.63	0.66	0.57	0.16	0.09	0.06

Different pension ages

43. The factors in the preceding tables assume retirement at age 65 for males and age 60 for females. It is not possible to calculate expected working life times assuming alternative retirement ages from the LFS data, since the employment data in the LFS are collected only for the working population, assumed aged between 16 and 64 for males and between 16 and 59 for females. Where the retirement age is different from age 65 for males or age 60 for females, it is suggested that this should be ignored and the reduction factor and the adjustments thereto be taken from the above tables for the age of the claimant as at the date of trial with no adjustment, i.e. assume that the retirement age is age 65 for males and age 60 for females. However, if the retirement age is close to the age at the date of trial, then it may be more appropriate to take into account the circumstances of the individual case.

44. It should be noted that the reduction factors in Tables A, B, C and D are based on data for the period 1998 to 2003. Whilst the reduction factors and adjustments allow for the age-specific probabilities of moving into, or out of, employment over future working life time, based on data for the period 1998–2003, the methodology assumes that these probabilities remain constant over time; there is no allowance for changes in these age-specific probabilities beyond this period. It is also assumed that there will be no change in disability status or educational achievement after the date of the accident. Future changes in the probabilities of moving into, and out of, employment are especially difficult to predict with any certainty. It is the intention that the factors should be reassessed from time to time as new data become available.

Section C: Summary of personal injury applications

45. To use the tables the guidance below should be followed:

(1) Choose the table relating to the appropriate sex of the claimant and period of loss or expense (e.g. loss for life, or loss of earnings to a set retirement age). Where loss of earnings is concerned, and none of the tables is relevant because the claimant's expected age of retirement differs from that assumed in the tables, the procedure in paragraphs 13 to 16 of the Explanatory Notes should be followed.

(2) Choose the appropriate discount column (currently 2½%).

(3) In that column find the appropriate figure for the claimant's age at trial ("the basic multiplier").

Loss of earnings

(4) When calculating **loss of earnings**, the tables should be used when a multiplier/multiplicand approach is appropriate. If it is, the basic multiplier should be adjusted to take account of contingencies other than mortality. These contingencies include the claimant's employment and disability status and educational qualifications. The basic multiplier should be multiplied by the appropriate figure taken from Tables A to D. It may be necessary at this stage to modify the resulting figure further to allow for circumstances specific to the claimant.

This process gives "the adjusted table multiplier".

(5) Multiply the net annual loss (the multiplicand) by the adjusted table multiplier to arrive at a figure which represents the capitalised value of the future loss of earnings.

(6) If the claimant has a residual earning capacity, allowance should be made for any post-accident vulnerability on the labour market: the following paragraphs show one way of doing this, although there may still be cases where a conventional *Smith v Manchester Corporation* award is appropriate.

Where it is appropriate to do so, repeat steps 1 to 5 above, replacing the pre-accident employment and disability status with the post-accident employment and disability status in step 4 and replacing the net annual loss by the assumed new level of net earnings at step 5. It will only be necessary to reconsider the claimant's educational attainments if these have changed between the accident and the date of trial or settlement.

The result will represent the capitalised value of the claimant's likely post-accident earnings. It is important to note that, when carrying out this exercise, the *degree* of residual disability may have a different effect on residual earnings depending on its relevance to the claimant's likely field of work. For example, the loss of a leg may have less effect on a sedentary worker's earnings than on a manual worker's.

(7) Deduct the sum yielded by step 6 from that yielded by step 5 to obtain the net amount of loss of earnings allowing for residual earning capacity. Where the above methodology is used there will usually be no need for a separate *Smith v Manchester Corporation* award.

Lifetime losses

(8) Where a **loss** will continue **for life**, follow steps 1 to 3 above to find the appropriate multiplier in the table.

Where the normal life expectancy given by the table is inapplicable the approach set out in paragraph 20, using the lifetime tables rather than Table 28, is the correct approach.

(9) This figure may need adjustment to allow for the particular circumstances of the claimant.

(10) Multiply the annual loss or expense by the multiplier as adjusted.

Variable annual losses

(11) In cases where there will be different losses at different periods it may be necessary to split the multiplier. The approach set out at paragraphs 22 to 24 should be followed.

Fixed period and Deferred losses

(12) Where a loss will continue over a fixed period, the appropriate multiplier can be found in Table 28.

(13) Where a loss will not commence until some future date, multiply the appropriate multiplier by a discount figure taken from Table 27 (the use of which is explained in paragraph 18). This paragraph does not apply to loss of pensions, which have their own tables.

46. The following are examples of the use of the tables in illustrative personal injury cases with simplified assumptions.

Example 3

47. The claimant is female, aged 35 at the date of the trial. She has three A levels, but not a degree, and was in employment at the date of the accident at a salary of £25,000 a year net of tax. She was not disabled before the accident. As a result of her injuries, she is now disabled and has lost her job but has found part-time employment at a salary of £5,000 a year net of tax. Her loss of earnings to retirement age of 60 is assessed as follows:

(1) Look up Table 8 for loss of earnings to pension age 60 for females.

(2) The appropriate rate of return is determined to be $2\frac{1}{2}$% (the rate currently set under Section 1 of the Damages Act 1996).

(3) Table 8 shows that, on the basis of a $2\frac{1}{2}$% rate of return, the multiplier for a female aged 35 is 18.39.

(4) Now take account of risks other than mortality. Allowing for the claimant being employed, not disabled and having achieved A levels at the date of trial, Table C would require 18.39 to be multiplied by 0.86, resulting in a revised multiplier of 15.82.

(5) The damages for loss of earnings are assessed as £395,500 (15.82 × £25,000).

(6) Allow for mitigation of loss of earnings in respect of post-injury earnings. As before, Table 8 shows that, on the basis of a $2\frac{1}{2}$% rate of return, the multiplier for a female aged 35 is 18.39.

(7) Now take account of risks other than mortality. Allowing for the claimant being employed, disabled and having achieved A levels at the date of trial, Table D would require 18.39 to be multiplied by 0.48, resulting in a revised multiplier of 8.83.

(8) The amount of mitigation for post-injury earnings is assessed as £44,150 (8.83 × £5,000).

(9) Hence award for loss of earnings after allowing for mitigation is
£395,500 − £44,150 = £351,350.

Example 4

48. The claimant is male, aged 48 at the date of the trial. He has no educational qualifications. His retirement age was 65, he was employed at the time of the accident and his pre-retirement multiplicand has been determined as £20,000 a year net of tax. He was not disabled before the accident. As a result of his injuries, he is now disabled and has lost his job. The multiplicand for costs of care is deemed to be £50,000 a year. He is unemployed at the date of trial but has been assessed as capable of finding work with possible future earnings of £5,000 a year net of tax. His loss of earnings to retirement age of 65 is assessed as follows:

(1) Look up Table 9 for loss of earnings to pension age 65 for males.

(2) The appropriate rate of return is determined to be 2½% (the rate currently set under Section 1 of the Damages Act 1996).

(3) Table 9 shows that, on the basis of a 2½% rate of return, the multiplier for a male aged 48 is 13.35.

(4) Now take account of risks other than mortality. Allowing for the claimant being employed, not disabled and having no educational qualifications at the date of trial, Table A would require 13.35 to be multiplied by 0.86, resulting in a revised multiplier of 11.48.

(5) The damages for loss of earnings are assessed as £229,600 (11.48 × £20,000).

(6) Allow for mitigation of loss of earnings in respect of post-injury earnings. As before, Table 9 shows that, on the basis of a 2½% rate of return, the multiplier for a male aged 48 is 13.35.

(7) Now take account of risks other than mortality. Allowing for the claimant being unemployed and disabled with no educational qualifications at the date of trial, Table B would require 13.35 to be multiplied by 0.11, resulting in a revised multiplier of 1.47.

(8) The amount of mitigation for post-injury earnings is assessed as £7,350 (1.47 × £5,000).

(9) Hence award for loss of earnings after allowing for mitigation is £229,600 − £7,350 = £222,250.

49. The damages for cost of care are assessed as follows:

(1) Look up Table 1 for the multiplier at age 48.

(2) The appropriate rate of return is 2½%.

(3) Table 1 shows that, on the basis of a 2½% rate of return, the multiplier at age 48 is 22.68.

(4) No adjustment is made for risks other than mortality.

(5) The damages for cost of care are assessed at £1,134,000 (22.68 × £50,000).

Example 5

50. The claimant is female, aged 14 at the date of the trial. She is expected to achieve a degree and to be in employment thereafter on a salary, in current terms, of £30,000 a year net of tax. She was not disabled before the accident. As a result of her injuries, she is now disabled—she is still expected to achieve a degree and to be in employment, but with an average salary in current terms of £20,000 net of tax. Her loss of earnings to retirement age of 60 is assessed as follows:

(1) Look up Table 8 for loss of earnings to pension age 60 for females.

(2) The appropriate rate of return is determined to be 2½% (the rate currently set under Section 1 of the Damages Act 1996).

(3) Table 8 shows that, on the basis of a 2½% rate of return, the multiplier for a female aged 16 is 26.60. This needs to be discounted back to age 14. The factor at 2½% for a period for deferment for 2 years is 0.9518 from Table 27, giving a total multiplier of 26.60 × 0.9518 = 25.32.

(4) Now take account of risks other than mortality. Allowing for the claimant assessed as achieving a degree, being employed and not disabled, Table C would require 25.32 to be multiplied by 0.87, resulting in a revised multiplier of 22.03.

(5) The damages for loss of earnings are assessed as £660,900 (22.03 × £30,000).

(6) Allow for mitigation of loss of earnings in respect of post-injury earnings. As before, Table 8 shows that, on the basis of a $2\frac{1}{2}$% rate of return, the multiplier for a female aged 16 is 26.60. As before, after discounting for two years to age 14 the multiplier is reduced to 26.60 × 0.9518 = 25.32.

(7) Now take account of risks other than mortality. Allowing for the claimant assessed as achieving a degree, being employed and disabled, Table D would require 25.32 to be multiplied by 0.65, resulting in a revised multiplier of 16.46.

(8) The amount of mitigation for post-injury earnings is assessed as £329,200 (16.46 × £20,000).

(9) Hence award for loss of earnings after allowing for mitigation is
£660,900 − £329,200 = £331,700.

Example 6

51. The claimant is male, aged 40 at the date of the trial. He has achieved O levels. He was unemployed at the time of the accident. His potential pre-retirement multiplicand has been determined as £15,000 a year net of tax. He was disabled before the accident. As a result of his injuries, he has been assessed as having no future prospect of employment. His loss of earnings to retirement age of 65 is assessed as follows:

(1) Look up Table 9 for loss of earnings to pension age 65 for males.

(2) The appropriate rate of return is determined to be $2\frac{1}{2}$% (the rate currently set under Section 1 of the Damages Act 1996).

(3) Table 9 shows that, on the basis of a $2\frac{1}{2}$% rate of return, the multiplier for a male aged 40 is 18.01.

(4) Now take account of risks other than mortality. Allowing for the claimant being unemployed, disabled and having achieved O levels at the date of trial, Table B would require 18.01 to be multiplied by 0.23, resulting in a revised multiplier of 4.14.

(5) The damages for loss of earnings are assessed as £62,100 (4.14 × £15,000).

(6) As the claimant has been assessed as having no future prospect of employment following the accident, there is no mitigation of loss of earnings in respect of post-injury earnings.

(7) Hence award for loss of earnings after allowing for mitigation is £62,100.

Section D: Application of tables to fatal accident cases

52. The approach of the courts is to assess the multiplier as at the date of death ***(Cookson v Knowles* [1979] A.C. 556)**.

53. That approach was criticised by the Law Commission in their Report 263 (*Claims for Wrongful Death*). The Law Commission recommended that multipliers should be assessed as at the date of trial and that the multipliers derived from the Ogden Tables should only take effect from the date of trial.

54. The Working Party, then under the Chairmanship of the late Sir Michael Ogden QC, considered that the Law Commission's criticism was valid. In the Fourth Edition of the Tables published in August 2000, the Working Party set out guidance in Section D of the Explanatory Notes on how damages should be calculated in such cases. That guidance was repeated in Section D of the Explanatory Notes to the Fifth Edition published in November 2004.

55. However the courts have considered themselves bound by ***Cookson v Knowles*** and hence have not followed the guidance offered (***White v Esab* [2002] P.I.Q.R. Q6** and ***H v S* [2003] Q.B. 965**).

56. The current approach also incorporates some actuarial flaws; in particular, it incorporates a discount for early receipt in the period prior to trial or assessment. Accordingly in these Notes, firstly we set out the current approach of the courts and secondly we repeat the suggestions for change already contained in the Fourth and Fifth Editions. An example is then provided which has been calculated using the current approach and also the two approaches set out in the Fifth Edition of the Ogden Tables.

Current law

57. Under the Fatal Accidents Act the loss is that of the dependants, i.e. those who relied upon the deceased for support. They may claim that part of the deceased's income (whether earnings, pension, unearned income or state benefits) that the deceased would have spent on them. They may also claim the loss of the services such as DIY, domestic/household or childcare which the deceased would have undertaken and from which they would have benefited. The position of each dependant must be considered separately.

58. Each head of dependency must be considered separately. For each head of claim for each dependant the court calculates a multiplicand. This is calculated on the basis of what is known at the date of trial. For pre-trial losses, the actual loss to date of trial is calculated. Interest is added. For post-trial losses the multiplicand is calculated as at the date of trial.

59. A multiplier for the period of dependency is applied to the multiplicand to arrive at an overall lump sum for each head of dependency.

Approach currently usually adopted by the courts

60. Under the approach currently usually followed by the courts, the multiplier is calculated as at the date of death. However, when making that calculation the court is entitled to take into account matters that have arisen between death and trial. For example, ***Williamson v Thorneycroft* [1940] 2 K.B. 658** in which the deceased's widow died after her husband but before trial. Her dependency terminated at her death. See also ***Corbett v Barking, Havering & Brentwood* HA [1991] 2 Q.B. 408**.

61. There are two periods to be determined:

(i) The expected period from date of death in which the deceased would have been capable of providing the dependency;

(ii) The expected period from the date of the death in which the dependant would have been able to receive the dependency.

The shorter of those two periods provides the basis for the multiplier.

62. In respect of each of those periods consideration must be given as to what discount should be made for contingencies other than mortality. The most obvious contingencies other than mortality fall into the following three categories:

(i) Factors relating to the deceased. For example, the deceased's health may have been such as to seriously affect his ability to provide services or work until retirement age. In relation to earnings the starting point for the adjustment factor should be the figures contained in Tables A to D.

(ii) Factors relating to the dependant. For example, at trial it may be proved that a dependant has a significantly reduced life expectancy.

(iii) Factors relating to the relationship of the deceased and the dependant. For example, an unmarried couple who were on the point of separation before the deceased died. See also section 3(4) of the Act and ***Drew v Abassi***, Court of Appeal 24 May 1995.

63. The assessment of the multiplier involves the following steps:

(1) Determine the expected period from the date of death for which the deceased would have been capable of providing the dependency.

(2) Discount that period for early receipt using the appropriate table as at the date of death and a discount rate of 2.5%.

(3) Apply any adjustment to the above figure to reflect contingencies other than mortality.

(4) Determine the expected period from date of death for which the dependant would have been able to receive the dependency.

(5) Discount that period for early receipt using the appropriate table as at the date of death at a discount rate of 2.5%.

(6) Apply any adjustment to the figure in (5) to reflect contingencies other than mortality.

(7) Take the lower of the figures in (3) and (6) above. That is the overall multiplier from date of death.

(8) Subtract the period elapsed from date of death to date of trial. Losses in this period will be treated as in effect special damages and will attract an award of interest.

(9) The balance of the multiplier will be the multiplier for the post-trial multiplicand.

Approach based on calculations as at date of trial

64. Whereas in personal injury cases the problem to be solved is that of setting a value on an income stream during the potential life of one person (the claimant), the situation is generally more complicated in fatal accident cases. Here the compensation is intended to reflect the value of an income stream during the lifetime of one or more dependants of the deceased (or the expected period for which the dependants would have expected to receive the dependency, if shorter) but limited according to the expectation of how long the deceased would have been able to provide the financial support, had he or she not been involved in the fatal accident.

65. In principle, therefore, the compensation for post-trial dependency should be based on the present value at the date of the trial of the dependency during the expected future joint lifetime of the deceased and the dependant or claimant (had the deceased survived naturally to the date of the trial), subject to any limitations on the period of dependency and any expected future changes in the level of dependency, for example, on attaining retirement age. In addition there should be compensation for the period between the date of accident and the date of trial.

66. A set of actuarial tables to make such calculations accurately would require tables similar to Tables 1 to 26 but for each combination of ages as at the date of the trial of the deceased and the dependant to whom compensation is to be paid. The Working Party concluded that this would not

meet the criterion of simplicity of application which was a central objective of these tables and recommends that, in complex cases, or cases where the accuracy of the multiplier is thought by the parties to be of critical importance and material to the resulting amount of compensation (for example in cases potentially involving very large claims where the level of the multiplicand is unambiguously established), the advice of a professionally qualified actuary should be sought. However, for the majority of cases, a certain amount of approximation will be appropriate, bearing in mind the need for a simple and streamlined process, and taking into consideration the other uncertainties in the determination of an appropriate level of compensation. The following paragraphs describe a methodology using Tables 1 to 26 which can be expected to yield satisfactory answers.

Damages for the period from the fatal accident to the date of trial

67. The period of pre-trial dependency will normally be equal to the period between the date of the fatal accident and the date of the trial, substituting where appropriate the lower figure of the expected period for which the deceased would have provided the dependency, had he or she not been killed in the accident, or if the period of dependency would have been limited in some way, for example if the dependant is a child.

68. A deduction may be made for the risk that the deceased might have died anyway, in the period between the date of the fatal accident and the date at which the trial takes place. In many cases this deduction will be small and could usually be regarded as *de minimis*. The need for a deduction becomes more necessary the longer the period from the date of accident to the date of trial and the older the deceased at the date of death. As an illustration of the order of magnitude of the deduction, Table E shows some examples of factors by which the multiplier should be multiplied for different ages of the deceased and for different periods from the date of accident to the date of the trial.

Table E
Factor by which pre-trial damages should be multiplied to allow for the likelihood that the deceased would not in any case have survived to provide the dependency for the full period to the date of trial

Age of deceased at date of accident	Period from date of accident to date of trial or date of cessation of dependency, if earlier (years)					
	Male deceased			Female deceased		
	3	6	9	3	6	9
10	1.00	1.00	1.00	1.00	1.00	1.00
20	1.00	1.00	1.00	1.00	1.00	1.00
30	1.00	1.00	0.99	1.00	1.00	1.00
40	1.00	0.99	0.99	1.00	1.00	0.99
50	0.99	0.99	0.98	1.00	0.99	0.99
60	0.98	0.96	0.94	0.99	0.98	0.96
65	0.98	0.94	0.90	0.99	0.96	0.94
70	0.96	0.91	0.84	0.98	0.94	0.89
75	0.93	0.85	0.75	0.95	0.90	0.83
80	0.89	0.77	0.64	0.92	0.83	0.73

N.B. The factor for a period of zero years is clearly 1.00. Factors for other ages and periods not shown in the table may be obtained approximately by interpolation.

69. The resultant multiplier, after application of any discount for the possibility of early death of the deceased before the date of trial, even had the accident not taken place, is to be applied to the multiplicand, which is determined in the usual way. Interest will then be added up to the date of trial on the basis of special damages.

Damages from the date of trial to retirement age

70. The assessment of the multiplier involves the following steps:

(1) Determine the expected period from the date of the trial for which the deceased would have been able to provide the dependency (see paragraph 71).

(2) Determine the expected period for which the dependant would have been able to receive the dependency (see paragraph 71).

(3) Take the lesser of the two periods.

(4) Treat the resulting period as a term certain for which the multiplier is to be determined and look up the figure in Table 28 for this period at the appropriate rate of interest.

(5) Apply any adjustment for contingencies other than mortality in accordance with Section B.

(6) If necessary, make an allowance for the risk that the deceased might have died anyway before the date of the trial (see paragraph 68).

71. The expected periods at (1) and (2) of paragraph 70 may be obtained from the 0% column of the appropriate table at the back of this booklet. For (1), Tables 3 to 14 will be relevant, according to the sex of the deceased and the expected age of retirement. The age at which the table should be entered is the age which the deceased would have been at the date of the trial. For (2) Tables 1 and 2 can be used, according to the sex of the dependant and looking up the table at the age of the dependant at the date of the trial.

72. If the period for which the dependency would have continued is a short fixed period, as in the case of a child, the figure at (2) would be the outstanding period at the date of the trial.

73. A deduction may be made for the risk that the deceased might have died anyway before the date of trial. The need for such a deduction becomes more necessary the longer the period from the date of accident to the date of trial and the older the deceased at the date of death. As an illustration of the order of magnitude of the deduction, Table F shows some examples of the factor by which the multiplier, determined as above, should be multiplied for different ages of the deceased and for different periods from the date of accident to the date of the trial.

Table F
Factor by which post-trial damages should be multiplied to allow for the likelihood that the deceased would not in any case have survived to the date of trial in order to provide any post-trial dependency

Age of deceased at date of accident	Period from date of accident to date of trial (years)					
	Male deceased			Female deceased		
	3	6	9	3	6	9
10	1.00	1.00	1.00	1.00	1.00	1.00
20	1.00	1.00	0.99	1.00	1.00	1.00
30	1.00	0.99	0.99	1.00	1.00	0.99
40	0.99	0.99	0.98	1.00	0.99	0.99
50	0.99	0.97	0.95	0.99	0.98	0.97
60	0.97	0.93	0.87	0.98	0.95	0.92
65	0.95	0.88	0.79	0.97	0.93	0.87
70	0.92	0.81	0.66	0.95	0.87	0.77
75	0.86	0.69	0.51	0.91	0.78	0.64
80	0.78	0.54	0.33	0.84	0.65	0.45

N.B. The factor for a period of zero years is clearly 1.00. Factors for other ages and periods not shown in the table may be obtained approximately by interpolation.

74. The resulting multiplier, after application of any discount for the possibility of early death of the deceased before the date of trial, even had the accident not taken place, is to be applied to the appropriate multiplicand, determined in relation to dependency as assessed for the period up to retirement age.

75. If there are several dependants, to whom damages are to be paid in respect of their own particular lifetime (or for a fixed period of dependency), separate multipliers should be determined for each

and multiplied by the appropriate multiplicand using the procedure in paragraphs 70 to 74. The total amount of damages is then obtained by adding the separate components. If a single multiplicand is determined, but the damages are to be shared among two or more dependants so long as they are each alive, or during a period of common dependency, then the multiplier will be calculated using the procedure in paragraphs 70 to 74. However, at step (2) of paragraph 70 the expected period will be the longest of the expected periods for which the dependency might last.

Damages for the period of dependency after retirement age

76. The method described in paragraphs 70 to 75 for pre-retirement age dependency cannot satisfactorily be applied directly to post-retirement age dependency with a sufficient degree of accuracy. We therefore propose a method which involves determining the multiplier by looking at dependency for the rest of life from the date of trial and then subtracting the multiplier for dependency up to retirement age.

77. The assessment of the multiplier for whole of life dependency involves the following steps:

(1) Determine the expectation of life which the deceased would have had as at the date of trial, or such lesser period for which the deceased would have been able to provide the dependency (see paragraph 78).

(2) Determine the expected period for which the dependant would have been able to receive the dependency (see paragraph 78).

(3) Take the lesser of the two periods.

(4) Treat the resulting period as a term certain for which the multiplier is to be determined and look up the figure in Table 28 for this period at the appropriate rate of interest.

78. The expected periods at (1) and (2) of paragraph 77 may be obtained from the 0% column of the appropriate table at the back of this booklet. For (1) Tables 1 or 2 will be relevant, according to the sex of the deceased. The age at which the table should be entered is the age which the deceased would have attained at the date of the trial. For (2) Tables 1 and 2 can be used, according to the sex of the dependant and looking up the table at the age of the dependant at the date of the trial.

79. Deduct the corresponding multiplier for post-trial pre-retirement dependency, as determined in paragraphs 70 to 75, but without any adjustment for contingencies other than mortality, or that the deceased may have died anyway before the date of trial. The result is the multiplier for post-retirement dependency, which must then be applied to the appropriate multiplicand, assessed in relation to dependency after retirement age. The adjustment for contingencies other than mortality in respect of the damages for the period of dependency after retirement age will often be less than that required for pre-retirement age damages (see paragraph 30).

80. A deduction may finally be made for the risk that the deceased might have died anyway before the date of trial. The need for such a deduction becomes more necessary the longer the period from the date of accident to the date of trial and the older the deceased at the date of death. As an illustration of the order of magnitude of the deduction, Table F shows some examples of the factor by which the multiplier, determined as above, should be multiplied for different ages of the deceased and for different periods from the date of accident to the date of the trial. The factors for this purpose are exactly the same deductions as used in the calculation at paragraphs 70 to 75.

Cases where dependency is not related to employment

81. The layout of paragraphs 70 to 80 is based on the assumption that the dependency provided by the deceased would have changed at retirement age. This may not be appropriate in some cases, particularly in the important case of the deceased wife and mother whose contribution has been solely in the home or in the case of an adult child caring for an elderly parent or parents. In cases like this, where the deceased might have provided the dependency throughout their lifetime, paragraphs 76 to 80 should be ignored and paragraphs 70 to 75 used, with the difference that the expected period required at step (1) of paragraph 70 should be a whole of life expectancy, taken from Tables 1 and 2. This is also the approach to use when the deceased was already a pensioner.

82. The following paragraphs give calculations of damages awards for the same example, but calculated on three different methodologies—the current approach adopted by the courts, the approach advocated in the Fifth Edition of the Ogden Tables and the alternative approach in the Fifth Edition of the Ogden Tables amended to use multipliers as at the date of death. In each case, the different methodology is applied to the following example:

Example 7

The dependant is female, aged 38 at the date of the trial, which is taking place 3 years after the date of the fatal accident which killed her husband, at that time aged 37, on whom she was financially dependent. The deceased had A levels, was in employment and in good health with no disability at the time of the fatal accident. The dependant was, at the date of death, and is at the date of trial, in good health. Their relationship was stable. The Court has determined a multiplicand of £30,000 up to the deceased's normal retirement age of 65 with no financial dependency post age 65, nor any services dependency. The damages are to be calculated as follows:

Current approach

83. (1) The deceased would have been capable of providing the financial dependency to the dependant for the period of 28 years from the date of his death aged 37 to his 65th birthday.

(2) The appropriate Table is 9. Using the 2.5% column the multiplier = 19.56.

(3) Adjustment factor for contingencies other than mortality (in accordance with Section B) for an employed male aged 37 with A levels and who is not disabled = 0.90 to give a multiplier of 19.56 × 0.90 = 17.60.

(4) The expected period for which the dependant would have been able to receive the dependency was between the ages of 35 and 63.

(5) The appropriate Tables are 8 and 10, and using the 2.5% column the multiplier = 19.86.

(6) The parties were married so section 3(4) does not apply. The relationship was stable. The dependant was and is in good health. The court is unlikely to make much of an adjustment to the figure in (5) above to reflect contingencies other than mortality.

(7) The lower of the two figures is that in (3) above, namely 17.60.

(8) The period that has elapsed between date of death and date of trial is 3 years. The pre-trial loss is therefore £30,000 × 3 = £90,000.

(9) Interest at half rate from date of death to date of trial: 3 years at 3% a year = 9%.
£90,000 × 9% = £8,100.

(10) The post-trial multiplier is 14.60 (17.60 − 3).

(11) The post-trial loss is therefore 14.60 × £30,000 = £438,000.

(12) Total financial dependency therefore £90,000 + £8,100 + £438,000 = £536,100.

Fifth edition approach

84. *Pre-trial damages*:

(1) Period between fatal accident and trial: 3 years.

(2) Factor for possible early death (Table E for male aged 37 and 3 years) = 1.00.

(3) Pre-trial damages = 3 × 1.00 × £30,000 = £90,000 (plus interest as special damages).

(4) Interest at half rate from date of death to date of trial: 3 years at 3% a year = 9%. £90,000 × 9% = £8,100.

Post-trial damages:

(1) Expected period for which the deceased would have provided the dependency (Table 9 at 0% for male aged 40, the age as at the date of trial): 24.00.

(2) Expected period for which the dependant would have been able to receive the dependency (Table 2 at 0% for female aged 38): 49.14.

(3) Lesser of two periods at (1) and (2) = 24.00.

(4) Multiplier for term certain of 24.00 years at 2½% rate of return = 18.11.

(5) Adjustment factor for contingencies other than mortality (in accordance with Section B) for an employed male aged 40 with A levels and who was not disabled = 0.88 to give a multiplier of 18.11 × 0.88 = 15.94.

(6) Adjustment factor for the risk that the deceased might have died anyway before the date of trial (Table F for male aged 37 and 3 years): 0.99 to give a multiplier of 15.94 × 0.99 = 15.78.

(7) Post-trial damages = 15.78 × £30,000 = £473,400.

(8) Total financial dependency therefore £90,000 + £8,100 + £473,400 = £571,500.

Alternative Fifth edition approach amended to use multipliers as at the date of death

85. If the court wishes to select multipliers from the date of death instead of following the guidance given above, it is essential to ensure that the period before the trial does not include a discount for early receipt. This could be achieved by selecting multipliers from the 0% columns of the appropriate tables and then applying the discount for early receipt to the period after the trial (using the discount rate set under Section 1 of the Damages Act 1996). Thus, the calculations for example 7 above would then be:

(1) Expected period for which the deceased would have provided the dependency (Table 9 at 0% for male aged 37, the age as at the date of death): 26.93.

(2) Deduct period between accidental death and date of trial of 3 years to give post-trial period: 23.93.

(3) Expected post-trial period for which the dependant would have been able to receive the dependency (Table 2 at 0% for female aged 38): 49.14.

(4) Lesser of two periods at (2) and (3) = 23.93.

(5) Multiplier for term certain of 23.93 years at 2.5% rate of return (Table 28) = 18.07.

(6) Adjustment factor for contingencies other than mortality (in accordance with Section B) for an employed male aged 37 with A levels and who was not disabled = 0.90 to give a multiplier of 18.07 × 0.90 = 16.26.

(7) Pre-trial damages = 3 × £30,000 = £90,000 (plus interest as special damages of £8,100).

(8) Post-trial damages = 16.26 × £30,000 = £487,800.

(9) Total financial dependency therefore £90,000 + £8,100 + £487,800 = £585,900.

86. As can be seen the three methodologies give three different amounts of damages, namely £536,100 for the current approach used by the courts, £571,500 using the methodology set out in the Fifth Edition and £585,900 using the alternative methodology set out in the Fifth Edition with multipliers as at the date of death. The size of the disparities between the three methods depends on the length of the period between the date of death and the date of trial; if the example had assumed a period of 6 years the differences would have been greater.

87. The following paragraphs show extensions of the methodology set out in the Fifth Edition to more complex examples. The other methodologies detailed earlier can be extended similarly.

Example 8

88. The dependant is female, aged 50 at the date of the trial, which is taking place 4 years after the date of the fatal accident which killed the man, at that time aged 47, on whom she was financially dependent. The deceased was in employment at the time of the fatal accident, was not disabled and had achieved A levels. The Court has determined a multiplicand, up to the deceased's normal retirement age of 60, of £50,000 and has decided that post-retirement damages should be payable based on a multiplicand of £30,000. The damages are to be calculated as follows:

Pre-trial damages:

(1) Period between fatal accident and trial: 4 years.

(2) Factor for possible early death (Table E for male aged 47 and 4 years): 0.99.

(3) Pre-trial damages = 4 × 0.99 × £50,000 = £198,000 (plus interest as special damages).

Post-trial pre-retirement damages:

(1) Expected period for which the deceased would have provided the dependency (Table 7 at 0% for male aged 51, the age as at the date of trial): 8.80.

(2) Expected period for which the dependant would have been able to receive the dependency (Table 2 at 0% for female aged 50): 36.69.

(3) Lesser of two periods at (1) and (2) = 8.80.

(4) Multiplier for term certain of 8.80 years at $2\frac{1}{2}$% rate of return (interpolating between the values for 8 and 9 in Table 28) = (9 − 8.80) × 7.26 + (8.80 − 8) × 8.07 = 7.91.

(5) Adjustment factor for contingencies other than mortality (in accordance with Section B) for an employed male aged 51 with A levels and who was not disabled = 0.82 to give a multiplier of 7.91 × 0.82 = 6.49.

(6) Adjustment factor for the risk that the deceased might have died anyway before the date of trial (Table F for male aged 47 and 4 years): 0.99 to give a multiplier of 6.49 × 0.99 = 6.43.

(7) Post-trial pre-retirement damages = 6.43 × £50,000 = £321,500.

Post-retirement damages:

(1) Expectation of life of deceased at date of trial (Table 1 at 0% for male aged 51): 32.44.

(2) Expected period for which the dependant would have been able to receive the dependency (Table 2 at 0% for female aged 50): 36.69.

(3) Lesser of two periods at (1) and (2) = 32.44.

(4) Multiplier for time certain of 32.44 years at $2\frac{1}{2}$% rate of return (interpolating between the values for 32 and 33 in Table 28) = (33 − 32.44) × 22.12 + (32.44 − 32) × 22.57 = 22.32.

(5) Deduct multiplier for post-trial pre-retirement damages before application of adjustment factors for contingencies other than mortality and for the risk that the deceased might have died anyway before the date of trial: 22.32 − 7.91 = 14.41.

(6) Adjustment factor for the risk that the deceased might have died anyway before the date of trial (Table F for male aged 47 and 4 years): 0.99 to give a multiplier of 14.41 × 0.99 = 14.27.

(7) Post-retirement damages = 14.27 × £30,000 = £428,100.

Example 9

89. There are two dependants, respectively a child aged 10 and a male aged 41 at the date of the trial, which is taking place 3 years after the date of the fatal accident which killed the woman, at that time aged 35, on whom both were financially dependent. She had a degree and worked in London for a computer company. The Court has determined a multiplicand, up to the deceased's normal retirement age of 62, of £50,000 for the male dependant and £10,000 for the child, up to the age of 21, and has decided that post-retirement damages should be payable based on a multiplicand of £20,000. The damages are to be calculated as follows:

Pre-trial damages:

1) Period between fatal accident and trial: 3 years.

(2) Factor for possible early death (Table E for female aged 35 and 3 years): 1.00.

(3) Pre-trial damages = 3 × 1.00 × (£50,000 + £10,000) = £180,000 (plus interest as special damages).

Post-trial pre-retirement damages:

(1) Expected period for which the deceased would have provided the dependency should be based on female aged 38 at the date of trial with retirement age of 62. First calculate as though deceased were aged 36 and had retirement age of 60 (Table 8 at 0% for female aged 36): 23.61.

Then calculate as though deceased were aged 41 and had retirement age of 65 (Table 10 at 0% for female aged 41): 23.37.

Interpolate for age 38 with retirement age of 62 = (3 × 23.61 + 2 × 23.37)/5 = 23.51.

(2) Expected period for which the male dependant would have been able to receive the dependency (Table 1 at 0% for male aged 41): 42.48.

Expected period for which child would have been able to receive the dependency = 11.00.

(3) Lesser of two periods at (1) and (2) = 11.00 (in case of child)

= 23.51 (in case of man).

(4) Multiplier for term certain of 11 years at $2\frac{1}{2}$% (Table 28): 9.63.

Multiplier for term certain of 23.51 years at $2\frac{1}{2}$% rate of return (interpolating between the values for 23 and 24 in Table 28)

= (24 − 23.51) × 17.55 + (23.51 − 23) × 18.11 = 17.84.

(5) Adjustment factor for contingencies other than mortality (in accordance with Section B) for an employed female aged 38 with a degree and who was not disabled = 0.89 (does not apply to child) to give a multiplier of 17.84 × 0.89 = 15.88.

(6) Adjustment factor for the risk that the deceased might have died anyway before the date of trial (Table F for female aged 35 and 3 years): 1.00, so multipliers are 9.63 and 15.88 respectively.

(7) Pre-retirement damages = 9.63 × £10,000 + 15.88 × £50,000

= £96,300 + £794,000 = £890,300.

Post-retirement damages:

(1) Expectation of life of deceased at date of trial (Table 2 at 0% for female aged 38): 49.14.

(2) Expected period for which the dependant would have been able to receive the dependency (Table 1 at 0% for male aged 41): 42.48 (no post-retirement dependency for child).

(3) Lesser of two periods at (1) and (2) = 42.48.

(4) Multiplier for time certain of 42.48 years at $2\frac{1}{2}$% rate of return (interpolating between the values for 42 and 43 in Table 28)

= (43 − 42.48) × 26.14 + (42.48 − 42) × 26.49 = 26.31.

(5) Deduct multiplier for post-trial pre-retirement damages before application of adjustment factors for contingencies other than mortality and for the risk that the deceased might have died anyway before the date of trial: 26.31 − 17.84 = 8.47.

(6) Adjustment factor for the risk that the deceased might have died anyway before the date of trial (Table F for female aged 35 and 3 years) = 1.00, so multiplier is 8.47 × 1.00 = 8.47.

(7) Post-retirement damages = 8.47 × £20,000 = £169,400.

Section E: Concluding remarks

90. These tables are designed to assist the courts to arrive at suitable multipliers in a range of possible situations. However, they do not cover all possibilities and in more complex situations, such as where there are significant pension rights, advice should be sought from a Fellow of the Institute of Actuaries or a Fellow of the Faculty of Actuaries.

CHRISTOPHER DAYKIN CB, MA, FIA
Government Actuary
London
March 2007

Table 1: Multipliers for pecuniary loss for life (males)

Age at date of trial	Multiplier calculated with allowance for projected mortality from the 2004-based population projections and rate of return of											Age at date of trial
	0.0%	*0.5%*	*1.0%*	*1.5%*	*2.0%*	*2.5%*	*3.0%*	*3.5%*	*4.0%*	*4.5%*	*5.0%*	
0	86.63	69.86	57.39	47.98	40.76	35.15	30.72	27.17	24.28	21.91	19.94	0
1	85.96	69.49	57.21	47.91	40.76	35.19	30.77	27.24	24.36	21.99	20.01	1
2	84.86	68.78	56.74	47.60	40.55	35.05	30.68	27.17	24.32	21.96	19.99	2
3	83.76	68.05	56.26	47.28	40.34	34.90	30.58	27.10	24.27	21.93	19.97	3
4	82.65	67.32	55.77	46.95	40.12	34.75	30.48	27.03	24.22	21.89	19.94	4
5	81.53	66.58	55.27	46.61	39.89	34.59	30.37	26.95	24.16	21.85	19.91	5
6	80.42	65.83	54.77	46.27	39.65	34.43	30.25	26.87	24.10	21.81	19.88	6
7	79.30	65.08	54.26	45.92	39.41	34.26	30.13	26.79	24.04	21.76	19.85	7
8	78.18	64.32	53.74	45.56	39.16	34.08	30.01	26.70	23.98	21.71	19.81	8
9	77.06	63.56	53.22	45.20	38.91	33.91	29.88	26.61	23.91	21.66	19.78	9
10	75.95	62.79	52.69	44.83	38.65	33.72	29.75	26.51	23.84	21.61	19.74	10
11	74.83	62.02	52.16	44.46	38.39	33.53	29.61	26.41	23.77	21.56	19.70	11
12	73.71	61.25	51.62	44.08	38.11	33.34	29.47	26.31	23.69	21.50	19.65	12
13	72.59	60.47	51.07	43.69	37.84	33.14	29.33	26.20	23.61	21.44	19.61	13
14	71.48	59.69	50.52	43.30	37.56	32.93	29.18	26.09	23.52	21.38	19.56	14
15	70.36	58.90	49.96	42.90	37.27	32.72	29.02	25.97	23.44	21.31	19.51	15
16	69.25	58.12	49.40	42.50	36.97	32.51	28.86	25.85	23.35	21.24	19.45	16
17	68.14	57.33	48.83	42.09	36.68	32.29	28.70	25.73	23.26	21.17	19.40	17
18	67.04	56.55	48.27	41.68	36.38	32.07	28.54	25.61	23.16	21.10	19.34	18
19	65.95	55.77	47.71	41.27	36.08	31.85	28.37	25.49	23.07	21.03	19.29	19
20	64.87	54.99	47.14	40.86	35.78	31.63	28.21	25.36	22.98	20.96	19.23	20
21	63.79	54.21	46.58	40.44	35.47	31.40	28.40	25.23	22.88	20.88	19.17	21
22	62.71	53.42	46.00	40.02	35.16	31.16	27.86	25.10	22.77	20.80	19.11	22
23	61.63	52.63	45.42	39.59	34.83	30.92	27.68	24.96	22.67	20.72	19.05	23
24	60.55	51.84	44.83	39.15	34.51	30.67	27.49	24.81	22.55	20.63	18.98	24
25	59.47	51.03	44.23	38.70	34.17	30.42	27.29	24.66	22.44	20.54	18.90	15
26	58.38	50.23	43.63	38.25	33.82	30.15	27.09	24.50	22.31	20.44	18.83	26
27	57.31	49.42	43.03	37.79	33.47	29.89	26.88	24.34	22.19	20.34	18.75	27
28	56.24	48.62	42.42	37.33	33.12	29.61	26.67	24.18	22.06	20.24	18.67	28
29	55.17	47.82	41.81	36.86	32.76	29.33	26.45	24.01	21.92	20.13	18.58	29
30	54.10	47.00	41.19	36.39	32.39	29.05	26.23	23.83	21.78	20.02	18.49	30
31	53.03	46.19	40.56	35.90	32.02	28.75	26.00	23.65	21.64	19.90	18.40	31
32	51.97	45.37	39.93	35.41	31.64	28.46	25.76	23.46	21.48	19.78	18.30	32
33	50.91	44.55	39.30	34.92	31.25	28.15	25.52	23.26	21.33	19.65	18.19	33
34	49.85	43.73	38.66	34.42	30.85	27.83	25.27	23.06	21.17	19.52	18.08	34
35	48.78	42.90	38.01	33.91	30.45	27.51	25.01	22.86	21.00	19.38	17.97	35
36	47.73	42.08	37.36	33.39	30.04	27.18	24.74	22.64	20.82	19.24	17.85	36
37	46.67	41.24	36.70	32.87	29.62	26.85	24.47	22.42	20.64	19.09	17.73	37
38	45.62	40.41	36.04	32.34	29.19	26.50	24.19	22.19	20.45	18.93	17.60	38
39	44.56	39.57	35.37	31.80	28.76	26.15	23.90	21.95	20.26	18.77	17.46	39
40	43.52	38.74	34.70	31.26	28.32	25.79	23.61	21.71	20.05	18.60	17.32	40
41	42.48	37.90	34.02	30.71	27.87	25.42	23.30	21.46	19.84	18.43	17.17	41
42	41.44	37.06	33.34	30.15	27.41	25.05	22.99	21.20	19.63	18.24	17.02	42
43	40.40	36.22	32.65	29.59	26.95	24.67	22.68	20.93	19.41	18.06	16.86	43
44	39.37	35.38	31.97	29.03	26.49	24.28	22.35	20.66	19.18	17.86	16.69	44
45	38.35	34.55	31.28	28.46	26.01	23.88	22.02	20.38	18.94	17.66	16.52	45
46	37.34	33.71	30.59	27.89	25.54	23.49	21.69	20.10	18.70	17.46	16.35	46
47	36.34	32.89	29.90	27.32	25.06	23.08	21.35	19.81	18.45	17.25	16.17	47
48	35.34	32.06	29.22	26.74	24.58	22.68	21.00	19.52	18.20	17.03	15.98	48
49	34.37	31.25	28.54	26.17	24.09	22.27	20.65	19.22	17.95	16.81	15.79	49
50	33.40	30.44	27.86	25.60	23.61	21.86	20.30	18.92	17.69	16.59	15.60	50
51	32.44	29.63	27.18	25.02	23.12	21.44	19.95	18.62	17.43	16.36	15.40	51
52	31.49	28.84	26.50	24.45	22.63	21.02	19.58	18.30	17.16	16.12	15.19	52
53	30.55	28.04	25.82	23.87	22.13	20.59	19.21	17.98	16.88	15.88	14.98	53
54	29.61	27.23	25.13	23.28	21.62	20.15	18.83	17.65	16.59	15.63	14.76	54

Table 1: Multipliers for pecuniary loss for life (males) *continued*

Age at date of trial	Multiplier calculated with allowance for projected mortality from the 2004-based population projections and rate of return of											Age at date of trial
	0.0%	***0.5%***	***1.0%***	***1.5%***	***2.0%***	***2.5%***	***3.0%***	***3.5%***	***4.0%***	***4.5%***	***5.0%***	
55	28.66	26.42	24.44	22.67	21.10	19.70	18.44	17.31	16.29	15.36	14.52	55
56	27.71	25.60	23.73	22.06	20.57	19.23	18.03	16.95	15.97	15.08	14.28	56
57	26.76	24.78	23.02	21.44	20.03	18.76	17.62	16.58	15.65	14.79	14.02	57
58	25.82	23.96	22.31	20.82	19.48	18.28	17.19	16.21	15.31	14.50	13.75	58
59	24.89	23.15	21.59	20.19	18.93	17.79	16.76	15.82	14.97	14.19	13.48	59
60	23.97	22.35	20.89	19.57	18.38	17.30	16.33	15.44	14.62	13.88	13.20	60
61	23.08	21.56	20.19	18.96	17.84	16.82	15.90	15.05	14.28	13.57	12.92	61
62	22.20	20.79	19.51	18.35	17.30	16.34	15.47	14.67	13.93	13.26	12.64	62
63	21.34	20.03	18.83	17.75	16.76	15.86	15.03	14.28	13.58	12.94	12.36	63
64	20.50	19.27	18.16	17.15	16.22	15.37	14.60	13.88	13.23	12.62	12.06	64
65	19.66	18.52	17.49	16.54	15.68	14.88	14.16	13.48	12.86	12.29	11.76	65
66	18.82	17.77	16.81	15.94	15.13	14.39	13.70	13.07	12.49	11.95	11.45	66
67	17.99	17.02	16.14	15.32	14.57	13.88	13.24	12.65	12.11	11.60	11.13	67
68	17.16	16.27	15.45	14.70	14.01	13.36	12.77	12.22	11.71	11.23	10.79	68
69	16.33	15.51	14.76	14.07	13.43	12.84	12.29	11.77	11.30	10.85	10.44	69
70	15.50	14.75	14.07	13.43	12.85	12.30	11.79	11.32	10.87	10.46	10.08	70
71	14.67	14.00	13.38	12.80	12.26	11.76	11.29	10.85	10.44	10.06	9.70	71
72	13.86	13.25	12.69	12.16	11.67	11.21	10.78	10.38	10.00	9.65	9.32	72
73	13.07	12.52	12.01	11.53	11.09	10.67	10.28	9.91	9.56	9.24	8.94	73
74	12.31	11.81	11.35	10.92	10.51	10.13	9.78	9.44	9.13	8.83	8.55	74
75	11.57	11.13	10.71	10.32	9.95	9.61	9.29	8.98	8.70	8.42	8.17	75
76	10.86	10.47	10.09	9.74	9.41	9.10	8.81	8.53	8.27	8.03	7.79	76
77	10.19	9.84	9.50	9.19	8.89	8.61	8.35	8.10	7.86	7.64	7.42	77
78	9.55	9.24	8.94	8.66	8.39	8.14	7.90	7.68	7.46	7.26	7.06	78
79	8.95	8.67	8.40	8.15	7.91	7.69	7.47	7.27	7.08	6.89	6.71	79
80	8.38	8.13	7.89	7.67	7.45	7.25	7.06	6.88	6.70	6.53	6.38	80
81	7.83	7.61	7.40	7.20	7.01	6.83	6.66	6.49	6.34	6.19	6.04	81
82	7.31	7.12	6.93	6.75	6.58	6.42	6.27	6.12	5.98	5.85	5.72	82
83	6.81	6.64	6.47	6.32	6.17	6.02	5.89	5.75	5.63	5.51	5.39	83
84	6.32	6.17	6.03	5.89	5.76	5.63	5.51	5.39	5.28	5.17	5.07	84
85	5.87	5.73	5.61	5.49	5.37	5.26	5.15	5.05	4.95	4.85	4.76	85
86	5.44	5.33	5.22	5.11	5.01	4.91	4.81	4.72	4.64	4.55	4.47	86
87	5.05	4.95	4.85	4.76	4.67	4.58	4.50	4.42	4.34	4.27	4.19	87
88	4.68	4.60	4.51	4.43	4.35	4.27	4.20	4.13	4.06	4.00	3.93	88
89	4.35	4.28	4.20	4.13	4.06	4.00	3.93	3.87	3.81	3.75	3.69	89
90	4.05	3.99	3.92	3.86	3.80	3.74	3.68	3.63	3.57	3.52	3.47	90
91	3.76	3.71	3.65	3.59	3.54	3.49	3.44	3.39	3.34	3.30	3.25	91
92	3.49	3.44	3.39	3.34	3.30	3.25	3.21	3.16	3.12	3.08	3.04	92
93	3.26	3.21	3.17	3.12	3.08	3.04	3.00	2.96	2.93	2.89	2.86	93
94	3.06	3.02	2.98	2.94	2.91	2.87	2.83	2.80	2.77	2.73	2.70	94
95	2.88	2.85	2.81	2.78	2.75	2.71	2.68	2.65	2.62	2.59	2.56	95
96	2.71	2.68	2.65	2.62	2.59	2.56	2.53	2.51	2.48	2.45	2.43	96
97	2.55	2.52	2.49	2.46	2.44	2.41	2.39	2.36	2.34	2.32	2.29	97
98	2.38	2.36	2.33	2.31	2.29	2.26	2.24	2.22	2.20	2.18	2.16	98
99	2.22	2.20	2.18	2.15	2.13	2.12	2.10	2.08	2.06	2.04	2.02	99
100	2.06	2.04	2.02	2.01	1.99	1.97	1.95	1.94	1.92	1.90	1.89	100

Table 2: Multipliers for pecuniary loss for life (females)

Age at date of trial	Multiplier calculated with allowance for projected mortality from the 2004-based population projections and rate of return of											Age at date of trial
	0.0%	0.5%	1.0%	1.5%	2.0%	2.5%	3.0%	3.5%	4.0%	4.5%	5.0%	
0	90.15	72.21	58.98	49.06	41.51	35.67	31.09	27.43	24.48	22.06	20.05	0
1	89.44	71.83	58.79	48.99	41.50	35.70	31.14	27.50	24.55	22.13	20.11	1
2	88.36	71.13	58.34	48.70	41.32	35.58	31.06	27.44	24.51	22.10	20.10	2
3	87.27	70.43	57.88	48.40	41.12	35.45	30.97	27.38	24.47	22.08	20.08	3
4	86.17	69.72	57.42	48.09	40.92	35.32	30.88	27.32	24.43	22.05	20.06	4
5	85.07	69.00	56.95	47.78	40.71	35.18	30.79	27.26	24.38	22.01	20.04	5
6	83.97	68.28	56.47	47.46	40.49	35.03	30.69	27.19	24.34	21.98	20.01	6
7	82.87	67.55	55.99	47.14	40.28	34.88	30.59	27.12	24.29	21.95	19.99	7
8	81.77	66.82	55.50	46.81	40.05	34.73	30.48	27.04	24.23	21.91	19.96	8
9	80.67	66.08	55.00	46.47	39.82	34.57	30.37	26.97	24.18	21.87	19.93	9
10	79.57	65.34	54.50	46.13	39.59	34.41	30.26	26.89	24.12	21.83	19.90	10
11	78.47	64.60	53.99	45.78	39.35	34.24	30.14	26.80	24.06	21.79	19.87	11
12	77.36	63.85	53.48	45.43	39.10	34.07	30.02	26.72	24.00	21.74	19.84	12
13	76.26	63.10	52.96	45.07	38.85	33.89	29.89	26.63	23.94	21.69	19.80	13
14	75.16	62.34	52.44	44.71	38.60	33.71	29.76	26.53	23.87	21.64	19.77	14
15	74.06	61.58	51.91	44.34	38.34	33.53	29.63	26.44	23.80	21.59	19.73	15
16	72.97	60.82	51.38	43.97	38.07	33.34	29.49	26.34	23.73	21.54	19.69	16
17	71.88	60.06	50.85	43.59	37.80	33.15	29.36	26.24	23.65	21.48	19.65	17
18	70.79	59.30	50.31	43.21	37.53	32.95	29.21	26.14	23.57	21.43	19.60	18
19	69.70	58.53	49.77	42.82	37.25	32.75	29.07	26.03	23.50	21.37	19.56	19
20	68.61	57.76	49.22	42.42	36.97	32.54	28.91	25.92	23.41	21.30	19.51	20
21	67.52	56.98	48.66	42.02	36.68	32.33	28.76	25.80	23.33	21.24	19.46	21
22	66.43	56.20	48.10	41.62	36.38	32.11	28.60	25.68	23.23	21.17	19.41	22
23	65.34	55.42	47.53	41.20	36.08	31.89	28.43	25.55	23.14	21.10	19.36	23
24	64.25	54.63	46.96	40.78	35.77	31.66	28.26	25.42	23.04	21.02	19.30	24
25	63.16	53.84	46.38	40.36	35.45	31.42	28.08	25.29	22.94	20.94	19.24	25
26	62.08	53.05	45.79	39.92	35.13	31.18	27.90	25.15	22.83	20.86	19.17	26
27	60.99	52.25	45.20	39.48	34.80	30.93	27.71	25.01	22.72	20.78	19.10	27
28	59.91	51.45	44.61	39.04	34.46	30.67	27.51	24.86	22.61	20.69	19.03	28
29	58.83	50.64	44.01	38.58	34.12	30.41	27.31	24.70	22.49	20.59	18.96	29
30	57.74	49.83	43.40	38.12	33.77	30.15	27.11	24.54	22.36	20.49	18.88	30
31	56.66	49.02	42.78	37.66	33.41	29.87	26.89	24.38	22.23	20.39	18.80	31
32	55.58	48.20	42.16	37.18	33.05	29.59	26.68	24.21	22.10	20.28	18.71	32
33	54.50	47.38	41.54	36.70	32.68	29.30	26.45	24.03	21.96	20.17	18.63	33
34	53.43	46.56	40.91	36.22	32.30	29.01	26.22	23.85	21.81	20.06	18.53	34
35	52.35	45.74	40.27	35.73	31.92	28.71	25.98	23.66	21.66	19.93	18.43	35
36	51.28	44.91	39.63	35.22	31.52	28.40	25.74	23.46	21.50	19.81	18.33	36
37	50.21	44.08	38.98	34.72	31.13	28.08	25.49	23.26	21.34	19.67	18.22	37
38	49.14	43.25	38.33	34.20	30.72	27.76	25.23	23.05	21.17	19.54	18.11	38
39	48.07	42.41	37.67	33.68	30.30	27.43	24.96	22.84	21.00	19.39	17.99	39
40	47.01	41.58	37.01	33.16	29.89	27.09	24.69	22.61	20.82	19.25	17.87	40
41	45.95	40.74	36.35	32.63	29.46	26.74	24.41	22.39	20.63	19.09	17.74	41
42	44.90	39.90	35.68	32.09	29.02	26.39	24.12	22.15	20.44	18.93	17.61	42
43	43.85	39.06	35.00	31.55	28.59	26.04	23.83	21.91	20.24	18.77	17.47	43
44	42.80	38.22	34.33	31.00	28.14	25.67	23.53	21.66	20.03	18.59	17.33	44
45	41.77	37.39	33.65	30.45	27.69	25.30	23.23	21.41	19.82	18.42	17.18	45
46	40.74	36.55	32.97	29.90	27.24	24.93	22.92	21.15	19.61	18.24	17.03	46
47	39.71	35.72	32.29	29.34	26.77	24.55	22.60	20.89	19.38	18.05	16.87	47
48	38.70	34.89	31.61	28.77	26.31	24.16	22.28	20.62	19.16	17.86	16.70	48
49	37.69	34.06	30.93	28.21	25.84	23.77	21.95	20.34	18.92	17.66	16.53	49
50	36.69	33.23	30.24	27.64	25.36	23.37	21.61	20.06	18.68	17.46	16.36	50
51	35.69	32.41	29.56	27.07	24.88	22.96	21.27	19.77	18.44	17.25	16.18	51
52	34.70	31.59	28.87	26.49	24.40	22.55	20.92	19.47	18.18	17.03	15.99	52
53	33.71	30.76	28.17	25.90	23.90	22.13	20.56	19.17	17.92	16.80	15.80	53
54	32.73	29.93	27.47	25.31	23.39	21.70	20.19	18.85	17.64	16.56	15.59	54

Table 2: Multipliers for pecuniary loss for life (females) *continued*

Age at date of trial	Multiplier calculated with allowance for projected mortality from the 2004-based population projections and rate of return of											Age at date of trial
	0.0%	*0.5%*	*1.0%*	*1.5%*	*2.0%*	*2.5%*	*3.0%*	*3.5%*	*4.0%*	*4.5%*	*5.0%*	
55	31.74	29.09	26.76	24.70	22.88	21.26	19.81	18.52	17.36	16.32	15.38	55
56	30.75	28.25	26.05	24.09	22.36	20.81	19.42	18.18	17.07	16.06	15.15	56
57	29.77	27.42	25.33	23.48	21.82	20.35	19.03	17.84	16.77	15.80	14.92	57
58	28.80	26.58	24.61	22.86	21.29	19.88	18.62	17.48	16.46	15.52	14.68	58
59	27.83	25.75	23.89	22.23	20.75	19.41	18.21	17.12	16.14	15.24	14.43	59
60	26.88	24.93	23.18	21.61	20.20	18.94	17.79	16.76	15.81	14.96	14.18	60
61	25.94	24.11	22.47	20.99	19.66	18.46	17.37	16.38	15.49	14.67	13.92	61
62	25.02	23.30	21.76	20.37	19.11	17.98	16.95	16.01	15.15	14.37	13.65	62
63	24.10	22.49	21.05	19.75	18.56	17.49	16.51	15.62	14.81	14.06	13.38	63
64	23.18	21.69	20.34	19.12	18.01	17.00	16.07	15.23	14.46	13.75	13.10	64
65	22.28	20.89	19.63	18.49	17.45	16.50	15.63	14.83	14.10	13.42	12.80	65
66	21.38	20.09	18.92	17.85	16.88	15.99	15.17	14.42	13.73	13.09	12.50	66
67	20.48	19.29	18.20	17.21	16.30	15.47	14.70	13.99	13.34	12.74	12.18	67
68	19.58	18.48	17.47	16.55	15.71	14.93	14.22	13.55	12.94	12.38	11.85	68
69	18.66	17.66	16.73	15.88	15.10	14.38	13.71	13.10	12.52	11.99	11.50	69
70	17.74	16.82	15.97	15.19	14.47	13.81	13.19	12.62	12.09	11.59	11.13	70
71	16.82	15.98	15.21	14.50	13.84	13.22	12.65	12.13	11.63	11.17	10.74	71
72	15.90	15.14	14.44	13.79	13.19	12.63	12.11	11.62	11.17	10.74	10.34	72
73	14.99	14.31	13.67	13.09	12.54	12.03	11.55	11.11	10.69	10.30	9.93	73
74	14.10	13.49	12.92	12.39	11.89	11.43	11.00	10.59	10.21	9.85	9.51	74
75	13.24	12.69	12.18	11.71	11.26	10.84	10.45	10.08	9.73	9.40	9.10	75
76	12.42	11.93	11.47	11.05	10.64	10.27	9.91	9.58	9.26	8.96	8.68	76
77	11.64	11.20	10.79	10.41	10.05	9.71	9.39	9.09	8.80	8.53	8.28	77
78	10.89	10.51	10.14	9.80	9.48	9.17	8.88	8.61	8.35	8.11	7.88	78
79	10.19	9.84	9.52	9.21	8.93	8.65	8.39	8.15	7.92	7.70	7.48	79
80	9.51	9.21	8.92	8.65	8.39	8.15	7.92	7.70	7.49	7.29	7.10	80
81	8.87	8.60	8.35	8.11	7.88	7.66	7.46	7.26	7.07	6.89	6.72	81
82	8.26	8.02	7.80	7.58	7.38	7.19	7.01	6.83	6.66	6.50	6.35	82
83	7.67	7.46	7.27	7.08	6.90	6.73	6.57	6.41	6.26	6.12	5.98	83
84	7.10	6.92	6.75	6.59	6.43	6.28	6.14	6.00	5.87	5.74	5.62	84
85	6.57	6.41	6.26	6.12	5.98	5.85	5.73	5.60	5.49	5.38	5.27	85
86	6.07	5.93	5.80	5.68	5.56	5.44	5.33	5.23	5.12	5.02	4.93	86
87	5.60	5.48	5.37	5.26	5.16	5.06	4.96	4.86	4.77	4.69	4.60	87
88	5.17	5.06	4.97	4.87	4.78	4.69	4.61	4.53	4.45	4.37	4.30	88
89	4.77	4.68	4.60	4.51	4.43	4.36	4.28	4.21	4.14	4.08	4.01	89
90	4.41	4.33	4.26	4.19	4.12	4.05	3.99	3.92	3.86	3.80	3.75	90
91	4.08	4.01	3.95	3.89	3.83	3.77	3.71	3.66	3.60	3.55	3.50	91
92	3.79	3.73	3.67	3.61	3.56	3.51	3.46	3.41	3.36	3.32	3.27	92
93	3.53	3.47	3.42	3.38	3.33	3.28	3.24	3.20	3.15	3.11	3.07	93
94	3.30	3.25	3.21	3.17	3.12	3.08	3.04	3.00	2.97	2.93	2.90	94
95	3.08	3.04	3.01	2.97	2.93	2.89	2.86	2.82	2.79	2.76	2.73	95
96	2.89	2.85	2.82	2.78	2.75	2.72	2.69	2.66	2.63	2.60	2.57	96
97	2.70	2.67	2.64	2.61	2.58	2.55	2.53	2.50	2.47	2.45	2.42	97
98	2.53	2.50	2.48	2.45	2.42	2.40	2.37	2.35	2.33	2.30	2.28	98
99	2.37	2.34	2.32	2.30	2.27	2.25	2.23	2.21	2.19	2.17	2.15	99
100	2.21	2.19	2.17	2.15	2.13	2.11	2.09	2.07	2.05	2.03	2.02	100

Table 3: Multipliers for loss of earnings to pension age 50 (males)

Age at date of trial	Multiplier calculated with allowance for projected mortality from the 2004-based population projections and rate of return of											Age at date of trial
	0.0%	***0.5%***	***1.0%***	***1.5%***	***2.0%***	***2.5%***	***3.0%***	***3.5%***	***4.0%***	***4.5%***	***5.0%***	
16	33.58	30.90	28.52	26.39	24.48	22.77	21.24	19.86	18.61	17.48	16.46	16
17	32.59	30.06	27.80	25.78	23.96	22.33	20.86	19.54	18.34	17.25	16.26	17
18	31.59	29.21	27.08	25.16	23.44	21.88	20.48	19.21	18.05	17.00	16.05	18
19	30.60	28.37	26.36	24.54	22.91	21.43	20.09	18.87	17.76	16.76	15.83	19
20	29.62	27.52	25.63	23.92	22.37	20.96	19.68	18.52	17.46	16.50	15.61	20
21	28.63	26.67	24.89	23.28	21.81	20.48	19.27	18.16	17.15	16.22	15.37	21
22	27.65	25.81	24.15	22.63	21.25	19.99	18.84	17.79	16.83	15.94	15.13	22
23	26.66	24.95	23.39	21.98	20.68	19.49	18.40	17.41	16.49	15.64	14.87	23
24	25.67	24.09	22.64	21.31	20.09	18.98	17.95	17.01	16.14	15.33	14.59	24
25	24.68	23.21	21.87	20.63	19.49	18.45	17.48	16.59	15.77	15.01	14.30	25
26	23.70	22.34	21.09	19.94	18.88	17.91	17.00	16.17	15.39	14.67	14.00	26
27	22.71	21.46	20.31	19.25	18.26	17.35	16.51	15.72	14.99	14.32	13.69	27
28	21.72	20.58	19.52	18.54	17.63	16.78	16.00	15.27	14.58	13.95	13.36	28
29	20.74	19.69	18.72	17.82	16.98	16.20	15.47	14.79	14.16	13.56	13.01	29
30	19.75	18.80	17.92	17.10	16.33	15.61	14.93	14.31	13.72	13.16	12.64	30
31	18.77	17.91	17.11	16.36	15.66	15.00	14.38	13.80	13.25	12.74	12.26	31
32	17.78	17.01	16.29	15.61	14.97	14.37	13.81	13.28	12.78	12.30	11.86	32
33	16.80	16.11	15.46	14.85	14.27	13.73	13.22	12.74	12.28	11.85	11.44	33
34	15.81	15.20	14.62	14.08	13.56	13.08	12.61	12.18	11.76	11.37	11.00	34
35	14.83	14.29	13.78	13.30	12.84	12.40	11.99	11.60	11.22	10.87	10.53	35
36	13.84	13.37	12.93	12.50	12.10	11.71	11.35	11.00	10.67	10.35	10.05	36
37	12.86	12.45	12.07	11.70	11.34	11.01	10.69	10.38	10.08	9.80	9.53	37
38	11.87	11.53	11.19	10.88	10.57	10.28	10.00	9.74	9.48	9.23	9.00	38
39	10.89	10.60	10.32	10.05	9.79	9.54	9.30	9.07	8.85	8.64	8.43	39
40	9.90	9.66	9.43	9.20	8.99	8.78	8.58	8.38	8.20	8.02	7.84	40
41	8.92	8.72	8.53	8.35	8.17	8.00	7.83	7.67	7.52	7.37	7.22	41
42	7.93	7.77	7.62	7.48	7.33	7.20	7.06	6.93	6.81	6.69	6.57	42
43	6.94	6.82	6.71	6.59	6.48	6.38	6.27	6.17	6.07	5.98	5.88	43
44	5.95	5.87	5.78	5.70	5.61	5.53	5.46	5.38	5.31	5.23	5.16	44
45	4.97	4.90	4.84	4.79	4.73	4.67	4.62	4.56	4.51	4.46	4.41	45
46	3.98	3.94	3.90	3.86	3.82	3.79	3.75	3.72	3.68	3.65	3.61	46
47	2.99	2.96	2.94	2.92	2.90	2.88	2.86	2.84	2.82	2.80	2.78	47
48	1.99	1.98	1.97	1.96	1.95	1.94	1.94	1.93	1.92	1.91	1.90	48
49	1.00	1.00	0.99	0.99	0.99	0.99	0.98	0.98	0.98	0.98	0.97	49

Table 4: Multipliers for loss of earnings to pension age 50 (females)

Age at date of trial	Multiplier calculated with allowance for projected mortality from the 2004-based population projections and rate of return of											Age at date of trial
	0.0%	***0.5%***	***1.0%***	***1.5%***	***2.0%***	***2.5%***	***3.0%***	***3.5%***	***4.0%***	***4.5%***	***5.0%***	
16	33.79	31.09	28.68	26.54	24.61	22.89	21.34	19.95	18.69	17.56	16.53	16
17	32.80	30.25	27.97	25.93	24.10	22.45	20.97	19.64	18.43	17.33	16.33	17
18	31.80	29.40	27.25	25.32	23.58	22.01	20.59	19.31	18.15	17.09	16.13	18
19	30.81	28.55	26.52	24.69	23.04	21.55	20.20	18.97	17.86	16.84	15.91	19
20	29.81	27.70	25.79	24.06	22.50	21.08	19.79	18.62	17.55	16.58	15.69	20
21	28.82	26.84	25.04	23.42	21.94	20.60	19.38	18.26	17.24	16.30	15.45	21
22	27.82	25.97	24.29	22.77	21.37	20.11	18.95	17.88	16.91	16.02	15.20	22
23	26.83	25.11	23.54	22.10	20.80	19.60	18.50	17.50	16.57	15.72	14.94	23
24	25.83	24.23	22.77	21.43	20.21	19.08	18.05	17.10	16.22	15.41	14.66	24
25	24.84	23.36	22.00	20.75	19.60	18.55	17.58	16.68	15.85	15.08	14.37	25
26	23.84	22.48	21.22	20.06	18.99	18.00	17.09	16.25	15.47	14.47	14.07	26
27	22.85	21.59	20.43	19.36	18.37	17.45	16.60	15.81	15.07	14.39	13.75	27
28	21.85	20.70	19.63	18.65	17.73	16.88	16.08	15.35	14.66	14.02	13.42	28
29	20.86	19.81	18.83	17.92	17.08	16.29	15.55	14.87	14.23	13.63	13.07	29
30	19.87	18.91	18.02	17.19	16.41	15.69	15.01	14.38	13.78	13.23	12.70	30
31	18.87	18.01	17.20	16.44	15.74	15.07	14.45	13.87	13.32	12.80	12.32	31
32	17.88	17.10	16.37	15.69	15.05	14.44	13.38	13.34	12.84	12.36	11.91	32
33	16.89	16.19	15.54	14.92	14.34	13.80	13.28	12.80	12.34	11.90	11.49	33
34	15.89	15.28	14.70	14.15	13.63	13.14	12.67	12.23	11.82	11.42	11.04	34
35	14.90	14.36	13.85	13.36	12.90	12.46	12.04	11.65	11.27	10.92	10.58	35
36	13.91	13.44	12.99	12.56	12.15	11.76	11.40	11.04	10.71	10.39	10.09	36
37	12.92	12.51	12.12	11.75	11.39	11.05	10.73	10.42	10.12	9.84	9.57	37
38	11.92	11.57	11.24	10.92	10.62	10.32	10.04	9.77	9.52	9.27	9.03	38
39	10.93	10.64	10.36	10.08	9.82	9.58	9.34	9.10	8.88	8.67	8.46	39
40	9.94	9.70	9.46	9.24	9.02	8.81	8.61	8.41	8.23	8.04	7.87	40
41	8.95	8.75	8.56	8.37	8.20	8.02	7.86	7.70	7.54	7.39	7.24	41
42	7.95	7.80	7.65	7.50	7.36	7.22	7.09	6.96	6.83	6.71	6.59	42
43	6.96	6.84	6.73	6.61	6.50	6.39	6.29	6.19	6.09	5.99	5.90	43
44	5.97	5.88	5.80	5.71	5.63	5.55	5.47	5.40	5.32	5.25	5.18	44
45	4.98	4.92	4.86	4.80	4.74	4.68	4.63	4.57	4.52	4.47	4.42	45
46	3.98	3.95	3.91	3.87	3.83	3.79	3.76	3.72	3.69	3.65	3.62	46
47	2.99	2.97	2.95	2.93	2.90	2.88	2.86	2.84	2.82	2.80	2.78	47
48	2.00	1.99	1.98	1.97	1.96	1.95	1.94	1.93	1.92	1.91	1.90	48
49	1.00	1.00	0.99	0.99	0.99	0.99	0.98	0.98	0.98	0.98	0.97	49

Table 5: Multipliers for loss of earnings to pension age 55 (males)

Age at date of trial	Multiplier calculated with allowance for projected mortality from the 2004-based population projections and rate of return of											Age at date of trial
	0.0%	***0.5%***	***1.0%***	***1.5%***	***2.0%***	***2.5%***	***3.0%***	***3.5%***	***4.0%***	***4.5%***	***5.0%***	
16	38.37	34.90	31.85	29.17	26.81	24.72	22.87	21.22	19.75	18.44	17.27	16
17	37.37	34.07	31.16	28.60	26.34	24.33	22.54	20.95	19.53	18.25	17.11	17
18	36.38	33.24	30.48	28.03	25.86	23.93	22.21	20.67	19.29	18.06	16.94	18
19	35.39	32.42	29.79	27.45	25.37	23.52	21.87	20.38	19.05	17.85	16.77	19
20	34.41	31.59	29.09	26.87	24.88	23.11	21.52	20.09	18.80	17.64	16.59	20
21	33.42	30.76	28.39	26.27	24.38	22.68	21.16	19.79	18.54	17.42	16.41	21
22	32.43	29.92	27.68	25.67	23.87	22.25	20.79	19.47	18.28	17.19	16.21	22
23	31.45	29.08	26.97	25.06	23.35	21.80	20.41	19.14	18.00	16.95	16.00	23
24	30.46	28.24	26.24	24.44	22.82	21.35	20.02	18.81	17.71	16.70	15.79	24
25	29.47	27.39	25.51	23.81	22.27	20.88	19.61	18.46	17.40	16.44	15.56	25
26	28.49	26.54	24.77	23.17	21.72	20.40	19.19	18.09	17.09	16.17	15.32	26
27	27.50	25.68	24.03	22.53	21.16	19.91	18.76	17.72	16.76	15.88	15.07	27
28	26.52	24.82	23.28	21.87	20.58	19.40	18.32	17.33	16.42	15.58	14.81	28
29	25.53	23.96	22.52	21.20	20.00	18.89	17.87	16.93	16.07	15.27	14.54	29
30	24.55	23.09	21.76	20.53	19.40	18.36	17.40	16.52	15.70	14.95	14.25	30
31	23.57	22.22	20.98	19.84	18.79	17.82	16.92	16.09	15.32	14.61	13.95	31
32	22.59	21.35	20.21	19.15	18.17	17.27	16.43	15.65	14.93	14.26	13.63	32
33	21.60	20.47	19.42	18.45	17.54	16.70	15.92	15.20	14.52	13.89	13.30	33
34	20.62	19.59	18.63	17.73	16.90	16.12	15.40	14.72	14.09	13.50	12.95	34
35	19.64	18.70	17.82	17.01	16.24	15.53	14.86	14.24	13.65	13.10	12.59	35
36	18.66	17.81	17.01	16.27	15.57	14.92	14.31	13.73	13.19	12.68	12.21	36
37	17.68	16.91	16.20	15.52	14.89	14.30	13.74	13.21	12.71	12.25	11.80	37
38	16.70	16.02	15.37	14.77	14.20	13.66	13.15	12.67	12.22	11.79	11.38	38
39	15.72	15.11	14.54	14.00	13.49	13.00	12.55	12.11	11.70	11.31	10.94	39
40	14.74	14.20	13.70	13.22	12.76	12.33	11.92	11.53	11.16	10.81	10.48	40
41	13.76	13.29	12.85	12.43	12.03	11.64	11.28	10.94	10.61	10.29	9.99	41
42	12.78	12.37	11.99	11.62	11.27	10.94	10.62	10.32	10.03	9.75	9.48	42
43	11.80	11.45	11.12	10.81	10.51	10.22	9.94	9.68	9.42	9.18	8.95	43
44	10.82	10.53	10.25	9.98	9.73	9.48	9.24	9.02	8.80	8.59	8.39	44
45	9.84	9.60	9.37	9.15	8.93	8.73	8.53	8.33	8.15	7.97	7.80	45
46	8.86	8.67	8.48	8.30	8.12	7.95	7.79	7.63	7.47	7.32	7.18	46
47	7.88	7.73	7.58	7.43	7.29	7.16	7.03	6.90	6.77	6.65	6.53	47
48	6.91	6.79	6.67	6.56	6.45	6.34	6.24	6.14	6.04	5.95	5.85	48
49	5.93	5.84	5.75	5.67	5.59	5.51	5.43	5.36	5.28	5.21	5.14	49
50	4.95	4.89	4.83	4.77	4.71	4.65	4.60	4.55	4.49	4.44	4.39	50
51	3.96	3.93	3.89	3.85	3.81	3.78	3.74	3.70	3.67	3.64	3.60	51
52	2.98	2.96	2.94	2.91	2.89	2.87	2.85	2.83	2.81	2.79	2.77	52
53	1.99	1.98	1.97	1.96	1.95	1.94	1.93	1.92	1.91	1.91	1.90	53
54	1.00	0.99	0.99	0.99	0.99	0.99	0.98	0.98	0.98	0.98	0.97	54

Table 6: Multipliers for loss of earnings to pension age 55 (females)

Age at date of trial	Multiplier calculated with allowance for projected mortality from the 2004-based population projections and rate of return of											Age at date of trial
	0.0%	*0.5%*	*1.0%*	*1.5%*	*2.0%*	*2.5%*	*3.0%*	*3.5%*	*4.0%*	*4.5%*	*5.0%*	
16	38.67	35.16	32.08	29.37	26.98	24.87	23.00	21.34	19.86	18.54	17.35	16
17	37.68	34.33	31.40	28.81	26.52	24.49	22.68	21.08	19.64	18.35	17.20	17
18	36.68	33.51	30.71	28.23	26.04	24.09	22.35	20.80	19.41	18.16	17.04	18
19	35.69	32.68	30.02	27.66	25.56	23.68	22.01	20.51	19.17	17.96	16.87	19
20	34.69	31.84	29.32	27.07	25.06	23.27	21.66	20.22	18.92	17.75	16.69	20
21	33.70	31.01	28.61	26.47	24.56	22.84	21.30	19.91	18.66	17.53	16.50	21
22	32.70	30.16	27.90	25.86	24.04	22.40	20.93	19.60	18.39	17.30	16.30	22
23	31.71	29.32	27.17	25.25	23.52	21.96	20.54	19.27	18.11	17.06	16.10	23
24	30.71	28.47	26.44	24.62	22.98	21.50	20.15	18.93	17.82	16.80	15.88	24
25	29.72	27.61	25.71	23.99	22.44	21.02	19.74	18.58	17.51	16.54	15.65	25
26	28.72	26.75	24.97	23.35	21.88	20.54	19.32	18.21	17.20	16.27	15.41	26
27	27.73	25.89	24.22	22.70	21.31	20.05	18.89	17.84	16.87	15.98	15.16	27
28	26.73	25.02	23.46	22.03	20.73	19.54	18.45	17.45	16.53	15.68	14.90	28
29	25.74	24.15	22.69	21.36	20.14	19.02	17.99	17.05	16.17	15.37	14.62	29
30	24.75	23.27	21.92	20.68	19.54	18.49	17.52	16.63	15.81	15.04	14.34	30
31	23.75	22.39	21.14	19.99	18.93	17.95	17.04	16.20	15.42	14.70	14.03	31
32	22.76	21.51	20.35	19.29	18.30	17.39	16.54	15.76	15.03	14.35	13.71	32
33	21.77	20.62	19.56	18.58	17.66	16.82	16.03	15.30	14.61	13.98	13.38	33
34	20.78	19.73	18.76	17.86	17.02	16.23	15.50	14.82	14.18	13.59	13.03	34
35	19.79	18.84	17.95	17.12	16.35	15.63	14.96	14.33	13.74	13.18	12.66	35
36	18.79	17.94	17.13	16.38	15.68	15.02	14.40	13.82	13.27	12.76	12.28	36
37	17.80	17.03	16.31	15.63	14.99	14.39	13.82	13.29	12.79	12.32	11.87	37
38	16.81	16.12	15.47	14.86	14.29	13.74	13.23	12.75	12.29	11.86	11.45	38
39	15.82	15.21	14.63	14.09	13.57	13.08	12.62	12.18	11.77	11.38	11.00	39
40	14.83	14.30	13.78	13.30	12.84	12.41	11.99	11.60	11.23	10.87	10.54	40
41	13.85	13.38	12.93	12.50	12.10	11.71	11.35	11.00	10.67	10.35	10.05	41
42	12.86	12.45	12.06	11.69	11.34	11.01	10.68	10.38	10.08	9.80	9.53	42
43	11.87	11.52	11.19	10.87	10.57	10.28	10.00	9.73	9.48	9.23	9.00	43
44	10.88	10.59	10.31	10.04	9.78	9.54	9.30	9.07	8.85	8.64	8.43	44
45	9.90	9.66	9.42	9.20	8.98	8.77	8.57	8.38	8.19	8.01	7.84	45
46	8.91	8.72	8.53	8.34	8.17	7.99	7.83	7.67	7.51	7.36	7.22	46
47	7.93	7.77	7.62	7.47	7.33	7.19	7.06	6.93	6.81	6.68	6.57	47
48	6.94	6.82	6.70	6.59	6.48	6.37	6.27	6.17	6.07	5.98	5.88	48
49	5.95	5.87	5.78	5.70	5.61	5.53	5.46	5.38	5.31	5.23	5.16	49
50	4.97	4.90	4.84	4.79	4.73	4.67	4.62	4.56	4.51	4.46	4.41	50
51	3.98	3.94	3.90	3.86	3.82	3.79	3.75	3.72	3.68	3.65	3.61	51
52	2.99	2.96	2.94	2.92	2.90	2.88	2.86	2.84	2.82	2.80	2.78	52
53	1.99	1.98	1.97	1.96	1.95	1.95	1.94	1.93	1.92	1.91	1.90	53
54	1.00	1.00	0.99	0.99	0.99	0.99	0.98	0.98	0.98	0.98	0.97	54

Table 7: Multipliers for loss of earnings to pension age 60 (males)

Age at date of trial	Multiplier calculated with allowance for projected mortality from the 2004-based population projections and rate of return of											Age at date of trial
	0.0%	***0.5%***	***1.0%***	***1.5%***	***2.0%***	***2.5%***	***3.0%***	***3.5%***	***4.0%***	***4.5%***	***5.0%***	
16	43.07	38.71	34.96	31.70	28.87	26.41	24.25	22.35	20.68	19.20	17.89	16
17	42.07	37.90	34.30	31.17	28.44	26.05	23.96	22.12	20.49	19.04	17.76	17
18	41.07	37.10	33.64	30.63	28.00	25.70	23.67	21.88	20.29	18.88	17.63	18
19	40.08	36.29	32.98	30.10	27.56	25.34	23.37	21.63	20.09	18.72	17.49	19
20	39.10	35.48	32.32	29.55	27.12	24.97	23.07	21.38	19.88	18.55	17.35	20
21	38.11	34.67	31.65	29.00	26.66	24.59	22.76	21.12	19.67	18.37	17.20	21
22	37.12	33.85	30.98	28.44	26.19	24.20	22.43	20.85	19.44	18.18	17.04	22
23	36.14	33.03	30.29	27.87	25.72	23.81	22.10	20.58	19.21	17.98	16.88	23
24	35.15	32.21	29.60	27.29	25.23	23.40	21.76	20.29	18.97	17.78	16.71	24
25	34.16	31.38	28.91	26.70	24.74	22.98	21.41	19.99	18.72	17.56	16.52	25
26	33.18	30.55	28.20	26.11	24.23	22.55	21.04	19.68	18.45	17.34	16.33	26
27	32.19	29.71	27.49	25.50	23.72	22.12	20.67	19.36	18.18	17.11	16.13	27
28	31.21	28.87	26.78	24.89	23.20	21.67	20.29	19.04	17.90	16.87	15.93	28
29	30.23	28.03	26.05	24.27	22.67	21.21	19.89	18.70	17.61	16.61	15.71	29
30	29.24	27.18	25.33	23.65	22.12	20.74	19.49	18.35	17.30	16.35	15.48	30
31	28.26	26.33	24.59	23.01	21.57	20.26	19.07	17.98	16.99	16.08	15.24	31
32	27.28	25.48	23.85	22.36	21.01	19.77	18.64	17.61	16.66	15.79	14.99	32
33	26.30	24.63	23.10	21.71	20.43	19.27	18.20	17.22	16.32	15.49	14.72	33
34	25.32	23.77	22.34	21.04	19.85	18.76	17.75	16.82	15.97	15.18	14.45	34
35	24.34	22.90	21.58	20.37	19.26	18.23	17.28	16.41	15.60	14.85	14.16	35
36	23.36	22.03	20.81	19.69	18.65	17.69	16.80	15.98	15.22	14.51	13.86	36
37	22.39	21.16	20.04	18.99	18.03	17.14	16.31	15.54	14.82	14.16	13.54	37
38	21.41	20.29	19.25	18.29	17.40	16.57	15.80	15.08	14.41	13.79	13.21	38
39	20.43	19.41	18.46	17.58	16.76	15.99	15.28	14.61	13.99	13.40	12.86	39
40	19.45	18.53	17.66	16.85	16.10	15.40	14.74	14.12	13.54	13.00	12.49	40
41	18.48	17.64	16.86	16.12	15.43	14.79	14.18	13.62	13.08	12.58	12.11	41
42	17.50	16.75	16.04	15.38	14.75	14.17	13.62	13.10	12.61	12.14	11.71	42
43	16.53	15.86	15.22	14.63	14.06	13.53	13.03	12.56	12.11	11.69	11.29	43
44	15.56	14.96	14.40	13.86	13.36	12.88	12.43	12.00	11.60	11.21	10.85	44
45	14.59	14.06	13.56	13.09	12.64	12.22	11.81	11.43	11.06	10.72	10.39	45
46	13.62	13.16	12.72	12.31	11.91	11.54	11.18	10.84	10.51	10.20	9.90	46
47	12.65	12.26	11.88	11.52	11.17	10.84	10.53	10.23	9.94	9.66	9.40	47
48	11.69	11.35	11.02	10.71	10.42	10.13	9.86	9.60	9.34	9.10	8.87	48
49	10.72	10.44	10.16	9.90	9.65	9.40	9.17	8.95	8.73	8.52	8.32	49
50	9.76	9.52	9.30	9.08	8.86	8.66	8.46	8.27	8.09	7.91	7.74	50
51	8.80	8.61	8.42	8.24	8.07	7.90	7.73	7.58	7.42	7.28	7.13	51
52	7.83	7.68	7.53	7.39	7.25	7.11	6.98	6.86	6.73	6.61	6.50	52
53	6.87	6.75	6.63	6.52	6.41	6.31	6.21	6.11	6.01	5.92	5.82	53
54	5.90	5.81	5.72	5.64	5.56	5.48	5.41	5.33	5.26	5.19	5.12	54
55	4.92	4.86	4.80	4.75	4.69	4.63	4.58	4.53	4.47	4.42	4.37	55
56	3.95	3.91	3.87	3.83	3.80	3.76	3.72	3.69	3.65	3.62	3.59	56
57	2.97	2.95	2.92	2.90	2.88	2.86	2.84	2.82	2.80	2.78	2.76	57
58	1.98	1.97	1.96	1.96	1.95	1.94	1.93	1.92	1.91	1.90	1.89	58
59	1.00	0.99	0.99	0.99	0.99	0.98	0.98	0.98	0.98	0.97	0.97	59

Table 8: Multipliers for loss of earnings to pension age 60 (females)

Age at date of trial	Multiplier calculated with allowance for projected mortality from the 2004-based population projections and rate of return of											Age at date of trial
	0.0%	***0.5%***	***1.0%***	***1.5%***	***2.0%***	***2.5%***	***3.0%***	***3.5%***	***4.0%***	***4.5%***	***5.0%***	
16	43.49	39.07	35.26	31.97	29.10	26.60	24.42	22.50	20.81	19.32	17.99	16
17	42.49	38.27	34.62	31.44	28.68	26.26	24.14	22.27	20.63	19.16	17.87	17
18	41.50	37.46	33.96	30.91	28.24	25.91	23.85	22.04	20.43	19.01	17.74	18
19	40.50	36.65	33.30	30.37	27.80	25.55	23.56	21.80	20.23	18.84	17.60	19
20	39.51	35.84	32.63	29.82	27.35	25.18	23.25	21.55	20.03	18.67	17.46	20
21	38.51	35.02	31.96	29.27	26.89	24.80	22.94	21.29	19.81	18.49	17.31	21
22	37.51	34.20	31.28	28.70	26.43	24.41	22.62	21.02	19.59	18.31	17.16	22
23	36.52	33.37	30.59	28.13	25.95	24.01	22.28	20.74	19.35	18.11	16.99	23
24	35.52	32.54	29.89	27.55	25.46	23.60	21.94	20.45	19.11	17.91	16.82	24
25	34.53	31.70	29.19	26.96	24.96	23.18	21.59	20.15	18.86	17.69	16.64	25
26	33.53	30.86	28.48	26.36	24.46	22.75	21.22	19.84	18.60	17.47	16.45	26
27	32.54	30.02	27.77	25.75	23.94	22.31	20.85	19.52	18.33	17.24	16.25	27
28	31.54	29.17	27.04	25.13	23.42	21.86	20.46	19.19	18.04	17.00	16.04	28
29	30.55	28.32	26.32	24.51	22.88	21.40	20.07	18.85	17.75	16.74	15.83	29
30	29.56	27.47	25.58	23.87	22.33	20.93	19.66	18.50	17.44	16.48	15.60	30
31	28.56	26.61	24.84	23.23	21.77	20.45	19.24	18.14	17.13	16.20	15.36	31
32	27.57	25.74	24.09	22.58	21.21	19.95	18.81	17.76	16.80	15.92	15.10	32
33	26.58	24.88	23.33	21.92	20.63	19.45	18.36	17.37	16.46	15.61	14.84	33
34	25.59	24.01	22.57	21.25	20.04	18.93	17.91	16.97	16.10	15.30	14.56	34
35	24.60	23.14	21.80	20.57	19.44	18.39	17.44	16.55	15.73	14.97	14.27	35
36	23.61	22.26	21.02	19.88	18.82	17.85	16.95	16.12	15.35	14.63	13.97	36
37	22.62	21.38	20.23	19.18	18.20	17.29	16.45	15.67	14.95	14.28	13.65	37
38	21.63	20.49	19.44	18.47	17.56	16.72	15.94	15.21	14.53	13.90	13.31	38
39	20.64	19.60	18.64	17.75	16.91	16.14	15.41	14.74	14.11	13.51	12.96	39
40	19.65	18.71	17.83	17.02	16.25	15.54	14.87	14.24	13.66	13.11	12.59	40
41	18.67	17.81	17.02	16.27	15.58	14.92	14.31	13.74	13.20	12.69	12.21	41
42	17.68	16.92	16.20	15.52	14.89	14.30	13.74	13.21	12.71	12.25	11.80	42
43	16.70	16.01	15.37	14.77	14.19	13.66	13.15	12.67	12.22	11.79	11.38	43
44	15.71	15.11	14.54	14.00	13.48	13.00	12.54	12.11	11.70	11.31	10.94	44
45	14.73	14.20	13.69	13.22	12.76	12.33	11.92	11.53	11.16	10.81	10.48	45
46	13.76	13.29	12.85	12.43	12.02	11.64	11.28	10.93	10.60	10.29	9.99	46
47	12.78	12.37	11.99	11.62	11.27	10.94	10.62	10.32	10.03	9.75	9.48	47
48	11.80	11.46	11.13	10.81	10.51	10.22	9.94	9.68	9.43	9.18	8.95	48
49	10.82	10.53	10.25	9.99	9.73	9.48	9.25	9.02	8.80	8.59	8.39	49
50	9.85	9.61	9.37	9.15	8.94	8.73	8.53	8.34	8.15	7.97	7.80	50
51	8.87	8.67	8.49	8.30	8.13	7.96	7.79	7.63	7.48	7.33	7.19	51
52	7.89	7.74	7.59	7.44	7.30	7.16	7.03	6.90	6.78	6.66	6.54	52
53	6.91	6.79	6.68	6.56	6.46	6.35	6.25	6.15	6.05	5.95	5.86	53
54	5.93	5.84	5.76	5.67	5.59	5.51	5.44	5.36	5.29	5.22	5.14	54
55	4.95	4.89	4.83	4.77	4.71	4.66	4.60	4.55	4.50	4.44	4.39	55
56	3.96	3.93	3.89	3.85	3.81	3.78	3.74	3.70	3.67	3.64	3.60	56
57	2.98	2.96	2.93	2.91	2.89	2.87	2.85	2.83	2.81	2.79	2.77	57
58	1.99	1.98	1.97	1.96	1.95	1.94	1.93	1.92	1.91	1.90	1.90	58
59	1.00	0.99	0.99	0.99	0.99	0.99	0.98	0.98	0.98	0.98	0.97	59

Table 9: Multipliers for loss of earnings to pension age 65 (males)

Age at date of trial	Multiplier calculated with allowance for projected mortality from the 2004-based population projections and rate of return of											Age at date of trial
	0.0%	***0.5%***	***1.0%***	***1.5%***	***2.0%***	***2.5%***	***3.0%***	***3.5%***	***4.0%***	***4.5%***	***5.0%***	
16	47.63	42.33	37.83	33.99	30.69	27.86	25.40	23.27	21.42	19.79	18.36	16
17	46.62	41.54	37.20	33.49	30.29	27.54	25.15	23.07	21.25	19.66	18.26	17
18	45.63	40.75	36.57	32.98	29.89	27.22	24.89	22.86	21.09	19.53	18.15	18
19	44.64	39.96	35.94	32.48	29.49	26.89	24.63	22.66	20.92	19.39	18.04	19
20	43.65	39.16	35.31	31.97	29.08	26.56	24.37	22.44	20.74	19.25	17.92	20
21	42.66	38.37	34.66	31.45	28.66	26.23	24.09	22.22	20.56	19.10	17.80	21
22	41.67	37.57	34.02	30.93	28.24	25.88	23.81	21.99	20.37	18.95	17.67	22
23	40.69	36.77	33.36	30.40	27.80	25.52	23.52	21.75	20.18	18.78	17.54	23
24	39.70	35.96	32.70	29.86	27.36	25.16	23.22	21.50	19.97	18.62	17.40	24
25	38.71	35.15	32.04	29.31	26.90	24.78	22.91	21.24	19.76	18.44	17.25	25
26	37.72	34.33	31.36	28.75	26.44	24.40	22.59	20.98	19.54	18.25	17.10	26
27	36.73	33.51	30.68	28.18	25.97	24.01	22.26	20.71	19.31	18.06	16.94	27
28	35.75	32.69	30.00	27.61	25.49	23.61	21.93	20.42	19.08	17.86	16.77	28
29	34.76	31.87	29.31	27.03	25.01	23.20	21.58	20.13	18.83	17.66	16.60	29
30	33.78	31.04	28.61	26.45	24.51	22.78	21.23	19.83	18.57	17.44	16.41	30
31	32.80	30.21	27.91	25.85	24.01	22.35	20.86	19.52	18.31	17.21	16.22	31
32	31.82	29.38	27.20	25.25	23.49	21.91	20.49	19.20	18.04	16.98	16.02	32
33	30.84	28.54	26.49	24.63	22.97	21.46	20.10	18.87	17.75	16.73	15.80	33
34	29.86	27.70	25.76	24.01	22.43	21.00	19.71	18.53	17.45	16.48	15.58	34
35	28.88	26.86	25.04	23.39	21.89	20.53	19.30	18.17	17.15	16.21	15.35	35
36	27.90	26.01	24.30	22.75	21.34	20.05	18.88	17.81	16.83	15.93	15.11	36
37	26.93	25.16	23.56	22.10	20.77	19.56	18.45	17.43	16.50	15.64	14.85	37
38	25.95	24.31	22.81	21.45	20.20	19.05	18.00	17.04	16.16	15.34	14.59	38
39	24.98	23.45	22.06	20.78	19.61	18.54	17.55	16.64	15.80	15.02	14.31	39
40	24.00	22.59	21.30	20.11	19.02	18.01	17.08	16.22	15.43	14.70	14.01	40
41	23.03	21.73	20.53	19.43	18.41	17.47	16.60	15.79	15.05	14.35	13.71	41
42	22.06	20.86	19.76	18.74	17.79	16.92	16.10	15.35	14.65	14.00	13.39	42
43	21.09	19.99	18.98	18.04	17.16	16.35	15.60	14.89	14.24	13.62	13.05	43
44	20.12	19.12	18.19	17.33	16.52	15.77	15.07	14.42	13.81	13.24	12.70	44
45	19.16	18.25	17.40	16.61	15.88	15.19	14.54	13.94	13.37	12.84	12.34	45
46	18.20	17.38	16.61	15.89	15.22	14.58	13.99	13.44	12.91	12.42	11.96	46
47	17.24	16.50	15.81	15.16	14.55	13.97	13.43	12.92	12.44	11.99	11.56	47
48	16.29	15.63	15.00	14.42	13.87	13.35	12.86	12.39	11.95	11.54	11.15	48
49	15.33	14.75	14.20	13.67	13.18	12.71	12.27	11.85	11.45	11.07	10.71	49
50	14.39	13.87	13.38	12.92	12.48	12.06	11.66	11.29	10.93	10.59	10.26	50
51	13.44	12.99	12.56	12.15	11.76	11.40	11.04	10.71	10.39	10.08	9.79	51
52	12.49	12.10	11.73	11.38	11.04	10.71	10.41	10.11	9.83	9.56	9.30	52
53	11.55	11.21	10.89	10.59	10.30	10.02	9.75	9.49	9.24	9.01	8.78	53
54	10.60	10.32	10.05	9.79	9.54	9.30	9.07	8.85	8.63	8.43	8.23	54
55	9.65	9.41	9.19	8.97	8.76	8.56	8.37	8.18	8.00	7.83	7.66	55
56	8.69	8.50	8.32	8.14	7.97	7.81	7.65	7.49	7.34	7.20	7.06	56
57	7.74	7.59	7.44	7.30	7.16	7.03	6.90	6.78	6.66	6.54	6.42	57
58	6.78	6.67	6.56	6.45	6.34	6.24	6.14	6.04	5.94	5.85	5.76	58
59	5.83	5.74	5.66	5.58	5.50	5.42	5.35	5.27	5.20	5.13	5.06	59
60	4.87	4.81	4.75	4.70	4.64	4.59	4.53	4.48	4.43	4.38	4.33	60
61	3.91	3.87	3.84	3.80	3.76	3.73	3.69	3.66	3.62	3.59	3.56	61
62	2.95	2.93	2.90	2.88	2.86	2.84	2.82	2.80	2.78	2.76	2.74	62
63	1.98	1.97	1.96	1.95	1.94	1.93	1.92	1.91	1.90	1.89	1.88	63
64	0.99	0.99	0.99	0.99	0.98	0.98	0.98	0.98	0.97	0.97	0.97	64

Table 10: Multipliers for loss of earnings to pension age 65 (females)

Age at date of trial	Multiplier calculated with allowance for projected mortality from the 2004-based population projections and rate of return of											Age at date of trial
	0.0%	*0.5%*	*1.0%*	*1.5%*	*2.0%*	*2.5%*	*3.0%*	*3.5%*	*4.0%*	*4.5%*	*5.0%*	
16	48.22	42.83	38.24	34.34	30.99	28.11	25.62	23.46	21.58	19.93	18.48	16
17	47.22	42.04	37.62	33.84	30.60	27.80	25.37	23.26	21.42	19.80	18.38	17
18	46.22	41.25	37.00	33.35	30.20	27.48	25.12	23.06	21.26	19.68	18.28	18
19	45.23	40.46	36.37	32.84	29.80	27.16	24.86	22.86	21.09	19.54	18.17	19
20	44.23	39.66	35.73	32.33	29.39	26.83	24.60	22.64	20.92	19.40	18.06	20
21	43.23	38.86	35.08	31.81	28.97	26.49	24.32	22.42	20.74	19.26	17.94	21
22	42.23	38.05	34.43	31.29	28.54	26.15	24.04	22.19	20.55	19.10	17.81	22
23	41.24	37.24	33.77	30.75	28.11	25.79	23.75	21.95	20.36	18.94	17.68	23
24	40.24	36.43	33.11	30.21	27.66	25.43	23.45	21.71	20.16	18.78	17.54	24
25	39.24	35.61	32.44	29.66	27.21	25.05	23.14	21.45	19.95	18.60	17.40	25
26	38.25	34.79	31.76	29.10	26.75	24.67	22.83	21.19	19.73	18.42	17.25	26
27	37.25	33.97	31.08	28.53	26.28	24.28	22.50	20.92	19.50	18.23	17.09	27
28	36.25	33.14	30.39	27.95	25.80	23.88	22.16	20.63	19.26	18.03	16.92	28
29	35.26	32.31	29.69	27.37	25.31	23.46	21.82	20.34	19.02	17.82	16.75	29
30	34.26	31.47	28.99	26.78	24.81	23.04	21.46	20.04	18.76	17.61	16.56	30
31	33.27	30.63	28.28	26.18	24.30	22.61	21.10	19.73	18.50	17.38	16.37	31
32	32.28	29.79	27.56	25.57	23.78	22.17	20.72	19.41	18.22	17.15	16.17	32
33	31.28	28.94	26.84	24.95	23.25	21.72	20.33	19.08	17.94	16.90	15.96	33
34	30.29	28.09	26.11	24.33	22.71	21.26	19.93	18.73	17.64	16.65	15.74	34
35	29.30	27.24	25.38	23.69	22.17	20.78	19.52	18.38	17.33	16.38	15.51	35
36	28.31	26.38	24.63	23.05	21.61	20.30	19.10	18.01	17.01	16.10	15.26	36
37	27.32	25.52	23.88	22.39	21.04	19.80	18.67	17.63	16.68	15.81	15.01	37
38	26.33	24.66	23.13	21.73	20.46	19.29	18.22	17.24	16.34	15.51	14.74	38
39	25.34	23.79	22.36	21.06	19.87	18.77	17.76	16.84	15.98	15.19	14.46	39
40	24.36	22.92	21.60	20.38	19.27	18.24	17.29	16.42	15.61	14.86	14.17	40
41	23.37	22.04	20.82	19.69	18.66	17.70	16.81	15.99	15.23	14.52	13.86	41
42	22.39	21.17	20.04	19.00	18.03	17.14	16.31	15.54	14.83	14.16	13.54	42
43	21.41	20.29	19.25	18.29	17.40	16.57	15.80	15.08	14.41	13.79	13.21	43
44	20.43	19.41	18.46	17.58	16.76	15.99	15.28	14.61	13.99	13.40	12.86	44
45	19.45	18.53	17.66	16.85	16.10	15.40	14.74	14.12	13.54	13.00	12.49	45
46	18.48	17.64	16.86	16.12	15.43	14.79	14.19	13.62	13.08	12.58	12.11	46
47	17.51	16.75	16.05	15.38	14.76	14.17	13.62	13.10	12.61	12.15	11.71	47
48	16.54	15.86	15.23	14.63	14.07	13.54	13.04	12.56	12.11	11.69	11.29	48
49	15.57	14.97	14.41	13.87	13.37	12.89	12.44	12.01	11.60	11.22	10.85	49
50	14.60	14.07	13.57	13.10	12.65	12.23	11.82	11.44	11.07	10.73	10.39	50
51	13.64	13.17	12.74	12.32	11.93	11.55	11.19	10.85	10.52	10.21	9.91	51
52	12.67	12.27	11.89	11.53	11.18	10.85	10.54	10.24	9.95	9.67	9.41	52
53	11.70	11.36	11.04	10.73	10.43	10.14	9.87	9.61	9.35	9.11	8.88	53
54	10.73	10.45	10.17	9.91	9.66	9.41	9.18	8.95	8.74	8.53	8.33	54
55	9.77	9.53	9.30	9.08	8.87	8.66	8.47	8.28	8.09	7.92	7.74	55
56	8.80	8.61	8.42	8.24	8.06	7.90	7.73	7.58	7.42	7.28	7.13	56
57	7.83	7.68	7.53	7.38	7.25	7.11	6.98	6.85	6.73	6.61	6.49	57
58	6.86	6.74	6.63	6.52	6.41	6.30	6.20	6.10	6.01	5.91	5.82	58
59	5.89	5.80	5.72	5.64	5.56	5.48	5.40	5.33	5.25	5.18	5.11	59
60	4.92	4.86	4.80	4.74	4.68	4.63	4.57	4.52	4.47	4.42	4.37	60
61	3.94	3.91	3.87	3.83	3.79	3.76	3.72	3.69	3.65	3.62	3.59	61
62	2.97	2.94	2.92	2.90	2.88	2.86	2.84	2.82	2.80	2.78	2.76	62
63	1.98	1.97	1.96	1.96	1.95	1.94	1.93	1.92	1.91	1.90	1.89	63
64	1.00	0.99	0.99	0.99	0.99	0.98	0.98	0.98	0.98	0.97	0.97	64

Table 11: Multipliers for loss of earnings to pension age 70 (males)

Age at date of trial	Multiplier calculated with allowance for projected mortality from the 2004-based population projections and rate of return of											Age at date of trial
	0.0%	***0.5%***	***1.0%***	***1.5%***	***2.0%***	***2.5%***	***3.0%***	***3.5%***	***4.0%***	***4.5%***	***5.0%***	
16	52.01	45.72	40.46	36.02	32.27	29.09	26.36	24.02	22.00	20.25	18.72	16
17	51.00	44.94	39.85	35.55	31.91	28.80	26.14	23.84	21.86	20.14	18.63	17
18	50.00	44.16	39.24	35.08	31.54	28.51	25.91	23.66	21.72	20.02	18.54	18
19	49.01	43.39	38.64	34.60	31.16	28.22	25.68	23.48	21.57	19.91	18.45	19
20	48.01	42.61	38.03	34.13	30.79	27.92	25.44	23.29	21.42	19.79	18.35	20
21	47.02	41.83	37.41	33.64	30.40	27.61	25.20	23.10	21.27	19.67	18.25	21
22	46.03	41.05	36.79	33.14	30.01	27.30	24.95	22.90	21.11	19.54	18.15	22
23	45.04	40.26	36.16	32.64	29.61	26.98	24.69	22.69	20.94	19.40	18.04	23
24	44.05	39.47	35.53	32.13	29.20	26.65	24.42	22.48	20.77	19.26	17.93	24
25	43.06	38.67	34.89	31.62	28.78	26.31	24.15	22.25	20.59	19.11	17.80	25
26	42.06	37.87	34.24	31.09	28.35	25.96	23.87	22.02	20.40	18.96	17.68	26
27	41.07	37.06	33.59	30.56	27.92	25.61	23.58	21.79	20.20	18.80	17.54	27
28	40.09	36.26	32.93	30.02	27.48	25.25	23.28	21.54	20.00	18.63	17.41	28
29	39.10	35.45	32.27	29.48	27.03	24.88	22.97	21.29	19.79	18.46	17.26	29
30	38.12	34.64	31.60	28.93	26.58	24.50	22.66	21.03	19.57	18.27	17.11	30
31	37.13	33.83	30.92	28.37	26.11	24.11	22.34	20.76	19.35	18.08	16.95	31
32	36.15	33.01	30.24	27.80	25.64	23.72	22.01	20.48	19.11	17.89	16.78	32
33	35.17	32.19	29.56	27.23	25.16	23.31	21.67	20.19	18.87	17.68	16.61	33
34	34.19	31.37	28.87	26.64	24.66	22.90	21.32	19.90	18.62	17.47	16.43	34
35	33.21	30.54	28.17	26.05	24.16	22.47	20.96	19.59	18.36	17.25	16.24	35
36	32.23	29.71	27.46	25.46	23.66	22.04	20.59	19.27	18.09	17.02	16.04	36
37	31.25	28.88	26.75	24.85	23.14	21.60	20.21	18.95	17.81	16.77	15.83	37
38	30.27	28.04	26.04	24.23	22.61	21.14	19.81	18.61	17.52	16.52	15.62	38
39	29.30	27.20	25.31	23.61	22.07	20.68	19.41	18.26	17.22	16.26	15.39	39
40	28.32	26.36	24.59	22.98	21.52	20.20	19.00	17.90	16.90	15.99	15.15	40
41	27.35	25.51	23.85	22.34	20.97	19.72	18.58	17.53	16.58	15.70	14.90	41
42	26.38	24.67	23.11	21.70	20.40	19.22	18.14	17.15	16.24	15.41	14.64	42
43	25.41	23.82	22.37	21.04	19.83	18.72	17.70	16.76	15.90	15.10	14.37	43
44	24.45	22.97	21.62	20.38	19.24	18.20	17.24	16.35	15.54	14.78	14.08	44
45	23.49	22.12	20.87	19.71	18.65	17.67	16.77	15.94	15.17	14.45	13.79	45
46	22.53	21.27	20.11	19.04	18.05	17.14	16.29	15.51	14.78	14.11	13.48	46
47	21.58	20.42	19.35	18.36	17.44	16.59	15.80	15.07	14.39	13.75	13.16	47
48	20.63	19.57	18.59	17.67	16.83	16.04	15.30	14.62	13.98	13.39	12.83	48
49	19.69	18.72	17.82	16.98	16.20	15.47	14.79	14.16	13.57	13.01	12.49	49
50	18.76	17.88	17.06	16.29	15.57	14.90	14.27	13.69	13.14	12.62	12.13	50
51	17.83	17.03	16.28	15.59	14.93	14.32	13.74	13.20	12.69	12.21	11.76	51
52	16.90	16.18	15.51	14.87	14.28	13.72	13.19	12.70	12.23	11.79	11.37	52
53	15.97	15.32	14.72	14.15	13.62	13.11	12.63	12.18	11.75	11.35	10.96	53
54	15.03	14.46	13.93	13.42	12.94	12.48	12.05	11.64	11.25	10.89	10.54	54
55	14.10	13.60	13.12	12.67	12.24	11.84	11.45	11.09	10.74	10.40	10.09	55
56	13.17	12.73	12.31	11.91	11.54	11.18	10.84	10.51	10.20	9.90	9.62	56
57	12.23	11.85	11.49	11.15	10.82	10.50	10.20	9.91	9.64	9.38	9.12	57
58	11.30	10.97	10.66	10.37	10.08	9.81	9.55	9.30	9.06	8.83	8.61	58
59	10.37	10.09	9.83	9.58	9.34	9.11	8.88	8.67	8.46	8.26	8.07	59
60	9.44	9.21	9.00	8.79	8.58	8.39	8.20	8.02	7.84	7.67	7.51	60
61	8.52	8.33	8.15	7.98	7.82	7.65	7.50	7.35	7.20	7.06	6.92	61
62	7.60	7.45	7.31	7.17	7.03	6.91	6.78	6.66	6.54	6.42	6.31	62
63	6.67	6.56	6.45	6.34	6.24	6.14	6.04	5.94	5.85	5.76	5.67	63
64	5.75	5.66	5.58	5.50	5.42	5.35	5.27	5.20	5.13	5.06	4.99	64
65	4.81	4.75	4.70	4.64	4.58	4.53	4.48	4.43	4.38	4.33	4.28	65
66	3.87	3.83	3.80	3.76	3.72	3.69	3.65	3.62	3.59	3.55	3.52	66
67	2.92	2.90	2.88	2.86	2.84	2.82	2.80	2.78	2.76	2.74	2.72	67
68	1.96	1.95	1.94	1.93	1.92	1.92	1.91	1.90	1.89	1.88	1.87	68
69	0.99	0.99	0.98	0.98	0.98	0.98	0.98	0.97	0.97	0.97	0.97	69

Table 12: Multipliers for loss of earnings to pension age 70 (females)

Age at date of trial	Multiplier calculated with allowance for projected mortality from the 2004-based population projections and rate of return of											Age at date of trial
	0.0%	*0.5%*	*1.0%*	*1.5%*	*2.0%*	*2.5%*	*3.0%*	*3.5%*	*4.0%*	*4.5%*	*5.0%*	
16	52.83	46.39	41.01	36.48	32.65	29.40	26.62	24.24	22.19	20.41	18.85	16
17	51.83	45.62	40.41	36.02	32.29	29.12	26.41	24.08	22.06	20.30	18.77	17
18	50.83	44.85	39.81	35.55	31.93	28.84	26.19	23.90	21.92	20.20	18.69	18
19	49.83	44.07	39.21	35.08	31.56	28.55	25.96	23.72	21.78	20.09	18.60	19
20	48.83	43.29	38.59	34.60	31.19	28.26	25.73	23.54	21.64	19.97	18.51	20
21	47.83	42.50	37.98	34.11	30.80	27.95	25.49	23.35	21.48	19.85	18.42	21
22	46.83	41.71	37.35	33.62	30.41	27.64	25.24	23.15	21.33	19.72	18.31	22
23	45.83	40.92	36.72	33.12	30.01	27.32	24.99	22.95	21.16	19.59	18.21	23
24	44.83	40.12	36.09	32.61	29.60	26.99	24.72	22.74	20.99	19.45	18.10	24
25	43.83	39.32	35.44	32.09	29.19	26.66	24.45	22.52	20.81	19.31	17.98	25
26	42.83	38.52	34.79	31.57	28.76	26.32	24.17	22.29	20.63	19.16	17.85	26
27	41.83	37.71	34.14	31.04	28.33	25.96	23.89	22.05	20.44	19.00	17.73	27
28	40.83	36.90	33.48	30.50	27.89	25.60	23.59	21.81	20.24	18.84	17.59	28
29	39.83	36.08	32.81	29.95	27.44	25.23	23.29	21.56	20.03	18.67	17.45	29
30	38.83	35.26	32.14	29.39	26.98	24.86	22.97	21.30	19.82	18.49	17.30	30
31	37.84	34.44	31.46	28.83	26.52	24.47	22.65	21.03	19.59	18.30	17.14	31
32	36.84	33.61	30.77	28.26	26.04	24.07	22.32	20.76	19.36	18.11	16.98	32
33	35.85	32.78	30.08	27.68	25.56	23.67	21.98	20.47	19.12	17.90	16.81	33
34	34.85	31.95	29.38	27.10	25.07	23.25	21.63	20.18	18.87	17.69	16.63	34
35	33.86	31.12	28.68	26.50	24.56	22.83	21.27	19.87	18.61	17.47	16.44	35
36	32.87	30.28	27.97	25.90	24.05	22.39	20.90	19.56	18.34	17.24	16.25	36
37	31.88	29.43	27.25	25.29	23.53	21.95	20.52	19.23	18.06	17.00	16.04	37
38	30.89	28.59	26.52	24.67	23.00	21.49	20.13	18.89	17.77	16.75	15.82	38
39	29.90	27.74	25.80	24.04	22.46	21.03	19.73	18.55	17.47	16.49	15.60	39
40	28.91	26.89	25.06	23.41	21.91	20.55	19.32	18.19	17.16	16.22	15.36	40
41	27.93	26.03	24.32	22.76	21.35	20.06	18.89	17.82	16.84	15.94	15.12	41
42	26.94	25.18	23.57	22.11	20.78	19.57	18.46	17.44	16.51	15.65	14.86	42
43	25.96	24.32	22.82	21.46	20.21	19.06	18.01	17.05	16.16	15.34	14.59	43
44	24.99	23.46	22.07	20.79	19.62	18.54	17.55	16.64	15.80	15.03	14.31	44
45	24.01	22.60	21.31	20.12	19.02	18.01	17.09	16.23	15.43	14.70	14.02	45
46	23.04	21.74	20.54	19.44	18.42	17.48	16.61	15.80	15.05	14.36	13.71	46
47	22.07	20.88	19.77	18.75	17.80	16.93	16.11	15.36	14.66	14.00	13.39	47
48	21.11	20.01	19.00	18.05	17.18	16.36	15.61	14.90	14.25	13.63	13.06	48
49	20.15	19.15	18.22	17.35	16.54	15.79	15.09	14.44	13.82	13.25	12.72	49
50	19.19	18.28	17.43	16.64	15.90	15.21	14.56	13.95	13.39	12.85	12.35	50
51	18.23	17.41	16.64	15.92	15.24	14.61	14.02	13.46	12.93	12.44	11.98	51
52	17.27	16.53	15.84	15.19	14.57	14.00	13.46	12.94	12.46	12.01	11.58	52
53	16.32	15.66	15.03	14.45	13.89	13.37	12.88	12.41	11.97	11.56	11.16	53
54	15.36	14.77	14.22	13.69	13.20	12.73	12.29	11.87	11.47	11.09	10.73	54
55	14.40	13.89	13.40	12.93	12.49	12.07	11.68	11.30	10.94	10.60	10.27	55
56	13.45	13.00	12.57	12.16	11.77	11.40	11.05	10.71	10.39	10.09	9.80	56
57	12.49	12.10	11.73	11.38	11.04	10.71	10.40	10.11	9.83	9.56	9.30	57
58	11.54	11.21	10.89	10.58	10.29	10.01	9.74	9.48	9.24	9.00	8.77	58
59	10.59	10.31	10.04	9.78	9.53	9.29	9.06	8.84	8.63	8.42	8.23	59
60	9.64	9.41	9.18	8.97	8.76	8.56	8.36	8.18	7.99	7.82	7.65	60
61	8.69	8.50	8.32	8.14	7.97	7.80	7.64	7.49	7.34	7.19	7.05	61
62	7.74	7.59	7.44	7.30	7.17	7.03	6.90	6.78	6.66	6.54	6.42	62
63	6.79	6.67	6.56	6.45	6.35	6.24	6.14	6.04	5.95	5.85	5.76	63
64	5.84	5.75	5.67	5.59	5.51	5.43	5.35	5.28	5.21	5.14	5.07	64
65	4.88	4.82	4.76	4.70	4.65	4.59	4.54	4.49	4.43	4.38	4.33	65
66	3.92	3.88	3.84	3.80	3.77	3.73	3.70	3.66	3.63	3.59	3.56	66
67	2.95	2.93	2.91	2.89	2.87	2.84	2.82	2.80	2.78	2.77	2.75	67
68	1.98	1.97	1.96	1.95	1.94	1.93	1.92	1.91	1.90	1.89	1.88	68
69	0.99	0.99	0.99	0.99	0.98	0.98	0.98	0.98	0.97	0.97	0.97	69

Table 13: Multipliers for loss of earnings to pension age 75 (males)

Age at date of trial	Multiplier calculated with allowance for projected mortality from the 2004-based population projections and rate of return of											Age at date of trial
	0.0%	***0.5%***	***1.0%***	***1.5%***	***2.0%***	***2.5%***	***3.0%***	***3.5%***	***4.0%***	***4.5%***	***5.0%***	
16	56.16	48.85	42.82	37.81	33.63	30.11	27.14	24.61	22.45	20.59	18.98	16
17	55.14	48.08	42.23	37.36	33.29	29.85	26.94	24.46	22.33	20.50	18.91	17
18	54.13	47.31	41.65	36.91	32.94	29.58	26.73	24.30	22.21	20.40	18.83	18
19	53.13	46.54	41.06	36.46	32.59	29.32	26.53	24.14	22.08	20.30	18.75	19
20	52.13	45.78	40.47	36.01	32.24	29.04	26.31	23.97	21.95	20.20	18.67	20
21	51.13	45.01	39.88	35.55	31.88	28.77	26.10	23.80	21.82	20.09	18.59	21
22	50.14	44.24	39.28	35.08	31.52	28.48	25.87	23.62	21.68	19.98	18.50	22
23	49.14	43.46	38.67	34.61	31.15	28.19	25.64	23.44	21.53	19.87	18.41	23
24	48.14	42.68	38.06	34.12	30.77	27.89	25.40	23.25	21.38	19.75	18.31	24
25	47.14	41.89	37.44	33.63	30.38	27.58	25.15	23.05	21.22	19.62	18.21	25
26	46.15	41.10	36.81	33.14	29.98	27.26	24.90	22.85	21.06	19.49	18.10	26
27	45.15	40.31	36.18	32.63	29.58	26.94	24.64	22.64	20.89	19.35	17.99	27
28	44.16	39.52	35.54	32.12	29.17	26.61	24.37	22.42	20.71	19.20	17.87	28
29	43.17	38.73	34.91	31.61	28.75	26.27	24.10	22.20	20.53	19.06	17.75	29
30	42.18	37.93	34.26	31.09	28.33	25.92	23.82	21.97	20.34	18.90	17.62	30
31	41.19	37.12	33.61	30.56	27.90	25.57	23.53	21.73	20.15	18.74	17.49	31
32	40.20	36.32	32.95	30.02	27.46	25.21	23.23	21.49	19.94	18.57	17.35	32
33	39.21	35.51	32.29	29.48	27.01	24.84	22.93	21.24	19.73	18.40	17.20	33
34	38.23	34.70	31.62	28.92	26.55	24.46	22.61	20.97	19.52	18.22	17.05	34
35	37.24	33.89	30.95	28.37	26.09	24.08	22.29	20.71	19.29	18.03	16.89	35
36	36.26	33.07	30.27	27.80	25.62	23.68	21.96	20.43	19.06	17.83	16.72	36
37	35.28	32.25	29.58	27.23	25.13	23.28	21.62	20.14	18.81	17.62	16.55	37
38	34.30	31.43	28.89	26.64	24.64	22.86	21.27	19.84	18.56	17.41	16.37	38
39	33.32	30.61	28.20	26.06	24.15	22.44	20.91	19.54	18.30	17.18	16.17	39
40	32.34	29.78	27.50	25.46	23.64	22.01	20.54	19.22	18.03	16.95	15.97	40
41	31.37	28.95	26.79	24.86	23.12	21.57	20.16	18.90	17.75	16.71	15.77	41
42	30.40	28.12	26.08	24.25	22.60	21.12	19.77	18.56	17.46	16.46	15.55	42
43	29.43	27.29	25.36	23.63	22.07	20.66	19.38	18.22	17.16	16.20	15.32	43
44	28.46	26.45	24.64	23.01	21.53	20.19	18.97	17.86	16.85	15.93	15.09	44
45	27.50	25.62	23.92	22.38	20.98	19.71	18.55	17.50	16.53	15.65	14.84	45
46	26.55	24.79	23.19	21.75	20.43	19.23	18.13	17.13	16.21	15.36	14.59	46
47	25.60	23.96	22.47	21.11	19.87	18.74	17.70	16.75	15.87	15.07	14.33	47
48	24.66	23.13	21.74	20.47	19.31	18.24	17.26	16.36	15.53	14.76	14.05	48
49	23.72	22.31	21.01	19.82	18.73	17.73	16.81	15.96	15.17	14.45	13.77	49
50	22.79	21.48	20.28	19.18	18.16	17.22	16.35	15.55	14.81	14.12	13.48	50
51	21.87	20.66	19.55	18.52	17.58	16.70	15.89	15.13	14.44	13.79	13.18	51
52	20.95	19.84	18.82	17.87	16.99	16.17	15.41	14.71	14.05	13.44	12.87	52
53	20.04	19.02	18.07	17.20	16.38	15.63	14.92	14.27	13.65	13.08	12.54	53
54	19.12	18.19	17.32	16.52	15.77	15.07	14.42	13.81	13.24	12.70	12.20	54
55	18.20	17.35	16.57	15.83	15.14	14.50	13.90	13.33	12.81	12.31	11.84	55
56	17.27	16.51	15.80	15.13	14.50	13.92	13.36	12.84	12.36	11.90	11.46	56
57	16.35	15.67	15.03	14.42	13.85	13.32	12.81	12.34	11.89	11.47	11.07	57
58	15.44	14.82	14.25	13.70	13.19	12.71	12.25	11.82	11.41	11.02	10.66	58
59	14.52	13.98	13.47	12.98	12.52	12.09	11.68	11.29	10.92	10.56	10.23	59
60	13.62	13.14	12.69	12.26	11.85	11.46	11.09	10.74	10.41	10.09	9.79	60
61	12.72	12.30	11.91	11.53	11.17	10.82	10.50	10.19	9.89	9.60	9.33	61
62	11.83	11.47	11.12	10.79	10.48	10.18	9.89	9.62	9.35	9.10	8.86	62
63	10.95	10.64	10.34	10.06	9.78	9.52	9.27	9.03	8.80	8.58	8.37	63
64	10.06	9.80	9.55	9.31	9.08	8.85	8.64	8.43	8.23	8.04	7.86	64
65	9.18	8.96	8.75	8.55	8.35	8.16	7.98	7.81	7.64	7.48	7.32	65
66	8.29	8.11	7.94	7.77	7.61	7.46	7.31	7.16	7.02	6.89	6.75	66
67	7.40	7.26	7.12	6.99	6.86	6.73	6.61	6.49	6.38	6.27	6.16	67
68	6.50	6.40	6.29	6.19	6.09	5.99	5.89	5.80	5.71	5.62	5.54	68
69	5.61	5.52	5.45	5.37	5.29	5.22	5.15	5.08	5.01	4.94	4.88	69
70	4.70	4.64	4.59	4.53	4.48	4.43	4.38	4.33	4.28	4.23	4.18	70
71	3.79	3.75	3.72	3.68	3.65	3.61	3.58	3.55	3.51	3.48	3.45	71
72	2.87	2.85	2.83	2.81	2.79	2.77	2.75	2.73	2.71	2.69	2.67	72
73	1.94	1.93	1.92	1.91	1.90	1.89	1.88	1.87	1.86	1.85	1.85	73
74	0.98	0.98	0.98	0.97	0.97	0.97	0.97	0.97	0.96	0.96	0.96	74

Table 14: Multipliers for loss of earnings to pension age 75 (females)

Age at date of trial	Multiplier calculated with allowance for projected mortality from the 2004-based population projections and rate of return of											Age at date of trial
	0.0%	*0.5%*	*1.0%*	*1.5%*	*2.0%*	*2.5%*	*3.0%*	*3.5%*	*4.0%*	*4.5%*	*5.0%*	
16	57.27	49.74	43.54	38.39	34.10	30.50	27.46	24.88	22.67	20.78	19.14	16
17	56.27	48.99	42.97	37.96	33.77	30.25	27.27	24.73	22.56	20.69	19.07	17
18	55.26	48.22	42.39	37.52	33.44	30.00	27.08	24.58	22.45	20.60	19.00	18
19	54.26	47.46	41.81	37.08	33.10	29.74	26.88	24.43	22.33	20.51	18.93	19
20	53.25	46.69	41.22	36.63	32.75	29.47	26.67	24.27	22.20	20.41	18.85	20
21	52.25	45.92	40.62	36.17	32.40	29.19	26.45	24.10	22.07	20.31	18.77	21
22	51.24	45.15	40.02	35.70	32.04	28.91	26.23	23.93	21.94	20.20	18.69	22
23	50.24	44.37	39.42	35.23	31.67	28.62	26.01	23.75	21.80	20.09	18.60	23
24	49.23	43.58	38.81	34.75	31.29	28.33	25.77	23.57	21.65	19.98	18.51	24
25	48.23	42.79	38.19	34.26	30.91	28.02	25.53	23.38	21.50	19.86	18.41	25
26	47.22	42.00	37.56	33.77	30.52	27.71	25.29	23.18	21.34	19.73	18.31	26
27	46.22	41.21	36.93	33.27	30.12	27.39	25.03	22.97	21.18	19.60	18.20	27
28	45.22	40.41	36.30	32.76	29.71	27.07	24.77	22.76	21.01	19.46	18.09	28
29	44.22	39.61	35.65	32.25	29.30	26.73	24.50	22.55	20.83	19.31	17.97	29
30	43.21	38.80	35.01	31.72	28.87	26.39	24.22	22.32	20.64	19.16	17.85	30
31	42.21	38.00	34.35	31.19	28.44	26.04	23.94	22.09	20.45	19.01	17.72	31
32	41.21	37.18	33.69	30.65	28.00	25.68	23.64	21.85	20.26	18.84	17.59	32
33	40.21	36.37	33.03	30.11	27.56	25.32	23.34	21.60	20.05	18.67	17.45	33
34	39.22	35.55	32.36	29.56	27.10	24.94	23.03	21.34	19.84	18.50	17.30	34
35	38.22	34.73	31.68	29.00	26.64	24.56	22.71	21.07	19.62	18.31	17.14	35
36	37.22	33.91	31.00	28.43	26.17	24.16	22.38	20.80	19.39	18.12	16.98	36
37	36.23	33.08	30.31	27.86	25.69	23.76	22.05	20.52	19.15	17.92	16.81	37
38	35.24	32.25	29.61	27.27	25.20	23.35	21.70	20.22	18.90	17.71	16.64	38
39	34.24	31.42	28.91	26.68	24.70	22.93	21.35	19.92	18.64	17.49	16.45	39
40	33.26	30.58	28.21	26.09	24.19	22.50	20.98	19.61	18.38	17.27	16.26	40
41	32.27	29.75	27.49	25.48	23.68	22.06	20.61	19.29	18.10	17.03	16.05	41
42	31.28	28.91	26.78	24.87	23.16	21.61	20.22	18.96	17.82	16.78	15.84	42
43	30.30	28.07	26.06	24.25	22.63	21.16	19.83	18.62	17.53	16.53	15.62	43
44	29.33	27.23	25.34	23.63	22.09	20.69	19.42	18.27	17.22	16.27	15.39	44
45	28.35	26.38	24.61	23.00	21.54	20.22	19.01	17.91	16.91	16.00	15.16	45
46	27.38	25.54	23.88	22.36	20.99	19.73	18.59	17.55	16.59	15.71	14.91	46
47	26.42	24.70	23.14	21.72	20.43	19.24	18.16	17.17	16.26	15.42	14.65	47
48	25.45	23.86	22.40	21.07	19.85	18.74	17.72	16.78	15.91	15.12	14.38	48
49	24.50	23.01	21.66	20.42	19.28	18.23	17.27	16.38	15.56	14.80	14.10	49
50	23.54	22.17	20.91	19.75	18.69	17.71	16.80	15.97	15.19	14.48	13.81	50
51	22.59	21.33	20.16	19.09	18.09	17.18	16.33	15.54	14.81	14.14	13.51	51
52	21.64	20.48	19.40	18.41	17.49	16.63	15.84	15.11	14.42	13.79	13.19	52
53	20.69	19.63	18.64	17.72	16.87	16.08	15.34	14.66	14.02	13.42	12.86	53
54	19.74	18.77	17.87	17.02	16.24	15.51	14.83	14.19	13.59	13.04	12.51	54
55	18.79	17.91	17.09	16.32	15.60	14.93	14.30	13.71	13.16	12.64	12.15	55
56	17.85	17.05	16.30	15.60	14.95	14.33	13.75	13.21	12.70	12.22	11.77	56
57	16.90	16.18	15.51	14.88	14.28	13.72	13.20	12.70	12.23	11.79	11.37	57
58	15.96	15.32	14.72	14.15	13.61	13.10	12.63	12.17	11.75	11.34	10.96	58
59	15.02	14.45	13.92	13.41	12.93	12.47	12.04	11.63	11.25	10.88	10.53	59
60	14.09	13.59	13.11	12.66	12.23	11.83	11.44	11.08	10.73	10.40	10.08	60
61	13.16	12.72	12.31	11.91	11.53	11.17	10.83	10.51	10.19	9.90	9.61	61
62	12.23	11.86	11.49	11.15	10.82	10.50	10.20	9.92	9.64	9.38	9.13	62
63	11.31	10.99	10.68	10.38	10.09	9.82	9.56	9.31	9.07	8.84	8.62	63
64	10.39	10.11	9.85	9.60	9.35	9.12	8.90	8.68	8.48	8.28	8.08	64
65	9.46	9.23	9.02	8.80	8.60	8.41	8.22	8.03	7.86	7.69	7.53	65
66	8.54	8.35	8.17	8.00	7.83	7.67	7.51	7.36	7.22	7.08	6.94	66
67	7.61	7.46	7.32	7.18	7.05	6.92	6.79	6.67	6.55	6.43	6.32	67
68	6.68	6.56	6.45	6.35	6.24	6.14	6.04	5.95	5.85	5.76	5.67	68
69	5.74	5.66	5.58	5.50	5.42	5.34	5.27	5.20	5.13	5.06	4.99	69
70	4.81	4.75	4.69	4.63	4.58	4.52	4.47	4.42	4.37	4.32	4.27	70
71	3.86	3.83	3.79	3.75	3.72	3.68	3.65	3.61	3.58	3.55	3.51	71
72	2.91	2.89	2.87	2.85	2.83	2.81	2.79	2.77	2.75	2.73	2.71	72
73	1.96	1.95	1.94	1.93	1.92	1.91	1.90	1.89	1.88	1.87	1.87	73
74	0.99	0.99	0.98	0.98	0.98	0.98	0.97	0.97	0.97	0.97	0.96	74

Table 15: Multipliers for loss of pension commencing age 50 (males)

Age at date of trial	Multiplier calculated with allowance for projected mortality from the 2004-based population projections and rate of return of											Age at date of trial
	0.0%	*0.5%*	*1.0%*	*1.5%*	*2.0%*	*2.5%*	*3.0%*	*3.5%*	*4.0%*	*4.5%*	*5.0%*	
0	37.30	26.17	18.48	13.13	9.38	6.75	4.87	3.54	2.58	1.90	1.40	0
1	37.37	26.36	18.71	13.36	9.60	6.94	5.04	3.68	2.70	1.99	1.47	1
2	37.27	26.42	18.85	13.54	9.77	7.10	5.18	3.80	2.80	2.08	1.54	2
3	37.16	26.49	19.00	13.71	9.95	7.26	5.33	3.93	2.91	2.17	1.62	3
4	37.04	26.54	19.14	13.88	10.13	7.43	5.48	4.06	3.02	2.26	1.70	4
5	36.93	26.60	19.28	14.05	10.30	7.60	5.63	4.19	3.14	2.36	1.78	5
6	36.81	26.66	19.42	14.23	10.49	7.77	5.79	4.33	3.26	2.46	1.87	6
7	36.70	26.71	19.56	14.41	10.67	7.95	5.95	4.47	3.38	2.57	1.96	7
8	36.58	26.77	19.70	14.59	10.86	8.13	6.12	4.62	3.51	2.68	2.05	8
9	36.47	26.82	19.85	14.77	11.05	8.31	6.29	4.78	3.65	2.79	2.15	9
10	36.35	26.88	19.99	14.95	11.25	8.50	6.46	4.93	3.78	2.92	2.26	10
11	36.24	26.93	20.14	15.14	11.45	8.70	6.64	5.10	3.93	3.04	2.36	11
12	36.12	26.99	20.28	15.33	11.65	8.90	6.83	5.27	4.08	3.17	2.48	12
13	36.01	27.04	20.43	15.52	11.85	9.10	7.02	5.44	4.24	3.31	2.60	13
14	35.89	27.10	20.58	15.71	12.06	9.31	7.22	5.62	4.40	3.45	2.72	14
15	35.78	27.15	20.73	15.91	12.27	9.52	7.42	5.81	4.56	3.60	2.86	15
16	35.66	27.21	20.88	16.11	12.49	9.74	7.62	6.00	4.74	3.76	3.00	16
17	35.55	27.27	21.03	16.31	12.71	9.96	7.84	6.20	4.92	3.92	3.14	17
18	35.45	27.33	21.19	16.52	12.94	10.19	8.06	6.40	5.11	4.09	3.29	18
19	35.35	27.40	21.35	16.73	13.17	10.42	8.29	6.62	5.31	4.27	3.45	19
20	35.25	27.47	21.52	16.95	13.41	10.67	8.52	6.84	5.51	4.46	3.62	20
21	35.16	27.54	21.68	17.17	13.66	10.92	8.77	7.07	5.73	4.66	3.80	21
22	35.07	27.61	21.85	17.39	13.90	11.17	9.02	7.31	5.95	4.86	3.99	22
23	34.98	27.68	22.02	17.61	14.16	11.43	9.27	7.55	6.18	5.07	4.18	23
24	34.88	27.75	22.20	17.84	14.41	11.70	9.54	7.81	6.42	5.30	4.39	24
25	34.78	27.82	22.36	18.07	14.67	11.97	9.81	8.07	6.67	5.53	4.60	25
26	34.69	27.89	22.54	18.30	14.94	12.25	10.09	8.34	6.92	5.77	4.83	26
27	34.60	27.96	22.71	18.54	15.21	12.53	10.37	8.62	7.19	6.02	5.06	27
28	34.51	28.04	22.90	18.79	15.49	12.83	10.67	8.91	7.47	6.29	5.31	28
29	34.43	28.12	23.08	19.04	15.78	13.13	10.98	9.21	7.76	6.57	5.57	29
30	34.35	28.20	23.27	19.29	16.07	13.44	11.29	9.53	8.07	6.86	5.85	30
31	34.27	28.28	23.45	19.54	16.36	13.76	11.62	9.85	8.38	7.16	6.13	31
32	34.19	28.36	23.64	19.80	16.66	14.08	11.95	10.18	8.71	7.47	6.44	32
33	34.11	28.44	23.84	20.07	16.97	14.42	12.30	10.53	9.05	7.81	6.75	33
34	34.03	28.53	24.03	20.34	17.29	14.76	12.65	10.89	9.40	8.15	7.09	34
35	33.96	28.61	24.23	20.61	17.61	15.11	13.02	11.26	9.77	8.51	7.44	35
36	33.88	28.70	24.43	20.89	17.94	15.47	13.39	11.64	10.16	8.89	7.81	36
37	33.81	28.79	24.63	21.17	18.27	15.84	13.78	12.04	10.56	9.28	8.19	37
38	33.74	28.88	24.84	21.46	18.62	16.22	14.19	12.45	10.97	9.70	8.60	38
39	33.68	28.98	25.05	21.75	18.97	16.61	14.60	12.88	11.40	10.13	9.03	39
40	33.62	29.08	25.27	22.05	19.33	17.01	15.03	13.33	11.86	10.58	9.48	40
41	33.56	29.18	25.49	22.36	19.70	17.43	15.47	13.79	12.33	11.06	9.95	41
42	33.51	29.29	25.72	22.68	20.08	17.85	15.93	14.27	12.82	11.56	10.45	42
43	33.46	29.40	25.95	23.00	20.47	18.29	16.40	14.76	13.33	12.08	10.98	43
44	33.42	29.52	26.19	23.33	20.87	18.74	16.89	15.28	13.87	12.63	11.53	44
45	33.38	29.64	26.43	23.67	21.29	19.21	17.40	15.82	14.43	13.20	12.12	45
46	33.36	29.78	26.69	24.03	21.72	19.70	17.94	16.39	15.02	13.81	12.73	46
47	33.35	29.92	26.96	24.40	22.16	20.21	18.49	16.98	15.64	14.45	13.39	47
48	33.35	30.08	27.25	24.78	22.62	20.73	19.07	17.59	16.29	15.12	14.08	48
49	33.37	30.25	27.54	25.18	23.11	21.28	19.67	18.24	16.97	15.83	14.82	49
50	33.40	30.44	27.86	25.60	23.61	21.86	20.30	18.92	17.69	16.59	15.60	50

Table 16: Multipliers for loss of pension commencing age 50 (females)

Age at date of trial	Multiplier calculated with allowance for projected mortality from the 2004-based population projections and rate of return of											Age at date of trial
	0.0%	*0.5%*	*1.0%*	*1.5%*	*2.0%*	*2.5%*	*3.0%*	*3.5%*	*4.0%*	*4.5%*	*5.0%*	
0	40.61	28.35	19.93	14.10	10.03	7.18	5.17	3.75	2.73	1.99	1.47	0
1	40.68	28.55	20.17	14.34	10.26	7.39	5.34	3.89	2.84	2.09	1.54	1
2	40.59	28.64	20.34	14.54	10.45	7.56	5.50	4.02	2.96	2.18	1.62	2
3	40.49	28.72	20.50	14.73	10.64	7.74	5.66	4.16	3.07	2.28	1.70	3
4	40.39	28.80	20.66	14.92	10.84	7.92	5.82	4.30	3.19	2.38	1.78	4
5	40.29	28.87	20.83	15.12	11.04	8.10	5.98	4.44	3.31	2.48	1.87	5
6	40.19	28.95	20.99	15.31	11.24	8.29	6.15	4.59	3.44	2.59	1.96	6
7	40.09	29.03	21.16	15.51	11.44	8.49	6.33	4.74	3.57	2.71	2.06	7
8	39.98	29.11	21.32	15.72	11.65	8.69	6.51	4.90	3.71	2.82	2.16	8
9	39.88	29.18	21.49	15.92	11.86	8.89	6.70	5.07	3.86	2.95	2.26	9
10	39.78	29.26	21.66	16.13	12.08	9.10	6.89	5.24	4.01	3.08	2.37	10
11	39.68	29.34	21.83	16.34	12.30	9.31	7.08	5.42	4.16	3.21	2.49	11
12	39.58	29.42	22.00	16.55	12.52	9.52	7.28	5.60	4.32	3.35	2.61	12
13	39.47	29.49	22.17	16.77	12.75	9.75	7.49	5.79	4.49	3.50	2.74	14
14	39.37	29.57	22.35	16.98	12.98	9.97	7.50	5.98	4.66	3.65	2.87	14
15	39.27	29.65	22.52	17.20	13.22	10.21	7.92	6.18	4.84	3.81	3.01	15
16	39.17	29.73	22.70	17.43	13.46	10.45	8.15	6.39	5.03	3.98	3.16	16
17	39.08	29.81	22.88	17.66	13.70	10.69	8.38	6.60	5.23	4.15	3.32	17
18	38.98	29.90	23.06	17.89	13.96	10.94	8.62	6.83	5.43	4.34	3.48	18
19	38.89	29.98	23.25	18.13	14.21	11.20	8.87	7.06	5.64	4.53	3.65	19
20	38.79	30.06	23.43	18.37	14.47	11.46	9.12	7.29	5.86	4.73	3.83	20
21	38.70	30.15	23.62	18.61	14.74	11.73	9.38	7.54	6.09	4.93	4.02	21
22	38.61	30.23	23.81	18.85	15.01	12.01	9.65	7.79	6.32	5.15	4.21	22
23	38.51	30.32	24.00	19.10	15.28	12.29	9.93	8.06	6.57	5.38	4.42	23
24	38.42	30.40	24.19	19.35	15.56	12.58	10.21	8.33	6.82	5.61	4.64	24
25	38.33	30.48	24.38	19.60	15.85	12.87	10.50	8.61	7.09	5.86	4.86	25
26	38.23	30.57	24.58	19.86	16.14	13.17	10.80	8.90	7.36	6.12	5.10	26
27	38.14	30.66	24.77	20.13	16.43	13.48	11.11	9.20	7.65	6.39	5.35	27
28	38.05	30.74	24.97	20.39	16.73	13.80	11.43	9.51	7.95	6.67	5.61	28
29	37.97	30.83	25.17	20.66	17.04	14.12	11.76	9.83	8.26	6.96	5.89	29
30	37.88	30.92	25.38	20.93	17.36	14.46	12.10	10.17	8.58	7.27	6.18	30
31	37.79	31.01	25.58	21.21	17.67	14.80	12.44	10.51	8.91	7.59	6.48	31
32	37.70	31.10	25.79	21.49	18.00	15.15	12.80	10.86	9.26	7.92	6.80	32
33	37.62	31.19	26.00	21.78	18.33	15.50	13.17	11.23	9.62	8.27	7.14	33
34	37.53	31.29	26.21	22.07	18.67	15.87	13.55	11.61	10.00	8.64	7.49	34
35	37.45	31.38	26.43	22.37	19.02	16.25	13.94	12.01	10.39	9.02	7.86	35
36	37.37	31.47	26.64	22.67	19.37	16.63	14.34	12.42	10.79	9.42	8.24	36
37	37.29	31.57	26.87	22.97	19.73	17.03	14.76	12.84	11.22	9.83	8.65	37
38	37.21	31.67	27.09	23.28	20.10	17.43	15.18	13.28	11.66	10.27	9.08	38
39	37.14	31.77	27.32	23.60	20.48	17.85	15.63	13.73	12.11	10.72	9.53	39
40	37.07	31.88	27.55	23.92	20.87	18.28	16.08	14.20	12.59	11.20	10.00	40
41	37.01	31.99	27.79	24.25	21.26	18.72	16.55	14.69	13.09	11.70	10.50	41
42	36.94	32.10	28.03	24.59	21.67	19.17	17.04	15.20	13.61	12.22	11.02	42
43	36.89	32.22	28.28	24.93	22.08	19.64	17.54	15.72	14.15	12.77	11.57	43
44	36.83	32.34	28.53	25.29	22.51	20.12	18.06	16.27	14.71	13.35	12.15	44
45	36.79	32.47	28.80	25.65	22.95	20.62	18.60	16.84	15.30	13.95	12.76	45
46	36.75	32.61	29.07	26.03	23.40	21.13	19.16	17.43	15.92	14.58	13.40	46
47	36.72	32.75	29.35	26.41	23.87	21.66	19.74	18.05	16.56	15.25	14.08	47
48	36.70	32.90	29.63	26.81	24.35	22.21	20.34	18.69	17.24	15.95	14.80	48
49	36.69	33.06	29.93	27.22	24.85	22.78	20.96	19.36	17.94	16.68	15.56	49
50	36.69	33.23	30.24	27.64	25.36	23.37	21.61	20.06	18.68	17.46	16.36	50

Table 17: Multipliers for loss of pension commencing age 55 (males)

Age at date of trial	Multiplier calculated with allowance for projected mortality from the 2004-based population projections and rate of return of											Age at date of trial
	0.0%	*0.5%*	*1.0%*	*1.5%*	*2.0%*	*2.5%*	*3.0%*	*3.5%*	*4.0%*	*4.5%*	*5.0%*	
0	32.51	22.49	15.64	10.94	7.69	5.43	3.86	2.75	1.97	1.42	1.03	0
1	32.56	22.64	15.83	11.13	7.86	5.59	3.99	2.86	2.06	1.49	1.08	1
2	32.45	22.68	15.94	11.27	8.00	5.71	4.10	2.95	2.14	1.55	1.13	2
3	32.35	22.73	16.06	11.40	8.14	5.84	4.21	3.05	2.22	1.62	1.19	3
4	32.23	22.77	16.17	11.54	8.28	5.97	4.33	3.15	2.30	1.69	1.25	4
5	32.12	22.81	16.28	11.68	8.43	6.11	4.45	3.25	2.39	1.76	1.31	5
6	32.01	22.84	16.39	11.82	8.57	6.24	4.57	3.36	2.48	1.84	1.37	6
7	31.89	22.88	16.51	11.97	8.72	6.38	4.70	3.47	2.57	1.92	1.43	7
8	31.78	22.92	16.62	12.11	8.87	6.53	4.83	3.58	2.67	2.00	1.50	8
9	31.67	22.96	16.73	12.26	9.02	6.67	4.96	3.70	2.77	2.09	1.57	9
10	31.55	23.00	16.85	12.41	9.18	6.82	5.09	3.82	2.88	2.17	1.65	10
11	31.44	23.03	16.96	12.55	9.34	6.98	5.23	3.95	2.99	2.27	1.73	11
12	31.33	23.07	17.08	12.71	9.50	7.13	5.38	4.07	3.10	2.37	1.81	12
13	31.21	23.11	17.19	12.86	9.66	7.29	5.53	4.21	3.22	2.47	1.90	13
14	31.10	23.14	17.31	13.01	9.83	7.45	5.68	4.34	3.34	2.57	1.99	14
15	30.99	23.18	17.43	13.17	9.99	7.62	5.83	4.49	3.46	2.68	2.09	15
16	30.88	23.22	17.55	13.33	10.17	7.79	6.00	4.63	3.59	2.80	2.19	16
17	30.77	23.26	17.67	13.49	10.34	7.97	6.16	4.78	3.73	2.92	2.29	17
18	30.66	23.30	17.80	13.65	10.52	8.15	6.33	4.94	3.87	3.04	2.40	18
19	30.56	23.35	17.92	13.82	10.71	8.33	6.51	5.10	4.02	3.18	2.52	19
20	30.47	23.40	18.05	13.99	10.90	8.52	6.69	5.27	4.17	3.31	2.64	20
21	30.37	23.45	18.18	14.17	11.09	8.71	6.88	5.45	4.33	3.46	2.77	21
22	30.28	23.50	18.32	14.35	11.29	8.91	7.07	5.63	4.50	3.61	2.90	22
23	30.19	23.55	18.45	14.53	11.49	9.12	7.27	5.82	4.67	3.76	3.04	23
24	30.09	23.60	18.59	14.71	11.69	9.33	7.47	6.01	4.85	3.93	3.19	24
25	29.99	23.64	18.72	14.89	11.89	9.54	7.68	6.21	5.03	4.10	3.34	25
26	29.90	23.69	18.86	15.07	12.10	9.75	7.89	6.41	5.23	4.27	3.51	26
27	29.81	23.74	19.00	15.26	12.32	9.98	8.12	6.62	5.43	4.46	3.68	27
28	29.72	23.80	19.14	15.46	12.54	10.21	8.34	6.85	5.63	4.65	3.86	28
29	29.64	23.85	19.29	15.66	12.76	10.45	8.58	7.07	5.85	4.86	4.04	29
30	29.55	23.91	19.43	15.86	12.99	10.69	8.82	7.31	6.08	5.07	4.24	30
31	29.47	23.97	19.58	16.06	13.22	10.93	9.07	7.55	6.31	5.29	4.45	31
32	29.38	24.02	19.73	16.26	13.46	11.19	9.33	7.81	6.55	5.52	4.67	32
33	29.30	24.08	19.88	16.47	13.71	11.45	9.59	8.07	6.81	5.76	4.89	33
34	29.22	24.14	20.03	16.69	13.95	11.71	9.87	8.34	7.07	6.02	5.13	34
35	29.14	24.20	20.18	16.90	14.21	11.98	10.15	8.62	7.34	6.28	5.38	35
36	29.07	24.27	20.34	17.12	14.46	12.26	10.43	8.91	7.63	6.55	5.65	36
37	28.99	24.33	20.50	17.34	14.73	12.55	10.73	9.21	7.93	6.84	5.92	37
38	28.92	24.40	20.66	17.57	15.00	12.84	11.04	9.52	8.23	7.14	6.22	38
39	28.85	24.46	20.83	17.80	15.27	13.15	11.36	9.84	8.55	7.46	6.52	39
40	28.78	24.54	21.00	18.04	15.55	13.46	11.68	10.18	8.89	7.79	6.84	40
41	28.72	24.61	21.17	18.28	15.84	13.78	12.02	10.52	9.24	8.13	7.18	41
42	28.66	24.69	21.35	18.53	16.14	14.11	12.37	10.88	9.60	8.50	7.54	42
43	28.60	24.77	21.53	18.78	16.44	14.45	12.73	11.26	9.98	8.87	7.91	43
44	28.55	24.85	21.72	19.04	16.76	14.80	13.11	11.65	10.38	9.27	8.31	44
45	28.51	24.95	21.91	19.31	17.08	15.16	13.50	12.05	10.79	9.69	8.73	45
46	28.48	25.05	22.11	19.59	17.42	15.54	13.90	12.47	11.23	10.13	9.17	46
47	28.45	25.16	22.33	19.88	17.77	15.93	14.32	12.92	11.68	10.59	9.63	47
48	28.44	25.28	22.55	20.18	18.13	16.33	14.76	13.38	12.16	11.08	10.13	48
49	28.44	25.41	22.78	20.50	18.50	16.76	15.22	13.87	12.67	11.60	10.65	49
50	28.45	25.55	23.03	20.83	18.90	17.20	15.70	14.37	13.20	12.15	11.21	50
51	28.48	25.71	23.29	21.17	19.31	17.66	16.21	14.91	13.76	12.72	11.80	51
52	28.51	25.88	23.57	21.53	19.74	18.15	16.73	15.47	14.34	13.33	12.42	52
53	28.56	26.06	23.85	21.90	20.18	18.65	17.28	16.06	14.96	13.98	13.08	53
54	28.61	26.24	24.14	22.29	20.64	19.17	17.85	16.67	15.61	14.65	13.78	54
55	28.66	26.42	24.44	22.67	21.10	19.70	18.44	17.31	16.29	15.36	14.52	55

Table 18: Multipliers for loss of pension commencing age 55 (females)

Age at date of trial	Multiplier calculated with allowance for projected mortality from the 2004-based population projections and rate of return of											Age at date of trial
	0.0%	***0.5%***	***1.0%***	***1.5%***	***2.0%***	***2.5%***	***3.0%***	***3.5%***	***4.0%***	***4.5%***	***5.0%***	
0	35.74	24.61	17.04	11.87	8.31	5.85	4.14	2.94	2.10	1.51	1.09	0
1	35.79	24.77	17.25	12.07	8.50	6.01	4.28	3.06	2.19	1.58	1.15	1
2	35.70	24.84	17.38	12.23	8.65	6.15	4.40	3.16	2.28	1.65	1.20	2
3	35.60	24.90	17.51	12.39	8.81	6.30	4.52	3.26	2.37	1.72	1.26	3
4	35.50	24.96	17.65	12.54	8.97	6.44	4.65	3.37	2.46	1.80	1.32	4
5	35.40	25.02	17.78	12.70	9.13	6.59	4.78	3.49	2.55	1.88	1.39	5
6	35.30	25.08	17.91	12.87	9.29	6.74	4.92	3.60	2.65	1.96	1.45	6
7	35.20	25.14	18.05	13.03	9.46	6.90	5.06	3.72	2.75	2.04	1.52	7
8	35.10	25.19	18.19	13.20	9.63	7.06	5.20	3.85	2.86	2.13	1.60	8
9	35.00	25.25	18.32	13.36	9.80	7.22	5.34	3.97	2.97	2.23	1.68	9
10	34.90	25.31	18.46	13.53	9.97	7.38	5.49	4.11	3.08	2.32	1.76	10
11	34.80	25.37	18.60	13.70	10.15	7.55	5.65	4.24	3.20	2.42	1.84	11
12	34.69	25.43	18.74	13.88	10.33	7.73	5.81	4.38	3.32	2.53	1.93	12
13	34.59	25.49	18.88	14.05	10.52	7.91	5.97	4.53	3.45	2.64	2.03	13
14	34.49	25.54	19.02	14.23	10.70	8.09	6.14	4.68	3.58	2.75	2.13	14
15	34.39	25.60	19.16	14.41	10.89	8.27	6.31	4.84	3.72	2.87	2.23	15
16	34.30	25.66	19.31	14.60	11.09	8.46	6.49	5.00	3.86	3.00	2.34	16
17	34.20	25.73	19.45	14.78	11.29	8.66	6.67	5.16	4.01	3.13	2.45	17
18	34.11	25.79	19.60	14.97	11.49	8.86	6.86	5.34	4.17	3.27	2.57	18
19	34.01	25.85	19.75	15.16	11.70	9.06	7.05	5.51	4.33	3.41	2.69	19
20	33.92	25.91	19.90	15.36	11.91	9.27	7.25	5.70	4.49	3.56	2.83	20
21	33.82	25.98	20.05	15.55	12.12	9.49	7.46	5.89	4.67	3.71	2.96	21
22	33.73	26.04	20.21	15.75	12.34	9.71	7.67	6.08	4.85	3.87	3.11	22
23	33.64	26.11	20.36	15.95	12.56	9.93	7.89	6.29	5.03	4.04	3.26	23
24	33.54	26.17	20.51	16.16	12.79	10.16	8.11	6.50	5.23	4.22	3.42	24
25	33.45	26.23	20.67	16.36	13.01	10.39	8.34	6.71	5.43	4.04	3.58	25
26	33.36	26.30	20.83	16.57	13.25	10.63	8.57	6.94	5.64	4.59	3.76	26
27	33.27	26.36	20.99	16.79	13.49	10.88	8.81	7.17	5.85	4.79	3.94	27
28	33.18	26.43	21.15	17.00	13.73	11.13	9.06	7.41	6.08	5.00	4.13	28
29	33.09	26.49	21.31	17.22	13.98	11.39	9.32	7.66	6.31	5.22	4.34	29
30	33.00	26.56	21.48	17.44	14.23	11.65	9.58	7.91	6.56	5.45	4.55	30
31	32.91	26.62	21.64	17.67	14.48	11.92	9.86	8.18	6.81	5.69	4.77	31
32	32.82	26.69	21.81	17.90	14.75	12.20	10.14	8.45	7.07	5.94	5.00	32
33	32.73	26.76	21.98	18.13	15.01	12.49	10.42	8.73	7.34	6.20	5.25	33
34	32.65	26.83	22.15	18.36	15.29	12.78	10.72	9.03	7.63	6.47	5.50	34
35	32.57	26.90	22.32	18.60	15.56	13.07	11.02	9.33	7.92	6.75	5.77	35
36	32.48	26.97	22.50	18.84	15.85	13.38	11.34	9.64	8.23	7.05	6.05	36
37	32.40	27.05	22.68	19.09	16.14	13.69	11.66	9.97	8.55	7.36	6.35	37
38	32.32	27.12	22.86	19.34	16.43	14.01	12.00	10.30	8.88	7.68	6.66	38
39	32.25	27.20	23.04	19.60	16.73	14.34	12.34	10.65	9.23	8.02	6.99	39
40	32.18	27.28	23.23	19.86	17.04	14.68	12.69	11.01	9.59	8.37	7.33	40
41	32.11	27.36	23.42	20.12	17.36	15.03	13.06	11.39	9.96	8.74	7.69	41
42	32.04	27.45	23.61	20.39	17.68	15.39	13.44	11.78	10.35	9.13	8.07	42
43	31.98	27.54	23.81	20.67	18.01	15.76	13.83	12.18	10.76	9.53	8.47	43
44	31.92	27.63	24.02	20.96	18.36	16.14	14.23	12.60	11.18	9.96	8.89	44
45	31.87	27.73	24.23	21.25	18.71	16.53	14.65	13.03	11.63	10.41	9.34	45
46	31.83	27.84	24.45	21.55	19.07	16.93	15.09	13.49	12.09	10.87	9.81	46
47	31.79	27.95	24.67	21.86	19.44	17.35	15.54	13.96	12.58	11.37	10.30	47
48	31.76	28.07	24.90	22.18	19.83	17.78	16.00	14.45	13.08	11.88	10.82	48
49	31.73	28.19	25.15	22.51	20.22	18.23	16.49	14.96	13.61	12.43	11.37	49
50	31.72	28.33	25.40	22.85	20.63	18.70	16.99	15.50	14.17	13.00	11.95	50
51	31.72	28.47	25.66	23.20	21.06	19.18	17.52	16.05	14.75	13.60	12.57	51
52	31.72	28.62	25.92	23.57	21.50	19.67	18.06	16.63	15.36	14.23	13.21	52
53	31.72	28.77	26.20	23.94	21.95	20.19	18.63	17.24	16.00	14.89	13.90	53
54	31.73	28.93	26.48	24.31	22.41	20.71	19.21	17.87	16.67	15.59	14.62	54
55	31.74	29.09	26.76	24.70	22.88	21.26	19.81	18.52	17.36	16.32	15.38	55

Table 19: Multipliers for loss of pension commencing age 60 (males)

Age at date of trial	Multiplier calculated with allowance for projected mortality from the 2004-based population projections and rate of return of											Age at date of trial
	0.0%	***0.5%***	***1.0%***	***1.5%***	***2.0%***	***2.5%***	***3.0%***	***3.5%***	***4.0%***	***4.5%***	***5.0%***	
0	27.80	18.95	12.98	8.94	6.18	4.29	3.00	2.10	1.48	1.04	0.74	0
1	27.83	19.07	13.13	9.09	6.32	4.41	3.09	2.18	1.54	1.09	0.78	1
2	27.72	19.10	13.22	9.19	6.42	4.51	3.18	2.25	1.60	1.14	0.82	2
3	27.62	19.12	13.31	9.30	6.53	4.61	3.27	2.32	1.66	1.19	0.86	3
4	27.51	19.15	13.39	9.41	6.64	4.71	3.35	2.40	1.72	1.24	0.90	4
5	27.40	19.17	13.48	9.52	6.76	4.81	3.45	2.48	1.79	1.29	0.94	5
6	27.28	19.19	13.56	9.63	6.87	4.92	3.54	2.55	1.85	1.35	0.98	6
7	27.17	19.21	13.65	9.74	6.98	5.03	3.63	2.64	1.92	1.40	1.03	7
8	27.06	19.24	13.74	9.85	7.10	5.14	3.73	2.72	1.99	1.46	1.08	8
9	26.95	19.26	13.82	9.97	7.22	5.25	3.83	2.81	2.07	1.53	1.13	9
10	26.84	19.28	13.91	10.08	7.34	5.36	3.94	2.90	2.14	1.59	1.18	10
11	26.73	19.30	14.00	10.20	7.46	5.48	4.04	2.99	2.22	1.66	1.24	11
12	26.62	19.32	14.09	10.31	7.58	5.60	4.15	3.09	2.31	1.73	1.30	12
13	26.51	19.34	14.17	10.43	7.71	5.72	4.26	3.19	2.39	1.80	1.36	13
14	26.40	19.36	14.26	10.55	7.84	5.85	4.38	3.29	2.48	1.88	1.43	14
15	26.29	19.38	14.35	10.67	7.97	5.97	4.50	3.40	2.57	1.96	1.49	15
16	26.18	19.40	14.44	10.79	8.10	6.10	4.62	3.50	2.67	2.04	1.56	16
17	26.08	19.43	14.53	10.92	8.24	6.24	4.74	3.62	2.77	2.13	1.64	17
18	25.97	19.45	14.63	11.05	8.38	6.37	4.87	3.73	2.87	2.22	1.72	18
19	25.87	19.48	14.72	11.18	8.52	6.52	5.00	3.85	2.98	2.31	1.80	19
20	25.78	19.51	14.82	11.31	8.66	6.66	5.14	3.98	3.09	2.41	1.89	20
21	25.68	19.54	14.92	11.44	8.81	6.81	5.28	4.11	3.21	2.51	1.98	21
22	25.59	19.57	15.02	11.58	8.96	6.96	5.43	4.24	3.33	2.62	2.07	22
23	25.50	19.60	15.13	11.72	9.12	7.12	5.57	4.38	3.46	2.73	2.17	23
24	25.40	19.63	15.23	11.86	9.27	7.27	5.73	4.52	3.59	2.85	2.27	24
25	25.30	19.65	15.33	12.00	9.43	7.43	5.88	4.67	3.72	2.97	2.38	25
26	25.21	19.68	15.43	12.14	9.59	7.60	6.04	4.82	3.86	3.10	2.50	26
27	25.12	19.71	15.53	12.29	9.75	7.77	6.21	4.98	4.01	3.23	2.62	27
28	25.03	19.75	15.64	12.43	9.92	7.94	6.38	5.14	4.16	3.37	2.74	28
29	24.95	19.79	15.75	12.59	10.09	8.12	6.56	5.31	4.23	3.52	2.87	29
30	24.86	19.82	15.86	12.74	10.27	8.31	6.74	5.49	4.48	3.67	3.01	30
31	24.77	19.85	15.97	12.89	10.45	8.49	6.92	5.66	4.65	3.82	3.16	31
32	24.69	19.89	16.08	13.05	10.63	8.68	7.12	5.85	4.82	3.99	3.31	32
33	24.61	19.93	16.20	13.21	10.81	8.88	7.31	6.04	5.01	4.16	3.47	33
34	24.52	19.96	16.31	13.37	11.00	9.08	7.52	6.24	5.20	4.34	3.64	34
35	24.44	20.00	16.43	13.54	11.19	9.28	7.73	6.45	5.40	4.53	3.81	35
36	24.36	20.04	16.54	13.70	11.39	9.49	7.94	6.66	5.60	4.72	3.99	36
37	24.28	20.08	16.66	13.87	11.59	9.71	8.16	6.88	5.82	4.93	4.19	37
38	24.21	20.12	16.78	14.05	11.79	9.93	8.39	7.11	6.04	5.14	4.39	38
39	24.13	20.17	16.91	14.22	12.00	10.16	8.62	7.34	6.27	5.37	4.60	39
40	24.06	20.21	17.03	14.40	12.22	10.39	8.87	7.59	6.51	5.60	4.83	40
41	24.00	20.26	17.16	14.59	12.44	10.63	9.12	7.84	6.76	5.84	5.06	41
42	23.93	20.31	17.30	14.77	12.66	10.88	9.38	8.10	7.02	6.10	5.31	42
43	23.87	20.36	17.43	14.97	12.89	11.13	9.64	8.38	7.29	6.37	5.57	43
44	23.81	20.42	17.57	15.17	13.13	11.40	9.92	8.66	7.58	6.65	5.85	44
45	23.76	20.48	17.72	15.37	13.37	11.67	10.21	8.96	7.88	6.94	6.14	45
46	23.72	20.55	17.87	15.58	13.63	11.95	10.51	9.26	8.19	7.25	6.44	46
47	23.68	20.63	18.03	15.80	13.89	12.24	10.82	9.59	8.52	7.58	6.77	47
48	23.66	20.72	18.20	16.03	14.16	12.55	11.14	9.92	8.86	7.93	7.11	48
49	23.64	20.81	18.37	16.27	14.45	12.86	11.48	10.28	9.22	8.29	7.47	49
50	23.64	20.91	18.56	16.52	14.74	13.20	11.84	10.65	9.60	8.67	7.86	50
51	23.64	21.03	18.76	16.78	15.06	13.54	12.21	11.04	10.00	9.08	8.26	51
52	23.66	21.15	18.97	17.06	15.38	13.90	12.60	11.45	10.42	9.51	8.70	52
53	23.68	21.29	19.19	17.34	15.72	14.28	13.01	11.88	10.87	9.96	9.16	53
54	23.71	21.42	19.41	17.63	16.06	14.67	13.43	12.32	11.33	10.44	9.64	54

Table 19: Multipliers for loss of pension commencing age 60 (males) *continued*

Age at date of trial	Multiplier calculated with allowance for projected mortality from the 2004-based population projections and rate of return of											Age at date of trial
	0.0%	***0.5%***	***1.0%***	***1.5%***	***2.0%***	***2.5%***	***3.0%***	***3.5%***	***4.0%***	***4.5%***	***5.0%***	
55	23.74	21.56	19.63	17.93	16.41	15.07	13.86	12.78	11.81	10.94	10.15	55
56	23.77	21.70	19.86	18.23	16.78	15.48	14.31	13.26	12.32	11.46	10.69	56
57	23.80	21.84	20.09	18.54	17.15	15.90	14.78	13.76	12.84	12.01	11.26	57
58	23.84	21.99	20.34	18.86	17.54	16.34	15.26	14.29	13.40	12.60	11.86	58
59	23.89	22.16	20.60	19.20	17.95	16.81	15.78	14.84	13.99	13.22	12.51	59
60	23.97	22.35	20.89	19.57	18.38	17.30	16.33	15.44	14.62	13.88	13.20	60

Table 20: Multipliers for loss of pension commencing age 60 (females)

Age at date of trial	Multiplier calculated with allowance for projected mortality from the 2004-based population projections and rate of return of											Age at date of trial
	0.0%	*0.5%*	*1.0%*	*1.5%*	*2.0%*	*2.5%*	*3.0%*	*3.5%*	*4.0%*	*4.5%*	*5.0%*	
0	30.93	20.99	14.32	9.82	6.77	4.69	3.26	2.28	1.60	1.13	0.80	0
1	30.96	21.12	14.49	9.99	6.92	4.81	3.37	2.36	1.67	1.18	0.84	1
2	30.86	21.17	14.59	10.11	7.04	4.92	3.46	2.44	1.73	1.23	0.88	2
3	30.77	21.21	14.70	10.24	7.16	5.04	3.56	2.52	1.80	1.28	0.92	3
4	30.67	21.25	14.81	10.36	7.29	5.15	3.66	2.60	1.86	1.34	0.97	4
5	30.57	21.30	14.91	10.49	7.42	5.27	3.76	2.69	1.94	1.40	1.01	5
6	30.47	21.34	15.02	10.62	7.55	5.39	3.86	2.78	2.01	1.46	1.06	6
7	30.37	21.38	15.13	10.75	7.68	5.51	3.97	2.87	2.08	1.52	1.11	7
8	30.27	21.42	15.23	10.88	7.81	5.63	4.08	2.96	2.16	1.59	1.17	8
9	30.17	21.46	15.34	11.02	7.95	5.76	4.19	3.06	2.25	1.65	1.22	9
10	30.07	21.50	15.45	11.15	8.09	5.89	4.31	3.16	2.33	1.73	1.28	10
11	29.97	21.54	15.56	11.29	8.23	6.02	4.43	3.27	2.42	1.80	1.34	11
12	29.87	21.58	15.67	11.43	8.37	6.16	4.55	3.37	2.51	1.88	1.41	12
13	29.77	21.62	15.78	11.57	8.52	6.30	4.67	3.48	2.61	1.96	1.48	13
14	29.67	21.66	15.89	11.71	8.66	6.44	4.80	3.60	2.71	2.04	1.55	14
15	29.57	21.70	16.00	11.85	8.82	6.58	4.94	3.72	2.81	2.13	1.62	15
16	29.48	21.75	16.12	12.00	8.97	6.73	5.07	3.84	2.92	2.22	1.70	16
17	29.38	21.79	16.23	12.15	9.13	6.89	5.22	3.97	3.03	2.32	1.78	17
18	29.29	21.84	16.35	12.30	9.29	7.04	5.36	4.10	3.14	2.42	1.87	18
19	29.20	21.88	16.47	12.45	9.45	7.20	5.51	4.23	3.26	2.52	1.96	19
20	29.10	21.92	16.59	12.60	9.61	7.36	5.66	4.37	3.38	2.63	2.05	20
21	29.01	21.96	16.70	12.76	9.78	7.53	5.82	4.51	3.51	2.74	2.15	21
22	28.92	22.01	16.82	12.91	9.95	7.70	5.98	4.66	3.65	2.86	2.25	22
23	28.82	22.05	16.95	13.07	10.13	7.88	6.15	4.82	3.79	2.99	2.36	23
24	28.73	22.10	17.07	13.24	10.31	8.05	6.32	4.97	3.93	3.11	2.48	24
25	28.64	22.14	17.19	13.40	10.49	8.24	6.49	5.14	4.08	3.25	2.60	25
26	28.55	22.18	17.31	13.56	10.67	8.42	6.67	5.31	4.23	3.39	2.72	26
27	28.46	22.23	17.44	13.73	10.86	8.61	6.86	5.48	4.40	3.54	2.85	27
28	28.37	22.28	17.56	13.90	11.05	8.81	7.05	5.66	4.56	3.69	2.99	28
29	28.28	22.32	17.69	14.07	11.24	9.01	7.25	5.85	4.74	3.85	3.13	29
30	28.19	22.37	17.82	14.25	11.44	9.21	7.45	6.04	4.92	4.01	3.29	30
31	28.10	22.41	17.95	14.42	11.64	9.42	7.66	6.24	5.10	4.19	3.44	31
32	28.01	22.46	18.08	14.60	11.84	9.64	7.87	6.45	5.30	4.37	3.61	32
33	27.93	22.51	18.21	14.79	12.05	9.86	8.09	6.66	5.50	4.56	3.79	33
34	27.84	22.55	18.34	14.97	12.26	10.08	8.32	6.88	5.71	4.75	3.97	34
35	27.76	22.60	18.48	15.16	12.48	10.31	8.55	7.11	5.93	4.96	4.16	35
36	27.67	22.65	18.61	15.35	12.70	10.55	8.79	7.34	6.16	5.17	4.36	36
37	27.59	22.70	18.75	15.54	12.93	10.79	9.03	7.59	6.39	5.40	4.57	37
38	27.51	22.75	18.89	15.74	13.16	11.04	9.29	7.84	6.64	5.63	4.80	38
39	27.43	22.81	19.03	15.94	13.39	11.29	9.55	8.10	6.89	5.88	5.03	39
40	27.36	22.87	19.18	16.14	13.63	11.55	9.82	8.37	7.16	6.14	5.27	40
41	27.29	22.92	19.33	16.35	13.88	11.82	10.10	8.65	7.43	6.40	5.53	41
42	27.22	22.98	19.48	16.56	14.13	12.10	10.38	8.94	7.72	6.68	5.80	42
43	27.15	23.05	19.63	16.78	14.39	12.38	10.68	9.24	8.02	6.98	6.09	43
44	27.09	23.12	19.79	17.00	14.66	12.67	10.99	9.56	8.33	7.29	6.39	44
45	27.03	23.19	19.96	17.23	14.93	12.97	11.31	9.88	8.66	7.61	6.70	45
46	26.98	23.27	20.13	17.47	15.21	13.28	11.64	10.22	9.00	7.95	7.04	46
47	26.94	23.35	20.30	17.71	15.50	13.61	11.98	10.57	9.36	8.30	7.39	47
48	26.90	23.43	20.48	17.96	15.80	13.94	12.33	10.94	9.73	8.68	7.76	48
49	26.86	23.53	20.67	18.22	16.11	14.28	12.70	11.32	10.12	9.07	8.15	49
50	26.84	23.63	20.87	18.49	16.43	14.64	13.08	11.72	10.53	9.48	8.56	50
51	26.82	23.74	21.07	18.76	16.76	15.01	13.48	12.14	10.96	9.91	8.99	51
52	26.81	23.85	21.28	19.05	17.10	15.39	13.89	12.57	11.40	10.37	9.45	52
53	26.80	23.96	21.49	19.34	17.44	15.78	14.32	13.02	11.87	10.85	9.94	53
54	26.80	24.08	21.71	19.63	17.80	16.19	14.76	13.49	12.36	11.35	10.45	54

Table 20: Multipliers for loss of pension commencing age 60 (females) *continued*

Age at date of trial	Multiplier calculated with allowance for projected mortality from the 2004-based population projections and rate of return of											Age at date of trial
	0.0%	***0.5%***	***1.0%***	***1.5%***	***2.0%***	***2.5%***	***3.0%***	***3.5%***	***4.0%***	***4.5%***	***5.0%***	
55	26.79	24.20	21.93	19.93	18.17	16.60	15.21	13.97	12.87	11.87	10.98	55
56	26.79	24.33	22.16	20.24	18.54	17.03	15.68	14.48	13.40	12.43	11.55	56
57	26.79	24.46	22.39	20.56	18.93	17.48	16.17	15.01	13.95	13.01	12.15	57
58	26.81	24.60	22.64	20.89	19.34	17.94	16.69	15.56	14.54	13.62	12.78	58
59	26.84	24.75	22.90	21.24	19.76	18.43	17.23	16.14	15.16	14.27	13.46	59
60	26.88	24.93	23.18	21.61	20.20	18.94	17.79	16.76	15.81	14.96	14.18	60

Table 21: Multipliers for loss of pension commencing age 65 (males)

Age at date of trial	Multiplier calculated with allowance for projected mortality from the 2004-based population projections and rate of return of											Age at date of trial
	0.0%	*0.5%*	*1.0%*	*1.5%*	*2.0%*	*2.5%*	*3.0%*	*3.5%*	*4.0%*	*4.5%*	*5.0%*	
0	23.20	15.58	10.51	7.12	4.85	3.31	2.27	1.56	1.08	0.75	0.52	0
1	23.21	15.67	10.63	7.24	4.95	3.40	2.34	1.62	1.13	0.79	0.55	1
2	23.11	15.68	10.69	7.32	5.03	3.47	2.41	1.67	1.17	0.82	0.58	2
3	23.00	15.69	10.75	7.40	5.11	3.55	2.47	1.73	1.21	0.85	0.60	3
4	22.90	15.70	10.82	7.48	5.20	3.62	2.54	1.78	1.26	0.89	0.63	4
5	22.79	15.71	10.88	7.56	5.28	3.70	2.60	1.84	1.30	0.93	0.66	5
6	22.68	15.72	10.94	7.65	5.36	3.78	2.67	1.89	1.35	0.96	0.69	6
7	22.58	15.73	11.00	7.73	5.45	3.86	2.74	1.95	1.40	1.00	0.72	7
8	22.47	15.73	11.06	7.81	5.54	3.94	2.81	2.02	1.45	1.05	0.76	8
9	22.36	15.74	11.13	7.90	5.63	4.02	2.89	2.08	1.50	1.09	0.79	9
10	22.25	15.75	11.19	7.98	5.72	4.11	2.96	2.14	1.56	1.13	0.83	10
11	22.15	15.75	11.25	8.07	5.81	4.19	3.04	2.21	1.61	1.18	0.87	11
12	22.04	15.76	11.31	8.15	5.90	4.28	3.12	2.28	1.67	1.23	0.91	12
13	21.93	15.77	11.38	8.24	5.99	4.37	3.20	2.35	1.73	1.28	0.95	13
14	21.83	15.77	11.44	8.33	6.09	4.46	3.29	2.43	1.80	1.34	1.00	14
15	21.72	15.78	11.50	8.42	6.18	4.56	3.37	2.50	1.86	1.39	1.04	15
16	21.62	15.78	11.57	8.51	6.28	4.66	3.46	2.58	1.93	1.45	1.09	16
17	21.52	15.79	11.63	8.60	6.38	4.75	3.55	2.66	2.00	1.51	1.14	17
18	21.42	15.80	11.70	8.70	6.49	4.85	3.65	2.75	2.08	1.57	1.20	18
19	21.32	15.81	11.77	8.79	6.59	4.96	3.74	2.83	2.15	1.64	1.25	19
20	21.22	15.82	11.84	8.89	6.70	5.06	3.84	2.92	2.23	1.71	1.31	20
21	21.13	15.84	11.91	8.99	6.81	5.17	3.94	3.02	2.31	1.78	1.37	21
22	21.04	15.85	11.98	9.09	6.92	5.29	4.05	3.11	2.40	1.85	1.44	22
23	20.95	15.86	12.06	9.19	7.03	5.40	4.16	3.21	2.49	1.93	1.51	23
24	20.85	15.87	12.13	9.30	7.15	5.51	4.27	3.31	2.58	2.01	1.58	24
25	20.76	15.88	12.20	9.40	7.26	5.63	4.38	3.42	2.67	2.10	1.65	25
26	20.67	15.90	12.27	9.50	7.38	5.75	4.50	3.53	2.77	2.19	1.73	26
27	20.58	15.91	12.34	9.61	7.50	5.88	4.62	3.64	2.87	2.28	1.81	27
28	20.49	15.93	12.42	9.72	7.63	6.00	4.74	3.75	2.98	2.37	1.89	28
29	20.41	15.94	12.50	9.83	7.75	6.14	4.87	3.87	3.09	2.47	1.98	29
30	20.32	15.96	12.58	9.94	7.88	6.27	5.00	4.00	3.21	2.58	2.08	30
31	20.23	15.97	12.65	10.05	8.01	6.40	5.13	4.13	3.33	2.69	2.18	31
32	20.15	15.99	12.73	10.17	8.14	6.54	5.27	4.26	3.45	2.80	2.28	32
33	20.07	16.01	12.81	10.28	8.28	6.69	5.41	4.40	3.58	2.92	2.39	33
34	19.99	16.03	12.89	10.40	8.42	6.83	5.56	4.54	3.71	3.04	2.50	34
35	19.90	16.04	12.97	10.52	8.56	6.98	5.71	4.68	3.85	3.17	2.62	35
36	19.82	16.06	13.05	10.64	8.70	7.13	5.86	4.83	3.99	3.31	2.74	36
37	19.74	16.08	13.14	10.76	8.85	7.29	6.02	4.99	4.14	3.45	2.88	37
38	19.67	16.10	13.22	10.89	8.99	7.45	6.18	5.15	4.30	3.59	3.01	38
39	19.59	16.12	13.31	11.02	9.15	7.61	6.35	5.31	4.46	3.75	3.16	39
40	19.52	16.15	13.40	11.15	9.30	7.78	6.53	5.49	4.62	3.91	3.31	40
41	19.45	16.17	13.49	11.28	9.46	7.95	6.71	5.67	4.80	4.07	3.47	41
42	19.38	16.20	13.58	11.42	9.62	8.13	6.89	5.85	4.98	4.25	3.63	42
43	19.31	16.23	13.68	11.56	9.79	8.32	7.08	6.04	5.17	4.43	3.81	43
44	19.25	16.26	13.77	11.70	9.96	8.50	7.28	6.24	5.37	4.62	3.99	44
45	19.19	16.30	13.88	11.85	10.14	8.70	7.48	6.45	5.57	4.82	4.18	45
46	19.14	16.34	13.98	12.00	10.32	8.90	7.69	6.67	5.79	5.03	4.39	46
47	19.10	16.39	14.10	12.16	10.51	9.11	7.91	6.89	6.01	5.26	4.61	47
48	19.06	16.44	14.22	12.32	10.71	9.33	8.15	7.13	6.25	5.49	4.83	48
49	19.03	16.50	14.34	12.50	10.92	9.56	8.39	7.37	6.50	5.74	5.08	49
50	19.01	16.57	14.48	12.68	11.13	9.80	8.64	7.63	6.76	6.00	5.33	50
51	19.00	16.65	14.62	12.87	11.36	10.04	8.90	7.91	7.04	6.28	5.61	51
52	19.00	16.73	14.77	13.07	11.59	10.30	9.18	8.19	7.33	6.57	5.90	52
53	19.00	16.82	14.93	13.28	11.84	10.57	9.47	8.49	7.63	6.87	6.20	53
54	19.01	16.92	15.09	13.49	12.09	10.85	9.76	8.80	7.95	7.20	6.53	54

Table 21: Multipliers for loss of pension commencing age 65 (males) *continued*

Age at date of trial	Multiplier calculated with allowance for projected mortality from the 2004-based population projections and rate of return of											Age at date of trial
	0.0%	***0.5%***	***1.0%***	***1.5%***	***2.0%***	***2.5%***	***3.0%***	***3.5%***	***4.0%***	***4.5%***	***5.0%***	
55	19.02	17.01	15.25	13.70	12.34	11.14	10.07	9.13	8.28	7.53	6.86	55
56	19.02	17.10	15.41	13.92	12.60	11.43	10.39	9.46	8.63	7.89	7.22	56
57	19.02	17.19	15.58	14.14	12.87	11.73	10.71	9.80	8.99	8.26	7.60	57
58	19.04	17.30	15.75	14.37	13.14	12.04	11.05	10.17	9.37	8.65	8.00	58
59	19.06	17.41	15.93	14.61	13.43	12.37	11.41	10.55	9.77	9.06	8.42	59
60	19.10	17.54	16.13	14.87	13.74	12.72	11.79	10.96	10.20	9.51	8.88	60
61	19.17	17.69	16.36	15.16	14.08	13.09	12.20	11.39	10.66	9.98	9.37	61
62	19.26	17.86	16.61	15.47	14.44	13.50	12.64	11.86	11.15	10.50	9.90	62
63	19.37	18.06	16.88	15.80	14.82	13.93	13.12	12.37	11.68	11.05	10.47	63
64	19.50	18.28	17.17	16.16	15.24	14.39	13.62	12.91	12.25	11.65	11.09	64
65	19.66	18.52	17.49	16.54	15.68	14.88	14.16	13.48	12.86	12.29	11.76	65

Table 22: Multipliers for loss of pension commencing age 65 (females)

Age at date of trial	Multiplier calculated with allowance for projected mortality from the 2004-based population projections and rate of return of											Age at date of trial
	0.0%	***0.5%***	***1.0%***	***1.5%***	***2.0%***	***2.5%***	***3.0%***	***3.5%***	***4.0%***	***4.5%***	***5.0%***	
0	26.18	17.52	11.78	7.95	5.39	3.67	2.51	1.72	1.19	0.82	0.57	0
1	26.20	17.62	11.91	8.08	5.51	3.77	2.59	1.79	1.24	0.86	0.60	1
2	26.10	17.65	11.99	8.18	5.60	3.85	2.66	1.85	1.29	0.90	0.63	2
3	26.01	17.68	12.07	8.28	5.70	3.94	2.74	1.91	1.33	0.94	0.66	3
4	25.91	17.70	12.15	8.37	5.80	4.03	2.81	1.97	1.38	0.98	0.69	4
5	25.81	17.73	12.23	8.47	5.89	4.12	2.89	2.03	1.44	1.02	0.72	5
6	25.72	17.75	12.31	8.57	5.99	4.21	2.97	2.10	1.49	1.06	0.76	6
7	25.62	17.78	12.39	8.67	6.10	4.30	3.05	2.17	1.55	1.11	0.79	7
8	25.52	17.80	12.47	8.77	6.20	4.40	3.13	2.24	1.60	1.15	0.83	8
9	25.42	17.83	12.55	8.88	6.30	4.49	3.21	2.31	1.66	1.20	0.87	9
10	25.33	17.85	12.64	8.98	6.41	4.59	3.30	2.38	1.73	1.25	0.91	10
11	25.23	17.88	12.72	9.09	6.52	4.69	3.39	2.46	1.79	1.31	0.96	11
12	25.13	17.90	12.80	9.19	6.63	4.80	3.48	2.54	1.86	1.36	1.00	12
13	25.03	17.92	12.88	9.30	6.74	4.90	3.58	2.62	1.93	1.42	1.05	13
14	24.94	17.95	12.97	9.41	6.85	5.01	3.67	2.70	2.00	1.48	1.10	14
15	24.84	17.97	13.05	9.52	6.97	5.12	3.77	2.79	2.07	1.54	1.15	15
16	24.75	18.00	13.14	9.63	7.09	5.23	3.88	2.88	2.15	1.61	1.21	16
17	24.66	18.02	13.23	9.74	7.21	5.35	3.98	2.98	2.23	1.68	1.27	17
18	24.56	18.05	13.31	9.86	7.33	5.47	4.09	3.07	2.31	1.75	1.33	18
19	24.47	18.07	13.40	9.98	7.45	5.59	4.20	3.17	2.40	1.82	1.39	19
20	24.38	18.10	13.49	10.09	7.58	5.71	4.32	3.27	2.49	1.90	1.46	20
21	24.29	18.13	13.58	10.21	7.71	5.84	4.43	3.38	2.58	1.98	1.52	21
22	24.20	18.15	13.67	10.33	7.84	5.96	4.55	3.49	2.68	2.07	1.60	22
23	24.11	18.18	13.76	10.45	7.97	6.10	4.68	3.60	2.78	2.15	1.67	23
24	24.01	18.20	13.85	10.58	8.10	6.23	4.81	3.72	2.89	2.25	1.75	24
25	23.92	18.23	13.94	10.70	8.24	6.37	4.94	3.84	2.99	2.34	1.84	25
26	23.83	18.25	14.03	10.83	8.38	6.51	5.07	3.96	3.11	2.44	1.92	26
27	23.74	18.28	14.13	10.95	8.52	6.65	5.21	4.09	3.22	2.55	2.02	27
28	23.66	18.31	14.22	11.08	8.67	6.80	5.35	4.22	3.34	2.65	2.11	28
29	23.57	18.34	14.31	11.21	8.81	6.95	5.50	4.36	3.47	2.77	2.21	29
30	23.48	18.36	14.41	11.35	8.96	7.10	5.65	4.50	3.60	2.88	2.32	30
31	23.39	18.39	14.50	11.48	9.11	7.26	5.80	4.65	3.73	3.01	2.43	31
32	23.30	18.41	14.60	11.61	9.27	7.42	5.96	4.80	3.87	3.14	2.55	32
33	23.22	18.44	14.70	11.75	9.43	7.58	6.12	4.95	4.02	3.27	2.67	33
34	23.14	18.47	14.80	11.89	9.59	7.75	6.29	5.11	4.17	3.41	2.79	34
35	23.05	18.50	14.90	12.03	9.75	7.92	6.46	5.28	4.33	3.55	2.93	35
36	22.97	18.53	15.00	12.18	9.92	8.10	6.64	5.45	4.49	3.71	3.07	36
37	22.89	18.56	15.10	12.32	10.09	8.28	6.82	5.63	4.66	3.86	3.21	37
38	22.81	18.59	15.20	12.47	10.26	8.47	7.00	5.81	4.83	4.03	3.37	38
39	22.73	18.62	15.31	12.62	10.44	8.65	7.20	6.00	5.02	4.20	3.53	39
40	22.65	18.66	15.42	12.78	10.62	8.85	7.40	6.20	5.21	4.38	3.70	40
41	22.58	18.70	15.53	12.93	10.80	9.05	7.60	6.40	5.40	4.57	3.88	41
42	22.51	18.73	15.64	13.09	10.99	9.25	7.81	6.61	5.61	4.77	4.07	42
43	22.44	18.77	15.75	13.26	11.19	9.46	8.03	6.83	5.82	4.98	4.26	43
44	22.37	18.82	15.87	13.42	11.39	9.68	8.26	7.06	6.05	5.19	4.47	44
45	22.31	18.86	15.99	13.60	11.59	9.91	8.49	7.29	6.28	5.42	4.69	45
46	22.26	18.91	16.12	13.77	11.80	10.14	8.73	7.54	6.52	5.66	4.92	46
47	22.21	18.97	16.25	13.95	12.02	10.38	8.98	7.79	6.78	5.91	5.16	47
48	22.16	19.03	16.38	14.14	12.24	10.62	9.24	8.06	7.04	6.17	5.41	48
49	22.12	19.09	16.52	14.34	12.47	10.88	9.51	8.33	7.32	6.44	5.68	49
50	22.08	19.16	16.67	14.54	12.71	11.14	9.79	8.62	7.61	6.73	5.97	50
51	22.06	19.23	16.82	14.74	12.96	11.42	10.08	8.92	7.91	7.03	6.26	51
52	22.03	19.31	16.98	14.96	13.21	11.70	10.38	9.23	8.23	7.35	6.58	52
53	22.01	19.40	17.13	15.18	13.47	11.99	10.69	9.56	8.56	7.69	6.91	53
54	21.99	19.48	17.30	15.40	13.74	12.29	11.02	9.90	8.91	8.04	7.26	54

Table 22: Multipliers for loss of pension commencing age 65 (females) ***continued***

Age at date of trial	Multiplier calculated with allowance for projected mortality from the 2004-based population projections and rate of return of											Age at date of trial
	0.0%	***0.5%***	***1.0%***	***1.5%***	***2.0%***	***2.5%***	***3.0%***	***3.5%***	***4.0%***	***4.5%***	***5.0%***	
55	21.97	19.56	17.46	15.62	14.01	12.60	11.35	10.24	9.27	8.40	7.63	55
56	21.96	19.65	17.63	15.85	14.29	12.91	11.69	10.61	9.64	8.79	8.02	56
57	21.94	19.74	17.80	16.09	14.58	13.24	12.05	10.99	10.04	9.19	8.43	57
58	21.94	19.84	17.98	16.34	14.88	13.58	12.42	11.38	10.45	9.61	8.86	58
59	21.94	19.95	18.17	16.60	15.19	13.93	12.81	11.80	10.89	10.06	9.32	59
60	21.96	20.07	18.38	16.87	15.52	14.31	13.22	12.23	11.35	10.54	9.81	60
61	22.00	20.20	18.60	17.16	15.87	14.70	13.65	12.70	11.83	11.05	10.33	61
62	22.05	20.36	18.84	17.47	16.23	15.12	14.11	13.19	12.35	11.59	10.89	62
63	22.11	20.52	19.09	17.79	16.62	15.55	14.59	13.71	12.90	12.16	11.49	63
64	22.19	20.70	19.35	18.13	17.02	16.01	15.09	14.25	13.48	12.77	12.12	64
65	22.28	20.89	19.63	18.49	17.45	16.50	15.63	14.83	14.10	13.42	12.80	65

Table 23: Multipliers for loss of pension commencing age 70 (males)

Age at date of trial	Multiplier calculated with allowance for projected mortality from the 2002-based population projections and rate of return of											Age at date of trial
	0.0%	*0.5%*	*1.0%*	*1.5%*	*2.0%*	*2.5%*	*3.0%*	*3.5%*	*4.0%*	*4.5%*	*5.0%*	
0	18.76	12.41	8.24	5.50	3.68	2.47	1.67	1.13	0.77	0.52	0.36	0
1	18.75	12.47	8.32	5.58	3.75	2.53	1.72	1.17	0.80	0.55	0.37	1
2	18.65	12.47	8.37	5.64	3.81	2.59	1.76	1.20	0.83	0.57	0.39	2
3	18.55	12.47	8.41	5.69	3.87	2.64	1.81	1.24	0.86	0.59	0.41	3
4	18.45	12.46	8.45	5.75	3.93	2.69	1.85	1.28	0.89	0.62	0.43	4
5	18.35	12.46	8.49	5.81	3.99	2.75	1.90	1.32	0.92	0.64	0.45	5
6	18.24	12.45	8.53	5.87	4.05	2.80	1.95	1.36	0.95	0.67	0.47	6
7	18.14	12.45	8.57	5.93	4.11	2.86	2.00	1.40	0.98	0.69	0.49	7
8	18.04	12.44	8.61	5.98	4.17	2.92	2.05	1.44	1.02	0.72	0.51	8
9	17.94	12.44	8.65	6.04	4.24	2.98	2.10	1.49	1.06	0.75	0.54	9
10	17.84	12.43	8.70	6.10	4.30	3.04	2.15	1.53	1.09	0.78	0.56	10
11	17.74	12.43	8.74	6.16	4.36	3.10	2.21	1.58	1.13	0.81	0.59	11
12	17.64	12.42	8.78	6.23	4.43	3.16	2.26	1.63	1.17	0.85	0.61	12
13	17.53	12.41	8.82	6.29	4.50	3.23	2.32	1.68	1.21	0.88	0.64	13
14	17.43	12.41	8.86	6.35	4.56	3.29	2.38	1.73	1.26	0.92	0.67	14
15	17.33	12.40	8.90	6.41	4.63	3.36	2.44	1.78	1.30	0.95	0.70	15
16	17.23	12.39	8.94	6.47	4.70	3.42	2.50	1.83	1.35	0.99	0.73	16
17	17.14	12.39	8.98	6.54	4.77	3.49	2.57	1.89	1.40	1.03	0.77	17
18	17.04	12.38	9.03	6.60	4.84	3.56	2.63	1.95	1.45	1.08	0.80	18
19	16.95	12.38	9.07	6.67	4.92	3.64	2.70	2.01	1.50	1.12	0.84	19
20	16.86	12.38	9.12	6.74	4.99	3.71	2.77	2.07	1.55	1.17	0.88	20
21	16.77	12.38	9.16	6.81	5.07	3.79	2.84	2.13	1.61	1.21	0.92	21
22	16.68	12.37	9.21	6.88	5.15	3.87	2.91	2.20	1.67	1.26	0.96	22
23	16.59	12.37	9.26	6.95	5.23	3.95	2.99	2.27	1.72	1.32	1.01	23
24	16.50	12.37	9.30	7.02	5.31	4.03	3.06	2.34	1.79	1.37	1.05	24
25	16.41	12.37	9.35	7.09	5.39	4.11	3.14	2.41	1.85	1.43	1.10	25
26	16.32	12.36	9.39	7.16	5.47	4.19	3.22	2.48	1.92	1.48	1.15	26
27	16.23	12.36	9.44	7.23	5.55	4.28	3.30	2.56	1.99	1.54	1.21	27
28	16.15	12.36	9.49	7.31	5.64	4.37	3.39	2.64	2.06	1.61	1.26	28
29	16.07	12.36	9.54	7.38	5.73	4.46	3.48	2.72	2.13	1.68	1.32	29
30	15.99	12.36	9.59	7.46	5.82	4.55	3.57	2.80	2.21	1.74	1.38	30
31	15.90	12.36	9.64	7.54	5.91	4.64	3.66	2.89	2.29	1.82	1.44	31
32	15.82	12.36	9.69	7.61	6.00	4.74	3.75	2.98	2.37	1.89	1.51	32
33	15.74	12.36	9.74	7.69	6.09	4.84	3.85	3.07	2.46	1.97	1.58	33
34	15.66	12.36	9.79	7.77	6.19	4.94	3.95	3.17	2.54	2.05	1.65	34
35	15.58	12.37	9.84	7.85	6.28	5.04	4.05	3.26	2.64	2.13	1.73	35
36	15.50	12.37	9.89	7.93	6.38	5.14	4.16	3.37	2.73	2.22	1.81	36
37	15.42	12.37	9.95	8.02	6.48	5.25	4.26	3.47	2.83	2.31	1.90	37
38	15.34	12.37	10.00	8.10	6.58	5.36	4.37	3.58	2.93	2.41	1.98	38
39	15.27	12.37	10.05	8.19	6.69	5.47	4.49	3.69	3.04	2.51	2.08	39
40	15.20	12.38	10.11	8.28	6.79	5.59	4.61	3.81	3.15	2.61	2.17	40
41	15.13	12.39	10.17	8.37	6.90	5.71	4.73	3.93	3.27	2.72	2.27	41
42	15.06	12.39	10.23	8.46	7.01	5.83	4.85	4.05	3.39	2.84	2.38	42
43	14.99	12.40	10.29	8.55	7.13	5.95	4.98	4.18	3.51	2.96	2.49	43
44	14.92	12.41	10.35	8.65	7.24	6.08	5.11	4.31	3.64	3.08	2.61	44
45	14.86	12.43	10.41	8.75	7.36	6.21	5.25	4.45	3.77	3.21	2.73	45
46	14.81	12.44	10.48	8.85	7.49	6.35	5.39	4.59	3.92	3.35	2.86	46
47	14.76	12.47	10.55	8.96	7.62	6.49	5.54	4.74	4.06	3.49	3.00	47
48	14.71	12.49	10.63	9.07	7.75	6.64	5.70	4.90	4.22	3.64	3.15	48
49	14.67	12.52	10.71	9.19	7.89	6.79	5.86	5.06	4.38	3.80	3.30	49
50	14.64	12.56	10.80	9.31	8.04	6.95	6.03	5.24	4.55	3.97	3.47	50
51	14.61	12.61	10.90	9.44	8.19	7.12	6.20	5.42	4.74	4.15	3.64	51
52	14.60	12.66	11.00	9.57	8.35	7.30	6.39	5.61	4.93	4.34	3.82	52
53	14.59	12.71	11.10	9.71	8.52	7.48	6.58	5.80	5.12	4.53	4.02	53
54	14.57	12.77	11.21	9.86	8.69	7.67	6.78	6.01	5.33	4.74	4.22	54

Table 23: Multipliers for loss of pension commencing age 70 (males) *continued*

Age at date of trial	Multiplier calculated with allowance for projected mortality from the 2004-based population projections and rate of return of											Age at date of trial
	0.0%	***0.5%***	***1.0%***	***1.5%***	***2.0%***	***2.5%***	***3.0%***	***3.5%***	***4.0%***	***4.5%***	***5.0%***	
55	14.56	12.82	11.31	10.00	8.86	7.86	6.99	6.22	5.55	4.96	4.43	55
56	14.55	12.88	11.42	10.15	9.03	8.06	7.20	6.44	5.77	5.18	4.66	56
57	14.53	12.93	11.53	10.30	9.21	8.26	7.41	6.67	6.01	5.42	4.89	57
58	14.52	12.99	11.64	10.45	9.40	8.47	7.64	6.90	6.25	5.67	5.14	58
59	14.52	13.06	11.76	10.61	9.59	8.69	7.88	7.15	6.51	5.93	5.41	59
60	14.53	13.13	11.89	10.79	9.80	8.92	8.13	7.42	6.78	6.21	5.69	60
61	14.56	13.23	12.04	10.97	10.02	9.17	8.40	7.70	7.08	6.51	6.00	61
62	14.61	13.34	12.20	11.18	10.26	9.43	8.69	8.01	7.40	6.84	6.33	62
63	14.67	13.47	12.38	11.41	10.52	9.72	9.00	8.34	7.74	7.19	6.69	63
64	14.75	13.61	12.58	11.65	10.80	10.03	9.33	8.69	8.10	7.56	7.07	64
65	14.85	13.77	12.79	11.90	11.09	10.35	9.68	9.06	8.49	7.97	7.49	65
66	14.95	13.94	13.02	12.18	11.41	10.70	10.05	9.45	8.90	8.40	7.93	66
67	15.07	14.12	13.26	12.46	11.73	11.06	10.45	9.88	9.35	8.86	8.41	67
68	15.20	14.32	13.51	12.77	12.08	11.45	10.86	10.32	9.82	9.35	8.92	68
69	15.34	14.53	13.78	13.09	12.45	11.86	11.31	10.80	10.33	9.89	9.47	69
70	15.50	14.75	14.07	13.43	12.85	12.30	11.79	11.32	10.87	10.46	10.08	70

Table 24: Multipliers for loss of pension commencing age 70 (females)

Age at date of trial	Multiplier calculated with allowance for projected mortality from the 2004-based population projections and rate of return of											Age at date of trial
	0.0%	*0.5%*	*1.0%*	*1.5%*	*2.0%*	*2.5%*	*3.0%*	*3.5%*	*4.0%*	*4.5%*	*5.0%*	
0	21.54	14.21	9.41	6.25	4.17	2.80	1.88	1.27	0.86	0.58	0.40	0
1	21.54	14.28	9.50	6.35	4.26	2.87	1.94	1.31	0.89	0.61	0.42	1
2	21.45	14.29	9.56	6.42	4.33	2.93	1.99	1.36	0.93	0.64	0.44	2
3	21.35	14.30	9.62	6.49	4.40	2.99	2.04	1.40	0.96	0.66	0.46	3
4	21.26	14.31	9.68	6.57	4.47	3.06	2.10	1.44	1.00	0.69	0.48	4
5	21.17	14.32	9.73	6.64	4.54	3.12	2.15	1.49	1.03	0.72	0.50	5
6	21.07	14.34	9.79	6.71	4.62	3.19	2.21	1.54	1.07	0.75	0.53	6
7	20.98	14.35	9.85	6.79	4.69	3.26	2.27	1.59	1.11	0.78	0.55	7
8	20.88	14.36	9.91	6.86	4.77	3.33	2.33	1.64	1.15	0.81	0.58	8
9	20.79	14.37	9.96	6.94	4.85	3.40	2.39	1.69	1.19	0.85	0.60	9
10	20.70	14.38	10.02	7.01	4.93	3.47	2.45	1.74	1.24	0.88	0.63	10
11	20.60	14.39	10.08	7.09	5.00	3.54	2.52	1.80	1.28	0.92	0.66	11
12	20.51	14.39	10.14	7.17	5.09	3.62	2.59	1.85	1.33	0.96	0.69	12
13	20.41	14.40	10.20	7.25	5.17	3.70	2.65	1.91	1.38	1.00	0.73	13
14	20.32	14.41	10.26	7.33	5.25	3.78	2.72	1.97	1.43	1.04	0.76	14
15	20.23	14.42	10.32	7.41	5.33	3.86	2.80	2.03	1.48	1.08	0.80	15
16	20.14	14.43	10.38	7.49	5.42	3.94	2.87	2.10	1.54	1.13	0.83	16
17	20.05	14.44	10.44	7.57	5.51	4.02	2.95	2.16	1.59	1.18	0.87	17
18	19.96	14.45	10.50	7.66	5.60	4.11	3.02	2.23	1.65	1.23	0.91	18
19	19.87	14.46	10.56	7.74	5.69	4.20	3.10	2.30	1.71	1.28	0.96	19
20	19.78	14.47	10.62	7.82	5.78	4.28	3.19	2.37	1.78	1.33	1.00	20
21	19.69	14.48	10.69	7.91	5.87	4.38	3.27	2.45	1.84	1.39	1.05	21
22	19.60	14.49	10.75	8.00	5.97	4.47	3.36	2.53	1.91	1.45	1.10	22
23	19.52	14.50	10.81	8.09	6.07	4.56	3.44	2.61	1.98	1.51	1.15	23
24	19.43	14.51	10.87	8.17	6.16	4.66	3.54	2.69	2.05	1.57	1.20	24
25	19.34	14.52	10.94	8.26	6.26	4.76	3.63	2.77	2.13	1.63	1.26	25
26	19.25	14.53	11.00	8.35	6.36	4.86	3.72	2.86	2.20	1.70	1.32	26
27	19.17	14.54	11.07	8.45	6.47	4.97	3.82	2.95	2.29	1.77	1.38	27
28	19.08	14.55	11.13	8.54	6.57	5.07	3.92	3.05	2.37	1.85	1.44	28
29	18.99	14.56	11.20	8.63	6.68	5.18	4.03	3.14	2.46	1.92	1.51	29
30	18.91	14.57	11.26	8.73	6.79	5.29	4.13	3.24	2.55	2.01	1.58	30
31	18.82	14.58	11.33	8.82	6.89	5.40	4.24	3.34	2.64	2.09	1.66	31
32	18.74	14.59	11.39	8.92	7.01	5.52	4.36	3.45	2.74	2.18	1.73	32
33	18.66	14.60	11.46	9.02	7.12	5.64	4.47	3.56	2.84	2.27	1.82	33
34	18.57	14.61	11.53	9.12	7.24	5.76	4.59	3.67	2.94	2.36	1.90	34
35	18.49	14.62	11.60	9.22	7.35	5.88	4.71	3.79	3.05	2.46	1.99	35
36	18.41	14.63	11.67	9.32	7.47	6.00	4.84	3.90	3.16	2.56	2.08	36
37	18.33	14.65	11.74	9.43	7.59	6.13	4.96	4.03	3.28	2.67	2.18	37
38	18.25	14.66	11.81	9.53	7.72	6.26	5.10	4.16	3.40	2.78	2.29	38
39	18.17	14.67	11.88	9.64	7.84	6.40	5.23	4.29	3.52	2.90	2.39	39
40	18.10	14.69	11.95	9.75	7.97	6.54	5.37	4.43	3.65	3.02	2.51	40
41	18.03	14.70	12.03	9.86	8.11	6.68	5.52	4.57	3.79	3.15	2.62	41
42	17.95	14.72	12.10	9.98	8.24	6.83	5.67	4.71	3.93	3.28	2.75	42
43	17.88	14.74	12.18	10.09	8.38	6.97	5.82	4.86	4.08	3.42	2.88	43
44	17.82	14.76	12.26	10.21	8.52	7.13	5.98	5.02	4.23	3.57	3.02	44
45	17.75	14.79	12.35	10.33	8.67	7.29	6.14	5.19	4.39	3.72	3.16	45
46	17.70	14.81	12.43	10.46	8.82	7.45	6.31	5.36	4.55	3.88	3.31	46
47	17.64	14.84	12.52	10.59	8.97	7.62	6.49	5.53	4.73	4.05	3.47	47
48	17.59	14.88	12.61	10.72	9.13	7.79	6.67	5.71	4.91	4.22	3.64	48
49	17.54	14.91	12.71	10.86	9.29	7.97	6.86	5.91	5.10	4.41	3.82	49
50	17.50	14.96	12.81	11.00	9.46	8.16	7.05	6.10	5.29	4.60	4.01	50
51	17.46	15.00	12.92	11.15	9.64	8.35	7.25	6.31	5.50	4.80	4.20	51
52	17.43	15.05	13.03	11.30	9.82	8.55	7.47	6.53	5.72	5.02	4.41	52
53	17.40	15.10	13.14	11.45	10.01	8.76	7.68	6.75	5.94	5.24	4.63	53
54	17.37	15.15	13.25	11.61	10.20	8.97	7.91	6.98	6.18	5.47	4.86	54

Table 24: Multipliers for loss of pension commencing age 70 (females) *continued*

Age at date of trial	Multiplier calculated with allowance for projected mortality from the 2004-based population projections and rate of return of											Age at date of trial
	0.0%	***0.5%***	***1.0%***	***1.5%***	***2.0%***	***2.5%***	***3.0%***	***3.5%***	***4.0%***	***4.5%***	***5.0%***	
55	17.33	15.20	13.36	11.77	10.39	9.19	8.14	7.22	6.42	5.72	5.10	55
56	17.30	15.26	13.48	11.93	10.58	9.41	8.38	7.47	6.67	5.97	5.36	56
57	17.28	15.31	13.60	12.10	10.79	9.63	8.62	7.73	6.94	6.24	5.62	57
58	17.26	15.37	13.72	12.27	11.00	9.87	8.88	8.00	7.22	6.52	5.91	58
59	17.24	15.44	13.85	12.45	11.22	10.12	9.15	8.28	7.51	6.82	6.21	59
60	17.24	15.52	14.00	12.65	11.45	10.38	9.43	8.58	7.82	7.14	6.52	60
61	17.25	15.61	14.15	12.85	11.69	10.66	9.73	8.90	8.15	7.47	6.87	61
62	17.27	15.71	14.31	13.07	11.95	10.95	10.04	9.23	8.49	7.83	7.23	62
63	17.31	15.82	14.49	13.29	12.22	11.25	10.37	9.58	8.86	8.21	7.62	63
64	17.35	15.94	14.68	13.53	12.50	11.57	10.72	9.95	9.25	8.61	8.03	64
65	17.40	16.07	14.87	13.79	12.80	11.90	11.09	10.34	9.66	9.04	8.47	65
66	17.46	16.21	15.08	14.05	13.11	12.26	11.47	10.76	10.10	9.49	8.94	66
67	17.53	16.36	15.30	14.32	13.44	12.62	11.88	11.19	10.56	9.98	9.44	67
68	17.60	16.51	15.52	14.61	13.77	13.00	12.30	11.64	11.04	10.48	9.97	68
69	17.67	16.66	15.74	14.90	14.12	13.40	12.73	12.12	11.55	11.02	10.53	69
70	17.74	16.82	15.97	15.19	14.47	13.81	13.19	12.62	12.09	11.59	11.13	70

Table 25: Multipliers for loss of pension commencing age 75 (males)

Age at date of trial	Multiplier calculated with allowance for projected mortality from the 2004-based population projections and rate of return of											Age at date of trial
	0.0%	*0.5%*	*1.0%*	*1.5%*	*2.0%*	*2.5%*	*3.0%*	*3.5%*	*4.0%*	*4.5%*	*5.0%*	
0	14.52	9.46	6.18	4.06	2.67	1.76	1.17	0.78	0.52	0.35	0.23	0
1	14.50	9.49	6.24	4.11	2.72	1.81	1.20	0.80	0.54	0.36	0.24	1
2	14.41	9.48	6.26	4.15	2.76	1.84	1.23	0.83	0.56	0.38	0.26	2
3	14.31	9.47	6.29	4.19	2.80	1.88	1.26	0.85	0.58	0.39	0.27	3
4	14.22	9.46	6.31	4.23	2.84	1.91	1.29	0.88	0.60	0.41	0.28	4
5	14.12	9.44	6.33	4.26	2.88	1.95	1.33	0.90	0.62	0.42	0.29	5
6	14.03	9.43	6.36	4.30	2.92	1.99	1.36	0.93	0.64	0.44	0.30	6
7	13.93	9.41	6.38	4.34	2.96	2.03	1.39	0.96	0.66	0.46	0.32	7
8	13.84	9.40	6.40	4.38	3.00	2.06	1.42	0.99	0.68	0.48	0.33	8
9	13.74	9.38	6.42	4.41	3.04	2.10	1.46	1.01	0.71	0.49	0.35	9
10	13.65	9.36	6.45	4.45	3.08	2.14	1.49	1.04	0.73	0.51	0.36	10
11	13.56	9.35	6.47	4.49	3.13	2.18	1.53	1.07	0.76	0.53	0.38	11
12	13.46	9.33	6.49	4.53	3.17	2.22	1.57	1.11	0.78	0.56	0.40	12
13	13.37	9.32	6.51	4.57	3.21	2.27	1.60	1.14	0.81	0.58	0.41	13
14	13.27	9.30	6.53	4.61	3.26	2.31	1.64	1.17	0.84	0.60	0.43	14
15	13.18	9.28	6.56	4.65	3.30	2.35	1.68	1.20	0.87	0.62	0.45	15
16	13.09	9.27	6.58	4.69	3.35	2.40	1.72	1.24	0.90	0.65	0.47	16
17	13.00	9.25	6.60	4.73	3.39	2.44	1.76	1.28	0.93	0.67	0.49	17
18	12.91	9.24	6.63	4.77	3.44	2.49	1.81	1.31	0.96	0.70	0.51	18
19	12.83	9.22	6.65	4.81	3.49	2.54	1.85	1.35	0.99	0.73	0.54	19
20	12.74	9.21	6.67	4.85	3.54	2.58	1.89	1.39	1.02	0.76	0.56	20
21	12.66	9.19	6.70	4.89	3.59	2.63	1.94	1.43	1.06	0.79	0.59	21
22	12.57	9.18	6.72	4.94	3.64	2.68	1.99	1.47	1.10	0.82	0.61	22
23	12.49	9.17	6.75	4.98	3.69	2.74	2.04	1.52	1.13	0.85	0.64	23
24	12.41	9.16	6.77	5.03	3.74	2.79	2.08	1.56	1.17	0.88	0.67	24
25	12.32	9.14	6.80	5.07	3.79	2.84	2.13	1.61	1.21	0.92	0.70	25
26	12.24	9.12	6.82	5.11	3.84	2.89	2.19	1.66	1.26	0.96	0.73	26
27	12.16	9.11	6.85	5.16	3.90	2.95	2.24	1.70	1.30	0.99	0.76	27
28	12.08	9.10	6.87	5.21	3.95	3.01	2.29	1.75	1.34	1.03	0.79	28
29	12.00	9.09	6.90	5.25	4.01	3.07	2.35	1.81	1.39	1.07	0.83	29
30	11.92	9.08	6.93	5.30	4.06	3.12	2.41	1.86	1.44	1.12	0.87	30
31	11.85	9.06	6.95	5.35	4.12	3.18	2.47	1.91	1.49	1.16	0.91	31
32	11.77	9.05	6.98	5.39	4.18	3.25	2.53	1.97	1.54	1.21	0.95	32
33	11.69	9.04	7.01	5.44	4.24	3.31	2.59	2.03	1.59	1.25	0.99	33
34	11.62	9.03	7.03	5.49	4.30	3.37	2.65	2.09	1.65	1.30	1.03	34
35	11.54	9.02	7.06	5.54	4.36	3.44	2.72	2.15	1.71	1.36	1.08	35
36	11.46	9.00	7.09	5.59	4.42	3.50	2.78	2.21	1.76	1.41	1.13	36
37	11.39	8.99	7.11	5.64	4.48	3.57	2.85	2.28	1.83	1.47	1.18	37
38	11.32	8.98	7.14	5.69	4.55	3.64	2.92	2.35	1.89	1.52	1.23	38
39	11.25	8.97	7.17	5.74	4.61	3.71	2.99	2.42	1.96	1.59	1.29	39
40	11.18	8.96	7.20	5.80	4.68	3.78	3.06	2.49	2.02	1.65	1.35	40
41	11.11	8.95	7.23	5.85	4.75	3.86	3.14	2.56	2.09	1.72	1.41	41
42	11.04	8.94	7.26	5.91	4.81	3.93	3.22	2.64	2.17	1.78	1.47	42
43	10.97	8.94	7.29	5.96	4.89	4.01	3.30	2.72	2.24	1.86	1.54	43
44	10.91	8.93	7.33	6.02	4.96	4.09	3.38	2.80	2.32	1.93	1.61	44
45	10.85	8.93	7.36	6.08	5.03	4.17	3.47	2.89	2.41	2.01	1.68	45
46	10.79	8.93	7.40	6.14	5.11	4.26	3.56	2.97	2.49	2.09	1.76	46
47	10.74	8.93	7.44	6.21	5.19	4.35	3.65	3.07	2.58	2.18	1.84	47
48	10.69	8.93	7.48	6.27	5.27	4.44	3.74	3.16	2.68	2.27	1.93	48
49	10.64	8.94	7.53	6.35	5.36	4.54	3.84	3.26	2.78	2.36	2.02	49
50	10.60	8.95	7.57	6.42	5.45	4.64	3.95	3.37	2.88	2.47	2.11	50
51	10.57	8.97	7.63	6.50	5.54	4.74	4.06	3.48	2.99	2.57	2.22	51
52	10.54	8.99	7.69	6.58	5.64	4.85	4.17	3.60	3.10	2.68	2.32	52
53	10.52	9.02	7.75	6.67	5.75	4.96	4.29	3.72	3.22	2.80	2.44	53
54	10.49	9.04	7.81	6.75	5.85	5.08	4.41	3.84	3.35	2.92	2.56	54

Table 25: Multipliers for loss of pension commencing age 75 (males) *continued*

Age at date of trial	Multiplier calculated with allowance for projected mortality from the 2004-based population projections and rate of return of											Age at date of trial
	0.0%	***0.5%***	***1.0%***	***1.5%***	***2.0%***	***2.5%***	***3.0%***	***3.5%***	***4.0%***	***4.5%***	***5.0%***	
55	10.47	9.07	7.87	6.84	5.96	5.20	4.54	3.97	3.48	3.05	2.68	55
56	10.44	9.09	7.93	6.93	6.07	5.32	4.67	4.10	3.61	3.19	2.81	56
57	10.41	9.11	7.99	7.02	6.18	5.44	4.80	4.24	3.75	3.33	2.95	57
58	10.39	9.14	8.06	7.11	6.29	5.57	4.94	4.39	3.90	3.47	3.10	58
59	10.37	9.17	8.13	7.21	6.41	5.70	5.08	4.54	4.05	3.63	3.25	59
60	10.36	9.21	8.20	7.32	6.53	5.84	5.23	4.70	4.22	3.79	3.41	60
61	10.36	9.26	8.29	7.43	6.67	6.00	5.40	4.87	4.39	3.97	3.59	61
62	10.37	9.32	8.39	7.56	6.82	6.16	5.57	5.05	4.58	4.1	3.78	62
63	10.40	9.39	8.49	7.69	6.98	6.34	5.76	5.24	4.78	4.36	3.99	63
64	10.43	9.47	8.61	7.84	7.15	6.52	5.96	5.45	5.00	4.58	4.21	64
65	10.48	9.56	8.74	8.00	7.33	6.72	6.17	5.68	5.23	4.82	4.44	65
66	10.53	9.66	8.87	8.16	7.52	6.93	6.40	5.91	5.47	5.07	4.70	66
67	10.59	9.77	9.02	8.33	7.71	7.15	6.63	6.16	5.73	5.33	4.97	67
68	10.65	9.87	9.16	8.51	7.92	7.38	6.88	6.42	6.00	5.61	5.25	68
69	10.72	9.99	9.32	8.70	8.14	7.62	7.14	6.70	6.29	5.91	5.56	69
70	10.80	10.11	9.48	8.90	8.36	7.87	7.41	6.99	6.60	6.23	5.89	70
71	10.88	10.25	9.66	9.11	8.61	8.14	7.71	7.30	6.93	6.58	6.25	71
72	10.99	10.41	9.86	9.35	8.88	8.44	8.03	7.65	7.29	6.96	6.65	72
73	11.14	10.60	10.09	9.63	9.19	8.78	8.40	8.04	7.70	7.39	7.09	73
74	11.33	10.83	10.37	9.94	9.54	9.16	8.81	8.48	8.16	7.87	7.59	74
75	11.57	11.13	10.71	10.32	9.95	9.61	9.29	8.98	8.70	8.42	8.17	75

Table 26: Multipliers for loss of pension commencing age 75 (females)

Age at date of trial	Multiplier calculated with allowance for projected mortality from the 2004-based population projections and rate of return of											Age at date of trial
	0.0%	*0.5%*	*1.0%*	*1.5%*	*2.0%*	*2.5%*	*3.0%*	*3.5%*	*4.0%*	*4.5%*	*5.0%*	
0	17.05	11.07	7.22	4.72	3.10	2.04	1.35	0.90	0.60	0.40	0.27	0
1	17.03	11.12	7.29	4.79	3.16	2.10	1.39	0.93	0.62	0.42	0.28	1
2	16.94	11.12	7.33	4.84	3.21	2.14	1.43	0.96	0.64	0.43	0.29	2
3	16.85	11.12	7.36	4.89	3.26	2.18	1.47	0.99	0.67	0.45	0.31	3
4	16.76	11.12	7.40	4.94	3.31	2.23	1.50	1.02	0.69	0.47	0.32	4
5	16.67	11.11	7.44	4.99	3.36	2.27	1.54	1.05	0.72	0.49	0.34	5
6	16.58	11.11	7.47	5.04	3.41	2.32	1.58	1.08	0.74	0.51	0.35	6
7	16.49	11.11	7.51	5.09	3.47	2.37	1.62	1.11	0.77	0.53	0.37	7
8	16.40	11.11	7.55	5.15	3.52	2.42	1.66	1.15	0.79	0.55	0.38	8
9	16.31	11.10	7.58	5.20	3.57	2.46	1.70	1.18	0.82	0.57	0.40	9
10	16.22	11.10	7.62	5.25	3.63	2.51	1.75	1.22	0.85	0.60	0.42	10
11	16.14	11.10	7.66	5.30	3.68	2.57	1.79	1.26	0.88	0.62	0.44	11
12	16.05	11.09	7.70	5.35	3.74	2.62	1.84	1.29	0.91	0.65	0.46	12
13	15.96	11.09	7.73	5.41	3.79	2.67	1.88	1.33	0.95	0.67	0.48	13
14	15.87	11.09	7.77	5.46	3.85	2.72	1.93	1.37	0.98	0.70	0.50	14
15	15.78	11.08	7.81	5.52	3.91	2.78	1.98	1.42	1.02	0.73	0.53	15
16	15.70	11.08	7.84	5.57	3.97	2.84	2.03	1.46	1.05	0.76	0.55	16
17	15.61	11.08	7.88	5.63	4.03	2.89	2.08	1.50	1.09	0.79	0.58	17
18	15.53	11.07	7.92	5.68	4.09	2.95	2.14	1.55	1.13	0.82	0.60	18
19	15.44	11.07	7.96	5.74	4.15	3.01	2.19	1.60	1.17	0.86	0.63	19
20	15.36	11.07	8.00	5.80	4.22	3.07	2.25	1.65	1.21	0.89	0.66	20
21	15.27	11.06	8.04	5.86	4.28	3.14	2.30	1.70	1.25	0.93	0.69	21
22	15.19	11.06	8.08	5.91	4.34	3.20	2.36	1.75	1.30	0.97	0.72	22
23	15.10	11.06	8.12	5.97	4.41	3.26	2.42	1.80	1.34	1.00	0.75	23
24	15.02	11.05	8.15	6.03	4.48	3.33	2.48	1.86	1.39	1.05	0.79	24
25	14.94	11.05	8.19	6.09	4.54	3.40	2.55	1.91	1.44	1.09	0.82	25
26	14.85	11.04	8.23	6.15	4.61	3.47	2.61	1.97	1.49	1.13	0.86	26
27	14.77	11.04	8.27	6.21	4.68	3.54	2.68	2.03	1.55	1.18	0.90	27
28	14.69	11.04	8.31	6.28	4.75	3.61	2.74	2.09	1.60	1.23	0.94	28
29	14.61	11.03	8.35	6.34	4.82	3.68	2.81	2.16	1.66	1.28	0.99	29
30	14.53	11.03	8.39	6.40	4.90	3.75	2.89	2.22	1.72	1.33	1.03	30
31	14.45	11.02	8.43	6.46	4.97	3.83	2.96	2.29	1.78	1.38	1.08	31
32	14.37	11.02	8.47	6.53	5.04	3.91	3.03	2.36	1.84	1.44	1.13	32
33	14.29	11.01	8.51	6.59	5.12	3.99	3.11	2.43	1.91	1.50	1.18	33
34	14.21	11.01	8.55	6.66	5.20	4.07	3.19	2.51	1.97	1.56	1.23	34
35	14.13	11.01	8.59	6.73	5.28	4.15	3.27	2.58	2.04	1.62	1.29	35
36	14.05	11.00	8.63	6.79	5.36	4.23	3.35	2.66	2.12	1.69	1.35	36
37	13.98	11.00	8.68	6.86	5.44	4.32	3.44	2.74	2.19	1.76	1.41	37
38	13.90	11.00	8.72	6.93	5.52	4.41	3.53	2.83	2.27	1.83	1.47	38
39	13.83	10.99	8.76	7.00	5.60	4.50	3.62	2.91	2.35	1.90	1.54	39
40	13.75	10.99	8.81	7.07	5.69	4.59	3.71	3.00	2.44	1.98	1.61	40
41	13.68	10.99	8.85	7.14	5.78	4.68	3.80	3.10	2.52	2.06	1.69	41
42	13.61	10.99	8.90	7.22	5.87	4.78	3.90	3.19	2.61	2.15	1.77	42
43	13.54	11.00	8.95	7.29	5.96	4.88	4.00	3.29	2.71	2.23	1.85	43
44	13.48	11.00	8.99	7.37	6.05	4.98	4.11	3.39	2.81	2.33	1.93	44
45	13.42	11.00	9.04	7.45	6.15	5.09	4.21	3.50	2.91	2.42	2.02	45
46	13.36	11.01	9.10	7.53	6.25	5.19	4.32	3.61	3.02	2.52	2.12	46
47	13.30	11.02	9.15	7.62	6.35	5.30	4.44	3.72	3.13	2.63	2.22	47
48	13.24	11.03	9.21	7.70	6.45	5.42	4.56	3.84	3.24	2.74	2.32	48
49	13.19	11.05	9.27	7.79	6.56	5.54	4.68	3.96	3.36	2.86	2.43	49
50	13.14	11.06	9.33	7.88	6.67	5.66	4.81	4.09	3.49	2.98	2.55	50
51	13.10	11.08	9.40	7.98	6.79	5.79	4.94	4.23	3.62	3.11	2.67	51
52	13.06	11.11	9.46	8.08	6.91	5.92	5.08	4.37	3.76	3.24	2.80	52
53	13.02	11.13	9.53	8.18	7.03	6.05	5.22	4.51	3.90	3.38	2.93	53
54	12.98	11.16	9.60	8.28	7.15	6.19	5.37	4.66	4.05	3.53	3.08	54

Table 26: Multipliers for loss of pension commencing age 75 (females) *continued*

Age at date of trial	Multiplier calculated with allowance for projected mortality from the 2004-based population projections and rate of return of											Age at date of trial
	0.0%	***0.5%***	***1.0%***	***1.5%***	***2.0%***	***2.5%***	***3.0%***	***3.5%***	***4.0%***	***4.5%***	***5.0%***	
55	12.94	11.18	9.67	8.38	7.28	6.33	5.52	4.81	4.21	3.68	3.23	55
56	12.91	11.20	9.74	8.49	7.41	6.48	5.67	4.97	4.37	3.84	3.38	56
57	12.87	11.23	9.82	8.60	7.54	6.62	5.83	5.14	4.53	4.01	3.55	57
58	12.84	11.26	9.89	8.71	7.68	6.78	5.99	5.31	4.71	4.18	3.72	58
59	12.81	11.30	9.98	8.83	7.82	6.94	6.17	5.49	4.89	4.37	3.90	59
60	12.79	11.34	10.06	8.95	7.97	7.11	6.35	5.68	5.09	4.56	4.10	60
61	12.78	11.39	10.16	9.08	8.13	7.29	6.54	5.88	5.29	4.77	4.30	61
62	12.78	11.44	10.26	9.22	8.29	7.47	6.74	6.09	5.51	4.99	4.53	62
63	12.79	11.51	10.38	9.37	8.47	7.67	6.95	6.31	5.74	5.22	4.76	63
64	12.80	11.58	10.49	9.52	8.65	7.88	7.18	6.55	5.98	5.47	5.01	64
65	12.82	11.66	10.62	9.69	8.85	8.09	7.41	6.80	6.24	5.74	5.28	65
66	12.84	11.74	10.75	9.86	9.05	8.32	7.66	7.06	6.51	6.01	5.56	66
67	12.87	11.83	10.89	10.03	9.26	8.55	7.91	7.33	6.79	6.31	5.86	67
68	12.90	11.91	11.02	10.21	9.47	8.79	8.17	7.61	7.09	6.61	6.18	68
69	12.92	12.00	11.15	10.38	9.68	9.03	8.44	7.90	7.40	6.94	6.51	69
70	12.94	12.07	11.29	10.56	9.90	9.28	8.72	8.20	7.72	7.27	6.86	70
71	12.95	12.16	11.42	10.74	10.12	9.54	9.01	8.51	8.05	7.63	7.23	71
72	12.98	12.25	11.57	10.94	10.36	9.82	9.32	8.85	8.41	8.01	7.63	72
73	13.03	12.36	11.74	11.16	10.62	10.12	9.65	9.21	8.81	8.42	8.07	73
74	13.11	12.50	11.94	11.41	10.91	10.45	10.02	9.62	9.24	8.88	8.55	74
75	13.24	12.69	12.18	11.71	11.26	10.84	10.45	10.08	9.73	9.40	9.10	75

Table 27: Discounting factors for term certain

Factor to discount value of multiplier for a period of deferment

Term	*0.5%*	*1.0%*	*1.5%*	*2.0%*	*2.5%*	*3.0%*	*3.5%*	*4.0%*	*4.5%*	*5.0%*	Term
1	0.9950	0.9901	0.9852	0.9804	0.9756	0.9709	0.9662	0.9615	0.9569	0.9524	1
2	0.9901	0.9803	0.9707	0.9612	0.9518	0.9426	0.9335	0.9246	0.9157	0.9070	2
3	0.9851	0.9706	0.9563	0.9423	0.9286	0.9151	0.9019	0.8890	0.8763	0.8638	3
4	0.9802	0.9610	0.9422	0.9238	0.9060	0.8885	0.8714	0.8548	0.8386	0.8227	4
5	0.9754	0.9515	0.9283	0.9057	0.8839	0.8626	0.8420	0.8219	0.8025	0.7835	5
6	0.9705	0.9420	0.9145	0.8880	0.8623	0.8375	0.8135	0.7903	0.7679	0.7462	6
7	0.9657	0.9327	0.9010	0.8706	0.8413	0.8131	0.7860	0.7599	0.7348	0.7107	7
8	0.9609	0.9235	0.8877	0.8535	0.8207	0.7894	0.7594	0.7307	0.7032	0.6768	8
9	0.9561	0.9143	0.8746	0.8368	0.8007	0.7664	0.7337	0.7026	0.6729	0.6446	9
10	0.9513	0.9053	0.8617	0.8203	0.7812	0.7441	0.7089	0.6756	0.6439	0.6139	10
11	0.9466	0.8963	0.8489	0.8043	0.7621	0.7224	0.6849	0.6496	0.6162	0.5847	11
12	0.9419	0.8874	0.8364	0.7885	0.7436	0.7014	0.6618	0.6246	0.5897	0.5568	12
13	0.9372	0.8787	0.8240	0.7730	0.7254	0.6810	0.6394	0.6006	0.5643	0.5303	13
14	0.9326	0.8700	0.8118	0.7579	0.7077	0.6611	0.6178	0.5775	0.5400	0.5051	14
15	0.9279	0.8613	0.7999	0.7430	0.6905	0.6419	0.5969	0.5553	0.5167	0.4810	15
16	0.9233	0.8528	0.7880	0.7284	0.6736	0.6232	0.5767	0.5339	0.4945	0.4581	16
17	0.9187	0.8444	0.7764	0.7142	0.6572	0.6050	0.5572	0.5134	0.4732	0.4363	17
18	0.9141	0.8360	0.7649	0.7002	0.6412	0.5874	0.5384	0.4936	0.4528	0.4155	18
19	0.9096	0.8277	0.7536	0.6864	0.6255	0.5703	0.5202	0.4746	0.4333	0.3957	19
20	0.9051	0.8195	0.7425	0.6730	0.6103	0.5537	0.5026	0.4564	0.4146	0.3769	20
21	0.9006	0.8114	0.7315	0.6598	0.5954	0.5375	0.4856	0.4388	0.3968	0.3589	21
22	0.8961	0.8034	0.7207	0.6468	0.5809	0.5219	0.4692	0.4220	0.3797	0.3418	22
23	0.8916	0.7954	0.7100	0.6342	0.5667	0.5067	0.4533	0.4057	0.3634	0.3256	23
24	0.8872	0.7876	0.6995	0.6217	0.5529	0.4919	0.4380	0.3901	0.3477	0.3101	24
25	0.8828	0.7798	0.6892	0.6095	0.5394	0.4776	0.4231	0.3751	0.3327	0.2953	25
26	0.8784	0.7720	0.6790	0.5976	0.5262	0.4637	0.4088	0.3607	0.3184	0.2812	26
27	0.8740	0.7644	0.6690	0.5859	0.5134	0.4502	0.3950	0.3468	0.3047	0.2678	27
28	0.8697	0.7568	0.6591	0.5744	0.5009	0.4371	0.3817	0.3335	0.2916	0.2551	28
29	0.8653	0.7493	0.6494	0.5631	0.4887	0.4243	0.3687	0.3207	0.2790	0.2429	29
30	0.8610	0.7419	0.6398	0.5521	0.4767	0.4120	0.3563	0.3083	0.2670	0.2314	30
31	0.8567	0.7346	0.6303	0.5412	0.4651	0.4000	0.3442	0.2965	0.2555	0.2204	31
32	0.8525	0.7273	0.6210	0.5306	0.4538	0.3883	0.3326	0.2851	0.2445	0.2099	32
33	0.8482	0.7201	0.6118	0.5202	0.4427	0.3770	0.3213	0.2741	0.2340	0.1999	33
34	0.8440	0.7130	0.6028	0.5100	0.4319	0.3660	0.3105	0.2636	0.2239	0.1904	34
35	0.8398	0.7059	0.5939	0.5000	0.4214	0.3554	0.3000	0.2534	0.2143	0.1813	35
36	0.8356	0.6989	0.5851	0.4902	0.4111	0.3450	0.2898	0.2437	0.2050	0.1727	36
37	0.8315	0.6920	0.5764	0.4806	0.4011	0.3350	0.2800	0.2343	0.1962	0.1644	37
38	0.8274	0.6852	0.5679	0.4712	0.3913	0.3252	0.2706	0.2253	0.1878	0.1566	38
39	0.8232	0.6784	0.5595	0.4619	0.3817	0.3158	0.2614	0.2166	0.1797	0.1491	39
40	0.8191	0.6717	0.5513	0.4529	0.3724	0.3066	0.2526	0.2083	0.1719	0.1420	40
41	0.8151	0.6650	0.5431	0.4440	0.3633	0.2976	0.2440	0.2003	0.1645	0.1353	41
42	0.8110	0.6584	0.5351	0.4353	0.3545	0.2890	0.2358	0.1926	0.1574	0.1288	42
43	0.8070	0.6519	0.5272	0.4268	0.3458	0.2805	0.2278	0.1852	0.1507	0.1227	43
44	0.8030	0.6454	0.5194	0.4184	0.3374	0.2724	0.2201	0.1780	0.1442	0.1169	44
45	0.7990	0.6391	0.5117	0.4102	0.3292	0.2644	0.2127	0.1712	0.1380	0.1113	45
46	0.7950	0.6327	0.5042	0.4022	0.3211	0.2567	0.2055	0.1646	0.1320	0.1060	46
47	0.7910	0.6265	0.4967	0.3943	0.3133	0.2493	0.1985	0.1583	0.1263	0.1009	47
48	0.7871	0.6203	0.4894	0.3865	0.3057	0.2420	0.1918	0.1522	0.1209	0.0961	48
49	0.7832	0.6141	0.4821	0.3790	0.2982	0.2350	0.1853	0.1463	0.1157	0.0916	49
50	0.7793	0.6080	0.4750	0.3715	0.2909	0.2281	0.1791	0.1407	0.1107	0.0872	50
51	0.7754	0.6020	0.4680	0.3642	0.2838	0.2215	0.1730	0.1353	0.1059	0.0831	51
52	0.7716	0.5961	0.4611	0.3571	0.2769	0.2150	0.1671	0.1301	0.1014	0.0791	52
53	0.7677	0.5902	0.4543	0.3501	0.2702	0.2088	0.1615	0.1251	0.0970	0.0753	53
54	0.7639	0.5843	0.4475	0.3432	0.2636	0.2027	0.1560	0.1203	0.0928	0.0717	54
55	0.7601	0.5785	0.4409	0.3365	0.2572	0.1968	0.1508	0.1157	0.0888	0.0683	55

Table 27: Discounting factors for term certain *continued*

Term	Factor to discount value of multiplier for a period of deferment									Term
	0.5%	***1.0%***	***1.5%***	***2.0%***	***2.5%***	***3.0%***	***3.5%***	***4.0%***	***4.5%***	***5.0%***	
56	0.7563	0.5728	0.4344	0.3299	0.2509	0.1910	0.1457	0.1112	0.0850	0.0651	56
57	0.7525	0.5671	0.4280	0.3234	0.2448	0.1855	0.1407	0.1069	0.0814	0.0620	57
58	0.7488	0.5615	0.4217	0.3171	0.2388	0.1801	0.1360	0.1028	0.0778	0.0590	58
59	0.7451	0.5560	0.4154	0.3109	0.2330	0.1748	0.1314	0.0989	0.0745	0.0562	59
60	0.7414	0.5504	0.4093	0.3048	0.2273	0.1697	0.1269	0.0951	0.0713	0.0535	60
61	0.7377	0.5450	0.4032	0.2988	0.2217	0.1648	0.1226	0.0914	0.0682	0.0510	61
62	0.7340	0.5396	0.3973	0.2929	0.2163	0.1600	0.1185	0.0879	0.0653	0.0486	62
63	0.7304	0.5343	0.3914	0.2872	0.2111	0.1553	0.1145	0.0845	0.0625	0.0462	63
64	0.7267	0.5290	0.3856	0.2816	0.2059	0.1508	0.1106	0.0813	0.0598	0.0440	64
65	0.7231	0.5237	0.3799	0.2761	0.2009	0.1464	0.1069	0.0781	0.0572	0.0419	65
66	0.7195	0.5185	0.3743	0.2706	0.1960	0.1421	0.1033	0.0751	0.0547	0.0399	66
67	0.7159	0.5134	0.3688	0.2653	0.1912	0.1380	0.0998	0.0722	0.0524	0.0380	67
68	0.7124	0.5083	0.3633	0.2601	0.1865	0.1340	0.0964	0.0695	0.0501	0.0362	68
69	0.7088	0.5033	0.3580	0.2550	0.1820	0.1301	0.0931	0.0668	0.0480	0.0345	69
70	0.7053	0.4983	0.3527	0.2500	0.1776	0.1263	0.0900	0.0642	0.0459	0.0329	70
71	0.7018	0.4934	0.3475	0.2451	0.1732	0.1226	0.0869	0.0617	0.0439	0.0313	71
72	0.6983	0.4885	0.3423	0.2403	0.1690	0.1190	0.0840	0.0594	0.0420	0.0298	72
73	0.6948	0.4837	0.3373	0.2356	0.1649	0.1156	0.0812	0.0571	0.0402	0.0284	73
74	0.6914	0.4789	0.3323	0.2310	0.1609	0.1122	0.0784	0.0549	0.0385	0.0270	74
75	0.6879	0.4741	0.3274	0.2265	0.1569	0.1089	0.0758	0.0528	0.0368	0.0258	75
76	0.6845	0.4694	0.3225	0.2220	0.1531	0.1058	0.0732	0.0508	0.0353	0.0245	76
77	0.6811	0.4648	0.3178	0.2177	0.1494	0.1027	0.0707	0.0488	0.0337	0.0234	77
78	0.6777	0.4602	0.3131	0.2134	0.1457	0.0997	0.0683	0.0469	0.0323	0.0222	78
79	0.6743	0.4556	0.3084	0.2092	0.1422	0.0968	0.0660	0.0451	0.0309	0.0212	79
80	0.6710	0.4511	0.3039	0.2051	0.1387	0.0940	0.0638	0.0434	0.0296	0.0202	80

Table 28: Multipliers for pecuniary loss for term certain

Term	Multiplier for regular frequent payments for a term certain at rate of return of										Term
	0.5%	***1.0%***	***1.5%***	***2.0%***	***2.5%***	***3.0%***	***3.5%***	***4.0%***	***4.5%***	***5.0%***	
1	1.00	1.00	0.99	0.99	0.99	0.99	0.98	0.98	0.98	0.98	1
2	1.99	1.98	1.97	1.96	1.95	1.94	1.93	1.92	1.91	1.91	2
3	2.98	2.96	2.93	2.91	2.89	2.87	2.85	2.83	2.81	2.79	3
4	3.96	3.92	3.88	3.85	3.81	3.77	3.74	3.70	3.67	3.63	4
5	4.94	4.88	4.82	4.76	4.70	4.65	4.59	4.54	4.49	4.44	5
6	5.91	5.82	5.74	5.66	5.58	5.50	5.42	5.35	5.27	5.20	6
7	6.88	6.76	6.65	6.54	6.43	6.32	6.22	6.12	6.02	5.93	7
8	7.84	7.69	7.54	7.40	7.26	7.12	6.99	6.87	6.74	6.62	8
9	8.80	8.61	8.42	8.24	8.07	7.90	7.74	7.58	7.43	7.28	9
10	9.75	9.52	9.29	9.07	8.86	8.66	8.46	8.27	8.09	7.91	10
11	10.70	10.42	10.15	9.88	9.63	9.39	9.16	8.93	8.72	8.51	11
12	11.65	11.31	10.99	10.68	10.39	10.10	9.83	9.57	9.32	9.08	12
13	12.59	12.19	11.82	11.46	11.12	10.79	10.48	10.18	9.90	9.63	13
14	13.52	13.07	12.64	12.23	11.84	11.46	11.11	10.77	10.45	10.14	14
15	14.45	13.93	13.44	12.98	12.54	12.12	11.72	11.34	10.98	10.64	15
16	15.38	14.79	14.24	13.71	13.22	12.75	12.30	11.88	11.48	11.11	16
17	16.30	15.64	15.02	14.43	13.88	13.36	12.87	12.41	11.97	11.55	17
18	17.22	16.48	15.79	15.14	14.53	13.96	13.42	12.91	12.43	11.98	18
19	18.13	17.31	16.55	15.83	15.17	14.54	13.95	13.39	12.87	12.38	19
20	19.03	18.14	17.30	16.51	15.78	15.10	14.46	13.86	13.30	12.77	20
21	19.94	18.95	18.03	17.18	16.39	15.65	14.95	14.31	13.70	13.14	21
22	20.84	19.76	18.76	17.83	16.97	16.17	15.43	14.74	14.09	13.49	22
23	21.73	20.56	19.48	18.47	17.55	16.69	15.89	15.15	14.46	13.82	23
24	22.62	21.35	20.18	19.10	18.11	17.19	16.34	15.55	14.82	14.14	24
25	23.50	22.13	20.87	19.72	18.65	17.67	16.77	15.93	15.16	14.44	25
26	24.38	22.91	21.56	20.32	19.19	18.14	17.18	16.30	15.48	14.73	26
27	25.26	23.68	22.23	20.91	19.71	18.60	17.59	16.65	15.80	15.01	27
28	26.13	24.44	22.90	21.49	20.21	19.04	17.97	16.99	16.09	15.27	28
29	27.00	25.19	23.55	22.06	20.71	19.47	18.35	17.32	16.38	15.52	29
30	27.86	25.94	24.20	22.62	21.19	19.89	18.71	17.64	16.65	15.75	30
31	28.72	26.67	24.83	23.17	21.66	20.30	19.06	17.94	16.91	15.98	31
32	29.58	27.41	25.46	23.70	22.12	20.69	19.40	18.23	17.16	16.19	32
33	30.43	28.13	26.07	24.23	22.57	21.08	19.73	18.51	17.40	16.40	33
34	31.27	28.85	26.68	24.74	23.01	21.45	20.04	18.78	17.63	16.59	34
35	32.12	29.56	27.28	25.25	23.43	21.81	20.35	19.04	17.85	16.78	35
36	32.95	30.26	27.87	25.74	23.85	22.16	20.64	19.28	18.06	16.96	36
37	33.79	30.95	28.45	26.23	24.26	22.50	20.93	19.52	18.26	17.13	37
38	34.62	31.64	29.02	26.70	24.65	22.83	21.20	19.75	18.45	17.29	38
39	35.44	32.32	29.58	27.17	25.04	23.15	21.47	19.97	18.64	17.44	39
40	36.26	33.00	30.14	27.63	25.42	23.46	21.73	20.19	18.81	17.58	40
41	37.08	33.67	30.69	28.08	25.78	23.76	21.97	20.39	18.98	17.72	41
42	37.89	34.33	31.23	28.52	26.14	24.06	22.21	20.59	19.14	17.86	42
43	38.70	34.98	31.76	28.95	26.49	24.34	22.45	20.78	19.30	17.98	43
44	39.51	35.63	32.28	29.37	26.83	24.62	22.67	20.96	19.44	18.10	44
45	40.31	36.27	32.80	29.78	27.17	24.88	22.89	21.13	19.58	18.21	45
46	41.10	36.91	33.30	30.19	27.49	25.15	23.10	21.30	19.72	18.32	46
47	41.90	37.54	33.80	30.59	27.81	25.40	23.30	21.46	19.85	18.43	47
48	42.69	38.16	34.30	30.98	28.12	25.64	23.49	21.62	19.97	18.53	48
49	43.47	38.78	34.78	31.36	28.42	25.88	23.68	21.77	20.09	18.62	49
50	44.25	39.39	35.26	31.74	28.72	26.11	23.86	21.91	20.20	18.71	50
51	45.03	40.00	35.73	32.10	29.00	26.34	24.04	22.05	20.31	18.79	51
52	45.80	40.60	36.20	32.47	29.28	26.56	24.21	22.18	20.42	18.87	52
53	46.57	41.19	36.66	32.82	29.56	26.77	24.37	22.31	20.51	18.95	53
54	47.34	41.78	37.11	33.17	29.82	26.97	24.53	22.43	20.61	19.03	54
55	48.10	42.36	37.55	33.51	30.08	27.17	24.69	22.55	20.70	19.10	55

Table 28: Multipliers for pecuniary loss for term certain *continued*

Term	Multiplier for regular frequent payments for a term certain at rate of return of										Term
	0.5%	***1.0%***	***1.5%***	***2.0%***	***2.5%***	***3.0%***	***3.5%***	***4.0%***	***4.5%***	***5.0%***	
56	48.86	42.93	37.99	33.84	30.34	27.37	24.83	22.66	20.79	19.16	56
57	49.61	43.50	38.42	34.17	30.59	27.56	24.98	22.77	20.87	19.23	57
58	50.36	44.07	38.84	34.49	30.83	27.74	25.12	22.88	20.95	19.29	58
59	51.11	44.63	39.26	34.80	31.06	27.92	25.25	22.98	21.03	19.34	59
60	51.85	45.18	39.67	35.11	31.29	28.09	25.38	23.07	21.10	19.40	60
61	52.59	45.73	40.08	35.41	31.52	28.26	25.50	23.17	21.17	19.45	61
62	53.33	46.27	40.48	35.70	31.74	28.42	25.62	23.26	21.24	19.50	62
63	54.06	46.81	40.88	36.00	31.95	28.58	25.74	23.34	21.30	19.55	63
64	54.79	47.34	41.26	36.28	32.16	28.73	25.85	23.42	21.36	19.59	64
65	55.52	47.86	41.65	36.56	32.36	28.88	25.96	23.50	21.42	19.64	65
66	56.24	48.39	42.02	36.83	32.56	29.02	26.07	23.58	21.47	19.68	66
67	56.95	48.90	42.40	37.10	32.75	29.16	26.17	23.65	21.53	19.72	67
68	57.67	49.41	42.76	37.36	32.94	29.30	26.27	23.73	21.58	19.75	68
69	58.38	49.92	43.12	37.62	33.13	29.43	26.36	23.79	21.63	19.79	69
70	59.09	50.42	43.48	37.87	33.31	29.56	26.45	23.86	21.68	19.82	70
71	59.79	50.91	43.83	38.12	33.48	29.68	26.54	23.92	21.72	19.85	71
72	60.49	51.41	44.17	38.36	33.65	29.80	26.63	23.98	21.76	19.88	72
73	61.19	51.89	44.51	38.60	33.82	29.92	26.71	24.04	21.80	19.91	73
74	61.88	52.37	44.85	38.83	33.98	30.03	26.79	24.10	21.84	19.94	74
75	62.57	52.85	45.18	39.06	34.14	30.15	26.87	24.15	21.88	19.97	75
76	63.26	53.32	45.50	39.29	34.30	30.25	26.94	24.20	21.92	19.99	76
77	63.94	53.79	45.82	39.51	34.45	30.36	27.01	24.25	21.95	20.02	77
78	64.62	54.25	46.14	39.72	34.60	30.46	27.08	24.30	21.99	20.04	78
79	65.29	54.71	46.45	39.93	34.74	30.56	27.15	24.35	22.02	20.06	79
80	65.97	55.16	46.75	40.14	34.88	30.65	27.21	24.39	22.05	20.08	80

ACTUARIAL FORMULAE AND BASIS

The functions tabulated are:

Tables 1 and 2	$\bar{a}_x$
Tables 3 and 4	$\bar{a}_{x:\overline{50-x}|}$
Tables 5 and 6	$\bar{a}_{x:\overline{55-x}|}$
Tables 7 and 8	$\bar{a}_{x:\overline{60-x}|}$
Tables 9 and 10	$\bar{a}_{x:\overline{65-x}|}$
Tables 11 and 12	$\bar{a}_{x:\overline{70-x}|}$
Tables 13 and 14	$\bar{a}_{x:\overline{75-x}|}$
Tables 15 and 16	$(50-x)|\bar{a}_x$
Tables 17 and 18	$(55-x)|\bar{a}_x$
Tables 19 and 20	$(60-x)|\bar{a}_x$
Tables 21 and 22	$(65-x)|\bar{a}_x$
Tables 23 and 24	$(70-x)|\bar{a}_x$
Tables 25 and 26	$(75-x)|\bar{a}_x$
Table 27	$1 / (1+i)^n$
Table 28	$a_{\overline{n}|}$

- Mortality assumptions for 2004-based official population projections for England and Wales
- Loadings: None
- Rate of return: As stated in the Tables

A9: The Lord Chancellor's statement, July 27, 2001

THE LORD CHANCELLOR'S DEPARTMENT
Discount Rate
Setting the Discount Rate
Lord Chancellor's Reasons
27th July 2001

Introduction

On 25 June 2001 I made the Damages (Personal Injury) Order 2001 ("the 2001 Order") pursuant to section 1 of the Damages Act 1996. In setting a rate of 2.5% in the 2001 Order I had regard to what I believed to be the accurate figure for the average gross redemption yield on Index-Linked Government Stock for the 3 years leading up to 8 June 2001. Following my announcement of the discount rate, questions were raised as to the correctness of the 3-year average yield figure upon which I had relied.

These questions led me to have the information about the 3-year average yield figure checked thoroughly. Those checks revealed certain limited inaccuracies in the information underlying the average yield figure on which I had based my reasoning in making the 2001 Order. In the light of the correction of that average yield figure, I think it right that I should consider completely afresh, on the basis of the accurate average yield figure, what rate I should have set when I made the 2001 Order on 25 June 2001, in order to determine whether the 2001 Order should be withdrawn.

Decision

Having considered all the material available to me, including the accurate, corrected average yield figure, I have come to the conclusion that a discount rate of 2.5% was the appropriate rate to set. Therefore, I do not consider that the 2001 Order should be withdrawn. This statement sets out my reasons for coming to that conclusion.

Reasons

In determining the discount rate, I have applied the appropriate legal principle laid down authoritatively by the courts, and in particular by the House of Lords in *Wells v Wells* [1999] 1 AC 345.

I also consider that it is highly desirable to exercise my powers under the Act so as to produce a situation in which claimants and defendants may have a reasonably clear idea about the impact of the discount rate upon their cases, so as to facilitate negotiation of settlements and the presentation of cases in court. In order to promote this objective, I have concluded that I should:

a set a single rate to cover all cases. This accords with the solution adopted by the House of Lords in *Wells v Wells*. It will eliminate scope for uncertainty and argument about the applicable rate. Similarly, I consider it is preferable to have a fixed rate, which promotes certainty and which avoids the complexity and extra costs that a formula would entail;

b set a rate which is easy for all parties and their lawyers to apply in practice and which reflects the fact that the rate is bound to be applied in a range of different circumstances over a period of time. For this reason, I consider it appropriate to set the discount rate to the nearest half per cent, so as to ensure that the figure will be suitable for use in conjunction with the Ogden Tables, which are a ready means for parties to take into account actuarial factors in computing the quantum of damages;

c set a rate which should obtain for the foreseeable future. I consider it would be very detrimental to the reasonable certainty which is necessary to promote the just and efficient resolution of disputes (by settlement as well as by hearing in court) to make frequent changes to the discount rate. Therefore, whilst I will remain ready to review the discount rate whenever I find there is a significant and established change in the relevant real rates of return to be expected, I do not propose to tinker with the rate frequently to take account of every transient shift in market conditions.

(I consider that the reasoning and conclusions in the above paragraph, which appeared in my original reasons for setting the discount rate in the 2001 Order, continue to apply.)

The principle which I must strive to apply is clear: ". . .the object of the award of damages for future expenditure is to place the injured party as nearly as possible in the same financial position he or she would have been in but for the accident. The aim is to award such a sum of money as will amount to no more, and at the same time no less, than the net loss." (*Wells v Wells* at 390A-B per Lord Hope of Craighead). I acknowledge that claimants who have suffered severe injuries are not in the position of ordinary investors. Such claimants have a pressing need for a dependable source of income to meet the costs of their future care. It is accordingly unrealistic to require severely injured claimants to take even moderate risks when they invest their damages awards.

Setting a single rate to cover all cases, whilst highly desirable for the reasons given above, has the effect that the discount rate has to cover a wide variety of different cases, and claimants with widely differing personal and financial characteristics. Moreover, as has become clear from the consultation exercise (including responses by expert financial analysts to questions which I posed them), the real rate of return on investments of any character (including investments in Index-Linked Government Securities) involves making assumptions for the future about a wide variety of factors affecting the economy as a whole, including for example the likely rate of inflation. In these circumstances, it is inevitable that any approach to setting the discount rate must be fairly broad-brush. Put shortly, there can be no single "right" answer as to what rate should be set. Since it is in the context of larger awards, intended to cover longer periods, that there is the greatest risk of serious discrepancies between the level of compensation and the actual losses incurred if the discount rate set is not appropriate, I have had this type of award particularly in mind when considering the level at which the discount rate should be set. (The above paragraphs also formed a part of my original reasons for setting the discount rate, and I consider that they continue to apply.)

The House of Lords in *Wells v Wells* determined the real rate of return obtainable by claimants through low-risk investment by reference to the gross redemption yields on Index-Linked Government Stock. Their Lordships assumed that a claimant would use his damages award to purchase the right portfolio of Index-Linked Government Stock to ensure that in future years the sums which he received from his portfolio by way of coupon payments and payments on redemption would be sufficient to meet his financial needs. The risk that an early sale of Index-Linked Government Stock might cause capital losses was removed by assuming that such a claimant would hold all his Index-Linked Government Stock until redemption.

The House of Lords thought it appropriate to set the discount rate by reference to the average yields on Index-Linked Government Stock. There is no single correct method by which this average yield may be calculated. Among other factors, the calculation will depend upon the length of the period under consideration, the stocks which are to be included within the average, the inflation assumption made and the form of average taken.

The majority of their Lordships considered it appropriate to set a discount rate by taking a 3-year average of Index-Linked Government Stock yields. I agree that, having regard to the benefits to be obtained in setting the discount rate for the foreseeable future, 3 years is an appropriate period over which to take an average. I note that Lord Lloyd of Berwick preferred a one year period; this confirms the need for judgements to be made in determining the appropriate average yield.

It appears from the speech of Lord Hope at 393E-F that his Lordship had regard to an average of gross redemption yields on Index-Linked Government Stock with lives of over 5 years. He did not give reasons for adopting that particular approach. I am aware that this approach has also been favoured by the Ogden Working Party. However, having regard to the basic reasoning of the House of Lords in *Wells v Wells*, I do not consider that I am obliged to follow it. As noted above, the House of Lords in *Wells v Wells* assumed that a claimant would generally hold all his Index-Linked Government Stock until redemption. Further, as was stated by Lord Clyde at 395H-396A, it was to be assumed that in each year of loss a proportion of the capital would have to be used. If these two assumptions are to be rendered consistent then it will be necessary for the claimant to purchase Index- Linked Government Stock which will mature in the short term, for otherwise the claimant would have to sell a proportion of his Index-Linked Government Stock prior to redemption in order to realise, in the short term, some of the capital value of his investments. Some claimants, whose losses extend over periods of about 5 years or so or less, would have to purchase all or most of their Index-Linked Government Stock (if that is what they chose to do with the damages paid to them) in this category of stock. I have therefore decided that it is proper to take an average over all Index-Linked Government Stock rather than to exclude Index-Linked Government Stock with less than 5 years to maturity.

Nevertheless, I consider that it would be inappropriate to include the gross redemption yields of such stock which is very near maturity ("near maturity ILGS" – which is stock for which the nominal value of the final coupon and redemption payments have become known with certainty). The gross redemption yield on such near maturity ILGS is a nominal yield rather than a real yield. Accordingly, I asked for a calculation of the size of the real yield element in the gross redemption yields of the near maturity ILGS and have included those real yields within my calculation of the average yield.

The average yield figure upon which Lord Hope relied at 393E-F in *Wells v Wells* was based on an inflation assumption of 5%. I consider that, given both the current rate of inflation and the Government's policy aim of maintaining that rate within an upper limit of 2.5%, an assumption of 3% is to be preferred for present purposes.

The House of Lords in *Wells v Wells* did not discuss what form of average should be taken of Index-Linked Government Stock yields. One method is to take an average which is weighted in accordance with the market value of each stock. To my mind, such a weighted average is not relevant to the present circumstances, as the choice of Index-Linked Government Stock portfolio which is necessary to ensure that the future financial needs of a claimant are adequately and promptly met does not depend upon the prevailing market values of Index-Linked Government Stock. I have therefore decided that it is appropriate to take a simple average of Index-Linked Government Stock yields.

A calculation of the simple average of the gross redemption yields of an Index-Linked Government Stock (with an appropriate adjustment for the yields of near maturity ILGS) at an assumed rate of inflation of 3% produces an average yield figure of 2.46%. Accordingly, I conclude that the net average yield on Index-Linked Government Stock, as adjusted to take account of tax, lies in the range between 2% and 2.5%. In my opinion, following *Wells v Wells*, the discount rate should be set within this range. Further, given that the rate is to be set to the nearest 0.5%, it is clear that the discount rate should either be 2% or 2.5%. I do not consider that the choice whether a rate of 2% or one of 2.5% is appropriate is a simple arithmetical matter, nor that *Wells v Wells* requires me to set one rate or the other. I must have regard to the basic principle to which I have referred above, and I have taken account of matters which I consider are relevant to the setting of a discount rate which is just as between claimants as a group and defendants as a group.

In the light of all the information now available to me, and considering the matter completely afresh, I have decided that on 25 June 2001 I should have set the discount rate at 2.5%.

In doing so, I have noted that the real rate of return to be expected from Index-Linked Government Securities tends to be higher the lower the rate of inflation is assumed to be (figures at assumed rates of inflation of 3% and 5% are readily available for comparison). The average gross redemption yield figure of 2.46% assumes an inflation figure of 3% extending into the future. But over recent years inflation has been kept close to or below the 2.5% target set by the Government, and Government policy and the function of the Bank of England remains firmly to maintain inflation according to that target. Although economists differ as to what inflation rates may be expected for the future, I note that the market's general expectation as to the rate of inflation for the future (as implied by market valuations of gilts) is well below 3%. I consider that it is reasonable to assume an inflation rate for the foreseeable future somewhere below 3%, and this in turn provides comfort that a discount rate set at 2.5% is reasonable. (The above paragraph and the larger part of the following four paragraphs were contained in my original reasons for setting the discount rate. They set out considerations which I consider continue to apply).

I am further supported in my conclusion that a discount rate of 2.5% is reasonable by indications that the rate of return in respect of Index-Linked Government Securities does not represent a pure and undistorted measure of the real rate of return which markets would afford in relation to investments with minimal risk which have emerged from the information which was provided in the responses to the consultation paper and the responses from expert financial analysts which I obtained, and by consideration of rates of return on other investments which are available at low risk to claimants. I have treated the following points as significant.

First, some responses to the consultation maintained that the market in Index-Linked Government Securities is at present distorted so that the prevailing yields are artificially low, and do not necessarily give a reliable indication of the real rate of return which markets would afford in relation to investments with minimal risk. The expert financial analysts whom I consulted concurred that the market is distorted at present. This appears to be a result of the minimum funding requirement introduced by the Pensions Act 1995 (which has, in effect, created additional demand for such securities on the part of pension funds) combined with a reduced supply of government securities generally, as the Government has reduced the national debt. The market in Index-Linked Government Securities has changed significantly since *Wells v Wells* was argued and decided. It is widely held that the continuing high demand for Index-Linked Government Stock and the scarcity of supply has led to yields being artificially low as compared with both past record and the yields presently available on similar investment instruments issued by other, comparable, national governments. I consider that the fact that yields in Index-Linked Government Stock appear to be artificially low at present militates against the suggestion that these yields over recent years should be taken as the sole indication of the rates of return that can be achieved through low risk investment in the market. Also, I consider that there is some reasonable prospect of a return to higher rates of return in respect of Index-Linked Government Stock when the Government's already announced plans to abolish the minimum funding requirement are carried into effect. Any distorting effect of the minimum funding requirement would be expected to be particularly pronounced in relation to the longer maturity stocks, whose yields have recently been lower than shorter maturity stocks.

Second, I have noted that the Court of Protection, even in the wake of *Wells v Wells,* has continued to invest, on the behalf of claimants, in multi-asset portfolios, including an equity element. Investment in this manner could be expected to produce real rates of return well in excess of 2.5%. The Court of

Protection has specific responsibility to ensure that the financial needs of those for whose benefit it acts will be met, ie its investment objectives are closely similar to those of the prudent claimant which the House of Lords identified in *Wells v Wells*. The Court of Protection takes competent financial advice as to the investment strategy which will best secure those objectives. Despite the decision of the House of Lords in *Wells v Wells* to set the discount rate by reference to yields on Index-Linked Government Securities, the Court of Protection has continued its former policy, with the agreement of the families concerned, of investing in portfolios comprising of a mixture of equities, gilts and cash. Master Lush of the Court of Protection has stated that none of the families of the Court's patients have chosen to invest in Index-Linked Government Stock since *Wells v Wells*, despite having been offered that option. Thus it appears that there are sensible, low risk investment strategies available to claimants which would enable them comfortably to achieve a real rate of return at 2.5% or above, without their being unduly exposed to risk in the equity markets. Although the House of Lords in *Wells v Wells* chose not to be guided by the practice of the Court of Protection, this was principally on the grounds that what the Court of Protection might do in the future was uncertain, and not on the grounds that its practice was irrelevant. I consider it is appropriate to take account of what has happened in the period since that decision.

Third, I consider that it is likely that real claimants with a large award of compensation, who sought investment advice and instructed their advisers as to the particular investment objectives which they needed to fulfil (as they could reasonably be expected to do) would not be advised to invest solely or even primarily in Index-Linked Government Securities, but rather in a mixed portfolio, in which any investment risk would be managed so as to be very low. This view is supported by the experience of the Court of Protection as to the independent financial advice they receive. It is also supported by the responses of the expert financial analysts whom I have consulted. No one responding to the consultation identified a single case in which the claimant had invested solely in Index-Linked Government Securities and doubts were expressed as to whether there was any such case. This suggests that setting the discount rate at 2.5% would not place an intolerable burden on claimants to take on excessive, i.e. moderate or above, risk in the equity markets, and would be a rate more likely to accord with real expectations of returns, particularly at the higher end of awards.

Finally, in deciding that a single rate of 2.5% should have been set by me on 25 June 2001, I have borne in mind that it will, of course, remain open for the Courts under section 1(2) of the Damages Act 1996 to adopt a different rate in any particular case if there are exceptional circumstances which justify it in doing so.

Irvine of Lairg
Lord Chancellor
July 27, 2001

Group B
Damages

B

B1: General Damages Table following *Heil v Rankin*

General Introduction

On the following pages are two tables for use in updating awards of general damages in the light of the Court of Appeal's judgment in *Heil v Rankin*.[1] At Table E2 will be found an inflation table.

Notes to Tables

Annexed to the Court of Appeal's judgment in *Heil* was a rather smudged graph provided to show "very approximately" the scale of the increase.

1. The difficulty comes in applying the tapered increase in the graph. Putting a straight-edge along the top line of the court's graph (the "uplifted" line) shows the line to be a shallow curve. In discussion after judgment was given, their Lordships said that they had not intended to lay down a mathematical formula. We must therefore assume that the top line was intended to fit around what had actually been done in *Heil* (i.e. nothing) and the other seven cases.

2. Despite this, and with a little diffidence (though some confidence) we suggest the following formula. It is calculated on the following assumptions—

   a. The highest award of general damages at March 23, 2000 was around £150,000: awards of this amount or higher were increased by $33\frac{1}{3}$ per cent;

   b. There is no increase in awards that were worth up to £10,000 before that date;

   c. The uplift is 0 per cent at £10,000 and rises *in a straight line* to $33\frac{1}{3}$ per cent.

3. To find the value of an *old* award in *new* terms, that award must first be updated to March 23, 2000 using the Retail Price Index (reproduced below), in the usual way. Let us call this £A. The formula is:

   $$£A + [{}^{£A-10,000}/_{420,000} \times £A]$$

   The part in square brackets is the uplift.

4. For example:

   a. On January 26, 1988, McNeill J. awarded the claimant in *Chan v Chan* general damages of £75,000.

   b. Updating £75,000 to March 23, 2000 in line with the Retail Price index gives £120,800.

   c. Subtract £10,000 from £120,800, and divide it by 420,000. This gives ${}^{110,800}/_{420,000} = 0.26$. This is the percentage uplift.

   d. Applying this uplift to the original award gives [0.26 × £120,800] = £31,400.

   e. The award in *Chan v Chan* was therefore worth [£120,800 + £31,400] = **£152,200** on March 23, 2000.

   f. Chan should then be updated from March 23, 2000 to present.

5. Because the degree of uplift varies with the size of the old award it is inaccurate to apply the *Heil v Rankin* uplift to a figure already adjusted for inflation to a date later than March 23, 2000. In June 2009 the RPI was 213.4.

[1] [2000] 2 W.L.R. 1173.

TABLES FOR UPDATING GENERAL DAMAGES

The table on this page shows the factor to allow for inflation from an earlier judgment date to March 23, 2000. The table overleaf shows the appropriate new figure, following *Heil v Rankin* in relation to the conventional level of damages at £1,000 intervals up to £150,000.

Note that the uplift should be applied to the damages adjusted for inflation to March 23, 2000, thus:

(1) Damages awarded January 1990 × Inflation increase January 1, 1990–March 23, 2000 (from first table)
= Old award as at March 23, 2000

(2) Award uplifted under *Heil v Rankin* (from second table)

(3) Then multiply by an inflation uplift from March 23, 2000 onwards to the date of trial.

TABLE TO UPDATE FOR INFLATION TO MARCH, 2000

	J	F	M	A	M	J	J	A	S	O	N	D	
1980	2.708	2.670	2.634	2.547	2.424	2.500	2.480	2.474	2.459	2.443	2.424	2.411	1980
1981	2.396	2.374	2.339	2.274	2.259	2.246	2.236	2.220	2.207	2.188	2.165	2.151	1981
1982	2.139	2.138	2.120	2.078	2.063	2.057	2.057	2.056	2.057	2.047	2.037	2.041	1982
1983	2.038	2.030	2.026	1.998	1.990	1.985	1.974	1.965	1.957	1.950	1.943	1.938	1983
1984	1.939	1.931	1.925	1.900	1.893	1.888	1.890	1.872	1.869	1.857	1.852	1.853	1984
1985	1.846	1.832	1.815	1.777	1.769	1.765	1.768	1.764	1.764	1.762	1.756	1.753	1985
1986	1.750	1.743	1.741	1.724	1.721	1.722	1.727	1.722	1.713	1.711	1.696	1.690	1986
1987	1.684	1.677	1.674	1.654	1.653	1.653	1.650	1.649	1.645	1.637	1.629	1.630	1987
1988	1.630	1.624	1.618	1.592	1.586	1.580	1.578	1.561	1.554	1.538	1.531	1.527	1988
1989	1.517	1.506	1.500	1.473	1.464	1.459	1.458	1.454	1.444	1.433	1.421	1.418	1989
1990	1.409	1.401	1.387	1.346	1.334	1.329	1.328	1.315	1.302	1.292	1.295	1.296	1990
1991	1.293	1.286	1.282	1.265	1.261	1.256	1.259	1.256	1.251	1.246	1.242	1.241	1991
1992	1.242	1.236	1.232	1.213	1.209	1.209	1.213	1.212	1.208	1.204	1.205	1.210	1992
1993	1.221	1.213	1.209	1.198	1.193	1.194	1.197	1.192	1.187	1.188	1.189	1.187	1993
1994	1.192	1.185	1.182	1.168	1.164	1.164	1.169	1.164	1.161	1.160	1.159	1.153	1994
1995	1.153	1.146	1.142	1.130	1.126	1.124	1.129	1.123	1.118	1.124	1.124	1.117	1995
1996	1.121	1.116	1.112	1.104	1.101	1.101	1.105	1.100	1.095	1.095	1.094	1.091	1996
1997	1.091	1.086	1.084	1.077	1.073	1.069	1.069	1.062	1.057	1.056	1.055	1.053	1997
1998	1.056	1.051	1.047	1.036	1.030	1.031	1.033	1.029	1.024	1.024	1.024	1.024	1998
1999	1.031	1.029	1.029	1.019	1.017	1.017	1.020	1.018	1.013	1.011	1.010	1.007	1999
2000	1.010	1.005											2000
	J	F	M	A	M	J	J	A	S	O	N	D	

UPLIFT FOR INFLATION FROM MARCH, 2000 TO THE DATE OF TRIAL

The Retail Prices Index on March 23, 2000 was 168.4. In June 2009 it was 213.4.
Uplift for inflation from March 2000 to June 2009 = 213.4 ÷ 168.4 = 1.267

	2009						2010						
Month	Jul	Aug	Sep	Oct	Nov	Dec	Jan	Feb	Mar	Apr	May	Jun	Jul
Current RPI													
Uplift (current RPI ÷ 168.4)													

TABLE OF UPLIFTS FOLLOWING *HEIL v RANKIN*

Old	New	Old	New	Old	New
0–10,000	No change	57,000	63,378	104,000	127,276
11,000	11,026	58,000	64,628	105,000	128,745
12,000	12,057	59,000	65,883	106,000	130,229
13,000	13,092	60,000	67,142	107,000	131,712
14,000	14,133	61,000	68,407	108,000	133,200
15,000	15,178	62,000	69,676	109,000	134,693
16,000	16,228	63,000	70,949	110,000	136,190
17,000	17,283	64,000	72,228	111,000	137,693
18,000	18,342	65,000	73,511	112,000	139,200
19,000	19,407	66,000	74,799	113,000	140,712
20,000	20,476	67,000	76,092	114,000	142,229
21,000	21,549	68,000	77,390	115,000	143,750
22,000	22,628	69,000	78,692	116,000	142,276
23,000	23,711	70,000	79,999	117,000	146,807
24,000	24,799	71,000	81,311	118,000	148,343
25,000	25,892	72,000	82,628	119,000	149,883
26,000	26,990	73,000	83,950	120,000	151,428
27,000	28,092	74,000	85,276	121,000	152,979
28,000	29,199	75,000	86,607	122,000	154,533
29,000	30,311	76,000	87,942	123,000	156,093
30,000	31,428	77,000	89,283	124,000	157,657
31,000	32,550	78,000	90,629	125,000	159,226
32,000	33,676	79,000	91,979	126,000	160,800
33,000	34,807	80,000	93,333	127,000	162,379
34,000	35,942	81,000	94,693	128,000	163,962
35,000	37,083	82,000	96,057	129,000	165,549
36,000	38,228	83,000	97,426	130,000	167,143
37,000	39,378	84,000	98,800	131,000	168,740
38,000	40,533	85,000	100,179	132,000	170,343
39,000	41,692	86,000	101,562	133,000	171,950
40,000	42,857	87,000	102,945	134,000	173,562
41,000	44,026	88,000	104,343	135,000	175,179
42,000	45,199	89,000	105,740	136,000	176,800
43,000	46,378	90,000	107,142	137,000	178,426
44,000	47,561	91,000	108,549	138,000	180,057
45,000	48,750	92,000	109,961	139,000	181,692
46,000	49,942	93,000	111,378	140,000	183,333
47,000	51,140	94,000	112,800	141,000	184,978
48,000	52,342	95,000	114,226	142,000	186,628
49,000	53,549	96,000	115,657	143,000	188,283
50,000	54,761	97,000	117,092	144,000	189,942
51,000	55,978	98,000	118,533	145,000	191,607
52,000	57,200	99,000	119,978	146,000	193,276
53,000	58,426	100,000	121,428	147,000	194,949
54,000	59,657	101,000	122,883	148,000	196,628
55,000	60,892	102,000	124,342	149,000	198,311
56,000	62,133	103,000	125,807	150,000	200,000

B2: Bereavement Damages

1. Damages for bereavement are awarded under s.1A of the Fatal Accidents Act 1976. This is a fixed sum, set by statute as amended (see below).

2. The claim for bereavement damages can only be brought:

   (i) By a bereaved spouse, or

   (ii) Where the deceased was a minor who never married, by:
   (a) either of his parents if the deceased was legitimate.
   (b) the mother if the deceased was illegitimate.

3. Where there is a claim for damages for bereavement for the benefit of the parents of the deceased, s.1A(4) of Fatal Accidents Act 1976 provides that:

   "The sum awarded shall be divided equally between them (subject to any deduction falling to be made in respect of costs not recovered from the defendant)."

   Where the parents are divorced or separated and only one parent makes the claim, that parent will hold half of the bereavement damages on trust for the other parent.

4. The Administration of Justice Act 1982 contains a provision (at s.1A(5)) for the Lord Chancellor to vary the statutory sum. The original statute fixed the sum at £3,500, and that was raised by three subsequent statutory instruments (SI 1990/2575, SI 2002/644 and SI 2007/3489). Hence the relevant dates and statutory sums are as follows:

   – if the death was before January 1, 1983, the award is **nil**

   – if the death was between January 1, 1983 and March 31, 1991, the award is **£3,500**

   – if the death was between April 1, 1991 and March 31, 2002, the award is **£7,500**

   – If the death was on or after April 1, 2002, the award is **£10,000**

   – if the death was on or after January 1, 2008, the award is **£11,800**

5. The claimant is entitled to interest on bereavement damages from the date of death to the date of trial or settlement of the action – see *Prior v Hastie.*[1]

[1] [1987] C.L.Y. 1219.

B3: *Auty* Analysis (Pension claims)

In *Wells v Wells*, the House of Lords made only passing reference to the calculation of future pension losses. The implication is that the multipliers for such losses are to be taken from the Ogden Tables, as are those for pecuniary losses for life and for loss of earnings. There is no justification for adopting a different approach. Since the mid-1980s, however, such claims have been based on the principles set out in *Auty v National Coal Board.*[1] This Analysis is a guide to those principles, but is included with the caution that it has almost certainly been superseded by *Wells v Wells.*

It is important to remember that the trial judge in *Auty* was not working from the Ogden Tables, but from a table of life expectation.

1. The net annual pension loss after tax: £433.
2. The claimant and his wife were both aged 34 at the date of trial.
3. The life tables showed that the claimant's life expectation beyond the age of 65 was 6.68 years, and his wife's life expectation beyond the age of 65 was 10.4 years. She was therefore expected to survive him by 3.75 years.
4. ***First discount***: the judge rounded 10.4 years down to 7. This is the equivalent of the discounting calculation (now 2.5 per cent) that has already been performed for one when one uses the Ogden Tables.
5. The basic pension loss at 65 was therefore [7 × £443] = £3,101.
6. Loss of lump sum gratuity: £1,899.
7. Total capital value of loss at retirement age [£3,101 + £1,899] = £5,000.
8. ***Second discount***: Mr Auty was 34 years old. He was therefore being compensated for his pension loss 31 years prematurely. The judge discounted the sum of £5,000 at 5 per cent over 31 years, leaving £1,100. This discount would now be performed by Ogden Table 27 at 2.5 per cent.
9. ***Third discount***: The Ogden Tables are based on mortality figures, discounted by 0.5–5 per cent. The Tables do not take the other contingencies of life—e.g. sickness, injury at work, redundancy —into account. Section B and C of the Explanatory Notes to the Tables shows how to adjust for "Contingencies other than Mortality". *These contingencies apply only to claims for loss of earnings, not to pension losses.* However, in *Auty* the judge discounted the pension claim by a further 27 per cent for contingencies. This brought the sum of £1,100 down to £800. Of this stage the Court of Appeal said[2]:

   "The discount for imponderables which the judge made in Auty's case was 27%. The judge said that the imponderables included voluntary wastage, redundancy, dismissal, supervening ill-health, disablement or death before 65, and said that death was the major discount."
10. Add value of loss of death in service benefit (£200).
11. Total value of award: **£1,000**.

Note: The three discounts bring the pension element alone (ignoring the lump sum and the death in service benefit) down to £500. If one simply applied Ogden Table 21 and a 2.5 per cent discount to the above pension loss the claimant would receive [6.83 × £433] = £2,853.

Employment tribunals have developed a different approach to the calculation of pension loss. Those interested are referred to the guidelines in Sneath, Sara, Daykin and Gallop, *Industrial Tribunals: Compensation for loss of pension rights* (2003, 3rd ed.) HMSO, approved by the Employment Appeal Tribunal in *Benson v Dairy Crest.*[3]

[1] [1985] 1 All E.R. 930.
[2] Waller L.J. in *Auty* at p.937.
[3] (EAT/192/89).

B4: *Roberts v Johnstone* Analysis (Accommodation claims)

1. Seriously injured claimants will often need special accommodation which may need to be adapted for their particular needs. This will often mean that they have to move to a more expensive house. The applicable principles of law were set out by the Court of Appeal in *Roberts v Johnstone*.[1]

2. **Example:** A paraplegic claimant lives in an unsuitable house with a market value of £50,000. She wishes to buy a more suitable house for £90,000 and alter it (because of her disabilities) at a cost of £20,000. The alterations will not (in themselves) make any difference to the value of the adapted house. The claimant will continue to live in the adapted house for the rest of her life and the agreed life multiplier is 10. Following *Roberts v Johnstone*, the claim for accommodation costs is calculated as follows:

   (i) Costs of adaption: **£20,000**
   Recovered in full because wholly attributable to injuries and will not add value to the house.

   (ii) Costs of moving house: **£5,000**
   Recovered in full if the Claimant would not have moved house but for the accident.

   (iii) Loss of Use of Capital:
   As a result of the move, the Claimant is obliged to invest in the house, thereby foregoing the use of a part of her capital. The discount rate of 2.5 per cent is taken as the annual loss caused by this. Hence the claim is:

   £40,000 (extra cost of the house) × 2.5% (discount rate) × 10 (agreed life multiplier) = **£10,000**

   Note that the Claimant does not recover the full additional capital cost of the house; if she did, the estate would derive a windfall benefit.

   (iv) Extra Annual Costs of Accommodation:
   If the costs of living in the more expensive house are higher, the Claimant can claim them. Items might include council tax, decorating costs and water charges. If these costs were £500 p.a., the claim would be:

   £500 (extra annual costs) × 10 (agreed life multiplier) = **£5,000**

3. The total claim for accommodation in the example is therefore **£40,000.**

[1] [1989] Q.B. 878

B5: Notes on Periodical Payments

1. Practitioners will be aware that the Court now has the power to order periodical payments in a suitable case. The principal rules are set on in CPR Rule 41.4 to 41.10 and in CPR Practice Direction 41B.

2. Section 2(8) of the Damages Act (as amended by the Courts Act 2003), provides that an order for periodical payments shall be treated as providing for the amount of the payment to vary by reference to the Retail Price Index ("the RPI"). However, Section 2(9) of the Damages Act 1996 states that an order for periodical payments may include provision for the disapplication or modification of Section 2 (8).

3. The issue which has arisen is whether and in what circumstances it will be appropriate for the courts to disapply or modify Section 2(8) so that the periodical payment will be varied by reference to an index or measure other than the RPI.

4. There have been a series of cases in which claimants with substantial claims for future losses (usually care and case management) have successfully argued that the RPI is not an appropriate index if the loss in question is not a goods-based loss.

5. The point is significant because (on the basis of past trends) it is likely that the costs of earnings (and hence the cost of care) will rise at a faster rate than the cost of goods. Over the past few decades, that differential has amounted to an average of between 1.5 and 2.5 per cent per year. The precise figure will depend upon the exact period of years and other factors.

6. These issues were first canvassed before the Court of Appeal in *Flora v Wakom* [2006] EWCA Civ 1103. Brooke L.J. held that it was permissible for the claimant to argue that periodical payments should be indexed according to a suitable earnings measure and dismissed the defendants' various arguments that it was not appropriate to depart from the RPI save in exceptional circumstances.

7. Brooke L.J. envisaged that there would be a "basket" of appeals to test the point since Flora had come to the Court of Appeal on a preliminary issue. Three of the four cases that were heard sub nom *Tameside and Others v Thompstone and Others* [2008] EWCA Civ 5, had involved full argument of the indexation points at first instance.

8. The Court of Appeal dismissed the defendants' appeals in all of the cases and held that where it could be shown that the RPI was not a suitable index, the court could properly substitute an alternative. Leave to appeal was given by the House of Lords but in June 2008, the defendants decided to abandon the appeals. This means that the Court of Appeal judgments in *Tameside* define the way in which the courts must approach indexation issues.

9. In the *Tameside* cases, the claimants had substantial post-trial life expectancies and large annual care claims which were to be met by periodical payments. All of the judges (both at first instance and in the Court of Appeal) accepted that if the periodical payments were varied by reference to an index which did not accurately match the change in future costs of care, there was a risk that the claimants would be unable to pay for their care in later life. The value of that shortfall (in 2008 money) might well exceed £1 million in each case.

10. The effect of the Court of Appeal's judgment in *Tameside* is that a claimant should now instruct an Independent Financial Adviser to advise both as to the suitability of periodical payments in general and as to the indexation point. They can also assist with drafting the schedule to an order.

11. Claimants (as in the three of the *Tameside* cases) have tended to seek periodical payments for care which are varied by reference to the Annual Survey of Hours and Earnings ("ASHE"). This is an annual survey published by the Office of National Statistics which samples the actual earnings of employees. The data is disaggregated so that each group of similar workers are classified together. The group which is involved in care assistants and home carers is designated "6115".

12. A brief guide as to how readers can access the ASHE data is set out below. However, in each case the selection of the appropriate part of the index will depend upon finding the appropriate centile. It is first necessary to calculate the weighted average hourly rate of pay for carers (and sometimes nurses) in the care package. Depending on the complexity of the package, this can sometimes be a complicated calculation. It is impossible to fix the centile until the weighted hourly rate has been determined.

13. The calculation of the year-on-year growth rate for the appropriate centile is included in the schedule to the order and this will need to be drafted by someone with financial qualifications.

14. Practitioners representing defendants should note that while the views of the defendants must be considered by the court, the Court of Appeal in *Tameside* discouraged defendants from obtaining a report from a financial adviser.

B6: Step-by-step guide to finding the annual estimates for hourly pay in ASHE 6115

The data collection point for the Annual Survey of Hours and Earnings (ASHE) is April each year. The data are collected over the summer and the first release of estimates takes place in November/December of that year. These are provisional estimates which are revised and published as final estimates the following November/December. The following estimates were published for ASHE 6115 2006 on November 7, 2007 and for ASHE 6115 2008 on December 4, 2008. The final estimates for 2006 and 2007 relate to earnings in April 2006 and April 2007 respectively and the provisional estimates for 2008 relate to earnings in April 2008.

ASHE 6115 2006–2008 centile estimates for hourly earnings £ for UK employees

Centile	10	20	25	30	40	50	60	70	75	80	90
ASHE 6115 2006 Final release	5.37	5.84	6.05	6.24	6.65	7.15	7.70	8.33	8.71	9.25	10.67
ASHE 6115 2007 Final release	5.65	6.15	6.36	6.55	7.01	7.53	8.12	8.80	9.21	9.79	11.38
ASHE 6115 2008 First release	5.85	6.29	6.48	6.69	7.19	7.71	8.32	9.11	9.55	10.11	11.68

Source: ONS ASHE 2006 final published November 7, 2007
ASHE 2007 final and 2008 first published December 4, 2008

ASHE estimates are only available online. They can be found on the website of the UK Statistics Authority. This requires some navigation from the Home page. Step-by-step instructions follow. You need not follow all these instructions each time you consult the tables as you can either download the tables as an Excel file or you can save the web link to the tables in bookmarks.

1. Find the home page of the UK Statistics Authority at *www.statistics.gov.uk*
2. Select the Office for National Statistics (ONS) option at the right hand side of the page and click.
3. Type in ASHE in the search box at the top of this page and click Go.
4. At the ASHE page, scroll down to Product Results and click on ASHE—2008 Results. This produces a list of options to web links to different pages of statistics. At the bottom of this list is some useful information on methodology changes, the ASHE questionnaire and the web link to all the annual ASHE estimates. Click Annual Survey of Hours and Earnings (ASHE) (web link) at the bottom of the list to get the list of ASHE tables by year. Save the link in bookmarks for future reference (*www.statistics.gov.uk/statBase/product.asp?vlnk=13101*).
5. At the list of options for annual ASHE tables, click on ASHE Results 2008.
6. Click on Table 14: Occupation—4 digit SOC.
7. Click on Table 14.5a Hourly Pay: Gross. Either save or open this Excel file.
8. Once in the Excel file, check the bottom tab. "All" refers to all employees (male and female, part and full time).
9. Scroll down to Description = Care Assistants and Home Carers and Code = 6115. Read across the centile estimates.

   The shading indicates the reliability of the estimate. Where the estimate of the error is less than 5 per cent, there is no shading. The key to the shading can be found at the bottom and at the right hand side of the table.

10. If you have not already saved this file at step 7 above, this table can be saved now either in part or in full. If the file is saved make a note that the 2008 estimates are provisional. They will be replaced in the final release in December 2009 under the same title.

This guide has been prepared by Dr Victoria Wass, Cardiff Business School, April 2009.

Group C
Interest Rates

C

C1: Interest base rates

Introductory notes

1. The data for this table are obtained from retail banks Barclays, Lloyds TSB, HSBC and National Westminster.

2. Where these banks' base rates did not change on the same day, an average rate is shown (and asterisked in the table).

3. Since August 3, 2006, these retail banks' base rates have been identical to the Bank of England's Official Bank Rate.

Date	New rate (%)
1982	
August 2	11.50
August 18	11.00
August 31	10.50
October 7	10.00
October 14	9.50
November 4	9.00
November 26	10.125*
1983	
January 12	11.00
March 15	10.50
April 15	10.00
June 15	9.50
October 4	9.00
1984	
March 7	8.875*
March 15	8.625*
May 10	9.125*
June 27	9.25
July 9	10.00
July 11	11.00*
July 12	12.00
August 9	11.50
August 10	11.00
August 20	10.50
November 7	10.00
November 20	9.875*
November 23	9.625*
1985	
January 11	10.50
January 14	12.00
January 28	14.00
March 20	13.75*
March 21	13.50
March 29	13.25*
April 2	13.125*
April 12	12.875*
April 19	12.675*
June 12	12.50
July 7	12.25*
July 16	12.00
July 29	11.75*
July 30	11.50
1986	
January 9	12.50
March 19	11.50
April 8	11.25*
April 9	11.00
April 24	10.50
May 27	10.00
October 14	11.00
1987	
March 10	10.50
March 19	10.00
April 29	9.50
May 11	9.00
August 7	10.00
October 26	9.50
November 5	9.00
December	8.50
1988	
February 2	9.00
March 17	8.50
April 11	8.00
May 18	7.50
June 3	8.00
June 6	8.25*
June 7	8.50
June 22	9.00
June 29	9.50
July 5	10.00
July 19	10.50
August 8	10.75*
August 9	11.00
August 25	11.50
August 26	12.00
November 25	13.00
1989	
May 24	14.00
October 5	15.00
1990	
October 8	14.00
1991	
February 13	13.50
February 27	13.00
March 25	12.50
April 12	12.00
May 24	11.50
July 12	11.00
September 4	10.50
1992	
May 5	10.00
September 16	12.00
September 17	10.00
September 22	9.00
October 16	8.00
November 13	7.00
1993	
January 26	6.00
November 23	5.50
1994	
February 8	5.25
September 12	5.75
December 7	6.25
1995	
February 2	6.75
December 13	6.50
1996	
January 18	6.25
March 8	6.00
June 6	5.75
October 30	6.00
1997	
May 7	6.25
June 9	6.50
July 11	6.75
August 8	7.00
November 7	7.25
1998	
June 5	7.50
October 9	7.25
November 6	6.75
December 1	6.25
1999	
January 8	6.00
February 5	5.50
April 8	5.25
June 10	5.00
September 8	5.25
November 4	5.50
2000	
January 13	5.75
February 10	6.00
2001	
February 8	5.75
April 5	5.50
May 10	5.25
August 2	5.00
September 18	4.75

cont.

Date	New rate (%)
October 4	4.50
November 8	4.00
2003	
February 7	3.75
July 10	3.50
November 6	3.75
2004	
February 5	4.00
May 6	4.25
June 10	4.50
August 5	4.75
2005	
August 4	4.50
2006	
August 10	4.75
November 9	5.00
2007	
January 11	5.25
May 10	5.50
July 5	5.75
December 6	5.50
2008	
February 7	5.25
April 10	5.00
October 8	4.50
November 6	3.00
December 4	2.00
2009	
January 8	1.50
February 5	1.00
March 5	0.50

C2: Real and nominal interest rates and price inflation

Introductory notes

1. Price inflation is calculated as the rate of change of the Retail Price Index.
2. The nominal interest rate is based on the rate on 20-year British Government Securities.
3. No account has been taken of tax in these figures.

	Price Inflation %	Nominal Interest Rate %	Real Interest Rate %
1970	6.52	9.21	2.69
1971	9.18	8.85	(0.33)
1972	7.48	8.90	1.42
1973	9.13	10.71	1.58
1974	15.94	14.77	(1.17)
1975	24.05	14.39	(9.66)
1976	16.62	14.43	(2.19)
1977	15.91	12.73	(3.18)
1978	8.20	12.47	4.27
1979	13.45	12.99	(0.46)
1980	18.03	13.78	(4.25)
1981	11.88	14.74	2.86
1982	8.70	12.88	4.18
1983	4.44	10.80	6.36
1984	5.01	10.69	5.68
1985	6.04	10.62	4.58
1986	3.40	9.87	6.47
1987	4.16	9.47	5.31
1988	4.92	9.36	4.44
1989	7.79	9.58	1.79
1990	9.44	11.08	1.64
1991	5.91	9.92	4.01
1992	3.73	9.12	5.39
1993	1.57	7.87	6.30
1994	2.48	8.05	5.57
1995	3.41	8.26	4.85
1996	2.44	8.10	5.66
1997	3.12	7.09	3.97
1998	3.42	5.45	2.03
1999	1.56	4.70	3.14
2000	2.93	4.68	1.75
2001	1.84	4.78	2.94
2002	1.62	4.83	3.21
2003	2.91	4.64	1.73
2004	2.96	4.77	1.81
2005	2.84	4.39	1.55
2006	3.20	4.27	1.07
2007	4.26	4.73	0.47
2008	4.00	4.68	0.68
Averages:			
1970–79	12.65	11.95	(0.70)
1980–89	7.44	11.18	3.74
1990–99	3.71	7.96	4.26
2000–08	2.95	4.64	1.69

Real interest rates 1970–2008

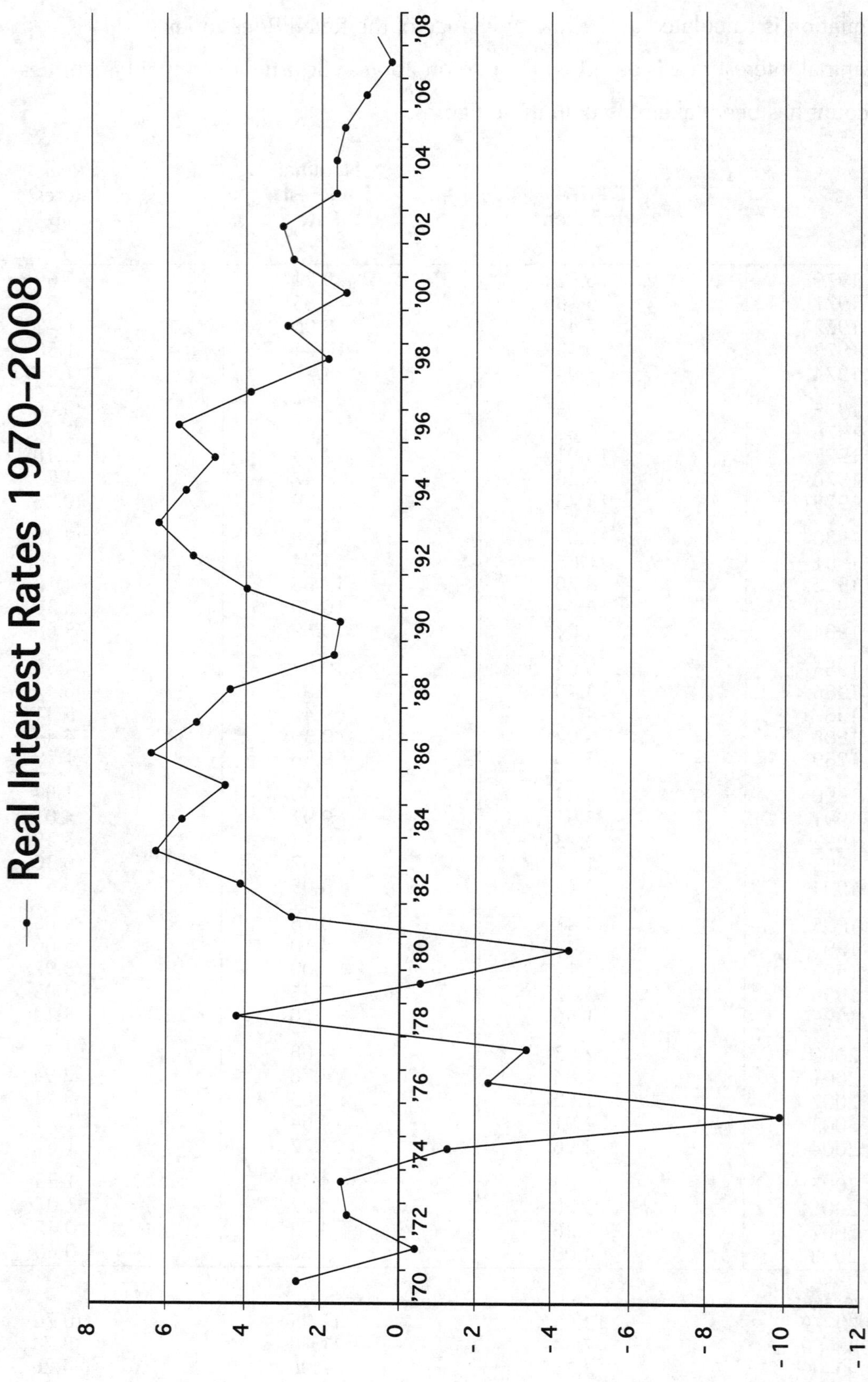

C3: Special investment account rates

Introductory notes

This is a composite table including both the Short Term Investment Account rate and the succeeding High Court Special Investment Account rate.

The manner of crediting interest is set out in Court Fund Rules 1987, r.27. Interest accruing to a special investment account is credited without the deduction of income tax.

From:		%
October 1	1965	5.0
September 1	1966	5.5
March 1	1968	6.0
March 1	1969	6.5
March 1	1970	7.0
April 1	1971	7.5
March 1	1973	8.0
March 1	1974	9.0
February 1	1977	10.0
March 1	1979	12.5
January 1	1980	15.0
January 1	1981	12.5
December 1	1981	15.0
March 1	1982	14.0
July 1	1982	13.0
April 1	1983	12.5
April 1	1984	12.0
August 1	1986	11.5
January 1	1987	12.25
April 1	1987	11.75
November 1	1987	11.25
December 1	1987	11.0
May 1	1988	9.5
August 1	1988	11.0
November 1	1988	12.25
January 1	1989	13.0
November 1	1989	14.25
April 1	1991	12.0
October 1	1991	10.25
February 1	1993	8.0
August 1	1999	7.0
February 1	2002	6.0
February 1	2009	3.0
June 1	2009	1.5
July 1	2009	0.5

C4: Special and general damages interest

Introductory notes

Special damages

The appropriate rate of interest for special damages is the rate, over the period for which the interest is awarded, which is payable on the court special account. This rate was reduced to 0.5 per cent on July 1, 2009. Interest since June 1987 has been paid daily on a 1/365th basis, even in a leap year such as 2004.

In cases of continuing special damages, half the appropriate rate from the date of injury to the date of trial is awarded. In cases where the special damages have ceased and are thus limited to a finite period, there are conflicting Court of Appeal decisions as to whether the award should be half the appropriate rate from injury to trial (*Dexter v Courtaulds*[1]) or the full special account rate from the date within the period to which the special damages are limited (*Prokop v DHSS*[2]).

The relevant rates since 1965 are set out in Table C3.

The table overleaf records the total of these rates from January 1980. The left hand column shows the month from the first day of which interest is assumed to run. The right hand column shows the percentage interest accumulated from the first day of each month to July 1, 2009.

Continued use may be made of this table by adding to the figures in it 1/365th of the special account rate for each day from July 1, 2009 onwards, using Table C6 which records the number of days between two dates in a two-year period.

Suppose that interest runs from January 1, 2001 to October 13, 2009. The total to July 1, 2009 is 50.65 per cent. From Table C6, July 1 to October 13 is 286 − 182 days. If the rate remains at 0.5 per cent p.a., the appropriate addition will be 0.5 per cent × 104/365 = 0.14 per cent. Thus the grand total from January 1, 2001 to October 13, 2009 will be 50.65 + 0.14 = 50.79 per cent.

General damages

In personal injury cases, the normal rate of interest on general damages for pain, suffering and loss of amenity was by convention 2 per cent per annum. In *Lawrence v Chief Constable of Staffordshire*[3] the Court of Appeal held that in spite of *Wells v Wells*,[4] the rate should remain at 2 per cent. Interest runs from the date of service of proceedings.

1 [1984] 1 All E.R. 70.

2 [1985] C.L.Y. 103.7

3 CA, transcript June 29, 2000.

4 [1999] A.C. 345.

Table of cumulative interest at the special account rate from the first day of each month to July 1, 2009.

	1980	1981	1982	1983	1984	1985	1986	1987	1988	1989
January	275.85	260.85	248.13	234.48	221.85	209.73	197.73	185.94	174.17	163.31
February	274.57	259.79	246.86	233.37	220.79	208.70	196.71	184.90	173.24	162.21
March	273.42	258.83	245.71	232.38	219.93	207.79	195.79	183.96	172.36	161.21
April	272.15	257.76	244.52	231.27	218.77	206.77	194.77	182.92	171.43	160.11
May	270.92	256.74	243.37	230.24	217.79	205.79	193.79	181.95	170.53	159.04
June	269.64	255.68	242.18	229.18	216.77	204.77	192.77	180.96	169.72	157.93
July	268.41	254.65	241.03	228.14	215.78	203.78	191.78	179.99	168.94	156.86
August	267.13	253.59	239.93	227.09	214.76	202.76	190.76	178.99	168.13	155.76
September	265.86	252.53	238.82	226.03	213.74	201.74	189.78	177.99	167.20	154.66
October	264.63	251.50	237.75	225.00	212.76	200.76	188.84	177.03	166.29	153.59
November	263.35	250.44	236.65	223.94	211.74	199.74	187.86	176.03	165.36	152.48
December	262.12	249.41	235.58	222.92	210.75	198.75	186.92	175.11	164.35	151.31
	1990	**1991**	**1992**	**1993**	**1994**	**1995**	**1996**	**1997**	**1998**	**1999**
January	150.10	135.85	123.74	113.46	105.27	97.27	89.27	81.25	73.25	65.25
February	148.89	134.64	123.87	112.59	104.59	96.59	88.59	80.57	72.57	64.57
March	147.79	133.54	122.05	111.97	103.97	95.97	87.95	79.95	71.95	63.95
April	146.59	132.34	121.18	111.29	103.29	95.29	87.27	79.27	71.27	63.27
May	145.42	131.35	120.34	110.64	102.64	94.64	86.62	78.62	70.62	62.62
June	144.22	130.33	119.47	109.96	101.96	93.96	85.94	77.94	69.94	61.94
July	143.04	129.35	118.63	109.30	101.30	93.30	85.28	77.28	69.28	61.28
August	141.82	128.33	117.75	108.62	100.62	92.62	84.60	76.60	68.60	60.60
September	140.61	127.31	116.88	107.94	99.94	91.94	83.92	75.92	67.92	60.01
October	139.44	126.32	116.04	107.28	99.28	91.28	83.26	75.26	67.26	59.43
November	138.23	125.45	115.17	106.60	98.60	90.60	82.58	74.58	66.58	58.84
December	137.06	124.61	114.33	105.95	97.95	89.95	81.93	73.93	65.93	58.26
	2000	**2001**	**2002**	**2003**	**2004**	**2005**	**2006**	**2007**	**2008**	**2009**
January	57.67	50.65	43.65	37.57	31.57	25.55	19.56	13.56	7.56	1.62
February	57.08	50.06	43.06	37.06	31.06	25.04	19.05	13.05	7.05	1.11
March	56.62	49.60	42.60	36.60	30.58	24.58	18.59	12.59	6.57	0.88
April	55.93	49.09	42.09	36.09	30.07	24.07	18.08	12.08	6.06	0.62
May	55.35	48.60	41.60	35.60	29.58	23.58	17.58	11.58	5.56	0.38
June	54.76	48.09	41.09	35.09	29.07	23.07	17.07	11.07	5.05	0.12
July	54.18	47.59	40.59	34.59	28.58	22.58	16.58	10.58	4.64	
August	53.59	47.08	40.08	34.08	28.07	22.07	16.07	10.07	4.13	
September	52.99	46.58	39.58	33.58	27.56	21.56	15.56	9.56	3.62	
October	52.42	46.08	39.08	33.08	27.07	21.07	15.07	9.07	3.13	
November	51.82	45.57	38.57	32.57	26.56	20.56	14.56	8.56	2.62	
December	51.25	45.08	38.08	32.08	26.06	20.06	14.06	8.06	2.13	

If the rate remains at 0.5 per cent, interest **up to** the first day of successive later months can be found by adding the following figures.

	2009 (%)		2010 (%)
August	0.04	January	0.25
September	0.08	February	0.29
October	0.13	March	0.33
November	0.17	April	0.38
December	0.21	May	0.42
		June	0.46
		July	0.50

C5: Base rate + 10 per cent

Introductory notes

1. Under the Civil Procedure Rules 1998, rule 36.21, where the judgment against a defendant is more advantageous to the claimant than the proposals in a claimant's Part 36 offer, the court may order interest on the sum awarded and on the costs, for some or all of the period starting with the latest date on which the defendant could have accepted the Part 36 offer without needing the permission of the court, at a rate not exceeding 10 per cent above base rate. In *All-in-One Design & Build Ltd v Motcomb Estates Ltd, The Times,* April 4, 2000, it was held that rule 36.21 is not *ultra vires.*

2. Rule 36.21(4) provides that where the rule applies, the court will make those orders unless it considers it unjust to do so; sub-rule (5) sets out the factors to be considered in deciding whether it would be unjust.

3. Since 1998 base rates have been as follows:

		Rate	Rate + 10%
1997	November 7	7.25%	17.25%
1998	June 4	7.50%	17.50%
	October 8	7.25%	17.25%
	November 5	6.75%	16.75%
	December 10	6.25%	16.25%
1999	January 7	6.00%	16.00%
	February 4	5.50%	15.50%
	April 8	5.25%	15.25%
	June 10	5.00%	15.00%
	September 8	5.25%	15.25%
	November 4	5.50%	15.50%
2000	January 13	5.75%	15.75%
	February 10	6.00%	16.00%
2001	February 8	5.75%	15.75%
	April 5	5.50%	15.50%
	May 10	5.25%	15.25%
	August 2	5.00%	15.00%
	September 18	4.75%	14.75%
	October 4	4.50%	14.50%
	November 8	4.00%	14.00%
2003	February 6	3.75%	13.75%
	July 10	3.50%	13.50%
	November 6	3.75%	13.75%
2004	February 5	4.00%	14.00%
	May 6	4.25%	14.25%
	June 10	4.50%	14.50%
	August 5	4.75%	14.75%
2005	August 4	4.50%	14.50%
2006	August 3	4.75%	14.75%
	November 9	5.00%	15.00%
2007	January 11	5.25%	15.25%
	May 10	5.50%	15.50%
	July 5	5.75%	15.75%
	December 6	5.50%	15.50%
2008	February 7	5.25%	15.25%
	April 10	5.00%	15.00%
	October 8	4.50%	14.50%
	November 6	3.00%	13.00%
	December 4	2.00%	12.00%
2009	January 8	1.50%	11.50%
	February 5	1.00%	10.50%
	March 5	0.50%	10.50%

The following table shows cumulative interest at 10% above base rate from the first day of each month until July 1, 2009. Interest for parts of a month can be found by following the method in the notes to Table C4.

	1999	2000	2001	2002	2003	2004	2005	2006	2007	2008	2009
January	153.45	138.10	122.09	106.97	92.97	79.28	64.86	50.21	35.57	20.06	5.35
February	152.08	136.77	120.73	105.78	91.78	78.11	63.61	48.98	34.28	18.75	4.36
March	150.89	135.51	119.52	104.71	90.73	77.00	62.48	47.87	33.11	17.53	3.52
April	149.57	134.15	118.18	103.52	89.56	75.81	61.22	46.64	31.82	16.23	2.62
May	148.32	132.83	116.91	102.37	88.43	74.66	60.01	45.45	30.57	15.00	1.75
June	147.02	131.47	115.60	101.18	87.26	73.46	58.76	44.21	29.26	13.72	0.86
July	145.78	130.16	114.35	100.03	86.13	72.27	57.55	43.02	27.98	12.49	
August	144.51	128.80	113.06	98.84	84.98	71.04	56.29	41.79	26.65	11.22	
September	143.23	127.44	111.78	97.65	83.83	69.79	55.06	40.54	25.31	9.94	
October	141.98	126.13	110.56	96.50	82.72	68.58	53.87	39.33	24.01	8.71	
November	140.69	124.77	109.32	95.31	81.58	67.32	52.64	38.07	22.68	7.47	
December	139.42	123.45	108.16	94.16	80.45	66.11	51.44	36.85	21.38	6.38	

If there are no further changes of rate after that on March 5, interest **up to** the first day of successive later months can be found by adding the figure from the following table:

	2009 (%)
August	0.89
September	1.78
October	2.65
November	3.54
December	4.40

	2010 (%)
January 2009	5.29
Feburary	6.18
March	6.99
April	7.88
May	8.75
June	9.64
July	10.50

C6: Number of days between two dates

Introductory notes

Deduct the number of the opening date from the number of the closing date (where necessary adding a day for February 29).
Example: October 14th–March 19th is 443 − 287 = 156 days.

Day of month	Day numbers																								Day of month
	Jan	Feb	Mar	Apr	May	Jun	Jul	Aug	Sep	Oct	Nov	Dec	Jan	Feb	Mar	Apr	May	Jun	Jul	Aug	Sep	Oct	Nov	Dec	
1	1	32	60	91	121	152	182	213	244	274	305	335	366	397	425	456	486	517	547	578	609	639	670	700	**1**
2	2	33	61	92	122	153	183	214	245	275	306	336	367	398	426	457	487	518	548	579	610	640	671	701	**2**
3	3	34	62	93	123	154	184	215	246	276	307	337	368	399	427	458	488	519	549	580	611	641	672	702	**3**
4	4	35	63	94	124	155	185	216	247	277	308	338	369	400	428	459	489	520	550	581	612	642	673	703	**4**
5	5	36	64	95	125	156	186	217	248	278	309	339	370	401	429	460	490	521	551	582	613	643	674	704	**5**
6	6	37	65	96	126	157	187	218	249	279	310	340	371	402	430	461	491	522	552	583	614	644	675	705	**6**
7	7	38	66	97	127	158	188	219	250	280	311	341	372	403	431	462	492	523	553	584	615	645	676	706	**7**
8	8	39	67	98	128	159	189	220	251	281	312	342	373	404	432	463	493	524	554	585	616	646	677	707	**8**
9	9	40	68	99	129	160	190	221	252	282	313	343	374	405	433	464	494	525	555	586	617	647	678	708	**9**
10	10	41	69	100	130	161	191	222	253	283	314	344	375	406	434	465	495	526	556	587	618	648	679	709	**10**
11	11	42	70	101	131	162	192	223	254	284	315	345	376	407	435	466	496	527	557	588	619	649	680	710	**11**
12	12	43	71	102	132	163	193	224	255	285	316	346	377	408	436	467	497	528	558	589	620	650	681	711	**12**
13	13	44	72	103	133	164	194	225	256	286	317	347	378	409	437	468	498	529	559	590	621	651	682	712	**13**
14	14	45	73	104	134	165	195	226	257	287	318	348	379	410	438	469	499	530	560	591	622	652	683	713	**14**
15	15	46	74	105	135	166	196	227	258	288	319	349	380	411	439	470	500	531	561	592	623	653	684	714	**15**
16	16	47	75	106	136	167	197	228	259	289	320	350	381	412	440	471	501	532	562	593	624	654	685	715	**16**
17	17	48	76	107	137	168	198	229	260	290	321	351	382	413	441	472	502	533	563	594	625	655	686	716	**17**
18	18	49	77	108	138	169	199	230	261	291	322	352	383	414	442	473	503	534	564	595	626	656	687	717	**18**
19	19	50	78	109	139	170	200	231	262	292	323	353	384	415	443	474	504	535	565	596	627	657	688	718	**19**
20	20	51	79	110	140	171	201	232	263	293	324	354	385	416	444	475	505	536	566	597	628	658	689	719	**20**
21	21	52	80	111	141	172	202	233	264	294	325	355	386	417	445	476	506	537	567	598	629	659	690	720	**21**
22	22	53	81	112	142	173	203	234	265	295	326	356	387	418	446	477	507	538	568	599	630	660	691	721	**22**
23	23	54	82	113	143	174	204	235	266	296	327	357	388	419	447	478	508	539	569	600	631	661	692	722	**23**
24	24	55	83	114	144	175	205	236	267	297	328	358	389	420	448	479	509	540	570	601	632	662	693	723	**24**
25	25	56	84	115	145	176	206	237	268	298	329	359	390	421	449	480	510	541	571	602	633	663	694	724	**25**
26	26	57	85	116	146	177	207	238	269	299	330	360	391	422	450	481	511	542	572	603	634	664	695	725	**26**
27	27	58	86	117	147	178	208	239	270	300	331	361	392	423	451	482	512	543	573	604	635	665	696	726	**27**
28	28	59	87	118	148	179	209	240	271	301	332	362	393	424	452	483	513	544	574	605	636	666	697	727	**28**
29	29		88	119	149	180	210	241	272	302	333	363	394		453	484	514	545	575	606	637	667	698	728	**29**
30	30		89	120	150	181	211	242	273	303	334	364	395		454	485	515	546	576	607	638	668	699	729	**30**
31	31		90		151		212	243		304		365	396		455		516		577	608		669		730	**31**

C7: Decimal years

An alternative way of calculating interest is with a table expressing intervals as decimals of a year. It is in some respects a simpler method than the Number of Days Table (Table C6) as it avoids the need to divide by 365.

The first table below gives days, weeks and months as decimals of a year.

The second table gives the period between corresponding days of two months, with the earlier month down the left hand side and the later month across the top. Thus from the two figures in bold one sees that from April 1 to June 1 is 0.167 years; from June 1 to the next April 1 is 0.833 years.

Days, weeks and months expressed as decimals of a year

Days

1	0.003	2	0.005	3	0.008	4	0.011	5	0.014	6	0.016	7	0.019	8	0.022	9	0.025	10	0.027
11	0.030	12	0.033	13	0.036	14	0.038	15	0.041	16	0.044	17	0.047	18	0.049	19	0.052	20	0.055
21	0.058	22	0.060	23	0.063	24	0.066	25	0.068	26	0.071	27	0.074	28	0.077	29	0.079	30	0.082

Weeks

1	0.019	2	0.038	3	0.058	4	0.077	5	0.096	6	0.115	7	0.134	8	0.153	9	0.173	10	0.192

Months

28 days	0.077	29 days	0.079	30 days	0.082	31 days	0.085

Intervals between corresponding days of months as decimals of a year

Later month

Earlier month	Jan	Feb	Mar	Apr	May	Jun
Jan	1.000	0.085	0.162	0.247	0.329	0.414
Feb	0.915	1.000	0.077	0.162	0.244	0.329
Mar	0.838	0.923	1.000	0.085	0.167	0.252
Apr	0.753	0.838	0.915	1.000	0.082	**0.167**
May	0.671	0.756	0.833	0.918	1.000	0.085
Jun	0.586	0.671	0.748	**0.833**	0.915	1.000
Jul	0.504	0.589	0.666	0.751	0.833	0.918
Aug	0.419	0.504	0.581	0.666	0.748	0.833
Sept	0.334	0.419	0.496	0.581	0.663	0.748
Oct	0.252	0.337	0.414	0.499	0.581	0.666
Nov	0.167	0.252	0.329	0.414	0.496	0.581
Dec	0.085	0.170	0.247	0.332	0.414	0.499

Earlier month	Jul	Aug	Sept	Oct	Nov	Dec
Jan	0.496	0.581	0.666	0.748	0.833	0.915
Feb	0.411	0.496	0.581	0.663	0.748	0.830
Mar	0.334	0.419	0.504	0.586	0.671	0.753
Apr	0.249	0.334	0.419	0.501	0.586	0.668
May	0.167	0.252	0.337	0.419	0.504	0.586
Jun	0.082	0.167	0.252	0.334	0.419	0.501
Jul	1.000	0.085	0.170	0.252	0.337	0.419
Aug	0.915	1.000	0.085	0.167	0.252	0.334
Sept	0.830	0.915	1.000	0.082	0.167	0.249
Oct	0.748	0.833	0.918	1.000	0.085	0.167
Nov	0.663	0.748	0.833	0.915	1.000	0.082
Dec	0.581	0.666	0.751	0.833	0.918	1.000

Example: to calculate interest at 8 per cent from 3 June 2006 to 15 April 2007

3.6.06–15.6.06	=	12 days	=	0.033 years		
15.6.06–15.4.07	=			0.833		
Total 3.6.06–15.4.07			=	0.866 years		
Interest at 8 per cent from 3.6.06–15.4.07			=	0.866 × 8	=	6.928 per cent

C8: Judgment debt interest rates (England and Wales)

Introductory notes

Interest rates under the Judgments Act 1838, s.17.

This table sets out the interest rates as determined by the Judgment Debts (Rate of Interest) Orders. Such orders are made under the Administration of Justice Act 1970, s.44.

By virtue of The County Courts (Interest on Judgment Debts) Order 1991, the general rule is that every judgment debt of not less than £5,000 carries interest from the date on which it was given, at the same rate as that payable on High Court judgments.

From	At %	Order
April 20, 1971	7.5	SI 1971/491
March 1, 1977	10	SI 1977/141
December 3, 1979	12.5	SI 1979/1382
June 9, 1980	15	SI 1980/672
June 8, 1982	14	SI 1982/696
November 10, 1982	12	SI 1982/1427
April 16, 1985	15	SI 1985/437
April 1, 1993 to date	8	SI 1993/564

C9: Judicial rates of interest (Scotland)

From	At %	Act of Sederunt
May 4, 1965 – January 5, 1970	5	SI 1965/321
January 6, 1970 – January 6, 1975	7	SI 1969/1819
January 7, 1975 – April 4, 1983	11	SI 1974/2090
April 5, 1983 – August 15, 1985	12	SI 1983/398
August 16, 1985 – March 31, 1993	15	SI 1985/1178
April 1, 1993 to date	8	SI 1993/770 and SI 1994/1443

Group D
Investment

D

D1: **Share Price Index (FTSE 100)**

D2: **Barclays Equity Index**

D3: **Index-linked stock**

D1: Share price index

FTSE® 100 (on last day of month)

	1986	1987	1988	1989	1990	1991	1992	1993
January	1435.00	1808.20	1790.80	2052.10	2337.30	2170.30	2571.20	2807.20
February	1543.90	1979.20	1768.80	2002.40	2255.40	2380.90	2562.10	2868.00
March	1668.80	1997.50	1742.50	2075.00	2247.90	2456.50	2440.10	2878.70
April	1660.50	2050.50	1802.20	2118.00	2103.40	2486.20	2654.10	2813.10
May	1602.80	2203.00	1784.40	2114.40	2345.10	2499.50	2707.60	2840.70
June	1649.80	2284.10	1857.60	2151.00	2374.60	2414.80	2521.20	2900.00
July	1558.10	2360.90	1853.60	2297.00	2326.20	2588.80	2399.60	2926.50
August	1661.20	2249.70	1753.60	2387.90	2162.80	2645.70	2312.60	3100.00
September	1555.80	2366.00	1826.50	2299.40	1990.20	2621.70	2553.00	3037.50
October	1632.20	1749.80	1852.40	2142.60	2050.30	2566.00	2658.30	3171.00
November	1636.60	1579.90	1792.40	2276.80	2149.40	2420.20	2778.80	3166.90
December	1679.00	1712.70	1793.10	2422.70	2143.50	2493.10	2846.50	3418.40
	1994	**1995**	**1996**	**1997**	**1998**	**1999**	**2000**	**2001**
January	3491.80	2991.60	3759.30	4275.80	5458.50	5896.00	6268.50	6297.50
February	3328.10	3009.30	3727.60	4308.30	5767.30	6175.10	6232.60	5917.90
March	3086.40	3137.90	3699.70	4312.90	5932.20	6295.30	6540.20	5633.70
April	3125.30	3216.70	3817.90	4436.00	5928.30	6552.20	6327.40	5966.90
May	2970.50	3319.40	3747.80	4621.30	5870.70	6226.20	6359.30	5796.10
June	2919.20	3314.60	3711.00	4604.60	5832.50	6318.50	6312.70	5642.50
July	3082.60	3463.30	3703.20	4907.50	5837.00	6231.90	6365.30	5529.10
August	3251.30	3477.80	3867.60	4817.50	5249.40	6246.40	6672.70	5345.00
September	3026.30	3508.20	3953.70	5244.20	5064.40	6029.80	6294.20	4903.40
October	3097.40	3529.10	3979.10	4842.30	5438.40	6255.70	6438.40	5039.70
November	3081.40	3664.30	4058.00	4831.80	5743.90	6597.20	6142.20	5203.60
December	3065.50	3689.30	4118.50	5135.50	5882.60	6930.20	6222.50	5217.40
	2002	**2003**	**2004**	**2005**	**2006**	**2007**	**2008**	**2009**
January	5164.80	3567.40	4390.70	4852.30	5760.30	6203.10	5879.78	4149.64
February	5101.00	3655.60	4492.20	4968.50	5791.50	6171.50	5818.62	3830.09
March	5271.80	3613.30	4385.70	4894.40	5964.60	6308.00	5852.58	3926.14
April	5165.60	3926.00	4489.70	4801.70	6023.10	6449.20	6087.25	4243.71
May	5085.10	4048.10	4430.70	4964.00	5723.80	6621.40	6053.50	4417.94
June	4656.40	4031.20	4464.10	5113.20	5833.40	6607.90	5625.90	4249.21
July	4246.20	4157.00	4413.10	5282.30	5928.30	6360.10	5411.90	
August	4227.30	4161.10	4459.30	5296.90	5906.10	6303.30	5636.61	
September	3721.80	4091.30	4570.80	5477.70	5960.80	6466.80	4902.45	
October	4039.70	4287.60	4624.20	5317.30	6129.20	6721.60	4377.34	
November	4169.40	4342.60	4703.20	5423.20	6048.80	6432.50	4288.01	
December	3940.40	4476.90	4814.30	5618.80	6220.80	6456.90	4434.17	

D2: Barclays Equity Index

Year	Equity Price Index December	%	Equity Income Index December	%	Income Yield %	Equity Price Index Adjusted for Cost of Living	%	Equity Income Index Adjusted for Cost of Living	%
1955	256	+5.8	179	+15.4	4.8	74	−0.0	53	+9.1
1956	220	−13.9	183	+2.2	5.7	62	−16.5	53	−0.8
1957	205	−7.0	188	+2.8	6.3	55	−11.1	52	−1.7
1958	289	+41.1	202	+7.5	4.8	76	+38.5	55	+5.5
1959	432	+49.5	227	+12.1	3.6	113	+49.5	61	+12.1
1960	421	−2.6	276	+21.7	4.5	108	−4.4	73	+19.5
1961	409	−3.0	286	+3.5	4.8	101	−7.0	73	−0.8
1962	391	−4.4	285	−0.4	5.0	94	−6.9	71	−3.0
1963	450	+15.2	266	−6.5	4.1	106	+13.1	65	−8.2
1964	405	−10.0	303	+13.7	5.1	91	−14.2	70	+8.5
1965	428	+5.9	326	+7.7	5.2	92	+1.3	73	+3.1
1966	389	−9.3	328	+0.5	5.8	81	−12.5	70	−3.1
1967	500	+28.7	319	−2.5	4.4	101	+25.6	67	−4.8
1968	718	+43.5	339	+6.1	3.2	137	+35.4	67	+0.2
1969	609	−15.2	342	+0.8	3.9	111	−19.0	65	−3.7
1970	563	−7.5	360	+5.5	4.4	95	−14.3	63	−2.3
1971	799	+41.9	379	+5.1	3.3	124	+30.2	61	−3.6
1972	901	+12.8	414	+9.3	3.2	130	+4.8	62	+1.6
1973	619	−31.4	430	+3.9	4.8	81	−37.9	58	−6.0
1974	276	−55.3	472	+9.6	11.7	30	−62.5	53	−8.0
1975	653	+136.3	521	+10.4	5.5	57	+89.2	47	−11.6
1976	628	−3.9	588	+12.8	6.4	48	−16.5	46	−2.0
1977	886	+41.2	682	+16.1	5.3	60	+25.9	48	+3.5
1978	910	+2.7	768	+12.6	5.8	57	−5.3	50	+3.9
1979	949	+4.3	951	+23.8	6.9	51	−11.0	53	+5.6
1980	1206	+27.1	1073	+12.8	6.1	56	+10.4	52	−2.0
1981	1294	+7.2	1111	+3.5	5.9	54	−4.3	48	−7.6
1982	1579	+22.1	1211	+9.0	5.3	62	+15.8	49	+3.4
1983	1944	+23.1	1309	+8.1	4.6	73	+16.9	51	+2.7
1984	2450	+26.0	1578	+20.6	4.4	88	+20.5	58	+15.3
1985	2822	+15.2	1781	+12.8	4.3	95	+9.0	62	+6.8
1986	3452	+22.3	2033	+14.1	4.0	112	+17.9	68	+10.0
1987	3596	+4.2	2264	+11.4	4.3	113	+0.4	74	+7.4
1988	3829	+6.5	2628	+16.1	4.7	113	−0.3	80	+8.7
1989	4978	+30.0	3076	+17.0	4.2	136	+20.7	87	+8.7
1990	4265	−14.3	3401	+10.5	5.5	107	−21.6	88	+1.1
1991	4907	+15.1	3591	+5.6	5.0	117	+10.1	89	+1.1
1992	5635	+14.8	3573	−0.5	4.4	131	+11.9	86	−3.0
1993	6951	+23.3	3414	−4.4	3.4	159	+21.0	81	−6.2
1994	6286	−9.6	3684	+7.9	4.0	140	−12.1	85	+4.9
1995	7450	+18.5	4127	+12.0	3.8	161	+14.8	92	+8.5
1996	8320	+11.7	4536	+9.9	3.7	175	+9.0	99	+7.3
1997	9962	+19.7	4690	+3.4	3.2	202	+15.5	98	−0.2
1998	11048	+10.9	4026	−14.2	2.5	218	+7.9	82	−16.5
1999	13396	+21.2	4140	+2.8	2.1	260	+19.1	83	+1.0
2000	12329	−8.0	4007	−3.2	2.2	233	−10.6	78	−5.9
2001	10428	−15.4	3998	−0.2	2.6	195	−16.0	77	−0.9
2002	7825	−25.0	4049	+1.3	3.6	142	−27.1	76	−1.6
2003	9121	+16.6	4121	+1.8	3.1	161	+13.4	75	−1.0
2004	9961	+9.2	4428	+7.5	3.1	170	+5.5	78	+3.8
2005	11764	+18.1	5058	+14.2	3.0	197	+15.5	87	+11.8
2006	11311	+13.2	5549	+9.7	2.9	213	+8.3	92	+5.0
2007	13580	+2.0	5978	+7.7	3.0	209	−1.9	95	+3.5
2008	9129	−32.8	5974	−0.1	4.5	139	−33.5	94	−1.1

Note: original investment of £100 December 1945, gross income reinvested.
Reproduced here with the kind permission of Barclays Capital.

D3: Index-linked stock

Return on index-linked government securities

	1999		2000		2001		2002		2003	
	Gross %	Net %	Gross %	Net %	Gross %	Net %	Gross %	Net %	Gross %	Net %
January	1.88	1.60	2.05	1.74	1.90	1.62	2.28	1.94	1.90	1.62
February	1.88	1.60	1.91	1.62	1.93	1.64	2.26	1.92	1.78	1.51
March	1.76	1.50	1.87	1.59	2.24	1.90	2.28	1.94	1.85	1.57
April	1.85	1.57	1.88	1.60	2.51	2.13	2.30	1.95	1.91	1.62
May	1.86	1.58	1.94	1.65	2.47	2.10	2.26	1.92	1.73	1.47
June	1.90	1.62	1.83	1.56	2.41	2.05	2.14	1.82	1.76	1.50
July	1.95	1.66	1.98	1.68	2.32	1.97	2.32	1.97	1.97	1.67
August	2.15	1.83	2.01	1.71	2.12	1.80	2.03	1.73	1.93	1.64
September	2.13	1.81	2.02	1.72	2.37	2.01	2.01	1.71	1.84	1.56
October	2.01	1.71	2.03	1.73	2.12	1.80	2.13	1.81	2.09	1.78
November	1.84	1.56	1.87	1.59	2.17	1.84	2.26	1.92	2.09	1.78
December	1.80	1.53	1.92	1.63	2.30	1.95	2.02	1.72	1.83	1.56

	2004		2005		2006		2007		2008	
	Gross %	Net %	Gross %	Net %	Gross %	Net %	Gross %	Net %	Gross %	Net %
January	1.88	1.60	1.61	1.37	0.99	0.84	1.43	1.22	0.92	0.78
February	1.75	1.49	1.60	1.36	1.00	0.85	1.21	1.03	0.89	0.76
March	1.67	1.42	1.61	1.37	1.19	1.01	1.38	1.17	0.81	0.69
April	1.82	1.55	1.56	1.33	1.37	1.16	1.46	1.24	0.93	0.79
May	1.90	1.61	1.54	1.31	1.35	1.15	1.62	1.38	1.00	0.85
June	1.87	1.59	1.39	1.18	1.43	1.22	1.67	1.42	0.86	0.73
July	1.91	1.62	1.50	1.27	1.25	1.06	1.48	1.26	0.95	0.81
August	1.75	1.49	1.32	1.12	1.12	0.95	1.31	1.11	0.59	0.50
September	1.71	1.45	1.33	1.13	1.16	0.99	1.33	1.13	0.96	0.82
October	1.69	1.44	1.31	1.11	1.05	0.89	1.30	1.11	1.56	1.33
November	1.62	1.38	1.24	1.05	1.06	0.90	1.11	0.94	1.68	1.43
December	1.54	1.31	1.09	0.93	1.23	1.05	1.00	0.85	0.97	0.82

	2009	
	Gross %	Net %
January	0.99	0.84
February	1.21	1.03
March	1.01	0.86
April	1.04	0.88
May	0.95	0.81
June	0.84	0.71

Notes:

1. The index used to compile the above table is the month end FTSE Actuaries Government Securities Index for index-linked stock with over five years to maturity assuming 5 per cent inflation. It is not the index created by the UK Government Debt Management Office for the Lord Chancellor when, on June 25, 2001, he prescribed a rate under s.1(1) of the Damages Act 1996.

2. The net percentage yield is stated after deduction of tax at an assumed average rate of 15 per cent: see *Wells v Wells.*[1] The actual average rate of tax will vary from case to case depending on the amount of taxable income. This will be affected both by the size of the award and the fact that only the interest element of the total return is taxable, with any capital loss or gain on redemption being exempt from tax.

[1] [1999] A.C. 345.

Index-linked stock (April 1999–April 2009)

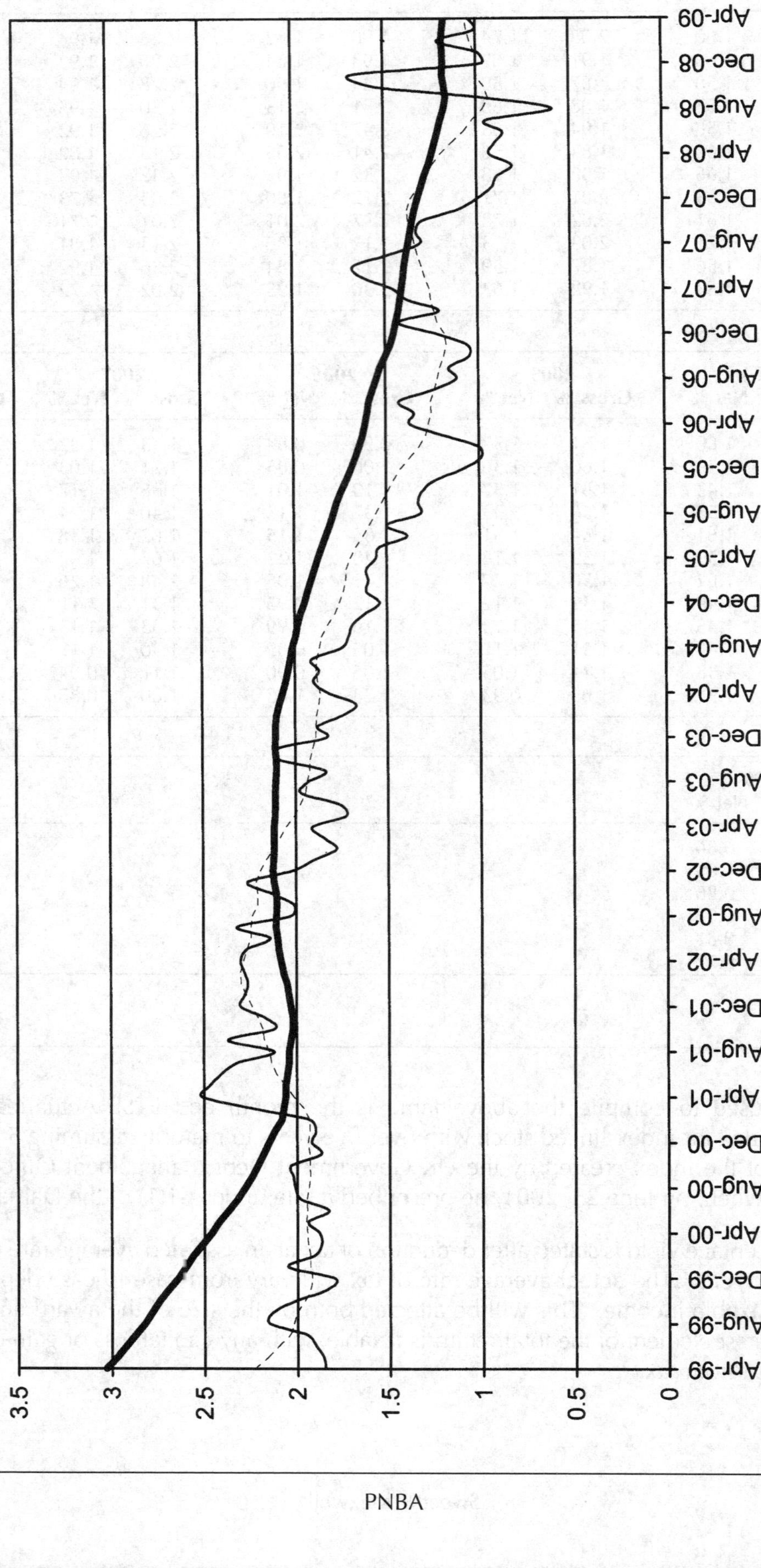

Group E

Prices

E

E1: Retail prices index

	Jan	Feb	Mar	Apr	May	June	July	Aug	Sept	Oct	Nov	Dec	
2009	210.10	211.40	211.30	211.50	212.80	213.40							**2009**
2008	209.80	211.40	212.10	214.00	215.10	216.80	216.50	217.20	218.40	217.70	216.00	212.90	**2008**
2007	201.60	203.10	204.40	205.40	206.20	207.30	206.10	207.30	208.00	208.90	209.70	210.90	**2007**
2006	193.40	194.20	195.00	196.50	197.70	198.50	198.50	199.20	200.10	200.40	201.10	202.70	**2006**
2005	188.90	189.60	190.50	191.60	192.00	192.20	192.20	192.60	193.10	193.30	193.60	194.10	**2005**
2004	183.10	183.80	184.60	185.70	186.50	186.80	186.80	187.40	188.10	188.60	189.00	189.90	**2004**
2003	178.40	179.30	179.90	181.20	181.50	181.30	181.30	181.60	182.50	182.60	182.70	183.50	**2003**
2002	173.30	173.80	174.50	175.70	176.20	176.20	175.90	176.40	177.60	177.90	178.20	178.50	**2002**
2001	171.10	172.00	172.20	173.10	174.20	174.40	173.30	174.00	174.60	174.30	173.60	173.40	**2001**
2000	166.60	167.50	168.40	170.10	170.70	171.10	170.50	170.50	171.70	171.60	172.10	172.20	**2000**
1999	163.40	163.70	164.10	165.20	165.60	165.60	165.10	165.50	166.20	166.50	166.70	167.30	**1999**
1998	159.50	160.30	160.80	162.60	163.50	163.40	163.00	163.70	164.40	164.50	164.40	164.40	**1998**
1997	154.40	155.00	155.40	156.30	156.90	157.50	157.50	158.50	159.30	159.50	159.60	160.00	**1997**
1996	150.20	150.90	151.50	152.60	152.90	153.00	152.40	153.10	153.80	153.80	153.90	154.40	**1996**
1995	146.00	146.90	147.50	149.00	149.60	149.80	149.10	149.90	150.60	149.80	149.80	150.70	**1995**
1994	141.30	142.10	142.50	144.20	144.70	144.70	144.00	144.70	145.00	145.20	145.30	146.00	**1994**
1993	137.90	138.80	139.30	140.60	141.10	141.00	140.70	141.30	141.90	141.80	141.60	141.90	**1993**
1992	135.60	136.30	136.70	138.80	139.30	139.30	138.80	138.90	139.40	139.90	139.70	139.20	**1992**
1991	130.20	130.90	131.40	133.10	133.50	134.10	133.80	134.10	134.60	135.10	135.60	135.70	**1991**
1990	119.50	120.20	121.40	125.10	126.20	126.70	126.80	128.10	129.30	130.30	130.00	129.90	**1990**
1989	111.00	111.80	112.30	114.30	115.00	115.40	115.50	115.80	116.60	117.50	118.50	118.80	**1989**
1988	103.30	103.70	104.10	105.80	106.20	106.60	106.70	107.90	108.40	109.50	110.00	110.30	**1988**
1987	100.00	100.40	100.60	101.80	101.90	101.90	101.80	102.10	102.40	102.90	103.40	103.30	**1987**
1986	96.25	96.60	96.73	97.67	97.85	97.79	97.52	97.82	98.30	98.45	99.29	99.62	**1986**
1985	91.20	91.94	92.80	94.78	95.21	95.41	95.23	95.49	95.44	95.59	95.92	96.05	**1985**
1984	86.84	87.20	87.48	88.64	88.97	89.20	89.10	89.94	90.11	90.67	90.95	90.87	**1984**
1983	82.61	82.97	83.12	84.28	84.64	84.84	85.30	85.68	86.06	86.36	86.67	86.89	**1983**
1982	78.73	78.76	79.44	81.04	81.62	81.85	81.88	81.90	81.85	82.26	82.66	82.51	**1982**
1981	70.29	70.93	71.99	74.07	74.55	74.98	75.31	75.87	76.30	76.98	77.79	78.28	**1981**
1980	62.18	63.07	63.93	66.11	66.72	67.35	67.91	68.06	68.49	68.92	69.48	69.86	**1980**
1979	52.52	52.95	53.38	54.30	54.73	55.67	58.07	58.53	59.11	59.72	60.25	60.68	**1979**
1978	48.04	48.31	48.62	49.33	49.61	49.99	50.22	50.54	50.75	50.98	51.33	51.76	**1978**
1977	43.70	44.13	44.56	45.70	46.06	46.54	46.59	46.82	47.07	47.28	47.50	47.76	**1977**
1976	37.49	37.97	38.17	38.91	39.34	39.54	39.62	40.18	40.71	41.44	42.03	42.59	**1976**
1975	30.39	30.90	31.51	32.72	34.09	34.75	35.11	35.31	35.61	36.12	36.55	37.01	**1975**
1974	25.35	25.78	26.01	26.89	27.28	27.55	27.81	27.83	28.14	28.69	29.20	29.63	**1974**
1973	22.64	22.78	22.92	23.35	23.52	23.64	23.75	23.82	24.03	24.50	24.69	24.87	**1973**
1972	21.01	21.12	21.19	21.38	21.49	21.63	21.70	21.87	21.99	22.30	22.37	22.49	**1972**
1971	19.43	19.53	19.69	20.11	20.25	20.39	20.51	20.52	20.55	20.67	20.79	20.89	**1971**
1970	17.91	18.00	18.11	18.38	18.44	18.49	18.62	18.61	18.70	18.90	19.03	19.16	**1970**
	Jan	Feb	Mar	Apr	May	June	July	Aug	Sept	Oct	Nov	Dec	

	Jan	Feb	Mar	Apr	May	June	July	Aug	Sept	Oct	Nov	Dec	
1969	17.06	17.15	17.22	17.41	17.38	17.46	17.46	17.42	17.47	17.60	17.64	17.76	**1969**
1968	16.07	16.15	16.20	16.49	16.51	16.57	16.59	16.61	16.63	16.71	16.74	16.97	**1968**
1967	15.66	15.67	15.67	15.79	15.78	15.85	15.75	15.71	15.70	15.82	15.91	16.02	**1967**
1966	15.11	15.12	15.15	15.33	15.44	15.48	15.41	15.50	15.48	15.52	15.61	15.63	**1966**
1965	14.47	14.47	14.52	14.80	14.85	14.89	14.89	14.92	14.93	14.95	15.01	15.08	**1965**
1964	13.84	13.85	13.90	14.02	14.14	14.19	14.19	14.25	14.25	14.26	14.38	14.43	**1964**
1963	13.57	13.69	13.71	13.74	13.73	13.73	13.65	13.61	13.65	13.71	13.74	13.77	**1963**
1962	13.22	13.23	13.28	13.47	13.51	13.60	13.55	13.43	13.41	13.40	13.45	13.52	**1962**
1961	12.63	12.63	12.68	12.74	12.78	12.89	12.89	13.01	12.99	13.01	13.15	13.17	**1961**
1960	12.36	12.36	12.34	12.41	12.41	12.47	12.50	12.42	12.43	12.53	12.59	12.62	**1960**
1959	12.42	12.41	12.41	12.32	12.27	12.29	12.26	12.29	12.23	12.28	12.37	12.40	**1959**
1958	12.16	12.10	12.19	12.33	12.28	12.40	12.20	12.18	12.19	12.31	12.35	12.40	**1958**
1957	11.74	11.73	11.71	11.75	11.77	11.89	11.99	11.97	11.93	12.05	12.11	12.17	**1957**
1956	11.25	11.25	11.39	11.55	11.53	11.52	11.47	11.51	11.48	11.55	11.60	11.63	**1956**
1955	10.70	10.70	10.70	10.76	10.74	10.97	11.00	10.93	11.00	11.11	11.29	11.29	**1955**
1954	10.28	10.26	10.35	10.39	10.36	10.42	10.60	10.53	10.51	10.56	10.61	10.66	**1954**
1953	10.14	10.17	10.24	10.33	10.30	10.35	10.35	10.29	10.27	10.27	10.30	10.26	**1953**
1952	9.71	9.72	9.77	9.93	9.93	10.09	10.08	10.02	10.00	10.09	10.08	10.15	**1952**
1951	8.60	8.68	8.74	8.88	9.10	9.13	9.27	9.31	9.38	9.44	9.48	9.54	**1951**
1950	8.28	8.30	8.32	8.35	8.37	8.33	8.33	8.30	8.35	8.44	8.47	8.52	**1950**
1949	7.99	8.01	7.98	7.96	8.11	8.14	8.15	8.16	8.19	8.23	8.23	8.25	**1949**
1948	7.64	7.78	7.80	7.91	7.90	8.04	7.92	7.92	7.93	7.95	7.97	7.98	**1948**
1947	–	–	–	–	–	7.33	7.38	7.34	7.37	7.43	7.58	7.60	**1947**
	Jan	Feb	Mar	Apr	May	June	July	Aug	Sept	Oct	Nov	Dec	

Note:

To calculate the equivalent value of a lump sum, divide by the RPI at the time and multiply the result by the current RPI. Thus £460.00 in June 1981 would be calculated as:

$$\left(\frac{460}{74.98}\right) \times \text{current RPI}$$

to show the relative value of that amount in 'today's money'.

E2: Inflation table

Introductory notes

Showing the value of the £ at various dates.

In the left-hand column of this table is the year and in the right-hand column the multiplier which should be applied to the £ in January of that year to show its value in terms of the £ in January 2009.

This table has been calculated from the Official Retail Prices Index, the value of the £ being taken from the figures published in January of each year, ending with January 2009.

Year	Multiplier	Year	Multiplier
1948	27.46	1981	2.98
1949	26.26	1982	2.66
1950	25.34	1983	2.54
		1984	2.42
1951	24.40	1985	2.30
1952	21.61		
1953	20.69	1986	2.18
1954	20.41	1987	2.10
1955	19.61	1988	2.03
		1989	1.89
1956	18.65	1990	1.76
1957	17.87		
1958	17.25	1991	1.61
1959	16.89	1992	1.55
1960	16.97	1993	1.52
		1994	1.49
1961	16.61	1995	1.44
1962	15.87		
1963	15.46	1996	1.40
1964	15.16	1997	1.36
1965	14.50	1998	1.32
		1999	1.29
1966	13.88	2000	1.26
1967	13.40		
1968	13.06	2001	1.23
1969	12.30	2002	1.21
1970	11.71	2003	1.18
		2004	1.15
1971	10.80	2005	1.11
1972	9.99		
1973	9.27	2006	1.09
1974	8.28	2007	1.04
1975	6.90	2008	1.00
		2009	1.00
1976	5.60		
1977	4.80		
1978	4.37		
1979	3.99		
1980	3.37		

E3: House price indices

Introductory notes

1. There are several price indices available in April 2009. These include the Halifax, Nationwide, the Financial Times, the Royal Institute of Chartered Surveyors, Hometrack, Rightmove, the Government Index and the Land Registry index.

2. The editors of "Facts & Figures" have used the Halifax table in previous editions and continue to do so. The Index Year for the Halifax table is 1983. In certain circumstances, the data offered by other indices may be useful. For example the Land Registry figures are broken down regionally and contain information about the numbers of first-time buyers. However, they exclude cash purchases which account for about a quarter of all transactions. Each table has strengths and weaknesses of this sort.

3. None of the indices should be treated as definitive. They can only be used as guides to the movement of prices over longer periods of time. Readers should be cautious about over-interpreting the analysis of short-term price changes.

All Houses

	U.K.			North		Yorks/Humb		N. West	
Year	Index	%	Average Price £	Index	%	Index	%	Index	%
91	220.5	−1.2	68,130	213.5	2.8	240.4	1.2	236.3	3.9
92	208.1	−5.6	64,309	210.1	−1.6	231.9	−3.6	226.1	−4.3
93	202.1	−2.9	62,455	206.3	−1.8	228.3	−1.6	219.3	−3.0
94	203.1	0.5	62,750	203.6	−1.3	226.3	−0.9	215.8	−1.6
95	199.6	−1.7	61,666	195.9	−3.8	219.2	−3.1	207.8	−3.7
96	208.6	4.5	64,441	201.9	3.1	224.5	2.4	210.7	1.4
97	221.7	6.3	68,504	206.5	2.3	228.5	1.8	216.7	2.9
98	233.7	5.4	72,196	211.2	2.3	229.8	0.5	220.4	1.7
99	250.5	7.2	77,405	220.1	4.2	236.5	2.9	231.0	4.8
00	275.1	9.8	85,005	221.9	0.8	243.9	3.2	242.6	5.0
01	298.6	8.5	92,256	234.0	5.5	257.5	5.6	255.7	5.4
02	350.6	17.4	108,342	271.4	16.0	297.7	15.6	292.8	14.5
03	429.1	22.4	132,589	370.6	36.5	395.6	32.9	366.3	25.1
04	507.6	18.3	156,831	490.3	32.3	495.0	25.1	472.8	29.1
05	536.6	5.7	165,807	533.3	8.8	549.3	11.0	523.7	10.8
06	581.3	8.3	179,601	567.3	6.4	602.4	9.7	565.1	7.9
07	635.9	9.4	196,478	601.8	6.1	640.5	6.3	596.8	5.6
08	585.9	−7.9	181,032	547.2	−9.1	580.0	−9.5	558.3	−6.5

	E. Midlands		W. Midlands		E. Anglia		S. West		S. East	
Year	Index	%	Index	%	Index	%	Index	%	Index	%
91	227.9	−2.8	240.4	1.0	214.4	−5.0	210.4	−5.1	210.8	−6.1
92	214.4	−5.9	229.4	−4.6	198.5	−7.4	193.9	−7.8	192.8	−8.5
93	208.3	−2.8	219.1	−4.5	193.2	−2.7	185.9	−4.1	186.4	−3.3
94	209.1	0.4	218.3	−0.4	195.8	1.3	186.6	1.5	189.8	1.8
95	203.9	−2.5	215.6	−1.2	193.5	−1.1	186.1	−1.3	190.3	0.3
96	209.4	2.7	224.6	4.2	197.7	2.1	195.1	4.8	199.9	5.0
97	221.5	5.8	237.3	5.6	211.0	6.7	209.7	7.5	221.2	10.7
98	229.9	3.8	250.0	5.4	224.4	6.4	226.4	8.0	244.2	10.4
99	244.8	6.5	254.7	1.9	241.1	7.5	248.8	9.9	271.2	11.0
00	265.0	8.2	282.2	10.8	279.7	16.0	291.0	17.0	318.3	17.4
01	287.3	8.4	301.5	6.8	322.6	15.4	327.8	12.6	354.7	11.4
02	361.7	25.9	363.7	20.7	386.0	19.6	403.4	23.0	413.7	16.6
03	457.5	26.5	460.7	26.7	465.0	20.5	477.7	18.4	483.8	17.0
04	541.4	18.3	540.5	17.3	522.3	12.3	545.4	14.2	528.8	9.3
05	564.9	4.3	565.4	4.6	536.0	2.6	552.6	1.3	537.0	1.5
06	599.4	6.1	602.8	6.6	581.1	8.4	587.5	6.3	571.2	6.4
07	632.4	5.5	640.4	6.2	637.3	9.7	641.9	9.3	636.9	11.5
08	582.0	−8.0	591.9	−7.6	600.8	−5.7	583.2	−9.1	588.6	−7.6

	Gr. London		Wales		Scotland		N. Ireland	
Year	Index	%	Index	%	Index	%	Index	%
91	222.9	−5.8	217.1	−1.1	192.8	5.9	146.9	11.2
92	202.0	−9.4	207.7	−4.3	193.2	0.2	145.5	−1.0
93	192.0	−4.9	204.5	−1.6	196.4	1.6	151.7	4.3
94	195.5	1.8	201.9	−1.2	199.4	1.6	162.1	6.9
95	194.9	−0.4	194.2	−3.8	199.4	0.0	172.8	6.6
96	212.4	9.0	205.5	5.9	204.9	2.8	204.5	18.3
97	246.3	16.0	212.0	3.1	204.7	−0.1	210.6	3.0
98	272.3	10.5	220.2	3.8	209.8	2.5	235.6	11.9
99	317.9	16.8	232.3	5.5	212.8	1.4	248.8	5.6
00	373.6	17.5	245.0	5.5	214.2	0.7	264.4	6.3
01	428.3	14.7	263.8	7.7	220.0	2.7	296.8	12.2
02	499.4	16.6	299.8	13.6	238.5	8.4	307.4	3.6
03	563.3	12.8	397.2	32.5	274.5	15.1	340.3	10.7
04	608.5	8.0	516.3	30.0	330.6	20.4	397.9	16.9
05	621.4	2.1	553.7	7.3	375.7	13.6	486.0	22.1
06	680.9	9.6	589.7	6.5	421.7	12.2	581.3	32.6
07	777.6	14.2	640.7	8.7	488.2	15.8	844.5	31.1
08	705.3	−9.3	579.4	−9.6	478.2	−2.1	679.2	−19.6

New Houses

Year	U.K. Index	U.K. %	Average Price £	North Index	North %	Yorks/Humb Index	Yorks/Humb %	N. West Index	N. West %
91	204.0	−1.8	70,987	198.3	3.1	214.0	1.7	206.5	4.2
92	197.8	−3.3	68,634	200.6	1.1	210.1	−1.8	199.7	−3.3
93	195.0	−1.1	67,856	200.6	0.0	210.6	0.3	195.3	−2.2
94	195.5	0.3	68,032	196.8	−1.9	208.7	−0.9	189.1	−3.2
95	196.0	0.2	68,183	199.4	1.3	206.5	−1.0	185.3	−2.0
96	199.6	1.9	69,453	195.5	−1.9	216.1	4.6	187.7	1.3
97	204.8	2.6	71,248	197.4	1.0	211.8	−2.0	191.1	1.8
98	217.9	6.4	75,806	212.7	7.7	220.2	4.0	203.5	6.5
99	228.1	4.7	79,384	221.2	4.0	238.0	8.0	202.7	−0.4
00	257.8	13.0	89,709	215.5	−2.6	274.1	15.2	232.5	14.7
01	276.6	7.3	96,252	228.2	5.9	291.4	6.3	237.5	2.2
02	318.5	15.1	110,832	260.1	14.0	302.9	3.9	270.2	13.8
03	380.5	19.4	132,383	316.3	21.6	392.2	29.5	311.2	15.2
04	443.3	16.5	154,235	382.4	20.9	450.3	14.8	441.1	41.8
05	461.6	4.1	160,615	454.5	18.9	501.8	11.4	453.5	2.8
06	497.3	7.7	173,026	459.0	1.0	526.0	4.8	448.3	−1.2
07	550.0	10.6	191,372	517.0	12.6	564.3	7.3	528.5	17.9
08	547.5	−0.4	190,517	520.4	0.7	501.1	−11.2	542.4	2.6

Year	E. Midlands Index	E. Midlands %	W. Midlands Index	W. Midlands %	E. Anglia Index	E. Anglia %	S. West Index	S. West %	S. East Index	S. East %
91	213.5	−1.6	214.4	−0.4	210.1	−6.7	209.4	−5.1	209.9	−6.1
92	204.3	−4.3	213.0	−0.6	199.8	−4.9	194.8	−7.0	194.3	−7.4
93	204.3	0.0	213.7	0.3	196.0	−1.9	191.2	−1.8	190.1	−2.1
94	201.5	−1.3	214.5	0.4	198.8	1.4	189.4	−0.9	194.8	2.4
95	205.9	2.2	210.0	−2.1	202.7	1.9	187.5	−1.0	192.1	−1.3
96	210.7	2.4	220.4	5.0	196.8	−2.9	190.3	1.5	200.0	4.1
97	221.3	5.0	228.5	3.7	211.3	7.4	207.2	8.8	215.5	7.8
98	232.2	4.9	243.6	6.6	219.7	4.0	217.2	4.8	235.8	9.4
99	243.7	4.9	239.8	−1.6	232.7	5.9	229.5	5.7	257.4	9.2
00	253.4	4.0	279.3	16.5	279.6	20.2	260.9	13.7	295.9	15.0
01	266.6	5.2	314.8	12.7	315.3	12.8	293.9	12.7	318.9	7.8
02	346.0	29.8	343.5	9.1	383.6	21.7	345.9	17.7	377.1	18.3
03	417.5	20.7	414.9	20.8	414.6	8.1	408.6	18.1	452.5	20.0
04	501.0	20.0	500.6	20.6	460.3	11.0	460.6	12.7	486.5	7.5
05	518.6	3.5	507.9	1.5	544.8	18.4	461.6	0.2	507.3	4.3
06	576.7	11.2	546.9	7.7	541.9	−0.6	497.7	7.8	514.2	1.4
07	596.6	3.5	614.4	12.3	604.7	11.7	518.0	4.1	569.4	10.7
08	583.5	−2.2	637.7	3.8	640.1	5.9	533.4	3.0	562.5	−1.2

Year	Gr. London Index	Gr. London %	Wales Index	Wales %	Scotland Index	Scotland %	N. Ireland Index	N. Ireland %
91	209.4	−6.4	203.2	−2.8	179.9	6.8	156.7	7.0
92	198.2	−5.4	201.0	−1.1	185.8	3.3	158.3	1.0
93	194.4	−1.9	198.7	−1.2	188.5	1.5	160.2	1.2
94	190.0	−2.3	200.1	0.7	191.7	1.7	172.2	7.5
95	188.1	−1.0	200.2	0.0	194.0	1.2	187.8	9.1
96	194.2	3.3	203.4	1.6	190.2	−2.0	208.5	11.0
97	202.2	4.1	205.4	1.0	190.0	−0.1	216.4	3.8
98	221.6	9.6	220.0	7.1	210.9	11.0	244.8	13.1
99	240.4	8.5	221.3	0.6	212.7	0.8	238.5	−2.6
00	302.6	25.9	243.6	10.1	214.2	0.7	269.4	13.0
01	364.1	20.3	253.8	4.2	218.4	2.0	267.3	−0.7
02	394.9	8.4	279.9	10.3	240.8	10.2	231.4	−13.0
03	480.3	21.6	366.1	30.8	270.4	12.3	324.2	40.1
04	492.5	2.6	471.4	28.8	324.4	20.0	384.8	18.7
05	330.5	7.7	529.6	12.3	361.8	11.5	487.9	26.8
06	597.0	12.5	507.8	−4.1	386.4	6.8	557.3	14.2
07	741.4	24.2	574.4	13.1	463.3	19.9	550.0	10.6
08	714.0	−3.7	481.4	−16.2	491.2	6.0	639.3	−13.3

Existing Houses

Year	U.K. Index	U.K. %	U.K. Average Price £	North Index	North %	Yorks/Humb Index	Yorks/Humb %	N. West Index	N. West %
91	223.1	−1.2	67,717	217.0	2.3	243.3	1.0	241.1	3.4
92	210.2	−5.8	63,797	212.1	−2.3	234.5	−3.6	230.2	−4.5
93	204.0	−3.0	61,911	208.5	−1.7	230.0	−1.9	222.8	−3.2
94	205.1	0.5	62,250	205.6	−1.4	227.9	−0.9	219.5	−1.5
95	201.3	−1.8	61,099	197.1	−4.1	220.0	−3.5	211.1	−3.8
96	211.0	4.8	64,044	204.1	3.5	225.7	2.6	214.1	1.5
97	225.2	6.7	68,334	209.4	2.6	230.3	2.0	220.9	3.2
98	237.3	5.4	72,030	212.6	1.5	231.1	0.3	224.5	1.6
99	255.0	7.5	77,396	222.7	4.8	237.6	2.8	235.5	4.9
00	280.3	9.9	85,061	226.5	1.7	246.8	3.9	245.1	4.1
01	305.8	9.1	92,795	240.2	6.1	259.9	5.3	261.3	6.6
02	360.1	17.8	109,274	278.9	16.1	303.4	16.8	299.5	14.6
03	440.9	22.5	133,808	383.4	37.5	402.6	32.7	377.0	25.8
04	521.0	18.2	158,111	508.5	32.6	505.5	25.6	483.8	28.4
05	549.6	5.5	166,810	550.7	8.3	557.8	10.3	536.1	10.8
06	596.6	8.6	181,081	590.0	7.1	613.0	9.9	580.0	8.2
07	650.4	9.0	197,384	621.1	5.3	650.9	6.2	610.7	5.3
08	592.5	−8.9	179,826	560.9	−9.7	588.7	−9.6	564.1	−8.1

Year	E. Midlands Index	E. Midlands %	W. Midlands Index	W. Midlands %	E. Anglia Index	E. Anglia %	S. West Index	S. West %	S. East Index	S. East %
91	230.7	−2.9	244.9	0.7	215.4	−4.5	210.4	−5.4	210.8	−5.8
92	216.3	−6.2	232.0	−5.3	198.9	−7.7	194.2	−7.7	192.7	−8.6
93	210.2	−2.8	220.6	−4.9	193.6	−2.6	186.1	−4.2	186.2	−3.4
94	210.7	0.2	220.8	0.1	197.1	1.8	189.5	1.8	189.9	2.0
95	205.1	−2.6	217.9	−1.3	193.6	−1.8	187.1	−1.3	190.7	0.4
96	211.4	3.0	227.8	4.6	198.7	2.6	197.1	5.3	200.9	5.3
97	223.6	5.8	240.9	5.7	212.5	7.0	212.6	7.9	223.8	11.4
98	232.0	3.7	252.8	4.9	226.5	6.6	230.3	8.3	247.8	10.7
99	246.6	6.3	259.1	2.5	244.1	7.7	254.5	10.5	274.8	10.9
00	267.0	8.2	285.7	10.3	283.4	16.1	298.6	17.3	324.4	18.1
01	294.3	10.3	308.9	8.1	331.7	17.1	336.7	12.8	361.9	11.6
02	371.5	26.2	377.0	22.0	398.2	20.1	413.1	22.7	422.2	16.7
03	468.8	26.2	475.0	26.0	481.5	20.9	492.0	19.1	489.9	16.0
04	553.0	18.0	552.7	16.3	540.8	12.3	561.1	14.0	535.3	9.3
05	576.5	4.3	577.5	4.5	546.2	1.0	568.6	1.3	542.9	1.4
06	605.8	5.1	614.6	6.4	591.3	8.3	605.5	6.5	577.8	6.4
07	640.9	5.8	647.6	5.4	647.0	9.4	663.6	9.6	642.4	11.2
08	582.9	−9.1	594.4	−8.2	601.0	−7.1	595.0	−10.3	592.8	−7.7

Year	Gr. London Index	Gr. London %	Wales Index	Wales %	Scotland Index	Scotland %	N. Ireland Index	N. Ireland %
91	223.6	−5.6	220.0	−1.2	197.1	5.7	144.9	11.8
92	202.7	−9.4	208.8	−5.1	197.6	0.2	144.2	−0.4
93	192.6	−5.0	206.2	−1.3	199.4	0.9	152.6	5.8
94	196.5	2.0	203.3	−1.4	201.8	1.2	162.6	6.6
95	195.3	−0.6	195.0	−4.1	201.5	−0.1	173.8	6.9
96	213.0	9.1	207.5	6.4	208.6	3.5	206.4	18.7
97	248.6	16.7	214.8	3.5	208.0	−0.3	214.0	3.7
98	274.8	10.5	223.0	3.8	214.1	2.9	240.8	12.5
99	319.7	16.3	235.8	5.7	216.7	1.2	256.7	6.6
00	377.9	18.2	247.7	5.1	219.2	1.1	275.3	7.2
01	433.2	14.6	269.6	8.8	228.8	4.4	310.5	12.8
02	507.2	17.1	307.9	14.2	249.3	9.0	322.7	3.9
03	569.8	12.4	408.5	32.7	289.2	16.0	349.2	8.2
04	614.1	7.8	534.0	30.7	347.4	20.1	409.3	17.2
05	623.9	1.6	571.3	7.0	394.7	13.6	489.9	19.7
06	686.8	10.1	604.6	5.8	443.2	12.3	668.4	36.4
07	786.9	14.6	653.7	8.1	507.9	14.6	871.2	30.3
08	692.9	−11.9	593.1	−9.3	493.5	−2.8	677.0	−22.3

Reproduced here with the kind permission of Halifax Plc.

E4: Average semi-detached house prices by region

Prices are as of the first quarter of 2009.

Region	£
North	120,739
North West	134,346
West Midlands	132,738
South East	212,077
Greater London	282,700
Yorkshire & Humberside	122,098
East Midlands	116,562
East Anglia	159,230
South West	165,487
Scotland	138,469
Wales	125,536
Northern Ireland	144,393

Group F
Earnings

F1: Earnings losses in personal injury and fatal accident cases

1. **Purpose of note**

The purpose of this note is to provide some basic guidance on what information to request from a Claimant in order to make an initial assessment as to whether an earnings loss is likely to arise.

2. **Nature of occupation**

Identify at an early stage into which category of occupation the Claimant falls:

Employment
— Employee without ownership rights
— Director/shareholder (of private company)

Self-employment
— Sole trader
— Partner

3. **Relevant dates**

For the purposes of proposing the periods for which information should be requested, relevant dates will be identified as follows:

For an individual in employment
(References here are to tax years ending on April 5, although the tax for many salaried employees will often effectively run from April 1 to March 31.)

D1 April 6 three years before D2
D2 April 5 immediately preceding D3
D3 Incident date
D4 April 5 immediately preceding D5
D5 Present time

For business accounts
D6 Date of beginning of accounting period three years before D7
D7 Date of end of accounting period immediately preceding D3
D8 Date of end of accounting period immediately preceding D5

A full three years' pre-accident financial information should often be sufficient (having regard to the need for proportionality), although documentation for a longer period may be appropriate if it emerges that business results have been volatile.

For an individual in employment

D1		D2	D3		D4	D5
			Incident			
April 6 April 5	April 6 April 5	April 6 April 5	April 6 April 5	April 6 April 5	April 6 April 5	April 6 Present time
Tax year −3	Tax year −2	Tax year −1	Tax year 0	Tax year +1	Current tax year −1	Current tax year

The shaded area represents the minimum period for which pay advices should be requested.

For business accounts

D6					D7	D3 Incident					D8		D5
Beginning	End	Beginning	End	Beginning	End	Beginning	End	Beginning	End	Beginning	End	Beginning	Present time
Accounts year −3		Accounts year −2		Accounts year −1		Accounts year 0		Accounts year +1		Current accounts year −1		Current accounts year	

The shaded area represents the minimum period for which business accounts should be requested.

4. **Employment: Employee without ownership rights**

This is the likely category for most employees—but excluding in particular those who are directors and/or shareholders with a degree of control over private companies.

In the absence of detailed representations from the employer, or from an employment expert, the earnings history may be the only useful guide to potential earnings but for the incident giving rise to the claim.

The most useful documentation will usually be a comprehensive set of pay advices (monthly, sometimes 4-weekly, or weekly) because these may be expected to show:

- Basic pay level (and dates/amounts of periodic increases)
- Overtime (if paid) and any other regular or periodic enhancements
- Bonuses (and dates/amounts paid)
- Sick pay (and dates)
- Employee pension contributions

Request:

- **Pay advices (whether from employment or subsequent pension) from D1* to D5***
- **Details of benefits other than pay for each tax year between D1* and D2* and for each tax year since D2***

* See 3 above

5. **Employment : Director/shareholders**

This category relates mainly to those individuals who have a degree of ownership or control, probably in a private company, and whose remuneration as such may not be a fair reflection of the personal reward available from the business.

For instance:

- Profits may have been drawn by way of dividend for reasons of tax efficiency; or
- Profits (which the Claimant could have drawn) have been re-invested in the business.

It may well be appropriate to assess loss along the lines that would be adopted in relation to a sole trader or partner, that is:

- Firstly to identify whether a business loss has occurred that is attributable to the claim incident.
- If so, go on to identify the share of the business loss suffered personally by the Claimant.

In such a case, it will often be appropriate to review not only the remuneration history of the individual but also the dividend history. Benefits history may also be important.

Request:

Regarding the Business

- **Full accounts (including detailed profit and loss accounts) from D6* to D8***

  and consider requesting

- **Figures for monthly (preferably) or quarterly sales from D6* to D5***
  (important if the Claimant's role is likely to have influenced Sales levels; the figures should show up trends and seasonality etc)

Regarding the Claimant

- **Pay advices (whether from employment or pension) from D1* to D5***
- **Tax returns from D1* to D4***
  (mainly to check remuneration and dividends received in each tax year, but also benefits and any personal pension contributions etc)

6. **Self-employment : Sole trader**

Request:

- **Full accounts from D6* to D8***
- **Figures for monthly or quarterly sales from D6* to D5***
- **Tax returns from D1* to D4***
  (mainly to check private usage deductions from business expenses, capital allowances, personal pension contributions etc)

7. **Self-employment : Partner**

Approach will be:

- Firstly to identify whether a business loss has occurred that is attributable to the claim incident.
- If so, go on to identify the share of the business loss suffered personally by the Claimant.

Request:

Regarding the Business

- **Full partnership accounts from D6* to D8***
- **Figures for monthly (preferably) or quarterly sales from D6* to D5***

Regarding the Claimant

- **Personal tax returns from D1* to D4***
  (mainly to check personal pension contributions etc)

8. **Benefits other than pay (employees)**

In the first instance, it is probably sufficient simply to ask, in relation to any employee (including a company director), for:

- **Details of any non-pecuniary benefits in employment, and any pension benefits**

9. **Other points**

- **Company searches**

Searches of small UK limited companies seldom yield helpful results as regards accounts because the contents of the accounts to be filed are invariably in shortened form, sometimes only a balance sheet.

In cases where there are doubts about full disclosure, a search may be useful in identifying whether a Claimant has more directorships than advised, or possibly a history of connections with insolvent companies.

- **Permanent Health Insurance income**

Where a Claimant receives insurance money through his employer, this will usually be evident from review of the pay advices.

As to whether credit needs to be given by the Claimant for such insurance money for claim purposes will probably depend on the nature of the underlying policy.

- **Ill-health pension**

Where a Claimant receives an ill-health pension following an incident, this should again be evident from review of the pay advices.

Generally, no credit is to be given for actual pension in a loss of earnings claim: *Parry v Cleaver* [1970] A.C. 1.

- **Partnerships**

There may be cases where the profit-sharing arrangements do not reflect the realistic commercial input of the respective partners. This issue may arise particularly where spouses are business partners. The Court may be prepared to put aside the historic arrangements in assessing loss: *Ward v Newall Insulation Co Ltd* [1998] 1 W.L.R. 1722.

F2: How to read a payslip

SPECIMEN PAY ADVICE

Employee name		Employer name
Mr G BROWN		FirstLord Limited
Pay Date	Tax period	Tax Code
31 MARCH 2009	12	603L

Pay and allowances (* non-taxable)	£	Deductions/(Refunds)	£	Totals to date	£
Salary	2,500.00			Taxable gross	33,800.00
Car allowance *	275.00			Car allowance *	1,650.00
		Income tax	379.40	Income tax	5,553.00
		National insurance	192.44	National insurance	2,430.00
		Pension	100.00	Pension	1,200.00
Total	2,775.00	Total	671.84	Net pay	2,103.16

Points to note

1 As good a starting point as any is usually a pay advice for the **last full tax year**, but try also to obtain all subsequent pay advices whether to date of trial in a personal injury case or to date of death if a fatal accident.

2 It is worth bearing in mind that some employers pay every 4 weeks, and on rare occasions every 2 weeks, rather than necessarily monthly or weekly. The **tax period** should help to identify payment frequency.

3 The tax code, 603L, represents the basic tax allowance of £6,035. This indicates that the tax inspector has no reason to make any adjustment to the standard code to collect additional tax due in the year.

This in turn implies that the employee has no taxable benefits from the employer.

The most common taxable benefits are probably health insurance cover and those related to private use of motor vehicles.

By way of example, were the employee enjoying benefits to a value of £1,000 pa, the code could be expected to be 503L. Application of this code would result in the tax due on the benefit being collected under PAYE over the course of the tax year.

4 In the illustration shown above, the **gross taxable income** figure requires some reconciliation to other figures.

The year-end figures suggest that salary has probably been running consistently at £2,500 per month, with a £100 per month pension contribution; that would be a net total of £28,800 in the year, suggesting that there has been additional pay of £5,000.

The figure for the year's total **National Insurance** for the year is consistent with a salary of £2,500 per month, with a single addition of £5,000.

So the gross taxable appears likely to comprise £30,000 salary, a one-off addition of £5,000 less £1,200 pension.

5. The combination of a **pension deduction** which appears to represent exactly 4% of salary, together with the fact that it can readily be established that the national insurance contributions are at contracted out rates, suggests that the employee is a member of a final salary pension scheme which may give rise to a pension loss claim.

   (In the case of a money purchase pension scheme, the deductions are made less basic rate tax, 20% in 2008/09, so a monthly contribution of £100.00 to such a scheme is improbable.)

6. **A car allowance** is shown but it is marked as non-taxable.

   Note also that the totals to date suggest that the allowance has been in payment for only 6 months in the year.

   Generally, if an allowance is non-taxable, it is unlikely to represent a valuable benefit. Perhaps the car allowance in this case is a fixed level reimbursement of business costs on a prescribed formula which will be adjusted after the year-end in accordance with actual business mileage or the like.

   Nevertheless it would be worth establishing why the car allowance was not in payment throughout the year.

F3: National Minimum Wage

Introductory notes

1. The National Minimum Wage became law on April 1, 1999.
2. The National Minimum Wage is the minimum amount of pay to which workers over a specified age are entitled. Up to September 30, 2004, the minimum age was 18. Since October 1, 2004 a new rate has been available to workers under 18 who are no longer of compulsory school age.
3. Most adult workers who are resident in the UK, who have a written, oral or implied contract and who are not genuinely self-employed, are entitled to the National Minimum Wage.
4. The National Minimum Wage is enforced by HM Revenue and Customs.
5. There are three levels of National Minimum Wage: a development rate for those aged between 18 and 21; a main rate for workers aged 22 or over; and, from October 1, 2004, a development rate for workers under 18 who are no longer of compulsory school age.
6. A development rate available, subject to various conditions, to workers aged 22 or over who started a new job with a new employer and did accredited training, being a course approved by the UK government to obtain a vocational qualification, was abolished for pay reference periods starting on or after October 1, 2006. When applicable, the accredited training rate can only be paid for the first six months of the new job, after which the National Minimum Wage main rate applied.

Rates

Workers under 18 who are no longer of compulsory school age (notes 2 and 5)
Pay reference periods starting on or after:

	1/6/00	**1/10/01**	**1/10/02**	**1/10/03**	**1/10/04**
	£ per hour	£ per hour	£ per hour	£ per hour	£ per hour
Hourly rate	–	–	–	–	3.00
	1/10/05	**1/10/06**	**1/10/07**	**1/10/08**	**1/10/09**
	£ per hour	£ per hour	£ per hour	£ per hour	£ per hour
Hourly rate	3.00	3.30	3.40	3.53	3.57

Development rate for workers aged 18 to 21 years (note 5)
Pay reference periods starting on or after:

	1/6/00	**1/10/01**	**1/10/02**	**1/10/03**	**1/10/04**
	£ per hour	£ per hour	£ per hour	£ per hour	£ per hour
Hourly rate	3.20	3.50	3.60	3.80	4.10
	1/10/05	**1/10/06**	**1/10/07**	**1/10/08**	**1/10/09**
	£ per hour	£ per hour	£ per hour	£ per hour	£ per hour
Hourly rate	4.25	4.45	4.60	4.77	4.83

Main rate for workers aged 22 or over (note 5)

Pay reference periods starting on or after:

	1/10/00	**1/10/01**	**1/10/02**	**1/10/03**	**1/10/04**
	£ per hour	£ per hour	£ per hour	£ per hour	£ per hour
Hourly rate	3.70	4.10	4.20	4.50	4.85
	1/10/05	**1/10/06**	**1/10/07**	**1/10/08**	**1/10/09**
	£ per hour	£ per hour	£ per hour	£ per hour	£ per hour
Hourly rate	5.05	5.35	5.52	5.73	5.80

Development rate for workers aged 22 years or over doing accredited training (note 6)

Pay reference periods starting on or after:

	1/10/00	**1/10/01**	**1/10/02**	**1/10/03**	**1/10/04**
	£ per hour	£ per hour	£ per hour	£ per hour	£ per hour
Hourly rate	3.20	3.50	3.60	3.80	4.10
	1/10/05	**1/10/06**	**1/10/07**	**1/10/08**	**1/10/09**
	£ per hour	£ per hour	£ per hour	£ per hour	£ per hour
Hourly rate	4.25	4.65	N/A	N/A	N/A

F4: Regional unemployment statistics

The following tables show the average duration of claims for benefits, terminating the quarter ending October 2008. They are taken from the Office of National Statistics Economic and Labour Market Review, January 2009 edition. They should be used with caution: they can only give the broadest of indications of what is actually happening in any region, and their interpretation is a matter for experts.

Generally, unemployment is rising. Before the recent recession, the pattern appeared to be that those in work who lost a job, while experiencing some time on the labour market, returned to work quickly. Those who became "long-term unemployed" (i.e. those who had been without work for 52 weeks or more) experienced difficulty in finding work. Those who had an accident or injury might typically fall into the latter category.

Using the "Summary Regional Labour Market Unemployment Statistics" as well, a good picture can be built up for the overall economic climate of an area, and whether there are exceptional difficulties, particularly for the hardcore or long-term unemployed.

United Kingdom

AGE	Mean Duration (weeks)			Median Duration (weeks)		
(years)	Female	Male	All	Female	Male	All
16–17	10	9	10	7	6	7
18–19	12	12	12	8	8	8
20–24	13	14	14	8	8	8
25–29	15	19	18	8	11	10
30–34	17	23	22	9	12	11
35–39	19	25	23	10	13	12
40–44	20	26	24	10	13	12
45–49	20	26	24	10	13	12
50–54	22	30	27	10	13	12
55–59	30	42	38	12	15	14
60 & over	102	35	36	37	12	12
All ages	16	21	19	9	10	10

North East

	Mean Duration (weeks)			Median Duration (weeks)		
(years)	Female	Male	All	Female	Male	All
16–17	8	8	8	5	6	6
18–19	12	12	12	8	8	8
20–24	13	14	13	8	9	8
25–29	15	19	18	9	10	10
30–34	18	23	22	10	12	11
35–39	19	24	23	10	12	11
40–44	20	25	23	10	12	11
45–49	19	24	22	10	11	10
50–54	19	28	25	11	11	11
55–59	32	46	42	14	13	13
60 & over	0	28	30	0	9	9
All ages	16	20	19	9	10	9

North West & Merseyside (GOR)

AGE	Mean Duration (weeks)			Median Duration (weeks)		
(years)	Female	Male	All	Female	Male	All
16–17	10	9	9	7	6	7
18–19	12	12	12	7	7	7
20–24	13	14	13	8	8	8
25–29	15	19	18	8	10	10
30–34	16	22	21	9	11	11
35–39	17	24	22	9	12	11
40–44	18	25	23	10	12	11
45–49	19	24	22	9	12	11
50–54	19	27	24	9	12	11
55–59	25	37	33	10	13	12
60 & over	0	32	32	0	10	10
All ages	15	19	18	8	10	9

Yorks & Humberside

	Mean Duration (weeks)			Median Duration (weeks)		
(years)	Female	Male	All	Female	Male	All
16–17	9	8	8	6	5	6
18–19	13	13	13	8	8	8
20–24	13	14	14	8	9	8
25–29	16	19	19	9	11	10
30–34	18	23	22	10	13	12
35–39	19	24	23	10	13	12
40–44	19	24	23	9	13	12
45–49	19	24	22	10	13	11
50–54	21	29	26	10	13	12
55–59	27	46	39	12	14	13
60 & over	0	38	38	0	11	11
All ages	16	20	19	9	10	10

East Midlands

AGE (years)	Mean Duration (weeks) Female	Male	All	Median Duration (weeks) Female	Male	All
16–17	10	9	9	7	6	6
18–19	13	13	13	8	8	8
20–24	14	15	15	9	11	10
25–29	17	21	20	8	11	10
30–34	17	23	22	9	12	11
35–39	18	24	22	10	13	12
40–44	19	26	24	10	13	12
45–49	18	26	23	10	13	11
50–54	21	29	26	10	13	11
55–59	30	36	33	13	14	13
60 & over	0	28	28	0	13	13
All ages	17	21	20	9	11	10

Eastern

AGE (years)	Mean Duration (weeks) Female	Male	All	Median Duration (weeks) Female	Male	All
16–17	12	10	11	8	7	8
18–19	13	12	12	8	7	8
20–24	13	14	14	8	9	8
25–29	16	20	19	9	11	10
30–34	18	23	22	10	12	11
35–39	17	25	23	9	14	12
40–44	18	25	23	10	13	12
45–49	20	25	23	9	13	12
50–54	21	28	25	11	13	12
55–59	26	35	32	12	14	14
60 & over	51	33	34	53	13	13
All ages	16	21	19	9	11	10

South East (GOR)

AGE (years)	Mean Duration (weeks) Female	Male	All	Median Duration (weeks) Female	Male	All
16–17	10	9	9	7	6	7
18–19	12	11	11	7	7	7
20–24	11	13	12	7	8	7
25–29	13	17	16	7	9	9
30–34	15	20	19	8	10	10
35–39	17	22	21	9	11	10
40–44	18	22	21	9	11	11
45–49	19	24	22	10	11	11
50–54	19	26	24	10	11	11
55–59	24	34	30	11	13	12
60 & over	57	25	25	23	11	11
All ages	15	19	18	8	0	9

West Midlands

(years)	Mean Duration (weeks) Female	Male	All	Median Duration (weeks) Female	Male	All
16–17	11	10	11	8	7	7
18–19	14	13	14	8	8	8
20–24	15	16	16	8	9	9
25–29	18	23	22	9	12	11
30–34	22	27	26	12	14	13
35–39	21	30	28	11	15	14
40–44	22	30	27	10	14	13
45–49	21	29	26	11	14	13
50–54	22	33	29	10	14	13
55–59	31	38	35	13	15	14
60 & over	570	41	41	570	14	14
All ages	18	23	22	9	11	11

London

(years)	Mean Duration (weeks) Female	Male	All	Median Duration (weeks) Female	Male	All
16–17	12	11	12	9	8	8
18–19	12	12	12	8	8	8
20–24	14	15	14	8	9	9
25–29	18	21	20	9	12	11
30–34	20	26	24	9	14	13
35–39	22	29	27	12	16	15
40–44	26	31	30	14	17	16
45–49	28	32	31	15	17	16
50–54	30	40	36	15	20	18
55–59	43	55	50	18	21	20
60 & over	79	58	59	50	17	18
All ages	20	9	9	7	6	7

South West

(years)	Mean Duration (weeks) Female	Male	All	Median Duration (weeks) Female	Male	All
16–17	11	10	10	7	6	6
18–19	10	11	10	6	6	6
20–24	10	12	11	6	7	7
25–29	13	15	15	6	9	8
30–34	14	18	17	8	10	9
35–39	15	20	18	8	10	9
40–44	15	20	19	8	10	9
45–49	15	21	19	8	11	10
50–54	17	22	20	8	10	9
55–59	22	31	28	10	12	11
60 & over	24	23	23	24	10	10
All ages	13	17	16	7	9	8

Wales

AGE (years)	Mean Duration (weeks) Female	Male	All	Median Duration (weeks) Female	Male	All
16–17	7	7	7	6	5	5
18–19	12	11	12	8	7	7
20–24	11	13	13	7	8	8
25–29	14	17	16	8	10	9
30–34	14	20	18	7	11	10
35–39	16	22	21	8	11	10
40–44	18	23	21	9	11	11
45–49	15	21	19	9	11	10
50–54	19	29	25	9	12	11
55–59	25	39	34	11	14	12
60 & over	433	23	25	433	9	9
All ages	14	18	17	8	9	9

Scotland

(years)	Mean Duration (weeks) Female	Male	All	Median Duration (weeks) Female	Male	All
16–17	11	10	10	8	6	7
18–19	12	12	12	8	8	8
20–24	12	13	13	7	8	8
25–29	14	18	17	8	10	9
30–34	15	20	19	8	10	10
35–39	17	23	21	9	12	11
40–44	19	23	22	9	12	11
45–49	18	26	23	9	12	11
50–54	20	30	27	10	13	12
55–59	36	52	46	12	17	15
60 & over	93	38	38	93	13	13
All ages	16	20	19	8	10	9

Northern Ireland

AGE (years)	Mean Duration (weeks) Female	Male	All	Median Duration (weeks) Female	Male	All
16–17	6	8	7	4	4	4
18–19	12	13	13	7	8	8
20–24	11	14	13	7	8	8
25–29	13	19	17	7	10	9
30–34	14	25	22	8	11	10
35–39	18	28	26	9	13	11
40–44	21	31	28	10	14	13
45–49	21	33	28	9	14	12
50–54	26	48	40	10	16	13
55–59	58	100	85	13	25	20
60 & over	0	94	94	0	15	15
All ages	16	25	22	8	10	9

England

(years)	Mean Duration (weeks) Female	Male	All	Median Duration (weeks) Female	Male	All
16–17	10	9	10	7	6	7
18–19	12	12	12	8	8	8
20–24	13	14	14	8	9	8
25–29	16	20	19	8	11	10
30–34	18	23	22	9	12	11
35–39	19	25	23	10	13	12
40–44	20	26	24	10	13	12
45–49	21	26	24	10	13	12
50–54	22	30	27	10	13	12
55–59	29	40	36	12	14	14
60 & over	86	34	35	32	12	12
All ages	17	21	20	9	10	10

Regional labour market summary 1

Labour Force Survey (November 2008 to January 2009)

	Total aged 16 & over	Economically active				Employment						Unemployment					
	Total	Total		Men	Women	Total		Men		Women		Total		Men		Women	
	Level	Level	Rate (%)	Level	Level	Level	Rate (%)	Level	Rate (%)	Level	Rate (%)	Level	Rate (%)	Level	Rate (%)	Level	Rate (%)
	1	2	3	4	5	6	7	8	9	10	11	12	13	14	15	16	17
North East	2,081	1,260	77.0	683	577	1,151	70.2	615	72.9	536	67.2	109	8.6	68	9.9	41	7.0
North West	5,503	3,414	77.7	1,834	1,579	3,152	71.6	1,672	73.9	1,479	69.0	262	7.7	162	8.8	100	6.3
Yorkshire & the Humber	4,192	2,615	77.8	1,431	1,184	2,428	72.1	1,320	75.6	1,109	68.3	186	7.1	111	7.8	75	6.3
East Midlands	3,580	2,311	81.2	1,262	1,049	2,164	75.9	1,180	79.8	984	71.5	147	6.4	83	6.6	65	6.2
West Midlands	4,303	2,663	77.9	1,467	1,196	2,452	71.5	1,333	75.5	1,120	67.1	210	7.9	134	9.2	76	6.4
East	4,576	3,007	82.8	1,629	1,377	2,842	78.1	1,530	81.9	1,312	73.9	165	5.5	100	6.1	65	4.7
London	6,112	4,094	77.6	2,266	1,828	3,787	71.7	2,107	78.5	1,680	64.4	307	7.5	159	7.0	148	8.1
South East	6,681	4,413	82.6	2,382	2,032	4,201	78.5	2,259	82.5	1,942	74.2	212	4.8	123	5.2	89	4.4
South West	4,235	2,720	82.6	1,453	1,267	2,581	78.2	1,366	80.4	1,216	75.8	139	5.1	87	6.0	52	4.1
England	**41,263**	**26,496**	**79.8**	**14,408**	**12,089**	**24,759**	**74.4**	**13,380**	**78.3**	**11,378**	**70.1**	**1,738**	**6.6**	**1,027**	**7.1**	**710**	**5.9**
Wales	2,409	1,431	76.1	765	666	1,322	70.0	695	71.9	628	67.9	109	7.6	71	9.2	38	5.8
Scotland	4,197	2,670	79.7	1,417	1,253	2,535	75.5	1,332	78.4	1,203	72.5	135	5.1	85	6.0	50	4.0
Great Britain	**47,868**	**30,598**	**79.6**	**16,590**	**14,008**	**28,616**	**74.3**	**15,407**	**78.0**	**13,209**	**70.2**	**1,982**	**6.5**	**1,183**	**7.1**	**799**	**5.7**
N Ireland	1,376	811	72.2	444	367	7865	68.0	4209	71.1	356	64.7	46	5.7	35	7.8	11	3.1
United Kingdom	**49,244**	**31,408**	**79.4**	**17,034**	**14,374**	**29,379**	**74.1**	**15,816**	**77.8**	**13,563**	**70.1**	**2,029**	**6.5**	**1,218**	**7.1**	**811**	**5.6**

Figures in thousands.

Claimant Count v ILO Unemployment

Along with a large number of other countries, the UK publishes two defined measures of unemployment that complement each other.

One comes from a monthly count of those claiming unemployment-related benefits. This administrative measure is known as the *Claimant Count.*

The other comes from a quarterly survey of households, the Labour Force Survey. This survey measure is accepted as an international standard because it is based on methods recommended by the International Labour Organisation. It is known as the *p* and is used by the European Union (EU) and the Organisation for Economic Co-operation and Development (OECD).

Both measures have their advantages and disadvantages.

The advantage of the claimant count is that it is available quickly and monthly and because it is a 100 per cent count, it also provides precise information on very small areas.

The ILO measure on the other hand as well as being internationally standard, springs from a data source (the Labour Force Survey) which allows unemployment to be analysed in the context of other labour market information and a variety of demographic characteristics.

A disadvantage of the Claimant Count is that it can be affected if there are changes to the benefit system from which it is derived.

Although changes in the benefit system may also affect the labour market behaviour of respondents to the LFS, the ILO definition itself is entirely independent of the benefit system. Comparatively the LFS results, based on the ILO measure, are not reliable for areas smaller than counties or the larger local authority districts, because of sample size restrictions. Estimates of less than 10,000 persons unemployed (after grossing up) are not shown in published tables because they are subject to unacceptably high sampling error and are, therefore, unreliable.

This said, government statistics apply recognised statistical procedures in order to minimise these disadvantages and maintain the relevance of both measures as accurate labour market indicators.

Claimant count rates

Area	1993	1994	1995	1996	1997	1998	1999	2000	2001	2002	2003	2004	2005	2006	2007	2008
United Kingdom	9.7	8.8	7.6	7.0	5.3	4.5	4.2	3.6	3.2	3.2	3.1	2.7	2.7	2.9	2.7	2.8
North East	12.1	11.7	10.8	10.0	8.1	7.2	7.0	6.3	5.7	5.1	4.9	4.0	3.9	4.1	4.0	4.3
North West	10.0	9.3	8.1	7.5	5.9	5.1	4.6	4.1	3.7	3.6	3.4	2.9	2.8	3.3	3.2	3.4
Yorkshire and the Humber	9.7	9.1	8.1	7.6	6.1	5.4	5.0	4.4	4.0	3.7	3.5	2.9	2.9	3.3	3.1	3.3
East Midlands	9.0	8.3	7.1	6.5	4.7	4.0	3.7	3.5	3.1	2.9	2.9	2.5	2.5	2.8	2.7	2.8
West Midlands	10.3	9.4	7.7	6.9	5.3	4.6	4.5	4.0	3.7	3.5	3.6	3.3	3.3	3.9	3.7	3.8
East	8.8	7.6	6.2	5.7	4.0	3.2	2.9	2.5	2.1	2.1	2.2	2.0	2.0	2.3	2.2	2.2
London	10.9	10.1	8.9	8.2	6.2	5.0	4.5	3.8	3.3	3.6	3.7	3.5	3.5	3.4	3.0	2.9
South East	8.1	6.9	5.6	4.9	3.3	2.6	2.3	1.9	1.6	1.7	1.8	1.6	1.6	1.8	1.6	1.7
South West	9.0	7.7	6.5	5.9	4.2	3.4	3.1	2.5	2.1	2.0	1.9	1.6	1.6	1.8	1.6	1.7
England	9.7	8.7	7.5	6.8	5.1	4.3	3.9	3.4	3.0	3.0	3.0	2.6	2.6	2.9	2.7	2.8
Wales	9.8	8.9	8.1	7.7	6.2	5.4	5.0	4.4	4.0	3.6	3.5	3.0	3.0	3.1	2.8	3.1
Scotland	9.2	8.7	7.5	7.3	6.2	5.5	5.1	4.6	4.0	4.2	3.8	3.5	3.3	3.1	2.8	2.8
Northern Ireland	13.6	12.6	11.2	10.7	8.1	7.3	6.4	5.3	4.9	4.8	4.3	3.6	3.4	3.2	2.8	3.2

Seasonally adjusted annual averages – percentages

ILO Unemployment Rates

Area	1993	1994	1995	1996	1997	1998	1999	2000	2001	2002	2003	2004	2005	2006	2007	2008
United Kingdom	10.3	9.6	8.6	8.2	7.1	6.1	6.0	5.6	4.8	5.1	5.1	4.8	4.7	5.6	5.3	6.5
North East	12.0	12.5	11.4	10.8	9.8	8.2	10.1	9.2	7.4	7.5	6.5	6.3	5.5	6.6	5.8	8.6
North West	9.8	9.5	8.3	7.3	6.3	5.6	5.5	5.4	5.1	5.2	4.5	4.9	4.8	5.2	5.9	7.7
Yorkshire and the Humber	10.0	9.9	8.7	8.1	8.1	7.0	6.6	6.1	4.9	5.2	4.6	5.0	4.2	5.7	5.5	7.1
East Midlands	9.1	9.1	7.5	7.4	6.3	4.9	5.2	5.2	4.9	4.2	4.3	4.5	4.3	5.2	5.7	6.4
West Midlands	11.8	11.8	9.0	9.2	6.8	6.3	6.8	6.3	5.0	5.5	5.6	5.5	4.6	5.8	6.3	7.9
East	9.2	9.2	7.5	6.2	5.9	5.0	4.2	3.6	3.6	3.8	4.1	3.3	3.9	4.8	5.0	5.5
London	13.2	13.2	11.5	11.3	9.1	8.1	7.5	7.1	5.8	7.0	6.6	6.9	6.7	7.8	6.4	7.5
South East	8.0	8.0	6.4	6.0	5.2	4.3	3.6	3.4	3.0	3.4	3.8	3.8	3.7	4.5	4.6	4.8
South West	9.2	9.2	7.8	6.3	5.2	4.5	4.7	4.2	3.5	3.7	3.7	2.8	3.5	3.7	3.9	5.1
England	10.3	10.3	8.6	8.1	6.9	6.0	5.8	5.3	4.6	4.9	5.0	4.7	4.6	5.5	5.4	6.6
Wales	9.6	9.6	8.8	8.3	8.4	6.7	7.1	6.2	5.7	5.4	4.8	4.9	4.5	3.7	5.1	7.6
Scotland	10.2	10.2	8.3	8.7	8.5	7.4	7.4	7.7	5.8	6.8	5.7	5.7	5.5	5.2	4.6	5.1
Northern Ireland	12.5	12.5	11.0	9.7	7.5	7.3	7.2	7.2	6.2	6.3	5.5	5.6	4.7	4.4	4.0	5.7

Percentages, Spring each year, seasonally adjusted

F5: Average earnings index

Average earnings index
All employees: main industrial sectors (not seasonally adjusted)

	1996	1997	1998	1999	2000	2001	2002
Jan	81.2	84.9	89.0	93.0	99.0	103.4	106.4
Feb	83.2	86.2	90.8	95.4	100.8	107.7	110.8
Mar	84.8	89.1	93.8	98.5	103.9	108.4	111.6
Apr	82.9	86.0	91.0	94.4	98.5	103.3	107.2
May	82.3	85.7	91.0	94.7	98.4	102.7	106.5
Jun	83.1	86.3	90.8	95.7	99.2	104.0	107.8
Jul	83.9	87.2	92.0	95.9	99.4	103.7	107.6
Aug	82.4	86.1	90.2	94.5	98.5	102.8	106.3
Sep	82.9	86.3	90.5	94.5	98.3	102.6	106.3
Oct	82.7	86.3	90.4	95.0	98.7	103.0	107.3
Nov	83.6	87.4	91.3	95.8	99.7	103.4	108.1
Dec	86.3	90.6	94.5	100.4	105.6	107.8	111.3
Yearly Average	83.3	86.8	91.3	95.7	100.0	104.4	108.1

	2003	2004	20055	2006	2007	2008	2009
Jan	109.9	118.2	123.3	127.2	133.3	138.4	137.5
Feb	113.8	118.1	124.9	131.6	138.8	144.4	141.5
Mar	116.8	122.2	127.5	133.2	137.8	144.1	146.1
Apr	110.0	115.0	119.9	124.1	128.0	132.0	137.1
May	110.0	114.8	119.2	124.5	129.0	133.0	135.9
Jun	111.2	116.1	120.4	126.4	130.5	134.9	
Jul	111.8	115.4	120.5	125.2	129.7	134.3	
Aug	110.2	114.8	119.0	123.5	128.7	132.8	
Sep	110.4	114.9	118.8	123.7	128.8	132.9	
Oct	110.9	115.7	119.1	123.9	128.2	132.7	
Nov	111.2	116.2	119.9	124.6	130.2	133.5	
Dec	114.7	119.5	124.6	129.4	134.4	138.8	
Yearly Average	111.7	116.7	121.4	126.4	131.5	135.9	

Index 2000 = 100

F6: Average weekly earnings

These figures are the average (mean) gross weekly earnings of full-time employees on adult rates whose pay was not affected by absence.

	Men	Women
	£	£
1985	192.40	126.40
1986	207.50	137.20
1987	224.00	148.10
1988	245.80	164.20
1989	269.50	182.30
1990	295.60	201.50
1991	318.90	222.40
1992	340.10	241.10
1993	353.50	252.60
1994	362.10	261.50
1995	374.60	269.80
1996	391.60	283.00
1997	408.70	297.20
1998	427.10	309.60
1999	442.40	326.50
2000	453.30	337.60
2001	490.50	366.80
2002	513.80	383.20
2003	525.00	396.00
2004	556.80	420.20
2005	568.00	435.60
2006	589.80	450.00
2007	606.10	462.80
2008	631.10	485.50

Until 2004 these figures were taken from the New Earnings Survey.
In 2004 the Annual Survey of Hours and Earnings (ASHE) was developed to replace the New Earnings Survey.
Both the New Earnings Survey and ASHE are published by HMSO.

F7: Average earnings statistics

Analyses of earnings by occupation

Introductory notes:

1. It will usually be possible to obtain agreement, or a direction, that the earnings shown in the Annual Survey of Hours and Earnings may be adduced in evidence without formal proof but occasionally it is necessary to adduce formal proof. This is done by calling a witness from the Office for National Statistics.
2. These tables have been compiled from the Department of Employment's New Earnings Survey, by kind permission of the Controller of Her Majesty's Stationery Office. Due to the re-classification of occupations in the 2003 survey (using SOC 2000), only the 2003 classifications are shown in this table.
3. The average gross weekly earnings shown are for employees whose pay for the survey pay-period was not affected by absence.
4. Average gross annual earnings have only been published since April 2000.

   Annual earnings figures are only provided for those employees who have been in the same job for at least 12 months, regardless of whether or not their pay was affected by absence.
5. Results are generally given only for those occupations represented by at least 30 persons in the same sample and which have a standard error of 5 per cent or less.
6. n.e.c. stands for "not elsewhere classified".

Full-Time Males on Adult Rates (where pay was not affected by absence)

Occupation SOC 2000	Gross Weekly Pay (in April) 2008 Median £	Gross Weekly Pay (in April) 2008 Mean £	Gross Annual Earnings (in April) 2008 Median £	Gross Annual Earnings (in April) 2008 Mean £
Managers and Senior Officials	766.6	937.9	40,612	56,999
Corporate Managers	792.3	970.8	42,000	59,078
Corporate Managers and Senior Officials	1,584.6	2,115.8	X	151,214
Senior officials in national government	1,321.4	1,310.3	X	69,303
Directors and chief executives of major organisations	1,916.5	2,619.5	X	193,313
Senior officials in local government	1,011.9	1,012.1	53,904	55,977
Senior officials of special interest organisations	674.2	776.5	33,804	38,778
Production Managers	768.0	884.6	40,000	49,410
Production, works and maintenance managers	768.2	883.0	39,999	49,062
Managers in construction	766.6	861.3	39,550	48,638
Managers in mining and energy	X	1,249.7	X	69,278
Functional Managers	925.9	1,096.1	50,000	70,065
Financial managers and chartered secretaries	1,171.6	1,352.4	65,000	103,487
Marketing and sales managers	863.6	1,016.0	48,168	61,781
Purchasing managers	845.8	1,022.8	42,753	53,020
Advertising and public relations managers	803.7	959.3	44,965	54,080
Personnel, training and industrial relations managers	896.9	1,146.3	48,062	66,837
Information and communication technology managers	881.0	970.9	46,945	54,031
Research and development managers	913.2	997.5	47,060	57,570
Quality and Customer Care Managers	669.8	757.0	36,205	40,768
Quality assurance managers	670.4	741.2	36,877	39,044
Customer care managers	664.1	765.5	35,893	41,682
Financial Institution and Office Managers	757.3	875.0	40,746	50,661
Financial institution managers	799.6	978.1	45,861	61,560
Office managers	740.4	812.5	38,649	43,980
Managers in Distribution, Storage and Retailing	544.3	628.0	28,880	35,118
Transport and distribution managers	624.9	741.4	32,950	43,902
Storage and warehouse managers	565.7	612.7	29,626	32,654
Retail and wholesale managers	504.6	601.1	26,838	33,428
Protective Service Officers	900.5	920.7	50,197	49,052
Officers in armed forces				
Police officers (inspectors and above)	998.4	1,084.7	52,617	54,118
Senior officers in fire, ambulance, prison and related services	727.3	840.6	43,410	46,472
Security managers	623.7	744.0	32,866	40,766
Health and Social Services Managers	757.0	782.8	38,657	40,909
Hospital and health service managers	842.5	889.2	43,056	45,071
Pharmacy managers	936.7	1,001.5	50,029	55,656
Healthcare practice managers	677.1	684.0	36,148	34,740
Social services managers	738.5	807.1	39,988	43,067
Residential and day care managers	543.3	583.9	28,786	31,011
Managers and proprietors in agriculture and services	574.5	692.7	32,056	X
Managers in Farming, Horticulture, Forestry and Fishing	532.3	580.7	30,065	33,003
Farm Managers	458.7	501.8	26,609	28,874
Natural environment and conservation managers	753.6	809.0	40,533	43,385
Managers in animal husbandry, forestry and fishing n.e.c.	X	668.1	X	X

Full-Time Males on Adult Rates (where pay was not affected by absence)

Occupation SOC 2000	Gross Weekly Pay (in April) 2008 Median £	Gross Weekly Pay (in April) 2008 Mean £	Gross Annual Earnings (in April) 2008 Median £	Gross Annual Earnings (in April) 2008 Mean £
Managers and Proprietors In Hospitality and Leisure Services	438.5	503.1	24,708	27,623
Hotel and accommodation managers	487.2	626.8	X	35,656
Conference and exhibition managers	X	629.8	25,527	27,221
Restaurant and catering managers	403.8	451.0	22,128	24,359
Publicans and managers of licensed premises	382.1	405.4	20,215	22,724
Leisure and sports managers	525.2	593.3	27,601	32,075
Travel agency managers	X	616.2	X	X
Managers and Proprietors In Other Service Industries	664.5	799.6	35,747	X
Property, housing and land managers	667.3	782.8	35,981	X
Garage managers and proprietors	551.6	598.4	29,378	34,252
Hairdressing and beauty salon managers and proprietors	X	X	X	X
Shopkeepers and wholesale/retail dealers	539.6	600.5	31,165	34,195
Recycling and refuse disposal managers	610.6	696.1	31,601	X
Managers and proprietors in other services n.e.c.	715.3	882.6	37,480	53,804
Professional Occupations	724.4	818.4	37,733	43,519
Science and Technology Professionals	707.7	760.8	37,270	40,154
Science Professionals	683.9	768.4	37,541	41,863
Chemists	665.7	745.4	36,372	40,698
Biological scientists and biochemists	668.8	752.1	36,113	41,045
Physicists, geologists and meteorologists	760.0	847.8	39,581	45,734
Engineering Professionals	687.1	731.8	35,999	38,108
Civil engineers	695.0	748.6	36,731	39,017
Mechanical engineers	742.4	755.5	37,828	39,926
Electrical engineers	801.4	846.9	41,949	43,596
Electronics engineers	887.3	855.8	44,155	43,769
Chemical engineers	X	548.7	X	X
Design and development engineers	689.8	727.2	35,544	37,589
Production and process engineers	638.8	659.2	34,147	34,793
Planning and quality control engineers	587.2	638.5	X	32,650
Engineering professionals n.e.c.	674.9	737.9	36,085	38,386
Information and Communication Technology Professionals	732.4	792.3	39,047	42,256
IT strategy and planning professionals	920.4	957.1	49,994	52,180
Software professionals	699.5	740.0	36,876	39,191
Health Professionals	1,235.2	1,420.3	74,744	81,591
Medical practitioners	1,455.4	1,544.8	90,940	91,421
Psychologists	1,014.8	913.1	49,205	45,264
Pharmacists/pharmacologists	745.6	712.4	39,746	38,690
Ophthalmic opticians	855.3	814.8	X	41,997
Dental practitioners	1,171.9	1,183.8	66,644	66,907
Veterinarians	X	X	X	X
Teaching and Research Professionals	705.7	765.4	37,212	38,896
Teaching Professionals	728.1	784.7	37,747	39,647
Higher education teaching professionals	820.1	905.6	42,592	46,474
Further education teaching professionals	641.0	692.0	32,772	35,793
Education officers, school inspectors	759.5	821.1	36,640	X
Secondary education teaching professionals	725.0	790.8	36,640	X
Primary and nursery education teaching professionals	686.0	709.8	35,479	35,876
Special needs education teaching professionals	682.6	703.4	35,146	35,644
Registrars and senior administrators of educational establishments	768.1	864.7	40,592	45,699
Teaching professionals n.e.c.	583.9	652.4	X	31,368

Full-Time Males on Adult Rates (where pay was not affected by absence)

Occupation SOC 2000	Gross Weekly Pay (in April) 2008 Median £	Gross Weekly Pay (in April) 2008 Mean £	Gross Annual Earnings (in April) 2008 Median £	Gross Annual Earnings (in April) 2008 Mean £
Research Professionals	592.3	624.1	30,909	32,855
Scientific researchers	651.0	692.6	34,683	36,421
Social science researchers	421.8	457.2	X	25,019
Researchers n.e.c.	575.2	609.4	29,509	31,442
Business and public service professionals	708.8	819.4	36,870	46,922
Legal Professionals	956.1	1,133.7	51,907	62,849
Solicitors and lawyers, judges and coroners	958.2	1,150.2	53,837	64,346
Legal professionals n.e.c.	X	1,002.0	X	X
Business and Statistical Professionals	774.9	880.0	40,992	51,161
Chartered and certified accountants	743.2	798.3	39,175	44,303
Management accountants	694.0	740.6	38,318	39,833
Management consultants, actuaries, economists and statisticians	819.2	966.4	44,764	58,722
Architects, Town Planners, Surveyors	690.0	748.7	36,866	46,516
Architects	742.6	846.0	38,222	X
Town Planners	630.7	685.3	33,356	37,548
Quantity surveyors	709.3	728.0	37,697	38,544
Chartered surveyors (not quantity surveyors)	675.4	724.6	36,003	44,855
Public Service Professionals	559.2	573.9	27,981	28,972
Public service administrative professionals	862.5	871.3	42,644	44,687
Social workers	590.4	587.0	30,615	29,906
Probation officers	557.5	555.7	28,787	28,618
Clergy	411.9	447.5	21,070	22,611
Librarians and Related Professionals	546.2	557.3	28,726	29,294
Librarians	489.5	528.1	27,583	28,062
Archivists and curators	565.6	603.8	30,134	30,794
Associate Professional and Technical Occupations	574.9	641.8	30,695	35,256
Science and Technology Associate Professionals	522.8	561.4	27,498	29,642
Science and Engineering Technicians	508.8	547.8	26,688	28,342
Laboratory technicians	464.7	490.9	24,977	26,282
Electrical/electronics technicians	540.8	566.4	29,567	30,535
Engineering technicians	598.0	613.2	30,547	31,508
Building and civil engineering technicians	481.0	534.2	24,513	27,139
Quality assurance technicians	486.9	540.6	25,882	28,902
Science and engineering technicians n.e.c.	465.1	503.6	24,167	25,528
Draughtspersons and Building Inspectors	525.4	525.9	27,191	27,536
Architectural technologists and town planning technicians	539.6	537.5	28,368	28,866
Draughtspersons	489.2	513.0	25,846	26,603
Building inspectors	556.3	553.0	28,942	29,052
IT Service Delivery Occupations	546.3	593.9	29,592	32,342
IT operations technicians	582.5	623.9	31,025	34,193
IT users support technicians	486.7	547.9	26,353	29,185
Health and Social Welfare Associate Professionals	535.7	548.3	27,621	28,086
Health Associate Professionals	590.9	597.0	30,583	30,410
Nurses	575.0	588.9	29,572	29,234
Midwives	561.2	596.7	26,762	29,826
Paramedics	704.6	727.2	36,054	37,551
Medical radiographers	704.3	699.8	37,290	37,586
Chiropodists	626.3	640.0	X	X
Dispensing opticians	X	X	X	X
Pharmaceutical dispensers	362.0	398.0	X	22,252
Medical and dental technicians	515.1	544.9	27,665	28,879

Full-Time Males on Adult Rates (where pay was not affected by absence)

Occupation SOC 2000	Gross Weekly Pay (in April) 2008 Median £	Gross Weekly Pay (in April) 2008 Mean £	Gross Annual Earnings (in April) 2008 Median £	Gross Annual Earnings (in April) 2008 Mean £
Therapists	554.3	589.0	27,850	29,588
Physiotherapists	559.0	609.1	29,493	32,196
Occupational therapists	463.1	496.9	23,974	25,313
Speech and language therapists				
Therapists n.e.c.	X	539.2	X	27,163
Social Welfare Associate Professionals	437.9	457.8	22,912	24,005
Youth and community workers	451.1	469.3	23,093	24,524
Housing and welfare officers	428.2	450.1	22,598	23,620
Protective Service Occupations	677.1	703.9	35,240	35,918
NCOs and other ranks				
Police officers (sergeant and below)	740.5	771.8	38,686	38,573
Fire service officers (leading fire officer and below)	590.1	618.1	30,096	30,698
Prison service officers (below principal officer)	526.2	515.4	26,850	27,041
Protective service associate professionals n.e.c.	577.8	590.5	29,386	29,548
Culture, media and sports occupations	520.7	633.5	27,196	34,010
Artistic and Literary Occupations	603.3	648.3	29,746	34,840
Artists	575.4	576.4	X	30,948
Authors, writers	585.9	636.5	27,851	32,449
Actors, entertainers	X	306.6	X	19,176
Dancers and choreographers				
Musicians	548.4	550.3	X	27,187
Arts officers, producers and directors	712.7	771.9	33,944	41,130
Design Associate Professionals	498.2	524.5	27,062	27,911
Graphic designers	468.7	501.7	25,040	25,765
Product, clothing and related designers	561.9	574.4	30,000	32,664
Media Associate Professionals	576.3	719.4	30,508	38,680
Journalists, newspaper and periodical editors	589.1	731.8	33,116	39,459
Broadcasting associate professionals	764.4	954.4	39,348	51,034
Public relations officers	517.2	626.2	X	X
Photographers and audio-visual equipment operators	486.1	558.1	26,252	29,762
Sports and Fitness Occupations	383.9	590.5	20,087	X
Sports players	X	X	X	X
Sports coaches, instructors and officials	437.1	478.7	22,445	24,931
Fitness instructors	320.2	350.1	X	18,351
Sports and fitness occupations n.e.c.	X	314.7		
Business and public service associate professionals	582.0	686.3	32,383	40,636
Transport Associate Professionals	778.1	978.7	39,868	45,709
Air traffic controllers	1,114.0	1,233.6	57,772	60,159
Aircraft pilots and flight engineers	1,281.6	1,419.9	X	62,394
Ship and hovercraft officers	X	655.8	X	X
Train drivers	37.0	759.3	39,008	39,445
Legal Associate Professionals	535.9	590.7	28,395	31,432
Business and Finance Associate Professionals	632.4	801.5	34,832	54,918
Estimators, valuers and assessors	554.5	613.3	29,450	33,495
Brokers	1,169.8	1,355.7	X	135,142
Insurance underwriters	722.6	876.6	X	54,389
Finance and investment analysts/advisers	678.5	824.3	39,395	59,000
Taxation experts	654.5	721.5	32,491	40,438
Importers, exporters	464.7	517.6	23,752	24,575

Full-Time Males on Adult Rates (where pay was not affected by absence)

Occupation SOC 2000	Gross Weekly Pay (in April) 2008 Median £	Gross Weekly Pay (in April) 2008 Mean £	Gross Annual Earnings (in April) 2008 Median £	Gross Annual Earnings (in April) 2008 Mean £
Financial and accounting technicians	729.9	925.6	X	54,122
Business and related associate professionals n.e.c.	567.6	600.3	29,829	31,893
Sales and Related Associate Professionals	530.4	615.7	30,349	34,796
Buyers and purchasing officers	552.5	618.5	28,378	33,492
Sales representatives	530.1	617.0	30,543	34,935
Marketing associate professionals	542.2	623.1	30,750	35,149
Estate agents, auctioneers	412.5	527.6	X	35,890
Conservation Associate Professionals	486.3	509.3	25,607	27,077
Conservation and environmental protection officers	548.2	557.8	28,874	29,916
Countryside and park rangers	396.8	412.5	21,369	21,918
Public Service and Other Associate Professionals	558.7	604.1	30,603	33,086
Public service associate professionals	623.6	679.7	34,154	36,572
Personnel and industrial relations officers	483.6	559.0	28,283	35,574
Vocational and industrial trainers and instructors	483.6	513.2	25,565	26,672
Careers advisers and vocational guidance specialists	506.9	542.7	26,125	28,119
Inspectors of factories, utilities and trading standards	576.3	715.2	X	38,928
Statutory examiners	544.4	564.0	31,058	30,304
Occupational hygienists and safety officers (health and safety)	641.4	687.1	X	X
Environmental health officers	591.8	628.5	29,607	30,516
Administrative and secretarial occupations	397.4	440.3	21,327	23,550
Administrative occupations	398.5	442.0	21,368	23,596
Administrative Occupations: Government and Related Organisations	409.7	431.5	21,622	22,345
Civil Service executive officers	483.1	495.5	25,244	26,023
Civil Service administrative officers and assistants	338.9	364.7	17,717	18,741
Local government clerical officers and assistants	437.6	468.2	22,845	23,750
Officers of non-governmental organisations	561.9	613.4	X	31,239
Administrative Occupations: Finance	408.9	481.5	22,620	26,880
Credit controllers	368.0	431.4	20,162	24,121
Accounts and wages clerks, book-keepers, other financial clerks	450.4	514.5	24,492	28,719
Counter clerks	377.2	437.6	20,903	24,249
Administrative Occupations: Records	402.5	438.0	21,410	23,147
Filing and other records assistants/clerks	408.4	439.8	21,800	23,363
Pensions and insurance clerks	374.7	434.1	20,654	23,935
Stock control clerks	388.8	414.8	20,642	21,907
Transport and distribution clerks	460.6	491.2	23,621	24,923
Library assistants/clerks	313.2	356.1	X	18,419
Database assistants/clerks	376.2	434.6	20,025	23,444
Market research interviewers	321.2	342.8	17,154	18,389
Administrative Occupations: Communications	477.2	501.2	25,296	26,784
Telephonists	364.2	437.2	X	22,184
Communications operators	496.2	520.1	26,212	28,062
Administrative Occupations: General	363.9	412.1	19,737	21,622
General office assistants/clerks	363.9	412.1	19,737	21,622
Secretarial and related occupations	353.1	396.0	20,223	22,156

Full-Time Males on Adult Rates (where pay was not affected by absence)

Occupation SOC 2000	Gross Weekly Pay (in April) 2008 Median £	Mean £	Gross Annual Earnings (in April) 2008 Median £	Mean £
Secretarial and related occupations	353.1	396.0	20,223	22,156
Medical secretaries	357.6	393.2		
Legal secretaries	313.0	351.4	X	X
School secretaries	358.3	404.9	X	22,706
Company secretaries	468.9	584.2	X	31,391
Personal assistants and other secretaries	435.7	451.2	X	X
Receptionists	305.9	316.4	15,612	16,840
Typists				
Skilled trades occupations	460.0	491.0	24,024	25,173
Skilled agricultural trades	326.3	351.9	17,444	18,298
Agricultural Trades	326.3	351.9	17,444	18,298
Farmers	330.3	367.6	19,003	19,482
Horticultural trades	313.7	318.8	17,199	19,539
Gardeners and groundsmen/groundswomen	325.0	348.9	17,245	18,012
Agricultural and fishing trades n.e.c.	359.4	411.6	X	21,336
Skilled metal and electrical trades	499.2	531.5	26,105	27,142
Metal Forming, Welding and Related Trades	478.6	510.0	24,775	25,811
Smiths and forge workers	446.6	458.2	24,377	23,446
Moulders, core makers, die casters	451.8	470.5	24,518	25,629
Sheet metal workers	409.9	445.5	21,248	22,409
Metal plate workers, shipwrights, riveters	526.5	559.7	26,747	26,380
Welding trades	466.3	499.3	24,731	25,791
Pipe fitters	602.3	642.7	33,525	33,291
Metal Machining, Fitting and Instrument Making Trades	525.5	546.0	26,873	27,796
Metal machining setters and setter-operators	494.7	511.7	25,385	25,833
Tool makers, tool fitters and markers-out	520.8	530.8	25,412	26,466
Metal working production and maintenance fitters	532.7	555.8	27,629	28,401
Precision instrument makers and repairers	493.5	519.5	24,778	26,795
Vehicle Trades	439.7	461.8	23,542	24,281
Motor mechanics, auto engineers	442.7	466.8	24,032	24,802
Vehicle body builders and repairers	423.8	458.0	22,461	22,572
Auto electricians	412.6	453.0	23,760	23,589
Vehicle spray painters	422.1	432.5	22,624	23,256
Electrical Trades	517.4	559.0	27,255	28,414
Electricians, electrical fitters	538.6	576.1	28,172	29,206
Telecommunications engineers	510.4	544.8	26,351	27,613
Lines repairers and cable jointers	576.9	694.5	31,813	33,285
TV, video and audio engineers	370.1	427.9	19,968	20,522
Computer engineers, installation and maintenance	500.1	540.7	27,665	27,978
Electrical/electronics engineers n.e.c.	483.9	531.4	25,849	27,408
Skilled construction and building trades	454.6	484.4	23,157	24,275
Construction Trades	460.0	491.1	23,540	24,636
Steel erectors	486.3	537.8	24,717	25,702
Bricklayers, masons	463.7	507.8	24,382	25,017
Roofers, roof tilers and slaters	400.0	467.7	20,901	21,735
Plumbers, heating and ventilating engineers	520.6	533.4	26,215	27,232
Carpenters and joiners	457.5	483.6	23,367	24,151
Glaziers, window fabricators and fitters	398.4	420.7	20,934	21,178
Construction trades n.e.c.	453.2	472.9	22,589	24,455
Building Trades	409.2	448.1	21,463	22,418
Plasterers	406.3	432.9	21,055	21,586
Floorers and wall tilers	380.0	416.8	20,802	21,631
Painters and decorators	425.0	461.7	21,980	22,907

Full-Time Males on Adult Rates (where pay was not affected by absence)

Occupation SOC 2000	Gross Weekly Pay (in April) 2008 Median £	Gross Weekly Pay (in April) 2008 Mean £	Gross Annual Earnings (in April) 2008 Median £	Gross Annual Earnings (in April) 2008 Mean £
Textiles, printing and other skilled trades	361.2	394.7	19,104	20,888
Textiles and Garments Trades	378.0	413.1	20,870	21,660
Weavers and knitters	360.6	370.2	18,182	19,624
Upholsterers	405.6	423.2	20,885	21,112
Leather and related trades	333.5	377.7	20,786	22,237
Tailors and dressmakers				
Textiles, garments and related trades n.e.c.	507.6	538.0	X	27,120
Printing Trades	432.0	474.8	22,575	24,725
Originators, compositors and print preparers	X	510.8	X	26,137
Printers	480.0	509.7	25,494	27,374
Bookbinders and print finishers	424.9	456.4	22,270	23,381
Screen printers	355.6	345.1	17,672	17,773
Food Preparation Trades	323.4	359.5	17,230	19,061
Butchers, meat cutters	319.6	371.2	16,927	17,146
Bakers, flour confectioners	317.8	347.7	16,904	18,336
Fishmongers, poultry dressers	271.0	303.9	14,186	16,186
Chefs, cooks	326.6	361.2	17,323	19,646
Skilled Trades n.e.c.	393.0	416.9	19,636	20,668
Glass and ceramics makers, decorators and finishers	425.9	429.1	19,640	21,096
Furniture makers, other craft woodworkers	380.0	400.6	18,727	19,046
Pattern makers (moulds)	579.5	617.8	28,173	31,952
Musical instrument makers and tuners	X	X	X	X
Goldsmiths, silversmiths, precious stone workers	X	476.0	X	25,255
Floral arranger, florists				
Hand craft occupations n.e.c.	362.2	380.3	18,753	19,154
Personal service occupations	353.1	389.2	18,649	19,720
Caring personal service occupations	341.1	367.2	17,905	18,503
Healthcare and Related Personal Services	352.8	374.5	18,272	18,724
Nursing auxiliaries and assistants	340.8	374.6	17,938	18,597
Ambulance staff (excluding paramedics)	415.6	459.1	20,958	23,110
Dental nurses				
Houseparents and residential wardens	375.2	401.3	X	X
Care assistants and home carers	348.3	359.6	17,730	17,796
Childcare and Related Personal Services	303.8	330.0	16,195	16,983
Nursery nurses	260.3	291.1	12,742	15,070
Childminders and related occupations				
Playgroup leaders/assistants	324.7	352.7	X	17,528
Educational assistants	304.4	332.5	16,345	17,174
Animal Care Services	325.2	357.6	18,260	19,997
Veterinary nurses and assistants	X	626.9	X	29,970
Animal care occupations n.e.c.	310.5	306.6	16,560	17,562
Leisure and Other Personal Service Occupations	370.4	414.0	19,729	21,001
Leisure and Travel Service Occupations	402.5	462.6	21,896	23,205
Sports and leisure assistants	297.1	322.6	16,276	17,389
Travel agents	413.0	399.8	21,876	22,181
Travel and tour guides	308.0	308.8	X	X
Air travel assistants	504.3	544.6	28,050	28,486
Rail travel assistants	508.4	622.3	25,873	27,008
Leisure and travel service occupations n.e.c.	X	549.4	X	X
Hairdressers and Related Occupations	229.5	276.4	X	X
Hairdressers, barbers	231.1	281.6	X	X
Beauticians and related occupations				

Full-Time Males on Adult Rates (where pay was not affected by absence)

Occupation SOC 2000	Gross Weekly Pay (in April) 2008 Median £	Gross Weekly Pay (in April) 2008 Mean £	Gross Annual Earnings (in April) 2008 Median £	Gross Annual Earnings (in April) 2008 Mean £
Housekeeping Occupations	346.3	367.0	18,207	19,083
Housekeepers and related occupations	311.3	321.4	18,524	19,131
Caretakers	348.7	369.5	18,183	19,081
Personal Services Occupations n.e.c.	416.3	419.9	20,731	20,819
Undertakers and mortuary assistants	412.9	404.0	20,607	19,984
Pest control officers	416.5	459.9	21,150	22,880
Sales and customer service occupations	302.7	339.8	16,182	17,777
Sales occupations	293.8	335.7	15,741	17,512
Sales Assistants and Retail Cashiers	287.5	325.1	15,028	16,635
Sales and retail assistants	287.5	327.9	15,119	16,780
Retail cashiers and check-out operators	251.2	268.3	13,024	13,843
Telephone salespersons	350.0	375.9	19,036	20,680
Sales Related Occupations	346.1	403.3	19,470	22,525
Collector salespersons and credit agents	X	455.1	21,771	25,092
Debt, rent and other cash collectors	303.0	328.2	16,635	17,551
Roundsmen/women and van salespersons	377.8	394.6	18,964	20,311
Market and street traders and assistants				
Merchandisers and window dressers	349.1	409.4	X	20,477
Sales related occupations n.e.c.	384.0	466.8	24,207	28,697
Customer Service Occupations	320.8	350.5	17,248	18,498
Call centre agents/operators	309.2	333.2	X	17,425
Customer care occupations	322.3	354.8	17,664	18,752
Process, plant and machine operatives	429.2	460.0	22,419	23,592
Process, plant and machine operatives	434.5	472.8	22,943	24,307
Process operatives	402.9	445.0	21,750	23,404
Food, drink and tobacco process operatives	355.3	388.2	18,967	20,569
Glass and ceramics process operatives	383.3	418.0	22,533	21,083
Textile process operatives	344.5	431.4	19,483	21,613
Chemical and related process operatives	524.4	554.2	27,382	28,824
Rubber process operatives	458.4	480.8	23,163	23,701
Plastics process operatives	361.2	414.1	19,044	21,019
Metal making and treating process operatives	499.1	524.0	29,029	28,542
Electroplaters	390.3	428.9	19,670	20,826
Process operatives n.e.c.	473.6	505.8	24,429	26,055
Plant and Machine Operatives	448.0	494.1	23,567	25,003
Paper and wood machine operatives	421.7	454.1	21,724	22,911
Coal mine operatives	938.4	972.3	43,122	45,008
Quarry workers and related operatives	515.7	550.9	27,532	29,385
Energy plant operatives	X	660.0	35,393	35,803
Metal working machine operatives	436.3	478.1	22,899	23,855
Water and sewerage plant operatives	459.3	524.0	25,562	27,183
Plant and machine operatives n.e.c.	437.9	471.6	22,380	24,037
Assemblers and Routine Operatives	409.3	430.6	21,202	22,408
Assemblers (electrical products)	360.2	381.3	18,351	19,527
Assemblers (vehicles and metal goods)	500.8	525.5	27,007	27,251
Routine inspectors and testers	424.7	449.9	22,659	23,557
Weighers, graders, sorters	392.0	401.5	20,583	20,477
Tyre, exhaust and windscreen fitters	337.6	359.1	17,841	19,074
Clothing cutters	X	450.6	19,215	22,534
Sewing machinists	289.3	324.2	X	17,908
Routine laboratory testers	X	415.9	X	20,524
Assemblers and routine operatives n.e.c.	355.4	384.1	18,891	19,690
Construction Operatives	523.1	562.1	27,275	28,314
Scaffolders, stagers, riggers	576.5	651.8	30,857	30,830
Road construction operatives	446.2	486.0	24,171	24,931
Rail construction and maintenance operatives	590.2	627.4	X	30,874

Full-Time Males on Adult Rates (where pay was not affected by absence)

Occupation SOC 2000	Gross Weekly Pay (in April) 2008 Median £	Gross Weekly Pay (in April) 2008 Mean £	Gross Annual Earnings (in April) 2008 Median £	Gross Annual Earnings (in April) 2008 Mean £
Construction operatives n.e.c.	528.1	564.8	27,723	28,811
Transport and mobile machine drivers and operatives	424.1	446.1	21,925	22,779
Transport Drivers and Operatives	422.4	440.7	21,823	22,495
Heavy goods vehicle drivers	477.7	485.5	24,436	24,470
Van drivers	359.7	378.1	18,714	19,346
Bus and coach drivers	403.6	439.8	21,149	22,762
Taxi, cab drivers and chauffeurs	312.7	353.9	16,579	17,950
Driving instructors	438.7	469.9	22,888	25,913
Rail transport operatives	493.8	534.0	26,230	26,386
Seafarers (merchant navy); barge, lighter and boat operatives	502.6	556.4	27,600	28,351
Air transport operatives	448.2	520.9	22,896	25,177
Transport operatives n.e.c.	441.7	495.9	25,896	25,887
Mobile Machine Drivers and Operatives	446.8	483.2	22,257	24,794
Crane drivers	620.2	657.1	28,021	30,193
Fork-lift truck drivers	355.4	389.3	18,359	19,758
Agricultural machinery drivers	395.1	417.2	22,313	22,123
Mobile machine drivers and operatives n.e.c.	500.0	532.8	24,842	28,385
Elementary occupations	341.7	367.1	18,460	19,294
Elementary trades, plant and storage related occupations	344.3	374.9	18,329	19,554
Elementary Agricultural Occupations	331.6	362.0	17,480	18,503
Farm workers	337.5	370.9	17,682	18,678
Forestry workers	377.2	404.1	18,847	20,211
Fishing and agriculture related occupations n.e.c.	298.3	319.0	15,711	16,898
Elementary Construction Occupations	366.3	401.4	19,276	20,555
Labourers in building and woodworking trades	365.2	398.5	19,317	20,544
Labourers in other construction trades n.e.c.	374.3	419.7	18,666	20,621
Elementary Process Plant Occupations	337.0	372.8	18,202	20,026
Labourers in foundries	402.5	395.7	20,235	21,062
Industrial cleaning process occupations	330.5	402.3	18,086	20,114
Printing machine minders and assistants	419.8	473.0	23,021	24,942
Packers, bottlers, canners, fillers	312.9	347.3	16,952	18,787
Labourers in process and plant operations n.e.c.	334.4	365.6	18,022	19,564
Elementary Goods Storage Occupations	340.7	368.3	18,226	19,138
Stevedores, dockers and slingers	469.6	493.4	25,180	26,281
Other goods handling and storage occupations n.e.c.	338.1	366.3	18,119	19,010
Elementary administration and service occupations	339.0	356.1	18,684	18,932
Elementary Administration Occupations	408.7	431.0	22,186	22,828
Postal workers, mail sorters, messengers, couriers	415.3	437.7	22,380	23,092
Elementary office occupations n.e.c.	281.4	334.5	17,215	18,218
Elementary Personal Services Occupations	253.9	270.5	13,095	13,741
Hospital porters	317.1	358.2	17,501	17,972
Hotel porters	266.9	287.6	13,333	13,912
Kitchen and catering assistants	246.1	259.5	12,840	13,364
Waiters	250.0	276.4	11,611	12,812
Bar staff	257.2	263.8	X	13,179
Leisure and theme park attendants	226.5	235.9	10,871	11,390
Elementary personal service occupations n.e.c.	255.3	275.1	X	X

Full-Time Males on Adult Rates (where pay was not affected by absence)

Occupation SOC 2000	Gross Weekly Pay (in April) 2008 Median £	Gross Weekly Pay (in April) 2008 Mean £	Gross Annual Earnings (in April) 2008 Median £	Gross Annual Earnings (in April) 2008 Mean £
Elementary Cleaning Occupations	297.7	311.3	15,703	16,019
Window cleaners	317.3	342.5	X	X
Road sweepers	319.9	352.9	17,560	18,436
Cleaners, domestics	282.7	296.3	14,462	14,994
Launderers, dry cleaners, pressers	242.6	260.6	11,720	12,172
Refuse and salvage occupations	339.5	352.9	18,226	18,608
Elementary cleaning occupations n.e.c.	308.7	337.3	17,892	18,868
Elementary Security Occupations	386.4	401.8	20,222	20,636
Security guards and related occupations	389.7	405.8	20,301	20,812
Traffic wardens	488.9	465.3	X	24,783
School crossing patrol attendants	X	X	X	X
School mid-day assistants	X	277.0	X	X
Car park attendants	305.8	347.6	17,209	18,671
Elementary security occupations n.e.c.	345.7	381.1	18,352	19,481
Elementary Sales Occupations	282.4	286.7	13,915	14,544
Shelf fillers	288.1	292.6	14,154	14,627
Elementary sales occupations n.e.c.	221.6	252.0	X	13,892
ALL EMPLOYEES	**521.2**	**631.1**	**27,500**	**35,122**

Full-Time Females on Adult Rates (where pay was not affected by absence)

Occupation SOC 2000	Gross Weekly Pay (in April) 2008		Gross Annual Earnings (in April) 2008	
	Median £	Mean £	Median £	Mean £
Managers and Senior Officials	574.9	670.7	29,938	36,568
Corporate Managers	601.8	697.0	31,089	38,335
Corporate Managers and Senior Officials	1,001.4	1,171.4	56,319	X
Senior officials in national government	1,223.9	1,241.7	67,066	68,903
Directors and chief executives of major organisations	1,564.4	1,738.6	X	X
Senior officials in local government	768.0	914.8	X	48,131
Senior officials of special interest organisations	630.4	703.9	X	39,490
Production Managers	656.7	729.9	33,316	38,017
Production, works and maintenance managers	659.4	732.0	33,106	38,154
Managers in construction	632.2	714.5	33,050	36,903
Managers in mining and energy	X	723.2		
Functional Managers	733.3	847.6	38,551	47,005
Financial managers and chartered secretaries	813.4	937.7	41,247	52,248
Marketing and sales managers	703.3	819.0	38,036	44,172
Purchasing managers	752.5	831.5	X	47,742
Advertising and public relations managers	692.2	840.5	35,219	X
Personnel, training and industrial relations managers	730.6	828.0	37,292	44,779
Information and communication technology managers	726.8	806.0	39,264	44,779
Research and development managers	697.9	757.9	36,499	44,116
Quality and Customer Care Managers	587.6	656.4	30,924	33,707
Quality assurance managers	702.9	779.2	32,635	38,855
Customer care managers	576.5	631.2	30,001	32,756
Financial Institution and Office Managers	536.6	609.6	28,439	32,719
Financial institution managers	622.6	715.3	35,567	41,841
Office managers	511.8	583.5	26,845	30,493
Managers in Distribution, Storage and Retailing	382.4	427.5	19,915	22,305
Transport and distribution managers	606.0	610.4	34,268	33,498
Storage and warehouse managers	417.5	488.4	22,164	25,530
Retail and wholesale managers	363.5	409.9	19,371	21,220
Protective Service Officers	739.7	823.5	X	39,158
Officers in armed forces				
Police officers (inspectors and above)	1,164.7	1,244.1	51,355	54,625
Senior officers in fire, ambulance, prison and related services	664.4	737.2	35,427	34,965
Security managers	584.0	594.3	X	29,314
Health and Social Services Managers	640.9	671.1	32,169	34,087
Hospital and health service managers	750.1	810.2	38,246	41,302
Pharmacy managers	625.2	593.0	35,538	32,580
Healthcare practice managers	543.3	560.5	27,207	29,166
Social services managers	637.8	650.0	33,379	33,566
Residential and day care managers	565.7	600.0	X	30,040
Managers and proprietors in agriculture and services	445.6	525.8	22,926	27,186
Managers in Farming, Horticulture, Forestry and Fishing	460.2	500.0	X	25,770
Farm Managers	427.9	442.6	22,171	22,783
Natural environment and conservation managers	X	605.7	X	32,748
Managers in animal husbandry, forestry and fishing n.e.c.	340.6	416.0	X	21,460

Full-Time Females on Adult Rates (where pay was not affected by absence)

	Gross Weekly Pay (in April) 2008		Gross Annual Earnings (in April) 2008	
Occupation SOC 2000	Median £	Mean £	Median £	Mean £
Managers and Proprietors In Hospitality and Leisure Services	390.1	432.7	19,219	22,290
Hotel and accommodation managers	362.5	472.4	18,311	24,375
Conference and exhibition managers	515.2	563.9	X	31,791
Restaurant and catering managers	368.9	390.1	18,642	19,833
Publicans and managers of licensed premises	351.7	385.3	17,633	19,674
Leisure and sports managers	425.6	482.8	21,880	25,001
Travel agency managers	365.6	438.2	X	23,359
Managers and Proprietors In Other Service Industries	536.2	615.7	28,177	31,722
Property, housing and land managers	586.8	710.8	30,657	35,843
Garage managers and proprietors	X	592.7	X	X
Hairdressing and beauty salon managers and proprietors	363.5	412.2	21,965	20,826
Shopkeepers and wholesale/retail dealers	371.7	428.6	X	24,475
Recycling and refuse disposal managers	518.2	569.0	27,038	29,460
Managers and proprietors in other services n.e.c.	531.2	592.6	27,690	30,552
Professional Occupations	633.9	694.9	32,702	35,057
Science and Technology Professionals	603.4	657.4	31,556	34,892
Science Professionals	598.1	642.3	32,711	34,572
Chemists	X	656.6	X	X
Biological scientists and biochemists	598.8	633.1	32,033	34,074
Physicists, geologists and meteorologists	609.3	708.5	X	34,323
Engineering Professionals	588.1	616.2	29,977	32,020
Civil engineers	528.7	632.9	27,128	31,210
Mechanical engineers	579.3	618.5	X	30,792
Electrical engineers	584.0	598.5	30,692	32,368
Electronics engineers				
Chemical engineers				
Design and development engineers	645.7	670.9	34,071	36,329
Production and process engineers	602.8	658.3	31,769	33,574
Planning and quality control engineers	594.9	623.4	31,350	33,934
Engineering professionals n.e.c.	534.0	566.0	26,987	29,150
Information and Communication Technology Professionals	614.0	691.3	32,005	36,818
IT strategy and planning professionals	782.3	868.3	41,240	48,927
Software professionals	592.2	632.8	30,605	33,317
Health Professionals	806.2	954.6	42,811	53,626
Medical practitioners	956.3	1,128.0	64,254	68,406
Psychologists	675.9	719.2	36,597	37,822
Pharmacists/pharmacologists	689.0	693.0	36,853	37,642
Ophthalmic opticians	656.5	680.2	X	X
Dental practitioners	526.3	643.1	X	28,156
Veterinarians	611.1	660.9	X	32,139
Teaching and Research Professionals	633.6	669.0	32,720	33,005
Teaching Professionals	640.8	674.3	32,788	33,122
Higher education teaching professionals	704.7	741.1	37,103	38,128
Further education teaching professionals	610.9	632.3	31,230	31,843
Education officers, school inspectors	757.8	772.3	35,977	37,997
Secondary education teaching professionals	657.0	692.0	33,578	33,260
Primary and nursery education teaching professionals	633.6	667.7	32,200	32,526
Special needs education teaching professionals	657.0	635.0	34,578	32,717
Registrars and senior administrators of educational establishments	547.3	625.9	29,734	33,882
Teaching professionals n.e.c.	458.4	507.6	23,517	26,843

Full-Time Females on Adult Rates (where pay was not affected by absence)

Occupation SOC 2000	Gross Weekly Pay (in April) 2008 Median £	Gross Weekly Pay (in April) 2008 Mean £	Gross Annual Earnings (in April) 2008 Median £	Gross Annual Earnings (in April) 2008 Mean £
Research Professionals	533.2	569.2	28,156	30,327
Scientific researchers	594.2	661.3	31,435	34,083
Social science researchers	387.5	455.3	X	24,429
Researchers n.e.c.	514.6	552.4	27,977	29,620
Business and public service professionals	610.3	686.9	31,371	36,125
Legal Professionals	766.6	901.8	40,585	50,298
Solicitors and lawyers, judges and coroners	785.8	930.6	42,005	52,418
Legal professionals n.e.c.	619.4	647.7	33,570	32,953
Business and Statistical Professionals	640.4	691.4	32,900	37,212
Chartered and certified accountants	615.2	649.4	32,215	34,872
Management accountants	631.8	660.6	32,153	35,149
Management consultants, actuaries, economists and statisticians	679.1	741.9	34,144	40,134
Architects, Town Planners, Surveyors	648.4	668.5	32,897	34,447
Architects	627.7	687.0	32,607	36,357
Town Planners	573.6	674.5	30,385	33,464
Quantity surveyors	X	541.1	19,634	26,898
Chartered surveyors (not quantity surveyors)	763.2	747.9	X	39,542
Public Service Professionals	574.6	583.9	29,194	29,518
Public service administrative professionals	729.3	744.0	34,454	36,698
Social workers	574.4	582.0	29,259	29,447
Probation officers	573.2	558.9	30,587	29,470
Clergy	362.3	410.7	X	21,674
Librarians and Related Professionals	479.2	491.5	24,592	25,158
Librarians	469.1	486.5	23,975	24,836
Archivists and curators	484.9	506.1	25,333	26,126
Associate Professional and Technical Occupations	502.1	535.0	26,126	27,777
Science and Technology Associate Professionals	447.3	477.3	23,204	24,855
Science and Engineering Technicians	385.1	429.5	19,669	21,720
Laboratory technicians	350.8	406.3	18,854	21,332
Electrical/electronics technicians				
Engineering technicians	568.1	602.6	27,437	28,089
Building and civil engineering technicians	360.9	400.0	X	19,005
Quality assurance technicians	409.5	413.0	19,906	20,765
Science and engineering technicians n.e.c.	415.4	438.0	20,232	21,559
Draughtspersons and Building Inspectors	482.8	503.1	25,592	26,306
Architectural technologists and town planning technicians	514.6	542.5	26,928	27,671
Draughtspersons	457.5	454.7	24,173	25,275
Building inspectors				
IT Service Delivery Occupations	476.0	523.5	25,382	27,862
IT operations technicians	497.7	548.2	26,923	29,347
IT users support technicians	449.2	488.7	24,235	25,577
Health and Social Welfare Associate Professionals	524.8	539.9	26,682	27,033
Health Associate Professionals	549.0	561.6	27,747	27,899
Nurses	551.3	567.2	27,858	28,060
Midwives	598.4	619.3	31,940	31,644
Paramedics	611.5	667.0	32,112	33,402
Medical radiographers	682.5	683.6	35,536	34,344
Chiropodists	557.4	583.1	28,143	29,210
Dispensing opticians	390.5	426.5	19,045	20,706
Pharmaceutical dispensers	296.7	329.4	15,171	16,948
Medical and dental technicians	467.6	464.7	22,600	23,520

Full-Time Females on Adult Rates (where pay was not affected by absence)

Occupation SOC 2000	Gross Weekly Pay (in April) 2008 Median £	Gross Weekly Pay (in April) 2008 Mean £	Gross Annual Earnings (in April) 2008 Median £	Gross Annual Earnings (in April) 2008 Mean £
Therapists	562.7	560.3	29,032	28,760
Physiotherapists	549.2	563.5	29,507	29,272
Occupational therapists	578.0	561.3	29,057	28,849
Speech and language therapists	479.2	520.8	25,461	27,749
Therapists n.e.c.	584.8	577.5	28,790	28,031
Social Welfare Associate Professionals	437.8	454.4	22,538	23,399
Youth and community workers	428.9	448.7	21,821	23,099
Housing and welfare officers	438.9	456.6	22,845	23,517
Protective Service Occupations	589.4	612.7	30,901	31,618
NCOs and other ranks				
Police officers (sergeant and below)	635.1	660.6	32,431	33,089
Fire service officers (leading fire officer and below)	530.4	585.3	28,046	28,000
Prison service officers (below principal officer)	428.4	438.7	23,354	23,032
Protective service associate professionals n.e.c.	575.9	577.3	30,066	29,354
Culture, media and sports occupations	479.1	563.9	25,201	32,045
Artistic and Literary Occupations	517.5	583.2	24,359	29,472
Artists	X	506.7	X	X
Authors, writers	517.3	610.3	X	29,853
Actors, entertainers				
Dancers and choreographers	615.4	619.7		
Musicians				
Arts officers, producers and directors	547.3	583.3	X	29,819
Design Associate Professionals	425.4	483.7	23,408	31,135
Graphic designers	421.6	456.1	21,710	24,246
Product, clothing and related designers	459.9	527.4	X	X
Media Associate Professionals	530.0	650.6	28,898	36,121
Journalists, newspaper and periodical editors	528.9	577.0	26,691	29,109
Broadcasting associate professionals	797.4	1,022.7	40,753	56,495
Public relations officers	507.3	591.9	26,372	34,384
Photographers and audio-visual equipment operators	403.6	430.5	X	24,065
Sports and Fitness Occupations	331.3	345.4	X	16,983
Sports players				
Sports coaches, instructors and officials	382.5	403.2	17,641	19,596
Fitness instructors	286.7	292.5	13,551	13,696
Sports and fitness occupations n.e.c.	345.6	349.3		
Business and public service associate professionals	478.9	524.8	25,191	28,162
Transport Associate Professionals	754.1	855.4	39,884	45,029
Air traffic controllers	X	943.1	45,472	50,082
Aircraft pilots and flight engineers				
Ship and hovercraft officers				
Train drivers	722.8	741.3	34,691	39,502
Legal Associate Professionals	479.1	493.2	24,507	25,873
Business and Finance Associate Professionals	521.5	603.8	27,195	32,418
Estimators, valuers and assessors	458.0	502.3	23,441	25,515
Brokers	762.3	918.4	X	X
Insurance underwriters	485.6	507.7	24,292	26,584
Finance and investment analysts/advisers	605.9	687.2	33,455	39,178
Taxation experts	575.0	626.7	27,361	30,627
Importers, exporters	346.3	341.3	X	X

Full-Time Females on Adult Rates (where pay was not affected by absence)

	Gross Weekly Pay (in April) 2008		Gross Annual Earnings (in April) 2008	
Occupation SOC 2000	**Median £**	**Mean £**	**Median £**	**Mean £**
Financial and accounting technicians	627.7	721.6	32,493	36,013
Business and related associate professionals n.e.c.	474.5	498.4	25,380	26,366
Sales and Related Associate Professionals	449.4	494.8	23,437	26,749
Buyers and purchasing officers	519.7	553.1	26,729	29,408
Sales representatives	421.1	479.3	22,180	25,708
Marketing associate professionals	475.7	502.9	24,380	27,472
Estate agents, auctioneers	X	506.9	X	X
Conservation Associate Professionals	465.0	488.4	24,225	25,572
Conservation and environmental protection officers	486.1	508.6	24,914	26,472
Countryside and park rangers	419.2	437.3	22,056	23,259
Public Service and Other Associate Professionals	467.1	502.6	24,877	26,754
Public service associate professionals	506.6	535.1	28,589	29,422
Personnel and industrial relations officers	441.0	495.3	23,837	26,412
Vocational and industrial trainers and instructors	438.9	473.1	22,778	24,692
Careers advisers and vocational guidance specialists	469.6	517.0	26,638	27,521
Inspectors of factories, utilities and trading standards	497.0	537.9	X	27,857
Statutory examiners	511.4	517.5	28,441	27,953
Occupational hygienists and safety officers (health and safety)	499.6	502.5	25,334	26,070
Environmental health officers	563.7	616.4	29,679	30,427
Administrative and secretarial occupations	351.5	382.1	18,417	19,725
Administrative occupations	349.9	379.8	18,326	19,539
Administrative Occupations: Government and Related Organisations	358.7	386.8	18,880	19,938
Civil Service executive officers	448.0	448.0	23,126	23,320
Civil Service administrative officers and assistants	334.8	346.4	17,533	17,924
Local government clerical officers and assistants	377.1	402.5	19,189	20,330
Officers of non-governmental organisations	412.9	438.6	22,932	22,374
Administrative Occupations: Finance	360.8	400.3	19,187	20,665
Credit controllers	351.5	365.3	19,032	19,533
Accounts and wages clerks, book-keepers, other financial clerks	369.5	402.0	19,150	20,691
Counter clerks	349.9	403.3	19,272	20,814
Administrative Occupations: Records	342.0	365.1	17,602	18,729
Filing and other records assistants/clerks	345.8	365.0	17,858	18,754
Pensions and insurance clerks	345.0	381.9	18,087	20,093
Stock control clerks	325.9	355.8	16,673	18,066
Transport and distribution clerks	381.8	404.3	19,716	20,679
Library assistants/clerks	332.1	350.2	16,573	17,402
Database assistants/clerks	314.7	339.1	16,809	17,557
Market research interviewers	363.6	391.9	X	18,523
Administrative Occupations: Communications	427.2	452.2	21,904	23,154
Telephonists	350.6	367.2	17,845	18,480
Communications operators	493.3	529.0	27,212	28,159
Administrative Occupations: General	330.7	363.5	17,185	18,555
General office assistants/clerks	330.7	363.5	17,185	18,555
Secretarial and related occupations	355.8	389.4	18,626	20,315

Full-Time Females on Adult Rates (where pay was not affected by absence)

Occupation SOC 2000	Gross Weekly Pay (in April) 2008 Median £	Gross Weekly Pay (in April) 2008 Mean £	Gross Annual Earnings (in April) 2008 Median £	Gross Annual Earnings (in April) 2008 Mean £
Medical secretaries	368.2	379.4	18,904	19,300
Legal secretaries	351.0	388.1	18,451	20,786
School secretaries	318.0	346.3	16,521	17,827
Company secretaries	462.1	519.0	24,974	29,492
Personal assistants and other secretaries	431.2	450.8	22,187	23,398
Receptionists	289.0	303.2	14,893	15,541
Typists	320.9	330.4	16,304	16,994
Skilled trades occupations	308.1	340.7	16,478	17,332
Skilled agricultural trades	313.6	330.5	X	15,421
Agricultural Trades	313.7	330.5	X	15,421
Farmers				
Horticultural trades	279.0	296.4	14,875	13,831
Gardeners and groundsmen/groundswomen	281.9	291.0	13,195	13,718
Agricultural and fishing trades n.e.c.				
Skilled metal and electrical trades	442.3	452.2	21,323	22,278
Metal Forming, Welding and Related Trades	444.2	446.8	26,652	25,209
Smiths and forge workers				
Moulders, core makers, die casters				
Sheet metal workers				
Metal plate workers, shipwrights, riveters				
Welding trades				
Pipe fitters				
Metal Machining, Fitting and Instrument Making Trades	382.3	433.9	17,895	20,527
Metal machining setters and setter-operators	262.9	322.1	X	16,975
Tool makers, tool fitters and markers-out				
Metal working production and maintenance fitters	448.3	466.9	X	22,121
Precision instrument makers and repairers	X	X	X	X
Vehicle Trades	402.6	394.0	16,260	15,654
Motor mechanics, auto engineers	411.6	401.2	16,260	15,654
Vehicle body builders and repairers				
Auto electricians				
Vehicle spray painters				
Electrical Trades	460.2	486.0	23,869	25,157
Electricians, electrical fitters	X	455.5	X	23,697
Telecommunications engineers	445.5	457.4	22,246	23,842
Lines repairers and cable jointers				
TV, video and audio engineers				
Computer engineers, installation and maintenance	493.3	534.1	X	27,266
Electrical/electronics engineers n.e.c.	448.5	501.5	23,658	25,882
Skilled construction and building trades	337.0	373.0	X	X
Construction Trades	384.6	390.1	X	X
Steel erectors				
Bricklayers, masons				
Roofers, roof tilers and slaters				
Plumbers, heating and ventilating engineers	X	409.6	X	X
Carpenters and joiners				
Glaziers, window fabricators and fitters				
Construction trades n.e.c.	392.7	399.9		
Building Trades	317.7	326.9	X	X
Plasterers				
Floorers and wall tilers				
Painters and decorators	324.2	330.3	X	X

Full-Time Females on Adult Rates (where pay was not affected by absence)

Occupation SOC 2000	Gross Weekly Pay (in April) 2008 Median £	Gross Weekly Pay (in April) 2008 Mean £	Gross Annual Earnings (in April) 2008 Median £	Gross Annual Earnings (in April) 2008 Mean £
Textiles, printing and other skilled trades	285.5	306.6	14,452	15,942
Textiles and Garments Trades	300.9	310.1	15,196	15,700
Weavers and knitters				
Upholsterers	X	315.1	X	17,045
Leather and related trades	339.7	348.9	16,031	16,626
Tailors and dressmakers	X	273.6	15,602	17,084
Textiles, garments and related trades n.e.c.	X	334.8	13,062	14,615
Printing Trades	342.7	358.2	15,707	17,846
Originators, compositors and print preparers	346.1	344.8	18,057	18,039
Printers	X	391.8	X	19,761
Bookbinders and print finishers	338.6	350.6	15,519	17,303
Screen printers				
Food Preparation Trades	285.0	302.4	14,378	15,691
Butchers, meat cutters				
Bakers, flour confectioners	268.4	285.8	X	14,479
Fishmongers, poultry dressers	246.5	280.2	13,371	13,826
Chefs, cooks	285.9	304.4	14,672	15,851
Skilled Trades n.e.c.	256.4	288.7	13,845	15,920
Glass and ceramics makers, decorators and finishers	282.4	306.2	16,632	17,678
Furniture makers, other craft woodworkers	243.1	268.9	X	14,636
Pattern makers (moulds)				
Musical instrument makers and tuners				
Goldsmiths, silversmiths, precious stone workers				
Floral arranger, florists	230.6	239.1	12,183	13,875
Hand craft occupations n.e.c.	288.2	349.8	X	X
Personal service occupations	305.0	324.6	15,477	16,136
Caring personal service occupations	304.3	320.3	15,413	15,851
Healthcare and Related Personal Services	315.5	333.1	15,976	16,381
Nursing auxiliaries and assistants	325.9	336.7	16,581	16,708
Ambulance staff (excluding paramedics)	385.4	417.3	20,886	21,673
Dental nurses	303.3	306.7	14,780	15,281
Houseparents and residential wardens	387.4	404.4	19,613	19,921
Care assistants and home carers	308.0	328.7	15,369	16,019
Childcare and Related Personal Services	280.1	297.7	14,492	14,882
Nursery nurses	276.9	293.0	14,859	15,149
Childminders and related occupations	314.5	347.1	15,394	16,807
Playgroup leaders/assistants	255.6	292.2	X	12,346
Educational assistants	279.2	296.5	14,398	14,661
Animal Care Services	262.2	293.0	13,938	15,874
Veterinary nurses and assistants	265.0	300.2	13,882	15,625
Animal care occupations n.e.c.	256.8	285.1	X	X
Leisure and Other Personal Service Occupations	310.8	350.1	16,111	17,747
Leisure and Travel Service Occupations	367.0	404.2	18,570	20,483
Sports and leisure assistants	298.5	311.2	15,138	15,837
Travel agents	346.2	367.8	18,121	19,574
Travel and tour guides	251.3	284.1	12,559	13,725
Air travel assistants	423.5	458.8	19,618	22,447
Rail travel assistants	461.3	531.1	24,389	24,917
Leisure and travel service occupations n.e.c.	X	518.7	X	X
Hairdressers and Related Occupations	251.2	284.3	12,720	14,444
Hairdressers, barbers	242.5	270.8	11,769	13,474
Beauticians and related occupations	285.9	308.9	15,145	16,543

Full-Time Females on Adult Rates (where pay was not affected by absence)

Occupation SOC 2000	Gross Weekly Pay (in April) 2008 Median £	Gross Weekly Pay (in April) 2008 Mean £	Gross Annual Earnings (in April) 2008 Median £	Gross Annual Earnings (in April) 2008 Mean £
Housekeeping Occupations	280.7	304.7	14,345	15,198
Housekeepers and related occupations	271.9	295.6	13,743	15,001
Caretakers	306.8	325.4	14,766	15,592
Personal Services Occupations n.e.c.	352.1	382.9	22,056	22,652
Undertakers and mortuary assistants	342.2	385.6	20,817	22,708
Pest control officers				
Sales and customer service occupations	274.5	296.8	14,090	15,123
Sales occupations	256.2	281.6	13,086	14,253
Sales Assistants and Retail Cashiers	252.0	273.8	12,793	13,687
Sales and retail assistants	251.0	272.1	12,748	13,492
Retail cashiers and check-out operators	234.3	245.8	11,917	12,512
Telephone salespersons	331.7	374.6	19,067	20,318
Sales related occupations	339.1	368.1	18,250	20,401
Collector salespersons and credit agents	324.1	316.5	18,552	18,157
Debt, rent and other cash collectors	280.8	314.0	15,514	16,534
Roundsmen/women and van salespersons	247.7	278.6		
Market and street traders and assistants				
Merchandisers and window dressers	372.2	409.7	19,895	22,066
Sales related occupations n.e.c.	347.7	373.6	19,363	21,488
Customer Service Occupations	315.1	332.8	16,665	17,314
Call centre agents/operators	303.9	322.2	15,893	16,460
Customer care occupations	316.8	335.0	16,973	17,503
Process, plant and machine operatives	302.1	327.8	15,755	16,680
Process, plant and machine operatives	296.9	319.6	15,487	16,403
Process operatives	288.9	316.0	15,607	16,404
Food, drink and tobacco process operatives	282.9	306.0	15,366	16,119
Glass and ceramics process operatives	251.8	299.6	X	X
Textile process operatives	251.5	269.9	13,037	13,353
Chemical and related process operatives	345.2	413.3	17,820	20,500
Rubber process operatives	312.9	367.4	X	X
Plastics process operatives	332.2	340.9	16,291	17,533
Metal making and treating process operatives	236.4	246.5	12,256	13,515
Electroplaters				
Process operatives n.e.c.	305.6	329.1	15,991	16,188
Plant and Machine Operatives	282.8	331.1	15,978	17,254
Paper and wood machine operatives	251.0	322.7	16,675	17,466
Coal mine operatives				
Quarry workers and related operatives				
Energy plant operatives				
Metal working machine operatives	274.7	300.7	13,962	15,354
Water and sewerage plant operatives	371.3	445.6	X	24,279
Plant and machine operatives n.e.c.	X	369.7	X	15,702
Assemblers and Routine Operatives	298.5	319.7	15,193	16,221
Assemblers (electrical products)	307.3	329.2	15,317	16,315
Assemblers (vehicles and metal goods)	325.1	342.4	16,923	18,354
Routine inspectors and testers	324.7	346.6	X	X
Weighers, graders, sorters	299.0	318.3	X	16,500
Tyre, exhaust and windscreen fitters				
Clothing cutters	X	X	13,862	15,701
Sewing machinists	279.1	300.4	13,917	14,293
Routine laboratory testers	300.0	331.8	15,819	16,794
Assemblers and routine operatives n.e.c.	274.6	300.3	14,649	15,840
Construction Operatives	337.1	354.6	17,805	18,381
Scaffolders, stagers, riggers				
Road construction operatives				
Rail construction and maintenance operatives				
Construction operatives n.e.c.	323.0	354.8	17,310	18,374

Full-Time Females on Adult Rates (where pay was not affected by absence)

Occupation SOC 2000	Gross Weekly Pay (in April) 2008 Median £	Mean £	Gross Annual Earnings (in April) 2008 Median £	Mean £
Transport and mobile machine drivers and operatives	342.8	376.0	17,260	18,565
Transport Drivers and Operatives	339.9	375.5	17,069	18,513
Heavy goods vehicle drivers	393.9	391.4	X	20,411
Van drivers	301.1	329.5	14,536	15,442
Bus and coach drivers	362.9	438.0	X	21,044
Taxi, cab drivers and chauffeurs	278.0	299.9	12,909	15,242
Driving instructors				
Rail transport operatives	X	538.5	X	29,450
Seafarers (merchant navy); barge, lighter and boat operatives				
Air transport operatives	X	363.9	X	16,342
Transport operatives n.e.c.	X	369.2	X	X
Mobile Machine Drivers and Operatives	340.4	383.6		
Crane drivers				
Fork-lift truck drivers				
Agricultural machinery drivers				
Mobile machine drivers and operatives n.e.c.	271.8	312.4		
Elementary occupations	262.5	288.3	13,541	14,447
Elementary trades, plant and storage related occupations	285.7	302.4	14,785	15,440
Elementary Agricultural Occupations	271.8	295.7	13,824	14,971
Farm workers	260.6	298.9	14,578	16,202
Forestry workers				
Fishing and agriculture related occupations n.e.c.	280.7	292.3	X	13,424
Elementary Construction Occupations	258.8	302.6		
Labourers in building and woodworking trades	217.5	262.3		
Labourers in other construction trades n.e.c.				
Elementary Process Plant Occupations	283.7	298.3	14,656	15,294
Labourers in foundries				
Industrial cleaning process occupations	296.8	291.0	X	14,981
Printing machine minders and assistants	323.9	338.5	14,870	18,748
Packers, bottlers, canners, fillers	283.9	297.4	14,604	15,223
Labourers in process and plant operations n.e.c.	271.9	293.9	14,503	14,948
Elementary Goods Storage Occupations	287.0	307.6	14,840	15,628
Stevedores, dockers and slingers				
Other goods handling and storage occupations n.e.c.	287.0	307.7	14,840	15,628
Elementary administration and service occupations	252.9	281.9	13,000	13,997
Elementary Administration Occupations	339.6	336.3	18,685	18,286
Postal workers, mail sorters, messengers, couriers	380.8	393.5	20,616	20,614
Elementary office occupations n.e.c.	229.2	246.8	11,547	12,904
Elementary Personal Services Occupations	233.9	252.9	11,900	12,229
Hospital porters	X	371.2	X	19,014
Hotel porters				
Kitchen and catering assistants	242.2	262.5	12,221	12,774
Waitresses	220.9	243.1	10,899	11,339
Bar staff	224.7	231.9	X	10,906
Leisure and theme park attendants	225.8	243.3	X	11,389
Elementary personal service occupations n.e.c.	239.6	250.1	13,522	13,925

Full-Time Females on Adult Rates (where pay was not affected by absence)

	Gross Weekly Pay (in April) 2008		Gross Annual Earnings (in April) 2008	
Occupation SOC 2000	Median £	Mean £	Median £	Mean £
Elementary Cleaning Occupations	251.6	270.1	12,579	13,032
Window cleaners				
Road sweepers				
Cleaners, domestics	252.2	271.3	12,515	12,931
Launderers, dry cleaners, pressers	232.8	247.6	12,642	12,943
Refuse and salvage occupations	429.0	437.9	19,634	23,328
Elementary cleaning occupations n.e.c.				
Elementary Security Occupations	367.2	400.5	19,725	19,542
Security guards and related occupations	399.6	430.0	21,467	20,999
Traffic wardens	354.2	381.9	18,512	19,683
School crossing patrol attendants				
School mid-day assistants	243.0	283.9	X	X
Car park attendants	380.1	411.8	20,124	21,091
Elementary security occupations n.e.c.	X	392.0	18,729	20,725
Elementary Sales Occupations	278.0	292.5	14,475	14,480
Shelf fillers	280.0	294.8	14,784	14,846
Elementary sales occupations n.e.c.	260.5	280.2	11,935	12,959
ALL EMPLOYEES	**412.0**	**485.5**	**21,447**	**25,304**

F8: Public sector comparable earnings

The gross income equivalent of net sums, and some comparable salaries

Net (£)	Gross equivalent (£)	Comparable gross salaries
10,000	11,976	
10,463	12,375	National Minimum Wage (adults) £12,375, Army (new entrant) £13,377
12,000	14,909	Healthcare Assistant £16,301, Army Private (B) £16,681
14,000	17,841	Nurse (newly qualified) £20,622
16,000	20,774	Junior Hospital Doctor (B) £22,190
18,000	23,706	Teacher (newly qualified, B) £24,168, Army Private (T) £25,887, Nurse Grade F £26,018
20,000	26,639	NHS Registrar (B) £29,411, Bishop (B) £30,350, Nurse (A) £30,450
22,500	30,305	Sister Grade G (T) £31,841, Dean (T) £32,040, Sergeant (B) £32,114, Teacher (Upper scale, B) £33,411
25,000	33,970	Sergeant (T) £36,205, Captain (B) £37,172, Head Teacher (B) £37,536
27,500	37,636	Bishop (T) £39,030
30,000	41,302	Captain (T) £44,206
32,500	44,848	NHS Registrar (T) £46,246, Major (B) £46,824
35,000	49,088	
37,500	53,459	Teacher (Advanced Skills, T) £55,669, Major (T) £56,077, Civil Service Band 1 (T) £57,300
40,000	57,829	Bishop of London £58,750, Archbishop of York £60,690
42,500	62,200	MP £64,766, Lieutenant Colonel (B) £65,717
45,000	66,570	
47,500	70,941	Archbishop of Canterbury £71,910, NHS Consultant (B) £74,504
50,000	75,312	Lieutenant Colonel (T) £76,096
52,500	79,682	Colonel (B) £79,716, Civil Service Band 2 (B) £81,600
55,000	84,053	Colonel (T) £87,656
57,500	88,424	
60,000	92,794	Junior Government Minister £94,228, Brigadier (B) £95,128, Major General (B) £96,835
62,500	97,165	Brigadier (T) £98,984, Civil Service Band 3 (B) £99,960
65,000	101,535	Minister of State £104,050
67,500	105,906	District Judge (PRFD) £106,921, Major General (T) £109,415
70,000	110,277	GP (A) £111,566, Lieutenant General (B) £114,213
72,500	114,647	Civil Service Band 1 (T) £117,740
75,000	119,018	NHS Consultant (A) £119,200
77,500	123,389	
80,000	127,759	Circuit Judge £128,296
82,500	132,130	
85,000	136,501	Senior Circuit Judge £138,548, Permanent Secretary (B) £139,740
87,500	140,871	Cabinet Minister £141,866, Lieutenant General (T) £142,539
90,000	145,242	
92,500	149,612	Head Teacher (T) £150,000
95,000	153,983	General (B) £154,700
97,500	158,354	
100,000	162,724	General (T) £170,791
105,000	171,466	High Court Judge £172,753
110,000	180,207	
115,000	188,948	Prime Minister £194,250, Lord Justice of Appeal £196,707
120,000	197,689	Civil Service Band 3 (T) £205,000, Lord of Appeal & Family Division President £206,857
130,000	215,171	Master of the Rolls £214,165, Chief of Defence Staff (B) £222,359
140,000	232,654	Chief of Defence Staff (T) £235,969, Lord Chief Justice £239,845
150,000	250,137	Permanent Secretary (T) £273,250
175,000	293,843	

Assumptions for the grossed-up equivalent 3% contributory pension; contracted out of SERPS for Class 1 NIC. Salaries effective April 2009 (teachers from September).

All are subject to diverse terms and conditions, and some to multifarious expenses.

(A), (B) and (T) indicate average, bottom and top of range or seniority for post or rank.

2009–10 tax rates are used for the figures in the second column.

F9: Public sector earnings websites

Websites that provide helpful information about pay and retirement benefits in the public sector include:

Sector (annual review date)	Sources of information
Armed forces (April 1)	*www.army.mod.uk* *www.rncom.mod.uk* *www.rafcom.co.uk*
Health service (April 1)	*www.nhscareers.nhs.uk* *www.nhsemployers.org*
Police (September 1)	*www.police-information.co.uk*
Teachers (September 1)	*www.teachers.org.uk* *www.atl.org.uk*
Local government (April 1)	*www.navca. org.uk* [National Association for Voluntary and Community Action] *www.lgps.org.uk* [Local Government Pension Scheme]
Civil service (April 1)	*www.civilservice.gov.uk*

Group G
Tax and National Insurance

G

G1: Net equivalents to a range of gross annual income figures

	1997/98 Net equivalent income				1998/99 Net equivalent income			
	Employed		Self-employed		Employed		Self-employed	
Gross income £pa	Single person £pa	Married man £pa	Single person £pa	Married man £pa	Single person £pa	Married man £pa	Single person £pa	Married man £pa
1,000	1,000	1,000	1,000	1,000	1,000	1,000	1,000	1,000
2,000	2,000	2,000	2,000	2,000	2,000	2,000	2,000	2,000
3,000	3,000	3,000	3,000	3,000	3,000	3,000	3,000	3,000
4,000	3,858	3,858	3,680	3,680	3,866	3,866	3,670	3,670
5,000	4,567	4,758	4,489	4,680	4,605	4,766	4,509	4,670
6,000	5,267	5,541	5,289	5,564	5,305	5,590	5,309	5,594
7,000	5,967	6,241	6,089	6,364	6,005	6,290	6,109	6,394
8,000	6,667	6,941	6,830	7,104	6,705	6,990	6,867	7,152
9,000	7,341	7,615	7,544	7,819	7,390	7,675	7,592	7,877
10,000	8,011	8,286	8,254	8,529	8,060	8,345	8,302	8,587
11,000	8,681	8,956	8,964	9,239	8,730	9,015	9,012	9,297
12,000	9,351	9,626	9,674	9,949	9,400	9,685	9,722	10,007
13,000	10,021	10,296	10,384	10,659	10,070	10,355	10,432	10,717
14,000	10,691	10,966	11,094	11,369	10,740	11,025	11,142	11,427
15,000	11,361	11,636	11,804	12,079	11,410	11,695	11,852	12,137
16,000	12,031	12,306	12,514	12,789	12,080	12,365	12,562	12,847
17,000	12,701	12,976	13,224	13,499	12,750	13,035	13,272	13,557
18,000	13,371	13,646	13,934	14,209	13,420	13,705	13,982	14,267
19,000	14,041	14,316	14,644	14,919	14,090	14,375	14,692	14,977
20,000	14,711	14,986	15,354	15,629	14,760	15,045	15,402	15,687
21,000	15,381	15,656	16,064	16,339	15,430	15,715	16,112	16,397
22,000	16,051	16,326	16,774	17,049	16,100	16,385	16,822	17,107
23,000	16,721	16,996	17,484	17,759	16,770	17,055	17,532	17,817
24,000	17,391	17,666	18,194	18,469	17,440	17,725	18,242	18,527
25,000	18,143	18,418	18,953	19,228	18,110	18,395	18,952	19,237
26,000	18,913	19,188	19,723	19,998	18,858	19,143	19,709	19,994
27,000	19,683	19,958	20,493	20,768	19,628	19,913	20,479	20,764
28,000	20,453	20,728	21,263	21,538	20,398	20,683	21,249	21,534
29,000	21,223	21,498	22,033	22,308	21,168	21,453	22,019	22,304
30,000	21,993	22,268	22,803	23,078	21,938	22,223	22,789	23,074
31,000	22,618	22,893	23,428	23,703	22,708	22,993	23,559	23,844
32,000	23,218	23,493	24,028	24,303	23,358	23,643	24,209	24,494
33,000	23,818	24,093	24,628	24,903	23,958	24,243	24,809	25,094
34,000	24,418	24,693	25,228	25,503	24,558	24,843	25,409	25,694
35,000	25,018	25,293	25,828	26,103	25,158	25,443	26,009	26,294
40,000	28,018	28,293	28,828	29,103	28,158	28,443	29,009	29,294
45,000	31,018	31,293	31,828	32,103	31,158	31,443	32,009	32,294
50,000	34,018	34,293	34,828	35,103	34,158	34,443	35,009	35,294
55,000	37,018	37,293	37,828	38,103	37,158	37,443	38,009	38,294
60,000	40,018	40,293	40,828	41,103	40,158	40,443	41,009	41,294
65,000	43,018	43,293	43,828	44,103	43,158	43,443	44,009	44,294
70,000	46,018	46,293	46,828	47,103	46,158	46,443	47,009	47,294
75,000	49,018	49,293	49,828	50,103	49,158	49,443	50,009	50,294
80,000	52,018	52,293	52,828	53,103	52,158	52,443	53,009	53,294
85,000	55,018	55,293	55,828	56,103	55,158	55,443	56,009	56,294
90,000	58,018	58,293	58,828	59,103	58,158	58,443	59,009	59,294
95,000	61,018	61,293	61,828	62,103	61,158	61,443	62,009	62,294
100,000	64,018	64,293	64,828	65,103	64,158	64,443	65,009	65,294
150,000	94,018	94,293	94,828	95,103	94,158	94,443	95,009	95,294
200,000	124,018	124,293	124,828	125,103	124,158	124,443	125,009	125,294
250,000	154,018	154,293	154,828	155,103	154,158	154,443	155,009	155,294
300,000	184,018	184,293	184,828	185,103	184,158	184,443	185,009	185,294

These figures are for persons under 65 in employment or self employment. Refer to table H1 for pensions for persons under 65 and for all income for persons aged 65 and over.

G1: Net equivalents to a range of gross annual income figures

	1999/00 Net equivalent income				2000/01 Net equivalent income			
	Employed		Self-employed		Employed		Self-employed	
Gross income £pa	Single person £pa	Married man £pa	Single person £pa	Married man £pa	Single person £pa	Married man £pa	Single person £pa	Married man £pa
1,000	1,000	1,000	1,000	1,000	1,000	1,000	1,000	1,000
2,000	2,000	2,000	2,000	2,000	2,000	2,000	2,000	2,000
3,000	3,000	3,000	3,000	3,000	3,000	3,000	3,000	3,000
4,000	3,943	3,943	3,659	3,659	3,995	3,995	3,896	3,896
5,000	4,776	4,843	4,592	4,659	4,834	4,834	4,791	4,791
6,000	5,555	5,743	5,471	5,659	5,622	5,622	5,610	5,610
7,000	6,225	6,422	6,241	6,438	6,302	6,302	6,320	6,320
8,000	6,895	7,092	6,983	7,180	6,982	6,982	7,030	7,030
9,000	7,565	7,762	7,693	7,890	7,662	7,662	7,740	7,740
10,000	8,235	8,432	8,551	8,748	8,342	8,342	8,450	8,450
11,000	8,905	9,102	9,113	9,310	9,022	9,022	9,160	9,160
12,000	9,575	9,772	9,823	10,020	9,702	9,702	9,870	9,870
13,000	10,245	10,442	10,533	10,730	10,382	10,382	10,580	10,580
14,000	10,915	11,112	11,243	11,440	11,062	11,062	11,290	11,290
15,000	11,585	11,782	11,953	12,150	11,742	11,742	12,000	12,000
16,000	12,255	12,451	12,663	12,860	12,422	12,422	12,710	12,710
17,000	12,925	13,122	13,373	13,570	13,102	13,102	13,420	13,420
18,000	13,595	13,792	14,083	14,280	13,782	13,782	14,130	14,130
19,000	14,265	14,462	14,793	14,990	14,462	14,462	14,840	14,840
20,000	14,935	15,132	15,503	15,700	15,142	15,142	15,550	15,550
21,000	15,605	15,802	16,213	16,410	15,822	15,822	16,260	16,260
22,000	16,275	16,472	16,923	17,120	16,502	16,502	16,970	16,970
23,000	16,945	17,142	17,633	17,830	17,182	17,182	17,680	17,680
24,000	17,615	17,812	18,343	18,540	17,862	17,862	18,390	18,390
25,000	18,285	18,482	19,053	19,250	18,542	18,542	19,100	19,100
26,000	18,955	19,152	19,763	19,960	19,222	19,222	19,810	19,810
27,000	19,725	19,922	20,533	20,730	19,902	19,902	20,520	20,520
28,000	20,495	20,692	21,303	21,500	20,600	20,600	21,243	21,243
29,000	21,265	21,462	22,073	22,270	21,380	21,380	22,023	22,023
30,000	22,035	22,232	22,843	23,040	22,160	22,160	22,803	22,803
31,000	22,805	23,002	23,613	23,810	22,940	22,940	23,583	23,583
32,000	23,575	23,772	24,383	24,580	23,720	23,720	24,363	24,363
33,000	24,232	24,429	25,040	25,237	24,461	24,461	25,104	25,104
34,000	24,832	25,029	25,640	25,837	25,061	25,061	25,704	25,704
35,000	25,432	25,629	26,240	26,437	25,661	25,661	26,304	26,304
40,000	28,432	28,629	29,240	29,437	28,661	28,661	29,304	29,304
45,000	31,432	31,629	32,240	32,437	31,661	31,661	32,304	32,304
50,000	34,432	34,629	35,240	35,437	34,661	34,661	35,304	35,304
55,000	37,432	37,629	38,240	38,437	37,661	37,661	38,304	38,304
60,000	40,432	40,629	41,240	41,437	40,661	40,661	41,304	41,304
65,000	43,432	43,629	44,240	44,437	43,661	43,661	44,304	44,304
70,000	46,432	46,629	47,240	47,437	46,661	46,661	47,304	47,304
75,000	49,432	49,629	50,240	50,437	49,661	49,661	50,304	50,304
80,000	52,432	52,629	53,240	53,437	52,661	52,661	53,304	53,304
85,000	55,432	55,629	56,240	56,437	55,661	55,661	56,304	56,304
90,000	58,432	58,629	59,240	59,437	58,661	58,661	59,304	59,304
95,000	61,432	61,629	62,240	62,437	61,661	61,661	62,304	62,304
100,000	64,432	64,629	65,240	65,437	64,661	64,661	65,304	65,304
150,000	94,432	94,629	95,240	95,437	94,661	94,661	95,304	95,304
200,000	124,432	124,629	125,240	125,437	124,661	124,661	125,304	125,304
250,000	154,432	154,629	155,240	155,437	154,661	154,661	155,304	155,304
300,000	184,432	184,629	185,240	185,437	184,661	184,661	185,304	185,304

From 2000–2001 onwards there is no difference between single and married people for tax purposes.

	2001/02 Net equivalent income		2002/03 Net equivalent income		2003/04 Net equivalent income	
	Employed	Self-employed	Employed	Self-employed	Employed	Self-employed
Gross income £pa	£pa	£pa	£pa	£pa	£pa	£pa
1,000	1,000	1,000	1,000	1,000	1,000	1,000
2,000	2,000	2,000	2,000	2,000	2,000	2,000
3,000	3,000	3,000	3,000	3,000	3,000	3,000
4,000	4,000	3,896	4,000	4,000	4,000	4,000
5,000	4,906	4,817	4,924	4,830	4,919	4,827
6,000	5,706	5,647	5,724	5,660	5,709	5,647
7,000	6,436	6,407	6,469	6,435	6,448	6,416
8,000	7,116	7,117	7,149	7,145	7,118	7,116
9,000	7,796	7,827	7,829	7,855	7,788	7,816
10,000	8,476	8,537	8,509	8,565	8,458	8,516
11,000	9,156	9,247	9,189	9,275	9,128	9,216
12,000	9,836	9,957	9,869	9,985	9,798	9,916
13,000	10,516	10,667	10,549	10,695	10,468	10,616
14,000	11,196	11,377	11,229	11,405	11,138	11,316
15,000	11,876	12,087	11,909	12,115	11,808	12,016
16,000	12,556	12,797	12,589	12,825	12,478	12,716
17,000	13,236	13,507	13,269	13,535	13,148	13,416
18,000	13,916	14,217	13,949	14,245	13,818	14,116
19,000	14,596	14,927	14,629	14,955	14,488	14,816
20,000	15,276	15,637	15,309	15,665	15,158	15,516
21,000	15,956	16,347	15,989	16,375	15,828	16,216
22,000	16,636	17,057	16,669	17,085	16,498	16,916
23,000	17,316	17,767	17,349	17,795	17,168	17,616
24,000	17,996	18,477	18,029	18,505	17,838	18,316
25,000	18,676	19,187	18,709	19,215	18,508	19,016
26,000	19,356	19,897	19,389	19,925	19,178	19,716
27,000	20,036	20,607	20,069	20,635	19,848	20,416
28,000	20,716	21,317	20,749	21,345	20,518	21,116
29,000	21,396	22,027	21,429	22,055	21,188	21,816
30,000	22,086	22,744	22,109	22,765	21,858	22,516
31,000	22,866	23,524	22,847	23,516	22,534	23,220
32,000	23,646	24,304	23,627	24,296	23,304	23,990
33,000	24,426	25,084	24,407	25,076	24,074	24,760
34,000	25,194	25,852	25,187	25,856	24,844	25,530
35,000	25,794	26,452	25,879	26,548	25,614	26,300
40,000	28,794	29,452	28,879	29,548	28,585	29,271
45,000	31,794	32,452	31,879	32,548	31,535	32,221
50,000	34,794	35,452	34,879	35,548	34,485	35,171
55,000	37,794	38,452	37,879	38,548	37,435	38,121
60,000	40,794	41,452	40,879	41,548	40,385	41,071
65,000	43,794	44,452	43,879	44,548	43,335	44,021
70,000	46,794	47,452	46,879	47,548	46,285	46,971
75,000	49,794	50,452	49,879	50,548	49,235	49,921
80,000	52,794	53,452	52,879	53,548	52,185	52,871
85,000	55,794	56,452	55,879	56,548	55,135	55,821
90,000	58,794	59,452	58,879	59,548	58,085	58,771
95,000	61,794	62,452	61,879	62,548	61,035	61,721
100,000	64,794	65,452	64,879	65,548	63,985	64,671
150,000	94,794	95,452	94,879	95,548	93,485	94,171
200,000	124,794	125,452	124,879	125,548	122,985	123,671
250,000	154,794	155,452	154,879	155,548	152,485	153,171
300,000	184,794	185,452	184,879	185,548	181,985	182,671

G1: Net equivalents to a range of gross annual income figures

	2004/05 Net equivalent income		2005/06 Net equivalent income		2006/07 Net equivalent income	
	Employed	**Self-employed**	**Employed**	**Self-employed**	**Employed**	**Self-employed**
Gross income £pa	**£pa**	**£pa**	**£pa**	**£pa**	**£pa**	**£pa**
1,000	1,000	1,000	1,000	1,000	1,000	1,000
2,000	2,000	2,000	2,000	2,000	2,000	2,000
3,000	3,000	3,000	3,000	3,000	3,000	3,000
4,000	4,000	4,000	4,000	4,000	4,000	4,000
5,000	4,946	4,847	4,977	4,872	5,000	4,891
6,000	5,736	5,657	5,767	5,692	5,797	5,717
7,000	6,498	6,459	6,556	6,511	6,587	6,537
8,000	7,168	7,159	7,226	7,211	7,280	7,260
9,000	7,838	7,859	7,896	7,911	7,950	7,960
10,000	8,508	8,559	8,566	8,611	8,620	8,660
11,000	9,178	9,259	9,236	9,311	9,290	9,360
12,000	9,848	9,959	9,906	10,011	9,960	10,060
13,000	10,518	10,659	10,576	10,711	10,630	10,760
14,000	11,188	11,359	11,246	11,411	11,300	11,460
15,000	11,858	12,059	11,916	12,111	11,970	12,160
16,000	12,528	12,759	12,586	12,811	12,640	12,860
17,000	13,198	13,459	13,256	13,511	13,310	13,560
18,000	13,868	14,159	13,926	14,211	13,980	14,260
19,000	14,538	14,859	14,596	14,911	14,650	14,960
20,000	15,208	15,559	15,266	15,611	15,320	15,660
21,000	15,878	16,259	15,936	16,311	15,990	16,360
22,000	16,548	16,959	16,606	17,011	16,660	17,060
23,000	17,218	17,659	17,276	17,711	17,330	17,760
24,000	17,888	18,359	17,946	18,411	18,000	18,460
25,000	18,558	19,059	18,616	19,111	18,670	19,160
26,000	19,228	19,759	19,286	19,811	19,340	19,860
27,000	19,898	20,459	19,956	20,511	20,010	20,560
28,000	20,568	21,159	20,626	21,211	20,680	21,260
29,000	21,238	21,859	21,296	21,911	21,350	21,960
30,000	21,908	22,559	21,966	22,611	21,020	22,660
31,000	22,578	23,259	22,636	23,311	22,690	23,360
32,000	23,276	23,979	23,306	24,011	23,360	24,060
33,000	24,046	24,749	23,976	24,728	24,030	24,760
34,000	24,816	25,519	24,646	25,498	24,746	25,492
35,000	25,586	26,288	25,541	26,268	25,516	26,262
40,000	28,742	29,444	28,904	29,631	29,066	29,812
45,000	31,692	32,394	31,854	32,581	32,016	32,762
50,000	34,642	35,344	34,804	35,351	34,966	35,712
55,000	37,592	38,294	37,754	38,481	37,916	38,662
60,000	40,542	41,244	40,704	41,431	40,866	41,612
65,000	43,492	44,194	43,654	44,381	43,816	44,562
70,000	46,442	47,144	46,604	47,331	46,766	47,512
75,000	49,392	50,094	49,554	50,281	49,716	50,462
80,000	52,342	53,044	52,504	53,231	52,666	53,412
85,000	55,292	55,994	55,454	56,181	55,616	56,392
90,000	58,242	58,944	58,404	59,131	58,566	59,312
95,000	61,192	61,894	61,354	62,081	61,516	62,262
100,000	64,142	64,844	64,304	65,031	64,466	65,212
150,000	93,642	94,344	93,804	94,531	93,966	94,712
200,000	123,142	123,844	123,304	124,031	123,466	124,212
250,000	152,642	153,344	152,804	153,531	152,966	153,712
300,000	182,142	183,844	182,304	183,031	182,466	183,212

	2007/08 Employed		
Gross income £pa	Net equivalent income £pa	Net per £100 extra £pa	Reason
1,000	1,000	100	
2,000	2,000	100	
3,000	3,000	100	
4,000	4,000	100	
5,000	5,000	100	
5,225	*5,225*	*79*	*← 10% tax payable and 11% NIC Class 1 payable*
6,000	5,837	79	
7,000	6,627	79	
7,455	*6,986*	*67*	*← 22% tax payable*
8,000	7,352	67	
9,000	8,022	67	
10,000	8,692	67	
11,000	9,362	67	
12,000	10,032	67	
13,000	10,702	67	
14,000	11,372	67	
15,000	12,042	67	
16,000	12,712	67	
17,000	13,382	67	
18,000	14,052	67	
19,000	14,722	67	
20,000	15,392	67	
21,000	16,062	67	
22,000	16,732	67	
23,000	17,402	67	
24,000	18,072	67	
25,000	18,742	67	
26,000	19,412	67	
27,000	20,082	67	
28,000	20,752	67	
29,000	21,422	67	
30,000	22,092	67	
31,000	22,762	67	
32,000	23,432	67	
33,000	24,102	67	
34,000	24,772	67	
34,840	*25,335*	*77*	*← NIC Class 1 reduced to 1%*
35,000	25,458	77	
37,500	27,382	77	
39,825	*29,172*	*59*	*← 40% tax payable*
40,000	29,276	59	
45,000	32,226	59	
50,000	35,176	59	
55,000	38,126	59	
60,000	41,076	59	
65,000	44,026	59	
70,000	46,976	59	
75,000	49,926	59	
80,000	52,876	59	
85,000	55,826	59	
90,000	58,776	59	
95,000	61,726	59	
100,000	64,676	59	
150,000	94,176	59	
200,000	123,676	59	
250,000	153,176	59	
300,000	182,676	59	

	2007/08 Self-employed		
Gross income £pa	Net equivalent income £pa	Net per £100 extra £pa	Reason
1,000	1,000	100	
2,000	2,000	100	
4,000	4,000	100	
4,635	*4,635*	*	*← £114 NIC Class 2 payable*
5,000	4,886	–	
5,225	*5,111*	*82*	*← 10% tax payable and 8% NIC Class 4 payable*
6,000	5,747	82	
7,000	6,567	82	
7,455	*6,940*	*70*	*← 22% tax payable*
8,000	7,321	70	
9,000	8,021	70	
10,000	8,721	70	
11,000	9,421	70	
12,000	10,121	70	
13,000	10,821	70	
14,000	11,521	70	
15,000	12,221	70	
16,000	12,921	70	
17,000	13,621	70	
18,000	14,321	70	
19,000	15,021	70	
20,000	15,721	70	
21,000	16,421	70	
22,000	17,121	70	
23,000	17,821	70	
24,000	18,521	70	
25,000	19,221	70	
26,000	19,921	70	
27,000	20,621	70	
28,000	21,321	70	
29,000	22,021	70	
30,000	22,721	70	
31,000	23,421	70	
32,000	24,121	70	
33,000	24,821	70	
34,000	25,421	70	
34,840	*26,109*	*77*	*← NIC Class 4 reduced to 1%*
35,000	26,233	77	
37,500	28,157	77	
39,825	*29,947*	*59*	*← 40% tax payable*
40,000	30,051	59	
45,000	33,001	59	
50,000	35,951	59	
55,000	38,901	59	
60,000	41,851	59	
65,000	44,801	59	
70,000	47,751	59	
75,000	50,701	59	
80,000	53,651	59	
85,000	56,601	59	
90,000	59,551	59	
95,000	62,501	59	* £2.20 × 52 weeks = £114 pa fixed for any level of income in excess of £4,635 pa. So net equivalent of £4,650 gross is £4,536.
100,000	65,451	59	
150,000	94,951	59	
200,000	124,451	59	
250,000	153,951	59	
300,000	183,451	59	

G1: Net equivalents to a range of gross annual income figures

	2008/09		
	Employed		
Gross income	Net equivalent income	Net per £100 extra	Reason
£pa	£pa	£pa	
1,000	1,000	100	
2,000	2,000	100	
3,000	3,000	100	
4,000	4,000	100	
5,000	5,000	100	
5,435	*5,435*	*89*	*← 11% NIC Class 1 payable*
6,000	5,938	89	
6,035	*5,969*	*69*	*← 20% tax payable*
7,000	6,635	69	
8,000	7,325	69	
9,000	8,015	69	
10,000	8,705	69	
11,000	9,395	69	
12,000	10,085	69	
13,000	10,775	69	
14,000	11,465	69	
15,000	12,155	69	
16,000	12,845	69	
17,000	13,535	69	
18,000	14,225	69	
19,000	14,915	69	
20,000	15,605	69	
21,000	16,295	69	
22,000	16,985	69	
23,000	17,675	69	
24,000	18,365	69	
25,000	19,055	69	
26,000	19,745	69	
27,000	20,435	69	
28,000	21,125	69	
29,000	21,815	69	
30,000	22,505	69	
31,000	23,195	69	
32,000	23,885	69	
33,000	24,575	69	
34,000	25,265	69	
35,000	25,955	69	
37,500	27,680	69	
40,000	29,405	69	
40,040	*29,432*	*79*	*← NIC Class 1 reduced to 1%*
40,835	*30,060*	*59*	*← 40% tax payable*
45,000	32,518	59	
50,000	35,468	59	
55,000	38,418	59	
60,000	41,368	59	
65,000	44,138	59	
70,000	47,268	59	
75,000	50,218	59	
80,000	53,168	59	
85,000	56,118	59	
90,000	59,068	59	
95,000	62,018	59	
100,000	64,968	59	
150,000	94,468	59	
200,000	123,968	59	
250,000	153,468	59	
300,000	182,968	59	

	2008/09		
	Self-employed		
Gross income	Net equivalent income	Net per £100 addition	Reason
£pa	£pa	£pa	
1,000	1,000	100	
2,000	2,000	100	
4,000	4,000	100	
4,825	*4,825*	*	*← £120 NIC Class 2 payable*
5,000	4,880	100	
5,435	*5,315*	*92*	*← 8% NIC Class 4 payable*
6,000	5,835	92	
6,035	*5,867*	*72*	*← 20% tax payable*
7,000	6,562	72	
8,000	7,282	72	
9,000	8,002	72	
10,000	8,722	72	
11,000	9,442	72	
12,000	10,162	72	
13,000	10,882	72	
14,000	11,602	72	
15,000	12,322	72	
16,000	13,042	72	
17,000	13,762	72	
18,000	14,482	72	
19,000	15,202	72	
20,000	15,922	72	
21,000	16,642	72	
22,000	17,362	72	
23,000	18,082	72	
24,000	18,802	72	
25,000	19,522	72	
26,000	20,242	72	
27,000	20,962	72	
28,000	21,682	72	
29,000	22,402	72	
30,000	23,122	72	
31,000	23,842	72	
32,000	24,562	72	
33,000	25,282	72	
34,000	26,002	72	
35,000	26,722	72	
37,500	28,522	72	
40,000	30,322	72	
40,040	*30,351*	*79*	*← NIC Class 4 reduced to 1%*
40,835	*30,979*	*59*	*← 40% tax payable*
45,000	33,436	59	
50,000	36,386	59	
55,000	39,336	59	
60,000	42,286	59	
65,000	45,236	59	
70,000	48,186	59	
75,000	51,136	59	
80,000	54,086	59	
85,000	57,036	59	
90,000	59,986	59	
95,000	62,936	59	
100,000	65,886	59	
150,000	95,386	59	
200,000	124,886	59	
250,000	154,386	59	
300,000	183,886	59	

* £2.30 × 52 weeks = £120 pa fixed for any level of income in excess of £4,825 pa. So net equivalent of £4,850 gross is £4,730.

Gross income £pa	2009/10 Employed: Net equivalent income £pa	Net per £100 extra £pa	Reason
1,000	1,000	100	
2,000	2,000	100	
3,000	3,000	100	
4,000	4,000	100	
5,000	5,000	100	
5,715	*5,715*	*89*	*← 11% NIC Class 1 payable*
6,000	5,969	89	
6,475	*6,391*	*69*	*← 20% tax payable*
7,000	6,754	69	
8,000	7,444	69	
9,000	8,134	69	
10,000	8,824	69	
11,000	9,514	69	
12,000	10,204	69	
13,000	10,894	69	
14,000	11,584	69	
15,000	12,274	69	
16,000	12,964	69	
17,000	13,654	69	
18,000	14,344	69	
19,000	15,034	69	
20,000	15,724	69	
21,000	16,414	69	
22,000	17,104	69	
23,000	17,794	69	
24,000	18,484	69	
25,000	19,174	69	
26,000	19,864	69	
27,000	20,554	69	
28,000	21,244	69	
29,000	21,934	69	
30,000	22,624	69	
31,000	23,314	69	
32,000	24,004	69	
33,000	24,694	69	
34,000	25,384	69	
35,000	26,074	69	
37,500	27,799	69	
40,000	29,524	69	
43,875	*32,197*	*59*	*← NIC Class 1 reduced to 1% and 40% tax payable*
45,000	32,861	59	
50,000	35,811	59	
55,000	38,761	59	
60,000	41,711	59	
65,000	44,661	59	
70,000	47,611	59	
75,000	50,561	59	
80,000	53,511	59	
85,000	56,461	59	
90,000	59,411	59	
95,000	62,361	59	
100,000	65,311	59	
150,000	94,811	59	
200,000	124,311	59	
250,000	153,811	59	
300,000	183,311	59	

Gross income £pa	2009/10 Self-employed: Net equivalent income £pa	Net per £100 addition £pa	Reason
1,000	1,000	100	
2,000	2,000	100	
3,000	4,000	100	
4,000	*4,000*	*100*	
5,075	5,075	*	*£125 NIC Class 2 ← payable*
5,715	*5,590*	*92*	*← 8% NIC Class 4 payable*
6,000	5,852	92	
6,475	*6,289*	*72*	*← 20% tax payable*
7,000	6,667	72	
8,000	7,387	72	
9,000	8,107	72	
10,000	8,827	72	
11,000	9,547	72	
12,000	10,267	72	
13,000	10,987	72	
14,000	11,707	72	
15,000	12,427	72	
16,000	13,147	72	
17,000	13,867	72	
18,000	14,587	72	
19,000	15,307	72	
20,000	16,027	72	
21,000	16,747	72	
22,000	17,467	72	
23,000	18,187	72	
24,000	18,907	72	
25,000	19,627	72	
26,000	20,347	72	
27,000	21,067	72	
28,000	21,787	72	
29,000	22,507	72	
30,000	23,227	72	
31,000	23,947	72	
32,000	24,667	72	
33,000	25,387	72	
34,000	26,107	72	
35,000	26,827	72	
37,500	28,627	72	
40,000	30,427	72	
43,875	*33,217*	*59*	*← NIC Class 4 reduced to 1% and 40% tax payable*
45,000	33,881	59	
50,000	36,831	59	
55,000	39,781	59	
60,000	42,731	59	
65,000	45,681	59	
70,000	48,631	59	
75,000	51,581	59	
80,000	54,531	59	
85,000	57,481	59	
90,000	60,431	59	
95,000	63,381	59	
100,000	66,331	59	
150,000	95,831	59	
200,000	125,331	59	
250,000	154,831	59	
300,000	184,331	59	

* £2.40 × 52 weeks = £125 pa fixed for any level of income in excess of £5,075 pa. So net equivalent of £5,100 gross is £4,975.

G2: Illustrative net earnings calculations

Person under 65 at 2005/06 tax rates

		Employed person				Self-employed person			
		£pa	**£pa**	**£pa**	**£pa**	**£pa**	**£pa**	**£pa**	**£pa**
Gross income	[a]	15,000	25,000	35,000	40,000	15,000	25,000	35,000	40,000
Income tax									
Gross		15,000	25,000	35,000	40,000	15,000	25,000	35,000	40,000
Personal allowance		(4,895)	(4,895)	(4,895)	(4,895)	(4,895)	(4,895)	(4,895)	(4,895)
Taxable		10,105	20,105	30,105	35,105	10,105	20,105	30,105	35,105
Tax payable									
– At 10%		209	209	209	209	209	209	209	209
– At 22%		1,763	3,963	6,163	6,668	1,763	3,963	6,163	6,668
– At 40%		–	–	–	1,082	–	–	–	1,082
	[b]	1,972	4,172	6,372	7,959	1,972	4,172	6,372	7,959
National Insurance									
Class 1									
– At 11%		1,112	2,212	3,065	3,065				
– At 1%				22	72				
Class 2						109	109	109	109
Class 4									
– At 8%						808	1,608	2,229	2,229
– At 1%								22	72
	[c]	1,112	2,212	3,087	3,137	917	1,717	2,360	2,410
Net income	[a-b-c]	11,916	18,616	25,541	28,904	12,111	19,111	26,268	29,631
Net % of gross		79.4%	74.4%	73.0%	72.2%	80.7%	76.4%	75.1%	74.1%

Person under 65 at 2006/07 tax rates

		Employed person				Self-employed person			
		£pa	£pa	£pa	£pa	£pa	£pa	£pa	£pa
Gross income	[a]	15,000	25,000	35,000	40,000	15,000	25,000	35,000	40,000
Income tax									
Gross		15,000	25,000	35,000	40,000	15,000	25,000	35,000	40,000
Personal allowance		(5,035)	(5,035)	(5,035)	(5,035)	(5,035)	(5,035)	(5,035)	(5,035)
Taxable		9,965	19,965	29,965	34,965	9,965	19,965	29,965	34,965
Tax payable									
– At 10%		215	215	215	215	215	215	215	215
– At 22%		1,719	3,919	6,119	6,853	1,719	3,919	6,119	6,853
– At 40%		–	–	–	666	–	–	–	666
	[b]	1,934	4,134	6,334	7,734	1,934	4,134	6,334	7,734
National Insurance									
Class 1									
– At 11%		1,096	2,196	3,135	3,135				
– At 1%				15	65				
Class 2						109	109	109	109
Class 4									
– At 8%						797	1,597	2,280	2,280
– At 1%								15	65
	[c]	1,096	2,196	3,150	3,200	906	1,706	2,404	2,454
Net income	[a-b-c]	11,970	18,670	25,516	29,066	12,160	19,160	26,262	29,812
Net % of gross		79.8%	74.7%	72.9%	72.7%	81.1%	76.6%	75.0%	74.5%

Person under 65 at 2007/08 tax rates

		Employed person				Self-employed person			
		£pa	£pa	£pa	£pa	£pa	£pa	£pa	£pa
Gross income	[a]	15,000	25,000	35,000	40,000	15,000	25,000	35,000	40,000
Income tax									
Gross		15,000	25,000	35,000	40,000	15,000	25,000	35,000	40,000
Personal allowance		(5,225)	(5,225)	(5,225)	(5,225)	(5,225)	(5,225)	(5,225)	(5,225)
Taxable		9,775	19,775	29,775	34,775	9,775	19,775	29,775	34,775
Tax payable									
– At 10%		223	223	223	223	223	223	223	223
– At 22%		1,660	3,860	6,060	7,121	1,660	3,860	6,060	7,121
– At 40%		–	–	–	70	–	–	–	70
	[b]	1,883	4,083	6,283	7,414	1,883	4,083	6,283	7,414
National Insurance									
Class 1									
– At 11%		1,075	2,175	3,258	3,258				
– At 1%				1	52				
Class 2						114	114	114	114
Class 4									
– At 8%						782	1,582	2,369	2,369
– At 1%								1	52
	[c]	1,075	2,175	3,259	3,310	896	1,696	2,484	2,535
Net income	[a-b-c]	12,042	18,742	25,458	29,276	12,221	19,221	26,233	30,051
Net % of gross		80.3%	75.0%	72.7%	73.2%	81.5%	76.9%	74.9%	75.1%

Person under 65 at 2008/09 tax rates

		Employed person				Self-employed person			
		£pa	**£pa**	**£pa**	**£pa**	**£pa**	**£pa**	**£pa**	**£pa**
Gross income	[a]	15,000	25,000	35,000	50,000	15,000	25,000	35,000	50,000
Income tax									
Gross		15,000	25,000	35,000	50,000	15,000	25,000	35,000	50,000
Personal allowance		(6,035)	(6,035)	(6,035)	(6,035)	(6,035)	(6,035)	(6,035)	(6,035)
Taxable		8,965	18,965	28,965	43,965	8,965	18,965	28,965	43,965
Tax payable									
– At 20%		1,793	3,739	5,793	6,960	1,793	3,739	5,793	6,960
– At 40%		–	–	–	3,666	–	–	–	3,666
	[b]	1,913	3,913	5,913	10,626	1,913	3,913	5,913	10,626
National Insurance									
Class 1									
– At 11%		1,052	2,152	3,252	3,806				
– At 1%					100				
Class 2						120	120	120	120
Class 4									
– At 8%						765	1,565	2,365	2,768
– At 1%									100
	[c]	1,052	2,152	3,252	3,906	885	1,685	2,485	2,988
Net income	[a-b-c]	12,155	19,109	25,955	35,468	12,322	19,576	26,722	36,386
Net % of gross		81.0%	76.4%	74.2%	70.9%	82.1%	78.3%	76.3%	72.8%

Person under 65 at 2009/10 tax rates

		Employed person				Self-employed person			
		£pa	£pa	£pa	£pa	£pa	£pa	£pa	£pa
Gross income	[a]	15,000	25,000	35,000	50,000	15,000	25,000	35,000	50,000
Income tax									
Gross		15,000	25,000	35,000	50,000	15,000	25,000	35,000	50,000
Personal allowance		(6,475)	(6,475)	(6,475)	(6,475)	(6,475)	(6,475)	(6,475)	(6,475)
Taxable		8,525	18,525	28,525	43,525	8,525	18,525	28,525	43,525
Tax payable									
– At 20%		1,705	3,705	5,705	7,480	1,705	3,705	5,705	7,480
– At 40%		–	–	–	2,450	–	–	–	2,450
	[b]	1,705	3,705	5,705	9,930	1,705	3,705	5,705	9,930
National Insurance									
Class 1									
– At 11%		1,021	2,121	3,221	4,198				
– At 1%					61				
Class 2						125	125	125	125
Class 4									
– At 8%						743	1,543	2,343	3,053
– At 1%									61
	[c]	1,021	2,121	3,221	4,259	868	1,668	2,468	3,239
Net income	[a-b-c]	12,274	19,174	26,074	35,811	12,427	19,627	26,827	36,831
Net % of gross		81.8%	76.7%	74.5%	71.6%	82.8%	78.5%	76.6%	73.7%

G3: Income tax reliefs and rates

Introductory notes

Personal allowance

Every taxpayer resident in the UK (as well as certain non-UK residents) is entitled to a personal allowance.

Age-related personal allowance

Higher personal allowances are available to taxpayers who are 65 or more in the tax year, subject to an income limit—£22,900 for 2009/10.

Where total income exceeds the prescribed income limit, the higher personal allowance is reduced by 50 per cent of the excess, although the allowance cannot be reduced below the ordinary personal allowance.

For 2009/10, the higher personal allowances available are:

Age 65 to 74 (at any time during the year)	£9,490
Age 75 and above	£9,640

Married couple's allowance

Relief in respect of the married couple's allowance, given at the taxpayer's marginal rate in years up to and including 1993/94, was restricted in subsequent years as follows:

Tax year 1994/95	20% of allowance
Tax years 1995/96 to 1998/99	15% of allowance
Tax year 1999/00	10% of allowance

Married couple's allowance was abolished with effect from 2000/01 onwards, except for couples at least one member of which was born before April 6, 1935. To reflect the abolition of the married couple's allowance (with the exception specified), the net equivalent incomes from 2000/01 onwards for a single person and a married person are identical in table G1.

A Children's Tax Credit was introduced from 2001/02 to replace the married couple's allowance [see below].

This in turn was replaced by Child Tax Credit from 2003/04 [see below].

Age-related married couple's allowance

As noted above, from 2000/01 onwards, married couple's allowance is only available where either spouse was born before April 6, 1935. Subject to this, married couple's allowances are available to taxpayers who are 65 or over at the end of the fiscal year, subject to the same income limit as the age-related personal allowance—£22,900 for 2009/10.

For 2009/10, the married couple's allowances available are:

Age 75 and above	£6,965

Where the husband's income exceeds the prescribed income limit, the married couple's allowance is reduced by 50 per cent of the excess less any reduction of the personal allowance (as above), until the allowance is equal to the ordinary married couple's allowance for years up to and including 1999/00, and the following amounts for subsequent years:

Tax year 2000/01	Minimum allowance £2,000
Tax year 2001/02	Minimum allowance £2,070
Tax year 2002/03	Minimum allowance £2,110
Tax year 2003/04	Minimum allowance £2,150
Tax year 2004/05	Minimum allowance £2,210
Tax year 2005/06	Minimum allowance £2,280
Tax year 2006/07	Minimum allowance £2,350
Tax year 2007/08	Minimum allowance £2,440
Tax year 2008/09	Minimum allowance £2,540
Tax year 2009/10	Minimum allowance £2,670

The level of the wife's income does not restrict the allowance available.

Children's Tax Credit
For 2001/02 and 2002/03, a Children's Tax Credit was available to parents who had at least one child under sixteen living with them. The credit was given through PAYE codes or tax calculations.

In 2002/03 the credit was £5,290 and the rate of relief 10 per cent, such that the value of the credit was £529. This was reduced if the main earner in the family was a higher rate taxpayer, by £2 for every £3 of taxable income above £29,900. No credit was therefore received when the total income reached £42,450.

For 2002/03 there was an increased Children's Tax Credit available for a child born in that year, for one year only—the baby rate. The increased credit was £10,490 and the rate of relief 10 per cent such that the value of the credit was £1,049. The baby rate was subject to the same reduction as the main rate. No credit was therefore available when the total income reached £50,250.

Child Tax Credit
Child Tax Credit replaced Children's Tax Credit, as well as the child elements of Working Families' Tax Credit and Disabled Person's Tax Credit, with effect from April 6, 2003.

Child Tax Credit is a means-tested benefit paid directly into the bank account of the main carer of the child(ren), on a weekly or 4-weekly basis.

Child Tax Credit neither is affected by, nor affects, Child Benefit, which continues to be paid in the usual way.

From 2004/05 onwards, Child Tax Credit is based initially on the income of the previous tax year.

For 2003/04 only, however, the initial claim was based on the income for the last tax year but one, 2001/02.

In all cases, the claim is corrected to actual income basis in due course.

For 2009/10, families (including single parents) with income up to £58,171 qualify for Child Tax Credit. If there are two children, the income limit is £113,703.

Taxation of savings income
Savings income is subdivided into dividends and other savings income, with dividends treated as the top slice of savings income.

From 1996/97 to 1998/99, the savings income of lower and basic rate taxpayers was taxed at 20 per cent at source. Higher rate taxpayers had to account for the 20 per cent difference between the 20 per cent deduction at source and their 40 per cent marginal rate.

From 1999/00 onwards, tax is payable on dividend income at the dividend ordinary rate of 10 per cent up to the basic rate limit, and at the dividend upper rate of 32½ per cent thereafter. Tax is payable on other savings income at 10 per cent on income in the starting rate band, at 20 per cent on income in the basic rate band, and at 40 per cent thereafter.

For 2008/09, there was a new 10% starting rate for savings income only, with a limit of £2,320. If the taxpayer's non-savings income exceeded this limit, the 10 per cent savings rate did not apply. This did not affect the dividend ordinary and upper rates applicable for the year.

For 2009/10, there is similarly a 10% starting rate for savings income only, with a limit of £2,440. If the taxpayer's non-savings income exceeds this limit, the 10% savings rate does not apply. This does not affect the dividend ordinary and upper rates applicable for the year.

1998/99 to 2009/10

Fiscal year:	1998/99 £	1999/00 £	2000/01 £	2001/02 £	2002/03 £	2003/04 £	2004/05 £	2005/06 £	2006/07 £	2007/08 £	2008/09 £	2009/10 £
Income tax reliefs												
Personal allowance	4,195	4,335	4,385	4,535	4,615	4,615	4,745	4,895	5,035	5,225	6,035	6,475
Married couple's allowance	1,900	1,970	–	–	–	–	–	–	–	–	–	–
Income tax rates												
Starting rate band – Payable at 10%	–	1,500	1,520	1,880	1,920	1,960	2,020	2,090	2,150	2,230	See note	See note
Lower rate band – Payable at 20%	4,300	–	–	–	–	–	–	–	–	–	–	–
Basic rate band – Payable at 20%	–	–	–	–	–	–	–	–	–	–	34,800	37,400
Basic rate band – Payable at 22%	–	–	26,880	27,520	27,980	28,540	29,380	30,310	31,150	32,370	–	–
Basic rate band – Payable at 23%	22,800	26,500	–	–	–	–	–	–	–	–	–	–
Higher rate band – Payable at 40%	Balance	Balance	Balance	Balance	Balance	Balance	Balance	Balance	Balance	Balance	Balance	Balance

Note

From 2008/09, there has been a 10% starting rate for savings income only. If non-savings taxable income exceeds the following limits, the starting rate is not available:

Tax year 2008/09	£2,320
Tax year 2009/10	£2,440

G4: National Insurance contributions

Introductory notes

1. Married women and widows could elect to pay a reduced contribution as follows:

   - 3.85% on earnings between lower earnings limit and upper earnings limit up to 1999/00
   - 3.85% on earnings between primary threshold and upper earnings limit in 2000/01 to 2002/03
   - 4.85% on earnings between primary threshold and upper earnings limit, and 1% on earnings above upper earnings limit in 2003/04 to 2007/08.

2. Class 1 employee contributions and Class 2 contributions cease to be payable when a man has reached 65 and a woman 60.

3. Class 4 contributions are not payable in respect of any fiscal year that starts after pensionable age has been reached.

4. Class 3 contributions are voluntary at a flat weekly rate (£12.05 pw in 2009/10).

1998/99 to 2003/04

Fiscal year:	1998/99 £	1999/00 £	2000/01 £	2001/02 £	2002/03 £	2003/04 £
Class 1 contributions (Employees)						
Lower earnings limit (LEL) (pa)	3,328	3,432	3,484	3,744	3,900	4,004
Primary threshold (PT) (pa)	N/A	N/A	3,952	4,535	4,615	4,615
Upper earnings limit (UEL) (pa)	25,220	26,000	27,820	29,900	30,420	30,940
Standard rate						
If earnings below LEL:	Nil	Nil	Nil	Nil	Nil	Nil
If earnings at or above LEL: – Contribution rate on earnings up to PT	2%	Nil	Nil	Nil	Nil	Nil
– Contribution rate on earnings between PT and UEL	10%	10%	10%	10%	10%	11%
– Contribution rate on earnings above UEL	Nil	Nil	Nil	Nil	Nil	1%
Maximum contribution (pa)	2,256	2,257	2,387	2,537	2,581	2,896 +1% of excess over UEL
Contracted out rate						
As standard rate except – Contribution rate on earnings between PT and UEL	8.4%	8.4%	8.4%	8.4%	8.4%	9.4%
Maximum contribution (pa)	1,905	1,896	2,005	2,132	2,167	2,475 +1% of excess over UEL
Class 2 contributions (Self-employed)						
Small earnings exception limit	3,590	3,770	3,825	3,955	4,025	4,095
Fixed weekly contributions (pw)	6.35	6.55	2.00	2.00	2.00	2.00
Class 4 contributions (Self-employed)						
Lower profits limit (LPL) (pa)	7,310	7,530	4,385	4,535	4,615	4,615
Upper profits limit (UPL) (pa)	25,220	26,000	27,820	29,900	30,420	30,940
Contribution rate on profits between LPL and UPL	6.0%	6.0%	7.0%	7.0%	7.0%	8.0%
Contribution rate on profits above UPL	Nil	Nil	Nil	Nil	Nil	1.0%
Maximum contribution (pa)	1,075	1,108	1,640	1,775	1,806	2,106 +1% of excess over UPL

2004/05 to 2009/10

Fiscal year:	**2004/05 £**	**2005/06 £**	**2006/07 £**	**2007/08 £**	**2008/09 £**	**2009/10 £**
Class 1 contributions (Employees)						
Lower earnings limit (LEL) (pa)	4,108	4,264	4,368	4,524	4,680	4,940
Primary threshold (PT) (pa)	4,745	4,895	5,035	5,225	5,435	5,715
Upper earnings limit (UEL) (pa)	31,720	32,760	33,540	34,840	40,040	43,875
Standard rate						
If earnings below LEL:	Nil	Nil	Nil	Nil	Nil	Nil
If earnings at or above LEL: – Contribution rate on earnings up to PT	Nil	Nil	Nil	Nil	Nil	Nil
– Contribution rate on earnings between PT and UEL	11%	11%	11%	11%	11%	11%
– Contribution rate on earnings above UEL	1%	1%	1%	1%	1%	1%
Maximum contribution (pa)	2,967 +1% of excess over UEL	3,065 +1% of excess over UEL	3,135 +1% of excess over UEL	3,258 +1% of excess over UEL	3,807 +1% of excess over UEL	4,198 +1% of excess over UEL
Contracted out rate						
As standard rate except – Contribution rate on earnings between PT and UEL	9.4%	9.4%	9.4%	9.4%	9.4%	9.4%
Maximum contribution (pa)	2,536 +1% of excess over UEL	2,619 +1% of excess over UEL	2,679 +1% of excess over UEL	2,784 +1% of excess over UEL	3,253 +1% of excess over UEL	3,587 +1% of excess over UEL
Class 2 contributions (Self-employed)						
Small earnings exception limit	4,215	4,345	4,465	4,635	4,825	5,075
Fixed weekly contributions (pw)	2.05	2.10	2.10	2.20	2.30	2.40
Class 4 contributions (Self-employed)						
Lower profits limit (LPL) (pa)	4,745	4,895	5,035	5,225	5,435	5,715
Upper profits limit (UPL) (pa)	31,720	32,760	33,540	34,840	40,040	43,875
Contribution rate on profits between LPL and UPL	8.0%	8.0%	8.0%	8.0%	8.0%	8.0%
Contribution rate on profits above UPL	1.0%	1.0%	1.0%	1.0%	1.0%	1.0%
Maximum contribution (pa)	2,158 +1% of excess over UPL	2,229 +1% of excess over UPL	2,280 +1% of excess over UPL	2,369 +1% of excess over UPL	2,768 +1% of excess over UPL	3,053 +1% of excess over UPL

G5: VAT registration limits

Registration is required when a person's turnover (taxable supplies from all the person's businesses) exceeds prescribed limits.

Past and future turnover limits apply (looking one year back and one year forward).

Registration is also required if a turnover limit is to be exceeded in a period of 30 days.

De-registration depends on satisfying HM Revenue & Customs that the future annual limit (e.g. £68,000 from May 1, 2009) will not be exceeded.

The registration levels are:

	Past turnover		Future turnover
	1 year	Unless turnover for next year will not exceed	30 days
	£	£	£
From May 1, 2009	68,000	66,000	68,000
April 1, 2008 to April 30, 2009	67,000	65,000	67,000
April 1, 2007 to March 31, 2008	64,000	62,000	64,000
April 1, 2006 to March 31, 2007	61,000	59,000	61,000
April 1, 2005 to March 31, 2006	60,000	58,000	60,000
April 1, 2004 to March 31, 2005	58,000	56,000	58,000
April 10, 2003 to March 31, 2004	56,000	54,000	56,000
April 25, 2002 to April 9, 2003	55,000	53,000	55,000
April 1, 2001 to April 24, 2002	54,000	52,000	54,000
April 1, 2000 to March 31, 2001	52,000	50,000	52,000

Note:
These limits can be of particular relevance in considering likely turnover levels for businesses such as taxis and driving schools, where VAT registration may render charges uncompetitive (because most such businesses operate below the registration limits).

Group H

Pension

H

H1: Net equivalents to a range of gross annual pension figures

Introductory notes

1. The following table sets out the net equivalents to a range of annual pension figures in 2009/10 distinguishing between:

   — a single person aged under 65;
   — a single person aged 65 to 74 at any time during the tax year;
   — a single person aged 75 or over at any time during the tax year;
   — a married person aged under 65;
   — a married person aged 65 to 74 at any time during the tax year; and
   — a married person aged 75 or over at any time during the tax year.

2. The tables are followed by illustrative net pension calculations for each marital status and age category, at income levels of £15,000, £20,000, £30,000 and £50,000 per annum.

3. The age ranges selected reflect the availability of age-related personal and married couple's allowances, as detailed in G3.

4. Since pensions are not subject to national insurance contributions, the net equivalent figures represent the gross pension less income tax. Given that liability to primary Class 1 national insurance contributions falls away when the earner has reached pensionable age [note 2 of G4], it follows that the net equivalent figures for those aged 65 and over apply equally to earnings from employment and pensions.

   Similarly, given that Class 4 contributions are not payable in respect of any fiscal year that starts after pensionable age has been reached [note 3 of G4], it follows that the net equivalent figures for those aged 65 and over apply also to earnings from self-employment where pensionable age has been reached in a prior fiscal year.

H1: Net equivalents to a range of gross annual pension figures

	2009/10 Net equivalent pension					
	Single, or married where neither spouse was born before 6.4.35			Married, where either spouse was born before 6.4.35		
Gross pension	**Aged under 65**	**Aged 65–74**	**Aged 75 or over**	**Aged under 65**	**Aged 65–74**	**Aged 75 or over**
£pa	**£pa**	**£pa**	**£pa**	**£pa**	**£pa**	**£pa**
1,000	1,000	1,000	1,000	1,000	1,000	1,000
2,000	2,000	2,000	2,000	2,000	2,000	2,000
3,000	3,000	3,000	3,000	3,000	3,000	3,000
4,000	4,000	4,000	4,000	4,000	4,000	4,000
5,000	5,000	5,000	5,000	5,000	5,000	5,000
6,000	6,000	6,000	6,000	6,000	6,000	6,000
7,000	6,895	7,000	7,000	6,895	7,000	7,000
8,000	7,695	8,000	8,000	7,695	8,000	8,000
9,000	8,495	9,000	9,000	8,495	9,000	9,000
10,000	9,295	9,898	9,928	9,295	9,898	10,000
11,000	10,095	10,698	10,728	10,095	10,698	11,000
12,000	10,895	11,498	11,528	10,895	11,498	12,000
13,000	11,695	12,298	12,328	11,695	12,298	13,000
14,000	12,495	13,098	13,128	12,495	13,098	13,825
15,000	13,295	13,898	13,928	13,295	13,898	14,625
16,000	14,095	14,698	14,728	14,095	14,698	15,425
17,000	14,895	15,498	15,528	14,895	15,498	16,225
18,000	15,695	16,298	16,328	15,695	16,298	17,025
19,000	16,495	17,098	17,128	16,495	17,098	17,825
20,000	17,295	17,898	17,928	17,295	17,898	18,625
21,000	18,095	18,698	18,728	18,095	18,698	19,425
22,000	18,895	19,498	19,528	18,895	19,498	20,225
23,000	19,695	20,288	20,318	19,695	20,288	21,015
24,000	20,495	20,988	21,018	20,495	20,988	21,715
25,000	21,295	21,688	21,718	21,295	21,688	22,415
26,000	22,095	22,388	22,418	22,095	22,388	23,115
27,000	22,895	23,088	23,118	22,895	23,088	23,815
28,000	23,695	23,788	23,818	23,695	23,788	24,515
29,000	24,495	24,495	24,518	24,495	24,495	25,215
30,000	25,295	25,295	25,295	25,295	25,295	25,953
31,000	26,095	26,095	26,095	26,095	26,095	26,703
32,000	26,895	26,895	26,895	26,895	26,895	27,453
33,000	27,695	27,695	27,695	27,695	27,695	28,203
34,000	28,495	28,495	28,495	28,495	28,495	28,953
35,000	29,295	29,295	29,295	29,295	29,295	29,703
40,000	33,295	33,295	33,295	33,295	33,295	33,562
45,000	37,070	37,070	37,070	37,070	37,070	37,337
50,000	40,070	40,070	40,070	40,070	40,070	40,337
55,000	43,070	43,070	43,070	43,070	43,070	43,337
60,000	46,070	46,070	46,070	46,070	46,070	46,337
65,000	49,070	49,070	49,070	49,070	49,070	49,337
70,000	52,070	52,070	52,070	52,070	52,070	52,337
75,000	55,070	55,070	55,070	55,070	55,070	55,337
80,000	58,070	58,070	58,070	58,070	58,070	58,337
85,000	61,070	61,070	61,070	61,070	61,070	61,337
90,000	64,070	64,070	64,070	64,070	64,070	64,337
95,000	67,070	67,070	67,070	67,070	67,070	67,377
100,000	70,070	70,070	70,070	70,070	70,070	70,377

H2: Illustrative net pension calculations

Single person aged under 65 at 2009/10 rates

		£pa	£pa	£pa	£pa
Gross pension	[a]	15,000	20,000	30,000	50,000
Income tax					
Gross		15,000	20,000	30,000	50,000
Personal allowance		(6,475)	(6,475)	(6,475)	(6,475)
Taxable		8,525	13,525	23,525	43,525
Tax payable					
– At 20%		1,705	2,705	4,705	7,480
– At 40%		–	–	–	2,450
	[b]	1,705	2,705	4,705	9,930
Net income	[a–b]	13,295	17,295	25,295	40,070
Net % of gross		88.6%	86.5%	84.3%	80.1%

Single person aged between 65 and 74 at 2009/10 rates

		£pa	£pa	£pa	£pa
Gross pension	[a]	15,000	20,000	30,000	50,000
Income tax					
Gross		15,000	20,000	30,000	50,000
Personal allowance (note 1)		(9,490)	(9,490)	(6,475)	(6,475)
Taxable		5,510	10,510	23,525	43,525
Tax payable					
– At 20%		1,102	2,102	4,705	7,480
– At 40%		–	–	–	2,450
	[b]	1,102	2,102	4,705	9,930
Net income	[a–b]	13,898	17,898	25,295	40,070
Net % of gross		92.7%	89.5%	84.3%	80.1%

Note 1: personal allowance

Allowance for age 65 to 74	9,490	9,490	9,490	9,490
Restriction for excess of income over limit*	–	–	(3,015)	(3,015)
Net allowance	9,490	9,490	6,475	6,475

*If gross pension does not exceed £22,900, no restriction.
If gross pension does exceed £22,900, restriction is the lower of:
(a) (gross pension—£22,900)/2; and
(b) £9,490–£6,475 = £3,015

Single person aged 75 or over at 2009/10 rates

		£pa	£pa	£pa	£pa
Gross pension	[a]	15,000	20,000	30,000	50,000
Income tax					
Gross		15,000	20,000	30,000	50,000
Personal allowance (note 1)		(9,640)	(9,640)	(6,475)	(6,475)
Taxable		5,360	10,360	23,525	43,525
Tax payable					
– At 20%		1,072	2,072	4,705	7,480
– At 40%		–	–	–	2,450
	[b]	1,072	2,072	4,705	9,930
Net income	[a–b]	13,928	17,928	25,295	40,070
Net % of gross		92.9%	89.6%	84.3%	80.1%

Note 1: personal allowance

Allowance for age 75 and over	9,640	9,640	9,640	9,640
Restriction for excess of income over limit*	–	–	(3,165)	(3,165)
Net allowance	9,640	9,640	6,475	6,475

*If gross pension does not exceed £22,900, no restriction.
If gross pension does exceed £22,900, restriction is the lower of:
(a) (gross pension – £22,900)/2; and
(b) £9,640–6,475 = £3,165

Married person aged under 65 at 2009/10 rates

		£pa	£pa	£pa	£pa
Gross pension	[a]	15,000	20,000	30,000	50,000
Income tax					
Gross		15,000	20,000	30,000	50,000
Personal allowance		(6,475)	(6,475)	(6,475)	(6,475)
Taxable		8,525	13,525	23,525	43,525
Tax payable					
– At 20%		1,705	2,705	4,705	7,480
– At 40%		–	–	–	2,450
	[b]	1,705	2,705	4,705	9,930
Net income	[a–b]	13,295	17,295	25,295	40,070
Net % of gross		88.6%	86.5%	84.3%	80.1%

Married person aged between 65 and 74 at 2009/10 rates

		£pa	£pa	£pa	£pa
Gross pension	[a]	15,000	20,000	30,000	50,000
Income tax					
Gross		15,000	20,000	30,000	50,000
Personal allowance (note 1)		(9,490)	(9,490)	(6,475)	(6,475)
Taxable		5,510	10,510	23,525	43,525
Tax payable					
– At 20%		1,102	2,102	4,705	7,480
– At 40%		–	–	–	2,450
	[b]	1,102	2,102	4,705	9,930
Net income	[a–b]	13,898	17,898	25,295	40,070
Net % of gross		92.7%	89.5%	84.3%	80.1%

Note 1: personal allowance

Personal allowance for age 65 to 74	9,490	9,490	9,490	9,490
Restriction for excess of income over limit*	–	–	(3,015)	(3,015)
Net allowance	9,490	9,490	6,475	6,475

*If gross pension does not exceed £22,900,
no restriction.
If gross pension does exceed £22,900,
restriction is the lower of:
(a) (gross pension – £22,900)/2; and
(b) £9,490−£6,475 = £3,015

Married person aged 75 or over at 2009/10 rates

		£pa	£pa	£pa	£pa
Gross pension	[a]	15,000	20,000	30,000	50,000
Income tax					
Gross		15,000	20,000	30,000	50,000
Personal allowance (note 1)		(9,640)	(9,640)	(6,475)	(6,475)
Taxable		5,360	10,360	23,525	43,525
Tax payable					
– At 20%		1,072	2,072	4,705	7,480
– At 40%		–	–	–	2,450
		1,072	2,072	4,705	9,930
Relief for married couple's allowance (note 2)		(697)	(697)	(658)	(267)
	[b]	375	1,375	4,047	9,663
Net income	[a–b]	14,625	18,625	25,953	40,337
Net % of gross		97.5%	93.1%	86.5%	80.7%

Note 1: personal allowance

Personal allowance for age 75 and over	9,640	9,640	9,640	9,640
Restriction for excess of income over limit*	–	–	(3,165)	(3,165)
Net allowance	9,640	9,640	6,475	6,475

*If gross pension does not exceed £22,900, no restriction.
If gross pension does exceed £22,900, restriction is the lower of:
(a) (gross pension—£22,900)/2; and
(b) £9,640–£6,475 = £3,165

Note 2: married couple's allowance

Assumption:
1 at least one spouse born before April 6, 1935 and
2 full married couple's allowance allocated to pensioner.

Married couple's allowance for age 75 and over	6,965	6,965	6,965	6,965
Restriction for excess of income over limit*	–	–	(385)	(4,295)
Net allowance	6,965	6,965	6,580	2,670
Relief at 10%	697	697	658	267

*If gross pension does not exceed £22,900, no restriction.
If gross pension does exceed £22,900, restriction is the lower of:
(a) (gross pension—£22,900)/2 **less** restriction of personal allowance; and
(b) £6,965–£2,670 = £4,295

H3: Note on pension losses

1. **Purpose of note**

The purpose of this note is to provide some basic guidance to practitioners who need to consider whether a pension loss is likely to arise in any specific case.

2. **"Final Salary" or "Money Purchase" scheme?**

Ascertain which type of scheme was being contributed to.

Final Salary schemes (also known as Deferred Benefit schemes)

- benefits are defined in advance, usually in terms of:
  - final salary
  - number of years of service
  - a factor (often 1/60th or 1/80th for each year of service)
- the financial risk (of ensuring that benefits are paid) lies with the employer.

Money Purchase schemes (also known as Personal Pensions and/or Defined Contribution schemes)

- benefits depend on a combination of:
  - the amounts paid in by the member
  - any amounts paid in by the employer (if there is one)
  - the investment returns achieved up to retirement
  - the annuity rates available on retirement
- the financial risk lies with the member

By definition, a self-employed person will have no employer contributions.

3. **Is there likely to be a loss?**

Start by assuming that there will be a loss to be evaluated, if:

- The claimant was contributing to a pension scheme; and
- There is a claim for loss of earnings; and
- There was an employer contribution.

4. **Final Salary scheme member**

Potential pension:

- Obtain a copy of the members' guide (which will often be in simple terms).
- Obtain a copy of the most recent statement of the individual members' scheme benefits (an estimate of pension at normal retirement age based on current salary).
- With these documents, and the projection of final salary being used for evaluating loss of earnings, it should be possible to calculate the expected pension at retirement date (at its present day value).

Actual pension:

- Establish the actual (reduced) pension that will be payable at normal retirement date (at its present day value).

Proceed by:

- Applying *Wells v Wells* principles ([1999] 1 A.C. 345). Table A10 refers.
- Calculating loss of annual pension (after tax). Table G1 will assist.
- Applying an appropriate multiplier drawn from the Ogden tables. Tables A1 and A10 refer.

Calculations incorporating a loss of lump sum benefit can be complex and will only be possible if the effect that taking the lump sum has on the annual pension can be ascertained with reasonable certainty. (Public pension schemes usually provide separately for lump sum and annual pension benefits, so the figures are generally straightforward to ascertain.)

5. Money Purchase scheme member

A forensic accountant will often approach evaluation of loss along the following lines:

Potential pension:

- Ascertain current value of pension fund
- Calculate contributions foregone (payable by member and by employer if applicable)
- Calculate value of potential pension fund at retirement, based on contributions foregone and an assumed rate of investment return within the fund
- Calculate in turn
  - the lump sum benefit available on retirement (discounted to present day value)
  - the gross annual pension (based on annuity tables)

Actual pension:

- Calculate value of actual pension fund at retirement, based on any future contributions to the scheme and the assumed rate of investment return within the fund
- Calculate in turn
  - the lump sum benefit available (discounted to present day value)
  - the gross annual pension

Proceed by:

- Calculating the loss of lump sum (at present day value)
- Calculating the loss of annual pension (after tax). Table G5 will assist
- Applying an appropriate multiplier drawn from the Ogden tables
- Consider whether any further adjustments should be applied, of the sort discussed at Table A10

6. Important cases

Have regard to:

- *Parry v Cleaver* [1970] A.C. 1

  briefly: pension loss only runs from anticipated retirement age

  so that: no credit need be given against earnings losses for an early/ill health pension

- *Longden v British Coal Corporation* [1998] A.C. 653

  briefly: explains how to apportion an actual tax-free lump sum received ahead of expected retirement age between pre- and post-retirement periods.

  so that: treatment of the actual lump sum is brought into line with *Parry v Cleaver* principles.

- *Aboul-Hosn v Trustees of the Italian Hospital* (1987) (unreported)

  briefly: allows for a simple calculation in which pension loss is based on the tax relief fore-gone on the claimant's potential personal pension contributions.

  (This would only be appropriate in a case where there are no employer contributions foregone.)

7. Further points

- Do not rely on quotations from pension providers; they invariably incorporate inflation and are not therefore compatible with conventional multipliers.
- Keep in mind the reality of life expectancy. If life expectancy is impaired, pension loss will be reduced.
- That said, do not overlook the possibility of a "lost years" claim in respect of pension losses between the end of the post-accident life expectancy and the end of the pre-accident life expectancy.
- Do not assume that males necessarily retire at 65 and females at 60.

  Bear in mind that, between April 2010 and April 2020, the state pension age for women will gradually increase from 60 to 65. The state pension age is then set to increase from 65 to 68 between 2024 and 2046. There is a state pension age calculator at *www.thepensionservice.gov.uk*.

- Claims for loss of state pension may arise, particularly in relation to the State Second Pension (S2P).
- Smaller pension losses may sometimes not be worth pursuing, given the safety net of the State Pension Credit. See Table I2.

Group I
Benefits, Allowances, Charges

I1: Social security benefits (non means-tested)

How they work

Generally, all these benefits may be claimed independently of each other. However, there are overlapping benefit rules which prevent more than one income replacement benefit being payable. If the claimant is entitled to more than one, then the amount of the highest will be payable.
Many benefits are contributory, entitlement being dependent on satisfying conditions as to amount of national insurance contributions paid.
Until April 2003, increases were payable for many benefits for dependent children, subject to an earnings limit. The increases have now been replaced by child tax credit (see section I2) but people in receipt of the increases on April 5, 2003 have transitional protection.
Entitlement to non means-tested benefits is frequently affected if claimants are in hospital or in full-time care.
Claims for all benefits must be made in writing. Claims can be backdated only to a limited extent (varying according to the type of benefit).

A. Income replacement

1. Retirement

Retirement Pension	**09–10**
Claimant (Category A)	£95.25
Spouse/adult dependant	£57.05

Either spouse may qualify in their own right, or as a dependent.
Special rules apply for married women, divorced people, widows and widowers.
Highly variable rates according to contribution history.
Contributory and taxable.
For details (e.g. for Form E) submit Form BR20 (for valuation of additional state pension); or Form BR19 (for benefit forecast): downloadable at *www.thepensionservice.gov.uk*.

Additional pension

An Additional Pension was introduced in 1978, the State Earnings-Related Pension (SERPS). This was replaced by the State Second Pension (S2P) from 2002. At present there is a link between the Additional Pension and past earnings. It is planned for this to change gradually so that, by 2030, S2P will be paid at a flat rate. When announced in 2006, this rate was put at the then level of £1.40 per week for each year's service (up to a maximum of 40 years) – equivalent to some £2,900 pa.
A useful note appears in Wikipedia under the heading of State Second Pension.

2. Ill Health

i. Statutory Sick Pay	**09–10**
Standard rate	£79.15

Paid by the employer for up to 168 days (28 six-day weeks), to employees earning not less than £95 gross p.w.
Taxable.

ii. Incapacity Benefit (IB) **09–10**
(From October 2008 new claimants claim Employment and Support Allowance (ESA) below; existing claimants will move to ESA at a later date)

Short-term (under pension age)		
Lower rate		£67.75
Higher rate		£80.15
Adult dependant – extra		£41.35
Short-term (over pension age)		
Lower rate		£86.20
Higher rate		£89.90
Adult dependant – extra		£51.10
Long-term		£89.80
Increase for age	Higher rate	£15.65
	Lower rate	£6.55
Adult dependant – extra		£53.10

Higher rate applies from week 29. Long-term IB payable after first 52 weeks (no new claimants over pension age).
Personal capability assessments apply (rather than ESA tests) for existing claimants for a transitional period.
Age increase is payable at higher rate when incapacity begins under 35; lower rate if under 45. Both to be reduced to come into line with ESA allowances.
Restrictions apply to dependants' allowances.
Contributory (save for those incapacitated in youth).
Taxable; except short-term lower rate and transitional benefits.

iii. Employment and Support Allowance (ESA) 09–10
(For new claimants from October 2008 replaces Incapacity Benefit and Income Support paid on incapacity grounds)

Maximum Basic Rate	
Single claimant	£64.30
Couple	£100.95
Work-related component (for those meeting work-related activity tests)	£25.50
Support component (for those assessed as unable to work)	£30.85
Premiums (Means-tested)	
Enhanced disability – single	£13.40
Enhanced disability – couple	£19.30

Entitlement to contributory benefits depends on payment of National Insurance Contributions. Amounts are per week.

Severe disability – single/couple (lower rate)	£52.85
Severe disability – couple (higher rate)	£105.70
Carer premium	£29.50
Pensioner premiums	
Single (work-related activity group	£40.20
Single (support group)	£34.85
Single (assessment phase)	£65.70
Couple (work-related activity group)	£72.00
Couple (support group)	£66.65
Couple (assessment phase)	£97.50

Includes both contributory and means-tested benefit, based on limited capacity for work ("work-related activity group") or incapacity ("support group").
Benefit paid at basic rate during 13-week assessment phase. No age or spouse's additions for contributory benefit.
No increased long-term rates. Lower rates for under 25s.
Means-tested assessment and housing costs modelled on Income Support (IS: Table 28). Up to £20 p.w. child maintenance disregarded. Capital rules for income-related ESA (IRESA) as for IS.
IRESA is a passport to other benefits including full Housing and Council Tax Benefit (HB & CTS: Table 28).
In youth neither contributory nor means-tested.
Contributory ESA taxable: means-tested ESA not.

iv. Carer's Allowance	**09–10**
Claimant	£53.10
Adult dependant – extra	£31.70

Paid to people over 16 who spend at least 35 hours p.w. caring for recipient of higher or middle rates of Care Component of Disability Living Allowance, or Attendance Allowance or Constant Attendance Allowance at or above the normal rate with a related pension. Can earn no more than £95 p.w. net and must not be in full-time education.

Non-contributory. Claimant's benefit is taxable; extra for adult dependant is not.

3. Unemployment – Jobseeker's Allowance (JSA)

i. Contribution-based JSA	**09–10**
Claimant	£53.10
Adult dependant – extra	£31.70

ii. Income-based JSA		**09–10**
Claimant	16–24	£50.95
	25 and over	£64.30
Couple	Both over 18	£100.95
Dependent children (existing claimants only – others see Child Tax Credit) till day before 20th birthday		£56.11
Premiums as for IS (Table 29) plus		
Pensioner	Single	£65.70
	Couple	£97.50

Contributory JSA is flat-rate based on age, without allowances for dependants, and paid for up to 26 weeks.
Income-based JSA is paid with, or from expiry of, contributory JSA and modelled on IS with similar rules for income, capital, premiums and mortgage interest.
Up to £20 p.w. child maintenance disregarded.
Claimants must be under State Pension age, available for and actively seeking work and have a current Jobseeker's Agreement: for these IBJSA is a passport to other benefits including full HB and CTB.
Men aged between 60 and 65 may claim Pension Credit instead.
Main rates only given. Not usually available for those under 18 or those working 16 hours a week or more.
Taxable.

4. Maternity/paternity/adoption

i. Statutory Maternity Pay[1]	**09–10**
Higher rate (first 6 weeks)	90% of average weekly wage
Average earnings threshold	£95.00
Lower rate (for up to next 20 weeks)	£123.06[2]

Paid by employer for a maximum of 39 weeks. Taxable.

ii. Statutory Paternity Pay[1]	**09–10**
Rate	£123.06[2]
Average earnings threshold	£95.00

Payable for up to 2 weeks.Taxable.

iii. Maternity Allowance	**09–10**
Standard rate	£123.06[2]
Adult dependant – extra	£41.35
Average earnings threshold	£30.00

Paid to claimants not entitled to Statutory Maternity Pay but above average earnings threshold.
39 weeks maximum. Non-taxable.

iv. Statutory Adoption Pay[1]	**09–10**
Standard rate	£123.06[2]
Average earnings threshold	£95.00

Paid by employer for a maximum of 39 weeks. Taxable.

[1] *Qualifying conditions based on length of service and average earnings*
[2] *Or (if less) 90% of the parent's weekly average earnings*

v. Surestart Maternity Grant	**09–10**
Standard one-off payment	£500.00

Available if mother or partner is in receipt of Income Support, Income-based Jobseeker's Allowance, Pension Credit, Child Tax Credit at higher than family element or Working Tax Credit where disabled or severe disabled element claimed.

Entitlement to contributory benefits depends on payment of National Insurance contributions.
Amounts are per week except for the Surestart Maternity Grant payment and Bereavement Benefit lump sum.

5. Bereavement

i. Bereavement Benefit	**09–10**
Lump sum	£2,000.00
ii. Bereavement Benefit (age related)	£28.58 to £95.25

Available to bereaved spouses/civil partners over 45 but under State Pension age who do not remarry or cohabit and who are not bringing up children.
Payable for up to 52 weeks from date of bereavement.

iii. Widowed Parent's Allowance	£95.25

Available to beareaved spouses/civil partners under State Pension age and in receipt of child benefit who do not remarry or cohabit.
Widowed Parent's Allowance and Bereavement Allowance cannot be claimed together.
All benefits are contributory and (save lump sum) taxable.

6. Additional child payments for specified benefits

	09–10
Oldest child with child benefit	£8.20
Each other child with child benefit	£11.35

Mostly replaced by Child Tax Credit (CTC: Table 28).

B. Special needs

1. Disability Living Allowance (DLA)

		09–10
Care Component	Highest	£70.35
	Middle	£47.10
	Lowest	£18.65
Mobility Component	Higher	£49.10
	Lower	£18.65

The claimant must qualify before reaching 65.

2. Attendance Allowance

	09–10
Higher rate	£70.35
Lower rate	£47.10

Paid for care needs of those over 65.
Although the range of both allowances is based on need, there are no restrictions on how they are used.
Non-contributory and non-taxable.

C. Children

1. Child Benefit

	2009
Only/elder/eldest child	£20.00
Each subsequent child	£13.20

A child must be under 16, or under 20 and in full-time secondary education.
Non-contributory and non-taxable.
Administered by HMRC.

2. Guardian's allowance

	09–10
Guardian's allowance	£14.10

Payable with child benefit to those raising the children of deceased (or sometimes, missing) parents.
Non-contributory and non-taxable.
Administered by HMRC.

I2: Social security benefits and tax credits (means-tested)

Income Support (IS) 2009–10

For reduced cohort of under 60s on low income, working less than 16 hrs p.w. (e.g. lone parents, carers, some disabled workers and students). Not for the unemployed or new claimants who are sick/disabled or childless people under 18. Children remain dependent while CB (ibid.) is payable, but replacement of allowances by CTC opposite continues.

With some exceptions for existing claimants, new conditions restrict entitlement for lone parents as youngest child reaches threshold age: 12 or over from 24 November 2008; 10 or over from 26 October 2009; and 7 or over from 25 October 2010. (Claims will be for JSA or ESA).

Main rates only are shown.

IS brings automatic entitlement on income gounds to other benefits including maximum HB & CTC *opposite.*

A need level is established from the allowances and premiums, plus mortgage interest (currently 6.08%) on loans of up to £200,000 (new claimants), with restrictions on increases during a claim and reduction for resident non-dependants. (Temporary new provisions assist homeowners.) IS is then paid to supplement other income to the need level. There are detailed rules on the application of premiums and disregarded income. Payments from a liable relative including child support may disqualify, including a lump sum payment of any amount (treated as income). Up to £20 p.w. child maintenance disregarded. No disregard for childcare costs (but New Deal programme has child care subsidy).

Capital up to £6,000 is disregarded (child, £3,000). Capital between £6,000 and £16,000 is deemed to produce tariff income of £1 for each £250 (or part) over £6,000. There is no entitlement to IS if capital exceeds £16,000, disregarding value of home. Different capital limits apply for those in residential homes. Notional capital rules penalise deliberate deprivation of capital to obtain IS.

Non-contributory. Rarely taxable.

Personal allowances		**p.w.**	**p.a.**
Single person	16–24	50.95	2,649.40
	25 or over	64.30	3,343.00
Lone parent	Under 18	50.95	2,649.40
	Over 18	64.30	3,343.60
Couple	Both over 18	100.95	5,249.40
Dependent children			
(existing untransferred claimants only – others see Child Tax Credit)			
till day before 20th birthday / end of secondary education (if earlier)		56.11	2,917.72
Premiums			
Carer		29.50	1,534.00
Pensioner (claimant's partner 60+)		97.50	5,070.00
Other pensioners, see Pension Credit			
Disability	Single	27.50	1,430.00
	Couple	39.15	2,035.80
Enhanced disability			
	Single	13.40	696.80
	Couple	19.30	1,003.60

Severe disability			
	Single	52.85	2,748.20
	Couple (both qualifiying)	105.70	5,496.40
Existing claimants only (others see Child Tax Credit):			
Family/lone parent family		17.30	899.60
Disabled child		51.24	2,664.48
Enhanced disability (child)		20.65	1,073.80

Pension Credit (PC) 2009–10

PC comprises 2 elements: Guarantee Credit for those 60 and over whose income is below the Standard Minimum Guarantee; and Savings Credit for those 65 and over with modest savings or income. Either or both are claimable.

Means-tested, some income disregarded. No upper capital limit. £6,000 disregarded (£10,000 for care home residents); thereafter tariff income is £1 for every complete £500 (or part). *£6,000 increases to £10,000 from November 2009.*

Not a tax credit. State pension is not affected. Administered by the Pensions Service, with typically 5-year awards. Child maintenance disregarded; other maintenance disregarded only for savings credit. No provision for childcare costs. Housing costs as for IS. Guarantee Credit is a passport to maximum HB & CTB.

Non-contributory. Not taxable.

Standard Minimum Guarantee			**p.w.**
	Single		130.00
	Couple		198.45
	Additional amount for severe disability		
	Single		52.85
	Couple (both qualify)		105.70
	Additional amount for carers		29.50
Savings Credit			
	Threshold	Single	96.00
		Couple	153.40
	Maximum	Single	20.40
		Couple	27.03

Working Tax Credit (WTC) 2009–10

			p.a.
First Income threshold			6,420.00
First withdrawal rate		39%	
Second Income threshold			50,000.00
Second withdrawal rate		6.67%	
Basic Credit			1,890.00
Additional couple's/lone parent element			1,860.00
30 hours element			775.00
Disabled worker element			2,530.00
Severe disability element			1,075.00
50+ return to work payment:			
	16–29 hours		1,300.00
	30+ hours		1,935.00

Childcare element		**p.w.**
Maximum eligible cost (maximum payable £240 p.w.)		300.00
Maximum eligible cost for one child (maximum pyable £140 p.w.)		175.00
Percentage of eligible costs covered	80%	

Based on gross annual income, in-work support for families with child/young person where adult works 16 hours per week or single/couple claimants over 25 where adult works 30 hours p.w. 16 hour condition also for those 50+ returning to work or with disability. Couple with children eligible for 30 hour element if jointly work 30 hours, provided at least one works 16 hours. Awards provisional until end of year notice identifies under/overpayments.

Elements are cumulative except for the 50+ return to work elements. Complex assessment rules. Maintenance ignored. Assessment on annual incomes, joint incomes for couples. Tapers as income rises. Up to First threshold, claimants receive the maximum. Above First threshold, the reduction applies last to the childcare element. Income threshold for child tax credit only: £16,040. Administered by HMRC.

Child Tax Credit (CTC) 2009–10

		p.a.
First Income threshold for those entitled to CTC only		16,040.00
First withdrawal rate	39%	
Second Income threshold		50,000.00
Second withdrawal rate	6.67%	
Family elements		
Family element		545.00
Family element, baby addition		545.00
Child elements		
Child element		2,235.00
Disabled child additional element		2,670.00
Severely disabled child additional element		1,075.00

Based on gross annual income, support for families with child/children. Tapers as income rises, but WTC is abated first. The per child element is reduced for income above £16,040. The family element is reduced for incomes above £50,000. Replaces most benefit additions for children and earlier tax credits.

One family element per family, including the baby addition where there is a child under one. The child elements are cumulative, including any disabled child or severely disabled child additional elements. Paid to nominated main carer. Administered by HMRC.

Housing (HB) & Council Tax (CTB) Benefits 2009–10

HB for housing costs, except mortgages. From 7 April 2008, new claims based on local housing allowance (LHA): flat rate using local median rents for household size/composition (bedrooms). Under 25s restricted to bedsit/shared accommodation rate. Capped at maximum housing allowance or £15 per week above liability if lower. LHA rate published monthly, see Rent Service or local websites.

Allowance for Council/social housing tenants based on contractual rent not LHA. Reduction for resident non-dependants.

CTB paid to those on low income to assist with payment of CT (so not under 18s or most full-time students).

Award for HB and CTB depends on: money coming in; amount of savings; personal circumstances (children, disability, others in household); eligible charge.

Those on IS or IBJSA or PC Guarantee or IRESA automatically eligible. For others, some income disregarded, e.g. £18.50 p.w of single parent's earnings. Child maintenance fully disregarded. Up to 80% of childcare costs paid by single parents and working/disabled couples may be disregarded, up to £175 p.w. for one child and £300 p.w. for more than one child.

If income is greater than the applicable amount, a tapered reduction applies. HB is reduced by 65% of excess income; CTB by 20%.

Usual upper savings limit £16,000; no upper limit or tariff income if on PC guarantee. Capital up to £6,000 is disregarded. *(£6,000 increases to £10,000 from November 2009 for pensioners.)* For claimants under 60: each £250 (or part) over £6,000 is deemed to produce tariff income of £1 p.w., not including value of home. For claimants 60 and over: rate is £1 per £500 (or part). Different capital limits for those in residential homes and for children.

Where other adult residents preclude the single person discount, an alternative CTB (Second Adult Rebate) may apply, based on their income and status.

Non-contributory and non-taxable. Administered by Local Authorities.

		p.w.
Claimant	18–24	50.95
	25 or over	64.30
Lone parent	Under 18	50.95
	18 or over	64.30
Couple	Both under 18	76.90
	One or both over 18	100.95
Dependent children to day before 20th birthday		56.11
Pensioner		
	Single 60–64	130.00
	Couple one or both 60–64	198.45
	Single 65 and over	150.40
	Couple one or both 65 and over	225.00

Premiums

As for Income Support **except**		
	Family premium	17.30
Protected lone parent family premium		22.20
Additional family premium for one or more		
	child(ren) under 1 year	10.50
ESA componenets		
	Work-related activity	25.50
	Support	30.95

I3: Effect of social security benefits and tax credits on damages

The Compensation Recovery Scheme

The DWP is entitled to recover certain "listed benefits" from a defendant liable to pay damages to a claimant, where the claimant has received social security benefits. The defendant is entitled to offset some of its liabilities against the claimant's damages awards. The financial consequences for parties can be profound and an awareness of the working of the scheme is essential.

The relevant legislation is the Social Security (Recovery of Benefits) Act 1997 and the Social Security (Recovery of Benefits) Regulations 1997. References to sections ("s.", "ss.", "reg.", or "regs") are to the corresponding parts of the 1997 Act and Regulations respectively. References commencing "*CCR*", "*CSCR*" and "*R(CR)*" are to decisions of Social Security Commissioners. They are available on the web at: *http://www.osscsc.gov.uk/pages/des.htm*

The liability of the defendant

The scheme applies to damages for "accident, injury or disease": s.1(1). Claims brought by parents for wrongful birth have been said not to come within that phrase: *Rand v E Dorset HA.*[1] The scheme applies to payments made on settlement or under a court order: s.1(3). It applies to the MIB: s.1(2)(b). It does not apply to certain categories of exempt payments: s.1(2)(b), Sch.1, reg.2.

Before making a compensation payment, a defendant must apply for a certificate of recoverable benefits ("CRB"): s.4, reg.7. The CRB specifies the benefits that are recoverable: s.5. The Secretary of State must provide clarification if required: s.5(6). If the Secretary of State fails to provide a certificate within a month of a request being made with the requisite information, then the liability to pay the benefits will not arise: s.21.

The Secretary of State has powers to require information to be provided by a compensator, claimant and the claimant's employer: s.23, regs 3–6.

The liability to pay arises on the making of the compensation payment (or the first of them, if more than one): s.6(2). Failing to apply for a CRB does not prevent the liability arising: s.7(1), (2). There are powers to enforce the liability through the County Court: s.7(4).

For cases where there is more than one defendant, see s.19 and reg.9. For modifications to the scheme in respect of structured settlements, see reg.10.

What benefits are recoverable?

The benefits recoverable are those which are "listed benefits" paid during the "relevant period" and which were paid "in respect of" the accident, etc: s.1(1)(a).

"Listed benefits" are those listed in Sch.2: s.29. The table from Sch.2 is reproduced below.

In the case of accidents or injuries, the "relevant period" is five years from the date of accident or injury: s.3(2). In the case of disease, the five year period runs from the date of the first claim for benefit on the basis of the disease: s.3(3). The relevant period may be brought to an end sooner by a payment being made in *final* discharge of a claim, or an agreement that an earlier payment is made in *final* discharge: s.3(4). Thus interim payments do not stop the relevant period running, and neither do payments into court: reg.8(1). The "relevant period" is not restricted by the length of period of the claimant's loss of earnings claim: *CCR/8023/1995.*

The words "in respect of" make it clear that there must be a link between the accident etc and the payment of the benefit. The accident etc need not be the sole cause of the payment of benefit. For example, if the claimant is incapable of work and receiving incapacity benefit, then the following rules apply:

[1] [2001] P.I.Q.R. Q1.

— the fact that the claimant was receiving incapacity benefit before the accident etc does not of itself mean that the benefit is not paid "in respect of" the accident: *Hassall v Secretary of State for Social Security*.[1] If the Claimant was before the accident receiving benefit A, and as a result of the accident ceases to be entitled to A, but becomes entitled to benefit B, which is recoupable under the Act, he has a claim for special damages in respect of the loss of benefit A, *Hassall*; *Neal v Bingle*.[2]

— if the claimant is permanently incapable of work as a result of the accident and then gets an unrelated ailment which would have rendered him incapable, the benefits remain recoverable from that date: *CCR/5336/1995*.

— if neither the accident etc nor the unrelated ailment individually render the claimant incapable of work but cumulatively they do so, the benefits are recoverable: *CCR/5336/1995*. That is so even if the unrelated ailment is the dominant cause: *CSCR/1/1995*.

— if the claimant's accident would not itself incapacitate the claimant but the unrelated ailment does, the accident is not an effective cause of the incapacity and the benefits are not recoverable: *CCR/4/1993*; *CCR/5336/1995*.

— in an "exacerbation" or "acceleration" case, where the evidence is that the accident only contributed to the claimant's symptoms for a limited period and thereafter the symptoms were attributable to some underlying disability, only benefits payable during the limited period are recoverable: *R(CR) 1/01*.

— it may be necessary to ascertain precisely what ailment the claim for damages relates to and in relation to what ailment benefit was awarded. The mere fact that both a disease forming the basis of the claim and one forming the basis of the award of benefit were related to asbestos exposure is insufficient to make benefit recoverable: *R(CR) 3/03*.

Generally, it is not possible to reduce the amount of benefit recoverable on the ground that part of it would have been paid anyway: *CCR/4/1993*. Nor can the amount payable be reduced where the claimant is contributorily negligent: *Williams v Devon CC*.[3] However, if a claimant would only have been paid industrial injuries disablement benefit as someone 20 per cent disabled following the accident and an unrelated accident increases disability to 50 per cent, and hence the amount of IIDB, the additional IIDB will not be recoverable: *R(CR) 1/03*.

Benefits which should not have been paid at all are not paid "in respect of" the accident etc: *R(CR) 1/02*; *R(CR) 2/02*. So if benefit is paid as a result of fraud, or a mistake by the DWP, a compensator can challenge the CRB.

The defendant's obligation to offset the liability

The scheme attempts to strike a fair balance between the interests of the public purse, the claimant and the defendant by requiring a defendant to deduct recoverable benefits from heads of loss which those benefits are, broadly speaking, supposed to compensate and to pay them to the state: s.8.

A table specifies the heads of loss and the recoverable benefits that may be deducted from it: Sch.2, which is reproduced below.

[1] [1995] 1 W.L.R. 812.
[2] [1998] Q.B. 466.
[3] [2003] P.I.Q.R. Q4.

Calculation of compensation payment

Head of compensation	Benefit
1. Compensation for earnings lost during the relevant period	Disablement pension payable under section 103 of the 1992 Act Incapacity benefit Income support Invalidity pension allowance Jobseeker's allowance Reduced earnings allowance Severe diablement allowance Sickness benefit Statutory sick pay Unemployment supplement Unemployment benefit
2. Compensation for cost of care incurred during the relevant period	Attendance allowance Care component of disability living allowance Disablement pension increase payable under section 104 or 105 of the 1992 Act
3. Compensation for loss of mobility during the relevant period	Mobility allowance Mobility component of disability living allowance

Notes

1. (1) References to incapacity benefit, invalidity pension and allowance, severe disablement allowance, sickness benefit and unemployment benefit also include any income support paid with each of those benefits on the same instrument of payment or paid concurrently with each of those benefits by means of an instrument for benefit payment.
   (2) For the purpose of this Note, income support includes personal expenses addition, special transitional additions and transitional addition as defined in the Income Support (Transitional) Regulations 1987.
2. Any reference to statutory sick pay—
   (a) includes only 80 per cent of payments made between 6th April 1991 and 5th April 1994, and
   (b) does not include payments made on or after 6th April 1994.
3. In this Schedule "the 1992 Act" means the Social Security Contributions and Benefits Act 1992.

It is to be noted that offsets may be made only against damages in so far as the claims are made in relation to the "relevant period". So there can be no offsetting against future losses.

"Compensation" in Sch.2 includes interest, so that an offset may be made against any interest payable on a head of loss in column 1 in addition to the damages: *Griffiths v British Coal Corporation.*[1]

"Compensation for loss of earnings" includes damages to compensate for loss of receipts as a self-employed individual running a business and not merely profit: *Chatwin v Lowther.*[2]

"Compensation for cost of care" includes claims for gratuitous care provided by relatives: *Griffiths*, not following *McManus v Babcock Energy Ltd.*[3]

[1] [2001] 1 W.L.R. 1493.
[2] [2003] P.I.Q.R. Q5.
[3] 1999 S.C. 569.

On the other hand, "compensation for loss of mobility" applies only to financial losses and not to any element of the general damages award which is attributable to loss of mobility: *Mitchell v Laing*.[1] This principle must also apply to the other heads of loss in column 1.

If, however, no claim is made for a certain head of loss, the defendant must still repay the benefit if such a claim should have been made, and may not deduct the benefit from any other head of loss: *CCR/3396/2000*.

It is unclear whether the deduction under s.8 is to be applied before or after a reduction for contributory negligence, or whether a compensator is entitled to deduct benefits paid over a different period to that over which the head of loss is claimed. In *CCR/427/2003*, a Commissioner suggested, *obiter*, that s.8 had to be applied before the reduction, and that if a loss of earnings claim was limited to eighteen months then the compensator may only deduct benefits paid during that period under s.8.

Interest is awarded on the full amount of special damages before any deductions under s.8: *Wisely v John Fulton (Plumbers) Ltd*.[2]

Offers to settle

The 1997 Act causes complications in relation to offers to settle and defendants need to ensure that Part 36 offers are correctly drawn. If CPR 36.23 and PD 36 para.10 are not complied with, the offer will not usually be capable of being relied upon when the court considers costs.

Williams v Devon CC[3] gives detailed guidance on the proper operation of these provisions and confirms that if the defendant does not take into account the proper operation of s.8, the Pt 36 offer will not be effective.

Challenging certificates

The DWP may review a certificate and issue a fresh one: s.10. However, it is not possible to increase the amount recoverable on a review unless the DWP was misled: s.10(3).

A compensator has a right to appeal to an Appeal Tribunal to challenge different types of error alleged to have been made in a CRB: s.11(1). An appeal may be made only once the claim has been finally settled and the payment due under the CRB made: s.11(3). A claimant may also appeal if his compensation has been reduced (see below).

Tribunals are administered by the Appeals Service and consist of a legally qualified chairman and a medical practitioner member. A Tribunal must take into account, but is not bound by, a court decision on similar issues such as the extent of the claimant's injury: s.12(3). The Tribunal may confirm the certificate, specify variations or order that it be revoked: s.12(4).

Most appeals will revolve around questions as to whether benefits were paid "in respect of" the accident etc. Opinions expressed in DWP medical reports are not binding: *CCR/12532/1996*; *R(CR) 1/04*. Such practitioners are often entirely unaware of a claimant's medical history or of unrelated ailments and Tribunals tend to regard full reports from consultants with sight of medical records as being of greater weight. For this reason, practitioners should ensure that medical experts are asked to express opinions on whether the conditions of entitlement for a particular benefit were met or whether the benefit was, or should have been, paid in respect of the accident etc. Where an expert changes his opinion at trial, a Tribunal will still be entitled to rely upon his original evidence in his reports if it finds it appropriate to do so: *CCR/2046/2002*.

Further appeals lie to a Social Security Commissioner on a point of law: s.13.

[1] 1998 S.C. 342.
[2] [2000] 1 W.L.R. 820.
[3] [2003] P.I.Q.R. Q4.

If a CRB is altered on review or appeal, then there are provisions for the amount payable by the defendant to the Secretary of State and the deduction under s.8 to be recalculated: s.12(4), reg.11. The Tribunals and Commissioners have no jurisdiction over such a question: *CCR/427/2003*. If a defendant fails or refuses to pay over a balance following a successful appeal, a claimant may either sue for it or make an application in the personal injury proceedings, even if the proceedings were settled by agreement: *Bruce v Genesis Fast Food Ltd.*[1]

Benefits Outside the Compensation Recovery Scheme

Many categories of benefit have not been listed in Sch.2. The question therefore arises as to whether those benefits can be offset by a defendant. They can be divided into two categories. Cases under the Law Reform (Miscellaneous Provisions) Act 1948 provide assistance.

Benefits specified in Schedule 2

In *Jackman v Corbett*,[2] it was held that since Parliament had set out a detailed statutory scheme in the 1948 Act specifically limiting the defendant's right to deduct benefits received to a period of five years, there was no right to offset benefits paid after that period.

There is as yet no authoritative decision, but there is County Court authority that in respect of those benefits specified in Sch. 2, the defendant's right to offset the benefits payable is exclusively that provided for in the 1997 Act: *Easton v Ellis*.[3] So it was not possible to deduct future entitlements to mobility allowance (or the mobility component of disability living allowance) from an award for the future cost of a wheelchair. See note on *Eagle v Chambers* (No.2) at I8.[7] It is suggested that the approach in *Jackman* should apply to benefits mentioned in the 1997 Act.

Benefits not mentioned in the 1997 Act

In *Hodgson v Trapp*[4] it was confirmed that where benefits were not dealt with in the 1948 Act, they should be deducted in full from a damages award if the claimant would otherwise receive dual compensation. There were only two recognised exceptions: payments received under insurance policies and charitable payments. This decision has now been applied in post-1997 cases.

Compensation under the Pneumoconiosis (Workers Compensation) Act 1979 is deductible in full from an award of damages: *Ballantine v Newalls Insulation Co Ltd.*[5]

Housing benefit administered by local authorities may be deducted in full from an award of damages if the claimant would not have received HB in the absence of being injured: *Clenshaw v Tanner*.[6] It is suggested that the same conclusion will follow in respect of council tax benefit. It is less clear whether it will follow in respect of other benefits administered by the DWP.

[1] [2004] P.I.Q.R. P9.
[2] [1988] Q.B. 154.
[3] [1999] 1 C.L.Y. 1525.
[4] [1989] A.C. 807.
[5] [2001] I.C.R. 25.
[6] [2002] EWCA Civ. 1848.
[7] [2004] EWCA Civ. 1033.

14: Personal injury trusts

Introduction

Personal injury solicitors cannot fulfil their remit to clients without enabling the client to carefully consider the possibility of founding a personal injury trust. Failure to secure this is a fast-track route to being hauled up in Court before the nearest professional indemnity specialist

The importance of personal injury trusts remains despite the October 2006 introduction of the *temporary* income-related means-tested benefits disregard for personal injury awards which are not shrouded within a trust. From April 2008, a further temporary disregard applies to local authority funded care but only in certain limited circumstances. It can fairly be said that these disregards are so restrictive, and so out of touch with the realities of litigation, that they provide very little help for many. Additionally, benefits retention is not the only relevant factor in considering whether or not a personal injury trust is appropriate. Even if it were the temporary disregard amounts to a time-limited game of roulette rather than a proper solution for the client.

Specialist advice on personal injury trusts must be made available to all injured clients who have a reasonable expectation of receiving an award of damages. The extensive changes to the taxation of trusts (personal injury trusts included) brought about by the Finance Act 2006 with the prospect of a further income tax "raid" on account of the Finance Act 2009 reinforce the point that dabblers in trusts should beware.

What exactly is a "personal injury trust"?

The multiple descriptive names applied to personal injury trusts have sometimes created sufficient confusion to deter further investigation into the use of personal injury trusts.

Do all personal injury clients really need advice on personal injury trusts?

The answer to this question is "Definitely". This is partly because of the fact that awards held within personal injury trusts are "disregarded" capital for means-testing purposes but also for other important reasons.

The personal injury trust secures the benefits, entitlements and the use of the award for the injured client but there are also other potential advantages.

In short, advice on personal injury trusts must be given in all cases concerning:

- accidental injuries;
- criminal injuries;
- clinical and other medical negligence causing injury; and
- compensation given for any disease or injury caused as a result of a disease.

That is irrespective of whether or not the harm caused to the client was physical or mental. It is irrespective of where the injury occurred. It may have occurred in the UK or abroad. It is also irrespective of the size of the payment made. That is unless the value of the award is miniscule in proportion to the client's other resources but even then care is required. Circumstances can change. Large but otherwise unprotected resources can be quickly eaten up by the cost of expensive care provision.

Does advice on personal injury trusts only need to be given to those already in receipt of means-tested benefits?

The answer to this question is "No".

Advice on personal injury trusts does not only need to be given if a person is *currently* in receipt of means-tested benefits. Indeed a person may not be in current need of benefits but might potentially have access to them in the future if their "assessable capital" for means-testing purposes is low enough.

The most important point to note is that a trust does not need to have a special generic title or be one sort of trust or another at law to be a personal injury trust. It is the *source* of the trust fund which determines the trust's nature. Client needs, their family circumstances and the relevant law should dictate the type of trust. But whatever legal type of trust it is if it is funded by an award of compensation for a personal injury then it will be a "personal injury trust".

It is particularly important to remember that long term care provision, either at home or in a care home, is a means-tested benefit provided by or through local authorities. An injured client may be more likely than others in the population to have need of such support in the future.

There are also other positive advantages of personal injury trusts apart from the retention of means-tested benefits. That is particularly, but not exclusively, in the case of older, very young, mentally incapable or other vulnerable clients:

- They may have no experience of handling a large sum of money.
- They may want the protection which trustees can offer against grasping relatives.
- They may have unstable mental conditions which renders the use of trustees helpful.
- They may just want to get on with their lives without having to concern themselves with financial administration.
- They may fear the impact of divorce and separation on their finances and want to try and "ring-fence" their resources in some way.

There are countless possibilities and the reader should note that a proper appreciation of these situations appears to have been singularly lacking in the drafting of the Finance Act 2006 to the potential detriment of many such clients.

It should be noted that:

- The award placed in the personal injury trust may be negotiated or mediated and no Court Order making an award is required to facilitate a personal injury trust unless the compensated person is either a minor or mentally incapable of managing their own affairs.
- Cases involving minors will involve the High Court agreeing to the foundation of a personal injury trust. (Civil Procedure Rule 21.11).
- Cases involving mentally incapable persons will involve the Court of Protection agreeing to the foundation of a personal injury trust (Mental Capacity Act 2005). This is the case despite the reorganisation and indeed regionalisation of the Court of Protection as a superior Court of Record which took place in October 2007.

Do personal injury trusts help clients retain entitlement to means-tested benefits?
The answer to this is definitely "yes".

Is it as simple as it sounds? "No".

The Department of Work and Pensions and local authority means-testing rules are very helpful to the compensated person but usually *only* if the option of a personal injury trust is taken. Personal injury trusts are "opt in" and not "opt out". Proactivity is required from the lawyer involved in advising the client.

Basically if a client does not opt into a personal injury trust the value of their personal injury award and the income generated from it will be assessable capital and assessable income. That can cost them their entitlement to means-tested benefits. If they fail to inform the authorities of the relevant change of circumstances which an award might create, it could also cost them their liberty.

Timing: When is it "too late" to found a personal injury trust?
The answer to this question is: "In theory, never".

If an interim payment or a single final payment is made to an injured client then unless a personal injury trust is founded they are highly likely to lose entitlement to means-tested benefits. Particular care must be taken in attempting to take any advantage of the new 52-week disregard. Remember that the first payment in consequence of a personal injury triggers the disregard. This is not necessarily an interim payment – it could be a critical illness payment or otherwise.

The recipient of the award has a duty to inform any relevant DWP and local authority office of that relevant "change of circumstances". This duty was reinforced in the new Social Security Fraud Act 2001 after which "prompt" notification has been required.

A personal injury trust can be set up "late" after funds are received but if a trust is not set up before receipt then lost benefits may take time to reinstate. It may become increasingly difficult to ascertain what arose from the award and what did not. So even if a late decision is made where a person is not actually in receipt of benefits an "audit trail" may be difficult to follow. This could lead to difficulties in the future when a claim for benefits is made.

The rule in respect of the giving advice upon personal injury trusts is to provide it "the sooner the better" if a benefits hiatus is not to occur. Furthermore, a rushed client cannot really take a balanced view and it avoids stress all round to secure positive forward planning.

A broad brush outline of the means-tested benefits position for mainstream income related benefits and personal injury trusts:

1. For income support purposes a claimant's "assessable capital", currently above £16,000, can dis-entitle them from receiving that benefit. Above £6,000 and up to (2009–10) £16,000 they will lose benefits on a sliding scale. Other means-tested benefits may also be lost as a "knock on" effect as entitlement is contingent upon being eligible for Income Support. Under £6,000 there will be full entitlement.

2. If a compensated person opts into a personal injury trust the capital held within it becomes "disregarded capital". Paragraph 12 of Schedule 10 of the Income Support (General) Regulations 1987 (IS(G) Regulations) applies and thus they can still claim means-tested benefits. But that is only if the claimant is both in receipt of a low income (income being means-tested as well as capital) *and* they are under the relevant capital threshold.

3. The capital threshold applies to "households" or "claimant units" with special rules being applicable to children.

4. The personal injury trust disregard does not apply to fatalities cases as the injury is to the deceased and not the benefits claimant.

5. The income support rules are reflected in the other means-tested benefits rules such as those for housing benefit and council tax benefit.

6. It is important to note that it is the *source* of the trust fund which triggers the applicability of the disregard for means-tested benefits purposes. Trust funds "derived from a payment made in consequence of any personal injury to the claimant" are disregarded. It is as simple as that. A personal injury trust can therefore be a bare trust, life interest type trust, discretionary type trust or otherwise. The choice of the type of personal injury trust used should therefore depend upon individual client

needs, their circumstances and, very importantly, the tax implications but *not* upon the means-tested benefits rules. Issues relating to the "availability" or not of the disregarded trust fund to the injured claimant or the trustees' distribution policy are irrelevant (although care should be taken so as not to inadvertently take the claimant above the lower capital threshold as a result of distributions). This is something which the benefits authorities often find confusing. They are more used to dealing with trust funds not comprising disregarded sums.

7. Normally "assessable capital" for means-tested benefits purposes includes the value of any trust fund which is "available" to a claimant, e.g. an "ordinary" bare trust which does not contain a payment made in consequence of a personal injury. A benefits claimant in normal circumstances can also be treated as having effected a "deprivation of capital" upon setting up a trust, which might exclude or restrict their entitlement to the settled trust fund. Such an act usually renders the trust fund assessable "notional" capital. They are treated as still owning it and accordingly it will not have the effect of enabling them to claim means-tested benefits. These rules do not apply to personal injury trusts. There is no relevant deprivation of capital upon the foundation of a personal injury trust. IS(G) Regulation 51(1)a disapplies the usual rules.

8. The Social Security (Miscellaneous Amendments) (No.4) Regulations 2006 (SI 2006/2378) did have one significant positive impact, despite the flaws in the temporary disregard which it introduced (referred to below). That was in respect of *income* from personal injury trusts. Formerly it could only be used to buy goods and services not met by means-tested benefits. That is things which were not ordinary expenses of daily living. Now it appears income type payments arising from a personal injury trust can be used for anything at all. This has the valuable effect of enabling the trustees to top up the income of the claimant, so that they are no longer required to manage on benefit rates for their everyday living costs. It can also potentially reduce certain aspects of trust related administration. However this may still be desirable from a budgetary perspective.

9. It should be noted that "periodical payments" arising from personal injury awards are treated in the same way as income from a personal injury trust. It makes good sense to pay such amounts into the personal injury trust to emphasis their separation from the claimant's general assessable assets and to ease administration.

10. There are special rules relating to older people and certain mainstream income related means-tested benefits which appear to render personal injury trusts redundant in such situations. However, those rules are complex and inconsistent with other benefits rules so it is usually best to assume that a personal injury trust should be put in place rather than should not be put in place. The rules relating to pension credit are particularly problematic.

11. The case of *Firth* v *George Ackroyd Junior Ltd and City of Bradford Metropolitan District Council* (March 28, 2000) involved an argument that the means-testing capital disregard only applied to damages for "pain and suffering". This was rejected as that did not fit with the regulations which are widely drafted. The value of the trust fund will all be disregarded. It has no top limit.

12. The existence of the personal injury trust fund does not affect entitlement to means-tested benefits of a partner or child in the same household/claimant unit as the injured party. That is per IS (G) Regulation 23(1) and its brethren for other means-tested benefits.

13. Once again fatalities cases do not obtain the benefit of the personal injury trust disregard.

A broad brush outline of the means-tested benefits position for those in long-term residential care in care homes and at home in the context of personal injury trusts:

1. The rules relating to the cost of care supplied by local authorities are extremely complex. Local authorities are responsible for securing residential accommodation (and associated services) for certain vulnerable people to the extent that the National Health Service has no responsibility. This arises under the National Assistance Act 1948 section 21(1) (as amended by the National Health

Service and Community Care Act 1990). But they also have an obligation undersection 22 to charge for those services in accordance with the National Assistance (Assessment of Resources) Regulations 1992 (as amended) (the NA(AR) Regulation).

2. Special rules apply to charges for temporary residents, those in care through provision of intermediate services and also those discharged (after "sectioning") under section 117 of the Mental Health Act 1983 where provision may be at a different rate or free of charge.

3. The NA(AR) Regulations means-test is an *individual* means-test and not a household/claimant unit based means test. Apart from an income based means test there is also a capital based means test. A resident with over £23,000 in properly assessable capital must pay for all their fees. There is a sliding scale down to £14,000. A resident can keep £14,000 of capital (the figures stated relate to England for 2009–10).

4. The NA(AR) Regulations disregard the value of personal injury trust funds from the local authority means test. The relevant regulation is found in Schedule 4 paragraph 10 NA(AR). As in the case of mainstream income related benefits it is the source of the trust fund and not the type of trust used which triggers the disregard. Regulation 25(1)(a) also disapplies the notional capital rules, mirroring the disapplication of those rules for income support and other income based benefits purposes.

5. The rules relating to the income aspect of the NA(AR) Regulations means test changed following the Social Security (Miscellaneous Amendments) (No.4) Regulations 2006 (SI 2006/2378). This is because the NA(AR) Regs incorporate provisions of the Income Support rules into the local authority means test. The former situation was that income type payments were broadly disregarded so far as they did not go towards meeting the "standard" or "contract rate" for care funded by the local authority (the care equivalent of ordinary expenses of daily living). It now appears that payments for such items is possible though there is no reason why it should be considered desirable. In practice the new provision ensures that trustees of personal injury trusts can top up the income of residents, enabling them to live in respect of their everyday needs, on a more generous basis.

6. It should be noted that under the NA(AR) Regulations periodical payments arising from personal injury awards are treated in the same way as income from a personal injury trust. It makes good administrative sense to pay such amounts into the personal injury trust.

7. Care at home, as opposed to in a home, should be assessed in accordance with the Fairer Charges Guidance. That was issued as mandatory guidance by the Department of Health as LAC (2001) 32 under section 7(1) of the Local Authority Social Services Act 1970. Section 17 of the Health and Social Services and Social Security Adjudications Act 1983 gives local authorities a discretionary power to make reasonable charges for adult service users, in England and Wales, for non-residential services but the Fairer Charges Guidance makes it clear that persons cared for at home should not be assessed financially in such a way as to disadvantage them when comparing their financial assessment with the one arising for a person in residential accommodation effected under the NA(AR) Regulations. This makes sense as it is government policy to secure care for people at home and not in an institutional type setting.

8. The Fairer Charges Guidance requires local authorities to take account of the provisions of the Charging for Residential Accommodation Guide (the CRAG). That is periodically issued by the Department of Health as mandatory guidance in relation to the NA(AR) Regulations. The current CRAG at time of writing is LAC (DH) 2000(3). It reiterates the point that the financial assessment of those cared for at home should mirror that of those who are residents in care homes. As the NA(AR) Regulations and the CRAG disregard personal injury trust funds in the context of residential care so should local authorities when addressing the means-tested cost of care provided at home.

9. The Court of Appeal case of *Crofton* v *NHSLA* on February 9, 2007 agreed with the above interpretation of the Fairer Charges Guidance so far as capital administered by the Court of Protection and/or in a personal injury trust was concerned. It also admitted some confusion over the treatment of income. It is submitted that the rules should be interpreted to disregard both capital and income. To suggest otherwise would be inconsistent. However, there is likely to be some local variation in the treatment of income which may require a formal challenge to resolve.

Minors and Mentally Incapable People
The High Court has the power under section 21.11 of the Civil Procedure Rules to establish a trust for a minor who is expected to be mentally capable when he or she reaches the age of eighteen. That is provided the Court is satisfied that this is the appropriate way to deal with the award of damages.

For people who lack capacity, including minors who on the balance of probabilities are considered not to be likely to have the capacity to deal with their own affairs at the age of eighteen, an application for a personal injury trust can be made to the Court of Protection. Although funds within the Court of Protection which relate to personal injury are disregarded for means-tested benefits and care purposes, there can be a number of factors, not least ease of administration and separation from the Court process, which can lead the family of a person without capacity to feel that a personal injury trust is a more effective mechanism of dealing with the award.

In both of these situations, the appropriate Court will require a suitably qualified and experienced professional trustee to be put in place and will also want to know details of the proposals for the investment award by the trustees. A report from an independent financial adviser in support of the application will also be necessary, again from a suitably qualified and experienced professional.

What about the temporary disregards for personal injury awards?
Temporary disregards for personal injury awards are contained within the Social Security (Miscellaneous Amendments) (No.4) Regulations 2006 (SI 2006/2378) commencing on October 1, 2006 and the National Assistance (Sums for Personal Requirements and Assessment of Resources) Amendment (England) Regulations 2008 (SI 2008/593) commencing on April 7, 2008. This put the value of using personal injury trusts into even sharper focus than before. It did not mitigate their usefulness.

Application of the temporary disregard to income related benefits (income support, housing benefit, JSA, council tax benefit) and funded care in some circumstances.

The temporary disregard applies to income related means-tested benefits. It also relates to care funded by the local authority, but in the context of care *"with the exception of any payment or any part of any payment that has been specifically identified by a court to deal with the cost of providing care"*. It is therefore easy at the outset to see how two people with substantially similar injuries and compensation could be treated completely differently, depending on the wording of the court order (consent order or otherwise).

The temporary disregards do not apply to the Pension Credit or Housing Benefit Council Tax Benefit regulations for people over 60 as these disregard payments made in compensation for personal injury anyway although in an over-complicated manner.

The relative simplicity of the personal injury trust disregard
As already noted the main capital disregard for funds held within a Personal Injury Trust is found at paragraph 12 of schedule 10 of the Income Support (General) Regulations 1987 (as amended) (the IS(G) Regulations).

It reads (with my words in square brackets):

> "Where the funds of a trust are derived from a payment made in consequence of any personal injury to the claimant, the value of the trust fund and the value of the right to receive any payment under that trust [are disregarded]."

This is simple, easy to understand and to apply in practice. The value of income from such trusts is also disregarded under paragraph 15 Schedule 9 of the IS(G) Regulations.

The complexity of the new temporary disregards

The temporary disregard, which so far as mainstream income-related benefits are concerned, appears as paragraph 12A of schedule 10 of the IS(G) Regulations is duplicated through the Jobseeker's Allowance, Housing Benefit and Council Tax Benefit regulations. It is also imported into the local authority means testing system (in that case subject to the restriction highlighted above). It is stated as follows (with the authors' words in square brackets):

"12A

1. Any payment made to the claimant or the claimant's partner in consequence of any personal injury to the claimant or as the case may be the claimant's partner [is disregarded]

2. But sub-paragraph 1–

   (a) applies only for the period of 52 weeks beginning with the day on which the claimant first receives any payment in consequence of that personal injury;

   (b) does not apply to any subsequent payment made to him in consequence of that injury (whether it is made by the same person or another);

   (c) ceases to apply to the payment or any part of the payment from the day on which the claimant no longer possesses it;

   (d) does not apply to any payment from a trust where the funds of the trust are derived from a payment made in consequence of any personal injury to the claimant.

3. For the purposes of sub-paragraph (2)(c) the circumstances in which the claimant no longer possesses a payment or a part of it include where the claimant has used a payment or part of it to purchase an asset.

4. References in sub-paragraphs (2) and (3) to the claimant are to be construed as including references to his partner (where applicable)."

These temporary disregards were effected as an *addition* to the existing personal injury trust disregard. They are couched around with a surprising number of qualifications, and are even more restricted in the case of care. There seems to be no logic behind this other than to overcomplicate what should surely be a simple 52-week exemption from assessment, a "period of grace" within which the person receiving their award can put their affairs into proper order.

Neither the main nor the temporary disregard applies in fatalities cases. Survivors on means-tested benefits or in care may accordingly lose those benefits and care funding. This is a discriminatory gap in the benefits aspect of the personal injury trust rules in general.

The 52-week disregard is triggered by the *first payment the claimant receives* in consequence of that personal injury. This has various implications:

1. An interim payment triggers the start of the 52-week period. If the claimant received an interim of (say) £3,000 two years ago and then receives damages of £50,000, they will not have the luxury of the 52-week disregard for the £50,000. Even if the £50,000 arrives a few weeks after the £3000, it appears that there is no period of grace whatsoever for the £50,000.

2. As the disregard relates to any payment in consequence of a personal injury, this also appears to be triggered by insurance payments such as those for critical illness if they were made as a result of the injury.
3. If there was an accident at work, the employer may have made an ex-gratia payment before settlement of the award proper. Again the 52-week disregard is apparently triggered.
4. At the widest definition even a payment from a family member or a friend or a charity to help the claimant over those difficult first few weeks could potentially trigger the 52-week period.

All these points are indicative of rather poor drafting and show little conception of the real lives of injured people.

While the money is sitting in the claimant's bank account it is disregarded. However, paragraph 12A(2)(c) says that once the claimant no longer possesses it, it is not disregarded anymore. Gifted awards are therefore assessable capital even within the 52-week period. Paragraph 12A(3) also points out that an exit from the disregard is triggered where the claimant has used a payment or part of it to purchase an "asset". That is neutral from the claimant's perspective where the asset purchased falls within one of the other means-tested benefits disregards such as for personal chattels. But a major concern is that any form of investment might be classed as a purchase of a non-disregarded assessable asset. This appears to encourage rushed expenditure as opposed to long term prudence.

The only reason that 12A is stated not to apply to personal injury trusts is because personal injury trusts retain their own disregard under paragraph 12.

In summary it would appear wisest to ignore the 12A disregard, other than for very temporary purposes (in the smallest of cases where the award is likely to be spent very quickly) and stick to the use of the far less restrictive personal injury trust vehicle.

The implications of the 2006 Budget upon the choice of type of personal injury trust

The Finance Act 2006 amended the Inheritance Tax Act 1984 (IHTA) in respect of many forms of trust founded after March 21, 2006. The result is that a full set of needs led choices is only available for the settlement into trust of awards of compensation amounting to no more than the amount of an injured client's available "nil rate band" for inheritance tax purposes. However, for most injured claimants the use of a bare trust should be adequate. They are unaffected.

For trusts other than bare trusts the cut off point is £325,000 less the injured client's cumulative total of lifetime chargeable transfers within the preceding seven years (tax year 2009–10).

Transfers of value into most forms of trust (notably discretionary and life interest trusts) in excess of that amount will now trigger an immediate inheritance tax charge on the surplus at the lifetime rate (20% for the tax year 2009–10) and potential further inheritance tax charges. That is something to be avoided.

In the case of larger awards, which for whatever reason need to be settled into a more protective arrangement than a personal injury bare trust, the choice of the type of trust is now largely inheritance tax driven.

Trust structures under Section 89 of the Inheritance Tax Act 1984 ("disabled trusts"), including the variants added to that arrangement by Finance Act 2006 may provide some relief. Sadly however, there are significant groups of people who do not fall within the definition of "disabled" in Section 89 but who would benefit from a trust other than a bare trust. They are the losers.

This is hardly a satisfactory state of affairs for the vulnerable. It has also added considerably to the technical demands placed upon the busy practitioner. A crash course on inheritance tax is unfortunately necessary. This is good news for trusts and tax lawyers seeking to eke out their meagre living but bad news for hard pressed injured clients wanting straight answers and simple solutions.

It is also noted that draft personal injury trusts supplied by CICA have recently evidenced the complexities inherent under the new arrangements. It is wise to involve an experienced trusts practitioner from an early stage especially in complex cases.

Making a decision over the choice of trust

For a mentally capable adult beneficiary, the simplest and most cost effective type of personal injury trust, where significant powers can be retained by the settlor, is generally a bare trust. It is also tax neutral and benefits efficient. Should unpredictable benefits related changes take place in the future, a different type of trust could potentially be created from such an arrangement at the behest of the injured settlor.

For mentally incapable adults and children, the Court of Protection will almost always require a bare trust. There may be some circumstances in which it is not appropriate for a bare trust to be founded but these will be exceptional. In all cases the Court retains its protective oversight which can support the trustees in their decision-making as appropriate.

In cases involving mentally capable minors and the jurisdiction of the ordinary High Court (as opposed to the Court of Protection), a CPR 21.11 bare trust is, the author submits, the only lawful trust-related alternative to allowing the Court Funds/Investment Division to handle the minor's funds.

There may be occasions, particularly in the case of mentally capable beneficiaries, where other types of trust are appropriate. The author considers that there are three scenarios in which this might be appropriate:

1. *Vulnerable but not mentally incapable clients who are afraid of their own irrational or impulsive behaviour.* The compensated person would like the trustees to be able to exercise more power to stop them "spending the lot". A life interest or a discretionary type arrangement will provide more braking power for the trustees.

2. *Vulnerable but not mentally incapable clients who fear the effect of third party pressure.* There is something in the beneficiary's personal or business life which renders a revocable bare trust inappropriate. A life interest or a discretionary arrangement will again provide more braking power for the trustees.

3. *Concerns about the settlor's heirs.* The intended beneficiaries under the compensated person's Will may be in receipt of means-tested benefits or have other personal circumstances which mean that they should not receive money outright. A discretionary trust may be appropriately founded by the compensated person which could continue for the benefit of others when they have died. However, the same effect can be achieved by a bare trust backed up by a discretionary Will trust subject to considerations 1 and/or 2 above also being relevant.

If a more protective type of trust arrangement would be of assistance to a vulnerable client then, if the amount involved is less than £325,000 (less the client's cumulative total of lifetime chargeable transfers within the preceding seven years), in the tax year 2009–10 the choice may be driven by no more than practical reasoning. That is with an *eye* to the modest impact of the income tax and capital gains tax consequences. The Income Tax and Capital Gains Tax rates were radically (and broadly favourably) overhauled in the 2007 Finance Act. The 2009 Finance Act holds out the prospect of a 50 per cent income tax rate on some protective type trusts for 2010–11 onwards, but refunds should be available in most cases.

In more usual circumstances the same practical reasoning must be weighed alongside the inheritance tax consequences. Great care should be taken in any event but even more care is required in those larger cases. The need for care is particularly well illustrated in the recent *Phelps v Stewarts* case.

The duties of the trustees of personal injury trusts

Taking up the role of a trustee is an onerous challenge. Many lay and professional people seriously underestimate the practical demands placed upon them and legal liabilities which can follow from an appointment as a trustee. It is important that such matters are not forgotten in the rush to secure a sensible post-settlement solution to fund administration.

Ideally, although apart from under pensions legislation the law does not strictly prohibit it, trustees should not be undischarged bankrupts. Also Trustees should voluntarily resign if they have *any* financial difficulties. This reduces the risk of both temptation and imputation of bad motives which can lead to difficulty. As a matter of law *Trustees must:*

1. Disclose any circumstances where they might have a conflict of interest with a beneficiary. If a beneficiary owes a trustee money this should be disclosed.
2. Not act in conflict with the interests of the beneficiaries or profit from their role as trustee.
3. Ensure they know what the terms of the trust are and that they are carried out.
4. Ensure that they do not act beyond the terms of the trust and their powers given by it.
5. Ensure that good trust records and accounts are kept and that tax due is paid on time.
6. Take independent financial advice. The trustees must also ensure that the advice taken is in accord with the Trustee Act 2000. Trustee investment is governed by different criteria as to the appropriateness of investments to private investment for oneself. In particular the difference between "investment" and "speculation" and the implications of the "active" versus "passive" investment debate should be taken seriously. Furthermore, the taking of financial advice does not preclude the use of common sense. (See generally *Coldrick on Modern Trustee* Investment – Ark 2007.) The ultimate decision over what to invest in is the trustees' decision. It cannot be delegated.
7. Act impartially and fairly between any multiple beneficiaries (less likely to be a problem in the case of a personal injury trust) and those who are beneficiaries now and those who will be in the future. This is the general rule but in the case of a personal injury settlement the compensated beneficiary will be expected to be the main if not sole beneficiary for life. That is allowed for under the powers of the trustees.
8. Take reasonable care. Professional trustees must take more care than others.
9. Act jointly. Trustees should not normally delegate functions to each other. Trustees are jointly liable for mistakes and should therefore act together.
10. Not charge fees. Only professional trustees can claim more than their out of pocket expenses.
11. Ensure that beneficiaries are kept fully informed. This avoids disputes.

To recap:

1. Personal Injury lawyers must actively ensure that their clients get advice and assistance on personal injury trusts.
2. All cases of accidental and criminal injuries, clinical and other negligence causing physical and/or mental harm to a person and where compensation is given for any disease or injury caused as a result of a disease are relevant.

3. Fatalities cases do not benefit from the personal injury trust disregard.
4. Advice must not be restricted to cases where clients are currently receiving means-tested benefits.
5. There are significant means-tested benefits advantages to having a personal injury trust and the possibility of the client needing expensive long term care in the future should not be forgotten or omitted from the advice being given.
6. There may be non-benefits related "peace of mind" and practical advantages to having a personal injury trust.
7. It is the source of the trust fund which determines the nature of a trust as a personal injury trust. Client needs/circumstances and the law of trusts/tax dictates the legal type of trust used.
8. Advice on personal injury trusts before interim or final payments is essential.
9. Do not simply accept draft trusts produced by CICA. They may be problematic or overly restrictive in a number of ways. Negotiation may be necessary.
10. Consider obtaining financial advice for the trustees as soon as it is clear there will be an award. Be aware of trustee involvement best practice principles.
11. The trust fund can be used for just about anything the compensated person needs or wants.
12. Before attempting to effect a personal injury trust ensure that you are fully acquainted with both trust law and the post March 21, 2006 inheritance tax rules as a means of enhancing client care and reducing professional risk.

15: Claims for Losses of Earnings and Maintenance at Public Expense

The Administration of Justice Act 1982, s.5 provides that where an injured claimant seeks to recover damages for losses of earnings, the defendant can set off against that claim any saving attributable to maintenance (either wholly or partly) at public expense in a hospital, nursing home or other institution.

This deduction is comparable to (but not the same as) the common law principle that where a claimant is in a private hospital or home (in respect of which damages are claimed from the defendant), credit must be giving for the domestic expenses thereby saved. This is the "domestic element" which was discussed in *Fairhurst v St Helens and Knowsley Health Authority*.[1]

16: Foster care allowances

Introductory notes:

These figures are an estimate of the cost of bringing up a child in its own home.

They are derived from the Fostering Network's recommended minimum weekly foster care allowances for the year commencing April 6, 2009, which incorporate a 50 per cent uplift over the cost of bringing up a child in its own home so as to reflect the additional cost involved in the care of a fostered child. The amounts shown incorporate a sum (equal to four weeks' extra payments) recommended by the Fostering Network to cover the cost of birthdays, holidays, and religious festivals.

The Fostering Network's full survey of foster care allowances paid by each local authority, Survey of Allowances 2008/09, is available free to members only from *www.fostering.net*.

Fostering Network recommended costs of bringing up a child in its own home for the year beginning April 6, 2009

Age of child (years)	National (£ per week)	London (£ per week)
0–4	90.00	106.00
5–10	103.00	121.00
11–15	128.00	150.00
16+	155.00	182.00

In *Spittle v Bunney* it was said that the cost of fostering services is not an appropriate measure for the value of the loss of a (deceased) mother's services, but the case is not uncontroversial.[2]

1 [1995] P.I.Q.R. Q1 at Q8 and Q9

2 [1988] 1 W.L.R. 847.

Group J

Court of Protection fees and costs

J

J1: Public Guardianship Office notice on personal injury damages, income support and care funding

This notice deals with the question whether income from an award of damages for personal injury held on trust must be taken into account for the purpose of eligibility for income support and for the purpose of assessment of resources by the local authority in relation to the funding of residential care. It replaces an earlier website notice with the same title, which is now out of date.

The law has recently been changed in the following respects:

- The treatment of income from personal injury damages held on trust
- The treatment of annuities where there is a structured settlement.

There has been **no change** in respect of:

- The treatment of the capital of a trust fund deriving from personal injury damages
- The treatment of personal injury damages held in the Court of Protection.

I will refer to the last two matters simply by way of a reminder.

INCOME SUPPORT

Treatment of capital

The income support regulations provide that the *capital* is not taken into account for income support purposes so long as the money is either held on trust or administered by the Court of Protection (*e.g.* held on Special Account). This has not changed.

Treatment of interest accruing to personal injury damages in court and payments out

Where the funds are in court, the Income Support regulations **treat the income accruing to the capital as capital**. In a case which came before Commissioner Powell on July 28, 2000 (CIS/4037/1999), it was decided that **payments out to the receiver were also to be treated as capital**. That case involved personal injury damages held in Court, where a monthly payment of £625 was made to the receiver. The result of the Commissioner's decision was that the applicant qualified for income support. Although the money withdrawn is treated as capital, it is no longer treated as disregarded capital when it leaves the Court. The effect of this is that the applicant will remain eligible for income support unless ruled out by the amounts of capital held *outside* the Court of Protection.

Commissioner Powell's decision is not affected by the recent change in the law, nor has it been affected by any subsequent decision of the courts. Another Commissioner made a similar decision in 2001 (CIS/929/00), and in November 2002 Commissioner Henty (CIS/2211/2002) held that monthly payments from a damages award held in court counted as capital, ie could not be disregarded, and, so far as the payments exceeded the income support capital threshold, they were subject to the "tariff income" rule. This made the claimant ineligible for income support.

Annuity payments under structured settlements

Prior to the recent change in the law, such payments ranked as income, with the result that the beneficiary would not be eligible for income support. This was confirmed by the Court of Appeal in *Beattie v Secretary of State for Social Security.*[1] **This decision has been reversed by an amendment to the Income Support Regulations**, as explained below.

Income from personal injury damages held on trust

Prior to the recent change in the law, income from such a trust ranked as income for the purposes of income support, so that the beneficiary would not normally be eligible. The rules differed from those applicable to personal injury damages held in court, although it was not easy to see why this should be so. However, the rules applicable to income from trusts have now been changed.

[1] [2001] 1 W.L.R. 1404.

The new rules
The Income Support Regulations have been amended as from 28 October 2002 by the Social Security Amendment (Personal Injury Payments) Regulations 2002 (No.2442). [This makes similar amendments to the regulations on housing benefit, council tax and jobseeker's allowance, but the details of those will not be given here].
The changes are as follows:

- Periodical payments received under an agreement (including an out of court settlement) or a court order to make personal injury payments are treated as income
- Payments under an annuity purchased with funds deriving from personal injury payments are **disregarded income** to the extent described below
- Payments received under an agreement or court order to make personal injury payments are **disregarded income** to the extent described below
- Payments of income from trusts whose funds derive from personal injury payments are **disregarded income** to the extent described below.

The new rule does not provided that these payments of income are automatically disregarded. **They are disregarded entirely when used for items other than everyday living expenses. If used for everyday living expenses, the first £20 is disregarded.** This means that the trustees will normally be able to ensure that the income is used in such a way that the beneficiary does not lose eligibility for income support.

ASSESSMENT OF RESOURCES FOR THE PURPOSE OF RESIDENTIAL CARE FUNDING
This is governed by the National Assistance (Assessment of Resources) Regulations 1992. The rules on the treatment of personal injury damages are the same as for income support, both as to capital and income. The changes described above come into operation in England on 28 October 2002 in relation to care funding, under the National Assistance (Assessment of Resources) (Amendment) (No.2) (England) Regulations 2002. Local Authorities have been advised of the changes by Local Authority Circular LAC (2002) 15, which may be accessed on the DOH website (www.doh.gov.uk/publications/coinh.html). Hard copies of the Circular may be obtained from Department of Health, PO Box 777, London SE1 6XH.

Jill Martin
Legal Adviser to the Public Guardianship Office
October 18, 2002 (updated April 2003)

Editor's note:
Similar changes to the care funding rules in Wales have been made by the National Assistance (Assessment of Resources) (Amendment) (Wales) Regulations 2003, with effect from April 7, 2003.

Part of the material dealt with in this notice has changed as a result of the Social Security (Miscellaneous Amendment) (No.4) Regulations 2006, SI 2006/2378.

J2: Editor's Note on the Court of Protection

1. The Mental Capacity Act 2005 and the Court of Protection

The Mental Capacity Act 2005 ("the Act") finally came into full effect from October 1, 2007 and has redefined the legal principles concerning people who may lack mental capacity to make decisions for themselves. The Act sets out rules for those who make decisions on behalf of people who are mentally unable to make decisions for themselves and enshrines in statute best practice and former common law principles concern decision making.

Accordingly, from the October 1, 2007 the new Court of Protection is established on the following basis:

(a) The former office of the Supreme Court known as the Court of Protection has been replaced with a new Court, also known as the Court of Protection.
(b) The new Court is designed to be a single specialised Court staffed by a number of appropriately trained judges.
(c) While the centre for the Court of Protection will remain at Archway Tower in London, with Senior Judge Lush sitting alongside several District Judges, the Court will also have a presence in cities across the country with the intention that it should be more accessible for attended hearings.
(d) The Court now has much wider powers to make decisions where a person is not able to make decisions for themselves about–

    (i) Their property and financial affairs.
    (ii) Their welfare, including medical treatment and care, where they are over 16 years of age.

(e) The Court will be able to make decisions as to whether or not a person lacks capacity to make a specific decision for themselves.
(f) If a person is unable to make a decision the Court will be able to either–

    (i) Make a single decision about that matter.
    (ii) Where a series of decisions are required it may appoint a Deputy to make decisions on behalf of that person.

(g) The former Public Guardianship Office is to be replaced by a new Office of the Public Guardian. Much of the executive decision making power of the old Office of the Public Guardian has been removed and decision making power is now vested almost entirely with the Court.
(h) While those appointed under old "Receivership" Orders will retain the powers of authority granted to them by the Court, it is likely that over time these orders will be replaced with "Deputyship Orders" where appropriate.

2. Who comes under the Jurisdiction of the Court of Protection?

It will be necessary to make an application to the Court of Protection where there is a need to make a decision for a person who lacks the mental capacity to make that decision for themselves, either with regard to their property and finances or welfare matters.

In cases of uncertainty or dispute the Court can be asked to make a decision as to whether or not a person lacks the mental capacity to make their own decisions.

The Act sets out the definition of when a person lacks mental capacity–

> "A person lacks capacity in relation to a matter if at the material time he is unable to make a decision for himself in relation to the matter because of an impairment of, or a disturbance in the functioning of, the mind or brain".

The Act also sets out principles to apply when considering whether a person lacks mental capacity–

(a) It does not matter if a mental impairment is permanent or temporary.
(b) Age, of itself, does not establish a lack of mental capacity.
(c) An "unjustified assumption" of a person's condition should not, of itself, establish a lack of mental capacity.
(d) Lack of ability to communicate, of itself, does not establish a lack of mental capacity.

Furthermore, the Act gives a four-step criteria, so that if a person does have capacity to make a decision they must be able to–

(a) Understand the information relevant to the decision.
(b) Retain that information.
(c) Use and weigh up that information as part of making the decision.
(d) Communicate their decision whether by talking, using sign language or any other means.

The Act makes the question of capacity "decision specific" and it is important to look at each individual decision in turn and consider the respective magnitude and complexity of the decision and circumstances surrounding it. For example, it is common experience that a client may be unable to manage their own financial affairs, due to the complexity of the series of decisions which would be necessary to do this, while that same client may in fact be able to give instructions for a Will if they have adequate understanding of their own circumstances, finances and the rights and claims of their friends and family members.

On the same basis, a particular client with a severe brain injury may well be able to make decisions with regard to their own bank account which may contain £300, but at the same time they may not be able to make decisions with regard to their personal injury award if it were as large as £300,000.

Therefore, the Court has the option of appointing a Deputy to make decisions for a person where that person will lack capacity to make some of their financial decisions.

The Court can also appoint a Deputy for welfare decisions, but it is envisaged that the authority given under such an Order would be defined at restrictively as possible and the Court is likely to prefer making "one off" decisions if appropriate in such circumstances.

3. Decisions made under the Act

The Act sets out principles that the Court will consider and will require Deputies and Attorneys to consider when dealing with the affairs of those who may be mentally incapable–

(a) There is to be a presumption of mental capacity unless it is proven otherwise.
(b) A person should have all practical steps taken to help them come to their decision without success before they are to be treated as incapable.
(c) There is not to be a presumption of the lack of mental capacity just because a person makes an "unwise" decision.
(d) Any acts done for a person lacking mental capacity should be done in their "best interests".
(e) Before taking an act for a person lacking mental capacity consideration should be given as to whether the desired act can be achieved in a less restrictive way.

Therefore, even in circumstances where a Deputy is appointed all steps should be taken to help the person come to their own decision before the Deputy steps in and makes a decision on their behalf.

In practice, this has made the duty of a Receiver/Deputy much more onerous. When a particular decision is required to be made the Deputy must first take "all practical steps" to help the person come to their own decision and it is only when that person is deemed to have been "unsuccessful" that the Receiver/Deputy can step in and make the decision on their behalf.

Furthermore, when a Deputy makes a decision on behalf of a person they need to consider the "best interests" criteria set out in the Act –

(a) The Deputy should consider as far as possible:

- (i) The person's past and present wishes and feelings (including any written statement made when he had capacity).
- (ii) The beliefs and values they would be likely to have if they had capacity.
- (iii) Factors they would consider "if able to do so".

(b) The Deputy should also consider consulting, if appropriate, the following people:

- (i) Anyone named by the person as someone to be consulted.
- (ii) Anyone caring for the person or interested in their welfare.
- (iii) Anyone appointed under a Power of Attorney.
- (iv) Any Deputy appointed by the Court.

While this gives a useful check-list for Deputies, and helps to define best practice, it also puts a wider obligation on the Deputy to research, carefully consider and consult before a decision is made on behalf of a person.

4. Approval of Damages Awards by the Court of Protection

Prior to October 2007 the Master of the Court of Protection would often provide email approval of a personal injury settlement, but this procedure is now to cease. The Civil Procedure (Amendment) Rules 2007 set out amendments to CPR Part 21 which provides that only a Master, designated Civil Judge or his nominee should normally hear applications for the approval of a settlement or compromise involving a "protected beneficiary" (a person who lacks capacity to manage or control any money recovered by them or on their behalf in the proceedings). Therefore, the approval of the Court of Protection is no longer required.

5. Appointment of a Deputy for Property and Financial Affairs

In cases where a substantial sum of damages is to be recovered for a person it may be necessary to ask the Court of Protection to appoint a Deputy if that person has suffered a severe head/brain injury or if they lack mental capacity owing to a pre-existing condition.

The appointment of a Deputy does not mean that a person is unable to make decisions for themselves, but rather that they may be unable to make some decisions with regard to their property and financial affairs. It will then be for that Deputy to try to enable that person to make their own decisions wherever possible and then "step in" to make a decision on behalf of the person in their best interests if they are unable to make their own decision.

The choice of who should be appointed as Deputy is one which should be given careful consideration. Traditionally this has been a role that has often been taken on by family members or friends, but the burden of the duties of a Deputy can be onerous and where a personal injury claim is being made consideration should be given to appointing a professional Deputy.

While many solicitors' firms will have the capability to deal with Deputy appointments, both assisting in making the application and taking on the role of Deputy, many firms will not have this facility available.

The Office of the Public Guardian does have a panel of professional Deputies who may be appointed if no-one else is available or suitable.

6. The Role of the Deputy

Being a Deputy can be an onerous responsibility and the requirements of the Act are likely to make this more of a burden in many circumstances. Guidance as to the duties of the Deputy, as well as concerning the implications of the Act, can be found in the Office of the Public Guardian documents "A Guide for Deputies appointed by the Court of Protection", being document COP43 and available on the Office of the Public Guardian website.

In summary, the work of a professional Deputy includes the following, amongst other things:

(a) Liaison with an application to the Court of Protection and the Office of the Public Guardian where necessary.
(b) Preparation of annual accounts/reports to the Office of the Public Guardian.
(c) Completion of tax returns and payment to the Inland Revenue as necessary.
(d) Dealing with requests for capital expenditure.
(e) Setting appropriate budgets and regular payments as appropriate.
(f) Considering and approving investment proposals.
(g) Overseeing and arranging the employment and retention of care workers, other employed staff and liaison as appropriate with the case manager.
(h) Overseeing and arranging payment of national insurance contributions and PAYE tax in respect of any employees' wages.
(i) Liaising with the person whose affairs are being dealt with and, wherever possible, taking all practical steps to enable them to make their own decisions.
(j) Liaising with the person's family, associates, care managers and other parties as appropriate (in accordance with the "best interest" criteria).
(k) Ensuring that the person receives the correct state benefits, council tax benefits and exemptions, housing benefit and local authority/public funding for care.
(l) Payment of bills, fees and regular expenses.

7. Charges for the Appointment of Deputies and Management of Professional Deputies

A solicitor who makes an application to the Court for the appointment of a Deputy, or indeed a one-off decision, may charge for his fees, and disbursements, and these costs should be claimed in the personal injury action.

Moreover, where a professional Deputy is appointed his annual costs of managing the person's property and financial affairs (or welfare decisions if appointed as a welfare Deputy) can be claimed and would be subject to the multiplier, depending upon the person's life expectancy.

The likely costs of a professional Deputy acting will vary from case to case, depending on the person's particular needs, requirements and disabilities. It is likely that the duties imposed by the Act will mean that more work is involved on an annual basis, as often straightforward decisions will now need to be considered with the person whose finances are being dealt with to see if they can come to their own decision before the Deputy makes the decision on their behalf. Furthermore, when a decision is made for a person who is deemed to be incapable, the duty to consider their views and consult with appropriate people means that more work will be required before a decision can be made.

When claiming costs consideration should be given to the time the Deputy will need to spend on an annual basis and whether it would be appropriate for some of that work to be undertaken by a more junior member of staff under the Deputy's supervision. Consideration should be given to the number of visits required in an average year, the time these will take, the travel time involved and the cost of mileage and any other expenses.

It is usual for a Deputy to visit the clients at least once a year at home, but it may be that such visits are necessary more frequently for some clients. It would be usual for more visits to be required in the early stages, particularly after settlement, owing to the number of decisions which will be required at that time.

It should also be borne in mind that a Deputy may need to make further applications from time to time to the Court. This may be the case if a Deputy needs to act beyond his general powers, for example if the person wishes to make a gift to a family member or if it is necessary to deal with Trusts of a property. In some such circumstances an additional Court application will need to be made and Court fees incurred.

8. Making a Will for a Person under the Court of Protection

Once a person turns 18 years of age they may make a Will and it will be necessary to consider whether they are able to make this particular decision for themselves.

In order to give instructions for a Will a person must be able to understand the following:

(a) The nature of the document to be executed.
(b) The extent of his property and estate.
(c) The nature of the claims of those he proposes to benefit or exclude from participation in the Will.

For a client who has suffered/brain injury it is good practice to obtain a written medical report from an appropriately qualified medical practitioner who has been properly instructed with regard to the full extent and nature of the person's state, family circumstances and the extent of their injuries. If it is confirmed that the person does have testamentary capacity then it is advised that his or her Will should be witnessed by that same medical practitioner who should keep a contemporaneous note in the medical records in case the Will is challenged after the person's death.

If a person is deemed to be unable to give his or her own instructions for a Will then the Court of Protection can be approached to put in place a Statutory Will on their behalf. This would require a new application and incur Court fees. The costs of a claim can be considerable, particularly because the Court will require thorough evidence with regard to the person's circumstances, finances, family tree and the reasons for the Will which is being proposed. Furthermore, the Court is likely to join as a party to the application any person who has an interest in the person's affairs or is adversely affected by the proposed Will. Where infants are adversely affected they would usually be represented by a Guardian Ad Litem. The person's interests will usually be separately represented by the Official Solicitor who can be appointed by the Court to act on his or her behalf.

The legal costs of all parties, as well as the application fee and hearing fee, are usually ordered to be paid from the person's estate unless the Court is presented with evidence or reasons why other parties should bear the legal costs.

9. Court Fees upon the Appointment of a Deputy

When a Deputy is appointed there is a one-off appointment fee payable to the Office of the Public Guardian of £125 for placing the Deputy's details on a register. In addition, the Office of the Public Guardian will set a Deputy Supervision fee (which incorporates the annual accounts fee of £105 which was payable previously). There are three types of annual supervision which attract the following fees:-

• Type I supervision (highest)	£800 per annum
• Type II supervision (lower)	£175 per annum
• Type III supervision (minimal)	no annual costs

It is difficult to estimate the level of fee payable following an application and this depends upon the Office of the Public Guardian's evaluation of the person's particular circumstances. The guidance given by the Office of the Public Guardian seems to indicate that in claims in excess of

£150,000 type I supervision will be allocated with the highest fee, but that this may be subject to review and reduction in later years.

10. Surety Bonds for Deputies

At the time of writing there is a degree of uncertainty with regard to the surety bonds being issued with new Deputyship Orders. In some cases the level of the bond has been set on the basis of the full amount of damages held, on the basis that the Deputy could in theory have full access to the funds.

This has resulted in incredibly large premiums of several thousands of pounds per annum for the surety bond. At the time of writing a number of separate appeals have been made against the setting of bonds in such circumstances and it is hoped that a universal and satisfactory position can be found across all cases.

11. Court of Protection Fees

Attached is a schedule of the Court of Protection fees which should be checked from time to time on the Office of the Public Guardian website.

12. Exemption and Fee Remissions

Attached is the Exemptions and Remissions advice from the Office of the Public Guardian website. Again, this should be checked from time to time on the website.

13. Solicitors' Fixed Costs

Attached is a copy of Practice Direction B concerning fixed costs in the Court of Protection.

Practitioners should be warned that these fixed costs may be easily exceeded in certain circumstances and careful consideration should be given before they are relied upon.

J3: Court of Protection Fees and Exemptions

Application fee	Payable on making an application to start Court proceedings, or on making an application for permission to start proceedings.		£400
Appeal fee	Payable on filing an appellant's notice appealing a Court decision or seeking permission to appeal a Court decision.		£400
Hearing fee	Payable where the Court has held a hearing to decide the application and has made the final order, declaration or decision.		£500
Copy of document fee	For additional copies of an order.		£5
Copy of certified document fee			£25
Enduring Power of Attorney (EPA) registration fee			£120
Lasting Power of Attorney (LPA) registration fee	A separate registration fee is payable for Property and Affairs LPAs and Personal Welfare LPAs when each application for registration is made.		£120
Appointment of Deputy fee	A one-off payment for placing the Deputy's details on a register and carrying out a risk assessment to determine the appropriate Deputy supervision regime.		£100
Application to search the registers fee	Covers a search of the three OPG registers. The register of registered LPAs, registered EPAs and the register of Court orders appointing Deputies.		£25
Deputy supervision fees	There are three types of supervision; each attracts a different annual fee, payable annually in arrears on 31 March. Each case will be reviewed regularly and the type of supervision allocated may change as circumstances change.	Type I (highest)	£800 p.a.
		Type IIA (intermediate)	£350 p.a.
		Type II (lower)	£175 p.a.
		Type III (minimal)	£0 p.a.

Notes

Applications and hearings relating to objections to the registration of EPAs and LPAs will not incur a fee, nor will some appeals. Please contact the Court of Protection for advice in particular cases.

Supervision fees will be calculated on a pro-rata basis if:

- there has been more than one type of supervision applied in a one-year period;
- or supervision has been in place for less than one year.

Details of pro-rata calculations will be shown on the annual invoice that the deputy receives.

Exemptions and remission

Patients are eligible for a fee ***exemption*** if they receive any of the following means-tested benefits and have not been awarded damages of more than £16,000, which were disregarded when determining their eligibility for the benefit:

- Income Support;
- Income-based Job-Seeker's Allowance;
- State Pension Guarantee Credit;
- A combination of Working Tax Credit and either Child Tax Credit, Disability Element or Severe Disability Element;
- Housing Benefit;
- or Council Tax Benefit.

A patient who does not qualify for a fee exemption may be eligible for a fee remission if his gross annual income is:

Income	Remission
up to £12,000	100%
£12,001 to £13,500	75% remission
£13,501 to £15,000	50% remission
£15,501 to £16,500	25% remission
> £16,501	No remission

To apply for a fee exemption or remission the patient should complete form OPG506A.

Fees can be found at: *http://www.publicguardian.gov.uk/about/CoP-fees.htm*

J4: Court of Protection and Deputy/Receiver's Fees

Sample calculation of fees for Schedules where there is a private receiver (i.e. not the Public Guardianship Office). It is assumed that the Claimant will live another 25 years.

(Please note that these calculations do not show all possibilities. Fees differ where the Court itself appoints an administrator.)

1.	Court of Protection Fees			
	a.	Past		
		i.	Commencement fee	£250
		ii.	Fee on appointment of receiver	£330
		iii.	Annual administration fee [2 × £250]	£500
		iv.	Account fee [2 × £200]	£400
		v.	Statutory will	£560
		vi.	Transaction fees, say [5 × £100]	£500
		vii.	Disbursements (doctors, process server, etc), say	£1,000
	b.	Future		
		i.	Annual administration fee [18.65 × £250]	£4,663
		ii.	Account fee [18.65 × £200]	£3,730
		iii.	Transaction fees, say [18.65 × average £150 pa]	£2,798
		iv.	Review of statutory will[1] (0.8203 × £560) + (0.6103 × £560)	£801
		v.	Appointment of new receiver[2] [3.51 × £300]	£1,053
		vi.	Winding-up fee on death of patient[3] [0.5394 × £300]	£162
2.	Professional receivership fees and costs			
	a.	Past		
		i.	First two years (see accounts)[4]	£10,000
		ii.	Security bond premium[5] [2 × £250]	£500
	b.	Future		
		i.	Annual fees [18.65 × £4,000]	£76,400
		ii.	Security bond premium [18.65 × £250]	£4,663
			Total	£108,410

[1] Once every ten years, discounted using Ogden Table 27.
[2] Assume a new Receiver is appointed every five years, with first replacement in five years' time, and use Table A5 in this book.
[3] Discount using Ogden Table 27.
[4] These costs will typically be higher in the first 18–24 months.
[5] The level of security is fixed when the application is considered. It will be at a level sufficient to cover the annual amount of the patient's funds that the receiver might be expected to handle, with an element of contingency. This figure will be the equivalent either to the patient's annual income or annual expenditure, whichever is the greater, plus a margin of approximately 50 per cent. The minimum figure will be £5,000, increasing in steps of £2,500.

Group K

Carer Rates and Rehabilitation

K1: Carer rates

Introductory notes

1. Assumptions and background

The following Tables are intended to help value claims for care, where that care has been provided gratuitously. They will not be appropriate in cases where the amount of care provided has been very substantial: in such cases it will usually be appropriate to instruct a nursing expert. The majority of such claims, however, concern relatively modest amounts of care, both past and future. The figures in the Tables represent the care rates for both London and elsewhere: only two rates are given, because outside London there is relatively little regional variation.

2. Where do the figures come from?

The British Nursing Association's rates are no longer relevant, for they have sold part of their businesses. There are a range of other rates both for qualified nurses and other carers. The rates are usually the Whitley scale rates which are used by the NHS and local authorities; the lowest, in some areas, are the "Crossroads: Caring for Carers" rates, based on another body which produces the "National Joint Council Rates". Other scales are provided by private nursing homes and other nursing and care agencies, which vary according to location.

It is not necessarily appropriate to ask a local Carers' Agency for a quotation, because their figures are likely to include charges that should not form part of a claim for gratuitous care, such as agency fees. Agencies may be reluctant to say how much of their total hourly charge is represented by the carer's salary.

3. Nature and extent of care

The range of care can be extensive:

a. Short Visit;
b. Care by the Hour;
c. Night Sleeper;
d. Night Sitter;
e. Residential Live-In.

All of the above can be carried out by a Home Care Assistant, Qualified Nurse and NNEB (Nursery Nurse).

4. What is being costed in these tables?

These tables cover the whole range of care, from occasional help with the housework or shopping, through assistance with personal hygiene (baths, showers, washing hair) to more conventional nursing activities such as changing dressings, administering drugs, or pushing wheelchairs.

5. The nature of Gratuitous Care

a. The test is whether the carer has provided services which the Claimant would not have needed but for the accident. In *Giambrone v Sunworld Holidays Ltd* [2004] EWCA Civ 158; [2004] P.I.Q.R. Q4 at Q36, the Court of Appeal upheld an award by Judge MacDuff Q.C., sitting as a High Court Judge, in which he held that awards for gratuitous care are not limited to "very serious cases" or cases in which the care provided is "well beyond the ordinary call of duty".
b. *Evans v Pontypridd Roofing* [2001] EWCA Civ 1657; [2002] P.I.Q.R. Q5, is the first time that the question of gratuitous care has been carefully examined since the classic decision of *Housecroft v Burnett* [1986] 1 All E. R. 322 (CA). It expressly declines to lay down any general

rules or guidance, but by the comments made, it does in fact do so. May L.J., in a careful judgment, explains the jurisprudential basis for such awards and then echoes the statement in *Hunt v Severs* [1994] 2 A.C. 350 at 363A, where Lord Bridge stated that what has to be quantified is the amount "to enable the voluntary carer to receive proper recompense for his and her services".

c. This is similar to O'Connor L.J.'s dictum in *Housecroft v Burnett* (ibid) in which he referred to "a capital sum . . . sufficient . . . to make recompense to the relative". He then says that: "On this basis, it seems to me that the guidance given as to quantification in *Housecroft v Burnett* remains helpful" (para.24).
d. May L.J. in *Evans v Pontypridd Roofing* (ibid) went on to say that: "In my judgment, this court should avoid putting first instance judges into too restrictive a straight-jacket, such as might happen if it was said that the means of assessing a proper recompense for services provided gratuitously by a family carer had to be assessed in a particular way or ways. Circumstances vary enormously and what is appropriate and just in one case may not be so in another . . . .".
e. He states that the first task is to determine the extent of the services and then decide the discount from the commercial rate, to take account of the fact that the gratuitous carer will not be paying tax or national insurance on the award. The trial judge had deducted 25%, and the Defendant was arguing that a standard discount should be set at 33%. May L.J. concluded that "there is no scientific basis for a strictly mathematical answer to this question. The assessment has to be a broad one, and what in the end is required is a single broad assessment to achieve a fair result in the particular case." He then says that: "But I do not consider that one possible element of a single broad assessment should be required to be a conventional figure. On the contrary it seems to me that first instance judges should have latitude to achieve a fair result." (para.37).
f. The Court of Appeal in Evans also made it clear that it was not appropriate to award damages for care for hospital visits, unless the visitors had actually provided nursing care during those visits.

6. This has been followed by another division of the Court of Appeal in *Newman v Folkes* [2001] EWCA Civ 591 (May 3, 2002) in which Ward, Sedley L.JJ., and Sumner J. followed the decision of May L.J. in *Evans v Pontypridd Roofing*. Their conclusions were:

a. Damages can be awarded to compensate a relative for nursing care, even if the carer has not lost wages of his/her own, but such an award will only be justified where that care has been well beyond the call of duty: *Mills v British Rail Engineering Ltd* [1992] P.I.Q.R. Q130, (CA); Brook L.J. in *Giambrone v Sunworld Holidays Ltd* expressly stated that he rejected the contention that *Mills* presents any binding authority for the proposition that such awards are reserved for "very serious cases".
b. The extra care and its extent should be such as results from the disability and which, but for that disability, would not be provided by the parents: *McDaid v Howletts & Port Lympne Estates Ltd* (May 17, 1996, QBD, Collins J., unreported).
c. To value such care has resulted in a normal practice of awarding gratuitous family care at about 75 per cent of the commercial rate: *Lamey v Wirral Health Authority* (September 22, 1993, Morland J., unreported, *Kemp & Kemp* A4–120).
d. The market rate is merely a guide and provides a ceiling. The Court may consider it unnecessary to discount that commercial rate.

7. Calculating the rates

The rates have been considered twice in the last year. In *A v B Hospitals Trust* [2006] EWHC 1178 (May 26, 2006), Lloyd Jones J. said "On balance, I favour the Claimant's approach because it is more likely to reflect the actual costs." He calculated a composite hourly rate spread out over the whole year. That approach was as follows:

a. Care costs to be calculated by reference to a 58-week year (so that the additional on-costs are included such as sickness, holidays); 58 weeks was chosen rather than the contended for period of 59 weeks, was regarded as sufficient to reflect holidays, sickness and staff training. This was a factual decision by the trial judge.

b. National insurance is added to the sums claimed.
c. Additional pay was added for bank holidays.
d. Payroll costs, including insurance, advertising and the cost of training carers was added.

In *Iqbal v Whipps Cross University Hospital NHS Trust* [2006] EWHC 3111(QB) (December 8, 2006), Sir Rodger Bell approved this decision of Lloyd Jones J. and awarded a composite hourly rate.

The rates that appear in the Tables below are therefore composite rates, calculated in accordance with the dicta in *A v B* and *Iqbal*. They avoid the need to calculate different rates for care provided during weekdays, at night, at weekends and on bank holidays, because they take into account that care may well be provided at all these times, though since they are weighted they take account of the fact that more care is provided during working weekdays and relatively little during e.g. bank holiday night-times.

8. Case management has been defined as:

"A collaborative process which assesses, plans, implements, co-ordinates, monitors and evaluates the options and services required to meet an individual's health, care, educational and employment needs, using communication and available resources to promote quality cost effective outcomes."

9. Case management is only necessary in the more serious cases. The claimant will need medical evidence to justify the employment of a case manager. A fully qualified case manager will plan the care, organise, hire and pay staff, supervise, organise or provide training and act as the first point of contact in a complex case. The case manager may also coordinate the purchase and replacement of aids and appliances, arrange the claimant's therapies, and pay the bills.

10. There are two Associations of Case Managers:

a. BABICM, which devised the case management concept from experience in management of brain injured patients. Its website can be found at *www.babicm.org.*
b. The Case Management Society UK (CMSUK) – *www.cmsuk.org.*

11. The cost of case management

Rates vary, but expect to pay up to £90 per hour plus travelling time. The number of hours varies from patient to patient. A new patient often requires a great deal of intensive work, and the first year of case management is usually more expensive than subsequent years: once a routine is established, the number of hours reduces. However, flexibility is paramount and staff training and other problems (e.g. recruitment, the organisation of holidays for carers, sourcing new carers, etc.) can be time expensive and complex.

12. The Case Manager in law

The Court of Appeal considered the role of the Case Manager in *Wright v Sullivan* [2006] 1 W.L.R. 172:

"It seems inevitable to me that the clinical case manager should owe her duties to her patient alone" (para.26).

"The role of a clinical case manager, if she is called to give evidence at the trial, will clearly be one of a witness of fact, as the BABICM guidelines suggest. She is there to give evidence of what she did and why she decided to do it" (para.33).

13. Other matters in respect of Care

There are other matters in respect of care, that need to be considered, in some cases, such as The Manual Handling Operations Regulations 1992 and The Care Standards Act 2000, which govern the activities of carers.

14. Carer rates

The table that follows gives rates that can be used to value care, when that care has been provided gratuitously.

In earlier editions of this book, we provided figures for three different levels: qualified nurses, carers, and home helps and companions. It was thought inappropriate to include the rate for qualified nurses, because that rate by definition will not usually apply where friends and family have provided the care — rather, it will apply to those cases in which the Claimant has needed and received the skilled services of a fully qualified nurse.

In most cases, the help that the Claimant has received will be a mixture of the services provided by carers, and by home helps and companions. The rates that follow are aggregate rates for those two levels.

The rate is also an aggregate for England and Wales. Rates in London will be slightly higher, and those outside London will be slightly lower. Outside London, there is not likely to be more than a few pence difference between the rates applying in different parts of the country. It was thought more appropriate and convenient to provide a unified rate, applicable for most gratuitous care throughout the country. Although there will be areas where recruitment will be particularly difficult, and it will be necessary to pay higher rates, this need not be reflected in the rates used where family and friends have rallied round, though it might well be where it has been necessary to pay an agency or a professional nurse the commercial rate.

Since September 1, 1990 the aggregate rate has been obtained by calculating the total cost of caring for a patient, 24 hours a day and seven days a week:

- There are 168 hours in a week, made up of:
  - 55 hours at the basic rate
  - 65 hours at the evening rate
  - 24 hours at the Saturday rate
  - 24 hours at the Sunday rate
- These multipliers are applied to the appropriate hourly rates, the products are added up, and the total is divided by 168.

The rates are, of course, to be reduced by the appropriate discount to reflect the fact that the carers will not have to pay tax or national insurance on the damages. There is a long line of authorities covering the topic, from *Housecroft v Burnett* [1986] 1 All E.R. 322 (CA) to *Evans v Pontypridd Roofing Ltd* [2001] EWCA Civ 1657. In the latter case the Defendant asked the Court of Appeal to set a definitive rate of discount. The Court expressly declined to do this, but gave a clear indication that it considered 25% to be the standard discount. (See paragraph 5e above.)

The figures are obtained from National Joint Council pay rates for local authorities, Spinal Point 8.

Year	Time of day	Hourly rate £	Hours pw	Cost pw £	Divided by hours pw	Aggregate rate
Nov 1976 to Oct 1977	Basic Time + ¼ Time + ½	£1.02 £1.28 £1.53	—	—	—	£1.23
Nov 1977 to Oct 1978	Basic Time + ¼ Time + ½	£1.12 £1.40 £1.68	—	—	—	£1.36
Nov 1978 to Jul 1979	Basic Time + ¼ Time + ½	£1.21 £1.51 £1.82	—	—	—	£1.47
Aug to Oct 1979	Basic Time + ¼ Time + ½	£1.29 £1.61 £1.94	—	—	—	£1.57
Nov 1979 to Mar 1980	Basic Time + ¼ Time + ½	£1.46 £1.83 £2.19	—	—	—	£1.78
Apr 1980 to Oct 1980	Basic Time + ¼ Time + ½	£1.54 £1.93 £2.31	—	—	—	£1.87
Nov to Dec 1980	Basic Time + ¼ Time + ½	£1.66 £2.08 £2.49	—	—	—	£2.02
Jan to Oct 1981	Basic Time + ¼ Time + ½	£1.88 £2.35 £2.02	—	—	—	£2.29
Nov 1981 to Oct 1982	Basic Time + ¼ Time + ½	£2.00 £2.50 £3.00	—	—	—	£2.43
Nov 1982 to Oct 1983	Basic Time + ¼ Time + ½	£2.10 £2.63 £3.15	—	—	—	£2.56
Nov 1983 to Oct 1984	Basic Time + ¼ Time + ½	£2.19 £2.74 £3.29	—	—	—	£2.67
Nov 1984 to Aug 1985	Basic Time + ¼ Time + ½	£2.29 £2.86 £3.44	—	—	—	£2.79
Sep 1985 to Aug 1986	Basic Time + ¼ Time + ½	£2.44 £3.05 £3.66	—	—	—	£2.97
Sep 1986 to Jun 1987	Basic Time + ¼ Time + ½	£2.60 £3.25 £3.90	—	—	—	£3.16
Jul 1987 to Aug 1988	Basic Time + ¼ Time + ½	£2.90 £3.63 £4.35	—	—	—	£3.53
Sep 1988 to Aug 1989	Basic Time + ¼ Time + ½	£3.07 £3.84 £4.61	—	—	—	£3.74
Sep 1989 to Aug 1990	Basic Time + ¼ Time + ½	£3.34 £4.18 £5.01	—	—	—	£4.07
Sep 1990 to Jun 1981	Basic Evening Weekend	£3.66 £4.58 £5.50	55 65 48	£201.30 + £297.70 + £266.00 = £763.00	168	£4.54
Jul 1991 to Jun 1992	Basic Evening Weekend	£3.89 £4.87 £5.84	55 65 48	£213.95 + £316.55 + £280.32 = £810.82	168	£4.83

Year	Time of day	Hourly rate £	Hours pw	Cost pw £	Divided by hours pw	Aggregate rate
Jul 1992 to Jun 1993	Basic Evening Weekend	£4.04 £5.05 £6.06	55 65 48	£222.20 + £328.25 + £290.88 = £841.33	168	£5.01
Jul 1993 to Aug 1994	Basic Evening Weekend	£4.21 £5.26 £6.32	55 65 48	£231.55 + £341.90 + £303.36 = £876.81	168	£5.22
Sep 1994 to May 1995	Basic Evening Saturday Sunday	£4.44 £5.55 £6.66 £8.88	55 65 24 24	£244.20 + £360.75 + £159.84 + £213.12 = £977.91	168	£5.82
Jun 1995 to Mar 1996	Basic Evening Saturday Sunday	£4.56 £5.70 £6.84 £9.12	55 65 24 24	£250.80 + £370.50 + £164.16 + £218.88 = £1,004.34	168	£5.98
Apr 1996 to Mar 1997	Basic Evening Saturday Sunday	£4.69 £5.86 £7.03 £9.38	55 65 24 24	£257.95 + £380.90 + £168.72 + £225.12 = £1,032.69	168	£6.15
Apr 1997 to Mar 1998	Basic Evening Saturday Sunday	£4.84 £6.05 £7.26 £9.68	55 65 24 24	£266.20 + £393.25 + £174.24 + £232.32 = £1,066.01	168	£6.35
Apr 1998 to Mar 1999	Basic Evening Saturday Sunday	£4.98 £6.22 £7.47 £9.96	55 65 24 24	£273.90 + £404.30 + £179.28 + £239.04 = £1,096.52	168	£6.53
Apr 1999 to Mar 2000	Basic Evening Saturday Sunday	£5.13 £6.41 £7.69 £10.26	55 65 24 24	£282.15 + £416.65 + £184.56 + £246.24 = £1,129.60	168	£6.72
Apr 2000 to Mar 2001	Basic Evening Saturday Sunday	£5.29 £6.61 £7.93 £10.58	55 65 24 24	£290.95 + £429.65 + £190.32 + £253.92 = £1,164.84	168	£6.93
Apr 2001 to Mar 2002	Basic Evening Saturday Sunday	£5.49 £6.86 £8.23 £10.97	55 65 24 24	£301.95 + £455.90 + £197.52 + £263.28 = £1,208.61	168	£7.19
Apr 2002 to Sep 2002	Basic Evening Saturday Sunday	£5.65 £7.06 £8.47 £11.30	55 65 24 24	£310.75 + £458.90 + £203.28 + £271.20 = £1,244.13	168	£7.41
Oct 2002 to Mar 2003	Basic Evening Saturday Sunday	£5.71 £7.14 £8.56 £11.42	55 65 24 24	£314.05 + £464.10 + £205.44 + £274.08 = £1,257.67	168	£7.49
Apr 2003 to Mar 2004	Basic Evening Saturday Sunday	£5.90 £7.37 £8.85 £11.80	55 65 24 24	£324.50 + £479.05 + £212.40 + £283.20 = £1,299.15	168	£7.73

Year	Time of day	Hourly rate £	Hours pw	Cost pw £	Divided by hours pw	Aggregate rate
Apr 2004 to Mar 2005	Basic Evening Saturday Sunday	£6.06 £7.57 £9.09 £12.12	55 65 24 24	£333.30 + £492.05 + £218.16 + £290.88 = £1,334.39	168	£7.94
Apr 2005 to Mar 2006	Basic Evening Saturday Sunday	£6.24 £7.80 £9.36 £12.48	55 65 24 24	£343.20 + £507.00 + £224.64 + £299.52 = £1,374.36	168	£8.18
Apr 2006 to Mar 2007	Basic Evening Saturday Sunday	£6.43 £8.04 £9.65 £12.86	55 65 24 24	£353.65 + £522.60 + £231.60 + £308.64 = £1,416.49	168	£8.43
Apr 2007 to Mar 2008*	Basic Evening Saturday Sunday	£6.62 £8.28 £9.93 £13.86	55 65 24 24	£364.10 + £538.20 + £238.32 + £317.76 = £1,458.38	168	£8.68
Apr 2008 to Mar 2009*	Basic Evening Saturday Sunday	£6.75 £8.44 £10.13 £13.50	55 65 24 24	£371.25 + £548.60 + £243.12 + £324.00 = £1,486.97	168	£8.85

* These figures are approximate as there is a lack of evidence to support them.

K2: Nannies, cleaners and school fees

The death or incapacity of a spouse frequently involves incurring the costs of a nanny or a housekeeper or of sending a child to boarding school so that the surviving parent can continue working. Also, with some employments, typically when they involve overseas postings or frequent moves, school fees are part of the remuneration and will be lost if the employee dies or is disabled from that particular employment.

Nannies

The following table is for weekly wages for nannies in 2009.

	Daily		Live-in	
	Weekly net	**Annual gross**	**Weekly net**	**Annual gross**
Central London	£ 449	£ 31,000	£ 347	£ 23,525
Outer London / Home Counties	£ 374	£ 25,559	£ 304	£ 20,277
Other cities / towns	£ 340	£ 22,988	£ 282	£ 18,618
Rural areas	£ 334	£ 22,544	£ 280	£ 18,466

The figures are derived from a survey by *Nannytax*. The total cost to the client will be more than the gross wage as it is necessary to pay for holidays, sickness, employer's national insurance contribution, agency fees and so on. (See the discussion of *A v B Hospitals Trust* [2006] EWHC 1178 at note 7 to Table K1: Carer rates.)

Cleaners

The services of cleaners in London are currently (April 2009) advertised at the following rates. These are commonly for 3 or more hours a week: one-off visits usually cost more.

Anyclean standard	£ 10.35 per hour	(£9.00 plus VAT)
Anyclean premium	£ 13.80 per hour	(£12.00 plus VAT)
MK Londyn	£ 9.78 per hour	(£8.50 plus VAT)
Amycleaners:	£ 9.24 per hour	(Average; the cleaner is paid separately avoiding VAT; there is also an agency fee.)

School fees

Annual school fees for a three-term year in 2008/09 are as follows.

	Public school
Boarders (Upper school)	£27,516
Day pupils (Upper school)	£19,056
Day pupils (Under school or preparatory school)	£13,236

Independent Schools Council (average)	
Boarder	£ 22,059
Day pupil (boarding school)	£ 12,330
Day pupil (day school)	£ 9,069

Notes:
1. Fees for pupils entering in the sixth form may be higher.
2. Fees for weekly as opposed to full-time boarders may be lower.

The information has been obtained from the websites of Nannytax, Anyclean, MK Londyn, Amycleaners, Westminster School, and the Independent Schools Council.

K3: DIY, gardening and housekeeping

1. Claimants are entitled to damages for the loss of the ability to do these tasks. Anyone who is responsible for the running of a house knows that there is a real cost in bringing in an electrician, tiler, carpenter, joiner, plumber or other skilled tradesmen to carry out tasks that they themselves cannot do. "The loss of ability to do work in the home is a recoverable head of damages and includes 'services' such as general housekeeping, gardening and maintenance".[1]

2. The same principle applies to loss of housekeeping skills. Claimants can be compensated for their inability to carry out the tasks which occur in most households—e.g. cleaning, shopping, laundry, ironing, cooking and washing up. Even sewing on buttons, cleaning the windows, and performing the mundane routines of daily existence, such as putting out the bins and dealing with the milkman, all have to be carried out by someone, though it is too easy to forget them.

3. The loss can be valued commercially, In *Phipps v Brooks Dry Cleaning Services*[2] Stuart-Smith L.J. says that such skills have "a real money value", and Brandon J. in *Daly v General Steam Navigation Co Ltd*[3] says "The loss occurred and the cost of employing someone else is no more than a way of measuring it".

4. The difficulty is always in finding an appropriate rate and working out a number of hours every week which such housekeeping tasks take to perform. Whether as a "jury award" or by using a multiplier/multiplicand approach, a judge is perfectly able to assess the evidence and make an award which reflects the reality of the loss to the claimant or the dependants. The courts have made a wide range of awards, which are analysed in Kemp & Kemp,Vol.1, Ch.17. In *Lawrence v Osborn,*[4] the defendant insurers accepted an annual rate of £750 pa as the standard figure for inability to perform DIY functions. In *Wells v Wells,*[5] the Court of Appeal accepted an award under this head of £1,000 pa. In *Dixon v Wene,*[6] Gross J. awarded £15,000 (a global sum), for loss of services: gardening and DIY.

5. Plainly, evidence is needed to support such a claim, photographs being an excellent addition to witness statement evidence. A report from a local surveyor and/or an independent agency can also strengthen this claim.

6. It should be borne in mind that often, as people get older, their appetite and energy for such tasks diminishes. This is not true for all, however; some 70 and 80 year olds seem to have an undiminished enthusiasm for these activities.

7. A Claimant need not prove an actual intention to employ replacement services (paid or unpaid). It is worth remembering the words of Bridge L.J. in *Daly v General Steam Navigation Co*:[7] "It has been energetically argued by Mr Bennett, for the defendants, that before future loss of capacity to undertake housekeeping duties can properly be assessed at the estimated cost of employing some third person to come in and do that which the plaintiff is unable to do for herself, the plaintiff has to satisfy the court that she has a firm intention in any event that such a person shall be employed. For my part, I am quite unable to see why that should be so. Once the judge had concluded, as this judge did, that, to put the plaintiff, so far as money could do so, in the position in which she would have been if she had never been injured, she was going to need, in the future, domestic

[1] Damages for Personal Injury: Medical, Nursing and Other Expenses; Law Commission, Law Com No 262 (1999), para 2.34.
[2] [1996] P.I.Q.R. Q 100.
[3] [1979] 1 Lloyds Rep. 257.
[4] (November 7, 1997), Anthony May J., QBD (unreported).
[5] [1997] 1 W.L.R. 652.
[6] [2004] EWHC 2273 (QB).
[7] [1981] W.L.R. 120, 127.

assistance for eight hours a week, it seems to me that it was entirely reasonable and entirely in accordance with principle in assessing damages, to say that the estimated cost of employing labour for that time, for an appropriate number of years having regard to the plaintiff's expectation of life, was the proper measure of her damages under this heading. It is really quite immaterial, in my judgment, whether having received those damages, the plaintiff chooses to alleviate her own housekeeping burden, which is an excessively heavy one, having regard to her considerable disability to undertake housekeeping tasks, by employing the labour which has been taken as the basis of the estimate on which damages have been awarded, or whether she chooses to continue to struggle with the housekeeping on her own and to spend the damages which have been awarded to her on other luxuries which she would otherwise be unable to afford".

Handyman Charges

	Hourly range	Daily range
London	£25 to £50	£180 to £240
Outside London	£15 to £35	£100 to £180

Gardening Charges

	Hourly range	Daily range
London	£20 to £30	n/a
Outside London	£15 to £20	n/a

Charges will vary depending on the complexity of the work undertaken.
Charges often increase for the first hour of work undertaken and/or at weekends.
Companies that cater exclusively to seniors or those on low income and consequently charge a much reduced rate have not been included in these ranges.
Handyman charges are exclusive of plumbing or electrical charges which are invariably set at a higher rate.

K4: Spire Healthcare hospital self-pay (uninsured) charges

The following figures are inclusive of hospital charges and surgeons' anaesthetists' fees. The charges are approximate, as certain factors affecting cost, such as length of stay or prosthesis used, vary from patient to patient.

Treatment	**Cost**
Arthrodesis	from £4,800
Knee arthroscopy	£2,250–£2,870
Hernia treatment	£1,750–£3,010
Investigation — CT — single system	from £650
Investigation — MRI — single investigation	from £550
Investigation — X-ray	from £100–£185
Replacement — hip	£7,500–£11,000
Replacement — knee	£9,660–£11,000
Scar revision	£450–£2,500
Spine — discectomy — lumbar (including fusion)	from £6,200
Therapy — physiotherapy (hourly rate)	from £120
Outpatient consultation (consultant charge)	£130–£200

These rates are approximate only, because the amounts allowable by private healthcare insurers can vary from hospital to hospital and from policy to policy. Further, doctors' own charges may vary.

K5: NHS charges

NHS prescriptions (from April 1, 2009)

Charge per prescribed item		£7.20
Prescription prepayment certificate:	3 months	£28.25
	12 months	£104.00

For items dispensed in combination (duo) packs, there is a charge for each different drug in the pack.

Sight tests (from April 1, 2009)

NHS sight test	free
NHS sight test at home	free
Private sight test	see your optician
Private sight test at home	see your optician
Hospital Eye Department sight test	free

NHS dental treatment (from April 1, 2009)

If a patient is not exempt from charges, he should pay one of the following rates for each course of treatment he receives:

Course of treatment	Cost	Scope
Band 1	£16.50	This covers an examination, diagnosis (e.g. X-rays) , advice on how to prevent future problems, and a scale and polish if needed and application of fluoride varnish or fissure sealants. If you require urgent care, even if your urgent treatment needs more than one appointment to complete, you will only need to pay one Band 1 charge.
Band 2	£46.60	This covers everything listed in Band 1, plus any further treatment such as fillings, root canal work or extractions.
Band 3	£198.00	This covers everything listed in Bands 1 and 2 above, plus crowns, dentures or bridges.

Notes

1. These are the only charges for NHS dental treatment.
2. A patient only has to pay one charge for each course of treatment, even if it takes more than one visit to the dentist to finish it.
3. If the patient needs more treatment within the same or lower charge band (e.g. an additional filling), within two months of completing a course of treatment, there is no extra charge.
4. There is no charge for repairing dentures or for having stitches removed.
5. Children under 18, and many adults, do not have to pay NHS charges. (See form HC11, "Help with Health Costs", which can be found on the Department of Health website *www.dh.gov.uk*.)

NHS wigs and fabric supports (from April 1, 2008)

Stock modacrylic wig	£59.20
Partial wig — human hair	£156.60
Full bespoke wig — human hair	£229.05
Abdominal support	£36.30
Spinal support	£36.30
Surgical brassière	£24.00
Support stockings	£7.10 (each)
Support tights available from hospitals only	£14.20 (per pair)

K6: The 2007 Rehabilitation Code

(Code of Best Practice on Rehabilitation, Early Intervention and Medical Treatment in Personal Injury Claims)

The aim of this code is to promote the use of rehabilitation and early intervention in the compensation process so that the injured person makes the best and quickest possible medical, social and psychological recovery. This objective applies whatever the severity of the injuries sustained by the claimant. The Code is designed to ensure that the claimant's need for rehabilitation is assessed and addressed as a priority, and that the process of so doing is pursued on a collaborative basis by the claimant's lawyer and the compensator.

Therefore, in every case, where rehabilitation is likely to be of benefit, the earliest possible notification to the compensator of the claim and of the need for rehabilitation will be expected.

1. INTRODUCTION

1.1 The purpose of the personal injury claims process is to put the individual back into the same position as he or she would have been in had the accident not occurred, insofar as money can achieve that objective. The purpose of the rehabilitation code is to provide a framework within which the claimant's health, quality of life and ability to work are restored as far as possible before, or simultaneously with, the process of assessing compensation.

1.2 Although the Code is recognised by the Personal Injury Pre-Action Protocol, its provisions are not mandatory. It is recognised that the aims of the Code can be achieved without strict adherence to the terms of the Code, and therefore it is open to the parties to agree an alternative framework to achieve the early rehabilitation of the claimant.

1.3 However, the Code provides a useful framework within which claimant's lawyers and the compensator can work together to ensure that the needs of injured claimants are assessed at an early stage.

1.4 In any case where agreement on liability is not reached it is open to the parties to agree that the Code will in any event operate, and the question of delay pending resolution of liability should be balanced with the interests of the injured party. However, unless so agreed, the Code does not apply in the absence of liability or prior to agreement on liability being reached.

1.5 In this code the expression "the compensator" shall include any loss adjuster, solicitor or other person acting on behalf of the compensator.

2. THE CLAIMANT'S SOLICITOR

2.1 It should be the duty of every claimant's solicitor to consider, from the earliest practicable stage, and in consultation with the claimant, the claimant's family, and where appropriate the claimant's treating physician(s), whether it is likely or possible that early intervention, rehabilitation or medical treatment would improve their present and/or long term physical and mental well being. This duty is ongoing throughout the life of the case but is of most importance in the early stages.

2.2 The claimant's solicitors will in any event be aware of their responsibilities under section 4 of the Pre-Action Protocol for Personal Injury Claims.

2.3 It shall be the duty of a claimant's solicitor to consider, with the claimant and/or the claimant's family, whether there is an immediate need for aids, adaptations, adjustments to employment to enable the claimant to keep his/her existing job, obtain suitable alternative employment with the same employer or retrain for new employment, or other matters that would seek to alleviate problems caused by disability, and then to communicate with the compensators as soon as practicable about any such rehabilitation needs, with a view to putting this Code into effect.

2.4 It shall not be the responsibility of the solicitor to decide on the need for treatment or rehabilitation or to arrange such matters without appropriate medical or professional advice.

2.5 It is the intention of this Code that the claimant's solicitor will work with the compensator to address these rehabilitation needs and that the assessment and delivery of rehabilitation needs shall be a collaborative process.

2.6 It must be recognised that the compensator will need to receive from the claimants' solicitors sufficient information for the compensator to make a proper decision about the need for intervention, rehabilitation or treatment. To this extent the claimant's solicitor must comply with the requirements of the Pre-Action Protocol to provide the compensator with full and adequate details of the injuries sustained by the claimant, the nature and extent of any or any likely continuing disability and any suggestions that may have already have been made concerning the rehabilitation and/or early intervention.

2.7 There is no requirement under the Pre-Action Protocol, or under this code, for the claimant's solicitor to have obtained a full medical report. It is recognised that many cases will be identified for consideration under this code before medical evidence has actually been commissioned or obtained.

3. **THE COMPENSATOR**

3.1 It shall be the duty of the compensator, from the earliest practicable stage in any appropriate case, to consider whether it is likely that the claimant will benefit in the immediate, medium or longer term from further medical treatment, rehabilitation or early intervention. This duty is ongoing throughout the life of the case but is most important in the early stages.

3.2 If the compensator considers that a particular claim might be suitable for intervention, rehabilitation or treatment, the compensator will communicate this to the claimant's solicitor as soon as practicable.

3.3 On receipt of such communication, the claimant's solicitor will immediately discuss these issues with the claimant and/or the claimant's family pursuant to his duty set out above.

3.4 Where a request to consider rehabilitation has been communicated by the claimant's solicitor to the compensator, it will usually be expected that the compensator will respond to such request within 21 days.

3.5 Nothing in this or any other code of practice shall in any way modify the obligations of the compensator under the Protocol to investigate claims rapidly and in any event within 3 months (except where time is extended by the claimant's solicitor) from the date of the formal claim letter. It is recognised that, although the rehabilitation assessment can be done even where liability investigations are outstanding, it is essential that such investigations proceed with the appropriate speed.

4. **ASSESSMENT**

4.1 Unless the need for intervention, rehabilitation or treatment has already been identified by medical reports obtained and disclosed by either side, the need for and extent of such intervention, rehabilitation or treatment will be considered by means of an assessment by an appropriately qualified person.

4.2 An assessment of rehabilitation needs may be carried out by any person or organisation suitably qualified, experienced and skilled to carry out the task. The claimant's solicitor and the compensator should endeavour to agree on the person or organisation to be chosen.

4.3 No solicitor or compensator may insist on the assessment being carried out by a particular person or organisation if [on reasonable grounds] the other party objects, such objection to be raised within 21 days from the date of notification of the suggested assessor.

4.4 The assessment may be carried out by a person or organisation which has a direct business connection with the solicitor or compensator, only if the other party agrees. The solicitor or compensator will be expected to reveal to the other party the existence of and nature of such a business connection.

5. **THE ASSESSMENT PROCESS**

5.1 Where possible, the agency to be instructed to provide the assessment should be agreed between the claimant's solicitor and the compensator. The method of providing instructions to that agency will be agreed between the solicitor and the compensator.

5.2 The assessment agency will be asked to carry out the assessment in a way that is appropriate to the needs of the case and, in a simple case, may include, by prior appointment, a telephone interview but in more serious cases will probably involve a face to face discussion with the claimant. The report will normally cover the following headings:-

1. The Injuries sustained by the claimant.
2. The current disability/incapacity arising from those Injuries. Where relevant to the overall picture of the claimant's needs, any other medical conditions not arising from the accident should also be separately annotated.
3. The claimant's domestic circumstances (including mobility accommodation and employment) where relevant.
4. The injuries/disability in respect of which early intervention or early rehabilitation is suggested.
5. The type of intervention or treatment envisaged.
6. The likely cost.
7. The likely outcome of such intervention or treatment.

5.3 The report should not deal with issues relating to legal liability and should therefore not contain a detailed account of the accident circumstances.

5.4 In most cases it will be expected that the assessment will take place within 14 days from the date of the letter of referral to the assessment agency.

5.5 It must be remembered that the compensator will usually only consider such rehabilitation to deal with the effects of the injuries that have been caused in the relevant accident and will normally not be expected to fund treatment for conditions which do not directly relate to the accident unless the effect of such conditions has been exacerbated by the injuries sustained in the accident.

6. THE ASSESSMENT REPORT

6.1 The report agency will, on completion of the report, send copies on to both the claimant's solicitor and compensator simultaneously. Both parties will have the right to raise questions on the report, disclosing such correspondence to the other party.

6.2 It is recognised that for this assessment report to be of benefit to the parties, it should be prepared and used wholly outside the litigation process. Neither side can therefore, unless they agree in writing, rely on its contents in any subsequent litigation.

6.3 The report, any correspondence related to it and any notes created by the assessing agency to prepare it, will be covered by legal privilege and will not be disclosed in any legal proceedings unless the parties agree. Any notes or documents created in connection with the assessment process will not be disclosed in any litigation, and any person involved in the preparation of the report or involved in the assessment process, shall not be a compellable witness at court. This principle is also set out in paragraph 4.4 of the Pre-Action Protocol.

6.4 The provision in paragraph 6.3 above as to treating the report etc as outside the litigation process is limited to the assessment report and any notes relating to it. Any notes and reports created during the subsequent case management process will be covered by the usual principle in relation to disclosure of documents and medical records relating to the claimant.

6.5 The compensator will pay for the report within 28 days of receipt.

6.6 This code intends that the parties will continue to work together to ensure that the rehabilitation which has been recommended proceeds smoothly and that any further rehabilitation needs are also assessed.

7. RECOMMENDATIONS

7.1 When the assessment report is disclosed to the compensator, the compensator will be under a duty to consider the recommendations made and the extent to which funds will be made available to implement all or some of the recommendations. The compensator will not be required to pay for intervention treatment that is unreasonable in nature, content or cost or where adequate and timely provision is otherwise available. The claimant will be under no obligation to undergo intervention, medical or investigation treatment that is unreasonable in all the circumstances of the case.

7.2 The compensator will normally be expected to respond to the claimant's solicitor within 21 days from the date upon which the assessment report is disclosed as to the extent to which the recommendations have been accepted and rehabilitation treatment would be funded and will be expected to justify, within that same timescale, any refusal to meet the cost of recommended rehabilitation.

7.3 If funds are provided by the compensator to the claimant to enable specific intervention, rehabilitation or treatment to occur, the compensator warrants that they will not, in any legal proceedings connected with the claim, dispute the reasonableness of that treatment, nor the agreed costs, provided of course that the claimant has had the recommended treatment. The compensator will not, should the claim fail or be later discontinued, or any element of contributory negligence be assessed or agreed, seek to recover from the claimant any funds that they have made available pursuant to this Code.

K7: Rehabilitation: a Practitioner's Guide

Compiled by the Bodily Injury Claims Management Association

Norman W. Cottington The Injury Care Clinics (President)
David Blofeld, past Claims Manager, Hart Re
Christopher Crook, Solicitor, Edwards Duthie
Tony Goff, Solicitor, George Ide Phillips
Graham Plumb, Claims Manager, AXA Insurance
Keith O. Popperwell, Solicitor Silverbeck Rymer
Bernard Rowe, Solicitor, Lyons Davidson (Treasurer)
Martin Saunders, Allianz Cornhill Insurance
Martin Staples, Solicitor, Vizards
Janet Tilley, Solicitor, Colemans CTTS (Secretary)
Ian Walker, Solicitor, Russell Jones and Walker (Vice President)

CONTENTS

1. CASE MANAGEMENT

One of the first decisions to make is who will manage the rehabilitative process. The various specialist disciplines are outlined below. The task of organising so many disciplines may seem daunting, but help can be found.

One way is to use a case manager to act as case co-ordinator.

The appointment of a case manager at an early stage in the claim will need to be discussed and preferably agreed with the claimant and the insurer. A case manager must have close contact with the claimant and his/her family.

A case manager must have the time available to deal with the claimant and preferably be based close to the claimant.

Case managers can come from a variety of disciplines, but look for someone trained and committed to the standards laid down by the Case Management Society of the UK (CMSUK).

There are a number of specialist case management organisations in the UK, although the number of claimants is likely to outweigh the availability of specialists for some time to come.

A case manager will co-ordinate all of the available services and should be required as appropriate to:

- Assess the personal circumstances and needs of the claimant and his/her family;
- Monitor medical rehabilitation and, if necessary, provide for multi-disciplinary assessment;
- Liaise with the DSS and claim appropriate benefits;

- Liaise with the local authority for interim support prior to a statutory assessment (currently Community Care Act 1990); review such assessment and negotiate the provision of services and financial assistance from the local authority;
- Arrange for therapies;
- Monitor the needs of the claimant's family and arrange for respite care, if necessary;
- Assist the claimant in obtaining training and monitoring carers;
- Facilitate employment rehabilitation;
- Arrange appropriate accommodation;
- Review personal transport arrangements;
- Consider mobility issues;
- Consider funding arrangements for rehabilitation.

Cost

Following an initial assessment, case management will normally be charged on an hourly basis (expect to pay between £65 and £85 per hour). Input by a case manager should reduce once rehabilitation needs have been addressed.

2. IMMEDIATE NEEDS ASSESSMENT

Why?

Rehabilitation in the long term will be difficult, if not impossible, if short-term needs are overlooked. "First Aid" support is essential to overcome the immediate aftermath of an injury and to provide a platform on which to build long-term rehabilitation.

At What Level?

As a rule of thumb, an immediate needs assessment is applicable to claimants who have sustained injuries likely to cause incapacity for several months or longer.

When?

The assessment should be done as soon as possible, even before discharge from hospital, with a view to ensuring the home environment to which the claimant will be discharged is suitable at least for the basic needs of the claimant and his/her family. However, an assessment undertaken years after the event of the injury can still help.

What to Expect

The report should provide preliminary background information about the claimant's circumstances, including the following:

a. The nature and extent of the injury;
b. Any relevant medical background;
c. Family circumstances;
d. Immediate home adaptation needs;
e. Steps to improve the claimant's quality of life and support for family carers;
f. How, and at what cost, recommendations can be implemented.

Relatively simple and inexpensive measures can make a big difference, for example, stair handrails, ramps for wheelchair access, raised toilet seats, widened doorways, lowered light switches or doorknobs.

Recommendations should be capable of being put into immediate effect and at proportionate, reasonable cost.

Do not confuse an immediate needs assessment with long-term care needs and costs, which will be addressed by appropriate experts in the claim.

By Whom?
A case manager trained and committed to the standards laid down by the Case Management Society of the UK (CMSUK) is the most obvious choice.

An occupational therapist or anyone with a social care background, for example, a community care nurse, a social worker or a general practitioner, may similarly be able to conduct the assessment.

Cost
The Code requires that the insurer be responsible for the cost.

The charge will depend upon the complexity of the report and travel expenses, but expect to pay between £750 and £1,750.

The defendant's insurer should usually fund reasonable recommendations by way of an interim payment (see section 7 of the Code).

Liability
Only a complete denial of liability should prevent a defendant's insurer from considering an immediate needs assessment (but also consider an assessment via Social Services).

If the dispute is confined to contributory negligence, the comparatively low cost of an assessment will be justified.

3. EMOTIONAL AND PSYCHOLOGICAL CARE

Why?
Anyone who has suffered a serious injury has experienced a major life event. The injured person, his/her family and close friends will be totally unprepared for either the injury or what follows.

Those who have suffered a serious injury will need to come to terms with what has happened to them. There may also be psychological disorders triggered by the accident, which must be recognised and dealt with. Failure to do so may prevent other treatments from being effective and may hinder a return to work.

Emotional, and in many cases psychological, support needs to be given to help the claimant and those upon whom he/she depends.

When?
Support should be offered as soon as possible. Often this will be determined by the willingness of the injured claimant and/or his/her family to accept outside help. Many people are frightened by their feelings or by the idea of sharing them with someone. Proper counselling can also be of great assistance to relatives acting as carers.

An early assessment can in itself help identify problems or potential problems in time to prevent prolonged post-traumatic stress disorder.

An assessment and, where needed, counselling or psychological treatment are best considered soon after the injury and/or return home from hospital (*i.e.* within the first three months of injury). The need for emotional and psychological support may last much longer than the medical treatment.

By Whom?
Clinical psychologists should normally carry out an initial assessment. If there is any suggestion of brain injury, then a neuropsychologist should be used.

It is useful to check first whether the claimant's hospital team has already involved a psychologist to help with rehabilitation or whether there is a facility within the GP's practice.

Arrangements should be made with a clinical psychologist close to the claimant's home. Where necessary, appointments can be arranged at the claimant's home, which is important if the claimant is distressed by travel.

There are a number of agencies that have panels of psychologists available or you can contact the British Psychological Society at St. Andrew's House, 48 Princess Road East, Leicester LE1 7DR or by telephone on 0116 254 9568.

What to Expect
Most assessments involve some psychological testing. This is necessary to determine what help is needed. Better insight and understanding by the claimant and/or his/her family of what to expect of themselves and their feelings will help to achieve maximum recovery.

Cost
A clinical psychologist's assessment and recommendations will cost between £200 and £500.

A neuropsychologist's assessment will cost between £750 and £1,750.

Psychological therapy costs between £75 and £150 per session.

4. PHYSIOTHERAPY, OSTEOPATHY AND CHIROPRACTIC

Why?
Early mobilisation following injury is now widely recognised as an important part of treatment and needs to be encouraged, provided that it is consistent with medical advice. Damaged tissue needs careful handling. Injury victims need to be shown how to regain movement and function as soon as possible. Whilst treatment methods vary amongst the different professions, these all work towards maximising useful function and can help prevent an injury from becoming a permanent disability.

When?
In the case of serious injuries, this type of treatment is normally determined by the hospital medical team. After discharge from hospital, it is all too easy to overlook the benefit to be gained from continuing physiotherapy and other treatments. Treatment is not just about relieving pain, but equally about achieving the best possible recovery of movement, strength and function. In the case of soft tissue injuries, treatment should be assessed as soon as possible, i.e. within a few weeks, not months, of the injury. In more serious cases, initial treatment should be considered as part of the overall medical management of the patient. After discharge, treatment should be considered as part of the overall nursing plan or by direct referral to a practitioner.

By Whom?
This type of treatment is provided by chartered physiotherapists, osteopaths or chiropractors. Increasingly, it is possible to find that two or more of these disciplines are offered at the same clinic. There are a number of specialist agencies that will provide and co-ordinate treatment. Details of local practitioners can also be found in the Yellow Pages. Alternatively, information is available from:

- Chartered Society of Physiotherapists 0207 306 6666
- General Council of Osteopaths 0207 357 6655
- British Chiropractic Association 0118 950 5950

What to Expect
Make sure the practitioner is a member of a relevant professional body and that there are well-equipped treatment rooms. All practitioners will want to assess the patient before offering treatment. The assessment may involve x-rays as well as a physical examination.

If treatment is offered, a treatment plan should be prepared that identifies the number of treatments and when they are to be given. Often a patient will be taught exercises to help speed up the recovery process.

Cost
The cost will vary from clinic to clinic. Average costs for an assessment will be in the order of £40 to £60. Treatment is likely to cost in the order of £30 to £45 per session depending upon locality.

5. ACCOMMODATION

Why?
A secure, comfortable and accessible home is likely to be a prerequisite for any home-based rehabilitation plan. Accommodation that was suitable for a claimant before an injury may be unsuitable after injury.

When?
Assessment of accommodation needs should be undertaken as soon as possible. For many patients, the only obstacle to being discharged from hospital is their inability to access their own home.

The need for substantial adaptations to accommodation or even a purpose-built property is normally a long-term consideration. Permanent arrangements are best dealt with when it is reasonably clear what the long-term requirements will be.

Physical needs will be identified in medical, occupational therapist and nursing reports.

Short-term needs are as important a consideration as long-term needs. Short term may, in fact, mean several months or even longer. Immediate needs may have been dealt with under an immediate needs report, but this will need to be updated.

By Whom?
A case manager or occupational therapist may be able to advise upon minor alterations that are needed until permanent needs become clear. Once these needs have been identified, a good local builder will be able to carry out minor works such as installing rails, ramps and widening doorways.

If major alterations are needed, a report will be required from an accommodation expert, usually a surveyor or architect, and preferably one with experience of designing accommodation for use by people with disabilities. Whoever carries out the assessment should be familiar with and liaise with the local authority, from which grants may be available. This is particularly relevant in cases where damages may be reduced as a result of an apportionment of liability.

What to Expect
A visit to the claimant's home or proposed home, after consideration of the medical and other reports. This will lead to a report detailing the physical requirements of the property that are necessary in order for the claimant to maximise his/her potential for independent living. In addition, it will take into account the possibility that a carer might need accommodation.

The report should detail the work needed, together with costs, including likely maintenance and/or replacement costs.

Cost
The cost of this report will vary from case to case. Hourly charge-out rates will be in the order of £100 to £150 per hour. A detailed report is likely to cost £1,000 or more.

6. NURSING, CARE AND EQUIPMENT

Why?

The objective will be to establish the most beneficial regime, aimed at ensuring the health and welfare of the injured person, and optimising independence and self-esteem by the most cost-effective means.

When?

It is important to establish in advance what arrangements will be beneficial at each stage of the recovery process, and not address each stage as it occurs. At each stage, it is vital that the case manager, or those reporting, are fully aware of the current medical prognosis, including any anticipated changes.

By Whom?

The appointed case manager is likely to be the best choice, as they often possess all the relevant experience. The person chosen must have an understanding of the medical and physical needs of the claimant, and how to provide for them. Not all nursing/care experts may deal with aids and equipment. Separate advice may be needed from an occupational therapist.

What to Expect

The expert will need to see all existing reports and it may be beneficial for the different disciplines to confer.

The expert will need to speak to the claimant and his/her family and carers as well as those responsible for medical treatment. The report should address:

- The injured person's capacity for coping with the challenges of his/her injury and impairment;
- Existing care, by whom and in what environment;
- External features impacting on the situation, e.g. accommodation, social contact, locality and family dynamics;
- The level of nursing care required;
- Vulnerabilities—health and safety issues for the claimant and his/her carers at present and in the future;
- The need for an enabler;
- The need for domestic assistance;
- Details of equipment needed;
- Detailed cost of recommendations and suggested providers;
- Objectives and their timescales.

Cost

This will depend upon the circumstances and the complexity of each case. Reports will cost from £1,000. Hourly charging rates are likely to range from £65 to £90 per hour, but could possibly be higher.

7. SOCIAL SERVICES

Social services are provided pursuant to the National Health Service Community Care Act 1990 by local authorities' Social Services departments, which are entitled to call upon:

- Health Authorities; and
- Housing Departments

The trigger for support is an assessment by the local authority pursuant to Section 47 of the NHS and Community Care Act 1990. The right to an assessment is absolute.

Once an assessment has been carried out, a written copy must be provided to the Social Services department. A complaints and review procedure is available if the assessment is considered unsatisfactory.

Following assessment, the local authority will make a decision about whether to provide services and the type of services to be provided.

Social services available include:

- Home helps or carers;
- Respite breaks for carers;
- Laundry service;
- Therapies;
- Odd job scheme;
- Rehabilitation;
- Carer support;
- Residential care;
- Transport;
- Housing adaptation;
- Provision of accommodation suitable to the claimant's needs.

The provision of services may be dependent upon the resources of the local authority. Each local authority publishes eligibility criteria. Certain services must be provided under a legal duty. Other services may be provided on a discretionary basis, but there is no duty to do so.

Section 2 of the Chronically Sick and Disabled Persons Act sets out services that must be supplied as a legal duty:

- Home help;
- Provision of radio, television, library or residential services;
- Home adaptations for greater safety, comfort or convenience;
- Holidays;
- Meals;
- Telephone.

The local authority will formulate a case plan, which will be administered by a case manager. This will specify all needs, including those that cannot be met due to budget restraints.

Local authorities are empowered to make direct cash payments to disabled persons so that they can purchase care services for themselves (Community Care (Direct Payments) Act 1996). In addition, cash payments are available from Independent Living Funds and from the DWP.

If the claimant needs suitable accommodation, the local authority has a duty to provide this pursuant to Section 21 of the National Assistance Act.

Residential care can be arranged by both local authorities and health authorities. Provision of residential care by a health authority is free, but DWP benefits are treated as if the claimant were in hospital. Local authority residential care is subject to means testing. Residential care includes the provision of basic accommodation.

A claimant can choose his/her preferred accommodation and can ask a third party (e.g. an insurer or tortfeasor) to meet any shortfall if the cost is more than the local authority would normally pay.

If a local authority provides services free of charge, a claimant cannot make a claim against the insurer in respect of such services.

A local authority has discretion to charge for services other than residential care.

The right to charge for services is subject to a two-stage test:

1. Whether it is reasonable in all the circumstances;
2. Whether the claimant has sufficient means to pay for the services.

Where residential accommodation is provided by a local authority, there is a duty to charge, subject to means testing.

However, such charges can be avoided by the creation of a trust or if the damages are administered by the court (see Preservation of Benefits below).

8. SOCIAL SECURITY BENEFITS

Aim
To maximise benefits and to preserve the right to means-tested benefits.

Non Means-Tested Benefits
There are four main groups of non means-tested benefits that are payable as a consequence of disability:

1. Incapacity for Work
   Incapacity Benefit
   Severe Disablement Allowance

2. Care and Supervision
   Disability Living Allowance
   Care Component
   Constant Attendance Allowance

3. Mobility
   DLA Mobility Component

4. Degree of Disablement
   Severe Disablement Allowance
   Industrial Disablement Benefit

Income Support
This is paid to the claimant if he/she is incapable of working, and to a carer if regularly and substantially engaged in caring for another person.

If the claimant has capital in excess of £8,000 (or £16,000 if in residential care), he/she does not qualify for income support.

Disability Working Allowance
This is intended to encourage people with disabilities to return to work. It is paid to people who work 16 hours or more per week. If a claimant (or his/her partner) has capital of more than £16,000, the claimant does not qualify for this allowance.

Disability Living Allowance
The DLA is not means-tested.

This allowance comprises a care component and a mobility component. The care component is for personal care needs and is paid at three different rates. The mobility component is paid at two different rates.

Tests are administered by an Adjudication Officer.

Receipt of the DLA acts as a gateway to the following benefits:

- Disability Premium;
- Severe Disability Premium;
- Independent Living Funds;
- Motability Scheme.

Industrial Injuries Benefit
This benefit is paid to those who are disabled by a loss of physical and mental capacity caused by an industrial accident or disease.

It is paid in addition to any other non means-tested benefit.

Incapacity Benefit
This is paid to those who are unable to work due to disability. It is non means-tested, but it is only payable if sufficient national insurance contributions (NIC) have been made.

Severe Disablement Allowance
This allowance is paid for 28 weeks to those who are incapable of working but have made insufficient NIC to qualify for the incapacity benefit.

How to Claim
Benefit is generally paid from the date a claim is received by a DWP Office.

There is discretion to accept anything in writing "as sufficient" in the circumstances of a particular case.

The DLA is paid from the date a claim form is requested, so long as the claim form is returned within six weeks.

Income support is paid from the date of notifying the DWP, so long as the claim form is returned within one month. There is discretion to extend time limits in some cases.

Claims should be made to a local DWP Office or by telephoning the Benefit Enquiry Line on 0800 882200.

Appeals are made to the local DWP Office. An appeal can be made within three months of any decision. There is some discretion to extend the time limit up to six years, but it is difficult to make a late appeal.

The Effect of Receipt of Damages on Income-Related Benefits
Lump sum payments of compensation are treated as capital and are added to any other capital that the claimant may have. The effect is that:

- A claimant or partner may have up to £8,000 (£16,000 if in residential care) in capital and benefit will not be affected;
- Deductions are made on a sliding scale in Income Support, DLA, Housing Benefit and Council Tax Benefit, depending on the amount of capital;
- Income support is not payable where there is capital in excess of £8,000 (or £16,000 if in residential care);
- No Housing Benefit, Council Tax Benefit or DLA is payable if capital exceeds £16,000.

Preservation of Benefits
Benefits paid to a claimant can be managed by creating a trust or ensuring the damages fund is administered by the court.

Trusts

The trust may be set up by the claimant or someone acting on behalf of the claimant. If a trust is created:

- The capital value of the trust fund is wholly disregarded;
- Payments from the trust fund to the claimant or on his/her behalf will be treated as income or capital, depending on frequency of payment and the terms of the trust;
- Regular discretionary payments will be disregarded, provided they are used for needs other than those intended to be covered by benefits[1].

Funds Administered by the Court

A decision of the Social Security Commissioner (1996) 3 J.S.S.L.D. 136 makes it clear that money in the Court of Protection should not be taken into account for entitlement to Income Support under the terms of Paragraph 12 to Schedule 120 of the Income Support (General) Regulations (as amended).

9. MOBILITY

Why?

Restricted mobility emphasises impairment and threatens independence. Mobility contributes toward independence.

When?

Immediate thought should be given to mobility within the home, which is often effectively achieved by simple steps such as providing ramps and widening doorways for wheelchair users.

Longer-term projects, such as specialised wheelchairs or appropriate motor vehicles, may have to await medical recovery.

What to Expect?

A driving assessment can identify and address any barriers to independent driving ability, and can identify aids, adaptations or controls required to overcome those barriers.

The Disability Living centres identify and cost aids and equipment for mobility and dexterity.

By Whom?

Personal mobility can be assessed by an occupational therapist.

Disability Living centres exhibit and assist in identifying appropriate aids, including wheelchairs, vehicles and prosthetic appliances.

Driving Assessment centres can assist in determining the right choice of vehicle and wheelchair.

The claimant or his/her family can apply to the DWP for a Mobility Allowance and/or payment under the Motability Scheme to defray the cost of a vehicle.

Disabled living experts, usually architects, can advise on property alterations to ensure ease of access.

Cost

A driving assessment is unlikely to cost £50 to £100 or more, at a mobility centre.

The Disability Living centres provide their services at no cost, although the equipment they recommend can cost anything from a few pounds for a wide-handled toothbrush to more than £1,000 for a suitable wheelchair.

[1] This is no longer so. It was changed by the 2006 Regulations. See H4.

10. VOCATIONAL

Why?

A return to work is more likely to raise a claimant's self-esteem than anything else. It provides independence and self-respect.

When?

A claimant should be helped to return to work, if appropriate, as soon as possible.

It is vital to:

a. Take early steps to consider, with the involvement of the employer, the preservation of the claimant's pre-accident job, by adapting the workplace or duties in accordance with the Disability Discrimination Act 1997;
b. If remaining with the pre-accident employer is not possible, then consider all alternative avenues.

Insurers may be willing to fund the necessary steps to achieve these goals.

By Whom?

A vocational or employment rehabilitation expert should assess the claimant's suitability to return to work and his/her requirements.

A vocational report should not be confused with the reports commonly commissioned from employment consultants. The latter are generally designed to assist in the quantification of loss, whereas the former is intended to identify the injured person's potential and motivation for employment, and to recommend how to achieve a return to suitable work. The expert should know the local area and sympathetic employers, whilst having a good working relationship with the Disability Employment Advisor.

What to Expect

A detailed interview should be undertaken to identify the claimant's former work experience abilities and qualifications, his/her aspirations, and a general assessment of his/her current physical and mental ability.

The next stage should, ideally, be a meeting between the vocational assessor and the previous employer with a view to identifying whether re-employment is possible, either in full or reduced capacity; whether other placements may be available; and/or whether adaptations to the work place may be necessary to facilitate such employment.

If employment with the pre-accident employer is not possible for whatever reason, then consideration will be given to other suitable local job opportunities.

If no such opportunities exist, a more detailed vocational assessment, carried out over a period of one week, may be recommended.

There are numerous facilities nationwide where such assessments can take place either on a day or residential basis. Assessments take place in a working environment and measure dexterity, co-ordination, ability, communication skills, confidence and motivation. Speed, ability and quality of work is recorded, assessed and reported upon.

Following assessment, recommendations may include finding a work placement properly suited to the claimant's skills and abilities or sending the claimant on a training scheme to learn new skills. Another possibility is for the claimant to be supported by a trainer or friend, who would work alongside him/her in a work placement until confidence is gained in employment skills.

A return to some form of remunerative employment is the most effective way an injured person can regain his/her self-esteem and achieve an improved quality of life.

Cost
This will vary depending upon the type of assessment and the time it takes. Expect charges of £750 to £1,500 for a vocational interview and report. More detailed assessments will cost more. A residential five-day assessment is likely to cost £2,000 or more.

Case Management—the early days
As health care options, delivery methods and financing mechanisms became more complex, with inconsistent incentives and accountability, the need for assistance in obtaining timely and appropriate care to achieve recovery and optimal functioning has become increasingly evident.

The first Case Management Society was established in America in 1990 (CMSA) after recognition of the need for a supportive body for this rapidly expanding profession. In 1996, the Case Management Society International was established to provide an umbrella for global affiliation. Canada, Australia, South Africa and a number of European countries already have their own case management societies.

In response to this growth in case management, an informal group of care professionals involved in case management practice started meeting during 2000 to explore the possibility of a national, non-profit, professional membership association for case managers.

About CMSUK
The overall goals and ambitions are to:

- Advise on the development of a professional case management qualification;
- Develop and encourage consistent professional standards of best practice, competence, service and conduct of case managers;
- Provide comprehensive continuing education programmes;
- Provide support for its members;
- Instil confidence for purchasers when employing the services of a CMSUK member;
- Development of case managers within existing public/private health and social environment;
- One of our main aims is to be affiliated with and accredited by the main professional bodies that currently register practising case managers.

With evolving care structures, CMSUK will play an integral part in setting and upholding standards to ensure that cost-effective and timely outcomes are achieved.

If you would like to know more about CMSUK, please write to: CMSUK 100 Fetter Lane London EC4A 1BN Email *cmsukltd@yahoo.co.uk*

Group L
Motoring and Allied Material

L1: AA motoring costs

Petrol cars

	Cost New (£)				
	Up to £12,000	£12,000 to £14,000	£14,000 to £22,000	£22,000 to £30,000	Over £30,000
Standing charges per annum (£)					
Vehicle Excise Duty (Road tax)	120.00	120.00	150.00	215.00	405.00
Insurance	379.00	297.00	485.00	619.00	892.00
Cost of capital	140.00	179.00	224.00	330.00	620.00
Depreciation	1284.00	1937.00	2942.00	3845.00	7794.00
Breakdown cover	42.00	42.00	42.00	42.00	42.00
Total (£)	1965.00	2675.00	3843.00	5051.00	9753.00
Standing charges per mile (in pence)					
5,000	38.79	52.73	75.68	99.48	191.94
10,000	19.65	26.75	38.43	50.51	97.53
15,000	13.44	18.35	26.40	34.70	67.10
20,000	10.47	14.34	20.69	27.18	52.66
25,000	8.48	11.63	16.78	22.05	42.75
30,000	7.11	9.76	14.08	18.50	35.89
Running costs per mile (in pence)					
Petrol*	9.41	10.17	12.21	13.46	16.61
Tyres	0.95	0.79	0.78	1.14	1.68
Service labour costs	3.48	3.54	3.33	3.70	3.59
Replacement parts	1.85	2.03	2.00	2.13	2.52
Parking and tolls	1.80	1.80	1.80	1.80	1.80
Total (pence)	17.49	18.33	20.12	22.23	26.20
* Unleaded petrol @ 95.0p/litre. For every penny more or less, add or subtract	0.10	0.11	0.13	0.14	0.17

Total of standing and running costs (in pence) based on annual mileage of:

5,000 miles	56.27	71.06	95.80	121.71	218.14
10,000 miles	37.14	45.08	58.55	72.74	123.73
15,000 miles	30.93	36.68	46.52	56.92	93.30
20,000 miles	27.95	32.68	40.80	49.40	78.86
25,000 miles	25.96	29.96	36.90	44.27	68.96
30,000 miles	24.59	28.09	34.20	40.73	62.09

Please see the associated notes for more detail. These figures are typical but do not represent all types of vehicle and conditions of use. The figures change from time to time.

Diesel cars

Standing charges per annum (£)	Cost New (£) Up to £12,000	£12,000 to £16,000	£16,000 to £24,000	£24,000 to £32,000	Over £30,000
Vehicle Excise Duty (Road tax)	120.00	120.00	150.00	215.00	405.00
Insurance	379.00	397.00	485.00	619.00	892.00
Cost of capital	152.00	195.00	258.00	378.00	664.00
Depreciation (at 10,000 miles/annum)	1441.00	2284.00	3152.00	4114.00	8313.00
Breakdown cover	42.00	42.00	42.00	42.00	42.00
Total (£)	2170.00	3077.00	4060.00	5391.00	8928.00
Standing charges per mile (in pence)					
5,000	42.10	59.85	80.48	105.71	202.99
10,000	21.34	30.38	40.87	53.68	103.16
15,000	14.61	20.86	28.09	36.88	70.99
20,000	11.39	16.33	22.01	28.90	55.74
25,000	9.23	13.25	17.86	23.45	45.25
30,000	7.74	11.12	14.99	19.68	37.99
Running costs per mile (in pence)					
Diesel*	7.59	8.32	9.91	11.58	14.68
Tyres	0.78	0.80	0.86	1.19	2.03
Service labour costs	2.79	2.82	2.69	2.99	3.12
Replacement parts	2.29	2.30	2.37	2.46	3.01
Parking and tolls	1.80	1.80	1.80	1.80	1.80
Total (pence)	15.25	16.04	17.63	20.02	24.64
* Diesel @ 102.7p/litre. For every penny more or less, add or subtract	0.07	0.08	0.109	0.11	0.14

Total of standing and running costs (in pence) based on annual mileage of:					
5,000 miles	57.35	75.89	98.11	125.74	227.63
10,000 miles	36.59	46.42	58.50	73.70	127.80
15,000 miles	29.86	36.90	45.72	56.91	95.63
20,000 miles	26.64	32.37	39.64	48.92	80..38
25,000 miles	24.48	29.29	35.49	43.47	69.89
30,000 miles	22.99	27.16	32.62	39.70	62.63

Notes to the AA tables:

The AA tables are published annually as a guide to the likely cost to the average private user to run a car. (In previous years tables were also produced for motorcycles and scooters.) The figures given can only be a guide, as individual vehicles will vary: for instance fuel consumption will depend on traffic conditions and the type of journey, and repairs can be very unpredictable. The aim is to show a representative cost that reflects all the important items, so that the motorist can see how it all adds up. This should help make the most suitable choice of economical and environmentally less damaging transport.

Standing Charges The basic costs which you have to pay whether you use the car or not. They include the Road Tax (annual VED), insurance, the cost of the capital used for the vehicle, the loss of value of the vehicle or depreciation, and AA breakdown cover. They also include depreciation, which is affected by mileage.

Running Costs The actual costs of using the car include petrol, oil, tyres, routine servicing and repairs and replacements. The effects of warranties are also taken into account.

Vehicle Groups Cars are put into groups depending on the new car price, as this is a better guide to what they cost to run than for instance the engine size. Take the new car list price when it was first sold (including the main options such as automatic gearbox, air conditioning, etc. supplied with the car), not the current list price. If in doubt, used-car price guides will give the original list prices.

Claiming Mileage How much an employer pays for mileage is a matter for negotiation between him and the employees, as circumstances will vary. The Inland Revenue operates the Approved Mileage Allowance Payment (AMAP) system (in our Table L2) – further details from your local tax office or:

www.hmrc.gov.uk/mileage/index.htm and
www.inlandrevenue.gov.uk/cars/fuel_company_cars.htm

The figures given in our tables are VAT inclusive.

The AA Website The Motoring Costs tables are also on the AA website at *www.theaa.com*

Here some of the data will be updated throughout the year, and there is an interactive version that can tailor the costs to an individual car model and, for instance, the actual insurance premium paid.

Road Tax For cars registered after 1st March, 2001 the rate of Vehicle Excise Duty depends on their fuel type and their emissions of carbon dioxide in the legislated Type Approval tests. In the tables, averages for the price groups are used for the VED rate. For older (pre-March 2001) cars, if the engine capacity is 1,549 cc or less the duty is £125, and if it is over 1,549 cc the duty is £190.

Insurance The UK average cost for a comprehensive policy with a 60 per cent no-claims discount.

Cost of capital This represents the loss of income from the owner's having money tied up in a vehicle, which could otherwise be earning interest in a deposit account, calculated at 1.85 per cent (the AA's online saving rate) of the average value for the car cost group. If the money is borrowed, the cost of capital will instead consist of the charges for loans or hire-purchase finance.

Depreciation Cars lose value at different rates, depending on make, age, mileage, condition and even colour. Older cars will in general depreciate at a slower rate. The tables assume that depreciation costs are averaged over four years from purchase, and include typical adjustments for the different annual mileage in that period.

AA breakdown cover For AA "Roadside" annual vehicle-based cover.

Fuel cost Based on the average UK price, but can be adjusted for price changes using the factors given. The fuel consumption figures taken are typical for each of the car bands listed.

Tyres Based on a tyre life of 27,000 miles, varying with price band. Actual tyre life will vary with individual driving style. The prices are based on online prices; the prices at main dealers will be higher.

Service and labour costs Average cost for each car cost group for normal servicing and parts replacement at a dealer, taking average UK labour rates.

Replacement parts The replacement parts included cover those likely to be needed under normal driving conditions, such as brake materials, oils, filters, bulbs, wipers, and hoses.

Parking and tolls The allowance for parking and road tolls is based on a national average for an urban driver. You may pay more or less depending on patterns of use.

Editors' note:

1. The AA notes have been rearranged by us, with the AA's permission, in the interests of space.
2. Figures for the taxation of car and fuel benefits are at Table L2.
3. The current Vehicle Excise Duty bands are as follows:

Band	CO_2 Emission (g/km)	Petrol or Diesel Car £	Alternative Fuel Car £
Band A	Up to 100	Not applicable	Not applicable
Band B	101 – 110	35.00	15.00
Band C	111 – 120	35.00	15.00
Band D	121 – 130	120.00	100.00
Band E	131 – 140	120.00	100.00
Band F	141 – 150	125.00	105.00
Band G	151 – 165	150.00	130.00
Band H	166 – 175	175.00	155.00
Band I	176 – 185	175.00	155.00
Band J	186 – 200	215.00	200.00
Band K	200 – 225*	215.00	200.00
Band L	226 – 255	405.00	390.00
Band M	Over 255	405.00	390.00

Band K includes cars with a CO_2 figure over 225 g/km which were registered before 23 March 2006.

The CO_2 emission of a particular vehicle can be found at a website provided by the Vehicle Certification Agency (VCA): *www.vcacarfueldata.org.uk//ved_calculator.asp.* It is also on the V5 registration document.

L2: Taxation of car and fuel benefits

Car benefit 1990/91 to 1993/94

Year	*Car (Manufacturer's list price and engine capacity)*		*Age of car at end of tax year: Under 4 years*	*Age of car at end of tax year: 4 years +*
1990/91	Original market value up to £19,250	1400cc or less 1401cc–2000cc More than 2000cc	£1,700 2,200 3,550	£1,150 1,500 2,350
	Original market value up to £19,250; no cylinder capacity	Up to £5,999 £6,000–£8,499 £8,500–£19,249	1,700 2,200 3,550	1,150 1,500 2,350
	Original market value over £19,250	£19,250–£28,999 £29,000+	4,600 7,400	3,100 4,900
1991/92	Original market value up to £19,250	1400cc or less 1401cc–2000cc More than 2000cc	2,050 2,650 4,250	1,400 1,800 2,850
	Original market value up to £19,250; no cylinder capacity	Up to £5,999 £6,000–£8,499 £8,500–£19,249	2,050 2,650 4,250	1,400 1,800 2,850
	Original market value over £19,250	£19,250–£28,999 £29,000+	5,500 8,900	3,700 5,900
1992/93	Original market value up to £19,250	1400cc or less 1401cc–2000cc More than 2000cc	2,140 2,770 4,440	1,460 1,880 2,980
	Original market value up to £19,250; no cylinder capacity	Up to £5,999 £6,000–£8,499 £8,500–£19,249	2,140 2,770 4,440	1,460 1,880 2,980
	Original market value over £19,250	£19,250–£28,999 £29,000+	5,750 9,300	3,870 6,170
1993/94	Original market value up to £19,250	1400cc or less 1401cc–2000cc More than 2000cc	2,310 2,990 4,800	1,580 2,030 3,220
	Original market value up to £19,250; no cylinder capacity	Up to £5,999 £6,000–£8,499 £8,500–£19,249	2,310 2,990 4,800	1,580 2,030 3,220
	Original market value over £19,250	£19,250–£28,999 £29,000+	6,210 10,040	4,180 6,660

Notes: 1 If the business use is **less than 2,500 miles per annum**, multiply the figures by 1.5
2 If the business use is **more than 18,000 miles per annum**, divide the figures by 2

Car benefit 1994/95 to 2001/02

		Business use of car (miles p.a.)					
		0–2,500		*2,500–17,999*		*18,000+*	
	Age of car at end of tax year	*One car*	*More than one car*	*One car*	*More than one car*	*One car*	*More than one car*
1994/5 to 1998/9	Under 4 years old	35	35	23.33	35	11.67	23.33
	4 years or more	23.33	23.33	15.55	23.33	7.78	15.55
1999/00 to 2001/02	Under 4 years old	35	35	25	35	15	25
	4 years or more	26.25	26.25	18.75	26.25	11.25	18.75

Car benefit 2002/03 to 2009/10

CO_2 emissions (g/km)								Percentage of car's price taxed if car does not run solely on diesel (%)	Percentage of car's price taxed if car does run solely on diesel (%)
2002/03	2003/04	2004/05	2005/06	2006/07	2007/08	2008/09	2009/10		
N/A	N/A	N/A	N/A	N/A	N/A	120	120	10	13
165	155	145	140	140	140	135	135	15	18
170	160	150	145	145	145	140	140	16	19
175	165	155	150	150	150	145	145	17	20
180	170	160	155	155	155	150	150	18	21
185	175	165	160	160	160	155	155	19	22
190	180	170	165	165	165	160	160	20	23
195	185	175	170	170	170	165	165	21	24
200	190	180	175	175	175	170	170	22	25
205	195	185	180	180	180	175	175	23	26
210	200	190	185	185	185	180	180	24	27
215	205	195	190	190	190	185	185	25	28
220	210	200	195	195	195	190	190	26	29
225	215	205	200	200	200	195	195	27	30
230	220	210	205	205	205	200	200	28	31
235	225	215	210	210	210	205	205	29	32
240	230	220	215	215	215	210	210	30	33
245	235	225	220	220	220	215	215	31	34
250	240	230	225	225	225	220	220	32	35
255	245	235	230	230	230	225	225	33	35
260	250	240	235	235	235	230	230	34	35
265	255	245	240	240	240	235	235	35	35

Notes

1. From April 6, 2002, although the benefit of a company car is still to be calculated as a percentage of the price of the car (normally list price), the percentage is graduated according to carbon dioxide (CO_2) emissions and adjustments for business mileage and older cars no longer apply.
2. There are discounts for certain cleaner alternatively-propelled cars, which may reduce the minimum charge from that shown in the table.
3. The diesel supplement and the discounts for cleaner alternatives apply only to cars first registered on January 1, 1998 or later.
4. Cars without an approved CO_2 emissions figure are taxed according to engine size. This will include all cars registered before 1998 but only a tiny proportion of those registered in 1998 and later.
5. The exact CO_2 figure is rounded down to the nearest 5 grams per kilometre when using the above table.
6. From April 6, 2008 there is a new lower rate of 10 per cent (13 per cent for diesel) for cars with CO_2 emissions of 12 grams per kilometre or less.

Car fuel benefit – petrol – cash equivalent 1987/88 to 2002/03

	Cylinder Capacity cc		
Year	*0–1400*	*1401–2000*	*2001+*
1987/88–1991/92	480	600	900
1992/93	500	630	940
1993/94	600	760	1130
1994/95	640	810	1200
1995/96	670	850	1260
1996/97	710	890	1320

	Cylinder Capacity cc		
Year	*0–1400*	*1401–2000*	*2001+*
1997/98	800	1010	1490
1998/99	1010	1280	1890
1999/00	1210	1540	2270
2000/01	1700	2170	3200
2001/02	1930	2460	3620
2002/03	2240	2850	4200

Notes

1. From 1987/88 to 1993/94, where there is no cylinder capacity,

cars whose original market value is	Up to £5,999	£6,000–£8,499	£8,500+
are treated as having a capacity of	0–1400	1401–2000	2001+

   respectively.
2. The original market value means the manufacturer's list price.
   The editors do not claim to understand how a car with an engine can have no engine capacity.

Car fuel benefit – diesel – cash equivalent 1991/92 and earlier to 2002/03

	Cylinder Capacity cc	
Year	*0–2000*	*2001+*
1991/92 and earlier	As petrol	As petrol
1992/93	£460	£590
1993/94	£550	£710
1994/95	£580	£750
1995/96	£605	£780
1996/97	£640	£820

	Cylinder Capacity cc	
Year	*0–2000*	*2001+*
1997/98	740	940
1998/99	1280	1890
1999/00	1540	2270
2000/01	2170	3200
2001/02	2460	3620
2002/03	2850	4200

(For the years up to and including 1992/93, divide the cash equivalent by 2 if the taxpayer drove more than 18,000 miles pa on business.)

Car fuel benefit – petrol and diesel – cash equivalent 2003/04 to 2009/10

Notes

1. From April 6, 2003, the car fuel benefit is, like the car benefit, linked directly to the CO_2 emissions of the company car.
2. There are the same diesel supplement and discounts for cleaner alternatively-propelled cars as there are in calculating the car benefit.
3. To calculate the car fuel benefit the percentage in the table used for calculating car benefit is multiplied against a set figure for the year:

   For 2003/04 to 2007/08, the set figure is £14,400.
   For 2008/09 to 2009/10, the set figure is £16,900.

   Thus, if the car benefit percentage for 2009/10 is 23%, the fuel benefit would be £16,900 × 23% = £3,887.
4. For cars registered before January 1, 1998 and cars with no approved CO_2 emissions figure, the percentage to be applied is the same as that used to calculate the car benefit.

Fixed Profit Car Scheme – tax free rates in pence per mile 1990/91 to 2001/02

This applied when employers paid employees an allowance for using their own cars. The scheme was abolished with effect from April 6, 2002 and replaced by a system of mileage allowance payments applying equally for all cars. The tax-free mileage rates under the Fixed Profit Car Scheme are set out below.

Annual mileage	*Up to 4,000*				*4,001 +*			
Cylinder capacity cc Year	*0–1000*	*1001–1500*	*1501–2000*	*2001+*	*0–1000*	*1001–1500*	*1501–2000*	*2001+*
1990/91	24.5	30.0	34.0	43.0	9.5	11.5	13.5	16.5
1991/92	24.5	30.0	34.0	45.0	11.0	13.0	16.0	20.5
1992/93	25.0	30.0	38.0	51.0	14.0	17.0	21.0	27.0
1993/94	26.0	32.0	40.0	54.0	15.0	18.0	22.0	30.0
1994/95	27.0	33.0	41.0	56.0	15.0	19.0	23.0	31.0
1995/96	27.0	34.0	43.0	60.0	15.0	19.0	23.0	32.0
1996/97	27.0	34.0	43.0	61.0	16.0	19.0	23.0	33.0
1997/98	28.0	35.0	45.0	63.0	17.0	20.0	25.0	36.0
1998/99	28.0	35.0	45.0	63.0	17.0	20.0	25.0	36.0
1999/00	28.0	35.0	45.0	63.0	17.0	20.0	25.0	36.0
2000/01	28.0	35.0	45.0	63.0	17.0	20.0	25.0	36.0
2001/02	40.0	40.0	45.0	63.0	25.0	25.0	25.0	36.0

Authorised mileage allowance payments – tax-free rates in pence per mile 2002/03 to 2009/10

Annual mileage	*Pence per mile*
Up to 10,000	40p
10,001+	25p

L3: The Motability Scheme

Disabled people who need a motor vehicle may obtain one by utilising most if not all of the Higher Rate component of the Disability Living Allowance or the War Pensioner's Mobility Supplement. Motability is only available to those in receipt of either of these benefits who assign them to the Scheme for the duration of the contract. Because of the very wide range of physical and mental disabilities of those in receipt of them the Scheme does not require the person seeking to use it to be a driver: anyone in receipt of either allowance who is over three is entitled to use it. Under the Scheme there are three available options:

1. A new car can be obtained on a three-year hire lease contract.
2. A new, or used, car can be taken on hire purchase over two to five years.
3. A quadricycle can be obtained on a five-year lease (a quadricycle is a light steering three door vehicle that can be driven on a motorcycle licence).
4. A powered wheelchair or scooter may be taken on contract hire or on hire purchase.

A national network of some 4,500 dealers provides a wide range of suitably adapted new and used cars. In the case of option (1) (three-year contract hire), the Scheme requires a capital sum, which depending on the model can be as low as zero, and a monthly payment which is provided for by the assignment of the relevant state benefit to the Scheme. As well as the adapted vehicle all maintenance is provided to include the cost of tyres, as is insurance for two named drivers who are over 25 and roadside recovery. Fuel, oil and other incidentals are the responsibility of the driver. There is a 60,000 mile limit on use over the three years of the contract and an annual limit of 20,000 miles. Any mileage over that limit attracts a penalty of 5p per mile. At the end of the contract period the car reverts to the Scheme. In the case of option (2) (hire purchase) the Scheme provides only for the hire purchase of the vehicle, with any necessary adaptation, in return for a capital payment and the assignment of the relevant state benefit. It does not provide for maintenance, roadside recovery or insurance. There is no mileage restriction. At the end of the period the car belongs to the disabled person. In the case of option (4) (wheelchair or scooter) the periods available range from 1–5 years depending on whether contract hire or hire purchase is required. In the case of hire purchase the client is responsible for all costs save insurance while in the case of contract hire more generous benefits are provided.

When costing care must be taken to distinguish between the three elements of any claim:

(i) the capital cost of both purchase and adaptation which recur every three years;
(ii) the monthly running costs covered by the Motability Scheme;
(iii) the running costs not covered by the Scheme such as oil, petrol and car washes.

Not all cars are available and advice must be obtained as to whether what is available adequately meets the needs of the disabled person. When experts have recommended that a car be obtained under the Scheme practitioners should ensure that they are clear which option is being recommended and ensure that they compare like for like.

The condition precedent for using the Motability Scheme is that the beneficiary is in receipt of a state benefit which falls within the Second Schedule of the Social Security (Recovery of Benefits) Act 1997. It is now clear, following *Eagle v Chambers (No.2),*[1] that s.17 of the Act precludes a court from insisting that the mobility component of the Disabled Living Allowance should be used by any recipient to mitigate her loss. Henceforth no Defendant can insist that a Claimant use the mobility allowance to participate in the Motability Scheme.

Further reading and assistance in specific cases can be obtained at:
www.motability.co.uk and Customer Services (0845) 456 4566.

[1] [2004] EWCA Civ 1033.

L4: Calculations involving motor cars

There are a number of commonly encountered calculations involving the cost of motor cars. This section contains tables and examples of calculations dealing with the following and should be read along with the table of AA motoring costs in section L1:

1. New car prices
2. Cost of future replacements
3. Cost of more frequent replacement
4. Cost of automatic cars
5. Cost of additional mileage

We have categorised cars as follows:

Mini:	Most cars of 1.1 litre or under, such as Toyota Aygo 1.0, Vauxhall Corsa 1.0
Super mini:	Similar cars between 1.1 and 1.4, Ford Fiesta 1.25, Nissan Tekna 1.4
Small:	Cars of the smaller Ford Focus, VW Golf type, mostly 1.3–1.6
Medium:	The Ford Mondeo, VW Passat type, mostly cars from 1.6–1.9
Executive:	The larger Passat, Volvo S80 type, mostly 2.0–2.8 litre
Prestige:	The BMW 330i, Jaguar 3.0, mostly up to 3.5 litre
Luxury:	The Jaguar XJ8 4.2, Audi A8 4.2, mostly over 3.5 litre and expensive
Estate etc:	Self-explanatory

Notes:

1. The first table is intended to convey in broad terms the purchase costs of motor cars across a range of models. The material is taken from *Parker's Car Price Guide* and *What Car?* with the kind permission of the publishers.

   The *New Price* is the recommended retail price (including VAT) according to the latest manufacturer's price list: all prices stated are "on the road" and include delivery charges, 12 months' road fund licence, number plates and £25 registration tax. *VED band* is the vehicle excise duty band: where two letters are shown (as "E/F") the first refers to the manual and the second to the automatic version.

2. Depreciation: Different cars, even produced by the same manufacturer, depreciate at different rates. As a model of car may change after a few years even if the same name is retained, losses over a long period cannot be calculated for individual models but only by reference to the general position.

3. Automatics: The comparison of manual and automatic cars is similarly a generalisation. The calculation for depreciation assumes that the new price of the automatic is *higher* than for the manual model. There is considerable variation, even among cars of similar type with similar new prices, in the rate at which the premium for the automatic version is eroded. With some cars the gap disappears very quickly: with some the premium for the automatic version is actually greater for used cars than for new ones.

4. Where the current new price of the manual and automatic versions is the same, which is often the case with expensive cars, the used automatic tends to retain its value *better* than the manual model. It may nevertheless have a higher fuel consumption but whether it will be more expensive overall may depend on the mileage.

1. New Car Prices

	New Price (£)	VED band	Mileage adjustment
Mini			
Citroën C1 1.0i VT 3d	7,695	B	B
Toyota Aygo 1.0 3d	7,040	B	B
Vauxhall Corsa 1.0i Expression 3d	8,455	E	A
Super Mini			
Citroën C2 1.4 Rhythm 3d	10,695	F	B
Ford Fiesta 1.25 Studio 3d	9,995	D	A
Nissan Micra 1.4 Tekna 3d	10,845	G	B
Suzuki Swift 1.3 GL 3d	8,750	F	A
Vauxhall Corsa 1.2i Design 3d	12,020	E	B
Volkswagen Polo 1.2 E 70 3d	8,770	E	B
Small			
Citroën C4 1.6v SX 5d	14,895	G	C
Ford Focus 1.6i Zetec 5d	17,040	G	C
Honda Civic 1.4 Type S 5d	15,000	E	C
Renault Megane 1.6 16v Dyn 5d	14,985	G	B
Toyota Auris 1.6 TR 5d	14,395	E	C
Vauxhall Astra 1.6i Design 16v 5d	16,685	G	C
Volkswagen Golf 1.6 102 S 5d	15,075	H	D
Medium			
BMW 320i ES 4d	23,165	F	D
Ford Mondeo 2.0 Ghia 4d	20,840	J	D
Renault Megane 2.0 VVT Dyn 5d	16,295	F	B/C
Toyota Avensis 1.8 VVT S T2 4d	16,560	G	–
Vauxhall Insignia 1.8 5d	17,860	I	–
Volkswagen Passat 1.8 TSI S 4d	17,945	I	–
Volvo S40 1.6 S 4d	14,295	H	D
Executive			
BMW 325i SE 4d	26,980	F	F
Honda Accord 2.0i VTEC EX 4d	20,227	F	E
Saab 9-3 1.8t 4d Linear	20,612	I	B
Toyota Avensis 2.2 D-4D TR 4d	20,090	F	–
Volkswagen Passat 2.0 TDi SEL 4d	23,180	G	D
Volvo S60 2.0 T SE 4d	19,995	I	D
Prestige			
Audi Quattro A4 3.0 TDi SE 4d	29,565	H	F
BMW 330i SE 4d	30,340	H	F
Jaguar X 2.2D Sovereign 4d	28,898	G	E
Mercedes-Benz E350 Elegance Auto 4d	37,462	K	G
Saab 9-5 2.3 HDT Turbo 4d	24,718	K	–
Volvo S80 2.4 D SE Lux 5d	27,770	H	F
Luxury			
Audi Quattro A8 4.2 V8 TDI SE 4d	61,380	L	H
BMW 550i SE 5d	47,995	M	H
Jaguar XJ8 4.2 V8 Sovereign 4d	57,028	M	H
Mercedes-Benz E500 Elegance Auto 4d	47,160	M	H

Estate	New Price (£)	VED band	Mileage adjustment
Ford Mondeo Estate 2.0 Ghia 5d	22,090	J	D
Jaguar X 3.0 V6 Sovereign 5d	32,080	L	E
Mercedes-Benz E500 Elegance 5d	48,922	M	H
Saab 9-5 2.3 Turbo 5d	25,893	K	D
Vauxhall Insignia 2.oT Elite 5d	25,250	K	–
Volkswagen Passat 2.0 S TDi 5d	18,715	F	C
4 × 4			
Citroën C-Crosser 2.2 HDi VTR 5d	23,195	J	F
Nissan Patrol 3.0 Di Aventura 5d	28,300	M	E
Toyota Landcruiser 3.0 D-4D LC3 5d	28,640	L	G
Vauxhall 2.0T 4×4 Elite 5d	26,475	K	–
Volkswagen Touareg 2.5 TDi	30,320	L	G
Volvo XC90 2.4 DS SE Lux 5d	36,995	K	H
People carriers			
Chrysler Grand Voyager 3.8 LE Auto 5d	32,308	M	–
Citroën C8 2.0 HDi 120 SX 5d	23,295	I	D
Ford Galaxy 2.3 Zetec 5d	25,690	L	F
Mitsubishi Grandis 2.4 Equippe 5d	19,735	L	C
Renault Espace 2.0t 16v Dyn 5d	25,060	K	D
Toyota Verso 2.2 D-4D T2 5d	16,770	G	–
Vauxhall Zafira 2.0 T SRi 5d	21,082	L	D

2. Cost of future replacements

Table 1 below has representat ve trade-in values of used *manual* cars expressed as a proportion of the *current* new price (calculated from material in *Parker's Car Price Guide*). Automatic cars may depreciate faster. Where the new price of an automatic car is *higher* than that of the corresponding manual car, there is a tendency for the automatic to depreciate by about 1% more (altogether, not per year).

Table 1 Trade-in values of used manual cars

Age of car	Residual value	Loss of value	Equivalent annual depreciation
1	0.64	0.36	0.360
2	0.50	0.50	0.256
3	0.41	0.59	0.204
4	0.36	0.64	0.168
5	0.33	0.67	0.143
Adjustment for automatic cars	– 0.01	+ 0.01	

The table can be used to calcu late the future net costs of replacements where the replacements will be second hand as well as where they will be new.

Example 1: The claimant is 54 and needs a people carrier such as a Chrysler Grand Voyager 3.3 LE Auto 5d, automatic version. He will need to replace it every 4 years, the final replacement being when he is 70. He would not otherwise have had a car (or the car is additional to whatever vehicle would have been bought in any event).

Initial price of people carrier, say		£32,995.00
Proportion of price lost at each replacement (Table 1 above, + 0.01)	0.65	
Cost of each replacement	0.65 × 32,995 = 21,446.75	
Multiplier for 16 years (Table A5, 2.5%, 4-yearly)	3.14	
Cost of future replacements	3.14 × 21,446.75	= £67,342.80
Total		£100,337.80

Example 2: The same claimant currently runs a manual Volvo S80 2.4 SE and will replace it with the Chrysler people carrier. The additional cost is the future cost of the Chryslers *minus* the corresponding figure saved on Volvos. (If both cars are manual or both automatic the calculation is simpler.)

Initial price of Volvo saved, say		£28,245.00
Proportion of price saved at each replacement (Table 1 above, manual)	0.64	
Cost of each replacement	0.64 × 28,245.00 = 18,076.80	
Multiplier for 16 years (Table A5, 2.5%, 4-yearly)	3.14	
Cost of future replacements saved	3.14 × 18,076.80	= £56,761.15
Total saved		£85,006.15
Net future cost of Chryslers instead of Volvos (100,337.80–85,006.15)		= £15,331.65

3. Cost of more frequent replacement

A claimant is sometimes advised that because of his condition he needs a more reliable car and should therefore replace it more often than he needed to do before his injury. Table 2, which is derived from Table 1, shows the additional annual cost, expressed as a proportion of the new price. Find the row corresponding to the new interval in years and the column corresponding to the old interval.

Note that the table expresses the multiplier as an *annual* cost, not the cost *on each exchange*. Thus in row 2, column 4, the figure 0.088 means that the additional expense of replacing a car every 2 years, instead of every 4 years, is 8.8% of the price of the car per year for however long the claimant continues to drive.

Table 2 Multipliers for additional annual cost of replacing car more frequently

		Old interval in years				
		1	**2**	**3**	**4**	**5**
New interval in years	**1**	0	0.104	0.156	0.192	0.217
	2		0	0.052	0.088	0.113
	3			0	0.036	0.061
	4				0	0.025
	5					0

Example: The claimant is 40 and drives a car currently costing £11,995 new. She has just bought one. She can continue to drive a similar car, with modifications. She has been advised that because of her disability she should now change it every 3 years rather than every 5 as she has until now. She should stop driving at about 73, so the last change will be at about age 70.

Multiplier for additional annual cost from table above – new frequency 3 years, old frequency 5 years	0.061		
Multiplier for woman of 40 until age 70 (Ogden table 28, at 2.5%)	20.50		
Multiplier for additional cost of more frequent replacement	0.061 × 20.50	=	1.25
Current cost of car			£11,995.00
Additional cost of replacing car more frequently until age 70			£14,993.75

4. Cost of automatic cars

A claimant's injuries sometimes make it necessary for him to have an automatic car which he would not otherwise have needed. Generally this involves additional costs in three respects: the automatic car is more expensive to buy, is more expensive to run and tends to depreciate faster than the corresponding manual model (but see the notes in the introduction).

Table 3 Added cost of automatic cars

	Mini and Super mini	Small	Medium and Executive	Prestige and Luxury	Estate, 4 × 4 and MPV
Added cost of new car (in £)	850	1,075	1,145	1,275	1,245

Table 4 Added cost of petrol

	Mini and Super mini	Small	Medium and Executive	Prestige and Luxury
(in pence per mile) Petrol at 106.8p/litre	2.51	1.27	1.05	0.30
For every penny more or less add or subtract	0.030	0.015	0.012	0.004

Greater depreciation

Where the new price of an automatic model of a car is *higher* than that of the corresponding manual car, there is a tendency for the automatic to depreciate by about 1% more (altogether, not per year) – see Table 1 above. Thus:

New manual model	£11,000	3 year old manual	11,000 × 0.41 = £4,510
New automatic	£12,000	3 year old automatic	12,000 × 0.40 = £4,800

Example: The claimant is 48. He drives a manual car of medium type whose price new is about £16,000. He drives about 10,000 miles a year and changes his car every 3 years. Because of his injury he now needs an automatic. He is likely to stop driving in about 30 years.

Extra cost of automatic car:			
On first purchase (from Table 3 column 3 above):			£1,145.00
Cost at each replacement of automatic (Table 1 row 3): 17,145 × 0.60 =		10,293.00	
less cost at each replacement of manual 16,000 × 0.59 =		9,440.00	
Additional cost at each replacement		£ 853.00	
Crude multiplier for replacements (table A5, 27 years, 3-yearly)	6.33		
Multiplier for 27 years certain (table A5, cont's loss) 19.71			
Multiplier for man of 48 until age 75 (table A1) 18.24			
Multiplier discounted for mortality (6.33 × 18.24/19.71) =		5.86	£4,996.79
Extra cost per mile, petrol at 94.2 p/litre = 1.05 + (−0.8 × 0.012) = 1.04 pence			
Extra running cost 10,000 miles pa		£104.00	
Crude multiplier (table A5, 30 years, cont's loss)	21.19		
Multiplier discounted for mortality (21.19 × 18.24/19.71) =		19.61	£2,039.44
Total extra cost:			£8,181.23

Note: the treatment of the multipliers in the example is more sophisticated than in earlier editions of these tables. The approach is explained in paragraphs 20–24 of table A8 (the 6th edition of the Ogden Tables.)

5. Cost of additional mileage

The AA figures for *running* costs at Table L1 do not include depreciation. Mileage reduces the value of a car by a factor which varies with the type of car and its age on resale. Age on resale is not necessarily the length of time the claimant had the car. The categories A, B, C etc are derived from *Parker's Price Guide*.

The table may not be appropriate for mileages below 1,000 miles a year or above 30,000 miles a year.

Table 5 Adjustment for depreciation for extra mileage

Age on resale	Depreciation in pence per mile							
	A	B	C	D	E	F	G	H
1	3.00	4.00	5.00	6.00	7.00	8.50	10.50	13.50
2	2.50	3.50	4.50	5.50	6.50	7.50	9.00	11.00
3	2.00	3.00	3.50	4.50	5.00	6.00	7.50	10.00
4	1.20	2.00	2.50	3.50	4.00	5.00	6.00	8.00
5	1.00	1.50	2.00	2.50	3.00	4.00	5.00	7.00
6	0.70	1.20	1.50	2.00	2.50	3.00	4.00	6.00
7	0.50	0.90	1.00	1.50	2.00	2.50	3.50	5.00
8	0.40	0.60	0.90	1.00	1.50	2.00	2.50	4.00

Example: The claimant would have had a car anyway. His mileage is increased by 4,000 miles a year because of his injury. He buys at 1 year old and changes at 4 years old cars costing about £14,000 in category C in the mileage adjustment table. Petrol costs 96.1 pence per litre.

Running cost per mile from AA figures (Table L1)	20.12 pence
Adjustment for petrol price (from Table L1) (+1.1p × 0.13)	0.14
Adjustment for mileage (category C, 4 years old)	2.50
Total per mile	22.76 pence
Total annual cost (4,000 × 23.89)	£ 910.40

Based on figures in *Parker's Car Price Guide* and from the websites of the Vehicle Certification Agency and the United States Department of Transportation.

L5: Time, speed and distance

Table of speeds and distances

Speeds				Distances in yards																			
mph	km/h	yd/sec	m/sec	5	10	15	20	25	30	40	50	60	75	100	125	150	175	200	225	250	300	400	500
5	8.0	2.44	2.24	2.0	4.1	6.1	8.2	10.2	12.3	16.4	20.5	24.5	30.7	4.09	51.1	61.4	71.6	81.8	92.0	102.3	122.7	163.6	204.5
10	16.1	4.89	4.47	1.0	2.0	3.1	4.1	5.1	6.1	8.2	10.2	12.3	15.3	20.5	25.6	30.7	35.8	40.9	46.0	51.1	61.4	81.8	102.3
15	24.1	7.33	6.71	0.7	1.4	2.0	2.7	3.4	4.1	5.5	6.8	8.2	10.2	13.6	17.0	20.5	23.9	27.3	30.7	34.1	40.9	54.5	68.2
20	32.2	9.78	8.94	0.5	1.0	1.5	2.0	2.6	3.1	4.1	5.1	6.1	7.7	10.2	12.8	15.3	17.9	20.5	23.0	25.6	30.7	40.9	51.1
25	40.2	12.22	11.18	0.4	0.8	1.2	1.6	2.0	2.5	3.3	4.1	4.9	6.1	8.2	10.2	12.3	14.3	16.4	18.4	20.5	24.5	32.7	40.9
30	48.3	14.67	13.41	0.3	0.7	1.0	1.4	1.7	2.0	2.7	3.4	4.1	5.1	6.8	8.5	10.2	11.9	13.6	15.3	17.0	20.5	27.3	34.1
35	56.3	17.11	15.65	0.3	0.6	0.9	1.2	1.5	1.8	2.3	2.9	3.5	4.4	5.8	7.3	8.8	10.2	11.7	13.1	14.6	17.5	23.4	29.2
40	64.4	19.56	17.88	0.3	0.5	0.8	1.0	1.3	1.5	2.0	2.6	3.1	3.8	5.1	6.4	7.7	8.9	10.2	11.5	12.8	15.3	20.5	25.6
45	72.4	22.00	20.12	0.2	0.5	0.7	0.9	1.1	1.4	1.8	2.3	2.7	3.4	4.5	5.7	6.8	8.0	9.1	10.2	11.4	13.6	18.2	22.7
50	80.5	24.44	22.35	0.2	0.4	0.6	0.8	1.0	1.2	1.6	2.0	2.5	3.1	4.1	5.1	6.1	7.2	8.2	9.2	10.2	12.3	16.4	20.5
60	96.6	29.33	26.82	0.2	0.3	0.5	0.7	0.9	1.0	1.4	1.7	2.0	2.6	3.4	4.3	5.1	6.0	6.8	7.7	8.5	10.2	13.6	17.0
70	112.7	34.22	31.29	0.1	0.3	0.4	0.6	0.7	0.9	1.2	1.5	1.8	2.2	2.9	3.7	4.4	5.1	5.8	6.6	7.3	8.8	11.7	14.6
80	128.7	39.11	35.76	0.1	0.3	0.4	0.5	0.6	0.8	1.0	1.3	1.5	1.9	2.6	3.2	3.8	4.5	5.1	5.8	6.4	7.7	10.2	12.8
90	144.8	44.00	40.23	0.1	0.2	0.3	0.5	0.6	0.7	0.9	1.1	1.4	1.7	2.3	2.8	3.4	4.0	4.5	5.1	5.7	6.8	9.1	11.4
100	160.9	48.89	44.70	0.1	0.2	0.3	0.4	0.5	0.6	0.8	1.0	1.2	1.5	2.0	2.6	3.1	3.6	4.1	4.6	5.1	6.1	8.2	10.2

Seconds

Notes:

1. The table shows the time taken to cover a given distance at a given speed, to the nearest $\frac{1}{10}$ second.
2. The table can also be used to ascertain the approximate speed of a vehicle, if the time and distance are known.
3. As an example, to find how long it would take to cover 125 yards at 35 mph, follow the vertical column down from the figure 125 and follow the horizontal row across from the figure 35: they meet at the figure 7.3, which is the number of seconds taken to cover the distance.
4. A speed of z miles per hour approximately equals [0.5z] yards per second.
5. The general formula for the number of seconds to cover a given distance at a given speed is approximately:

$$\frac{\text{distance in yards} \times 2.04545}{\text{speed in miles per hour}}$$

Typical Stopping Distances (average car length = 4 metres)

Speed (mph)	Thinking Distance (metres)	Braking Distance (metres)	Total Stopping Distance (metres)	(car lengths)
20	6	6	12	3
30	9	14	23	6
40	12	24	36	9
50	15	38	53	13
60	18	55	73	18
70	21	75	96	24

Extracted from The Highway Code, published by the Stationery Office.

Group M
Other Information

M

M1: Conversion formulae

M2: Perpetual calendar

M3: Religious festivals

M4: Medical reference intervals and scales

M5: Websites

M6: Addresses of useful organisations

M1: Conversion formulae

	To convert	Multiply by
Area	Square inches to square centimetres	6.452
	Square centimetres to square inches	0.1555
	Square metres to square feet	10.7638
	Square feet to square metres	0.0929
	Square yards to square metres	0.8361
	Square metres to square yards	1.196
	Square miles to square kilometres	2.590
	Square kilometres to square miles	0.3861
	Acres to hectares	0.4047
	Hectares to acres	2.471
Length	Inches to centimetres	2.540
	Centimetres to inches	0.3937
	Feet to metres	0.3048
	Metres to feet	3.281
	Yards to metres	0.9144
	Metres to yards	1.094
	Miles to kilometres	1.609
	Kilometres to miles	0.6214
Temperature	Centigrade to Fahrenheit	$\times 9 \div 5 + 32$
	Fahrenheit to Centigrade	$-32 \times 5 \div 9$
Volume	Cubic inches to cubic centimetres	16.39
	Cubic centimetres to cubic inches	0.06102
	Cubic feet to cubic metres	0.02832
	Cubic metres to cubic feet	35.31
	Cubic yards to cubic metres	0.7646
	Cubic metres to cubic yards	1.308
	Cubic inches to litres	0.01639
	Litres to cubic inches	61.024
	Gallon to litres	4.545
	Litres to gallons	0.22

	To convert		Multiply by
Weight	Grains to grams		0.0647
	Grams to grains		15.43
	Ounces to grams		28.35
	Grams to ounces		0.03527
	Pounds to grams		453.592
	Grams to pounds		0.0022
	Pounds to kilograms		0.4536
	Kilograms to pounds		2.2046
	Tons to kilograms		1016.05
	Kilograms to tons		0.0009842
Speed	Miles per hour to kilometres per hour		1.6093
	Kilometres per hour to miles per hour		0.6214
Fuel cost	Pence per litre to pounds per gallon		0.045
	Pounds per gallon to pence per litre		22.00
USA measures	Dry	USA pint to UK pint	0.9689
		UK pint to USA pint	1.1032
		USA pint to litres	0.5506
		Litres to USA pint	1.816
		USA bushel to UK bushel	0.9689
		UK bushel to USA bushel	1.032
		USA bushel to litres	35.238
		Litres to USA bushel	0.0283
	Liquid	USA pint (16 fl oz) to UK pint	0.8327
		UK pint to USA pint	1.2
		USA pint to litres	0.4732
		Litres to USA pint	2.113
		USA gallon to UK gallon	0.8327
		UK gallon to USA gallon	1.2
		USA gallon to litres	3.7853
		Litres to USA gallons	0.2641

Clothing

Shirts

UK/USA	14	14½	15	15½	16	16½	17	17½
Europe	36	37	38	39	40	41	42	43

Ladies clothes

UK							
Size code	10	12	14	16	18	20	22
Bust/hip inches	32/34	34/36	36/38	38/40	40/42	42/44	44/46
Bust/hip cm	84/89	88/93	92/97	97/102	102/107	107/112	112/117
USA							
Size code	10	12	14	16	18	20	22
Bust/hip inches	35½/37	36½/38½	38½/39½	39½/41½	41½/42½	43½/45	45½/47

European sizes vary from country to country

Footwear – Men

British	6	7	8	9	10	11	12
American	6½	7½	8½	9½	10½	11½	12½
Continental	40	41	42	43	44	45	46

Footwear – Women

British	3	4	5	6	7	8	9
American	4½	5½	6½	7½	8½	9½	10½
Continental	36	37	38	39	40	41	41

Children's clothes

UK												
Age	1	2	3	4	5	6	7	8	9	10	11	12
Height/inches	32	36	38	40	43	45	48	50	53	55	58	60
Height/cm	80	92	98	104	110	116	122	128	134	140	146	152
USA												
Boys' size code	1	2	3	4	5	6	8		10		12	
Girls' size code	2	3	4	5	6	6x	7	8	10		12	
Europe												
Height/cm	80	92	98	104	110	116	122	128	134	140	146	152

M2: Perpetual calendar

The number opposite each of the years in the list below indicates which of the calendars on the following pages is the one for that year. Thus the number opposite 2000 is 14, so calendar 14 can be used as a 2000 calendar.

Leap years

Years divisible by four without remainder are leap years with 366 days instead of 365 (29 days in February instead of 28). However the last year of the century is not a leap year except when divisible by 400.

Easter Sunday

These dates apply unless there is a change to a fixed Easter.

1990	15 April	1997	30 March	2004	11 April
1991	31 March	1998	12 April	2005	27 March
1992	19 April	1999	4 April	2006	16 April
1993	11 April	2000	23 April	2007	8 April
1994	3 April	2001	15 April	2008	23 March
1995	16 April	2002	31 March	2009	12 April
1996	7 April	2003	20 April	2010	4 April

Year	Calendar	Year	Calendar	Year	Calendar	Year	Calendar	Year	Calendar	Year	Calendar
1980	10	1992	11	2004	12	2016	13	2028	14	2040	8
1981	5	1993	6	2005	7	2017	1	2029	2	2041	3
1982	6	1994	7	2006	1	2018	2	2030	3	2042	4
1983	7	1995	1	2007	2	2019	3	2031	4	2043	5
1984	8	1996	9	2008	10	2020	11	2032	12	2044	13
1985	3	1997	4	2009	5	2021	6	2033	7	2045	1
1986	4	1998	5	2010	6	2022	7	2034	1	2046	2
1987	5	1999	6	2011	7	2023	1	2035	2	2047	3
1988	13	2000	14	2012	8	2024	9	2036	10	2048	11
1989	1	2001	2	2013	3	2025	4	2037	5	2049	6
1990	2	2002	3	2014	4	2026	5	2038	6	2050	7
1991	3	2003	4	2015	5	2027	6	2039	7		

1

	January	February	March	April
M	2 9 16 23 30	6 13 20 27	6 13 20 27	3 10 17 24
T	3 10 17 24 31	7 14 21 28	7 14 21 28	4 11 18 25
W	4 11 18 25	1 8 15 22	1 8 15 22 29	5 12 19 26
T	5 12 19 26	2 9 16 23	2 9 16 23 30	6 13 20 27
F	6 13 20 27	3 10 17 24	3 10 17 24 31	7 14 21 28
S	7 14 21 28	4 11 18 25	4 11 18 25	1 8 15 22 29
S	1 8 15 22 29	5 12 19 26	5 12 19 26	2 9 16 23 30

	May	June	July	August
M	1 8 15 22 29	5 12 19 26	3 10 17 24 31	7 14 21 28
T	2 9 16 23 30	6 13 20 27	4 11 18 25	1 8 15 22 29
W	3 10 17 24 31	7 14 21 28	5 12 19 26	2 9 16 23 30
T	4 11 18 25	1 8 15 22 29	6 13 20 27	3 10 17 24 31
F	5 12 19 26	2 9 16 23 30	7 14 21 28	4 11 18 25
S	6 13 20 27	3 10 17 24	1 8 15 22 29	5 12 19 26
S	7 14 21 28	4 11 18 25	2 9 16 23 30	6 13 20 27

	September	October	November	December
M	4 11 18 25	2 9 16 23 30	6 13 20 27	4 11 18 25
T	5 12 19 26	3 10 17 24 31	7 14 21 28	5 12 19 26
W	6 13 20 27	4 11 18 25	1 8 15 22 29	6 13 20 27
T	7 14 21 28	5 12 19 26	2 9 16 23 30	7 14 21 28
F	1 8 15 22 29	6 13 20 27	3 10 17 24	1 8 15 22 29
S	2 9 16 23 30	7 14 21 28	4 11 18 25	2 9 16 23 30
S	3 10 17 24	1 8 15 22 29	5 12 19 26	3 10 17 24 31

2

	January	February	March	April
M	1 8 15 22 29	5 12 19 26	5 12 19 26	2 9 16 23 30
T	2 9 16 23 30	6 13 20 27	6 13 20 27	3 10 17 24
W	3 10 17 24 31	7 14 21 28	7 14 21 28	4 11 18 25
T	4 11 18 25	1 8 15 22	1 8 15 22 29	5 12 19 26
F	5 12 19 26	2 9 16 23	2 9 16 23 30	6 13 20 27
S	6 13 20 27	3 10 17 24	3 10 17 24 31	7 14 21 28
S	7 14 21 28	4 11 18 25	4 11 18 25	1 8 15 22 29

	May	June	July	August
M	7 14 21 28	4 11 18 25	2 9 16 23 30	6 13 20 27
T	1 8 15 22 29	5 12 19 26	3 10 17 24 31	7 14 21 28
W	2 9 16 23 30	6 13 20 27	4 11 18 25	1 8 15 22 29
T	3 10 17 24 31	7 14 21 28	5 12 19 26	2 9 16 23 30
F	4 11 18 25	1 8 15 22 29	6 13 20 27	3 10 17 24 31
S	5 12 19 26	2 9 16 23 30	7 14 21 28	4 11 18 25
S	6 13 20 27	3 10 17 24	1 8 15 22 29	5 12 19 26

	September	October	November	December
M	3 10 17 24	1 8 15 22 29	5 12 19 26	3 10 17 24 31
T	4 11 18 25	2 9 16 23 30	6 13 20 27	4 11 18 25
W	5 12 19 26	3 10 17 24 31	7 14 21 28	5 12 19 26
T	6 13 20 27	4 11 18 25	1 8 15 22 29	6 13 20 27
F	7 14 21 28	5 12 19 26	2 9 16 23 30	7 14 21 28
S	1 8 15 22 29	6 13 20 27	3 10 17 24	1 8 15 22 29
S	2 9 16 23 30	7 14 21 28	4 11 18 25	2 9 16 23 30

3

	January	February	March	April
M	7 14 21 28	4 11 18 25	4 11 18 25	1 8 15 22 29
T	1 8 15 22 29	5 12 19 26	5 12 19 26	2 9 16 23 30
W	2 9 16 23 30	6 13 20 27	6 13 20 27	3 10 17 24
T	3 10 17 24 31	7 14 21 28	7 14 21 28	4 11 18 25
F	4 11 18 25	1 8 15 22	1 8 15 22 29	5 12 19 26
S	5 12 19 26	2 9 16 23	2 9 16 23 30	6 13 20 27
S	6 13 20 27	3 10 17 24	3 10 17 24 31	7 14 21 28

	May	June	July	August
M	6 13 20 27	3 10 17 24	1 8 15 22 29	5 12 19 26
T	7 14 21 28	4 11 18 25	2 9 16 23 30	6 13 20 27
W	1 8 15 22 29	5 12 19 26	3 10 17 24 31	7 14 21 28
T	2 9 16 23 30	6 13 20 27	4 11 18 25	1 8 15 22 29
F	3 10 17 24 31	7 14 21 28	5 12 19 26	2 9 16 23 30
S	4 11 18 25	1 8 15 22 29	6 13 20 27	3 10 17 24 31
S	5 12 19 26	2 9 16 23 30	7 14 21 28	4 11 18 25

	September	October	November	December
M	2 9 16 23 30	7 14 21 28	4 11 18 25	2 9 16 23 30
T	3 10 17 24	1 8 15 22 29	5 12 19 26	3 10 17 24 31
W	4 11 18 25	2 9 16 23 30	6 13 20 27	4 11 18 25
T	5 12 19 26	3 10 17 24 31	7 14 21 28	5 12 19 26
F	6 13 20 27	4 11 18 25	1 8 15 22 29	6 13 20 27
S	7 14 21 28	5 12 19 26	2 9 16 23 30	7 14 21 28
S	1 8 15 22 29	6 13 20 27	3 10 17 24	1 8 15 22 29

4

	January	February	March	April
M	6 13 20 27	3 10 17 24	3 10 17 24 31	7 14 21 28
T	7 14 21 28	4 11 18 25	4 11 18 25	1 8 15 22 29
W	1 8 15 22 29	5 12 19 26	5 12 19 26	2 9 16 23 30
T	2 9 16 23 30	6 13 20 27	6 13 20 27	3 10 17 24
F	3 10 17 24 31	7 14 21 28	7 14 21 28	4 11 18 25
S	4 11 18 25	1 8 15 22	1 8 15 22 29	5 12 19 26
S	5 12 19 26	2 9 16 23	2 9 16 23 30	6 13 20 27

	May	June	July	August
M	5 12 19 26	2 9 16 23 30	7 14 21 28	4 11 18 25
T	6 13 20 27	3 10 17 24	1 8 15 22 29	5 12 19 26
W	7 14 21 28	4 11 18 25	2 9 16 23 30	6 13 20 27
T	1 8 15 22 29	5 12 19 26	3 10 17 24 31	7 14 21 28
F	2 9 16 23 30	6 13 20 27	4 11 18 25	1 8 15 22 29
S	3 10 17 24 31	7 14 21 28	5 12 19 26	2 9 16 23 30
S	4 11 18 25	1 8 15 22 29	6 13 20 27	3 10 17 24 31

	September	October	November	December
M	1 8 15 22 29	6 13 20 27	3 10 17 24	1 8 15 22 29
T	2 9 16 23 30	7 14 21 28	4 11 18 25	2 9 16 23 30
W	3 10 17 24	1 8 15 22 29	5 12 19 26	3 10 17 24 31
T	4 11 18 25	2 9 16 23 30	6 13 20 27	4 11 18 25
F	5 12 19 26	3 10 17 24 31	7 14 21 28	5 12 19 26
S	6 13 20 27	4 11 18 25	1 8 15 22 29	6 13 20 27
S	7 14 21 28	5 12 19 26	2 9 16 23 30	7 14 21 28

5

	January	February	March	April
M	5 12 19 26	2 9 16 23	2 9 16 23 30	6 13 20 27
T	6 13 20 27	3 10 17 24	3 10 17 24 31	7 14 21 28
W	7 14 21 28	4 11 18 25	4 11 18 25	1 8 15 22 29
T	1 8 15 22 29	5 12 19 26	5 12 19 26	2 9 16 23 30
F	2 9 16 23 30	6 13 20 27	6 13 20 27	3 10 17 24
S	3 10 17 24 31	7 14 21 28	7 14 21 28	4 11 18 25
S	4 11 18 25	1 8 15 22	1 8 15 22 29	5 12 19 26

	May	June	July	August
M	4 11 18 25	1 8 15 22 29	6 13 20 27	3 10 17 24 31
T	5 12 19 26	2 9 16 23 30	7 14 21 28	4 11 18 25
W	6 13 20 27	3 10 17 24	1 8 15 22 29	5 12 19 26
T	7 14 21 28	4 11 18 25	2 9 16 23 30	6 13 20 27
F	1 8 15 22 29	5 12 19 26	3 10 17 24 31	7 14 21 28
S	2 9 16 23 30	6 13 20 27	4 11 18 25	1 8 15 22 29
S	3 10 17 24 31	7 14 21 28	5 12 19 26	2 9 16 23 30

	September	October	November	December
M	7 14 21 28	5 12 19 26	2 9 16 23 30	7 14 21 28
T	1 8 15 22 29	6 13 20 27	3 10 17 24	1 8 15 22 29
W	2 9 16 23 30	7 14 21 28	4 11 18 25	2 9 16 23 30
T	3 10 17 24	1 8 15 22 29	5 12 19 26	3 10 17 24 31
F	4 11 18 25	2 9 16 23 30	6 13 20 27	4 11 18 25
S	5 12 19 26	3 10 17 24 31	7 14 21 28	5 12 19 26
S	6 13 20 27	4 11 18 25	1 8 15 22 29	6 13 20 27

6

	January	February	March	April
M	4 11 18 25	1 8 15 22	1 8 15 22 29	5 12 19 26
T	5 12 19 26	2 9 16 23	2 9 16 23 30	6 13 20 27
W	6 13 20 27	3 10 17 24	3 10 17 24 31	7 14 21 28
T	7 14 21 28	4 11 18 25	4 11 18 25	1 8 15 22 29
F	1 8 15 22 29	5 12 19 26	5 12 19 26	2 9 16 23 30
S	2 9 16 23 30	6 13 20 27	6 13 20 27	3 10 17 24
S	3 10 17 24 31	7 14 21 28	7 14 21 28	4 11 18 25

	May	June	July	August
M	3 10 17 24 31	7 14 21 28	5 12 19 26	2 9 16 23 30
T	4 11 18 25	1 8 15 22 29	6 13 20 27	3 10 17 24 31
W	5 12 19 26	2 9 16 23 30	7 14 21 28	4 11 18 25
T	6 13 20 27	3 10 17 24	1 8 15 22 29	5 12 19 26
F	7 14 21 28	4 11 18 25	2 9 16 23 30	6 13 20 27
S	1 8 15 22 29	5 12 19 26	3 10 17 24 31	7 14 21 28
S	2 9 16 23 30	6 13 20 27	4 11 18 25	1 8 15 22 29

	September	October	November	December
M	6 13 20 27	4 11 18 25	1 8 15 22 29	6 13 20 27
T	7 14 21 28	5 12 19 26	2 9 16 23 30	7 14 21 28
W	1 8 15 22 29	6 13 20 27	3 10 17 24	1 8 15 22 29
T	2 9 16 23 30	7 14 21 28	4 11 18 25	2 9 16 23 30
F	3 10 17 24	1 8 15 22 29	5 12 19 26	3 10 17 24 31
S	4 11 18 25	2 9 16 23 30	6 13 20 27	4 11 18 25
S	5 12 19 26	3 10 17 24 31	7 14 21 28	5 12 19 26

7

	January	February	March	April
M	3 10 17 24 31	7 14 21 28	7 14 21 28	4 11 18 25
T	4 11 18 25	1 8 15 22	1 8 15 22 29	5 12 19 26
W	5 12 19 26	2 9 16 23	2 9 16 23 30	6 13 20 27
T	6 13 20 27	3 10 17 24	3 10 17 24 31	7 14 21 28
F	7 14 21 28	4 11 18 25	4 11 18 25	1 8 15 22 29
S	1 8 15 22 29	5 12 19 26	5 12 19 26	2 9 16 23 30
S	2 9 16 23 30	6 13 20 27	6 13 20 27	3 10 17 24

	May	June	July	August
M	2 9 16 23 30	6 13 20 27	4 11 18 25	1 8 15 22 29
T	3 10 17 24 31	7 14 21 28	5 12 19 26	2 9 16 23 30
W	4 11 18 25	1 8 15 22 29	6 13 20 27	3 10 17 24 31
T	5 12 19 26	2 9 16 23 30	7 14 21 28	4 11 18 25
F	6 13 20 27	3 10 17 24	1 8 15 22 29	5 12 19 26
S	7 14 21 28	4 11 18 25	2 9 16 23 30	6 13 20 27
S	1 8 15 22 29	5 12 19 26	3 10 17 24 31	7 14 21 28

	September	October	November	December
M	5 12 19 26	3 10 17 24 31	7 14 21 28	5 12 19 26
T	6 13 20 27	4 11 18 25	1 8 15 22 29	6 13 20 27
W	7 14 21 28	5 12 19 26	2 9 16 23 30	7 14 21 28
T	1 8 15 22 29	6 13 20 27	3 10 17 24	1 8 15 22 29
F	2 9 16 23 30	7 14 21 28	4 11 18 25	2 9 16 23 30
S	3 10 17 24	1 8 15 22 29	5 12 19 26	3 10 17 24 31
S	4 11 18 25	2 9 16 23 30	6 13 20 27	4 11 18 25

8

	January	February	March	April
M	2 9 16 23 30	6 13 20 27	5 12 19 26	2 9 16 23 30
T	3 10 17 24 31	7 14 21 28	6 13 20 27	3 10 17 24
W	4 11 18 25	1 8 15 22 29	7 14 21 28	4 11 18 25
T	5 12 19 26	2 9 16 23	1 8 15 22 29	5 12 19 26
F	6 13 20 27	3 10 17 24	2 9 16 23 30	6 13 20 27
S	7 14 21 28	4 11 18 25	3 10 17 24 31	7 14 21 28
S	1 8 15 22 29	5 12 19 26	4 11 18 25	1 8 15 22 29

	May	June	July	August
M	7 14 21 28	4 11 18 25	2 9 16 23 30	6 13 20 27
T	1 8 15 22 29	5 12 19 26	3 10 17 24 31	7 14 21 28
W	2 9 16 23 30	6 13 20 27	4 11 18 25	1 8 15 22 29
T	3 10 17 24 31	7 14 21 28	5 12 19 26	2 9 16 23 30
F	4 11 18 25	1 8 15 22 29	6 13 20 27	3 10 17 24 31
S	5 12 19 26	2 9 16 23 30	7 14 21 28	4 11 18 25
S	6 13 20 27	3 10 17 24	1 8 15 22 29	5 12 19 26

	September	October	November	December
M	3 10 17 24	1 8 15 22 29	5 12 19 26	3 10 17 24 31
T	4 11 18 25	2 9 16 23 30	6 13 20 27	4 11 18 25
W	5 12 19 26	3 10 17 24 31	7 14 21 28	5 12 19 26
T	6 13 20 27	4 11 18 25	1 8 15 22 29	6 13 20 27
F	7 14 21 28	5 12 19 26	2 9 16 23 30	7 14 21 28
S	1 8 15 22 29	6 13 20 27	3 10 17 24	1 8 15 22 29
S	2 9 16 23 30	7 14 21 28	4 11 18 25	2 9 16 23 30

9

	January	February	March	April
M	1 8 15 22 29	5 12 19 26	4 11 18 25	1 8 15 22 29
T	2 9 16 23 30	6 13 20 27	5 12 19 26	2 9 16 23 30
W	3 10 17 24 31	7 14 21 28	6 13 20 27	3 10 17 24
T	4 11 18 25	1 8 15 22 29	7 14 21 28	4 11 18 25
F	5 12 19 26	2 9 16 23	1 8 15 22 29	5 12 19 26
S	6 13 20 27	3 10 17 24	2 9 16 23 30	6 13 20 27
S	7 14 21 28	4 11 18 25	3 10 17 24 31	7 14 21 28

	May	June	July	August
M	6 13 20 27	3 10 17 24	1 8 15 22 29	5 12 19 26
T	7 14 21 28	4 11 18 25	2 9 16 23 30	6 13 20 27
W	1 8 15 22 29	5 12 19 26	3 10 17 24 31	7 14 21 28
T	2 9 16 23 30	6 13 20 27	4 11 18 25	1 8 15 22 29
F	3 10 17 24 31	7 14 21 28	5 12 19 26	2 9 16 23 30
S	4 11 18 25	1 8 15 22 29	6 13 20 27	3 10 17 24 31
S	5 12 19 26	2 9 16 23 30	7 14 21 28	4 11 18 25

	September	October	November	December
M	2 9 16 23 30	7 14 21 28	4 11 18 25	2 9 16 23 30
T	3 10 17 24	1 8 15 22 29	5 12 19 26	3 10 17 24 31
W	4 11 18 25	2 9 16 23 30	6 13 20 27	4 11 18 25
T	5 12 19 26	3 10 17 24 31	7 14 21 28	5 12 19 26
F	6 13 20 27	4 11 18 25	1 8 15 22 29	6 13 20 27
S	7 14 21 28	5 12 19 26	2 9 16 23 30	7 14 21 28
S	1 8 15 22 29	6 13 20 27	3 10 17 24	1 8 15 22 29

10

	January	February	March	April
M	7 14 21 28	4 11 18 25	3 10 17 24 31	7 14 21 28
T	1 8 15 22 29	5 12 19 26	4 11 18 25	1 8 15 22 29
W	2 9 16 23 30	6 13 20 27	5 12 19 26	2 9 16 23 30
T	3 10 17 24 31	7 14 21 28	6 13 20 27	3 10 17 24
F	4 11 18 25	1 8 15 22 29	7 14 21 28	4 11 18 25
S	5 12 19 26	2 9 16 23	1 8 15 22 29	5 12 19 26
S	6 13 20 27	3 10 17 24	2 9 16 23 30	6 13 20 27

	May	June	July	August
M	5 12 19 26	2 9 16 23 30	7 14 21 28	4 11 18 25
T	6 13 20 27	3 10 17 24	1 8 15 22 29	5 12 19 26
W	7 14 21 28	4 11 18 25	2 9 16 23 30	6 13 20 27
T	1 8 15 22 29	5 12 19 26	3 10 17 24 31	7 14 21 28
F	2 9 16 23 30	6 13 20 27	4 11 18 25	1 8 15 22 29
S	3 10 17 24 31	7 14 21 28	5 12 19 26	2 9 16 23 30
S	4 11 18 25	1 8 15 22 29	6 13 20 27	3 10 17 24 31

	September	October	November	December
M	1 8 15 22 29	6 13 20 27	3 10 17 24	1 8 15 22 29
T	2 9 16 23 30	7 14 21 28	4 11 18 25	2 9 16 23 30
W	3 10 17 24	1 8 15 22 29	5 12 19 26	3 10 17 24 31
T	4 11 18 25	2 9 16 23 30	6 13 20 27	4 11 18 25
F	5 12 19 26	3 10 17 24 31	7 14 21 28	5 12 19 26
S	6 13 20 27	4 11 18 25	1 8 15 22 29	6 13 20 27
S	7 14 21 28	5 12 19 26	2 9 16 23 30	7 14 21 28

11

	January	February	March	April
M	6 13 20 27	3 10 17 24	2 9 16 23 30	6 13 20 27
T	7 14 21 28	4 11 18 25	3 10 17 24 31	7 14 21 28
W	1 8 15 22 29	5 12 19 26	4 11 18 25	1 8 15 22 29
T	2 9 16 23 30	6 13 20 27	5 12 19 26	2 9 16 23 30
F	3 10 17 24 31	7 14 21 28	6 13 20 27	3 10 17 24
S	4 11 18 25	1 8 15 22 29	7 14 21 28	4 11 18 25
S	5 12 19 26	2 9 16 23	1 8 15 22 29	5 12 19 26

	May	June	July	August
M	4 11 18 25	1 8 15 22 29	6 13 20 27	3 10 17 24 31
T	5 12 19 26	2 9 16 23 30	7 14 21 28	4 11 18 25
W	6 13 20 27	3 10 17 24	1 8 15 22 29	5 12 19 26
T	7 14 21 28	4 11 18 25	2 9 16 23 30	6 13 20 27
F	1 8 15 22 29	5 12 19 26	3 10 17 24 31	7 14 21 28
S	2 9 16 23 30	6 13 20 27	4 11 18 25	1 8 15 22 29
S	3 10 17 24 31	7 14 21 28	5 12 19 26	2 9 16 23 30

	September	October	November	December
M	7 14 21 28	5 12 19 26	2 9 16 23 30	7 14 21 28
T	1 8 15 22 29	6 13 20 27	3 10 17 24	1 8 15 22 29
W	2 9 16 23 30	7 14 21 28	4 11 18 25	2 9 16 23 30
T	3 10 17 24	1 8 15 22 29	5 12 19 26	3 10 17 24 31
F	4 11 18 25	2 9 16 23 30	6 13 20 27	4 11 18 25
S	5 12 19 26	3 10 17 24 31	7 14 21 28	5 12 19 26
S	6 13 20 27	4 11 18 25	1 8 15 22 29	6 13 20 27

12

	January	February	March	April
M	5 12 19 26	2 9 16 23	1 8 15 22 29	5 12 19 26
T	6 13 20 27	3 10 17 24	2 9 16 23 30	6 13 20 27
W	7 14 21 28	4 11 18 25	3 10 17 24 31	7 14 21 28
T	1 8 15 22 29	5 12 19 26	4 11 18 25	1 8 15 22 29
F	2 9 16 23 30	6 13 20 27	5 12 19 26	2 9 16 23 30
S	3 10 17 24 31	7 14 21 28	6 13 20 27	3 10 17 24
S	4 11 18 25	1 8 15 22 29	7 14 21 28	4 11 18 25

	May	June	July	August
M	3 10 17 24 31	7 14 21 28	5 12 19 26	2 9 16 23 30
T	4 11 18 25	1 8 15 22 29	6 13 20 27	3 10 17 24 31
W	5 12 19 26	2 9 16 23 30	7 14 21 28	4 11 18 25
T	6 13 20 27	3 10 17 24	1 8 15 22 29	5 12 19 26
F	7 14 21 28	4 11 18 25	2 9 16 23 30	6 13 20 27
S	1 8 15 22 29	5 12 19 26	3 10 17 24 31	7 14 21 28
S	2 9 16 23 30	6 13 20 27	4 11 18 25	1 8 15 22 29

	September	October	November	December
M	6 13 20 27	4 11 18 25	1 8 15 22 29	6 13 20 27
T	7 14 21 28	5 12 19 26	2 9 16 23 30	7 14 21 28
W	1 8 15 22 29	6 13 20 27	3 10 17 24	1 8 15 22 29
T	2 9 16 23 30	7 14 21 28	4 11 18 25	2 9 16 23 30
F	3 10 17 24	1 8 15 22 29	5 12 19 26	3 10 17 24 31
S	4 11 18 25	2 9 16 23 30	6 13 20 27	4 11 18 25
S	5 12 19 26	3 10 17 24 31	7 14 21 28	5 12 19 26

13

	January	February	March	April
M	4 11 18 25	1 8 15 22 29	7 14 21 28	4 11 18 25
T	5 12 19 26	2 9 16 23	1 8 15 22 29	5 12 19 26
W	6 13 20 27	3 10 17 24	2 9 16 23 30	6 13 20 27
T	7 14 21 28	4 11 18 25	3 10 17 24 31	7 14 21 28
F	1 8 15 22 29	5 12 19 26	4 11 18 25	1 8 15 22 29
S	2 9 16 23 30	6 13 20 27	5 12 19 26	2 9 16 23 30
S	3 10 17 24 31	7 14 21 28	6 13 20 27	3 10 17 24

	May	June	July	August
M	2 9 16 23 30	6 13 20 27	4 11 18 25	1 8 15 22 29
T	3 10 17 24 31	7 14 21 28	5 12 19 26	2 9 16 23 30
W	4 11 18 25	1 8 15 22 29	6 13 20 27	3 10 17 24 31
T	5 12 19 26	2 9 16 23 30	7 14 21 28	4 11 18 25
F	6 13 20 27	3 10 17 24	1 8 15 22 29	5 12 19 26
S	7 14 21 28	4 11 18 25	2 9 16 23 30	6 13 20 27
S	1 8 15 22 29	5 12 19 26	3 10 17 24 31	7 14 21 28

	September	October	November	December
M	5 12 19 26	3 10 17 24 31	7 14 21 28	5 12 19 26
T	6 13 20 27	4 11 18 25	1 8 15 22 29	6 13 20 27
W	7 14 21 28	5 12 19 26	2 9 16 23 30	7 14 21 28
T	1 8 15 22 29	6 13 20 27	3 10 17 24	1 8 15 22 29
F	2 9 16 23 30	7 14 21 28	4 11 18 25	2 9 16 23 30
S	3 10 17 24	1 8 15 22 29	5 12 19 26	3 10 17 24 31
S	4 11 18 25	2 9 16 23 30	6 13 20 27	4 11 18 25

14

	January	February	March	April
M	3 10 17 24 31	7 14 21 28	6 13 20 27	3 10 17 24
T	4 11 18 25	1 8 15 22 29	7 14 21 28	4 11 18 25
W	5 12 19 26	2 9 16 23	1 8 15 22 29	5 12 19 26
T	6 13 20 27	3 10 17 24	2 9 16 23 30	6 13 20 27
F	7 14 21 28	4 11 18 25	3 10 17 24 31	7 14 21 28
S	1 8 15 22 29	5 12 19 26	4 11 18 25	1 8 15 22 29
S	2 9 16 23 30	6 13 20 27	5 12 19 26	2 9 16 23 30

	May	June	July	August
M	1 8 15 22 29	5 12 19 26	3 10 17 24 31	7 14 21 28
T	2 9 16 23 30	6 13 20 27	4 11 18 25	1 8 15 22 29
W	3 10 17 24 31	7 14 21 28	5 12 19 26	2 9 16 23 30
T	4 11 18 25	1 8 15 22 29	6 13 20 27	3 10 17 24 31
F	5 12 19 26	2 9 16 23 30	7 14 21 28	4 11 18 25
S	6 13 20 27	3 10 17 24	1 8 15 22 29	5 12 19 26
S	7 14 21 28	4 11 18 25	2 9 16 23 30	6 13 20 27

	September	October	November	December
M	4 11 18 25	2 9 16 23 30	6 13 20 27	4 11 18 25
T	5 12 19 26	3 10 17 24 31	7 14 21 28	5 12 19 26
W	6 13 20 27	4 11 18 25	1 8 15 22 29	6 13 20 27
T	7 14 21 28	5 12 19 26	2 9 16 23 30	7 14 21 28
F	1 8 15 22 29	6 13 20 27	3 10 17 24	1 8 15 22 29
S	2 9 16 23 30	7 14 21 28	4 11 18 25	2 9 16 23 30
S	3 10 17 24	1 8 15 22 29	5 12 19 26	3 10 17 24 31

M3: Table of Religious Festivals

2009		
☬	Birthday of Guru Gobind Singh	January 5
✝	Ash Wednesday	February 25
☪	Mawlid	March 9
✡	Purim	March 10
☬	Hola Mohalla	March 11
ॐ	Holi	March 11
✡	Passover	April 9
✝	Good Friday	April 10
✝	Easter Sunday	April 12
✝	Easter Monday	April 13
☬	Baisakhi Day	April 13
✝	Ascension Day	May 21
✡	Shavuot	May 29
✝	Pentecost	May 31
☪	Ramadan begins	August 22
✡	Rosh Hashanah	September 19
☪	Eid al-Fitr	September 21
ॐ	Dasarah	September 28
✡	Yom Kippur	September 28
✡	Succot	October 3
ॐ	Diwali	October 17
☬	Birthday of Guru Nanak (lunar calendar)	November 2
☪	Eid al-Adha	November 28
✡	Chanukah	December 12
☪	Hijra – New Year	December 18
✝	Christmas Day	December 25
☪	Ashura	December 27

2010		
☬	Birthday of Guru Gobind Singh	January 5
✝	Ash Wednesday	February 17
☪	Mawlid	February 26
✡	Purim	February 28
☬	Hola Mohalla	March 1
ॐ	Holi	March 1
✡	Passover	March 30
✝	Good Friday	April 2
✝	Easter Sunday	April 4
✝	Easter Monday	April 5
☬	Baisakhi Day	April 13
☬	Birthday of Guru Nanak	April 14
✝	Ascension Day	May 13
✡	Shavuot	May 19
✝	Pentecost	May 23
☪	Ramadan begins	August 12
✡	Rosh Hashanah	September 9
☪	Eid al-Fitr	September 10
ॐ	Dasarah	October 9
✡	Yom Kippur	September 18
✡	Succot	September 22
ॐ	Diwali	November 5
☪	Eid al-Adha	November 17
✡	Chanukah	December 2
☪	Hijra – New Year	December 7
☪	Ashura	December 16
✝	Christmas Day	December 25

2011		
☬	Birthday of Guru Gobind Singh	January 5
☪	Mawlid-al-Nabi	February 15
✝	Ash Wednesday	March 9
ॐ	Holi	March 19
✡	Purim	March 20
☬	Hola Mohalla	March 20
☬	Baisakhi Day	April 14
✡	Passover	April 19
✝	Good Friday	April 22
✝	Easter Sunday	April 24
✝	Easter Monday	April 25
✝	Ascension Day	June 2
✡	Shavuot	June 8
✝	Pentecost	June 12
☪	Ramadan begins	August 1
☪	Eid al-Fitr	August 30
✡	Rosh Hashanah	September 29
ॐ	Dasarah	October 6
✡	Yom Kippur	October 8
✡	Succot	October 13
ॐ	Diwali	October 26
☪	Eid al-Adha	November 6
☬	Birthday of Guru Nanak	November 10
☪	Hijra – New year	November 26
☪	Ashurah	December 5
✡	Chanukah	December 21
✝	Christmas Day	December 25

✝ Christian
ॐ Hindu
✡ Jewish
☪ Muslim
☬ Sikh

Note: all Islamic and Jewish holidays begin at sundown on the preceding day.

M4: Medical reference intervals and scales

Haematology – reference intervals

Measurement		Reference interval
White cell count		$4.0–11.0 \times 10^9/l$
Red cell count –	Male:	$4.5–6.5 \times 10^{12}/l$
	Female:	$3.9–5.6 \times 10^{12}/l$
Haemoglobin –	Male:	13.5–18.0g/dl
	Female:	11.5–16.0g/dl
Platelet count		$150.0–400.0 \times 10^9/l$
Erythrocyte sedimentation rate (ESR) –	Male:	Up to age in years divided by 2.
	Female:	Up to (age in years plus 10) divided by 2.
Prothrombin time (factors II, VII, X)		10–14 seconds
Activated partial thromboplastin time (VIII, IX, XI, XII)		35–45 seconds

Proposed therapeutic ranges for prothrombin time (British Society for Haematology guidelines on oral anticoagulants, 1984)

British ratio (INR)	Clinical state
2.0–2.5	Prophylaxis of deep vein thrombosis including high risk surgery (e.g. for fractured femur).
2.5–3.0	Treatment of deep vein thrombosis, pulmonary embolism, transient ischaemic attacks.
3.0–4.5	Recurrent deep vein thrombosis and pulmonary embolism; arterial disease including myocardial infarction; arterial grafts; cardiac prosthetic valves and grafts.

Cerebrospinal fluid – reference intervals

Opening pressure (mmCSF)	Infants: < 80; children: < 90; adults: < 210

Substance	Reference interval
Glucose	3.3–4.4 mmol/l or $\geq 2/3$ of plasma glucose
Chloride	122–128 mmol/l
Lactate	< 2.8 mmol/l

Biochemistry – reference intervals

Substance	Specimen	Reference Interval
Albumin	P	*35–50 g/l
α-amylase	P	0–180 Somogyi U/dl
Bicarbonate	P	*24–30 mmol/l
Calcium (ionised)	P	1.0–1.25 mmol/l
Calcium (total)	P	*2.12–2.65 mmol/l
Chloride	P	95–105 mmol/l
Cholesterol	P	3.9–7.8 mmol/l
Creatinine	P	*70–150 mmol/l
Glucose (fasting)	P	3.5–5.5 mmol/l
Glycosylated haemoglobin	B	5–8%
Phosphate	P	0.8–1.45 mmol/l
Potassium	P	3.5–5.0 mmol/l
Protein (total)	P	60–80 g/l
Sodium	P	*135–145 mmol/l
Urea	P	*2.5–6.7 mmol/l

Key: P = plasma; B = whole blood

*Reference intervals for these substances differ in pregnancy. Reference intervals in pregnancy are not reproduced here.

Arterial blood gases – reference intervals

pH:	7.35–7.45
PaO_2:	> 10.6 kPa
$PaCO_2$:	4.7–6.0 kPa
Base excess	± 2 mmol/l

NB: 7.6 mmHg = 1 kPa (atmospheric pressure = 100 kPa)

Apgar scoring chart

A baby's condition is assessed at 1 and 5 minutes after birth by means of the Apgar score. This system observes five signs. A score of nought, one or two is awarded for each sign.

Sign	0	1	2
Heart rate	Absent	Slow (below 100)	Over 100
Respiratory effort	Absent	Weak cry, hypoventilation	Good cry
Muscle tone	Limp	Some flexion of extremities	Well flexed
Reflex irritability	No response	Some motion	Cry
Colour	Blue, pale	Body pink, extremities blue	Completely pink

NB: An Apgar score of 10 represents optimal condition. A score of 3 or less indicates a markedly asphyxiated infant.

Glasgow coma scale

Three types of response are assessed:

	Score	
Best motor response	6	Obeys commands
	5	Localises to pain
	4	Flexion/withdrawal to pain
	3	Abnormal flexion
	2	Abnormal extension
	1	None
Best verbal response	5	Oriented
	4	Confused
	3	Inappropriate words
	2	Incomprehensible sounds
	1	None
Eye opening	4	Spontaneously
	3	To speech
	2	To pain
	1	None

The overall score is the sum of the scores in each area, *e.g.* no response to pain + no verbal response + no eye opening = 3.

In severe injury the score is 8 or under.
In moderate injury the score is 9–12.
In minor injury the score is 13–15.

PULHHEEMS rating

This is a system of physical and mental grading used by all three branches of the British Armed Forces. It is taken from the Joint Services publication JSP 346 which is issued to all Service and civilian medical practitioners required to examine applicants for entry to the Armed Forces. It is carried out on new recruits, and repeated at five-yearly intervals after the age of 30. After the age of 50, it is performed biennially.

PULHHEEMS is an abbreviation for the factors to be tested. These include:

P	Physique
U	Upper limbs
L	Locomotion – i.e. lower limbs and back
H	Hearing in the left ear
H	Hearing in the right ear
E	Visual acuity – left eye
E	Visual acuity – right eye
M	Mental function
S	Stability (emotional)

The maximum score is 8 (excellent) and the minimum 1 (unfit for service). On the form, this appears in a table as follows (Lord Nelson taken as an example):

P	U	L	H	H	E	E	M	S
8	4	8	8	8	8	1	8	8

M4: FDI World Dental Federation notation

FDI Two-Digit Notation

Permanent Teeth

upper right								upper left							
18	17	16	15	14	13	12	11	21	22	23	24	25	26	27	28
48	47	46	45	44	43	43	41	31	32	33	34	35	36	37	38
lower right								lower left							

Deciduous teeth (baby teeth)

upper right					upper left				
55	54	53	52	51	61	62	63	64	65
85	84	83	82	81	71	72	73	74	75
lower right					lower left				

Codes, names and usual number of roots

Codes		Names	Usual number of roots
11	21	maxillary central incisor	1
41	31	mandibular central incisor	1
12	22	maxillary lateral incisor	1
42	32	mandibular lateral incisor	1
13	23	maxillary canine	1
43	33	mandibular canine	1
14	24	maxillary first premolar	2
44	34	mandibular first premolar	1
15	25	maxillary second premolar	1
45	35	mandibular second premolar	1
16	26	maxillary first molar	3
46	36	mandibular first molar	2
17	27	maxillary second molar	3
47	37	mandibular second molar	2
18	28	maxillary third premolar	3
48	38	mandibular third premolar	2

How the codes are constructed

Syntax: <quadrant code><tooth code>

Quadrant codes

1	upper right
2	upper left
3	lower left
4	lower right

Tooth codes

1	central incisors
2	lateral incisors
3	canines
4	1st premolars
5	2nd premolars
6	1st molars
7	2nd molars
8	3rd molars

M5 : Websites

Useful web sites

Site	Address
Acts of Parliament	*www.opsi.gov.uk/acts.htm*
Australasian Legal Information Institute	*www.austlii.edu.au*
Bank of England	*www.bankofengland.co.uk*
Bar Council	*www.barcouncil.org.uk*
British and Irish Legal Information Institute	*www.bailii.org*
CGT Indexation Allowance	*www.number7.demon.co.uk/cgt/allow.htm*
Child Support Agency	*www.csa.gov.uk*
Social Security and Child Support Commissioners' Decisions	*www.osscsc.gov.uk/decisions/decisions.htm*
Companies House	*www.companies-house.gov.uk*
Her Majesty's Court Service	*www.hmcourts-service.gov.uk/*
Crossroads Caring for Carers	*www.crossroads-wirral.org.uk*
Service Legal Information Portal	*www.hmcourts-service.gov.uk/elis/index.htm*
Delia Venables Legal Resources	*www.venables.co.uk*
DCA Human Rights site	*www.dca.gov.uk/hract/hramenu.htm*
Department of Health Social Security (Press Releases)	*www.gov.im/dhss/*
Electronic Share Information (iii)	*www.iii.co.uk*
European Court of Human Rights	*www.echr.coe.int*
Financial Times	*www.ft.com*
Government Actuary's Department	*www.gad.gov.uk*
Government Information Service	*www.direct.gov.uk*
Hague Conference on Private International Law	*www.hcch.net/index_en.php*
Hague Convention on Child Abduction	*www.hcch.e-vision.nl/index_en.php?act=text.display&tid=21*
Hansard: House of Commons Debates	*www.publications.parliament.uk/pa/cm/cmhansrd.htm*
House of Lords Debates	*www.parliament.the-stationery-office.co.uk/pa/ld/ldhansrd.htm*
H.M. Land Registry	*www.landreg.gov.uk*
H.M.S.O.	*www.opsi.gov.uk*
Home Office Human Rights Unit	*www.nationalarchives.gov.uk/ERO/records/ho415/hract/hramenu.htm*
House of Commons	*www.parliament.uk/about_commons/about_commons.CFM*
House of Lords	*www.parliament.uk/about-lords/about-lords.cfm*
Judgments	*www.privy-council.org.uk/output/Page31.asp*
House Price Indices (Halifax)	*www.halifax.co.uk*
Information for Lawyers	*www.infolaw.co.uk*
Inland Revenue	*www.hmrc.gov.uk/home.htm*
Law Society	*www.lawsociety.org.uk*
Legal Services Commission	*www.legalservices.gov.uk/*
Life Assurance quotations	*www.royalsunalliance.co.uk*
Ministry of Justice	*www.justice.gov.uk*
National Savings & Investments	*www.nsandi.com/*
Official Solicitor and Public Trustee Office	*www.officialsolicitor.gov.uk/index.htm*
Pension annuity quotes	*www.annuity-bureau.co.uk*
RPI (full table)	*www.devon.gov.uk/dris/economic/retprice.html*
Smith Bernal (transcripts of judgments)	*www.smithbernal.com*
The Stationery Office	*www.tso.co.uk*
Statutory Instruments	*www.opsi.gov.uk/stat.htm*
Sweet & Maxwell	*www.sweetandmaxwell.co.uk*
The Times	*www.timesonline.co.uk*
UK Parliament	*www.parliament.uk*
Upmystreet (regional data)	*www.upmystreet.com*

M6: Addresses of useful organisations

Part 1 – Medical

British Medical Association

BMA House
Tavistock Square
London WC1H 9JP
Tel: 020 7387 4499
Fax: 020 7383 6400
Website: www.bma.org.uk

General Medical Council

Regent's Place
350 Euston Road
London NW1 3JN
Tel: 0845 357 8001
Fax: 020 7189 5401
Email: gmc@gmc-uk.org

General Dental Council

37 Wimpole Street
London W1G 8DQ
Tel: 020 7887 3800
Fax: 020 7224 3294
Email: CAIT@gdc-uk.org

General Optical Council

41 Harley Street
London W1G 8DJ
Tel: 020 7580 3898
Fax: 020 7436 3525
Email: goc@optical.org

Accident and emergency

British Association for Accident and Emergency Medicine
The Royal College of Surgeons of England
35–43 Lincoln's Inn Fields
London WC2A 3PE
Tel: 020 7405 3474
Fax: 020 7405 0318
Email: baem1@emergencymedicine.uk.net

Accidents

Royal Society for the Prevention of Accidents (RoSPA)
RoSPA House
Edgbaston Park
353 Bristol Road
Edgbaston
Birmingham B5 7ST
Tel: 0121 248 2000
Fax: 0121 248 2001
Email: help@rospa.co.uk

Alcoholism

Medical Council on Alcohol
5 St. Andrew's Place
Regent's Park
London NW1 4LB
Tel: 020 7487 4445
Fax: 020 7935 4479
Email: mca@medicouncilalcol.demon.co.uk

Alzheimer's disease

Alzheimer's Disease Society
Devon House
58 St Katherine's Way
London E1W 1X
Tel: 020 7423 3500
Fax: 020 7306 0808
Email: enquiries@alzheimers.org.uk
Website: www.alzheimers.org.uk

Anaesthetics

Obstetric Anaesthetists' Association
PO Box 3219 Barnes
London SW13 9XR
Tel: 020 8741 1311
Fax: 020 8741 0611
Email: secretariat@oaa-anaes.ac.uk

Asthma

National Asthma Campaign
Summit House
70 Wilson Street
London EC2A 2DB
Tel: 020 7786 4900
Fax: 020 7256 6075
Email: info@asthma.org.uk

Bereavement

Child Bereavement Trust
Aston House
West Wycombe
High Wycombe
Buckinghamshire HP14 3AG
Tel: 01494 446 648
Fax: 01494 440 057
Email: enquiries@childbereavement.org.uk

The Compassionate Friends
(counselling for bereaved parents)
National Office
53 North Street
Bristol BS3 1EN
Tel: 08451 203785
Fax: 08451 203786
Email: info@tcf.org.uk

Biochemistry

Biochemical Society
Third Floor, Eagle House
16 Procter Street
London WC1V 6NX
Tel: 020 7280 4100
Fax: 020 7280 4170
Email: genadmin@biochemistry.org
Website: www.biochemsoc.org.uk

Blindness

Royal National Institute of the Blind
105 Judd Street
London WC1H 9NE
Tel: 020 7388 1266
Fax: 020 7388 2034
Email: helpline@rnib.org.uk

Brain

Brain Research Trust
PO Box
Bury BL8 9EJ
Tel:
Fax:
Email: babichsecretary@hotmail.com

British Association of Brain Injury Case
Managers (BABICM)
PO Box 134
Cranbrook
TN17 9AA
Tel: 0700 2222 426

Centre for Brain Injury, Rehabilitation and
Development (BIRD)
The Old Coach House
Church Road, Eccleston
Chester CH4 9HT
Tel: 01244 678 629
Fax: 01244 538 723
Email: admin@b-i-r-d.org.uk

Brittle bone disease

Brittle Bone Society
Grant Patterson House
30 Guthrie Street
Dundee DD1 5BS
Tel: 01382 204 446
Fax: 01382 206 771
Email: bbs@brittlebone.org

Cancer

British Association of Cancer United Patients
(BACUP)
3 Bath Place
Rivington Street
London EC2A 3RJ
Tel: 020 7840 7840
Fax: 020 7840 7841

The Association for Cancer Surgery
Royal College of Surgeons
35–43 Lincoln's Inn Fields
London WC2A 3PE
Tel: 020 7405 5612
Fax: 020 7404 6574
Email: admin@baso.org.uk

CancerLink
11–21 North Down Street
London N1 9BN
Tel: 020 7833 2818
Fax: 020 7833 4963
Email: cancerlink@cancerlink.org.uk

Macmillan Cancer Relief
89 Albert Embankment
London SE1 7UQ
Tel: 020 7840 7840
Fax: 020 7840 7841
Email: cancerline@macmillan.org.uk

Cancer Research UK
P.O. Box 123
Lincoln's Inn Fields
London WC2A 3PX
Tel: 020 7121 6699
Fax: 020 7269 3100

Marie Curie Cancer Care
89 Albert Embankment
London SE1 7TP
Tel: 020 7599 7777
Fax: 020 7599 7708
Email: info@mariecurie.org.uk

Cardiology

British Cardiac Society
9 Fitzroy Square
London W1T 5HW
Tel: 020 7383 3887
Fax: 020 7388 0903
Email: enquiries@bcs.com

British Heart Foundation
14 Fitzhardinge Street
London W1H 6DH
Tel: 020 7935 0185
Fax: 020 7487 5820
Email: internet@bhfs.org.uk

Society of Cardiothoracic Surgeons of Great Britain & Northern Ireland
The Royal College of Surgeons
35–43 Lincoln's Inn Fields
London WC2A 3PE
Tel: 020 7869 6893
Fax: 020 7869 6890
Email: sctsadmin@scts.org

Childbirth

The Association for Post-Natal Illness
145 Dawes Road
London SW6 7EB
Tel: 020 7386 0868
Fax: 020 7386 8885
Email: info@apni.org

The National Childbirth Trust
Alexandra House
Oldham Terrace
London W3 6NH
Tel: 0870 770 3236
Fax: 0870 770 3237
Email: enquiries@nct.org.uk

Royal College of Midwives
15 Mansfield Street
London W1G 9NH
Tel: 020 7312 3535
Fax: 020 7312 3536
Email: info@rcm.org.uk

Stillbirth and Neonatal Death Society (SANDS)
28 Portland Place
London W1B 1LY
Tel: 020 7436 7940
Fax: 020 7436 3715
Email: support@UK-sands.org

Children

The National Association for Children with Lower Limb Abnormalities (STEPS)
Warrington Lane
Lymm
Cheshire WA13 OSA
Tel: 0871 717 0045
Fax: 0192 575 0270
Email: info@steps-charity.org.uk

Barnardo's
Tanners Lane
Barkingside
Ilford
Essex IG6 1QG
Tel: 020 8550 8822
Fax: 020 8551 6870
Website: www.barnardos.org.uk

Baby Life Support Systems (Bliss)
9 Holyrood Street
London SE1 2EL
Tel: 020 7378 1122
Fax: 020 7403 0673
Email: information@bliss.org.uk
Website: www.bliss.org.uk

Child Accident Prevention Trust
Canterbury Court
1–3 Brixton Road
London SW9 6DE
Tel: 020 7608 3828
Fax: 020 7608 3674
Email: safe@capt.org.uk

Child Poverty Action Group (CPAG)
94 White Lion Street
London N1 9PF
Tel: 020 7837 7979
Fax: 020 7837 6414
Email: staff@cpag.org.uk
Website: www.cpag.org.uk

(see also **Paediatric**)

Chiropody

Institute of Chiropodists & Podiatrists
27 Wright Street
Southport
Merseyside PR9 0TL
Tel: 01704 546 141
Fax: 01704 500 477
Email: secretary@iocp.org.uk
Website: www.iocp.org.uk

Society of Chiropodists & Podiatrists
1 Fellmonger's Pass
Tower Bridge Road
London SE1 3LY
Tel: 020 7234 8620
Fax: 0845 450 3721
Website: www.feetforlife.org

Colostomy

Colostomy Association
2 London Court, East Street
Reading RG1 4QL
Tel: 0118 939 1537
Email: cass@colostomyassociation.org.uk
Website: www.colostomyassociation.org.uk

Counselling

British Association for Counselling and Psychotherapy
BACP House
15 St John's Business Park
Lutterworth LE17 4HB
Tel: 01455 883300
Fax: 01455 550243
Email: bacp@bacp.co.uk

Cystic fibrosis

Cystic Fibrosis Trust
11 London Road
Bromley
Kent BR1 1BY
Tel: 020 8464 7211
Fax: 020 8313 0472
Email: enquiries@cftrust.org.uk
Website: www.cftrust.org.uk

Day surgery

British Association of Day Surgery
The Royal College of Surgeons
35–43 Lincoln's Inn Fields
London WC2A 3PE
Tel: 020 7973 0308
Fax: 020 7973 0314
Email: bads@bads.co.uk
Website: www.daysurgery.uk.org

Deafness

Royal Association in Aid of Deaf People
Walsingham Road
Colchester CO2 7BP
Tel: 0845 588 2525
Minicom: 0845 688 2527
Fax: 01206 769 755
Email: info@royaldeaf.org.uk

Royal National Institute for Deaf People
19–23 Featherstone Street
London EC1Y 8SL
Tel: 020 7296 8000
Minicom: 020 7296 8001
Fax: 020 7296 8199
Email: informationline@rnid.org.uk
Website: www.rnid.org.uk

Dentists

British Dental Association
64 Wimpole Street
London W1G 8YS
Tel: 020 7935 0875
Fax: 020 7487 5232
Email: enquiries@bda.org
Website: www.bda.org

Dermatology

British Association of Dermatologists
19 Fitzroy Square
London W1T 5HQ
Tel: 020 7383 0266
Fax: 020 7388 5263
Email: admin@bad.org.uk
Website: www.bad.org.uk

Development

British Association for Developmental Disabilities
5 Handsworth Drive
Great Barr
Birmingham B43 6ED
Tel/Fax: 0121 360 2027

Diabetes

Diabetes UK Central Office
Macleod House
10 Parkway
London NW1 7AA
Tel: 0845 120 2966
Fax: 020 7424 1001
Email: info@diabetes.org.uk

Diagnostics

Cellmark Diagnostics
PO Box 265
Abingdon OX14 1YX
Tel: 0800 036 2522
Fax: 01235 528 141
Email: cellmark@orchid.co.uk
Website: www.cellmark.co.uk

University Diagnostics Ltd
Queens Road
Teddington
Middx TW11 0NJ
Tel: 020 8943 8400
Email: udl@lgc.co.uk
Website: www.applegate.co.uk

Dietetics

British Dietetic Association
5th Floor Charles House
148–9 Great Charles Street
Queensway

Birmingham B3 3HT
Tel: 0121 200 8080
Fax: 0121 200 8081
Email: info@bda.uk.com
Website: www.bda.uk.com

British Nutrition Foundation
High Holborn House
52–54 High Holborn
London WC1V 6RQ
Tel: 020 7404 6504
Fax: 020 7404 6747
Email: postbox@nutrition.org.uk
Website: www.nutrition.org.uk

Digestion

Digestive Disorders CORE Foundation
3 Saint Andrew's Place
London NW1 4LB
Tel: 020 7486 0341
Fax: 020 7224 2012
Email: info@corecharity.org.uk
Website: www.corecharity.org.uk

Disability

Disabled Living Foundation
380–384 Harrow Road
London W9 2HU
Tel: 020 7289 6111
Fax: 020 7226 2922 [111]
Email: info@dlf.org.uk
Website: www.dlf.org.uk

Royal Association for Disability and Rehabilitation (RADAR)
12 City Forum
250 City Road
London EC1V 8AF
Tel: 020 7250 3222
Fax: 020 7250 0212
Email: radar@radar.org.uk
Website: www.radar.org.uk

Changing Faces

(Charity for Facially Disfigured People)
The Squire Centre
33–37 University Street
London WC1E 6JN
Tel: 0845 4500 275
Fax: 0845 4500 276
Email: info@changingfaces.org.uk
Website: www.changingfaces.org.uk

Down's Syndrome

Down's Syndrome Association (DSA)
Langdon Down Centre
2a Langdon Park
Teddington TW11 9PS
Tel: 0845 230 0372
Fax: 0845 230 0373
Email: info@downs-syndrome.org.uk

Drugs

Committee on Safety of Medicines (for adverse reaction reports)
10–2 Market Towers
1 Nine Elms Lane
London SW8 5NQ
Tel: 020 7210 3000
Fax: 020 7084 2353
Email: info@mhra.gsi.gov.uk
Website: www.mhra.gov.uk

Narcotics Abusers' Register
Chief Medical Officer
Home Office Drugs Branch
Queen Anne's Gate
London SW1H 9AT
Tel: 020 7273 3302

Dyslexia

Dyslexia Institute
Park House
Wick Road
Egham
Surrey TW20 0HH
Tel: 01784 222 300
Fax: 01784 222 333
Email: training@dyslexia-inst.org.uk
Website: www.dyslexia-inst.org.uk

Ear, nose and throat

British Association of Otorhinolaryngologists
ENT UK at The Royal College of Surgeons
35–43 Lincoln's Inn Fields
London WC2A 3PE
Tel: 020 7404 8373
Fax: 020 7404 4200
Email: info@entuk.org

(see also **Deafness**)

Elderly

British Geriatrics Society
Marjory Warren House
31 St John's Square
London EC1M 4DN
Tel: 020 7608 1369
Fax: 020 7608 1041
Email: general.information@bgs.org.uk

British Association for Service to the Elderly (BASE)
The Guildford Institute
Ward Street
Guildford GU1 4LH
Tel: 01483 451036
Fax: 01483 451034
Email: enquiries@base.org.uk

Endocrinology

Society for Endocrinology
22 Apex Court
Woodlands
Bradley Stoke
Bristol BS32 4JT
Tel: 01454 642 200
Fax: 01454 642 222
Email: info@endocrinology.org
Website: www.endocrinology.org.uk

Epilepsy

British Epilepsy Association
New Anstey House
Gate Way Drive
Yeadon
Leeds LS19 7XY
Tel: 0808 800 5050
Fax: 0113 391 0300
Email: epilepsy@epilepsy.org.uk
Website: www.epilepsy.org.uk

Forensic science

British Academy of Forensic Sciences
Anaesthetic Unit
Royal London Hospital
London E1 1BB
Tel: 020 7377 9201
Website: www.bafs.org.uk

Gastroenterology

British Society of Gastroenterology
3 Saint Andrew's Place
Regent's Park
London NW1 4LB
Tel: 020 7935 2815
Fax: 020 7487 3734
Email: bsg@mailbox.ulcc.ac.uk

Glaucoma

International Glaucoma Association
Woodcote House
15 Highpoint Business Village
Henwood
Ashford
Kent TN24 8DH
Tel: 01233 64 81 70
Fax: 01233 64 81 79
Email: info@iga.org.uk
Website: www.glaucomaassociation.com

General information

Health Information (will provide a wide range of health information for both doctors and their patients)
The Mapels
Level 2
The Lister Hospital
Coreys Mill Lane
Stevenage
Hertfordshire SG1 4AB
Tel: 0800 665544

Haematology

British Society for Haematology
100 White Lion Street
London N1 9PF
Tel: 020 7837 5813
Fax: 020 7713 0990
Email: info@b-s-h.org.uk

Haemophilia

The Haemophilia Society
First Floor
Petersham House
57a Hatton Garden
London EC1N 8JG
Tel: 020 7831 1020
Fax: 020 7405 4824
Email: info@haemophilia.org.uk
Website: www.haemophilia.org.uk

Hand surgery

British Society of Surgery of the Hand
Royal College of Surgeons of England
37–43 Lincoln's Inn Fields
London WC2A 3PE
Tel: 020 7831 5162
Fax: 020 7831 4041
Email: secretariat@bssh.ac.uk
Website: www.bssh.ac.uk

Head injuries

Headway (The Brain Injuries Association)
4 King Edward Court
King Edward Street
Nottingham
NG1 1EW
Tel: 0115 924 0800
Fax: 0115 958 4446
Email: enquiries@headway.org.uk
Website: www.headway.org.uk

Health visitors

Community Practitioners' and Health Visitors Association (Amicus/CPHVA)
33–37 Moreland Street
London EC1 8HA
Tel: 020 7505 3000
Website: www.msfcphva.org

Hysterectomy

Hysterectomy Association
Prospect House
Peverell Avenue East

Dorchester
Dorset OT1 3WE
Tel: 0844 357591
Fax: 01305 260676
Email: info@hysterectomy-association.org.uk

Injury

(See **Rehabilitation**)

Kidneys

National Kidney Federation
The Point, Coach Road
Shireoaks, Worksop
Nottinghamshire S81 8BW
Tel: 01909 487 795
Fax: 01909 481 723
Email: webmaster@kidney.org.uk

The National Kidney Research Fund
Kings Chambers
Priestgate
Peterborough PE1 1FG
Tel: 0845 070 7601
Email: info@kidneyresearch.uk.org
Website: www.kidneyresearch.uk.org

Lungs

(See **Thoracic**)

Lupus

Lupus U.K.
St James House
Eastern Road
Romford
Essex RM1 3NH
Tel: 01708 731 251
Fax: 01708 731 252
Email: headoffice@lupusuk.org.uk
Website: www.lupusuk.com

Maxillofacial surgery

(See **Oral**)

M.E.

Myalgic Encephalomyelitis Association
7 Apollo Office Court
Radclive Road, Gawcott
Buckinghamshire MK18 4DF
Tel: 0870 444 8233
Fax: 01280 821 602
Email: enquiries@meassociation.org.uk
Website: www.meassociation.org.uk

Medicine

Committee on Safety of Medicines
Market Towers
1 Nine Elms Lane
London SW8 5NQ
Tel: 020 7084 2000
Fax: 020 7084 2353
Email: info@mhra.gsi.gov.uk

Medical Society of London
Lettsom House
11 Chandos Street
London W1G 9EB
Tel: 020 7580 1043
Fax: 020 7580 5793

Medicines Commission
1 Nine Elms Lane
London SW8 5NQ
Tel: 020 7084 2000
Fax: 020 7084 2353
Email: info@mhra.gsi.gov.uk

The Royal Society of Medicine
1 Wimpole Street
London W1G 0AE
Tel: 020 7290 2900
Fax: 020 7290 2989
Website: www.ism.ac.uk

Meningitis

The National Meningitis Trust
Fern House
Bath Road
Stroud
Gloucestershire GL5 3TJ
Tel: 01453 768 000
Fax: 01453 768 001
Email: info@meningitis-trust.org.uk
Website: www.meningitis-trust.org

Menopause (Premature)

The Amarant Trust
80 Lambeth Road
London SE1 7PW
Tel: 01293 413 000 (Advice Line)
Website: www.amarantmenopausetrust.org.uk

Mental health

National Association for Mental Health (MIND)
Granta House
15/19 Broadway
London E15 4BQ
Tel: 020 8519 2122
Fax: 020 8522 1725
Email: contact@mind.org.uk
Website: www.mind.org.uk

Royal Society for Mentally Handicapped Children and Adults (MENCAP)
Mencap National Centre
123 Golden Lane
London EC1Y 0RT
Tel: 020 7454 0454
Fax: 020 7608 3254
Email: information@mencap.org.uk
Website: www.mencap.org.uk

Midwives

(See **Childbirth**)

Migraine

Migraine Trust
2nd Floor
55–56 Russell Square
London WC1B 4HP
Tel: 020 7436 1336
Fax: 020 7436 2880
Email: info@migrainenetrust.org
Website: www.migrainetrust.org

Motor Neurone Disease

Motor Neurone Disease Association
PO Box 246
Northampton NN1 2PR
Tel: 01604 250505
Tel: 08457 626262 (helpline)
Fax: 01604 638289/624726
Email: enquiries@mndassociation.org
Website: www.mindassociation.org

Multiple Sclerosis

Multiple Sclerosis Society of Great Britain & Northern Ireland
372 Edgware Road
London NW2 6ND
Tel: 020 8438 0700
Fax: 020 8438 0701
Email: info@mssociety.org.uk
Website: www.mssociety.org.uk

Muscular Dystrophy

Muscular Dystrophy Group
61 Southwark Street
London SE1 0HL
Tel: 020 7803 4800
Fax: 020 7401 3495
Email: info@muscular-dystrophy.org
Website: www.muscular-dystrophy.org

Narcolepsy

The Narcolepsy Association (U.K.)
50 Culver Street
Newent
Gloucestershire GL18 1DA
Tel: 0845 450 0399
Fax: 0845 777 3039
Email: info@narcolepsy.org.uk
Website: www.narcolepsy.org.uk

Neurology

Association of British Neurologists
Ormond House
27 Boswell Street
London WC1W 3JZ
Tel: 020 7405 4060
Fax: 020 7405 4070
Email: info@theabn.org
Website: www.theabn.org

Neurosurgery

Society of British Neurological Surgeons
35–43 Lincoln's Inn Fields
London WC21 3PE
Tel: 020 7869 6892
Fax: 020 7869 6890
Email: admin@sbns.freeserve.co.uk
Website: www.sbns.org.uk

Nursing

Royal College of Nursing of the United Kingdom
20 Cavendish Square
London W1G 0RN
Tel: 020 7409 3333
Fax: 020 7647 3435
Website: rcn.org.uk

BNA Care Assessment Services
Beaconsfield Close
Beaconsfield Road
Hatfield
Hertfordshire AL10 8YD
Tel: 01707 255 658
Fax: 01707 255 660
Website: www.bna.co.uk

Crossroads Caring for Carers

10 Regent Place
Rugby
Warwickshire CV21 2PN
Tel: 0845 450 0350
Fax: 01788 565 498
Email: communications@crossroads.org.uk
Website: www.crossroads.org.uk

Occupational medicine

Society of Occupational Medicine
6 Saint Andrew's Place
Regent's Park
London NW1 4LB
Tel: 020 7486 2641
Fax: 020 7486 0028
Email: admin@som.org.uk
Website: ww,som.org.uk

Occupational therapy

British Association of Occupational Therapists/
College of Occupational Therapists
106–114 Borough High Street
Southwark
London SE1 1LB
Tel: 020 7357 6480
Website: www.cot.co.uk

Oncology

(See **Cancer**)

Oral

British Association of Oral & Maxillofacial Surgeons
Royal College of Surgeons
35–43 Lincoln's Inn Fields
London WC2A 3PE
Tel: 020 7405 8074
Fax: 020 7430 9997
Email: office@baoms.org.uk
Website: www.baoms.org.uk

British Society for Oral Medicine
Dr David Felix
Glasgow Dental Hospital
378 Sauchiehall Street
Glasgow G2 3GZ
Tel: 0141 211 9654
Fax: 0141 353 2899
Email: enquiries@BSOM.org.uk
Website: www.bsom.org.uk

Orthopaedic

British Orthopaedic Association
Royal College of Surgeons
35–43 Lincoln's Inn Fields
London WC2A 3PE
Tel: 020 7405 6507
Fax: 020 7831 2676
Email: secretary@boa.ac.uk
Website: www.boa.ac.uk

Osteoporosis

National Osteoporosis Society
Camerton
Bath BA2 OPJ
Tel: 01761 471 771
Fax: 01761 471 104
Website: nos.org.uk
Email: info@nos.org.uk

Pain

The British Pain Society
Third Floor, Churchill House
35 Red Lion Square
London WC1R 4SG
Tel: 020 7631 8870
Fax: 020 7831 0859
Email: info@britishpainsociety.org
Website: www.britishpainsociety.org

National Back Pain Association
Backcare
16 Elmtree Road
Teddington
Middlesex TW11 8ST
Tel: 020 8977 5474
Fax: 020 8943 5318
Email: info@backcare.org.uk
Website: www.backcare.org.uk

Banstead Mobility Centre
Damson Way
Fountain Drive
Carshalton
Surrey SM5 4NR
Tel: 020 8770 1151
Fax: 020 8770 1211
Email: info@mobility-ge.com

Parkinson's disease

Parkinson's Disease Society of the United Kingdom Ltd
215 Vauxhall Bridge Road
London SW1V 1EJ
Tel: 020 7931 8080
Fax: 020 7233 9908
Email: enquiries@parkinsons.org.uk
Website: www.parkinsons.org.uk

Pathology

Pathological Society of Great Britain & Ireland
2 Carlton House Terrace
London SW1Y 5AF
Tel: 020 7976 1260
Fax: 020 7976 1267
Email: administrator@pathsoc.org.uk
Website: www.pathsoc.org

Royal College of Pathologists
2 Carlton House Terrace
London SW1Y 5AF
Tel: 020 7451 6700
Fax: 020 7451 6701
Email: info@rcpath.org

Patients

Patients Association
PO Box 935
Harrow HA1 3YJ
Tel: 020 8423 9111
Fax: 020 8423 9119
Email: mailbox@patients-association.com
Website: www.patients-association.org.uk

Physiotherapy

Chartered Society of Physiotherapy
14 Bedford Row
London WC1R 4ED
Tel: 020 7306 6666
Fax: 020 7306 6611
Email: csp@csphysio.org.uk
Website: www.csp.org.uk

Plastic surgery

British Association of Plastic Surgeons
The Royal College of Surgeons
35–43 Lincoln's Inn Fields
London WC2A 3PE
Tel: 020 7831 5161
Fax: 020 7831 4041
Email: secretariat@bapras.com
Website: www.bapras.co.uk

Polio

British Polio Fellowship
Ground Floor
Unit A
Eagle Office Centre
The Runway
South Ruislip
Middlesex HA4 6SE
Tel: 020 8842 4999
Fax: 020 8842 0555
Email: info@britishpolio.org
Website: www.britishpolio.org.uk

Post-natal illness

(See **Childbirth**)

Psoriasis

Psoriasis Association
Dick Coles House, 2 Queensbridge
Northampton NN4 7BF
Tel: 0845 676 0076
Fax: 01604 251621
Email: psoriasis-association.org.uk
Website: www.psoriasis-association.org.uk

Psychiatry

Royal College of Psychiatrists
17 Belgrave Square
London SW1X 8PG
Tel: 020 7235 2351
Fax: 020 7245 1231
Email: rcpsyche@rcpsych.ac.uk
Website: www.rcpsych.ac.uk

Psychology

British Psychological Society
Saint Andrew's House
48 Princess Road East
Leicester LE1 7DR
Tel: 0116 254 9568
Fax: 0116 227 1314
Email: enquiries@bps.org.uk

David McGlown
Clinical Psychologist Public Trust Office
Stewart House
24 Kingsway
London WC2B 6JX
Tel: 020 7269 7085

Psychotherapy

British Association of Psychotherapists
37 Mapesbury Road
London NW2 4HJ
Tel: 020 8452 0310
Fax: 020 8452 5182
Email: mail@bap-psychotherapy.org

Radiography and Radiology

Society and College of Radiographers
207 Providence Square
Mill Street
London SE1 2EW
Tel: 020 7740 7200
Fax: 020 7740 7204
Email: info@sor.org
Website: www.sor.org

Royal College of Radiologists
38 Portland Place
London W1B 4JQ
Tel: 020 7636 4432
Fax: 020 7323 3100
Email: enquiries@rcr.ac.uk
Website: www.rcr.ac.uk

Rehabilitation

British Society of Rehabilitation Medicine
c/o Royal College of Physicians
11 Saint Andrew's Place
London NW1 4LE
Tel: 01992 638 865
Fax: 01992 638 905
Email: admin@bsrm.co.uk
Website: www.bsrm.co.uk

REMEDI (Rehabilitation and Medical
Research Trust for Relief of Disability)
14 Crondace Road
London SW6 4BB
Tel: 01761 470 662
Fax: 01761 470 662
Email: g.coles-remedi@btinternet.com

The Injury Care Clinics Ltd
1 St George's Business Centre
St George's Square
Portsmouth PO1 3EY
Tel: 08700 501 710
Fax: 08700 501 717
Email: info@ticcs.co.uk

Research

Medical Research Society
3 Littleton Road
Harrow
Middlesex HA1 3SY
Tel: 020 8743 2030
Fax: 020 8846 7447

Rheumatology

British Society for Rheumatology
Bride House
18–20 Bride Lane
London EC4Y 8EE
Tel: 020 7842 0900
Fax: 020 7842 0901
Email: bsr@rheumatology.org.uk
Website: www.rheumatology.org.uk

Schizophrenia

National Schizophrenia Fellowship
Rethink
89 Albert Embankment
London SE1 7TP
Tel: 020 7840 3188
Fax:
Email: info@rethink.org

SCOPE

Scope (formerly The Spastics Society)
6 Market Road
London N7 9PW
Tel: 020 7619 7100
0808 8003333 (Helpline: 11am–9pm Mon–Fri, 2–6pm weekend)
Fax: 020 7619 7399
Email: response@scope.org.uk

Speech

Royal College of Speech & Language Therapists
White Hart Yard
London SE1 1NX
Tel: 020 7378 1200
Fax: 020 7403 7254
Email: info@rcslt.org
Website: www.rcslt.org

Association for all Speech-Impaired Children (AFASIC)
First Floor, 20 Bowling Green Lane
London EC1R 0BD
Tel: 020 7490 9410
Fax: 020 7251 2834
Email: info@afasic.org.uk
Website: www.afasic.org.uk

Spinal injuries

Spinal Injuries Association
SIA House
2 Trueman Place
Oldbrook
Milton Keynes MK6 3HH
Tel: 0845 678 6633
Fax: 0845 070 6911
Freephone Helpline: 0800 980 0501
Email: sia@spinal.co.uk

(See also **Back pain** under **Pain**)

Stroke

The Stroke Association
Stroke House
240 City Road
London EC1V 2PR
Tel: 020 7566 0300
Fax: 020 7490 2686
Email: info@stroke.org.uk
Website: www.stroke.org.uk

Torture

Medical Foundation for the Care of Victims of Torture
111 Isledon Road
London N7 7JW
Tel: 020 7697 7777
Fax: 020 7697 7739
Website: www.torturecare.org.uk

Thoracic

British Thoracic Society
17 Doughty Street
London WC1N 2PL
Tel: 020 7831 8778
Fax: 020 7831 8766
Email: bts@brit-thoracic.org.uk
Website: www.brit-thoracic.org.uk

British Lung Foundation
Lung Foundation House
73–75 Goswell Road
London EC1V 7ER
Tel: 08458 50 50 20
Email: blf@britishlungfoundation.com
Website: www.lunguk.org

Society of Cardiothoracic Surgeons of Great Britain & Ireland
35–43 Lincoln's Inn Fields
London WC2A 3PE
Tel: 020 7869 6893
Fax: 020 7869 6890
Email: sctsadmin@scts.org
Website: www.scts.org

(See also **Asthma**)

Transplants

UK Transplant
Fox Den Road
Stoke Gifford BS34 8RR
Tel: 0117 975 7575
Fax: 0117 975 7577
Email: enquiries@uktransplant.nhs.uk
Website: www.uktransplant.org.uk

Tropical Medicine

Liverpool School of Tropical Medicine
Pembroke Place
Liverpool L3 5QA
Tel: 0151 708 9393
Fax: 0151 708 8733
Website: www.liv.ac.uk/lstm

London School of Hygiene and Tropical Medicine
Keppel Street
London WC1E 7HT
Tel: 020 7636 8636
Fax: 020 7436 5389
Website: www.lshtm.ac.uk

Malaria Reference Laboratory (for advice on prophylaxis)
Tel: 020 7636 7921
Website: www.malaria-reference.co.uk

Urology

British Association of Urological Surgeons
Royal College of Surgeons
35–43 Lincoln's Inn Fields
London WC2A 3PE
Tel: 020 7869 6950
Fax: 020 7404 5048
Email: admin@baus.org.uk
Website: www.baus.org.uk

Part 2 – Litigation

Action Against Medical Accidents (AvMA)

44 High St
Croydon
Surrey CR0 17B
Tel: 020 8688 9555
Fax: 020 8667 9065
Email: advice@avma.org.uk
Website: www.avma.org.uk

Association of Personal Injury Lawyers (APIL)

11 Castle Quay
Castle Boulevard
Nottingham NG7 1FW
Tel: 0115 958 0585
Fax: 0115 958 0885
Email: mail@apil.com
Website: www.apil.org.uk

Association of Trial Lawyers of America

777 6th Street NW
Suite 200
Washington DC 20001
Tel: 001 800 424 2725
Email: help@justice.org

Clinical Disputes Forum

Chairman: Dr Alastair Scotland
Medical Director and Chief Officer
National Clinical Assessment Authority
9th Floor, Market Towers
London SW8 5NQ
Tel: 0115 947 4700
Fax: 0115 958 0885
Email: margaret.dangoor@blueyonder.co.uk

Compensation Recovery Unit (CRU)

Compensation Recovery Unit
Durham House
Washington
Tyne & Wear NE38 7SF
Tel: 0191 225 2005
Fax: 0191 225 2048
Email: cru-info-management@dwp.gsi.gov.uk

Disability Law Service

(free advice for the disabled on legal matters, benefits and grants)
39–45 Cavell Street
London E1 2BP
Tel: 020 7791 9800
Fax: 020 7791 9802
Email: advice@dls.org.uk
Website: www.dis.org.uk

General Council of the Bar

289–293 High Holborn
London WC1V 7HZ
Tel: 020 7242 0082
Fax: 020 7831 9217
Email: generaloffice@barcouncil.org.uk
Website: www.barcouncil.org.uk

Incorporated Council of Law Reporting for England and Wales

Megarry House
119 Chancery Lane
London WC2A 1PP
Tel: 020 7242 6471
Fax: 020 7831 5247
Email: postmaster@iclr.co.uk
Website: www.lawreports.co.uk

Inquest

89–93 Fonthill Road
London N4 3JH
Tel: 020 7263 1111
Fax: 020 7561 0799
Email: inquest@inquest.org.uk
Website: www.inquest.gn.apc.org

Law Society

113 Chancery Lane
London WC2A 1PL
Tel: 020 7242 1222
Fax: 020 7831 0344
Email: contact@lawsociety.org.uk
Website: www.lawsociety.org.uk

Legal Services Commisson

Legal Services Commission Head Office
85 Gray's Inn Road
London WC1X 8TX
Tel: 020 7759 0000
Website: legalservices.gov.uk

Legal Services Commission London/South Eastern Group Area Offices (Area No. 1)
29–37 Red Lion Street
London WC1R 4PP
Tel: 020 759 1966
Email: london@legalservices.gov.uk

Legal Services Commission (Area No. 2)
Invicta House
Trafalgar Place
Cheapside
Brighton BN1 4FR
Tel: 01273 878800

Legal Services Commission (Area No. 3)
Dukesbridge House, 23 Duke Street
Reading RE1 4SA
Tel: 0118 955 8600

Legal Services Commission Wales and the West Group Area Offices (Area No. 4)
33–35 Queen Square
Bristol BS1 4LU
Tel: 0117 302 3000

Legal Services Commission (Area No. 5)
Marland House
Central Square
Cardiff CF10 1PF
Tel: 0845 608 7070
Fax: 02920 647 173

Legal Services Commission Midlands Group Area Offices (Area No. 6)
First Floor, Cannon House
18 The Priory, Queensway
Birmingham B4 6BS
Tel: 0121 232 5500

Legal Services Commission (Area No. 7)
2nd Floor Lee House
90 Great Bridewater Street
Manchester M1 5JW
Tel: 0161 244 5000

Legal Services Commission (Area No. 8)
Eagle Star House
Fenkle Street
Newcastle NE1 5RU
Tel: 0191 244 5800

Legal Services Commission (Area No. 9)
Harcourt House
Chanceller House
21 The Calls
Leeds LS2 7EH
Tel: 0113 390 7300
Email: leeds@legalservices.gov.uk

Legal Services Commission (Area No. 10)
1st Floor, Fothergill House
16 King Street
Nottingham NG1 2AS
Tel: 0115 908 4200
Fax: 0115 908 4399

Legal Services Commission (Area No. 11)
62–68 Hills Road
Cambridge CB2 1LA
Tel: 01223 417 991

Legal Services Commission North Western Group Area Offices (Area No. 12)
2nd Floor, Pepper House
Pepper Row
Chester CH1 1DW
Tel: 01244 404 500

Legal Services Commission (Area No. 15)
Cavern Court
8 Matthew Street
Liverpool L2 6RE
Tel: 0151 242 5200
Email: liverpool@legalservices.gov.uk

Medical Defence Union

230 Blackfriars Road
London SE1 8PJ
Tel: 020 7202 1500
Fax: 020 7202 5800
Email: advisory@the-mdu.com
Website: www.the-mdu.com

The Medical Protection Society Ltd

33 Cavendish Square
London W1G 0PS
Tel: 0845 605 4000
Fax: 0113 241 0500
Email: info@mps.org.uk
Website: www.medicalprotection.org.uk

Medico-Legal Society

Richard Griffin (1820) Ltd
XPL Publishing, 99 Hatfield Road
St Albans
Hertfordshire AL1 4EG

President's contact details:
Dr Robin Moffat
8A Bedford Towers
King's Road
Brighton BN1 2JG

Motor Insurers Bureau

Linford Wood House
6–12 Capital Drive
Milton Keynes MK14 6XT
Tel: 01908 830 001
Fax: 01908 671 681
Email: enquiries@MIB.org.uk
Website: www.mib.org.uk

National Association of Guardians ad Litem and Reporting Officers (NAGALRO)

PO Box 264
Esher
Surrey KT10 0WA
Tel: 01372 818 504
Fax: 01372 818 505
Email: nagalro@globalnet.co.uk
Website: NAGLRO: www.nagalro.com

Official Solicitor to the Supreme Court

81 Chancery Lane
London WC2A 1DD
Tel: 020 7911 7127
Fax: 020 7911 7105
Email: enquiries@offsol.gsi.gov.uk
Website: www.officialsolicitor.gov.uk

The Patients' Association

PO Box 935
Harrow HA1 3YJ
Tel: 020 8423 9111
Fax: 020 8423 9119
Email: mailbox@patients-association.com

Personal Injury Bar Association (PIBA)

Nigel Cooksley QC
Outer Temple Chambers
10–11 Bedford Row
London WC1R 4BU
Tel: 020 7353 5892
Email: cooksleyqc@oldsquare.co.uk

Professional Negligence Bar Association (PNBA)

Victoria Woodbridge
Crown Office Chambers
London EC4Y 7EP
Tel: 020 7797 8100
Email: woodbridge@crownofficechambers.com
Website: www.pnba.co.uk

Prevention of Professional Abuse Network

Delta House
175–177 Borough High Street
London SE1 1HR
Tel: 020 7939 9920
Email: info@witnessagainstabuse.org.uk

Smith Bernal Reporting Ltd

(Court of Appeal Transcribers)
190 Fleet Street
London EC4A 2AG
Tel: 020 7404 1400
Fax: 020 7831 8838
Email: mail@wordwave.co.uk
Website: www.wordwave.co.uk

Part 3 – Government

Commission for Local Administration in England

(Local Government Ombudsman)
10th Floor, Millbank Tower
Millbank
London SW1P 4QP
Tel: 020 7217 4620
Fax: 020 7217 4621

Department of Health

Richmond House
79 Whitehall
London SW1A 2NL
Tel: 020 7210 4850
Email: dhmail@doh.gov.uk

Department of Work and Pensions

Correspondence Unit
Room 112 The Adelphi
1–11 John Adam Street
London WC2N 6HT
Tel: 020 7712 2171
Fax: 020 7712 2386
Website: www.dwp.gov.uk

Department of Health Social Care Group

Richmond House
79 Whitehall
London SW1A 2NL
Tel: 020 7210 4850

Health & Safety Executive

2 Southwark Bridge
London SE1 9HS
Tel: 020 7556 2100
Fax: 020 7557 2102
Website: www.hse.gov.uk

HSE Information Centre

Caerphilly Business Park
Caerphilly CF83 3GG
Tel: 0845 345 0055
Fax: 0845 408 9577
Email: hse.infoline@natbrit.com

Health and Safety Executive – Health Policy Division

Rose Court
2 Southwark Bridge
London SE1 9HS
Tel: 020 7717 6000 (Head Office)
Fax: 020 7717 6717

Home Office

Home Office Direct Communications Unit
2 Marsham Street
London SW1P 4DF
Tel: 020 7035 4848
Fax: 020 7035 4745
Email: public.enquiries@homeoffice.gsi.gov.uk
Website: www.homeoffice.gov.uk

HM Inspector of Anatomy

Dept. of Health
Rm 630 Wellington House
135–153 Waterloo Road
London SE1 8UG
Tel: 020 7972 4551
Fax: 020 7972 4791
Email: karen.huscroft@dh.gsi.gov.uk

Mental Health Act Commission

Maid Marian House
56 Houndsgate
Nottingham NG1 6BG
Tel: 0115 943 7100
Fax: 0115 943 7101
Email: chiefexec@mhac.org.uk
Website: www.mhac.org.uk

Mental Welfare Commission for Scotland

K Floor, Argyle House
3 Lady Lawson Street
Edinburgh EH3 9SH
Tel: 0131 222 6111
Fax: 0131 222 6112
Email: enquiries@mwcscot.org.uk
Website: www.mwcscot.org.uk

Ministry of Defence Medical Services Directorate

Lacon House
Theobalds Road
London WC1X 8RY

Ministry of Justice

102 Petty France
London SW1H 69AJ
Tel: 020 3334 3555
Fax: 020 334 4455
Email: general.queries@justice.gsi.gov.uk
Website: www.justice.gov.uk

National Blood Authority

Oak House
Reeds Crescent
Watford WD24 4QN
Tel: 01923 486 800
Fax: 01923 486 801
Website: www.blooddonor.org.uk

Scottish Office Home and Health Department

St Andrew's House
Regent Road
Edinburgh EH1 3DG
Tel: 0131 244 9010
Fax: 0131 244 7059
Email: sharon.nicol@scotland.gov.uk

London Office: Dover House
Whitehall
London SW1A 2AU
Tel: 020 7270 6754
Fax: 020 7270 6812
Email: scottish.secretary@scotland.gsi.gov.uk

Scottish National Blood Transfusion Service

21 Ellen's Glen Road
Edinburgh EH17 7QT
Tel: 0131 536 5700
Fax: 0131 536 5781

Nursing and Midwifery Council

23 Portland Place
London W1B 1PZ
Tel: 020 7637 7181
Fax: 020 7436 2924
Email: advice@nmc-uk.org
Website: www.nmc-uk.org

Part 4 – Courts and Tribunals

Judicial Office of the House of Lords

London SW1A 0PW
Tel: 020 7219 3000
Website: www.parliament.uk

Court of Appeal

Civil Division
Room E330
Royal Courts of Justice
Strand
London WC2A 2LL
Tel: 020 7947 7882
Fax: 020 7947 6740

High Court of Justice

Royal Courts of Justice
Strand
London WC2A 2LL
Tel: 020 7947 6000 (General Office)

Court of Protection

Archway Tower
2 Junction Road
London N19 5SZ
Tel: 0845 330 2900
Fax: 020 7664 7551
Website: publictrust.gov.uk

Criminal Injuries Compensation Authority (CICA)

Tay House
300 Bath Street
Glasgow G2 4LN
Tel: 0800 358 3601
Fax: 0141 331 2287
Website: cica.gov.uk

Part 5 – Other

Child Poverty Action Group

94 White Lion Street
London N1 9PF
Tel: 020 7837 7979
Fax: 020 7837 6414
Email: staff@cpag.org.uk
Website: www.cpag.org.uk

Fostering Network

87 Blackfriars Road
London SE1 8HA
Tel: 020 7620 6400
Fax: 020 7620 6401
Email: info@fostering.net
Website: www.fostering.net

Leonard Cheshire Foundation

66 South Lambeth Road
London SW8 1RL
Tel: 020 3242 0200
Fax: 020 3242 0250
Email: info@lcdisabiltiy.org
Website: www.lcdisability.org

The Bank of England

Threadneedle Street
London EC2R 8AH
Tel: 020 7601 4444
Fax: 020 7601 5460
Email: enquries@bankofengland.co.uk
Website: www.bankofengland.co.uk